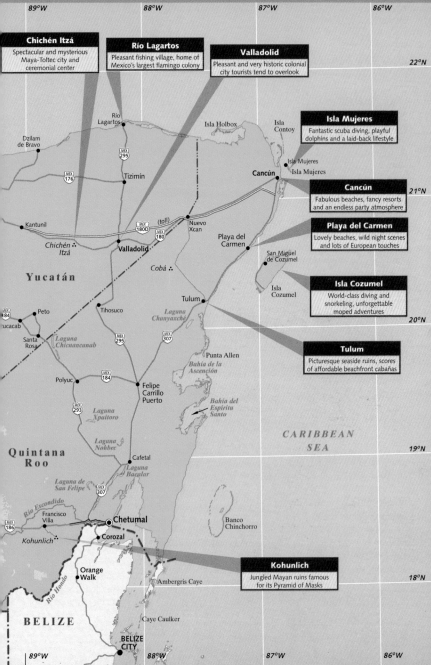

89°W · 88°W · 87°W · 86°W

Chichén Itzá
Spectacular and mysterious Maya-Toltec city and ceremonial center

Río Lagartos
Pleasant fishing village, home of Mexico's largest flamingo colony

Valladolid
Pleasant and very historic colonial city tourists tend to overlook

22°N

Isla Mujeres
Fantastic scuba diving, playful dolphins and a laid-back lifestyle

Cancún
Fabulous beaches, fancy resorts and an endless party atmosphere

21°N

Playa del Carmen
Lovely beaches, wild night scenes and lots of European touches

Isla Cozumel
World-class diving and snorkeling, unforgettable moped adventures

20°N

Tulum
Picturesque seaside ruins, scores of affordable beachfront cabañas

19°N

Kohunlich
Jungled Mayan ruins famous for its Pyramid of Masks

18°N

Dzilam de Bravo
Río Lagartos
Isla Holbox
Isla Contoy
Isla Mujeres
Isla Mujeres
Cancún

MEX 295
Tizimín
MEX 176

Kantunil
Nuevo Xcan
(toll)
MEX 180D
MEX 180
Playa del Carmen
San Miguel de Cozumel

Chichén Itzá
Valladolid
Cobá
Isla Cozumel

Yucatán

Tihosuco
Laguna Chunyaxché
Tulum

MEX 184
Peto
ucacab
Santa Rosa
Laguna Chicnancanab
MEX 295
MEX 307
Punta Allen
Bahía de la Ascensión

CARIBBEAN SEA

Polyuc
MEX 184
Felipe Carrillo Puerto
Bahía del Espíritu Santo

MEX 293
Laguna Xpaitoro

Laguna Nohbec

Quintana Roo

Cafetal
Laguna Bacalar
Laguna de San Felipe
MEX 307

Río Escondido
MEX 186
Francisco Villa
Chetumal
Banco Chinchorro

Kohunlich
Corozal

Orange Walk
Ambergris Caye

Río Hondo

BELIZE

Caye Caulker

BELIZE CITY

Yucatán
1st edition – August 2000

Published by
Lonely Planet Publications Pty Ltd A.C.N. 005 607 983
192 Burwood Rd, Hawthorn, Victoria 3122, Australia

Lonely Planet Offices
Australia PO Box 617, Hawthorn, Victoria 3122
USA 150 Linden St, Oakland, CA 94607
UK 10a Spring Place, London NW5 3BH
France 1 rue du Dahomey, 75011 Paris

Photographs
Most of the images in this guide are available for licensing from
Lonely Planet Images.
email: lpi@lonelyplanet.com.au

Front cover photograph
Replica of Chac-Mool, a Mayan ceremonial figure, Quintana Roo
(John Neubauer)

ISBN 1 86450 103 0

Printed by The Bookmaker Pty Ltd
Printed in China

**Although the authors
and Lonely Planet try
to make the informa-
tion as accurate as
possible, we accept
no responsibility for
any loss, injury or
inconvenience sus-
tained by anyone
using this book.**

Contents – Text

2   Contents

Contents – Maps

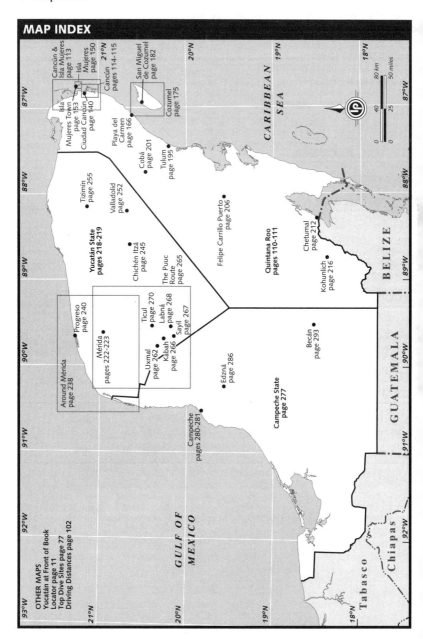

MAP INDEX

Cancún & Isla Mujeres page 113

Isla Mujeres page 150

Cancún pages 114-115

San Miguel de Cozumel page 182

Isla Mujeres Town page 153

Ciudad Cancún page 140

Cozumel page 175

Playa del Carmen page 166

Cobá page 201

Tulum page 195

Tizimín page 255

Valladolid page 252

Yucatán State pages 218-219

Chichén Itzá page 245

The Puuc Route page 265

Felipe Carrillo Puerto page 206

Quintana Roo pages 110-111

Chetumal page 212

Kohunlich page 216

B E L I Z E

Progreso page 240

Mérida pages 222-223

Ticul page 270

Labná page 268

Sayil page 267

Becán page 293

Around Mérida page 238

Uxmal page 262

Kabah page 266

Edzná page 286

Campeche State page 277

G U A T E M A L A

Campeche pages 280-281

G U L F   O F   M E X I C O

C A R I B B E A N   S E A

80 km

50 miles

40

25

T a b a s c o

C h i a p a s

93°W   92°W   91°W   90°W   89°W   88°W   87°W

20°N   19°N   18°N

21°N   20°N   19°N   18°N   21°N

The Author

Scott Doggett

Scott's interest in Latin America became personal when, in 1983, as a recent graduate of the University of California at Berkeley, he moved to El Salvador to work as a photojournalist. His initial career was followed by postgraduate study at Stanford University; reporting assignments for United Press International in Los Angeles, Pakistan and Afghanistan; and, most recently, seven years as an editor for the *Los Angeles Times* (he and his wife, Annette Haddad, currently cowrite a weekly business column for the newspaper). Scott is the author of Lonely Planet's *Panama* and *Las Vegas* and coauthor of Lonely Planet's *Mexico* and *Dominican Republic & Haiti*. He has also written guidebooks to Amsterdam and Los Angeles and is an author and coeditor of *Travelers' Tales: Brazil*. At the time this book went to press, Scott was writing Lonely Planet's guide to Havana.

FROM THE AUTHOR

During the writing of *Yucatán*, I lost my remarkable sister, Wendy, to a horrible accident. Her death threw me into the worst funk of my life and I missed my deadline by a wide margin. Most companies would show a bit of sympathy for a grieving contract employee, allow a brief recovery period and then apply the thumbscrews if the worker didn't 'get over it' *tout suite*. After all, contract employees are expendable. But Lonely Planet embraced me like a best friend when I needed an embrace most, and for that I will always be grateful.

Susan Charles Bush is the exceptional editor who received the material I occasionally submitted piecemeal, caught and corrected about a thousand discrepancies, and gave parts of the book the overhaul they so often needed. If this book has any polish on it, Susan deserves most of the credit. Overseeing her work as well as mine from planning through editing was senior editor Tom Downs, who is one of the keys to Lonely Planet's success. An author himself, Tom is the kind of project manager every LP writer likes – particular yet pragmatic, patient yet demanding.

I look forward to working with Susan and Tom on many future books.

This Book

Some of the information in this book was taken from portions of Lonely Planet's *Guatemala, Belize & Yucatán* by Tom Brosnahan.

FROM THE PUBLISHER
This book was produced in Lonely Planet's Oakland office. It was edited by Susan Charles Bush and Erin Corrigan, with guidance from Tom Downs. Erin and Christine Lee proofread the text and maps. All of the maps were done by cartographer Eric Thomsen, with help from Kimra McAfee, Andy Rebold, Mary Hagemann, Monica Lepe and Rachel Leising and oversight from Tracey Croom. The lovely design and layout was accomplished through the hard work of Wendy Yanagihara and guidance of Susan Rimerman. The catchy cover was designed by Rini Keagy. Illustrations appearing in these pages were drawn by Beca Lafore, Hugh D'Andrade, Lisa Summers, Hayden Foell, Mark Butler and Hannah Reineck. Ken DellaPenta produced the index with his usual professionalism. Beca and Justin Marler coordinated all the illustrations, and Maria Donohoe and Laura Harger also assisted with this book. Finally, a special thanks goes to Ben Greensfelder for his invaluable research in the field.

Foreword

ABOUT LONELY PLANET GUIDEBOOKS

The story begins with a classic travel adventure: Tony and Maureen Wheeler's 1972 journey across Europe and Asia to Australia. Useful information about the overland trail did not exist at that time, so Tony and Maureen published the first Lonely Planet guidebook to meet a growing need.

From a kitchen table, then from a tiny office in Melbourne (Australia), Lonely Planet has become the largest independent travel publisher in the world, an international company with offices in Melbourne, Oakland (USA), London (UK) and Paris (France).

Today Lonely Planet guidebooks cover the globe. There is an ever-growing list of books, and there's information in a variety of forms and media. Some things haven't changed. The main aim is still to help make it possible for adventurous travelers to get out there – to explore and better understand the world.

At Lonely Planet we believe travelers can make a positive contribution to the countries they visit – if they respect their host communities and spend their money wisely. Since 1986 a percentage of the income from each book has been donated to aid projects and human-rights campaigns.

Updates Lonely Planet thoroughly updates each guidebook as often as possible. This usually means there are around two years between editions, although for more unusual or more stable destinations the gap can be longer. Check the imprint page (following the color map at the beginning of the book) for publication dates.

Between editions, up-to-date information is available in two free newsletters – the paper *Planet Talk* and email *Comet* (to subscribe, contact any Lonely Planet office) – and on our website at www.lonelyplanet.com. The *Upgrades* section of the website covers a number of important and volatile destinations and is regularly updated by Lonely Planet authors. *Scoop* covers news and current affairs relevant to travelers. And, lastly, the *Thorn Tree* bulletin board and *Postcards* section of the site carry unverified, but fascinating, reports from travelers.

Correspondence The process of creating new editions begins with the letters, postcards and emails received from travelers. This correspondence often includes suggestions, criticisms and comments about the current editions. Interesting excerpts are immediately passed on via newsletters and the website, and everything goes to our authors to be verified when they're researching on the road. We're keen to get more feedback from organizations or individuals who represent communities visited by travelers.

Lonely Planet gathers information for everyone who's curious about the planet – and especially for those who explore it firsthand. Through guidebooks, phrasebooks, activity guides, maps, literature, newsletters, image library, TV series and website, we act as an information exchange for a worldwide community of travelers.

Research Authors aim to gather sufficient practical information to enable travelers to make informed choices and to make the mechanics of a journey run smoothly. They also research historical and cultural background to help enrich the travel experience and allow travelers to understand and respond appropriately to cultural and environmental issues.

Authors don't stay in every hotel because that would mean spending a couple of months in each medium-size city and, no, they don't eat at every restaurant because that would mean stretching belts beyond capacity. They do visit hotels and restaurants to check standards and prices, but feedback based on readers' direct experiences can be very helpful.

Many of our authors work undercover; others aren't so secretive. None of them accept freebies in exchange for positive write-ups. And none of our guidebooks contain any advertising.

Production Authors submit their raw manuscripts and maps to offices in Australia, the USA, the UK or France. Editors and cartographers – all experienced travelers themselves – then begin the process of assembling the pieces. When the book finally hits the shops, some things are already out of date, we start getting feedback from readers and the process begins again....

WARNING & REQUEST

Things change – prices go up, schedules change, good places go bad and bad places go bankrupt – nothing stays the same. So, if you find things better or worse, recently opened or long since closed, please tell us and help make the next edition even more accurate and useful. We genuinely value all the feedback we receive. Julie Young coordinates a well-traveled team that reads and acknowledges every letter, postcard and email and ensures that every morsel of information finds its way to the appropriate authors, editors and cartographers for verification.

Everyone who writes to us will find their name in the next edition of the appropriate guidebook. They will also receive the latest issue of *Planet Talk*, our quarterly printed newsletter, or *Comet*, our monthly email newsletter. Subscriptions to both newsletters are free. The very best contributions will be rewarded with a free guidebook.

Excerpts from your correspondence may appear in new editions of Lonely Planet guidebooks, the Lonely Planet website, *Planet Talk* or *Comet*, so please let us know if you *don't* want your letter published or your name acknowledged.

Send all correspondence to the Lonely Planet office closest to you:

Australia: PO Box 617, Hawthorn, Victoria 3122
USA: 150 Linden St, Oakland, CA 94607
UK: 10A Spring Place, London NW5 3BH
France: 1 rue du Dahomey, 75011 Paris

Or email us at: talk2us@lonelyplanet.com.au

For news, views and updates, see our website: www.lonelyplanet.com

HOW TO USE A LONELY PLANET GUIDEBOOK

The best way to use a Lonely Planet guidebook is any way you choose. At Lonely Planet, we believe the most memorable travel experiences are often those that are unexpected, and the finest discoveries are those you make yourself. Guidebooks are not intended to be used as if they provided a detailed set of infallible instructions!

Contents All Lonely Planet guidebooks follow the same format. The Facts about the Country chapters or sections give background information ranging from history to weather. Facts for the Visitor gives practical information on issues like visas and health. Getting There & Away gives a brief starting point for researching travel to and from the destination. Getting Around gives an overview of the transport options available when you arrive.

The peculiar demands of each destination determine how subsequent chapters are broken up, but some things remain constant. We always start with background, then proceed to sights, places to stay, places to eat, entertainment, getting there and away, and getting around information – in that order.

Heading Hierarchy Lonely Planet headings are used in a strict hierarchical structure that can be visualized as a set of Russian dolls. Each heading (and its following text) is encompassed by any preceding heading that is higher on the hierarchical ladder.

Entry Points We do not assume guidebooks will be read from beginning to end, but that people will dip into them. The traditional entry points are the list of contents and the index. In addition, however, some books have a complete list of maps and an index map illustrating map coverage.

There may also be a color map that shows highlights. These highlights are dealt with in greater detail later in the book, along with planning questions. Each chapter covering a geographical region usually begins with a locator map and another list of highlights. Once you find something of interest in a list of highlights, turn to the index.

Maps Maps play a crucial role in Lonely Planet guidebooks and include a huge amount of information. A legend is printed on the back page. We seek to have complete consistency between maps and text, and to have every important place in the text captured on a map. Map key numbers usually start in the top left corner.

Although inclusion in a guidebook usually implies a recommendation, we cannot list every good place. Exclusion does not necessarily imply criticism. In fact, there are a number of reasons why we might exclude a place – sometimes it is simply inappropriate to encourage an influx of travelers.

Introduction

The Yucatán Peninsula is the most intriguing region in all of Latin America. It is home to some of the most impressive archaeological sites in the world, including the ancient Mayan cities of Chichén Itzá, Uxmal and Cobá. The peninsula – often referred to simply as 'Yucatán' or 'the Yucatán' – also contains numerous colonial cities studded with pirate-thwarting fortifications, captivating Franciscan churches and stately government buildings that date back to the earliest years of the Spanish conquest of the New World.

The Yucatán's Caribbean coast offers thrill-seekers truly world-class snorkeling and scuba diving. Visitors can also choose from a broad array of unconventional water sports. Ever been given a lift by a pair of playful dolphins? Ever swum down a jungle-flanked river to its terminus at the edge of a sea the color of imperial jade? Ever peered upon a world-famous beach resort as you glided through the air simultaneously suspended from a parachute and pulled by a boat? You could answer *yes* to all three questions if you'd visited Yucatán lately.

Sun worshippers and party animals the world over have at the very least heard of Cancún, a long and narrow resort-lined island that's shaped like a Lucky 7 and hugs the eastern coast of the Yucatán like a bosom buddy. Mexico is home to Acapulco, Mazatlán and Cabo San Lucas, but Cancún receives more visitors each year than those three famous fun spots combined. Cancún's sugary beaches, its scandalous nightlife and its lengthy menu of restaurants have made it one of the hottest tourist destinations in the world.

A visit to Yucatán wouldn't be complete without at least a little wildlife adventure of the natural-world kind. Although humans have occupied Yucatán for thousands of years, most of the peninsula remains blanketed by tropical lowland forest. The forest is not the snake-dripping jungle of Amazonia, but it is home to jaguars, tapirs and crocodiles, hundreds of species of exotic birds and a dazzling array of butterflies. It is here, too, that Mexico's two largest flamingo sanctuaries can be found, and a trip to either is

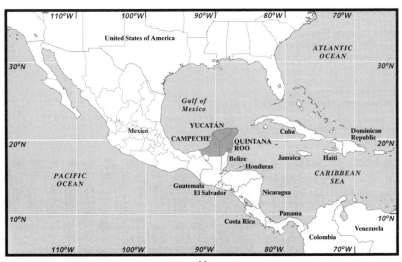

an unforgettable experience. Also found throughout the Yucatán are spectacular caves ripe for exploring and freshwater pools that take the bite out of the tropical midday sun.

As it has for hundreds of years, Yucatán remains the center of the *mundo Maya*, or Mayan world – a vast realm that includes portions of Mexico, Guatemala, Belize, Honduras and El Salvador. Not only are more Mayan ruins located in the Yucatán than anywhere else, but the Mayan way of life has endured here despite the best efforts of Spanish missionaries to destroy it. Mayan villages dot the peninsula like scattered kernels of corn, and in them the residents continue to live off the land and worship their gods as they have for at least 1800 years. The great cities mostly lay in ruin, but many aspects of Mayan culture live on.

Shoppers will appreciate the handicrafts found on the peninsula. In their handmade goods, the modern-day Maya have fused Old and New World forms and materials. Among the high-quality handicrafts produced in Yucatán are exquisite silver ornaments that reflect the filigree technique introduced by the Spanish, wonderful models of galleons carved from blocks of mahogany and Panama hats so tightly woven that they can hold water. The best hammocks in the world come from the Yucatán, as do the world's finest *guayaberas*.

Mexico is famous for its cuisine, which varies considerably from one part of the country to another. Even if you've eaten scores of Mexican dishes, chances are you're unfamiliar with Yucatecan food. Among the better-known regional dishes are *cochinita pibil* (pork slow-cooked in banana leaves and flavored with achiote paste, oregano leaves, salt, pepper, garlic, onion, sour orange and a single habanero pepper) and *pavo en escabeche oriental* (turkey marinated in sour orange juice, garlic and xcalic peppers, slow-cooked to perfection, then sliced and cooked in green oil and garlic). For dessert, how about candied papaya served with chunks of Edam cheese? Careful: This dessert is habit forming.

Splendid colonial architecture. Magnificent Mayan ruins. History galore. A fascinating people. Nightlife to fantasize about. Culture at every turn. Pristine beaches. Fantastic food. Sensational shopping. Superb snorkeling. Vast cave systems. Refreshing natural pools. World-class diving. Cancún, Cozumel, Playa del Carmen – fun, fun, fun! And reasonable prices most everywhere. Yucatán. It's got something for most everyone.

Facts about Yucatán

HISTORY
The First Americans

Homo sapiens first arrived in the Americas approximately 32,000 years ago via a land bridge that connected present-day Alaska with present-day Russia. Back then, much of the Earth's water supply was locked in glacial ice, permitting travel across valleys that are now on the ocean floor. During the next 25 millennia, the ice thawed, the oceans rose and the land bridge disappeared under a body of water we call the Bering Strait.

Campsites found in recent years indicate that these early inhabitants gradually worked their way south and east from the icy northwest reaches of the Americas, eventually reaching the Yucatán Peninsula about 30 millennia ago. Although quite different in appearance from contemporary Americans, these were true humans: They stood fully erect and were capable of higher thought processes, as indicated by the symbols they carved into mastodon bones found on the peninsula.

The first Americans were skilled hunters, stalking and slaying animals much larger than they. Anthropologists have found in the Yucatán the chipped-flint tips of spears inside the skulls of Pleistocene mammals, including the earth-trembling American elephant, the giant imperial mammoth and the awe-inspiring saber-toothed tiger – indisputable evidence of man's presence in southeastern Mexico dozens of millennia ago.

Exactly what happened to these extra-large mammals (and others, such as the American camel, the woolly mammoth and bison four times the size of today's American buffalo) is not known. Scientists theorize that the planetary thawing that occurred between 28,000 and 10,000 BC killed off the Pleistocene mammals and the first Americans who fed upon them – victims, apparently, of their inability to adapt to a changing environment.

The Second Wave of Americans

Around 8000 BC a second group of wanderers made their way across the narrow land bridge atop the Bering Sea. They wielded Stone Age tools like their predecessors, but theirs came in many different styles and served many purposes. In addition to the axes and spears of times past, they used knives, throwing darts, drills and a variety of picks and scrapers. They also painted and made music.

As they spread from west to east and north to south they developed an estimated 1200 distinct languages. And whereas the

---

Yucatán's Dinosaur-Killing Meteorite

For the past two decades there has been growing scientific agreement that a meteorite slammed into the Yucatán 65 million years ago, kicking up enough debris to block out the sun for a decade and trigger a global freeze that killed off two-thirds of the Earth's species.

This theory gained steam in late 1998, when Frank Kyte, a geochemist at the University of California, Los Angeles, found a sliver of an asteroid dating from the time of the dinosaurs. The tiny fossil meteorite discovered by Kyte is thought to have been part of the suspected 8km-wide cosmic fist that smashed into the Yucatán, producing a crater 300km wide.

No other pieces of the meteorite have yet been discovered, and for good reason: It struck the Earth with such force that it blasted itself to pieces and scattered like gunshot. The fragment Kyte came across was found within a deep ocean core taken from the waters northwest of Hawaii – more than 4000km from the Yucatán.

first Westerners went as far as Mesoamerica (Middle America) over a 2000-year period, the later group is known to have reached as far south as Peru by 7000 BC, a mere 1,000 years after they crossed the land bridge.

The newcomers were Mongoloid in bone structure and height and even featured the characteristic Asian eye fold. And it's the descendants of these indigenous peoples – Native Americans – who Christopher Columbus encountered 8500 years later.

Village People

From approximately 7000 BC until 2000 BC, the hunter-gatherers of Mesoamerica gradually put away their walking sticks and settled down. Like the first Americans, they initially went where the hunting was good and moved along when their prey migrated or when they had overhunted. Like the early peoples of Europe, they began planting crops and establishing villages; their nomadic days were numbered.

As 2000 BC neared, most Americans were cultivating corn, squash, avocados and beans, and raising chickens, turkeys and dogs. They continued to hunt and fish as they had for generations, but they became heavily dependent upon crops, which some anthropologists believe is why these people found gods. Even today, belief in a god of rain and a god of corn is widespread in Latin America. Whether or not their faith stemmed from their increasing dependence on rain or another factor, the second wave of Americans became true believers, attributing events such as floods and droughts to supernatural forces.

Perhaps the oldest Mesoamerican culture belongs to the Olmecs, who lived along the Gulf of Mexico near present-day Veracruz, 500k or so southwest of the Yucatán, from about 1500 to 200 BC. Known mostly for the colossal carved-stone heads they left behind, the Olmecs built the first ceremonial centers in Mesoamerica. As time passed, their religion became complex and increasingly relied upon shamans, who purportedly communicated with the supernatural world. Religious rituals, including human sacrifices to assuage an ever-increasing number of blood-thirsty gods, became common Olmec events.

Around 500 BC the Zapotecs of Oaxaca, who lived on the Pacific coast southwest of the Olmec territory, borrowed considerably from the Olmec culture, and in many ways took it a step further. Like the Olmecs, the Zapotecs built stone structures for religious uses, but they also produced fine headdresses and highly detailed terra-cotta objects with significant cult meanings. The same can be said for the Teotihuacán and El Tajín cultures that existed from 250 to 900 AD hundreds of kilometers north of the Zapotecs, who disappeared around 800 AD.

Enter the Maya

Around the same time the Teotihuacán and El Tajín civilizations flourished, another civilization was having its day in the sun on the Yucatán Peninsula and in the highlands to the south. These people were the ancient Maya, who existed as a civilization (that is, who lived in cities and performed tasks special to the maintenance of the cities) from about 250 to 1524 AD. The former date signifies the widely acknowledged start of the Mayan temple-building era. The latter date signifies the year the last major Mayan group, the Quiché Maya, was conquered by Spanish troops (at the Battle of Utatlán, in Guatemala).

Archaeologists believe Mayan-speaking people first appeared in the highlands of Guatemala as early as 1500 BC and that groups of Mayan farmers relocated to the lowlands of the Yucatán Peninsula between 1200 and 1000 BC. In the lowlands, the Maya formed villages and tended crops just as they had done in the highlands, and for the next 400 to 600 years they did little of archaeological value, though it was during this period that the early Maya invented the *na*, or thatched Mayan hut, which is still used today throughout the Yucatán. It was also between 1200 and 300 BC that the Maya placed a high value on cacao beans, using them to make chocolate and as a currency.

As agriculture played an increasing role in Mayan life, so too did the climate in which the Maya lived. By 300 BC, most Mayan

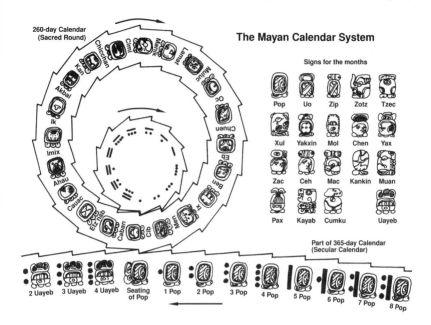

260-day Calendar
(Sacred Round)

The Mayan Calendar System

Signs for the months

Pop Uo Zip Zotz Tzec

Xul Yakkin Mol Chen Yax

Zac Ceh Mac Kankin Muan

Pax Kayab Cumku Uayeb

Part of 365-day Calendar
(Secular Calendar)

2 Uayeb 3 Uayeb 4 Uayeb Seating of Pop 1 Pop 2 Pop 3 Pop 4 Pop 5 Pop 6 Pop 7 Pop 8 Pop

villages were heavily dependent upon regular rains to feed their crops. A dry spell was cause for panic; a drought brought widescale death. Understanding when the rains came became a Mayan preoccupation, out of which some long-forgotten individual came up with a calendar that featured a year of 18 months, each 20 days long, with five days left over.

Of course, a calendar has yet to be created that forecasts every rain or foretells periods of drought. However, the Mayan calendar helped the Maya anticipate rainy and dry seasons, which aided them in planting. As a result, the Maya became better farmers, and those Maya who possessed knowledge of the calendar became leaders, as did shamans who supposedly could account for a late rain or other climate-related event by prescribing it to an angry god. As with many early cultures, the Mayan remedy for an angry god was sacrifice and worship. About the time of Christ, the highland Maya were building temples and sacrificing people like madmen.

Monumental Builders

From approximately 250 to 900 AD, the Maya became the most impressive civilization of pre-Columbian Mesoamerica. During these 650 years they produced the most sophisticated written language native to the Americas; they lived by not one but three calendars equal to our own; the so-called *stargazers* accurately predicted eclipses of the sun and moon and calculated, to within 14 seconds a year, the exact path of Venus; and they built and then abandoned more cities than existed in all of ancient Egypt.

Just how many Mayan cities once existed is anybody's guess. Lost Mayan cities continue to be discovered even today – more than a century after scientists and adventurers began a concerted effort to find them. The reason is simple: Most of the lost cities remain buried beneath jungle, and the territory ruled by the ancient Maya was vast, extending from the Yucatán Peninsula and the bordering Mexican states of Tabasco and Chiapas south through Guatemala and

Belize, and into northwestern El Salvador and Honduras.

Despite the Maya's growth as a culture and in population, armies from Teotihuacán, near modern-day Mexico City, invaded the Mayan highlands south of Yucatán, conquered the Maya there, and imposed their rule and their culture for some time. Eventually, waves of invaders conquered Teotihuacán, and the Teotihuacán people living in southern Mexico and in Guatemala were absorbed into Mayan daily life. The so-called Esperanza culture, a blend of Mexican and Mayan elements, was born of this integration.

The great Mayan ceremonial centers at Copán in present-day Honduras, Caracol in Belize, Yaxchilán and Palenque in Chiapas, Mexico, and Tikál, Quiriguá and Kaminaljuyú in present-day Guatemala prospered between 250 and 600 AD, which archaeologists define as the Early Classic period of Mayan history. But the great lost cities of the Yucatán – Uxmal, Chichén Itzá and Cobá among them – had only begun to blossom during that period. It wouldn't be until the next 300 years – from 600 to 900 AD, the Late Classic period – that high Mayan civilization would move into the jungled lowlands of Yucatán from the highlands of Guatemala, Belize, Honduras and southwestern Mexico.

It should be noted somewhere, and here's as good a place as any, that archaeologists, like scientists, don't like loose ends. So, they tend to lump events within *periods* and create classifications which may or may not paint an entirely accurate picture of a situation. With regard to the Maya, for example, archaeologists like to tidy them up by classifying their history as Preclassic, Classic and Postclassic, and then subclassifying those classifications; it adds a sense of orderliness to Mayan history. Since the experts do this, some classifying has been done here.

However, it's important to keep in mind that Mayan history, and Mayan construction in particular, does not fall neatly into labeled boxes. The Mayans tended to build upon earlier works, which complicates an archaeologist's work immensely. For example, while it's true that Chichén Itzá was an architecturally stunning city before 1000 to 1200 AD,

it wasn't until that period that the magnificent El Castillo pyramid was constructed. However, excavations of El Castillo revealed an inner stairway that led to the discovery of a smaller pyramid inside the one we see today. In fact, the earlier pyramid appears to have been carefully preserved prior to being covered. It is for this reason that the dates archaeologists sometimes attribute to the build up of Chichén Itzá (and other Mayan cities) can vary by hundreds of years.

Complicating matters is that very little is actually known about the ancient Maya; their written history is contained in rock carvings, many of which have worn smooth over time. Very few of the hieroglyphs have been deciphered – and many never will due to the damage they've sustained – and it's probable that most of the carved stones remain unearthed. Archaeologists studying the carvings have created a list of rulers and little else. Indeed, until recently most experts believed the Maya were a peaceful people; today, most experts believe they were a violent race who destroyed themselves as a culture with all their infighting. It's quite possible that the prevailing understanding of Mayan history a century from now will differ greatly from what it is today. Bear in mind, historians continue to debate the causes of the Fall of Rome.

Late Classic Period (600 to 900)

At its height, the Mayan lands were ruled not as an empire but as a collection of independent but also interdependent city-states. Each city-state had its noble house, headed by a king who was the social, political and religious focus of the city's life. The king propitiated the gods by shedding his blood in ceremonies where he pierced his tongue and/or penis with a sharp instrument. He also led his city's soldiers into battle against rival cities, capturing prisoners for use in human sacrifices. Many a king perished in a battle he was too old to fight; but the king, as sacred head of the community, was required to lead in battle for religious as well as military reasons.

King Pacal ruled at Palenque and King Bird-Jaguar at Yaxchilán during the early

part of this period, marking the height of civilization and power in these two cities. Mayan civilization in Tikal was also at its height during the Late Classic period. By the end of the period, however, the great Mayan cities of Tikal, Yaxchilán, Copán, Quiriguá and Caracol had reverted to little more than minor towns, or even villages. The focus of Mayan civilization had by then shifted to the Yucatán, where a new civilization developed at Chichén Itzá, Uxmal, Labná, Kabah, Edzná, Sayil and elsewhere.

Early Postclassic Period (900 to 1200)

Prevailing expert opinion has it that the collapse of classic Mayan civilization was as surprising as it was sudden. The upper classes are thought to have demanded ever more servants, acolytes and laborers, and though the Mayan population was growing rapidly, it did not furnish enough farmers to feed everyone. Thus weakened, the Maya were easy prey to invaders.

At the same time, a remarkable individual with the memorable birth name Ce Acatl Topiltzin (Our Prince, Born in the Year I-Reed) led the Toltecs from Teotihuacán to Tula, a city he founded 70km north of present-day Mexico City. There, Topiltzin was eventually deposed, but he and his followers went on to capture Cholula, 50km southeast of Mexico City and the site of the largest pyramid ever built. Archaeologists believe Topiltzin led the Toltecs of Cholula on a great invasion of the Yucatán in 987 AD, conquering the much-weakened Maya with little difficulty.

By then, Topiltzin had taken on legendary status, and soon his name became virtually inseparable from that of Quetzalcóatl, a great god whose name variously translates as Snake of Precious Feathers or, more commonly, Plumed Serpent. The Maya would come to call Topiltzin by yet another name, Kukulcán, who was one of their great gods. Regardless of his name, it was this man who established himself in Yucatán at Uucil-abnal (Chichén Itzá) near the end of the first millennium after Christ. Upon his death, it was said Topiltzin/Quetzalcóatl/Kukulcán

Legendary Ce Acatl Topiltzin, AKA Quetzalcóatl

would one day return from the direction of the rising sun and initiate a new era. It was a legend that haunted many Mesoamericans when Spanish conquistadors arrived four centuries later.

The culture at Uucil-abnal flourished after the late 9th century, when all of the great buildings were constructed, but by 1200 the city was abandoned. The cause of its decline and abandonment remains a mystery.

Late Postclassic Period (1200 to 1524)

Itzaes After the forsaking of Toltec Uucil-abnal, the site was occupied by a people called the Itzaes. Probably of Mayan race, the Itzaes had lived among the Putun Maya near Champotón in Mexico's Tabasco state until the early 13th century. Forced by other invaders to leave their traditional homeland, they headed southeast into El Petén, Guatemala, to the lake that became known as Petén Itzá after their arrival. Some continued to Belize, later making their way north along the coast and into northern Yucatán, where they settled at Uucil-abnal.

The Itzae leader styled himself Kukulcán, as had the city's Toltec founder, and recycled other Toltec lore as well. The Itzaes strengthened the belief in sacred *cenotes* (natural limestone caves that provided the Maya with their water supply on the riverless plains of

Yucatán Gets Its Name

A great many places in Latin America were named by Spanish conquistadors centuries ago, but Mexico's enormous eastern peninsula reportedly takes its name from the Mayan language. Legend has it that when Europeans first reached the region, some of them attempted to ask the natives how they called their land. The response was always the same – 'Yucatán' – and the name stuck. What the Spanish didn't know was that *'yucatán'* is Mayan for 'we don't understand you.'

the northern Yucatán Peninsula), and they even named their new home Chichén Itzá (At the Mouth of the Well of the Itzaes).

From Chichén Itzá, the ruling Itzaes traveled westwards and founded a new capital city at Mayapán (built during the latter half of the 13th century), which dominated the political life of northern Yucatán for several hundred years. From Mayapán, the Cocom lineage of the Itzaes ruled a fractious collection of Yucatecan city-states until the mid-15th century, when a subject people from Uxmal, the Xiú, overthrew Cocom power. Mayapán was pillaged, ruined and never re-populated. For the next century, until the coming of the Spanish conquistadors, northern Yucatán was alive with battles and power struggles among its city-states.

The Spaniards Cometh The Spaniards had had a presence in the Caribbean since the arrival of Christopher Columbus in 1492, with their main bases on the islands of Santo Domingo (modern-day Hispaniola) and Cuba. Realizing that they had not reached the East Indies, they began looking for a passage through the landmass to their west but were distracted by tales of a gold-rich empire somewhere in the area. Trading, slaving and exploring expeditions from Cuba, led by Francisco Hernández de Córdoba in 1517 and Juan de Grijalva in 1518, were unable to penetrate inland from Mexico's Gulf Coast, where they were driven back by hostile natives.

In 1518 the governor of Cuba, Diego Velázquez, asked officer Hernán Cortés to lead a new expedition westward. As Cortés gathered ships and men, Velázquez became uneasy about the costs of the venture and about Cortés' questionable loyalty, so he canceled the expedition. Cortés ignored the governor and set sail on February 15, 1519, with 11 ships, 550 men and 16 horses.

At this time, central Mexico was dominated by the Aztec empire, ruled from Mexico City. The story of the confrontation between the Spaniards and the Aztecs is one of the most bizarre in history. Aztec legends predicted the 'return' of fair-skinned gods from the east at just about the time of Cortés' arrival. Thrown off guard by these legends, the rulers of the mighty Aztec empire were toppled by the small Spanish expeditionary force. A detailed first-hand account may be found in the *True History of the Conquest of New Spain* by one of Cortés' soldiers, Bernal Díaz del Castillo.

Landing first at the island of Cozumel off the Yucatán Peninsula, the Spaniards were joined by Jerónimo de Aguilar, a Spaniard who had been shipwrecked there several years earlier. With Aguilar acting as translator and guide, Cortés' force moved west,

Hernán Cortés, the man Neil Young made famous.

along the coast to Tabasco. There they defeated an unknown number of natives, and Cortés delivered the first of many lectures to the Indians on the importance of Christianity and the greatness of King Carlos I of Spain. Cortés went on to conquer central Mexico, after which he turned his attentions – and his armies – to Yucatán.

The Cocoms and the Xiús were still battling when the conquistadors arrived. Yucatán's Maya could not present a united front to the invaders – indeed, they'd abandoned all of their cities except for Tulum prior to the arrival of the Spanish – and the European invaders triumphed. In less than a century after the conquest of Mayapán by the Xiú, the conquistadors had seized the Aztec capital of Tenochtitlán (1521; it's now Mexico City), founded Guatemala City (1527) and Mérida (1542), and wrested control of the once-mighty Mayan world.

Colonial Period (1524 to 1821)

Yucatán Despite the political infighting among the Yucatecan Maya, conquest by the Spaniards was not easy. The Spanish monarch commissioned Francisco de Montejo *(El Adelantado*, or the Pioneer) with the task, and he set out from Spain in 1527 accompanied by his son, also named Francisco de Montejo. Landing first at Cozumel on the Caribbean coast, then at Xel-ha on the mainland, the Montejos discovered that the local people wanted nothing to do with them. The Maya made it quite clear that they should go conquer somewhere else.

The Montejos then sailed around the peninsula, conquered Tabasco (1530) and established their base near Campeche, which could be easily supplied with necessities, arms and new troops from New Spain (that is, central Mexico). They pushed inland to conquer, but after four long, difficult years were forced to retreat and to return to Mexico City in defeat.

The younger Montejo *(El Mozo*, or the Lad) took up the cause again, with his father's support, and in 1540 he returned to Campeche with his cousin named – you got it – Francisco de Montejo. The two Francisco de Montejos pressed inland with speed

and success, allying themselves with the Xiús against the Cocoms, defeating the Cocoms and converting the Xiús to Christianity.

When the Xiú leader was baptized, he had to take a Christian name, so he chose what must have appeared to him to be the most popular name of the entire 16th century and became Francisco de Montejo Xiú.

The Montejos founded Mérida in 1542 and within four years had almost all of Yucatán subjugated to Spanish rule. The once-proud and independent Maya became peons, working for Spanish masters without hope of deliverance except in heaven. The attitude of the conquistadors toward the indigenous peoples is graphically depicted in the reliefs on the façade of the Montejo mansion in Mérida: In one scene, armor-clad conquistadors are shown with their feet upon the heads of two brutish savages, their faces twisted in and showing no trace of intelligent life.

Friar Diego de Landa The Maya recorded information about their history, customs and ceremonies in beautiful painted picture books made of beaten-bark paper coated with fine lime. These codices, as they are known, must have numbered in the hundreds when the conquistadors and missionary friars first arrived in the Mayan lands. But because the ancient rites of the Maya were seen as a threat to the adoption and retention of Christianity, the priceless books were set aflame upon the orders of the Franciscans. Only a handful of painted books survive, but these provide much insight into ancient Mayan life.

Among those Franciscans directly responsible for the burning of the Mayan books was Friar Diego de Landa, who, in July of 1562 at Maní (near present-day Ticul in Yucatán), ordered the destruction of 27 'hieroglyphic rolls' and 5000 idols. Landa went on to become bishop of Mérida from 1573 until his death in 1579.

Ironically, it was Landa, the great destroyer of Mayan cultural records, who wrote the most important book on Mayan customs and practices, the source for very much of what we know about the Maya. Landa's book, *Relación de las Cosas de Yucatán*, was

written about 1565. It covers virtually every aspect of Mayan life as it was in the 1560s, from the climate, Mayan houses, food and drink, wedding and funeral customs to the calendar and the counting system.

Landa's book is available in English as *Yucatán Before and After the Conquest*. You can buy it at a number of bookstores as well as shops at archaeological sites in the Yucatán.

Independence Period

During the colonial period, society in Spain's New World colonies was rigidly and precisely stratified, with Spanish natives, known as *peninsulares* or, derisively, *gachupines*, at the very top. Next on the ladder were the *criollos* (creoles), people born in the New World of Spanish stock. Below them were the *ladinos* or *mestizos*, people of mixed Spanish and Indian blood; and at the bottom were the Indians and blacks of pure race. Only the native Spaniards had real power, a fact deeply resented by the criollos.

The harshness of Spanish rule resulted in frequent revolts; however, none of them were successful for very long. Mexico's Miguel Hidalgo y Costilla gave the Grito de Dolores, or the 'Cry (of Independence) at Dolores,' at his church near Guanajuato in 1810, inciting his parishioners to revolt. With his lieutenant, a mestizo priest named José María Morelos, he brought large areas of central Mexico under his control. But this rebellion, like earlier ones, failed: The power of Spain was too great.

Napoleon's conquests in Europe changed all that, destabilizing the Spanish empire to its very foundations. When the French emperor deposed Spain's King Ferdinand VII and put his brother Joseph Bonaparte on the throne of Spain (1808), criollos in many New World colonies took the opportunity to rise in revolt. By 1821 both Mexico and Guatemala had proclaimed their independence. As with the American Revolution of 1776, the Latin American movements were conservative in nature, preserving control of politics, the economy and the military for the upper classes of European blood but native birth.

Independent Mexico urged the peoples of Yucatán, Chiapas and Central America to join it in the formation of one large new state. At first Yucatán and Chiapas refused and Guatemala accepted, but all later changed their minds. Yucatán and Chiapas joined the Mexican union, while Guatemala led the formation of the United Provinces of Central America (July 1, 1823), with El Salvador, Nicaragua, Honduras and Costa Rica. The latter union, torn by civil strife from the beginning, lasted only until 1840 before breaking up into its constituent states.

Though independence brought new prosperity to the criollos, it worsened the lot of the Maya. The end of Spanish rule meant that the Crown's few liberal safeguards, which had afforded the Indians minimal protection from the most extreme forms of exploitation, were abandoned. Mayan claims to ancestral lands were largely ignored and huge plantations were created for the cultivation of tobacco, sugarcane and henequen (agave rope fiber). The Maya, though legally free, were enslaved by debt peonage to the great landowners.

War of the Castes

Not long after independence from Spain, the Yucatecan ruling classes were again dreaming of independence – this time from Mexico, and perhaps of union with the USA. With these goals in mind, and in anticipation of an invasion from Mexico, the *hacendados* (landholders) made the mistake of arming and training their Mayan peons as local militias. Trained to use European weaponry, the common Maya envisioned a release from their own misery and boldly rebelled against their Yucatecan masters.

The War of the Castes of 1847 began in Valladolid, a city known for its particularly strict and oppressive laws. In Valladolid, the Maya were forbidden to enjoy the main plaza or the prominent streets, forced to keep to the back streets and the outskirts. The Mayan rebels quickly gained control of the city in an orgy of killing, looting and vengeance. Supplied with arms and ammunition by the British through Belize, they spread relentlessly across the Yucatán.

In little more than a year, the Mayan revolutionaries had driven their oppressors from every part of Yucatán except Mérida and the walled city of Campeche. Seeing the whites' cause as hopeless, Yucatán's governor was about to abandon Mérida when the rebels saw the annual appearance of the winged ant. In Mayan mythology, corn (the staff of life) must be planted at the first sighting of the winged ant. If the sowing is delayed, Chac, the rain god, will be affronted and respond with a drought. Thus, the rebels abandoned the attack and went home to plant the corn. This gave the whites and mestizos time to regroup and receive aid from their erstwhile adversary, the government in Mexico City.

The Talking Cross

The counterrevolution against the Maya was without quarter and vicious in the extreme. Between 1848 and 1855 the Indian population of Yucatán was halved. Some Mayan combatants sought refuge in the jungles of southern Quintana Roo. There, they were inspired to continue fighting by a religious leader working with a ventriloquist, who, in 1850 at Chan Santa Cruz, made a sacred cross 'talk' (the cross was an important Mayan religious symbol long before the coming of Christianity). The talking cross convinced the Maya that their gods had made them invincible, and they continued to fight until 1866.

The governments in Mexico City and Mérida largely ignored the Mayan rebels of Chan Santa Cruz until the beginning of the 20th century, when Mexican troops with modern arms subdued the region. The shrine of the talking cross at Chan Santa Cruz was destroyed, and the town was renamed Felipe Carrillo Puerto, in honor of a progressive Yucatecan governor, but the local Maya were allowed a good deal of autonomy. The region was declared a Mexican 'territory' only in 1936 and didn't become a state until 1974. Today, if you visit Felipe Carrillo Puerto, you can visit the restored shrine of the talking cross above a dried-up cenote in what is now a city park, though the local Maya are very protective of it.

High-Fiber Economy

From the 1880s until the end of WWII, the Yucatán was the world's top producer of rope and twine made from raw henequen, an agave also known as sisal that continues to be cultivated in parts of Mexico today. Over a period of 60 years, vast plantations of the gray-stalked plant with putrid-smelling flowers could be found scattered about Yucatán state and the northern region of Campeche state. (For a detailed description of this spiky plant and its cultivation, see the boxed text, 'Yucatán's Past Tied to Natural Rope,' in the Yucatán chapter.)

The fiber industry brought great wealth to many of Yucatán's cities, particularly Mérida, where the grand homes of wealthy plantation owners lined many of the grid-patterned streets of the White City, as the bustling colonial town has come to be known. The rope business provided thousands upon thousands of jobs, placed southeastern Mexico on the international map and created tremendous fortunes for more than a few individuals. For many years, the rope and twine business was the biggest industry on Mexico's eastern peninsula (Baja California being the country's western peninsula).

Foreign competition and synthetics, however, eventually destroyed the global market for Yucatecan rope and twine. Today, the northern half of the peninsula is littered with the dilapidated hulks of once-magnificent and typically colonnaded *casas de máquinas* (machine houses) where the henequen was processed. The sisal barons were often more concerned with the design of their factories than that of their living quarters, and the few old henequen factories that have been restored and made into hotels are usually as splendid as they are historic.

After the henequen boom went bust, most of the peninsula's residents returned to eking out a subsistence by harvesting corn on small, rain-dependent plots, just like many of their ancestors had done before them. And the former fields once studded with millions of sisal plants? Most are overgrown with weeds, though a few are now covered with citrus trees. Limes are

somewhat popular among growers, who sell the fruit to soft-drink companies, but no crops are doing particularly well due to the peninsula's nutrient-thin soil and unreliable water supply.

The Rich Get Richer

Of course, with Yucatán thriving as a tourist destination, there *are* many happy people on the peninsula. The vast majority are people who speak English and Spanish and have money to invest in a tourism-related project. Unfortunately, very few of the beneficiaries are Mayan.

What's more, even access to Yucatán's loveliest natural sites are becoming off-limits to Mayans in particular and Mexicans in general. The government has sold off every kilometer of public beach along the Caribbean coast to either a developer or a theme-park operator. Although the beaches are open to everyone, the darker skinned you are the less likely you are able to pass through a hotel lobby to get to the beach.

The peninsula's *cenotes* (freshwater pools) that once sustained Mayan life are increasingly being privatized and promoted as exotic swimming holes; the cost to take a refreshing dip in one exceeds the average daily wage in Mexico. The entry fee at every major restored Mayan ruin, as well as the price of admission to most of the Yucatán's theme parks, exceeds the average weekly wage of a Mexican.

Despite the Yucatán's relatively sudden popularity with international tourists, with a full 20% of Mexico's tourist revenue coming from Cancún alone, life for the average Yucatecan isn't getting any easier. And as the price of land and services continue to increase out of proportion with the incomes of the region's native population, it's probable that the Maya will be forced to leave the world that they and their ancestors have inhabited for more than two millennia.

Yucatán Today

The Yucatán Peninsula at the start of the third millennium after Christ is in a state of flux. Beginning with the development of Cancún during the late 1960s, all three states

dividing up the vast limestone landmass – Quintana Roo, Campeche and Yucatán – have been undergoing a radical transformation, from an agriculture-based economy to one that's driven by foreign visitors clamoring for a tan and a little fun in the sun.

For the tourist, the peninsula has never offered so many amenities nor so many natural and unnatural attractions and ease with which to reach them. For a variety of reasons, Yucatán is a world-class destination. Unfortunately, across the peninsula, from Campeche on the Gulf of Mexico to Cancún on the Caribbean coast, the countryside is emptying of indigenous peoples as the hardship of farming in a land with poor soil and few rivers appears increasingly bleak beside the specious 'easy money' of tourism. Throughout the Yucatán, and especially along the Caribbean coast, Yucatecans are heading to cities with the dream of making lots of *dinero* working in hotels, restaurants and bars.

Since the early 1970s, roughly one in four of the region's Maya have left their villages for Cancún to find work. Many others have sought employment in Cozumel, Playa del Carmen and other tourist haunts – most speaking only Yucatec when they arrive. Their weak or nonexistent grasp of Spanish, the sheer number of people seeking work and discrimination on the part of Mexican managers and employers result in relatively few Maya obtaining jobs viewed as 'good' by anyone's standards. Young Mayan women seeking work in tourist-popular Mérida actually stand a much better chance of hiring on as a piece-worker at one of the new foreign-owned apparel plants than at any tourism-related business.

For at least a few more years, construction will remain the Yucatán's latest boom, but some day this boom will go bust. Practically the entire Caribbean coast of Mexico is being developed, with dozens of resorts going up at water's edge simultaneously and many more appearing near restored ruins. The descendants of the people who built the great Mayan pyramids are now building the seaside resorts. But usually the workers live in camps far from tourists' view, 50 men or

so per unventilated tar-paper shack. Their US$5-a-day wages are bad even by Mexican standards.

GEOGRAPHY

The Yucatán Peninsula is situated in extreme southeastern Mexico, and its shape is not unlike that of an upturned big toe. Approximately a third of the peninsula is flanked by the Gulf of Mexico, another third meets the western edge of the Caribbean Sea and the remaining third is connected to the rest of the North American continent. Landwise, the Yucatán borders the Mexican state of Tabasco, a broad swatch of northern Guatemala and the northern tip of Belize.

There's very little about the Yucatán to excite a topographer. Nearly the entire peninsula is one vast, flat limestone shelf rising only 12m above sea level for many kilometers inland (the peninsula's average elevation is a mere 30m).

The limestone shelf extends outward and below sea level from the shoreline for several kilometers. If you reach the Yucatán during daylight hours via the Cancún airport, you should have no trouble seeing the barrier reef that marks the limit of the shelf.

On the landward side of the reef, the water is shallow (usually no more than 5 to 10m deep). On the seaward side of the reef, the water plunges to a depth of several thousand meters only 10km out.

The underwater shelf makes Yucatán's coastline wonderful for aquatic sports, keeping the waters warm and the marine life abundant, but it makes life difficult for traders: At Progreso, north of Mérida, the *muelle* (wharf) must extend 6.5km from dry land across the shallow water to reach water deep enough to receive ocean-going vessels.

The only anomaly in the flat, mountainless terrain of the Yucatán Peninsula are the low rolling hills in the Puuc region of Yucatán state, near Uxmal, which can attain heights of several hundred meters. ('Puuc,' incidentally, is Mayan for 'hill.') And there are hills – quite a few in fact – in the heavily forested southern section of the peninsula along the Mexico-Guatemala border.

A Cenote Is Born

Most of the Yucatán Peninsula rests on limestone, a rock formed chiefly by the accumulation of organic remains (such as shells and coral) and consisting mainly of calcium carbonate. The combination of rainwater and carbon dioxide dissolves limestone and makes fissures in the underground rock. Eventually, caverns appear at the level of the water table, with erosion continuing until a well-like hole appears in the ground, at the bottom of which is fresh, potable water. Over time the vertical walls erode away, and the result is a large freshwater pool called a cenote.

GEOLOGY

Until about 200 million years ago, the Earth's surface consisted of a single ocean and one great landmass. Then the landmass began to break apart under the strain of molten rock welling up from deep within the Earth. The planet's crust separated into thick plates that have been moving apart and colliding at a snail's pace ever since.

Beginning about 65 million years ago, the Caribbean plate separated from the Pacific plate, forcing the former plate downward and under the much larger plate. During this time, the Caribbean Sea filled a depression created by plate movement, and the Yucatán Peninsula, which had been submerged, rose out of the ocean. Today, the Caribbean plate is moving west and disappearing beneath both the North and South American plates at a rate of about 2cm each year.

Because the Yucatán rose from the ocean, its soil consists mostly of limestone – a rock that is formed chiefly by the accumulation of organic remains such as shells and coral. Because limestone dissolves when exposed to water and carbon dioxide, the Yucatán has few lakes and exposed rivers, although it has many underground rivers.

People living on the peninsula have traditionally drawn their fresh water from cenotes – limestone caverns with collapsed roofs that serve as natural cisterns. South of the Puuc region, in the Chenes region, there

are few cenotes, and the inhabitants there traditionally have resorted to drawing water from limestone pools more than 100m below ground. These deep wells *(chenes)* give the region its name.

CLIMATE

It is always hot in the Yucatán during the day, with outdoor temperatures often topping 40°C (100°F) at the height of the day's heat. At night it cools a little bit, but because the breeze drops then, the humidity increases. From May to October, the rainy season makes the air sticky as well as hot. From October to May the air is generally dry and parching. Violent but brief storms called *nortes* can roll in on any afternoon, their black clouds, high winds and torrents of rain typically followed within an hour by bright sun and utterly blue sky.

Hurricanes

The Yucatán's four-month-long hurricane season can be described in a rhyme: 'June – too soon; July – stand by; August – a must; September – remember.' Well, hurricanes aren't really a 'must' in August (this is a rhyme, for goodness sake, not scripture), but when they strike they are usually deadly. Hurricane Mitch of 1998, which devastated

Honduras and Nicaragua before winding its way up to the Yucatán Peninsula, killed more than 10,000 people.

If a hurricane is forecast when you're in the Yucatán, you'd be wise to leave the peninsula well before it arrives. At the very least go inland – far from the dangerous sea swell that usually accompanies hurricanes. Under no circumstances do you want to be within a kilometer of the beach due to the very real risk of being swept out to sea.

If you find yourself caught in a hurricane, try to keep your wits about you. This is not the time to get drunk and show your friends how 'brave' you are by running to the end of the pier or otherwise acting stupid. Avoid the urge to stand near windows, as hurricanes have a habit of shattering them and spraying glass fragments and other debris like bombs.

If you decide to ride out the storm, stock up on enough items to meet your needs for at least a week. These items should include packaged food, bottled water, flashlights and plenty of batteries. Remember: After a hurricane it could be weeks before tap water, electricity, phone service, natural gas and gasoline are available, and food can be in extremely short supply as well. Following Hurricane Mitch, many parts of Central America were without electricity for months.

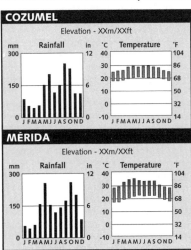

High-Velocity Winds

Hurricanes that strike the Yucatán Peninsula originate off the coast of Africa, forming as winds rush toward a low-pressure area and swirl around it due to the rotational forces of the Earth's spin. The storms move counter-clockwise across the Atlantic, fed by warm winds and moisture, building up force in their 3000-km run toward Central and North America.

A hurricane builds in stages, the first of which is called a tropical disturbance. The next stage is a tropical depression. When winds exceed 64km/h, the weather system is up-graded to a tropical storm and is usually ac-companied by heavy rains. The system is called a hurricane if wind speed exceeds 120km/h and intensifies around a low-pressure center, the so-called 'eye of the storm.'

Hurricane systems can range from 80km in diameter to devastating giants more than 1600km across. Their energy is prodigious – far more than the mightiest thermonuclear explosions ever unleashed on Earth. The area affected by winds of great destructive force may exceed 240km in diameter. Gale-force winds can prevail over an area twice as great.

The strength of a hurricane is rated from one to five. The mildest, a Category 1 hurricane, has winds of at least 120km/h. The strongest and rarest hurricane, the Category 5 monster, packs winds that exceed 250km/h; Hurricane Mitch, which killed more than 10,000 people in Central America and southeastern Mexico in late 1998, was a rare Category 5 hurricane. Hurricanes travel at varying speeds, from as little as 10km/h to more than 50km/h.

For current tropical-storm information, go to *The Miami Herald* website (www.herald.com) and scan the menu for hurricane and storm information. Another excellent source is the website main-tained by the US National Oceanic and Atmospheric Administration (www.esdim.noaa.gov/weather_page.html).

ECOLOGY & ENVIRONMENT

The Yucatán is home to some truly spectac-ular wildlife, both on land and in the shim-mering sea that brushes the eastern shore of the peninsula. Sadly, very little is being done to protect it.

Yes, there are private ecological groups on the peninsula such as Greenpeace and Friends of Sian Ka'an, but they are having minimal impact. Yes, the Mexican govern-ment has created national parks and the United Nations has funded two huge re-serves, but you need only spend a day in any

of them to witness illegal fishing, hunting or logging. If you speak about wildlife with people living on the edges of Yucatán's sup-posedly protected areas, you'll soon learn that most of it has been poached and what remains is being hunted down.

One of the great tragedies occurring all along the Caribbean coast of Mexico is the destruction of the reef. Laws to protect the coast and the reef have been in place since 1994, but hotels have been built and are being built up and down the coast in violation of those laws. The reason: It takes

the government *years* to issue building permits, and developers aren't willing to wait. Time and again they build and take their chances that some day they might have to pay a fine.

The overbuilding not only kills marine life, such as sea turtles that need protected beaches to nest, but the vast majority of the hotels have inadequate facilities to handle all the waste their guests produce. The overbuilding is also uprooting the coastal mangroves on which the reef depends for nutrients. So not only is the reef receiving fewer nutrients, but it's being subjected to tons upon tons of human waste. Most environmentalists give the reef only another 10 years or so to live.

FLORA & FAUNA
Plants
The plants found on the peninsula fall into four main categories: aquatic and subaquatic vegetation, and humid and subhumid forests. In other words, the Yucatán has mangroves, it's got sea plants, and it's got tropical forests – specifically tropical semievergreen medium forests, tropical subdeciduous medium forests, and tropical deciduous low and medium forests.

All that will mean something to you if you're a botanist. If you're not, what it means is that you can expect to see a wide variety of flora on the peninsula, ranging from swampy-looking mangrove forest along some stretches of the coast to a fairly dense forest characterized by mostly lower trees that shed their leaves in the winter, to a jungle-like forest with tall trees and climbing vegetation and more than a few air plants (but without the soggy underbrush and multiple canopies you'd find farther south).

In the Yucatán you can expect to see a wide variety of palms, scores of mango and avocado trees, and lots of annuals and perennials, such as the red-orange-flowering flamboyant tree and the purple-flowering jacaranda. There are 75 known species of orchid in the taller trees found on the southern half of the peninsula; for the really spectacular blooms, the avid orchid hunter will need to head into the highlands of Chiapas,

where the exotic plants thrive at an elevation of about 1000m.

Birds
What the Yucatán lacks in plant life, relative to the spectacular jungle foliage found in Chiapas and in many parts of Central America, it more than makes up for in bird life. The peninsula is home to many regional endemics (such as birds found only on Cozumel, for example), a startling variety of waterbirds and an impressive list of tropical species.

In her 1992 *Check-list of the Birds of the Yucatán Peninsula*, Barbara MacKinnon states that there are some 509 known species of bird on the peninsula and nearby islands.

The Mayan Pheasant

The so-called 'pheasant' of Mayan lore is actually a turkey – an ocellated turkey, to be specific – a beautiful bird that resembles a peacock.

Originally, turkeys were native to northeast USA and Yucatán, not to Turkey at all. How the birds came to be known as *turkeys* instead of *yucatáns* or *americans* makes for interesting reading.

The large birds were originally shipped from the US and Yucatán to the West Indies, where some were placed on English merchant ships that had come from Turkey and were bound for English galleons in what historians have dubbed the Triangle Trade. Although their last port of call was an island in the West Indies (usually Jamaica or Hispaniola), in England the galleons were commonly referred to as 'Turkey boats,' and the savory avifauna were known as Turkey-birds and, later, turkeys.

Most of the birds that weren't shipped to England were placed on galleons bound for Turkey. There, the feathery creatures were not known as Turkey-birds or turkeys, but rather they were called *hindis* (Indians), because – from a Turk's perspective – the birds came from the Indies (albeit, the *West* Indies, not India).

This figure represents 48% of the total number of bird species that have been recorded in all of Mexico. What's more, MacKinnon notes that most of the 509 species were recorded in areas that have been set aside for conservation.

Among some of the species birders on the peninsula would want to squint for are the Yucatan Woodpecker, the White-browed Wren and the Black-throated Blue Warbler. In addition to MacKinnon's field checklist, which can often be found in Cancún bookstores, serious birders will want to purchase a copy of Steve NG Howell's *A Bird-Finding Guide to Mexico* (1999, Cornell University Press), in which he devotes 30 info- and map-packed pages on 10 of the best birding sites in the Yucatán.

Land Animals

Mexican tourism offices go to great lengths to advertise the Yucatán's jaguars; the mug of a majestic jaguar is on every brochure the government publishes for the region. But speak with locals who live in the forests throughout the peninsula and you soon come to realize that if there are any wild jaguars left in the Yucatán, they're prowling far from human view in the dense forest along the Guatemalan border. Despite the Maya's traditional fascination with the New World's largest cat, poaching has all but wiped them out in southeastern Mexico.

The puma, ocelot, margay and the peninsula's other native wildcat, the jaguarundi, are also endangered, but sightings of pumas in the southern portion of the peninsula aren't all that unusual (the big cats find dogs rather tasty), and the author actually stood over a jaguarundi in 1999 not 2km from the Cancún airport; the weasel-resembling cat with a dark gray coat had been struck by a vehicle and landed at road's edge, in plain view of tourists heading from the airport into town. Margays and ocelots also can be seen occasionally.

Crocodiles still ply the mangroves near the towns of Río Lagartos and Celestún (home to two of Mexico's largest flamingo colonies) in Yucatán state, but their numbers are a fraction of what they were just 30 years ago. There are still plenty of the beady-eyed amphibious reptiles at the Reserva de la Biósfera Sian Ka'an (Sian Ka'an Biosphere Reserve), and there's no shortage of them in pens and on display at a touristy croc farm just south of Cancún.

Other regional natives include tapirs and peccaries, which live in southern Yucatán, as well as armor-plated armadillos. Somehow missing from the government's tourist brochures is the Western diamondback rattlesnake, two of which the author has seen near the Mayan ruins at Dzibilchaltún and Uxmal. Unless you're looking for them, you're only likely to see them as roadkill. Whatever you do, don't touch one – not even a dead rattlesnake. Experts say that at least one in five rattlesnake bites are inflicted by dead rattlesnakes; biting, they say, is a reflex action that takes a while to shut down in rattlesnakes.

Sea Creatures

The Great Maya Barrier Reef, which runs parallel to the Quintana Roo coast, from Cancún to beyond Tulum, is home to some of the finest snorkeling and diving in the world. It also protects the gorgeous white-sand coast of Quintana Roo from the fierce storms that frequent the Yucatán; this coastline is variously called the Maya Coast and the Riviera Maya.

What makes the snorkeling so incredible is the tremendous variety of colorful marine life that exists here. At times the fish look lit up. The coney grouper, for example, is impossible to miss in its bright-yellow suit (it varies in color from reddish brown to sun yellow). The redband parrotfish is easy to recognize by the striking red circle around the eye and the red band that runs from the eye to the gills. As their name suggests, butterflyfish are brilliantly colored (there are six species in the area), and the yellow stingray is covered with attractive spots that closely resemble the rosettes of a golden jaguar.

Providing an extraordinary backdrop to the colorful stars of the sea is a vast array of corals, which come in two varieties: hard corals, such as the great star coral, the boulder coral and numerous brain corals;

and soft corals, such as sea fans and sea plumes, which are particularly delicate and sway with the current. Successive generations of coral form a skin of living organisms over the limestone reef.

Complementing the experience is a water temperature that seldom dips below 27°C (77°F) and visibility that's often simply amazing. Because this coast contains not a single exposed river (many underground rivers do present themselves as they near the sea, but they carry very little soil), there's practically no sediment to muck up the water. Visibility is compromised only during or after a storm, and for several weeks around April/May and September/October, when reef animals and plants release zillions of eggs and droplets of sperm.

Endangered Species

Pollution, poaching, illegal traffic of rare species and the filling in of coastal areas for yet another resort are taking an enormous toll on Yucatán's wildlife. However, the biggest killer of all is deforestation. Since 1960, more than 5 million hectares of forest have been felled in the Yucatán. The lives of all the plants and animals that depend on the forest have also passed to another world. Species on the peninsula that are threatened with extinction include five species of cat, four species of sea turtle, the manatee, the tapir and hundreds of species of bird, in-

The endangered harpy eagle

cluding the harpy eagle, the red flamingo and the jabiru stork.

Parks & Reserves

There are many national parks on the peninsula, some scarcely larger than the ancient Mayan cities they contain (Parque Nacional Tulum is a good example of this), while others (such as those surrounding Río Lagartos and Celestún) spread across thousands of hectares. The Parque Nacional Río Lagartos and Parque Natural del Flamenco Mexicano de Celestún are famous throughout Mexico for the red flamingo nesting grounds located within them.

Much more impressive than the national parks are the two colossal biosphere reserves found in the Yucatán. Both were created by UNESCO (United Nations Educational, Scientific and Cultural Organization). The Reserva de la Biósfera Calakmul (Calakmul Biosphere Reserve), covering more than 7230 sq km in Campeche, Quintana Roo and Chiapas, as well as parts of Belize and Guatemala, is the largest of Mexico's 20 such reserves. It is home to more than 300 species of birds and can sustain jaguars, pumas and tapirs.

The Reserva de la Biósfera Sian Ka'an, located on the Costa Maya 150km south of Cancún, covers 6000 sq km, including 100 sq km of the Great Maya Barrier Reef. Its life forms range from more than 70 species of coral to 350 species of bird (by comparison, there are only 400 species of bird in all of Europe). Crocodiles, pumas and jaguars are said to make Sian Ka'an their home.

GOVERNMENT & POLITICS
National

In theory, the United Mexican States (Estados Unidos Mexicanos) is a multiparty democracy with an elected president, a bicameral legislature and an independent judiciary. In practice, the Partido Revolucionario Institucional (PRI, Institutional Revolutionary Party) has controlled all aspects of political life and society, including the government, the labor movement, the press and most of the small 'opposition' parties, since its foundation in the 1930s.

A Feminist First in Macho Mexico

In a sign of the times, in 1999 Amalia García became the first woman to head a major Mexican political party when the main leftist opposition force, the Partido de la Revolución Democrática (PRD), elected the federal senator as its president.

The July 1999 vote also marked the first time that Mexicans living in the US could play a part in domestic politics, with PRD members in US cities allowed to cast ballots. Outside of Mexico, more Mexicans reside in the US than anywhere else.

Widely condemned for corruption, mishandling the economy, and election fraud, the PRI was on the defensive during the mid-1990s but still in control. President Ernesto Zedillo was pressured to make the congressional elections of 1997 fairer than any in Mexican history. The result was a revolution in Mexican politics. Instead of its normal absolute majority, the PRI claimed less than 40% of the vote. The right-of-center Partido de Acción Nacional (PAN, National Action Party) garnered 27%, the Partido de la Revolución Democrática (PRD, Democratic Revolution Party) 26%, with another 10% going to splinter parties. The PRI lost 12 seats in the Senate and was forced to share power in the Chamber of Deputies, the lower house of Congress, which determines the country's budget.

The most symbolic opposition gains were in Mexico City. In earlier years, the mayor of the capital had been appointed by the president, but in the first elections ever for the post, the mayoralty was won by the PRD's standard-bearer, Cuauhtémoc Cárdenas, son of the late president Lázaro Cárdenas.

Lázaro Cárdenas, a young army general, was elected president of Mexico in 1934. He embarked on a vigorous, far-reaching program of reforms, which included giving Mexico's peasants greater rights in the land they cultivated and greatly reducing the power and influence of foreign corporations in Mexico's economy – especially in the petroleum industry. He also shaped the PRI to be the organ of control over all of Mexican society.

His son, Cuauhtémoc, named for the last Aztec emperor, was raised in the PRI and advanced to leadership positions easily. Uncomfortable with the authoritarian nature of the party, he attempted reforms from within, but finally broke with the PRI and began an opposition political movement during the 1980s.

In 1988, Cuauhtémoc Cárdenas challenged the PRI's handpicked presidential candidate, Carlos Salinas de Gortari, for the nation's highest office, but 'lost' when the PRI-controlled election computers mysteriously broke down during vote counting. With his victory in the Mexico City mayoralty race, Cárdenas is well positioned to run for the highest office when presidential elections are held in July 2000.

Mexico's main political parties are expected to spend US$1.06 billion in the 2000 general elections, more than any other country in the world. That amount of money, destined for campaign advertising and vote-winning gimmicks, is ridiculously high for a country where a third of the population lives below the poverty line, earning just

Ernesto Zedillo

US$2 a day. But such are the priorities in Mexican politics.

Cárdenas and his party, the PRD, have revived many of Lázaro Cárdenas' political themes, including empowerment of workers and a hard line toward foreign economic interests with influence in Mexico. But without the authoritarian powers of past presidents – including his revered father – Cuauhtémoc Cárdenas will have to pursue his goals through the messy, compromise-clouded organs of democracy.

Yucatán

'Traffickers Move Into Yucatán Peninsula: Mexican tourist paradise becoming "cocaine coast" as smugglers, aided by extensive corruption, expand their reach, US officials say.'

That headline, which appeared on the front page of the *Los Angeles Times* in August 1998, tells everyone familiar with Mexican politics and the power of Colombian druglords in Latin America all they need to know about the political scene on the peninsula today. Most notorious of the peninsula's three states is Quintana Roo, which 'has become a narco-state,' a US official told the *Times*. 'It's corrupt from the traffic cop to the governor.'

The governor at the time, Mario Villanueva, vehemently denied such allegations, calling them politically motivated slander. Several months later, Villanueva went into hiding. Mexico's justice ministry announced that an arrest warrant had been issued for him on charges of being involved in organized crime and drug trafficking, and Villanueva didn't want his day in court. The ex-governor was still in hiding when this was written.

ECONOMY

Tourism is the top industry in the states of Quintana Roo and Yucatán and is gaining steam in Campeche, where oil production and fishing remain the main revenue generators. The annual foreign visitor rate continues to climb across the peninsula at a steady, healthy rate of 3% each year.

Much more surprising than the rising popularity of Yucatán is the increase in the number of *maquiladoras* that have opened their doors on the peninsula. Maquiladoras are factories where foreign companies are allowed to import raw materials duty-free for processing or assembly by inexpensive Mexican labor, then re-export the finished products. Maquiladoras employ some 1 million Mexicans. Once seemingly restricted to border towns, foreign-owned and -operated factories are popping up right and left in southeastern Mexico. Despite the poor pay they offer, many Mayans have taken the attitude that a poor-paying job is better than no job.

For example, in the town of Motúl, 44km northeast of Mérida, there are now two clothing maquiladoras, up from none five years ago. Their employees earn only the minimum wage of US$35 a week, but before the factories arrived many of the town's residents were earning next to nothing – only what they could get as street vendors or doing odd jobs. Many had been sisal workers, and when the rope industry went slack, their meager but steady incomes dried up.

Today, many of the people of Motúl quietly admit that the work is hard and the pay disappointing, but most take the long view: There's simply little other work for them in Motúl, and it's good to have some pesos in the pocket.

Liz Claiborne slacks, Lee jeans and Maidenform bras are among a wide array of items being produced in Yucatán in late 1999.

POPULATION & PEOPLE

For more than a millennium, the Maya of Yucatán have intermarried with neighboring and/or invading peoples, especially those of central Mexico, with whom they had diplomatic and commercial relations. The descendants of Mayan and Spanish stock are called *mestizos*.

Most of Mexico's population is mestizo, but the Yucatán Peninsula has an especially high proportion of pure-blooded Maya. In many areas of Yucatán, Mayan languages prevail over Spanish, or Spanish may not be spoken at all. In remote jungle villages, some modern cultural practices descend almost directly from those of ancient Mayan civilization.

Thanks to the continuation of their unique cultural identity, the Maya of Yucatán are proud without being arrogant, confident without the machismo seen so frequently elsewhere in Mexico, and kind without being servile. And with the exception of those who have become jaded by the tourist hordes that descend on Cancún, Cozumel and other Yucatán cities, the Maya have a welcoming attitude toward foreign visitors.

People tend to go to where the jobs are, and today, as it's been for many years, the state of Yucatán provides the greatest employment opportunities of the three states on the peninsula. The state contains an estimated 1.4 million inhabitants, nearly half residing in the bustling capital of Mérida.

Quintana Roo has about 550,000 inhabitants, more than half in or around Ciudad Cancún. Another 115,000 or so people reside in Chetumal, the state's capital.

Though covering more than 51,000 sq km, Campeche is the peninsula's least progressive and least populated state, with 336,578 residents, just over half of whom live in the capital city of Campeche.

In all, there are approximately 3.2 million people living on the Yucatán Peninsula.

EDUCATION

The government boasts that more than 90% of Mexico's population can read and write, and perhaps that figure is accurate nationally. But on the Yucatán Peninsula, many primary- and secondary-school-age students fail to complete their education programs. Less than 20% of the children make it to high school, and less than 5% of Yucatecan youth go on to college. In a world that is becoming increasingly sophisticated and technologically driven, Mayan prospects in the global market appear increasingly limited to minimum-wage positions.

ARCHITECTURE & ARCHAEOLOGY

Mayan architecture is amazing for its achievements, but perhaps even more amazing because of what it did not achieve. Mayan architects never seem to have understood or to have used the true arch (a rounded arch

with a keystone), and they never thought to put wheels on boxes and use them as wagons to move the thousands of tons of construction materials needed in their tasks. They had no metal tools – they were technically in a Stone Age culture – yet they could build breathtaking temple complexes and align them so precisely that windows and doors were used as celestial observatories of great accuracy.

The arch used in most Mayan buildings is the corbeled vault (or corralled arch), which consists of large flat stones on either side set at an angle inward and topped by capstones. This arch served the purpose, but limited severely the amount of open space beneath. In effect, Mayan architects were limited to long, narrow vaulted rooms. True (Roman) arches and Gothic-style vaulting would have allowed them to build stone roofs above far larger halls.

Another important element they lacked was draught animals (horses, donkeys, mules, oxen). All the work had to be done by humans, on their feet, with their arms and with their backs, without wagons or even wheelbarrows.

The Celestial Plan

In Mayan architecture there was always a celestial plan. Temples were aligned in such a manner as to enhance celestial observation, whether of the sun, moon or certain stars, especially Venus. The alignment might not be apparent except at certain conjunctions of the celestial bodies (ie, at Venus Rising or at an eclipse), but the Maya knew each building was properly 'placed' and that this enhanced its sacred character.

Temples usually had other features that linked them to the stars. The doors and windows might be aligned in order to sight a celestial body at a certain exact point in its course on a certain day of a certain year. This is the case with the Governor's Palace at Uxmal, which is aligned in such a way that, from the main doorway, Venus would have been visible exactly on top of a small mound some 3.5km away, in the year 750 AD. At Chichén Itzá, the observatory building called El Caracol was aligned in order to sight Venus exactly in the year 1000 AD.

Furthermore, the main door to a temple might be decorated to resemble a huge mouth, signifying entry to Xibalba (the secret world or underworld). Other features might have significance in terms of the numbers of the Calendar Round, as at Chichén Itzá's El Castillo. This pyramid has 364 stairs to the top; with the top platform this makes 365, the number of days in the Mayan Vague Year. On the sides of the pyramid are 52 panels, signifying the 52-year cycle of the Calendar Round. The terraces on each side of each stairway total 18 (nine on either side), signifying the 18 'months' of the solar Vague Year. The alignment of El Castillo catches the sun and turns it into a sacred sky-serpent descending into the earth on the vernal equinox (March 21 or 22) and the autumnal equinox (September 21 or 22) each year. The serpent is formed perfectly only on that day, and descends during a short period of only 34 minutes.

Mayan temples were often built on top of smaller, older temples. In Mayan opinion, this doubling-up increased the temples' sacredness and preserved the alignment of each temple complex.

Mayan Architectural Styles

Mayan architecture's 1500-year history saw a fascinating progression of styles. The style of architecture changed not just with the times, but with the particular geographic area of Mesoamerica in which the architects worked. Not all of the styles can be seen in Yucatán.

Late Preclassic (300 BC to 250 AD) Late Preclassic architecture is perhaps best exhibited at Uaxactún, north of Tikal in Guatemala's Petén department. At Uaxactún, Pyramid E-VII-sub is a fine example of how the architects of what is known as the Chicanel culture designed their pyramid-temples in the time from around 100 BC to 250 AD. E-VII-sub is a square stepped-platform pyramid with central stairways on each of the four sides, each stairway flanked by large jaguar masks. The entire platform was covered in fine white stucco. The top platform is flat, and probably bore a temple

na made of wooden poles topped with palm thatch. This temple was well preserved because others had been built on top of it; these later structures were ruined by the ages, and were cleared away to reveal E-VII-sub. Chicanel-style temples similar to this one were built at Tikal and El Mirador in Guatemala and Lamanai in Belize.

By the end of the Late Preclassic period, simple temples such as E-VII-sub were being aligned and arranged around plazas, and all was prepared for the next phase of Mayan architecture.

Early Classic (250 to 600) The Esperanza culture typifies this phase. In Esperanza-style temples, the king was buried in a wooden chamber beneath the main staircase of the temple; successive kings were buried in similar places in the pyramids built on top of the first one. Among the largest Early Classic Esperanza sites is Kaminaljuyú in Guatemala City; unfortunately, most of the site was destroyed by construction crews or covered by their buildings, and urban sprawl engulfed the site before archaeologists could complete their work.

Of the surviving Early Classic pyramids, perhaps the best example is the step-pyramid at Acanceh, about 30km southeast of Mérida.

Late Classic (600 to 900) The most important Classic sites flourished during the latter part of the period, the so-called Late Classic. By this time the Mayan temple-pyramid had a masonry building on top, replacing the na of wood poles and thatch. Numbers of pyramids were built close together, sometimes forming contiguous or even continuous structures. Near them, different structures, now called palaces, were built. These palaces sat on lower platforms and held many more rooms, perhaps a dozen or more.

In addition to pyramids and palaces, Classic sites have carved stelae and round 'altar-stones' set in the plaza in front of the pyramids. Another feature of the Classic and later periods is the ball court, with sloping playing surfaces of stone covered in stucco.

Among the purest of the Classic sites is Copán in Honduras.

Of all the Classic sites, however, Tikal is the grandest so far uncovered and restored. Here the pyramids reached their most impressive heights, and were topped by superstructures (called roofcombs by archaeologists) that made them even taller. As in earlier times, these monumental structures were used as the burial places of kings.

If Tikal is the most impressive Classic Mayan city, Palenque, in Chiapas, is certainly the most beautiful. Mansard roofs and large relief murals characterize the great palace, with its unique watchtower and the harmonious Temple of the Inscriptions. Palenque exhibits the perfection of the elements of the Classic Mayan architectural style. The great stairways, the small sanctuaries on top of pyramids, and the lofty roofcombs were all brought to their finest proportions here. The tomb of King Pacal in the Temple of the Inscriptions, reached by a buried staircase, is unique in its Egyptian-like qualities: a secret chamber accessible without dismantling the pyramid, and a great carved slab covering the sarcophagus.

Puuc, Chenes & Río Bec Among the most distinctive of the Late Classic Mayan architectural styles are those that flourished in the western and southern regions of the Yucatán Peninsula. These styles valued exuberant display and architectural bravado more than they did proportion and harmony.

The Puuc style, named for the low Puuc Hills near Uxmal, used facings of thin limestone 'tiles' to cover the rough stone walls of buildings. The tiles were worked into geometric designs and stylized figures of monsters and serpents. Minoan-style columns and rows of engaged columns (half-round cylinders) were also a prominent feature of the style, and were used to good effect on façades of buildings at Uxmal and at the Ruta Puuc (Puuc Route) sites of Kabah, Sayil, Xlapak and Labná. Puuc architects were crazy about Chac, the rain god, and stuck his grotesque face on every temple, many times. At Kabah, the façade of the Codz Poop temple is completely covered in Chac masks.

The Chenes style, prevalent in areas to the south of the Puuc Hills in Campeche, is very similar to the Puuc style, but Chenes architects seem to have enjoyed putting huge masks as well as smaller ones on their façades.

The Río Bec style, epitomized in the richly decorated temples at the Río Bec archaeological site on the highway between Escárcega and Chetumal, used lavish decoration as in the Puuc and Chenes styles, but added huge towers to the corners of its low buildings, just for show. Río Bec buildings look like a combination of the Governor's Palace of Uxmal and Temple I at Tikal.

Early Postclassic (900 to 1200) The collapse of Classic Mayan civilization created a power vacuum that was filled by the invasion of the Toltecs from central Mexico. The Toltecs brought with them their own architectural ideas, and in the process of conquest these ideas were assimilated and merged with those of the Puuc style.

The foremost example of what might be called the Toltec-Maya style is Chichén Itzá. Elements of Puuc style – the large masks and decorative friezes – coexist with Toltec Atlantean warriors and *chac-mools*, the odd reclining statues that are purely Toltec and have nothing to do with Mayan art. Platform pyramids with very broad bases and spacious top platforms, such as the Temple of the Warriors, look as though they might have been imported from the ancient Toltec capital of Tula, or by way of Teotihuacán, with its broad-based pyramids of the sun and moon. Because Quetzalcóatl (Kukulcán in Mayan) was so important to the Toltecs, feathered serpents are used quite extensively as architectural decoration.

Late Postclassic (1200 to 1524) After the Toltecs came the Itzaes, who established their capital at Mayapán, south of Mérida, and ruled a confederation of Yucatecan states. After the golden age of Tikal and Palenque, even after the martial architecture of Chichén Itzá, the architecture of Mayapán is a disappointment. The pyramids and temples are small and crude compared

to the glorious Classic structures. Mayapán's only architectural distinction comes from its vast defensive city wall, one of the few such walls ever discovered in a Mayan city. The fact that the wall exists testifies to the weakness of the Itzá rulers and the unhappiness of their subject peoples.

Tulum, another walled city, on the coast east of Cobá, is also a product of this time. The columns of the Puuc style are used, and the painted decoration on the temples must have been colorful, but there is nothing to rival the Classic age.

Cobá has the finest architecture of this otherwise decadent period. The stately pyramids at Cobá had new little temples built atop them in the style of Tulum.

The finest and best preserved Late Postclassic sites are: Mixco Viejo, north of Guatemala City; Utatlán (or K'umarcaaj), the old Quiché Maya capital on the outskirts of Santa Cruz del Quiché; and Iximché, the last Cakchiquel capital on the Panamericana highway near Tecpan. All of these sites show pronounced central Mexican influences in their twin temple complexes, which probably descend from similar structures at Teotihuacán.

Spanish Colonial Architecture
During their domination of the Yucatán (1524 to 1821), the conquistadors, the Franciscans and the Dominicans brought with them the architecture of their native Spain and adapted it to the conditions they met in the Mayan lands. Churches in the largest cities were decorated with baroque elements, but in general the churches are simple and fortresslike. The exploitation of the Maya by the Spaniards led to frequent rebellions, and the strong, high stone walls of the churches worked well in protecting the upper classes from the wrath of the indigenous people.

As you travel in the Yucatán, you'll be surprised to find so many very plain churches – plain outside and plain inside. The crude and simple borrowings from Spanish architecture are eclipsed by the richness of the religious pageantry that takes place inside the buildings during patron saint festivals and half-Mayan, half-Catholic processions.

ARTS
The arts-and-crafts scene on the Yucatán Peninsula is enormously rich and varied. The influence of the Mayan and/or Spanish cultures appears in almost every facet of Yucatecan art, from their dance and music to the clothes they wear, such as the *huipiles*, the colorfully embroidered white cotton tunicdresses Mayan women have been wearing for centuries, and *panamás* – Panama hats – which were being woven in the state of Campeche long before their famous namesake received worldwide acclaim as stylish and practical headgear for the Tropics.

Dance
The Spanish influence on Mayan culture is quite evident in the *jarana*, the name Yucatecans have given to a dance they have been performing for centuries. In this dance, the men and women move separately, facing each other in two lines. At different stages of the jarana, the couples raise their arms and snap their fingers. The dancers move in precision to the music.

Although the music is different, the dance is quite similar to the *jota*, a folkloric dance performed in Spain's Alto Aragón region. The movements of the dancers, with their torsos held rigid and a formal distance separating men from women, are nearly identical; however, whereas the Spanish would punctuate elegant turns of their wrists with clicks of their castanets, the Mayan women snap their fingers. The similarity between dances cannot be coincidental.

Music
Latin jazz, Caribbean reggae, and English- and Spanish-language rock 'n' roll is often performed in the tourist haunts of Cancún, Mérida and Playa del Carmen, while the latest popular dance music fills the dance halls from Cancún to Chetumal, near the Belize border.

But to hear traditional Yucatecan music you must attend one of the folkloric shows put on for tourists in Cancún, or a *vaquería* in the lovely colonial city of Mérida, the cultural capital of the peninsula and the capital of Yucatán state. Vaquerías – traditional

Yucatecan parties where couples dance in unison to a series of songs – are held every Monday night in front of Mérida's Palacio Municipal.

Jarana music is generally provided by an orchestra consisting of at least two trumpets, two trombones, violins, kettledrums and a *güiro* (a percussion instrument made out of a gourd that is played by rasping its rough surface with a drumstick). A jarana orchestra always ends its performances with the traditional *torito*, a vivacious song that evokes the fervor of a bullfight. If you're in Mérida for a vaquería, be sure to stay till the very end.

Traditional Dress

Women throughout the Yucatán Peninsula traditionally wear straight, white cotton dresses called *huipiles*, the bodices of which are always embroidered. These tunics generally fall just below the knee; on formal occasions, a lacy white underskirt that reaches the ankle will be added to the dress. Huipiles are never worn with a belt, which would defeat it's airy, cool design.

Also commonly worn on the peninsula (and very similar to the huipil in appearance) is the *gala terno*, which is a straight, white, square-necked dress with an embroidered over-yoke and hem, worn over an underskirt, which sports an embroidered strip near the bottom. This attire is fancier than a huipil and is often accompanied by a delicately hand-knitted shawl.

In addition to huipiles, galas ternos and shawls, Mayan women throughout the peninsula are known for weaving lovely sashes, tablecloths and napkins.

The article of clothing most often associated with men of the Yucatán is the *guayabera*, a light linen shirt with four square pockets that's standard traditional business wear in southeast Mexico.

Guayaberas originally hail from Yucatán, where they are slowly being replaced by the button-down, single-pocketed Oxford-style shirt so popular with American businessmen. Still, they remain the uniform of local politicians. The best guayaberas can be purchased in Mérida; see the Yucatán chapter for further details.

Panama Hats

The classic woven straw hat that most people associate with Panama was made internationally famous in the late 19th century by Ferdinand de Lesseps, builder of the Suez Canal and the brains behind the failed French attempt to build a canal in Panama.

The much-photographed Lesseps was balding when he arrived in Panama, and he found that the light but durable hat provided excellent protection against the sun. Most newspaper photographs taken of him here showed the larger-than-life figure looking even more worldly in his exotic headgear. Soon men around the globe began placing orders for the 'Panama hat.'

The original hat was made in Ecuador and exported to Panama. However, at least as early as the 1880s, residents of Becal in the Mexican state of Campeche were producing the same style hat. Today, more than 1000 people in the small, quiet town of Becal are still making the hats, which they variously call *panamás* or *jipijapas* (the Mexican hats are made from *jipijapa* palm fronds).

Wooden Crafts

In handicrafts shops across the peninsula, you'll come across beautiful wooden crafts, such as carved wooden panels and wooden galleons.

The ancient Maya made wood carvings of their many gods, just as they carved the images of their deities in stone. The skill and techniques associated with the artistry survive to this day. The wooden panels are often a meter or more in height and feature a strange looking character of unmistakably Mayan imagination – the image will resemble figures you've seen at Mayan ruins. If the carved image is one of a heavily adorned man raising a chalice, most likely you're looking at a representation of Itzamná, lord of the heavens; he's a popular figure on the wooden panels of contemporary Maya.

Mayans – so impressed with the Spanish galleons that arrived on their shores that they made meter-long models of the ships, complete with tiny sails – have been making wooden galleons for generations. Today, the galleons that used to haul cargoes of

hardwood back to Europe are gone, but the craft of galleon model-making is alive and well in the Yucatán.

You can usually find carved wooden sailfish, carved wooden turtles and carved wooden parrots at the same crafts shops that you find the lovely wooden models of galleons. Campeche is the Mexican state that's most associated with such items, but in fact they are made by artisans in the states of Yucatán and Quintana Roo as well.

Silver Filigree

Silver has been mined in Mexico for hundreds of years and, indeed, the country is widely regarded for producing some of the world's finest silverware. The Spanish brought with them the filigree technique, in which openwork patterns are created from minute cable made of two or three twined or braided gold or silver wires.

Filigree was very popular in Europe during the 16th and 17th centuries, used to decorate vases and drinking glasses. But artisans on the Yucatán preferred to make filigree jewelry, and unlike the vases and glasses of Europe, they preferred the silver to stand alone – without a backing material. Today, there aren't more than a dozen silversmiths in the Yucatán producing silver filigree, but it's still usually available in the better jewelry stores on the peninsula.

SOCIETY & CONDUCT

The people of the Yucatán Peninsula are, by and large, being conquered again. Right and left the best land in southeast Mexico is being purchased by foreigners – either people from abroad or people from Mexico City (who are foreigners as far as most Yucatecans are concerned). With few exceptions, the people filling the desirable jobs are not Mayan. The people making infrastructure decisions, generally, are not Mayan. In many ways, the Maya are second-class citizens in their own land.

Yet, the Maya remain generally friendly to outsiders. And, whereas *machismo* (exaggerated masculinity) is a problem elsewhere in Mexico, on the Yucatán Peninsula it isn't much of a problem. In general, you'll find

that the Yucatecans will treat you as you treat them. If you're friendly, you can expect friendliness in return.

Making Contact

No Yucatecan expects an outsider to speak Yucatec (one of the 39 languages belonging to the Mayan family). But because Spanish *is* the official language of the region, don't expect Yucatecans to speak English – outside of the tourist areas of Cancún, Isla Mujeres, Cozumel and Playa del Carmen, anyway.

Just a few basic Spanish phrases will do the trick, and all of the important ones can be found in the Language chapter at the end of this book. Please take the time to at least learn how to say *Hello* and *Thank you* in Spanish. You'll find the phrases under the Greetings & Civilities section particularly useful, and they take only a few minutes to learn.

Time

The Mexican attitude toward time – *'mañana, mañana…'* – is legendary and it is real: In Mexico, a person might show up an hour late for an appointment and this action, generally, would not be considered rude. Gringos often have great difficulty dealing with the mañana syndrome, allowing it to elevate their blood pressure and trigger head pain every time. The foreign managers of maquiladoras typically contend with the mañana syndrome by closing the doors to their factories 15 minutes after the work day begins, thus preventing employees from straggling in whenever it suits them.

Unless you're running a business that permits you to shut out employees, you'll have to be a bit more diplomatic, yet firm. If you're making an appointment with a local and it's important to you that that person be prompt, be specific. Tell the Yucatecan to arrive at a specified time and not later. If you're arranging to go fishing and want to leave at 7 o'clock, for example, say '7, not 7:15, not 7:30 – 7 *on the dot.*' (If you speak Spanish, *'en punta'* is the Spanish equivalent for 'on the dot.') This heavy emphasis may sound condescending to you, but all you are really doing is clearly communicating to the

local that you are on gringo time, not local time. This clarification can reduce frustration and prevent hard feelings.

Dos & Don'ts

Politeness is a very important aspect of social interaction on the peninsula. When beginning to talk to someone, even in such routine situations as in a store or on the bus, it's polite to preface your conversation with a greeting to the other person. A simple *'Buenos días'* or *'Buenas tardes'* and a smile, answered by a similar greeting on the other person's part, gets a conversation off to a positive start.

When you enter a room, even a public place such as a restaurant or waiting room, it's polite to make a general greeting to everyone in the room – again, a *'Buenos días'* or *'Buenas tardes'* will do just fine. Handshakes are another friendly gesture and are used frequently.

Pay attention to your appearance when in the Yucatán. Mexicans, on the whole, are very conscious of appearance, grooming and dress; it's difficult for them to understand why a foreign traveler, who is naturally assumed to be rich, would go around looking scruffy when even poor Mexicans do their best to look neat. Try to present as clean an appearance as possible, especially if you're dealing with officialdom (police, immigration officers, etc); in such cases it's a good idea to look not only clean, but also as conservative and respectable as possible.

Dress modestly when entering churches (and do not chat inside them), as this shows respect for local people and their culture. Short pants are not allowed in government buildings. Some churches in heavily touristed areas will post signs at the door asking that shorts and tank tops not be worn in church, but in most places such knowledge is assumed.

Photographers should not assume that people like having their picture taken. Before snapping away, seek permission.

Treatment of Animals

In general, domestic animals are no worse off on the Yucatán Peninsula than they are in any other poverty stricken country. There is no shortage of stray cats or packs of mangy dogs, but they aren't especially mistreated the way they are in some Asian countries. And you can't very well expect people in a land where the minimum daily wage is only US$5 a day to spend money having their pets fixed.

On the other hand, most Mexican bullfights are purely sadistic displays. The *corrida de toros* (bullfight) begins with cape-waving toreros tiring the animal by luring him around the ring. After 10 minutes or so, a picador on a heavily padded horse enters the ring and stabs the bull in the shoulder with a lance. The lance slices into the bull's shoulder muscles, and usually a large artery or two, considerably weakening the confused animal.

The picador exits and replacing him in the ring are two or three toreros, who further 'soften up' the bull by jabbing three elongated darts into the animal's shoulder. Once the thoroughly confused and bloodied bull has been properly jabbed (ie, the darts go in deep and stay there), the brave matador enters the ring and the so-called fight begins.

The show hereafter contains the following: The matador exhausts the bull by baiting him with a cape, which bulls are predisposed to charge; the matador exchanges his cape for a smaller one and a sword, which the matador plunges into the heart of the bull when he's in a good position to do so; and, an assistant to the matador runs up to the dying bull and slashes his jugular, so the beast 'doesn't suffer.'

If the matador was deemed to have put on an exceptional display of agility and daring (a judge makes the determination), the judge will give the matador's assistant a signal to slice off one or both of the bull's ears, which are then presented to the matador. If the matador is deemed by the judge to have put on a spectacular show, he'll even be awarded the bull's tail for his trophy case.

RELIGION
The Ancient Maya

World-Tree & Xibalba For the ancient Maya, the world, the heavens and the mysterious underworld called Xibalba were all

one great, unified structure that operated according to the laws of astrology and ancestor worship. The towering ceiba tree was considered sacred, for it symbolized the Whack Chan, or world-tree, which united the 13 heavens, the surface of the Earth and the nine levels of the underworld. The world-tree had a sort of cruciform shape and was associated with the color blue-green. In the 16th century, when the Franciscan friars came bearing a cross and required the Indians to venerate it, the symbolism meshed easily with established Mayan beliefs.

Points of the Compass In Mayan cosmology, each point of the compass had special religious significance. East was most important, as it was where the sun was reborn each day; its color was red. West was black because it was where the sun disappeared. North was white and was the direction from which the all-important rains came, beginning in May. South was yellow because it was the 'sunniest' point of the compass.

Everything in the Mayan world was seen in relation to these cardinal points, with the world-tree at the center; but the cardinal points were only the starting point for the all-important astronomical and astrological observations that determined fate.

Bloodletting & Human Sacrifice Humans had certain roles to play within this great system. Just as the great cosmic dragon shed its blood, which fell as rain to the earth, so humans had to shed blood to link themselves with Xibalba.

Bloodletting ceremonies were the most important religious ceremonies, and the blood of kings was seen as the most acceptable for these rituals. Thus, when the friars said that the blood of Jesus, the King of the Jews, had been spilled for the common people, the Maya could easily understand the symbolism.

Sacred Places Mayan ceremonies were performed in natural sacred places as well as their human-made equivalents. Mountains, caves, lakes, cenotes, rivers and fields were

all sacred and had special importance in the scheme of things. Pyramids and temples were thought of as stylized mountains; sometimes these had secret chambers within them, like the caves in a mountain. A cave was the mouth of the creature that represented Xibalba, and to enter it was to enter the spirit of the secret world. This is why some Mayan temples have doorways surrounded by huge masks: As you enter the door of this 'cave' you are entering the mouth of Xibalba.

The plazas around which the pyramids were placed symbolized the open fields or the flat land of the tropical forest. What we call stelae were to the Maya 'tree-stones' – sacred tree-effigies echoing the sacredness of the world-tree. These tree-stones were often carved with the figures of great Mayan kings, for the king was the world-tree of Mayan society.

It made sense for succeeding Mayan kings to build new and ever grander temples directly over the older temples, as this enhanced the sacred character of the spot. The temple being covered was seen as a sacred artifact to be preserved. Certain features of these older temples, such as the large masks on the façade, were carefully padded and protected before the new construction was placed over them.

Ancestor worship and genealogy were very important to the Maya, and when they buried a king beneath a pyramid, or a commoner beneath the floor or courtyard of his na, the sacredness of the location was increased.

The Mayan 'Bible' Of the painted books destroyed by Friar Diego de Landa and other Franciscans, no doubt some of them were books of sacred legends and stories similar to the Bible. Such sacred histories and legends provide a worldview to believers and guide them in belief and daily action.

One such Mayan book, the *Popol Vuh*, survived not as a painted book but as a transcription into the Latin alphabet of a Mayan narrative text. In other words, it was written in Quiché Maya, but in Latin characters, not hieroglyphs. The *Popol Vuh* was apparently

written by Quiché Maya Indians of Guatemala who had learned Spanish and the Latin alphabet from the Dominican friars. The authors showed their book to Francisco Ximénez, a Dominican who lived and worked in Chichicastenango from 1701 to 1703. Friar Ximénez copied the Indians' book word for word, then translated it into Spanish. Both his copy and the Spanish translation survive, but the Indian original has been lost.

According to the *Popol Vuh*, the great god K'ucumatz created humankind first from mud. But these 'earthlings' were weak and dissolved in water, so K'ucumatz tried again using wood. The wood people had no hearts or minds and could not praise their Creator, so they were destroyed, all except the monkeys who lived in the forest, who are the descendants of the wood people. The Creator tried once again, this time successfully, using substances recommended by four animals – the gray fox, the coyote, the parrot and the crow. White and yellow corn was ground into meal to form the flesh, and stirred into water to make the blood.

The *Popol Vuh* legends include some elements that made it easier for the Maya to understand certain aspects of Christian belief, including virgin birth and sacrificial death followed by a return to life.

Animism & Catholicism The ceiba tree's cruciform shape was not the only correspondence the Maya found between their animist beliefs and Christianity. Both traditional Mayan animism and Catholicism have rites of baptism and confession, days of fasting and other forms of abstinence, religious partaking of alcoholic beverages, burning of incense and the use of altars.

Contemporary Yucatecans

Today's Maya identify themselves as Catholic but they practice a Catholicism that is a fusion of shamanist-animist and Christian ritual. The traditional religious ways are so important that often a Maya will try to recover from a malady by seeking the advice of a religious shaman rather than a medical doctor. Use of folk remedies linked with animist tradition is widespread in Mayan areas.

In addition to Roman Catholicism, which accounts for 85% of the religious orientation of contemporary Yucatecans, 12% of the peninsula's population identify themselves as Protestants or evangelicals. Congregations affiliated with churches such as the Assemblies of God, the Seventh Day Adventists, the Church of Jesus Christ of Latter Day Saints, and Jehovah's Witnesses can also be found in the Yucatán, though in much smaller numbers.

LANGUAGE

Technically speaking, today's Maya don't speak Mayan, though they might think they do. Yucatec is the language of today's Maya, and it is the closest language to what many ancient Mayas of Yucatán were speaking between 200 and 900 AD. (Indeed, 39 languages of the Mayan family are still used daily by millions of Indians. Most of the languages are as different from each other as English and Greek.)

Now, more than ever, scholars are looking to Yucatec to help them piece together the language spoken by the people who built Uxmal, Chichén Itzá, Mayapán and Yucatán's other lost cities. (It's good to keep in mind that an entire library of Mayan texts that could have given modern archaeologists tremendous insights into the codices was burned in the 1500s by the Spanish bishop of the Yucatán, Diego de Landa, who believed them to be heresy.)

Spanish is, of course, the official language of Mexico and is widely spoken on the peninsula. English is widely spoken in the major cities and at the better hotels and restaurants, but few people know the 'universal language' in the smaller cities and in the rural towns and villages. There is a Language chapter at the back of this book that can help you with your Spanish; it includes a section on Modern Mayan pronunciation and is followed by a Glossary.

Facts for the Visitor

HIGHLIGHTS

Most people who visit Yucatán stay at one of Cancún's many enormous resorts, where they soak up the sun on a white-sand beach during the day and dine, drink, dance and *dormirse* (sleep) at night. Some visitors to Cancún spice up their stay with excursions to the Mayan ruins of Chichén Itzá and Tulum, while others sign up for scuba diving with a local operator and see the Great Maya Barrier Reef as it really should be seen – up close and personal.

The majority of Yucatán's visitors, however, never stray from Cancún's Zona Hotelera (Hotel Zone) and/or the nearby downtown area. They arrive at the nearby airport, have a great time in Cancún, and return to the airport for their flight home. They leave exploration to others. There's certainly nothing wrong with that, and if melting away some of life's stress is your short-term goal, Cancún can definitely help you reach it. These highlights are intended for adventurous spirits who want to see Cancún and then some.

Cancún

Not to mention Cancún as a highlight of Yucatán – granted, a very commercial one – would be to do it an injustice. Cancún is not only one of the world's top tropical playpens, but it's also a great base from which to make day trips to the peninsula's top tourist attractions – of the natural and ancient-city varieties. An entire section of this book is devoted to Cancún, stuffed to the binding with news about the resorts' varied restaurant, excursion and nightlife options.

But wait, you say, *I haven't even decided on Cancún*. Perhaps this will help: If all you really want from your trip to Yucatán is a gorgeous Caribbean beach, lots of meal options and a vivacious nightlife that's hugely popular with twentysomethings and thirtysomethings, look no farther than Cancún. Cancún is Mexico's Party Central – if you're young and single and seeking that someone special for a night or two or – gasp – something even more substantial, Cancún's as good a place as any to find a fun-loving hardbodied type who's also wild at heart.

Of course, Cancún isn't just for Generation Xers and whatever the group after them is calling itself. There's a Club Med and other exclusive resorts in the hotel zone, and few Generation Xers – let's be honest – can afford to stay at such places, so if you're concerned about being surrounded by rowdies at your Cancún hotel, just treat yourself and stay at one of the pricier resorts.

Playa del Carmen & Cozumel

Most Yucatán visitors who aren't hanging out in Cancún are hanging out in Playa del Carmen or Cozumel – much smaller and less commercial versions of Cancún – soaking up the sun, sipping *piña coladas* and listening to beach music.

The beach/bar/disco scenes of Playa del Carmen and Cozumel aren't nearly as wild as the beach/bar/disco scenes of Cancún's Zona Hotelera and the slightly more 'authentic' downtown Cancún a few kilometers away, but that's one of the main reasons these two destinations appeal to so many people: Visitors here have many of the same options that they'd have in Cancún, the same luxury and excess, without feeling like they're part of a herd. (Few of Playa's hotels, for example, have more than 50 guest rooms.)

The island of Cozumel offers also some world-class snorkeling and scuba diving options. Adventurous types will want to rent a moped while on the island (a very easy, though not altogether safe, thing to do) and give the island a good look-see, as much of Cozumel is undeveloped and ripe for exploration, and the best beaches and snorkel sites are easily reached by moped. Separated only by a brief ferry ride, Cancún and Cozumel offer the visitor an attractive combination package.

Ancient Mayan Cities

From the Great Pyramid of Cheops in Egypt to the Great Stupa in India, from the five central towers of Angor Wat in Cambodia to the pyramid monument of Chavín de Huántar in the Andean highlands of Peru, our planet is freckled with outstanding feats of construction by people who lived long ago. But the vast majority of the works pale in comparison to the building done by the ancient Maya.

The Maya constructed with clarity of purpose. Mayan architecture didn't simply contain thousands upon thousands of fanciful glyphs carved into altars, stelae and temples that narrated tales of the ruling dynasties – which in itself is spectacular – but the exact positioning of each major building served a specific purpose. For example, El Palacio del Gobernador (the Governor's Palace) at Uxmal, in central Yucatán, was oriented in such a way that from the central doorway astronomers could observe Venus on the horizon as it rose across the sky to the tip of a pyramid situated several kilometers away.

Seemingly everything related to construction mattered to the ancient Maya. For example, Chichén Itzá's awesome El Castillo pyramid and a smaller, earlier pyramid deep inside it both feature four stairways, each consisting of 91 steps. The sum of all four stairways, plus the continuous step around the top of each pyramid, totals 365 – the number of days in the solar calendar. Given the importance the ancient Maya placed on calendars and astronomy, it's fair to assume that even the exact number of steps in each of these buildings was intentional.

Anyone who leaves Yucatán without seeing at least one ancient Mayan city is making a mistake. Among the most spectacular Mayan ruins on the Yucatán Peninsula are the abandoned cities of Chichén Itzá and Uxmal in Yucatán state; Tulum, Cobá and Kohunlich in the state of Quintana Roo; and Edzná and Calakmul in Campeche state. If time permits, visiting the lesser ancient sites along the Ruta Puuc in Yucatán state and the numerous sites along Hwy 186 between Escárcega and Xpujil would greatly add to your appreciation of the great Mayan people of time past.

See the National Parks, Reserves & Ruins map in the Facts for the Visitor chapter for the locations of Mayan ruins in the Yucatán Peninsula.

Colonial Mérida

Mérida is a fascinating city to visit for a variety of reasons. For starters, it is one of Mexico's great colonial cities. Its cathedral, which features a fantastic dome and flying buttresses, is the oldest mainland cathedral in North America (only the cathedral in Santo Domingo in the Dominican Republic is older). In fact, of the seven cathedrals begun in Mexico during the 16th century, Mérida's was the only one completed by the end of the century.

But Mérida's impressive colonial attractions don't stop with the cathedral. The cathedral faces Mérida's main square, the Plaza Mayor, around which are situated a splendid Palacio Municipal (Town Hall), which dates from 1542; the Palacio de Gobierno (State Government House), which was completed in 1892; and the Casa de Montejo (House of Montejo), built in 1549 and famous for its plateresque façade. Colonial homes and remnants of the city's original walls also distinguish Mérida.

Mérida, the capital of Yucatán state, is also its cultural center, priding itself on its traditions, such as the dances the city's residents have performed for generations. Every Monday evening the street in front of the Palacio Municipal is closed to vehicular traffic for the weekly *vaquería*, a regional festival that celebrates the branding of the cattle. The festival features dance performances by men and women dressed in traditional Yucatecan attire. The music is provided by an orchestra, and in the shadow of the tall cathedral, it's easy to imagine how Mérida might have been 200 years ago.

Red Flamingos

There are five species of flamingo on Earth, the largest of which is the greater flamingo, which may reach 155cm (61 inches) in height. The greater flamingo has two subspecies: the

Visit red flamingoes year round at natural parks along the Gulf coast.

red flamingo, which has breeding grounds from Yucatán and the West Indies to the coast of northeastern South America, and the paler rose flamingo, which inhabits parts of the Old World, India and Africa.

Red flamingos can be seen year-round at two national parks in the state of Yucatán. The park closest to Cancún is Parque Natural Río Lagartos, directly north of the city of Valladolid. The park closest to Mérida is Parque Natural Flamingo Mexicano de Celestún, directly west of the colonial city. Both flamingo colonies are also flanked by mangrove at the edge of the Gulf of Mexico.

A visit to either flamingo colony is an adventure you'll remember for years. To see the flamingos, you board a small boat that winds through placid salt water and ancient mangrove forests to shallow water where hundreds and occasionally thousands of the quirky-looking birds search for food. If some of the birds take flight, as they usually do when boats appear, you'll be in for a beautiful sight as the lanky *aves* (birds) expose the lovely, salmon-colored feathers on the underside of their wings. When a large flock of these birds lift off at once, the horizon fills with spectacular color. A visit to the red flamingos is definitely a highlight of any trip to Yucatán.

PLANNING
When to Go
The dry season (October to May) is generally preferred for travel in Yucatán, with November and early December perhaps the best times, as there are fewer tourists and prices are relatively low then. The busy winter tourism season runs from mid-December through March, and it's then that room rates are at their highest; on and near Christmas, New Year's and Easter, expect to pay twice or three times as much for a room as you would during the low season.

May, the end of the dry season, and June, when the rains begin, are the hottest and muggiest months. If you have a choice of months, don't choose them. July and August are hot, not too rainy and busy with the US summer travel crowd. September and October are pretty good for travel, as the traffic decreases markedly and so do the rains.

Maps
High-quality Yucatán Peninsula maps include ITMB Publishing's 1:1,000,000-scale *Yucatán Peninsula*, which is easy to read and very detailed (for example, it includes lots of minor Maya ruins and many more cenotes, or natural freshwater pools. than are found on other maps, and much of Tabasco and Chiapas are shown as well); and Guia Roji's 1:1,000,000-scale *Maya World*, which shows all of the peninsula and parts of Tabasco and Chiapas but isn't nearly as detailed as the ITMB map. Both maps are updated every couple of years. ITMB maps are published in Canada and can be ordered via their website (www.nas.com/travelmaps). Guia Roji publishes in Mexico and is reachable via their website (www.guiaroji.com.mx/).

Guia Roji also publishes an annual national road atlas called *Carreteras de México* that's widely available in Mexico, very detailed and in some ways easier to use than the ITMB map because it opens like a magazine (unlike ITMB's *Yucatán Peninsula*, which is a large foldout map). However,

Carreteras de México is considerably more expensive than the ITMB map and cannot fit conveniently into a back pocket.

There are lots of individual states and southeast Mexico maps available in Yucatán shops that are put out by the Instituto Nacional de Estadistica Geografía e Informacion, but at the time of this writing none had been published in recent years and, therefore, didn't show new roads or indicate the current status of roads that have been dramatically improved. Same goes for the maps published by Mexico's Secretaria de Comunicaciones y Transportes.

There is also a host of free city and regional maps available on the peninsula, most contained in small promotional publications such as *Cancún Tips*, *La Iguana* and *Passport*, which are given away at airports and stacked for the taking at resorts and restaurants. The maps generally are weak on details and, apparently, advertiser driven (the expensive places are always shown, while many good, low-priced restaurants rarely receive mention).

Two foldout maps published by an American couple – *Can-Do The Riviera Maya* and *Can-Do Cancún* – are extremely well done and are updated annually. In addition to containing multiple insert maps, these maps also contain dozens of color photos, many site-specific reviews and a very useful index for restaurants, hotels and attractions. To learn more about these superb maps and to order them, visit the couple's website (www.cancunmap.com).

What to Bring

Anything you are likely to need on the Yucatán Peninsula you can probably buy there, perhaps even more cheaply than you can back home. However, if you're short on time, try to bring everything you think you'll need with you so you won't have to spend time roaming store aisles when you could be touring ancient ruins, watching the waves roll in or putting a bartender to the test.

Toiletries such as shampoo, shaving cream, razors, soap and toothpaste are readily available throughout Yucatán in all but the smallest villages. You should bring your own contact lens solution, tampons, contraceptives, sunscreen and insect repellent – they are available in Mexico, but not always readily so.

Other recommended items are sunglasses, a hat, a flashlight, a pocket knife, a money belt or a money pouch that you can wear under your clothes, a small padlock, and a portable English-Spanish dictionary.

For carrying it all, a backpack is most convenient if you'll be doing much traveling on foot. You can make it reasonably theft-proof with small padlocks. A light day pack, too, is useful. When visiting ruins, you'll want to carry water with you. Unless you don't mind carrying a bottle of water in your hand, you might want to consider bringing something more user-friendly to put the water in. Such containers can be found at stores specializing in outdoor gear.

What to Wear

If you want to be treated with respect, don't dress like a bum. Only the poorest Yucatecans would wear cutoffs, and no locals strut around in bikini tops except at the beach. Due to the heat, the most climate-appropriate clothing for Yucatán cities is

Floss It

For the cost of a crummy cigar, you can buy a vacation-saving item. It's called dental floss, and its uses are innumerable. Got a fishhook but no line? Four words: green waxed dental floss. Need to secure a mosquito net? Reach for dental floss. Forgot to pack a clothesline? You're in luck if you've packed dental floss. Tear in your jeans, rip in your pack? A little dental floss and a sewing needle and life goes on.

Dental floss comes in 50m and 100m lengths and is sold in nifty little cases complete with built-in cutters. It's cheap, it's light, it's strong and it's outrageously useful. Some say dental floss can even remove decay-causing material from between teeth and under gums. Now in cinnamon, mint and grape flavors. No kidding.

made of 100% cotton fiber or (even better, but pricier) capilene – a material that wicks moisture away from skin. High-tech wear made of capilene usually can be found in stores that specialize in outdoor apparel.

If the nightclub scene is your thing, keep in mind that what you wear when you enter the club will likely be what you'll wear when you leave the establishment very late at night. Oftentimes *gringas* can be seen staggering down the streets of Cancún and Playa del Carmen after midnight wearing scarcely more than beachwear. Cancún is reputed to be safe, but in Playa del Carmen, at least one foreign woman is raped each week, according to people who live there (see the Women Travelers section later this chapter for more about this).

Yucatecans generally do not expect you to dress as formally as they do (they realize that you are probably on vacation, whereas they are usually dressed for work), but you should know that, except in beach resorts, shorts and T-shirts are the marks of the tourist; this comment is intended for those of you who don't like to stand out in crowds. Jeans are often uncomfortably heavy in typically hot Yucatán. A light rain jacket, or better yet a loose-fitting poncho (they're widely available on the peninsula), is good to have.

In general, it is better for women to dress conservatively in towns (except seaside resorts) and in off-the-beaten-track villages unaccustomed to tourists – no short shorts, no halter tops, etc. Lean toward the more respectful end of the dress spectrum when visiting churches.

Although people should know better, most usually arrive in Yucatán without sunscreen. Every day hundreds, if not thousands, of tourists spend their Yucatán vacation lying flat on their backs in bed because they got horrible sunburns their first day on the peninsula. Please note that many of the more ecological resorts on the Mayan Riviera require that the sunscreen you use is biodegradable. If you're fair skinned, consider wearing long sleeves and long pants while in Yucatán and leave sunbathing to people with olive skin.

RESPONSIBLE TOURISM

Many souvenirs sold in Yucatán are made from endangered plants and animals that have been acquired illegally. By collecting or purchasing these items you aid in their extinction. Avoid purchasing any items made from turtle shell or from coral. The sale and purchase of jaguar teeth and pelts is not only illegal, it's ethically criminal. Same goes for crocodile and ocelot and margay skins. Orchids are endemic and are also protected by domestic and international law; view but don't pick.

Assuming for a moment that you live in a country where the official language is not Spanish, how would you like it if visitors to your country frequently approached you and started speaking Spanish at you? You probably wouldn't like it much at all. Likewise, when in Mexico please bear in mind that Spanish is the local language. Please acquaint yourself with the Language chapter at the back of this book so that you can at least say 'Hello' and 'Thank you' in Spanish.

Lastly, please don't do anything you know you shouldn't – and you know what I mean: When you've drunk that last drink from your water bottle out at the hot Mayan ruin, don't toss it in the bushes like so many inconsiderate tourists before you. Don't take home anything that you pick up at the site of an ancient city or out on a coral reef. And please be careful what you touch and where you place your feet when you're snorkeling and scuba diving; not only can coral cut you, but it's extremely fragile and takes years to grow even a finger's length; see 'Considerations for Responsible Diving' section, later in the chapter.

TOURIST OFFICES
Local Tourist Offices

There are tourist offices in many of Yucatán's cities, but visitors should not expect much assistance from them. Sad but true, the people working in most of the tourist offices on the Yucatán Peninsula are pretty ignorant when it comes to things you'd assume they'd know. For example, you'll stump most any Yucatecan tourist official if you ask him/

Travel with a Conscience

It's not always possible to 'leave only footprints,' but the following five tips are good to remember if you're concerned about the environment.

1. *Don't litter.* There's no excuse for littering, and it never hurts to pick some up and put it in the garbage. Everyone benefits when trash is disposed of properly.

2. *Be hands off.* Never take 'souvenirs' such as shells, plants or artifacts from historical sites or natural areas. Treat shells, sea urchins, coral and other marine life as sacred.

3. *Think before you buy.* Many species of plants and animals are destroyed only to make trinkets for tourists. By buying products made of tortoiseshell, coral, bird feathers or similar materials, you contribute to the decimation of wildlife. Please, shop with a conscience.

4. *Keep to footpaths.* When you're hiking, always follow designated trails. Natural habitats are often quickly eroded, and animals and plants disturbed, by walkers who stray off the beaten path. Also, you're less likely to step on a rattlesnake if you stick to the trails.

5. *Don't touch or stand on coral.* Coral is extremely sensitive and is easily killed by snorkelers and divers who fail to honor this law of nature: Human contact is deadly.

her to name the best restaurant in town. Why? Because a meal at the best restaurant in town could possibly cost him/her at least several days' wages.

Likewise, if you ask a tourist official in Yucatán to name a reputable dive operator, don't expect anything more than a guess. Scuba diving is an activity most Mexicans cannot afford. Which is more spectacular, Chichén Itzá or Uxmal? It costs several days' wages for a Yucatecan tourist official to enter either. Chances are the official hasn't visited Chichén Itzá or Uxmal, although pride will likely move the official to name one of them. Also, most of the offices are staffed with people who don't speak English, despite the fact most of the people they 'attend to' speak English and very little Spanish. Finally, most of the offices have only mediocre maps and literature to hand out – if any at all.

The major exception to the rule are the two tourist offices in Mérida, which are generally staffed with friendly and knowledgeable people who usually even have a large assortment of helpful materials on hand. Details about Mérida's tourist offices and many of the other tourist offices on the Yucatán Peninsula can be found in the destination chapters.

Tourist Offices Abroad

The Mexican government has tourist offices in nine countries. Those in the USA seem to be staffed by people hired for their ability to steer inquiries elsewhere – to other tourist offices, to the Mexican embassy in Washington, DC, to their inept public relations firm in New York City. Perhaps those outside the USA are more helpful.

Mexican tourist offices abroad frequently change their telephone numbers. The information provided here was accurate at the time this book went to press:

Argentina
(☎ 541-821-7170, 541-825-7566, fax 541-821-7251)
Larrea No 1230, 1117 Buenos Aires

Canada
Vancouver: (☎ 604-669-2845, fax 604-669-3498)
999 W Hastings St, suite 1610, Vancouver, BC V6C 1M3
Toronto: (☎ 416-925-0704, fax 416-925-6061) 2 Bloor St W, suite 1801, Toronto, Ontario M4W 3E2
Montréal: (☎ 514-871-1052, fax 514-871-3825) 1 Place Ville Marie, suite 1526, Montréal, Québec H3B 2B5

France
(☎ 01-42-86-56-30, fax 01-42-86-05-80) 4 Rue Notre Dame des Victoires, 75002 Paris

Germany
(☎ 069-252-413, 069-253-541, fax 069-253-755)
Wiesenhüttenplatz 26, D60329 Frankfurt-am-Main

Italy
(☎ 06-487-2182, 06-482-7160, fax 06-482-3630)
Via Barberini 3, 00187 Rome

Japan
(☎ 813-580-2962, fax 813-581-5539) 2-15-1
Nagata-Cho, Chiyoda-Ku, Tokyo 100

Spain
(☎ 341-561-3520, fax 341-411-0759) Calle Velázquez 126, Madrid 28006

UK
(☎ 020-7839-3177, 020-7734-1058, fax 0171-930-9202) 60-61 Trafalgar Square, 3rd floor, London WC2N 5DS

USA
Los Angeles: (☎ 310-203-8191, fax 310-203-8316)
10100 Santa Monica Blvd, suite 224, Los Angeles, CA 90067
Coral Gables: (☎ 305-443-9160, fax 305-443-1186)
2333 Ponce de Leon Blvd, suite 710, Coral Gables, FL 33134
Chicago: (☎ 312-606-9252, fax 312-606-9012)
300 North Michigan Ave, 4th floor, Chicago, IL 60601
New York: (☎ 212-755-7261, fax 212-755-2874)
405 Park Ave, suite 1401, New York, NY 10022
Houston: (☎ 713-880-5153, fax 713-880-1833)
2707 North Loop West, suite 450, Houston, TX 77008
Washington, DC: (☎ 202-728-1750, fax 202-728-1758) 1911 Pennsylvania Ave NW, Washington, DC 20006

VISAS & DOCUMENTS
Passport
Visitors to Mexico should have a valid passport, whether or not one is required, because officials are used to passports and sometimes delay people who present other documents. Some nationalities must obtain visas; most Western nationalities require only the easily obtained Mexican government tourist card. Because regulations sometimes change, be sure to confirm them at a Mexican government tourist office or a Mexican embassy or consulate before you go.

Visas
Citizens of the following countries don't need to obtain a visa to enter Mexico: An-dorra, Argentina, Aruba, Australia, Austria, Bahamas, Belgium, Belize, Bermuda, Canada, Chile, Costa Rica, Denmark, Finland, France, Germany, Greece, Hungary, Iceland, Ireland, Israel, Italy, Japan, Liechtenstein, Luxembourg, Monaco, Netherlands, New Zealand, Norway, Poland, Portugal, San Marino, Singapore, Slovenia, South Korea, Spain, Sweden, Switzerland, United Kingdom, United States of America, Uruguay, Venezuela and Yugoslavia.

However, citizens of those countries must obtain a tourist card, which varies in price from $10 to $40 depending on your country of origin. A tourist card can be obtained upon arrival (see Tourist Cards, below).

To clear Mexican Immigrations, US citizens need to present one of the following documents at the port of entry: a valid passport; an original birth certificate, a certified copy of a birth certificate or a certificate of naturalization with an official photo identification (ie, a driver's license); a voter registration card with an official photo identification; or a notarized affidavit with official photo identification. Citizens from all other countries on the above list, except Canada, need to present a passport.

Canadian tourists may enter Mexico with an official photo identification plus a citizenship card, original birth certificate or notarized affidavit. Canadian landed immigrants, however, require a valid passport and their original landed immigration document (record of landing). Again, it is best to travel with a passport, because that is what Mexican immigration officers are accustomed to seeing.

Nationals from Ecuador, El Salvador and Jamaica are not required to have a visa to enter Mexico, but they have to obtain a tourist card stamped by the Mexican embassy in their home country.

Visitors from all countries not mentioned above need to have a valid passport and obtain a visa before entering Mexico. Visa requirements vary; if you need to obtain a visa to enter Mexico, be sure to contact the nearest Mexican embassy or consulate for requirements specific to your country of citizenship.

Tourist Cards

The tourist card (officially, the Forma Migratoria de Turista) is a brief paper document that you can obtain at any port of entry into Mexico. You are required to present it to an immigration officer when you enter and leave the country. At the US-Mexico border you won't usually be given one automatically – you have to ask for it.

At many US-Mexico border crossings you don't *have* to get the card stamped at the border itself (there are other immigration offices a little farther into Mexico, where it's possible to have the card stamped), but it's advisable in case there are difficulties elsewhere.

One section of the card deals with the length of your stay in Mexico. The normal maximum is 180 days, though for French, Austrian, Greek and Argentine passport holders it's 90 days. If you don't fill in this part yourself, Mexican immigration officials will often do it for you, putting '30 days' on the assumption you're there for a short vacation. If you want more time than that, fill in the number of days yourself or tell the officer before he or she does so.

In any case it's often advisable to put down more days than you think you'll need, in case you change your plans. Travelers entering Mexico from Guatemala or Belize may find that immigration officers will not put more than 15 or 30 days on their tourist card – as little as five days in some cases – but you should be able to get an extension once you are deeper inside Mexico (see Extensions & Lost Cards, below).

Look after your tourist card, as Mexican law requires you to carry it with you at all times while you're in Mexico and to hand it in when you leave the country. If you overstay the limit on your card, you may be subject to a fine (normally around US$50 for up to one month). If no one looks at your tourist card when you leave or reenter Mexico, as often happens at the US border, there would be nothing to stop you from using the same card more than once, provided it's still valid.

Extensions & Lost Cards If the limit on your tourist card is for less time than the maximum you're allowed (see previous section), its validity may be extended one or more times, at no cost, up to your maximum. But not everyone is automatically allowed the maximum – especially people applying for a second or subsequent extension. To get a card extended you have to apply at a Delegación de Servicios Migratorios (immigration office). These offices exist in many towns and cities on the peninsula, but the one in downtown Cancún processes extensions with the least hassle.

The procedure should be straightforward; you'll need your passport, tourist card, ticket out of Mexico (if you have one), and some evidence of 'sufficient funds' – a major credit card is OK, and at most offices US$300 in traveler's checks will suffice. Most offices will not extend a card until a few days before it is due to expire – it's not usually worth trying earlier.

If you lose your card or need further information, contact your embassy or consulate. They may be able to give you a letter enabling you to leave Mexico without your card, or at least an official note to take to your local Delegación de Servicios Migratorios, which will issue a duplicate. You can also call the SECTUR tourist office in Mexico City (☎ 01-800-714-9580 or 01-800-714-9562) for information.

Minors

Every year many parents try to run away from the USA or Canada to Mexico with their children to escape the legal machinations of the children's other parent. To prevent this, minors (people under 18) entering Mexico without one or both of their parents may be – and often are – required to show a notarized consent form, signed by the absent parent or parents, giving permission for the young traveler to enter Mexico.

In the case of divorced parents, a custody document may be needed, too. If one or both parents are dead, or the traveler has only one legal parent, a notarized statement saying so may be required.

These rules are aimed primarily at North Americans but apparently apply to all nationalities. Procedures vary from country to

country; if you or a traveling companion are younger than 18 years old, you should contact a Mexican consulate well ahead of your trip to find out exactly what you need to do.

Travel Insurance
See the Insurance section under Health, later in this chapter.

Driver's License & Permits
If you're thinking of renting a vehicle in Mexico, take your driver's license and a major credit card with you (preferably a gold or platinum American Express card, because of the auto coverage it provides that the other cards don't). For more information on rentals, see the Getting Around chapter. For the paperwork involved in taking your own vehicle into Mexico, see the Getting There & Away chapter.

Note that International Driving Permits generally are not considered valid driver's licenses by Mexican authorities.

Hostel, Student, Youth & Teacher Cards
A youth hostel card won't save you a peso at the few youth hostels on the Yucatán Peninsula, which are located in Playa del Carmen, Cancún and Chetumal and aren't too nice anyway. Notices at museums, archaeological sites and so on usually state that student prices apply to Mexicans only, but in practice the ISIC card will often result in a reduction. The same card may also get you discounts on some bus tickets, so take it along if you've got one. The GO25 card for travelers between ages 12 and 25, seniors' cards and the ITIC card for teachers generally are not recognized in Mexico.

Photocopies
Before you leave for Mexico, it's worthwhile making two photocopies of all important documents you're taking with you – things like the data pages of your passport and any important visas in it, plane tickets, insurance papers, traveler's check receipts or serial numbers, driver's license, vehicle papers, numbers of any credit or bank cards you're carrying, and contact telephone numbers for

replacing lost documents, checks or cards. Leave one set with someone at home, take the other with you, and keep it separate from the originals. When you get to Mexico, add a photocopy of your tourist card and, if you're driving, vehicle import papers. The copies can make things a whole lot easier if any of your documents are lost or stolen and you have to replace them.

It's also a good idea to store details of your vital travel documents in Lonely Planet's free online Travel Vault in case you lose the photocopies or can't be bothered with them. Your password-protected Travel Vault is accessible online anywhere in the world – create it at www.ekno.lonelyplanet.com.

EMBASSIES & CONSULATES
Mexican Embassies & Consulates
Unless otherwise noted, details are for embassies or their consular sections.

Argentina
Embassy: (☎ 01-821-7172) Larrea 1230, 1117 Buenos Aires

Australia
Embassy: (☎ 02-6273-3905) 14 Perth Ave, Yarralumla, Canberra, ACT 2600
Consulate: (☎ 02-9326-1311) Level 1, 135-153 New South Head Rd, Edgecliff, Sydney, NSW 2027

Austria
Embassy: (☎ 01-310-7383) Turkenstrasse 15, 1090 Vienna

Belgium
Embassy: (☎ 02-629-0711) Av Franklin Roosevelt 94, 1050 Brussels

Belize
Embassy: (☎ 02-30-193/194) 20 North Park St, Fort George Area, Belize City

Brazil
Embassy: (☎ 061-244-1011) SES Av das Nacoes Lote 18, 70412-900 Brasilia

Canada
Embassy: (☎ 613-233-8988/6665) 45 O'Connor St, suite 1500, Ottawa, ON K1P 1A4
Consulate: (☎ 514-288-2502) 2000 rue Mansfield, suite 1015, Montreal, PQ H3A 2Z7
Consulate: (☎ 416-368-2875) Commerce Court West, 199 Bay St, suite 4440, Toronto, ON M5L 1E9
Consulate: (☎ 604-684-1859) 810-1130 West Pender St, Vancouver, BC V6E 4A4

Costa Rica
Embassy: (☎ 225-4430) Av 7a No 1371, San José

Denmark
Embassy: (☎ 3961-0500) Strandvejen 64E, 2900 Hellerup, Copenhagen
El Salvador
Embassy: (☎ 243-0445) Calle Circunvalación y Pasaje No 12, Colonia San Benito, San Salvador
France
Embassy: (☎ 01-53-70-27-40) 9 rue de Longchamps, 75116 Paris
Consulate: (☎ 01-42-61-51-80) 4 rue Notre Dame des Victoires, 75002 Paris
Germany
Embassy: (☎ 0228-914-8620) Adenauerallee 100, 53113 Bonn
Consulate: (☎ 030-324-9047) Kurfurstendamm 72, 10709 Berlin
Consulate: (☎ 069-299-8750) Hochstrasse 35-37, 60330 Frankfurt-am-Main
Guatemala
Embassy: (☎ 333-7254) Edificio Centro Ejecutivo, 15a Calle No 3-20, 7th Nivel, Zona 10, Guatemala City
Consulate: (☎ 331-8165) 13a Calle No 7-30, Zona 9, Guatemala City
Consulate: (☎ 763-1312) 9a Av No 6-19, Zona 1, Quetzaltenango
Honduras
Embassy: (☎ 32-0138) Av República de México 2402, Colonia Palmira, Tegucigalpa
Ireland
Embassy: (☎ 01-260-0699) 43 Ailesbury Rd, Ballsbridge, Dublin 4
Israel
Embassy: (☎ 03-544-6705) Grand Beach Hotel, 250 Hayarkon, 63113 Tel Aviv
Italy
Embassy: (☎ 06-440-2309) Via Lazzaro Spallanzani 16, 00161 Rome
Consulate: (☎ 02-7602-0541) Via Cappuccini 4, 20122 Milan
Japan
Embassy: (☎ 03-3580-8734) 2-15-1 Nagata-Cho, Chiyoda-Ku, Tokyo 100
Netherlands
Embassy: (☎ 070-360-2900) Nassauplein 17, 2585 EB The Hague
New Zealand
Embassy: (☎ 04-472-5555) 8th floor, 111-115 Customhouse Quay, Wellington
Nicaragua
Embassy: (☎ 0-278-1860) Carretera a Masaya Km 4.5, 25 varas arriba (next to Optica Matamoros), Altamira, Managua

Norway
Embassy: (☎ 22-43-11-65) Drammensveien 108B, 0244 Oslo
South Africa
Embassy: (☎ 12-342-6190) Southern Life Plaza, 1st floor, CNR Schoeman and Festival Sts, Hatfield, 0083 Pretoria
Spain
Embassy: (☎ 91-369-2814) Carrera de San Jerónimo 46, 28014 Madrid
Consulate: (☎ 93-201-1822) Avinguda Diagonal 626, 08021 Barcelona
Consulate: (☎ 95-456-3944) Calle San Roque 6, 41001 Sevilla
Sweden
Embassy: (☎ 08-661-2213) Grevgatan 3, 11453 Stockholm
Switzerland
Embassy: (☎ 031-351-4060) Bernestrasse 57, 3005 Bern
UK
Embassy: (☎ 020-7235-6393) 8 Halkin St, London SW1X 7DW
USA
Embassy: (☎ 202-728-1694) 1911 Pennsylvania Ave NW, Washington, DC 20006
Consulate: (☎ 202-736-1000) 2827 16th St NW, Washington, DC 20009

Mexican Consulates in the USA There are consulates in many other US cities besides the one included above for Washington, DC, particularly in the border states.

Arizona
Douglas	☎ 520-364-3107
Nogales	☎ 520-287-2521
Phoenix	☎ 602-242-7398
Tucson	☎ 520-882-5595

California
Calexico	☎ 760-357-3863
Fresno	☎ 209-233-3065
Los Angeles	☎ 213-351-6800
Sacramento	☎ 916-441-2987
San Bernardino	☎ 909-889-9837
San Diego	☎ 619-231-9741
San Francisco	☎ 415-392-5554
San Jose	☎ 408-294-8334

Colorado
Denver	☎ 303-331-1110

Florida
Miami	☎ 305-716-4979
Orlando	☎ 407-894-0514

Georgia
Atlanta   ☎ 404-266-1913

Illinois
Chicago   ☎ 312-855-1380

Louisiana
New Orleans   ☎ 504-522-3596

Massachusetts
Boston   ☎ 617-426-4942

Michigan
Detroit   ☎ 313-567-7709

Missouri
St Louis   ☎ 314-436-3426

New Mexico
Albuquerque   ☎ 505-247-2139

New York
New York   ☎ 212-217-6400

Oregon
Portland   ☎ 503-274-1442

Pennsylvania
Philadelphia   ☎ 215-922-4262

Texas
Austin   ☎ 512-478-9031
Brownsville   ☎ 210-542-2051
Corpus Christi   ☎ 512-882-3375
Dallas   ☎ 214-630-1604
Del Rio   ☎ 830-775-2352
Eagle Pass   ☎ 830-773-9255
El Paso   ☎ 915-533-3644
Houston   ☎ 713-339-4701
Laredo   ☎ 956-723-6369
McAllen   ☎ 956-686-4684
Midland   ☎ 915-687-2334
San Antonio   ☎ 210-227-9145

Utah
Salt Lake City   ☎ 801-521-8502

Washington State
Seattle   ☎ 206-448-8435

Embassies & Consulates in Mexico

All embassies are in Mexico City, but many countries also have consulates in other cities around Mexico. Cancún is home to numerous foreign consulates, and several countries have diplomatic outposts in Mérida as well.

Many Mexican and foreign embassies and consulates have websites. Links to most of them can be found at the 'Embajadas' link on www.mexico.web.com.mx/. Two particularly useful sites, with tourist information and data on Mexican visas and tourist permits, are the Mexican embassy in Washington, DC (www.embassyofmexico.org) and the Mexican consulate in New York (www.quicklink.com/mexico).

As a tourist, it's important to realize what your embassy can and can't do. Generally speaking, it won't be much help in emergencies if the trouble you're in is remotely your own fault. Remember that you are bound by the laws of the country you are in. Your embassy will not be sympathetic if you end up in jail after committing a crime locally, even if such actions are legal in your own country.

In genuine emergencies you might get some assistance, but only if other channels have been exhausted. For example, if you need to get home urgently, a free ticket home is exceedingly unlikely – the embassy would expect you to have insurance. If you have all your money and documents stolen, it might assist in getting a new passport, but a loan for onward travel is out of the question.

The following is a selective list of embassies in Mexico City. They often keep limited business hours – usually 9 or 10 am to 1 or 2 pm Monday to Friday – and close on both Mexican and their own national holidays. Many do provide 24-hour emergency telephone contact. If you're telephoning from outside Mexico City, dial the long-distance access code 01 before the number given below. If you're visiting your embassy, it's best to call ahead to check hours and confirm that the address you're heading for is the right one for the service you want. The addresses below include the *colonias* (neighborhoods) of Mexico City in which the embassies are located, and any metro stations convenient to them.

Australia
(☎ 5-531-5225; Australians needing out-of-hours assistance can call reverse-charges the Australian number ☎ 61-2-6261-1446) Rubén Darío 55, Polanco

Belize
(☎ 5-520-1274) Bernardo de Gálvez 215, Lomas de Chapultepec

Canada
(☎ 5-724-7900, ☎ 800-706-2900) Schiller 529, Polanco

France
(☎ 5-282-9700) Lafontaine 32, Polanco

Germany
(☎ 5-283-2200) Lord Byron 737, Polanco

Guatemala
(☎ 5-540-7520) Av Explanada 1025, Lomas de Chapultepec

Netherlands
(☎ 5-258-9921, emergency ☎ 5-505-0752) Av Vasco de Quiroga 3000, 7th piso, Santa Fe

New Zealand
(☎ 5-281-5486) Lagrange 103, 10th piso, Los Morales

UK
(☎ 5-207-2089) Río Lerma 71, Colonia Cuauhté-moc, Independencia; consular section at rear (Río Usumacinta 30)

USA
(☎ 5-209-9100, always attended) Paseo de la Reforma 305 at Río Danubio, Colonia Cuauhté-moc; visa office (☎ 01-900-849-3737) at side of embassy on Río Danubio

A number of countries have consulates in the Yucatán Peninsula.

Austria
(☎ 9-984-7505) Calle Cantera No 4, Ciudad Cancún

Belgium
(☎ 9-925-2939/2996) Calle 25 No 159 between Calles 28 and 30, Mérida

Belize
(☎ 9-832-2871, 9-882-2100, fax 9-882-0100) Avenida Álvaro Obregon No 226A, Chetumal.

Canada
(☎ 9-983-3360, fax 9-983-3232) Plaza Caracol No 330, Zona Hotelera, Cancún

Denmark
(☎ 9-925-4488/4599) Calle 32 No 198 at Calle 17, Colonia Garcia Ginerés, Mérida

Finland
(☎ 9-984-1557/3712) Av Nader No 28, suite 2, Ciudad Cancún

France
(☎ 9-985-2924) Casa Turquesa, Blvd Kukulcán Km 13.5, Zona Hotelera, Cancún
(☎ 9-925-2291, fax 9-925-7009) Calle 33B No 528 between Calles 62 and 64, Mérida

Germany
(☎ 9-984-1898) Punta Conoco No 36, Ciudad Cancún
(☎ 9-981-2976) Calle 7 No 217 between Calles 20 and 20A, Colonia Chuburna de Hidalgo, Mérida

Great Britain
(☎ 9-985-0100, fax 9-985-1225) Royal Caribbean, Blvd Kukulcán Km 16.5, Zona Hotelera, Cancún

Guatemala
(☎ 9-832-3045) Retorno Numero 4, Casa 8, Fraccionamiento Bahía, Chetumal

Honduras
(☎ 9-944-8206) Calle 54 No 280, Fraccionamiento del Norte, Mérida

Italy
(☎ 9-984-1261, fax 9-984-5415) Calle Alcatraces No 39, Ciudad Cancún

Netherlands
(☎ 9-983-0200) Presidente Inter-Continental, Blvd Kukulcán Km 7, Zona Hotelera, Cancún
(☎ 9-924-3122, 9-924-4147, 9-946-1155) Calle 64 No 418 between Calles 47 and 49, Mérida

Spain
(☎ 9-983-2466, fax 9-983-2870) Edificio Oasis, Blvd Kukulcán Km 6.5, Zona Hotelera, Cancún
(☎ 9-927-1520, fax 9-923-0055) Calle 3 No 237, Fraccionamiento Campestre, Mérida

Switzerland
(☎ 9-981-8000, fax 9-981-8080) Caesar Park, Blvd Kukulcán Km 17, Zona Hotelera, Cancún

UK
(☎ 9-928-6152, fax 9-928-3962) Calle 53 No 489 at Calle 58, Fraccionamiento del Norte, Mérida; you can also obtain information about travel in Belize here

USA
(☎ 9-983-0272, fax 9-983-1373) Plaza Caracol, 3rd floor, Blvd Kukulcán Km 8.5, Zona Hotelera, Cancún
(☎ 9-925-5409, fax 9-925-6219) Paseo de Montejo 453 at Av Colón, Mérida

CUSTOMS

When entering Mexico, customs agents generally indicate a button for you to push on what looks like a traffic signal. If you get a green light, you go right through without inspection. If you get a red light, your luggage will be inspected, usually quickly and courteously. This system was instituted to discourage the former system, whereby the tediousness of the inspection was inversely proportional to the size of the 'tip' (ie, bribe) you paid the customs official.

MONEY
Currency

Officially, Mexico's currency is the *nuevo peso* (new peso), but everyone refers to it

simply as the peso. It is divided into 100 centavos. Coins come in denominations of five, 10, 20 and 50 centavos and one, two, five, 10, 20 and 50 pesos, and there are notes of 10, 20, 50, 100, 200 and 500 pesos.

The $ sign is used to refer to pesos in Mexico, and the designations 'N$,' 'NP' (both for nuevos pesos) and 'MN' *(moneda nacional)* all refer to pesos. Prices quoted in US dollars will normally be written 'US$X,' '$X Dlls' or 'X USD,' with the X representing an actual dollar amount.

Because the peso's exchange value is unpredictable, prices in this book are given in US dollar equivalents. Indeed, the value of the peso varies daily, sometimes fluctuating as much as 10% from one day to the next against foreign currencies. At the time this book was researched, the average daily exchange rate was N$10 for US$1.

Exchange Rates
Though banks and *casas de cambio* (exchange houses) change most major currencies, US dollars are always easiest to change due to their economic stability on the global market and the proximity of the United States. Bank automated teller machines (ATMs) give the best service (24 hours a day) and rates. The worst rates in all of Yucatán are found in Cancún's hotel zone. The next worst? Downtown Cancún.

In such heavily touristed areas as Cancún and Cozumel you can often spend US dollars as easily as pesos. Most of the time you won't get as good an exchange rate as if you had changed your dollars for pesos at a bank; sometimes the rates in hotels, restaurants and shops will be downright outrageous. However, in other establishments – to induce you to spend your money there – dollars are accepted at an exchange rate as good as or better than that of the banks.

At the time this book went to press, the following exchange rates applied:

country	unit		nuevos pesos
Australia	A$1	=	N$5.71
Canada	CN$1	=	N$6.35
euro	€1	=	N$9.00
France	FFr1	=	N$1.37
Germany	DM1	=	N$4.60
Italy	IL1000	=	N$4.65
Japan	J¥100	=	N$8.81
New Zealand	NZ$1	=	N$4.56
UK	UK£1	=	N$14.65
USA	US$1	=	N$9.31

Exchanging Money
You can change money in banks or at casas de cambio (which are often single-window kiosks). Banks go through a more time-consuming procedure than casas de cambio and have shorter exchange hours (typically 9 or 10 am to 1 or 2 pm Monday to Friday). Casas de cambio can easily be found in just about every large or medium-size town and in many smaller ones. They're quick and often open afternoons, evenings or weekends, but they may not accept traveler's checks, which rarely happens in banks.

Exchange rates vary a little from one bank or casa de cambio to another. Different rates are also often posted for *efectivo* (cash) and *documento* (traveler's checks). On the whole, though not invariably, banks give better rates for traveler's checks than for cash, and casas de cambio do the opposite.

If you have trouble finding a place to change money, particularly on a weekend, you can always try a hotel – though the exchange rate won't be the best.

Traveler's Checks & Cash Even if you have a credit card or debit card, you should still take along some major-brand traveler's checks (best denominated in US dollars) as a backup, or – less desirable for security reasons – cash US dollars. If you don't have a credit card or debit card, use US-dollar traveler's checks. American Express is a good brand to have because it's recognized everywhere, which can prevent delays. American Express in Mexico City maintains a 24-hour hot line (☎ 5-326-3625) for lost American Express traveler's checks; you can call it collect from anywhere in Mexico.

ATMs Not so long ago automated teller machines were uncommon in Yucatán. Today,

the majority of banks on the peninsula have at least one ATM out front.

ATMs are generally the easiest source of cash. Despite the handling charge that will normally appear on your account, by using ATMs you get a good exchange rate and avoid the commission you would pay when changing cash or traveler's checks.

Mexican banks call their ATMs by a variety of names – usually something like *caja permanente* or *cajero automático*. Each ATM displays the cards it will accept. To guard against robbery when using ATMs, try to use them during the bank's working hours and choose ones that are securely inside a bank building, rather than the glass-enclosed ones on the street.

Credit & Debit Cards The easiest money in Mexico is a major credit card or bank cash card (called debit card). Credit cards such as Visa and MasterCard (Eurocard, Access) are accepted by virtually all airlines, car-rental companies and travel agents in Mexico, and by many hotels, restaurants and shops; American Express cards are widely accepted too.

Equally convenient, you can use major credit cards and some bank cards, such as those on the Cirrus and Plus systems, to withdraw cash pesos from ATMs (bank cash machines) and over the counter at banks.

International Money Transfers If you need money wired to you in Mexico, an easy and quick method is the Western Union 'Dinero en Minutos' (Money in Minutes) service. It's offered by the approximately 300 Elektra electrical-goods stores around Mexico (most are open 9 am to 9 pm daily), and by the *telégrafos* (telegraph) offices in many cities. Your sender pays the money at the nearest Western Union branch, along with a fee, and gives the details on who is to receive it and where. When you go to pick up the money, take photo identification.

Western Union has offices worldwide; check a local telephone directory for the telephone number of an office nearest you. In the USA, call ☎ 800-325-6000.

Black Market The peso is exchanged freely, so there is no black market in Mexico. However, that doesn't stop some confidence artists from trying to cheat tourists with 'good black-market rates.'

Some years ago the Mexican government issued new currency (ie, the new peso) and withdrew from circulation the old currency. Some of the old bills are still around, though they usually only see the light of day these days when a con artist is pulling a scam.

Don't be a victim. If someone on the street solicits you with, 'Change money?' and a friendly smile, you'd be wise to say no, smile back and keep moving.

Security

Moneychangers Most moneychangers won't try to rip you off, but every once and a while one will try to shortchange you. Why? Because many tourists don't bother counting the pesos they've just exchanged, and that bad habit tempts some moneychangers to try to keep some of *your* pesos.

Be smart with your money. Whenever you exchange it, always take the time to count it – and count it right there at the counter, so that if there is a discrepancy, the moneychanger won't accuse you of trying to pull a fast one. The amount you receive should equal the total amount shown on a slip of paper that'll be handed to you with the pesos.

Be advised that the figure shown on the slip of paper is sometimes incorrect. For this reason, it's always good to use a calculator to do your own math when exchanging money, to ensure that you're not the victim of a 'calculating error.'

Carrying Money Ideally, when you're out and about, carry only what you'll need that day. Leave the rest in the *caja fuerte* (hotel safe). If there isn't a safe, you have to decide whether it's better to carry your funds with you or try to hide them in your room. Baggage that you can lock up is an advantage here. It's also a good idea to divide your funds into several stashes in different places.

See Dangers & Annoyances, later in this chapter, for more tips on safeguarding your money.

Receiving Change When paying for something, wait until all of the change has been counted out before picking it up. A favorite ruse of dishonest ticket clerks in particular is to hand over the change slowly, bit by bit, in the hope that you'll pick it up and go before you have it all.

Costs

Cancún and Cozumel are the two most expensive places in Mexico, far more expensive than Mexico City or even Acapulco. Small towns such as Tizimín and Izamal, not being heavily touristed, are much cheaper. Cities such as offer a good range of prices, with good values for your money.

In Cancún and Cozumel, a single traveler staying in budget or lower-middle-range accommodations and eating two meals a day in restaurants should plan to pay between US$50 and US$70 per day during the low tourist season (April to mid-December); expect to pay at least 50% more during the high season.

Elsewhere on the peninsula, food and accommodations cost considerably less. For budget purposes, figure on US$35 a day for two restaurant meals and a fan-only room and US$50 for two restaurant meals and an air-con room. Add in the other costs of travel (snacks, purified water, soft drinks, admission to archaeological sites, local transportation, etc), and you may find yourself spending an additional US$30 or so per day.

If there are two or more of you sharing accommodations, costs per person come down considerably. Double rooms are often only a few dollars more than singles, and triples or quadruples are only very slightly more expensive than doubles.

Rental-car rates and airfares range widely, but tend to fluctuate mostly with time of purchase and time of use. If you want to rent a car during the high tourist season, expect to pay as much as US$45 or more per day just for a Volkswagen Beetle – excluding insurance. If you decide to reserve a Beetle only a week in advance, you'll likely find that none are available, which means you'll have to rent a more expensive vehicle, if you intend to rent at all.

It's wise to make your car-rental reservation far in advance, and be sure to have a confirmation faxed or emailed to you indicating the amount you were quoted.

Of course, the prices cited here are only estimates. Inflation and currency fluctuations can dramatically effect your costs. Moreover, one person's 'budget' room will be another person's 'luxury' room. If your idea of a budget room includes air-con and a TV, you'll pay much more than someone who can easily do without both.

Tipping & Bargaining

In general, people on staff in the smaller, cheaper places don't expect much in the way of tips, while those in the expensive resort establishments expect you to be lavish in your largesse. In Yucatán, as well as elsewhere in México, a 5% tip is considered stingy or insulting, a 10% tip is viewed as a good one, and a 15% tip is seen as generous. Taxi drivers don't generally expect tips, but gas station attendants do.

Though you can attempt to bargain down the price of a hotel room, especially in cheaper places and in the off-season, the rates normally are set fairly firmly, particularly during the busy winter season. In markets, bargaining is the rule, and you may pay much more than the going rate if you accept the first price quoted. You should also bargain with drivers of unmetered taxis.

Taxes

Mexico's *Impuesto de Valor Agregado* (Value-Added Tax), abbreviated IVA (EE-bah), is levied at 15%. By law the tax must be included in virtually any price quoted to you and should not be added afterward. Signs in shops and notices on restaurant menus often state *'IVA incluido.'* Occasionally they state instead that IVA must be added to the quoted prices.

Impuesto Sobre Hospedaje (Lodging Tax), abbreviated ISH ('ee-ESS-e-AHCH-e'), is levied on the price of hotel rooms. Each Mexican state sets its own level of ISH, but in most places it's 2%.

Most budget and mid-range accommodations include both IVA and ISH in quoted

prices (though it's sometimes worth checking if the rate seems unusually low compared to others in the area or those listed in this book). But in top-end hotels a price may often be given as, say, 'US$100 *más impuestos*' (plus taxes), in which case you must add about 17% to the figure. When in doubt, ask, '*¿Están incluidos los impuestos?*' (Are taxes included?)

Prices in this book include IVA and ISH. See the Getting There & Away and Getting Around chapters for details of taxes on air travel. For information on the new-in-1999 visitor tax, please see the beginning of the Getting There & Away chapter.

POST & COMMUNICATIONS
Post
Almost every town in the Yucatán has an *oficina de correos* (post office) where you can buy stamps and send or receive mail. They're usually open Saturday mornings as well as long hours Monday to Friday.

Sending Mail An airmail letter weighing up to 20g costs US$0.50 to North America, US$0.60 to Europe and US$0.70 to Australasia. Post cards are slightly cheaper.

Delivery times are elastic, and packages in particular sometimes go missing. If you are sending something by airmail, be sure to clearly mark it 'Correo Aéreo.' *Certificado* (registered) service helps ensure delivery and costs less than US$1. An airmail letter from Mexico to the USA or Canada can take four to 14 days to arrive but often takes longer. Mail to Europe may take between one and three weeks, to Australasia a month or more.

If you're sending a package internationally from Mexico, be prepared to open it for customs inspection; take packing materials with you to the post office.

For assured and speedy delivery, you can use one of the expensive international courier services, such as United Parcel Service (UPS), Federal Express or DHL. Minimum rates from Mexico (for delivery of a package weighing up to 500g) are in the region of US$22 to North America or US$28 to Europe.

Receiving Mail You can receive letters and packages care of a post office if they're addressed as follows (for example):

Jane SMITH (last name in capitals)
Lista de Correos
Cozumel
Quintana Roo 00000 (post code)
MEXICO

When the letter reaches the post office, the addressee's name is put on a list. Try to check the list yourself – it's often pinned on the wall – because the letter may be listed under your first name instead of your last. To claim your mail, present your passport or other identification. There's no charge; the snag is that many post offices hold 'Lista' mail for only 10 days before returning it to the sender. If you think you're going to pick up mail more than 10 days after it has arrived, have it sent c/o Poste Restante (for example):

Jane SMITH (last name in capitals)
Poste Restante
Correo Central
Cozumel
Quintana Roo 00000 (post code)
MEXICO

Poste restante may hold mail for up to a month, but no list of what has been received is posted. Again, there's no charge for collection.

If you have an American Express card or American Express traveler's checks, you can have mail sent to you c/o any of the 50-plus American Express offices in Mexico. Take along your card or a traveler's check to show when you collect the mail.

Inbound mail usually takes as long to arrive as outbound mail does (see above), and international packages coming into Mexico may go missing, just like outbound ones.

Telephone
Local calls are cheap, but domestic long-distance and international calls can be very expensive. Generally, using a phone card at a public pay phone (see below) is the least expensive way to place a call in Mexico.

There's a wide range of local and international phonecards. Lonely Planet's eKno Communication Card (see the insert at the back of this book) is aimed specifically at independent travelers and provides budget international calls, a range of messaging services and free email and travel information – but for local calls, you're usually better off with a local card such as Ladatel. You can join eKno online at www.ekno .lonelyplanet.com or by phone from Mexico by dialing ☎ 001-800-514-0287.

Check the eKno Web site for joining and access numbers from other countries and updates on super budget local access numbers and new features.

There are three main types of places you can place a call from. Cheapest is a public pay phone. A bit more expensive is a *caseta de teléfono* or *caseta telefónica* – a call station, maybe in a shop or restaurant, where an operator connects the call for you and you take it in a booth. The third option is to call from your hotel, but hotels can – and do – charge what they like for this service; it's nearly always cheaper to go elsewhere.

Be advised that at the time of writing Mexico's telephone system was undergoing major changes. Until 1999, many phone numbers in Mexico were five, six or seven digits long. Likewise, the areas codes varied in length. Cancún, for example, had a 983 area code followed by a five-digit phone number. Today, the area code for Cancún is 9, and 83 has been added to the beginning of most of the telephone numbers.

You may still see phone numbers expressed the old way. In Mérida, the old way would be area code 99 followed by a six-digit number. Today, Mérida's area code is 9 (yes, same as Cancún's) followed by a seven-digit number beginning with a 9.

The changes are meant to create a more uniform numbering system whereby all telephone numbers in Mexico are seven digits long.

Public Pay Phones These are common in towns and cities: You'll usually find some at airports, bus stations and around the main square of any sizable town. Most work OK.

Those operated by Telmex are usually marked 'Ladatel,' 'Lada 91,' 'Lada 01' or 'Telmex.' 'Lada' stands for *larga distancia* (long distance), but these phones work for both local and long-distance calls.

Nearly all Telmex pay phones work exclusively on *tarjetas telefónicas* or *tarjetas Ladatel* (phone cards). The cards are sold at many kiosks and shops – look for the blue-and-yellow sign reading *'De Venta Aquí Ladatel'* – in denominations of 20, 50 or 100 pesos. See below for the average cost per call. As you talk, the display shows you how much credit you have left on the card. Only a few pay phones are still coin-operated.

Casetas Casetas de teléfono are more expensive than pay phones (anywhere from 10% to 100% more), but you don't need a phone card to use them, and they eliminate street noise. Casetas usually have a telephone symbol outside, or signs saying 'teléfono,' 'Lada' or 'Larga Distancia.'

Prefixes, Codes & Costs When dialing a call, you need to know what *prefijo* (prefix) and *claves* (country or area codes) to put before the number. If you are making a call in Mexico, the prefixes, codes and approximate costs of local and long-distance calls vary depending on where you are calling. General guidelines are as follows:

calls to city/town you are in – no need to dial a prefix or code; US$0.04 per minute

calls to other cities/towns in Mexico – dial 01 + area code; US$0.40 per minute

calls to USA or Canada – dial 00 + country code + area code; US$1.30 per minute

calls to Europe – dial 00 + country code + area code; US$2.75 per minute

calls to Australasia – dial 00 + country code + area code; US$3.50 per minute

Telmex international calls are 33% cheaper at the following times:

calls to the USA (except Alaska and Hawaii) and Canada: Monday to Friday 7 pm to 6.59 am, Saturday all day, Sunday till 4.59 pm

calls to Europe or Australasia: Monday to Friday 6 pm to 5.59 am (Europe), 5 am to 4.59 pm (Australasia), Saturday and Sunday all day (both)

If you need to speak to a domestic operator, call ☎ 020; for an international operator, call ☎ 090. For Mexican directory information, call ☎ 040. The country code for Mexico is 52.

To call a number in Mexico from another country, dial your international access code, then the Mexico country code – 52 – then the area code and number.

Toll-Free Numbers Mexican toll-free numbers – all ☎ 800 followed by five digits – always require the 01 prefix. Most US toll-free numbers are ☎ 800 or 888 followed by seven digits. In general you cannot call a toll-free number from outside the country where it is based, but in the US and Canada you can call any toll-free number in either of those two countries.

North American Calling Cards If you have an AT&T, MCI or Sprint card, a Canadian calling card or HELLO! phone pass or Call-Me service, you can use them for calls from Mexico to the USA or Canada by dialing the access numbers below. You can check with your phone company before going to Mexico to ask about costs and exactly what procedures you'll have to follow. Normally, after dialing the access number you either have to enter your calling card number or follow voice prompts or operator instructions.

AT&T	☎ 001-800-462-4240
Canada Direct	☎ 01-800-123-0200
MCI	☎ 01-800-021-8000
Sprint	☎ 001-800-877-8000

If you get an operator who asks for your Visa or MasterCard number instead of your calling card number, or says the service is unavailable, hang up and dial again. There are various scams in which calls are rerouted to credit card phone services (also see the Credit Card Phones section, below).

Collect Calls A *llamada por cobrar* (collect call) can cost the receiving party much more than if *they* call *you*, so it's cheaper for them if you find a phone where you can receive an incoming call, then pay for a

quick call to the other party to ask them to call you back. Be forewarned, collect calls from Mexico can be outrageously high. A collect call from Cancún to New York, for example, can cost as much as US$20 per minute. It's a good idea to ask the operator for the per-minute rate before you place your collect call.

If you do need to make a collect call, you can do so from pay phones without a card. Call an operator at ☎ 020 for domestic calls, or ☎ 090 for international calls. Mexican international operators can usually speak English.

Some telephone casetas and hotels will make collect calls for you, but they usually charge for the service.

Credit Card Phones In Cancún, Cozumel and Mérida, you'll find phones with signs urging you to charge calls to MasterCard, Visa or American Express. Some of them resemble Pacific Bell or AT&T phones. Beware that very high rates – as high as US$23 for the first minute, US$8 per minute thereafter – are charged on these devices, which require dialing only 0 to contact an international operator.

Fax, Email & Internet Access

It's generally possible to send faxes from hotels in Yucatán; the service is often available to guests. Where it's not, a tip will usually result in the service being rendered. Faxes can also usually be sent from Internet cafés, and there are many other businesses that provide the service; those that do generally post a *'Fax Público'* sign in their window.

Internet cafés can be found with little difficulty in Ciudad Cancún, Cozumel, Playa del Carmen, Mérida and Tulum; they're harder to locate elsewhere. These cafés typically charge around US$3 to US$5 for 30 minutes on a computer.

INTERNET RESOURCES

The World Wide Web is a rich resource for travelers. You can research your trip, hunt down bargain airfares, book hotels, check on weather conditions or chat with locals and

other travelers about the best places to visit (or avoid!).

There's no better place to start your web explorations than the Lonely Planet website (www.lonelyplanet.com). Here you'll find succinct summaries on traveling to most places on earth, postcards from other travelers and the Thorn Tree bulletin board, where you can ask questions before you go or dispense advice when you get back. You can also find travel news and updates to many of our most popular guidebooks, and the sub-WWWay section links you to the most useful travel resources elsewhere on the web.

There are dozens of websites touting accommodations and tourist-related services in and to Yucatán. All, of course, were created to sell something. So, buyer, beware; that website describing a 'hidden secret' in 'paradise' was most likely created by the owner of the so-called hidden secret in paradise. Don't be surprised if the hidden secret doesn't live up to its billing.

Likewise, the Official Home Page of the Ministry of Tourism of Mexico (www.mexico-travel.com/sectur.htm) contains all kinds of information on the country's archaeological sites, its individual states and so on, but keep in mind that the source has many vested interests in portraying Mexico in a certain light. The book you hold in your hands is one of the few places to turn for truly objective reporting on things Yucatecan.

For the latest positive news out of Quintana Roo, check out Novedades Quintana Roo (www.cancun.novenet.com.mx/), which bills itself as 'a daily newspaper of Cancún, Mexico.' You won't find any negative news at this site, but you will find plenty of informative updates as well as plenty of hotel, restaurant and reservation information for the entire Yucatán state.

Two other websites that may be of interest to you are: Cancún Online (www.cancun.com/), which offers even more information on Quintana Roo; and the US State Department Travel Advisory page (www.travel.state.gov/travel_warnings.html), which occasionally provides useful information concerning crime issues in various parts of Mexico.

BOOKS

Most books are published in different editions by different publishers in different countries. As a result, a book might be a hardcover rarity in one country while readily available in paperback in another. Fortunately, bookstores and libraries can search by title or author, so your local bookstore or library is the best place to find out about the availability of the following recommendations.

That said, the titles mentioned below can often be found in bookstores in Cancún, Mérida and Cozumel. However, they generally cost substantially more in Mexico than they do in the US, Canada or the UK.

Lonely Planet

Lonely Planet also publishes *Guatemala, Belize & Yucatán – La Ruta Maya*, which is well worth the cover price if you intend to visit Mayan sites outside the Yucatán Peninsula. In addition to the three Yucatán states covered in this book, *GBY* also covers the Mexican states of Tabasco and Chiapas. If you intend to travel in Mexico outside the five states covered in *GBY*, you might consider purchasing *Mexico*, which is *the* travel guide to the country. A handy companion for anyone traveling in Mexico is Lonely Planet's *Latin American Spanish phrasebook*, which contains practical, up-to-date words and expressions in Latin American Spanish. If you are going to be doing some diving and snorkeling, get Lonely Planet's

Internet Book Search Engines

The following Internet sites are helpful for locating hard-to-find books:

Advanced Book Exchange
    www.abebooks.com
Amazon.com
    www.amazon.com
Bibliofind
    www.bibliofind.com
Interloc
    www.interloc.com

Pisces guide *Diving & Snorkeling: Cozumel* – it has beautiful, full-color underwater shots and detailed accounts of the possible dives and dive outfitters.

Guidebooks

Those of you with a keen interest in pre-Hispanic sites should acquire *A Guide to Ancient Mexican Ruins* and *A Guide to Ancient Maya Ruins*, both by C Bruce Hunter. Between them, the two books provide maps and details on more than 40 sites.

Travel

Incidents of Travel in Central America, Chiapas & Yucatán and *Incidents of Travel in Yucatán*, by John L Stephens, are fascinating accounts of adventure and discovery by the enthusiastic 19th-century amateur archaeologist. The latter book is most always available in Cancún and Mérida bookstores. Both books contain superb illustrations by architect Frederick Catherwood, who accompanied Stephens in 1839 and 1841 as he explored a large part of the Mayan region. The two works have become classics in the literature on ancient Mayan cities.

Graham Greene's *Lawless Roads* traces his wanderings down the eastern side of Mexico to Chiapas in the 1930s, a time of conflict between Catholics and the atheistic state. Greene wasn't impressed with Mexican food, which he found to be 'all a hideous red and yellow, green and brown.' Aldous Huxley's *Beyond the Mexique Bay*, first published in 1934, has interesting observations on the Maya. It's also worth reading if you're going to be visiting Oaxaca.

Travelers' Tales Mexico, edited by James O'Reilly and Larry Habegger, is a very readable anthology containing about 50 recent articles and essays on all sorts of Mexican places and experiences, and it includes a number of compelling articles about Yucatecan adventures. The book makes for excellent in-country reading.

History & Society

Two books by Michael D Coe give a learned and well illustrated but not overly lengthy picture of the great cultures of ancient Mexico: *The Maya* traces the history, art and culture of the Maya, while *Mexico* concentrates on Mexico's other pre-Hispanic civilizations. Both have gone through several editions. Coe's 1992 book *Breaking the Maya Code* tells the fascinating story of the partial deciphering of ancient Mayan writing.

Maria Longhena's *Ancient Mexico*, published in 1998, is a large, hardbound, extremely presentable book that features history and culture of the Maya, Aztecs and other pre-Columbian peoples. The book contains scores of gorgeous color photographs of ruins, ancient art and artifacts. Due to its size and weight, this is not a book to travel with, but it is an excellent book to review prior to visiting the ancient Mayan cities.

TR Ferrenbach offers Mexico buffs a wealth of information presented in a compelling manner with his 1995 title, *Fire & Blood*. Though the book describes the entire history of Mexico, from man's arrival in Middle America up to the mid-1990s, it's worth buying if only for the first of its three parts; Part One takes the reader from the earliest peoples up to the Spanish Conquest, and in it Ferrenbach describes the ancient Maya and other Amerindians in spellbinding prose.

William Henry Prescott's mammoth *History of the Conquest of Mexico* remains a classic, even though it was published in 1843 by an author who never went to Mexico. Only with Hugh Thomas' *Conquest: Montezuma, Cortés & The Fall of Old Mexico* has the 20th century produced an equivalent tome. This book, the product of meticulous research, was published in Britain as *The Conquest of Mexico* in 1993.

Richard and Rosalind Perry present Yucatán history fans with a special treat with their 1988 paperback *Maya Missions: Exploring the Spanish Colonial Churches of Yucatán*. This is one book that's difficult to put down. It tells the spectacular histories of the peninsula's monasteries, many of which were built atop ancient Mayan pyramids. Over the years, the churches came under attack by pirates, by Mayan rebels and by zealous revolutionaries, and the Perrys do a superlative job of recounting these attacks,

as well as describing the architectural features unique to each of the missions.

Friar Diego de Landa's book *Yucatán Before and After the Conquest* can be bought in a number of bookstores and shops at archaeological sites in the Yucatán. Landa played a major role in wiping out Mayan culture and civilization; in July 1562, in the town of Maní, for example, he ordered the destruction of 5000 Mayan images and 27 hieroglyphics. But, somewhat amazingly, he wrote a superb book describing Mayan ceremonial festivals, daily life, history, clothing, human sacrifices, the Spanish conquest and more.

Yet another detailed, first-hand account of Mexico's colonization may be found in the *True History of the Conquest of New Spain*, by one of the conquistadors, Bernal Díaz del Castillo.

Artists Frida Kahlo and Diego Rivera

Art, Architecture & Crafts

Mask Arts of Mexico, by Ruth D Lechuga and Chloe Sayer, is a finely illustrated work by two experts. Sayer has also written two fascinating books tracing the evolution of crafts from pre-Hispanic times to the present, with dozens of beautiful photos: *Arts & Crafts of Mexico* is a wide-ranging overview, while *Mexican Textiles* is a comprehensive treatment of its absorbing topic, with a wealth of detail about Mexican life.

The Art of Mesoamerica, by Mary Ellen Miller, in the Thames & Hudson World of Art series, is a good survey of pre-Hispanic art and architecture. The most important single book on colonial architecture is George Kubler's *Mexican Architecture of the Sixteenth Century* (1948).

Good books on Mexico's great 20th-century artists include Diego Rivera's autobiography *My Art, My Life*; *The Fabulous Life of Diego Rivera*, by BD Wolfe; *Frida: A Biography of Frida Kahlo*, by Hayden Herrera; *Frida Kahlo*, another biography, by Malka Drucker; and *The Mexican Muralists*, by Alma M Reed.

Flora, Fauna & Environment

Roland H Wauer's *Naturalist's Mexico* (1992) is a guide to dozens of areas of natural interest all around Mexico, based on the author's three decades of annual trips exploring what he calls 'a biological paradise of enormous natural diversity.'

Defending the Land of the Jaguar (1995), by Lane Simonian, is the detailed but absorbing story of Mexico's long, if weak, tradition of conservation, from pre-Hispanic forest laws to the modern environmental movement.

Dedicated birders should seek out the Spanish-language *Aves de México*, by Roger Tory Peterson and Edward L Chalif, published by Mexico's Editorial Diana. The English-language version of this book, *A Field Guide to Mexican Birds*, omits pictures of birds that also appear in Peterson's guides to US birds. An alternative is *A Guide to the Birds of Mexico & Northern Central America*, by Steve NG Howell and Sophie Webb.

In 1999, Howell came out with an excellent book, *A Bird-Finding Guide to Mexico*, which breaks down the country by regions and then provides maps and instructions on how to see the most interesting birds within each region. The last chapter, for example, which is devoted to the Yucatán Peninsula, provides readers with 10 superior birding sites on the peninsula, with easy-to-follow directions, user-friendly maps and a list of species to look for at each site. In her 1992 *Check-list of the Birds of the Yucatán Peninsula*, Barbara MacKinnon identifies some 509 known species of bird on the peninsula and nearby islands. It's pretty much a must-have for serious birders.

Brimming with bright color photos, *The Pisces Guide to Caribbean Reef Ecology*, by William S Alevizon, introduces its subject with lively text.

NEWSPAPERS & MAGAZINES
English Language
The respected US newspapers *The Miami Herald* and *The New York Times*, along with *Time* and *Newsweek* magazines, are available in bookstores in Cancún, Mérida and Cozumel; elsewhere in Yucatán they're difficult or impossible to acquire.

The quarterly *Mundo Maya* (Maya World) contains articles in Spanish and English about the Mayan culture and natural attractions found in the Mayan-populated regions of Mexico, Belize, Honduras, Guatemala and El Salvador. The current edition of this excellent magazine can be read online, and back issues and upcoming issues can be ordered via the Internet.

The English-language, locally published *Mexico City News* is distributed throughout Mexico wherever tourists gather. The price varies with location, but is usually about US$1.

Spanish Language
Mexico has a thriving local Spanish-language press. Even small cities often have two or three newspapers of their own, each with their own political agenda. Many are controlled by political parties and the quality of their reporting cannot be trusted. In addition, most won't report on allegations of corruption or drug trafficking, due to very real threats such stories pose to the journalists who write them.

However, one of the finest newspapers in all of Mexico is Mérida's *El Diario de Yucatán*, which frequently reports on allegations of drug trafficking and governmental improprieties, despite expensive lawsuits, anonymous death threats and other pressures.

RADIO & TV
There's a broad range of radio programming available in Cancún, a fairly wide selection in Mérida and Campeche, and in Chetumal it's possible to pick up several of the English radio stations broadcasting in Belize. Outside of these areas there's scarcely a thing on the dial. If you'll be traveling around the peninsula in a rental car, you might want to consider bringing a portable tape/CD/minidisc player with you.

In the cities, the better hotels will provide in-room cable TV or satellite TV, and either will carry a host of Mexican and American programming. Outside of the cities, expect no more than three local stations on your in-room TV. Tube addicts needn't fret, however; most towns and all of the cities on the peninsula have bars, and they typically are rigged to receive satellite TV. Don't, however, expect the shows to be set to English-language programming unless you're in a very touristy locale.

PHOTOGRAPHY & VIDEO
Film & Equipment
Common print film manufactured by Kodak and Fuji is readily available in areas frequented by tourists, but it usually costs more that what you'd pay in the USA, Canada or Europe. Slide film is considerably rarer outside Cancún (where it's plentiful), usually limited to Kodak's Ektachrome and Agfachrome (although Fuji Velvia is available in downtown Cancún).

More important, film is heat sensitive, but it seems many Yucatecans are unaware of this fact. Often a store's entire stock of film will be on display in the front window – directly exposed to the intense tropical sun. Film that's been 'stored' this way usually

produces washed-out images. Fuji Velvia, a top choice among professionals, actually should be refrigerated during storage.

Beware that film remains heat sensitive inside your camera. Never leave your camera sitting in the sun, and before and after you've used a roll of film try to keep it in a cool place. Many people make the mistake of leaving film in glove compartments, which can get very hot and spoil your lovely images.

Camera equipment is available on the peninsula, but like film it tends to be pricey and limited in selection. If taking photographs is important to you, bring everything you think you'll need. Same goes with batteries: Because batteries lose power when heated, those found on shelves in the Tropics often have lost half their life before they've left the store.

Technical Tips

Your greatest potential disappointment when you get your processed photographs is a washed-out look. This is due to overexposure. The bright tropical light can fool even the most sophisticated light-metering systems.

To avoid this problem, consider purchasing a polarizing filter. A polarizing filter is primarily used to darken a pale blue sky and to remove reflections from glass and water surfaces. No serious photographer would visit a destination packed with gorgeous white-sand beaches and light-colored ruins without a polarizer.

If you mount a polarizer on your lens, you'll notice that it can be rotated within the filter ring. Its position determines the effectiveness of the polarizer. At a right angle to the sun, the effect is greatest, heightening the contrasts so that the subject is clearly visible – removing, for example, the glare off the ocean, bringing into sharp focus the sailboat you're aiming at.

If you intend to take most of your photos outside during daylight hours, consider purchasing a 'slow' film, which will provide the best color rendition. Fujichrome Velvia (ASA 50) is the pro's choice among slide films, followed closely by Kodachrome 25 and 64. For print film, avoid film with an ISO higher than 100.

A common mistake photographers make is failing to compensate for the contrast between dark faces and bright backgrounds. This failure generally produces a featureless black head silhouetted against a correctly exposed background. Most cameras these days have a fill-in flash feature that, if the subject is close enough, can eliminate this problem. If you aren't familiar with this feature on your camera, consider reading up on it in the camera's instruction manual.

Video

Video cameras and tapes are widely available at photo supply stores in the largest cities and in towns that receive many foreign visitors. Prices are significantly higher than you may be used to in North America or Europe. VHS is standard.

Be forewarned that there's a 'video fee' at many of the ruins and other attractions. In some instances, the user will be expected to pay US$20 or more if he/she intends to use a motion-picture camera while at a tourist site.

Restrictions

It is illegal to take pictures in Mexican airports and of police stations and penal institutions. Also, many police officers do not like having their pictures taken and they have the authority to arrest you for photographing them without authorization. When in doubt, ask before you shoot.

Photographing People

In general, Yucatecans enjoy having their pictures taken and will be happy to pose for your camera – if you ask. Just as you might not enjoy having someone photograph you without your permission, you should ask permission before opening fire.

Increasingly, you will be asked to pay for the photo. This is especially true in areas that see heavy tourist traffic. Many locals have grown tired of being treated like objects of art or even zoo animals, and have taken the attitude that they deserve compensation for being 'framed.'

If you intend to take lots of photos of Yucatecans, consider bringing a Polaroid

camera in addition to your 35mm camera. By presenting a stranger with a photo of themselves you usually are able to remove whatever tension may have initially existed between you and your subject, and you can now capture a warm and welcome expression.

If local people make any sign of being offended by your desire to photograph them, you should put your camera away and apologize immediately, both out of decency and for your own safety.

Airport Security

It's a good idea to avoid sending your film through airport x-ray machines. While most won't damage your film, there's no point in taking the chance. Most security personnel will hand-inspect your film if you ask them to, removing the necessity of having it x-rayed. Don't forget to have your camera hand-inspected if it has film inside.

Some people – particularly sales personnel at camera stores – swear by lead-lined film pouches which, incidentally, you can buy at most camera stores. Be advised the pouches are heavy and expensive, and nine times out of ten when an x-ray machine operator sees one on the screen, the operator does two things: cranks up the x-rays to penetrate the lead, and nearly always instructs a security officer to hand inspect the pouch.

TIME

The entire Yucatán Peninsula observes the Hora del Centro, which is same as US Central Time – GMT minus six hours in winter, and GMT minus five hours during daylight saving. Daylight saving time runs from the first Sunday in April to the last Sunday in October.

For the exact time, dial ☎ 030.

ELECTRICITY
Voltage & Cycle

The electrical current in Mexico is the same as in the USA and Canada: 110 volts, 60 cycles.

Plugs & Sockets

Though most plugs and sockets are the same as in the USA and Canada, Mexico actually has three different types of electrical socket: older ones with two equally sized flat slots, newer ones with two flat slots of differing sizes, and a few with two flat slots and a round hole for a grounding pin. If your plug doesn't fit the Mexican socket, get an adapter. Most Mexican supermarkets have an electrical-goods section in which adapters can be found.

WEIGHTS & MEASURES

Mexico uses the metric system. For conversion between metric and US or Imperial measures, see the inside back cover of this book.

LAUNDRY

Laundry service is widely available throughout Yucatán, but it never hurts to pack a small bottle or pouch of detergent so you don't waste time looking for a *lavandería* (laundry). Laundries throughout the peninsula generally work this way: You drop off your clothes in the morning, and by 4 or 5 pm your clothes are ready for pick up. The cost for the service, which typically includes washing, drying, folding and wrapping, is generally no more than US$4 for a large load of wash.

TOILETS

The Yucatán Peninsula is squarely situated within the Stand-Up Toilet Zone – no squatting here, please. In the better restaurants and hotels, expect toilets such as you'll find in every developed Western country.

However, the toilets in budget hotels and budget restaurants are often missing seats. Low-end and older establishments also frequently place a small wastepaper basket beside the toilet, which is the management's way of saying, 'Don't flush the TP;' the plumbing at such places generally can't handle toilet paper.

HEALTH
Predeparture Planning

Insurance Mexican medical treatment is generally inexpensive for common diseases and minor treatment, but if you suffer some serious disease or injury, you may want to

find a private hospital or fly out for treatment. Travel insurance can cover the costs of that. Insurance against theft, loss (including plane tickets), and delay or cancellation of a flight is also worth considering. Many US health insurance policies stay in effect, at least for a limited time, if you travel abroad, but it's worth checking exactly what you'll be covered for in Mexico.

For people whose medical insurance or national health systems don't extend to Mexico – which means most non-Americans – a travel policy is advisable. Your travel agent will be able to make recommendations. The international student travel policies handled by STA Travel or other student travel organizations are usually a good value. Check the fine print:

- Some policies specifically exclude 'dangerous activities,' which can mean scuba diving, for instance.
- You may prefer a policy that pays doctors or hospitals directly, rather than your having to pay on the spot and getting reimbursed later. If you have to claim later, make sure you keep all documentation.
- Check whether the policy covers the ambulance services and an emergency flight home.

Medical Kit It is always a good idea to travel with a small first-aid kit. Items it should contain include: antihistamine (such as Benadryl) – useful as a decongestant for colds and allergies, or to ease the itch from insect bites or stings; kaolin preparation, Imodium or Lomotil for diarrhea; rehydration mixture for severe diarrhea; antiseptic such as Dettol or Betadine; bandages and Band-Aids; scissors and tweezers; insect repellent; sunscreen and burn cream (Caladryl is good).

Don't forget an adequate supply of any medication you're already taking: The prescription may be difficult to match in Mexico.

Medical Information Services For advice on immunizations or other matters, talk to your doctor or an appropriate information service. In the USA, you can call the Centers for Disease Control & Prevention's

international travelers hot line (☎ 404-332-4559), or visit their website (www.cdc.gov). In Canada, there's Health Canada (☎ 613-957-8739). In the UK, you can obtain a printed health brief for any country by calling Medical Advisory Services for Travellers Abroad (☎ 0891-224100). In Australia, call the Australian Government Health Service or consult a clinic such as the Travelers Medical & Vaccination Centre, Level 2, 393 Little Bourke St, Melbourne (☎ 03-9670-3969).

Immunizations It's a good idea to be up-to-date on your tetanus, typhoid, polio and diphtheria shots and to check your immunity to measles (catching measles is not a pleasant prospect for an adult; those who had it as children are immune). You should also get vaccinated against hepatitis A. You'll need a yellow fever certificate to enter Mexico only if you'll be arriving from an infected country.

Basic Rules
Food & Water Food can be contaminated with any one of a number of bacteria when it is harvested, shipped, handled, washed or prepared. Make sure the food you eat is freshly cooked and still hot. Steer clear of salads and uncooked vegetables; raw or rare meat, fish and shellfish; and unpasteurized milk and milk products (including cheese). Squeezing lime on salads may help reduce your danger from bacterial dysentery, as may eating lots of raw garlic, but these habits are far from foolproof. In general, restaurants that are packed with customers will be fine; empty ones should be avoided.

Don't trust any water unless it has been boiled for at least five minutes, treated with purifiers or comes in an unopened bottle labeled *agua purificada*. Simple filtering will not remove all dangerous organisms. Most hotels have large bottles of purified water from which you can fill your water bottle or canteen. Inexpensive purified water is available at supermarkets, grocery stores and liquor stores.

If the waiter swears that the ice in your drink is made from agua purificada, it's certainly up to you whether or not to chance it.

A prudent person would request an altogether different drink, without ice, so the waiter won't be tempted to simply remove the ice from your drink. If that occurs, the ice will be gone but contamination of the beverage may have occurred. Canned or bottled carbonated beverages, including carbonated water, are usually safe, as are beer, wine and liquor.

If you plan to travel off-the-beaten track, you may have to purify water yourself. Tincture of iodine (2%), or water purification drops or tablets containing tetraglycine hydroperiodide are sold under brand names such as Globaline, Potable Aqua or Coghlan's in pharmacies and US sporting-goods stores such as REI (in the USA ☎ 800-426-4840), LL Bean (☎ 800-441-5713) and Campmor (in the USA ☎ 800-526-4784).

In Mexico ask for *gotas* (drops) or *pastillas* (tablets) *para purificar agua* (for purifying water) in pharmacies and supermarkets. For tincture of iodine, four drops per liter or quart of clear water is the recommended dosage; let the treated water stand for 20 to 30 minutes before drinking. Vigorously boiling water for five minutes is another way to purify the water, but at high altitudes water boils at a lower temperature, so germs are less likely to be killed. Boil it for longer in those environments.

Heat You can avoid heat-related problems by drinking lots of fluids and generally not overdoing things. Take time to acclimatize: Avoid excessive alcohol intake or strenuous activity when you first arrive. Remember that the sun is much fiercer in the middle of the day than in the morning or afternoon.

Take it easy climbing pyramids. Carry water and wear a hat and light, loose cotton clothing. Take frequent rest breaks in the shade. Use sun block. You can get burned surprisingly quickly, even through clouds. Near water the glare from the sand and water can double your exposure to the sun; you may want to wear a T-shirt and hat while swimming or boating. Calamine lotion is good for treating mild sunburns.

Dehydration or salt deficiency can cause heat exhaustion. Salt deficiency is characterized by fatigue, lethargy, headaches, giddiness and muscle cramps. In extreme cases you may develop heat stroke – see the Climatic & Geographical Considerations section, below, for more info on heat stroke. Be sure to add a little salt to your diet while in the Tropics.

Protection against Mosquitoes Some serious tropical diseases are spread by infected mosquitoes. In general, mosquitoes are most bothersome between dusk and dawn and most prevalent in lowland and coastal regions and during the rainy season (May to October). You can discourage them by:

* wearing light-colored clothing, long pants and long-sleeved shirts
* using mosquito repellents containing the compound DEET on exposed areas
* avoiding highly scented perfume or aftershave
* making sure your room has properly fitting mosquito screens over the windows
* using a mosquito net (it may be worth taking your own)

Medical Problems & Treatment
Before presenting the following somewhat alarming catalog of potential illnesses, it should be remembered that it is entirely possible to spend months – even years – in the Yucatán without getting anything worse than occasional traveler's diarrhea.

If you come down with a serious illness, be careful to find a competent doctor, and don't be afraid to get second opinions. Your embassy or consulate is a good place to turn for referrals. You may want to telephone your doctor at home as well.

Hospitals & Clinics Almost every town and city on the peninsula has either a hospital or a clinic, as well as Cruz Roja (Red Cross) emergency facilities (all of which are indicated by road signs showing a red cross). Most major hotels have a doctor available. Hospitals are generally inexpensive for common ailments (dysentery) and minor treatments (cuts and sprains). Clinics are often too overburdened with local problems to be of much help, but they are linked by radio to emergency services.

Insect Repellent

Mosquitoes generally are not a problem on the Yucatán Peninsula, but if you need some insect repellent you'll want to get some containing Deet. You can buy repellent with 15% to 90% of this proven ingredient. Lotions are best for direct contact with the skin, while pump sprays are best for applying repellent to clothes.

If you find that Deet irritates your skin, consider using a lower strength; most people find repellent containing 30% Deet to be effective and user-friendly. Everyone should avoid getting Deet in their eyes, on their lips and on other sensitive parts. Because Deet can dissolve plastic, try to keep it off camera equipment, plastic eyewear, etc.

Deet can be toxic to children and shouldn't be used on their skin. Instead, try Avon's Skin So Soft, which has insect-repellent properties, isn't toxic and generally can be found in supermarkets on the peninsula. Also, camping stores often sell insect repellents that don't contain any toxins, but some people find them to be less effective than Deet-based repellents.

Mosquito coils are widely available in Yucatán and are a godsend to have if you'll be staying at budget accommodations, such as the beach huts near Tulum. The coils burn like incense but release a smoke that insects hate. Be sure to follow the instructions that come with the coils; the smoke from them can be harmful when they are used without adequate ventilation.

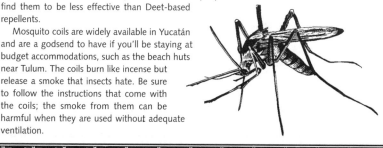

If you use these services, try to ascertain the competence of the staff treating you. In big cities and major tourist resorts you should be able to find an adequate hospital. Care in more remote areas is limited.

Most hospitals have to be paid at the time of service, and doctors usually require immediate cash payment. Some facilities may accept credit cards. It's always a good idea to ask before service is rendered.

If you should need an air ambulance to fly you to Mexico City or another city with top-notch medical facilities, the Mexico City-based Aeromed (☎ 5-294-4286) has been recommended by travelers. You'll have to spend thousands of dollars for the service, but if you need it, you need it.

Medicines Not to Take Pharmacies in Mexico sometimes sell medicines that are banned elsewhere for good reason. Incompetent doctors or pharmacists might recommend such medicines for gastrointestinal ailments, but these drugs may cause other problems, such as neurological damage. Medicines called halogenated hydroxyquinoline derivatives are among these; they may bear the chemical names clioquinol or iodoquinol, or brand names Entero-Vioform, Mexaform or Intestopan, or something similar. Stay away from them.

Climatic & Geographical Considerations

Heat Stroke Long, continuous periods of exposure to high temperatures can leave you vulnerable to this serious, sometimes fatal condition. The symptoms are feeling unwell, not sweating very much or at all, and a high body temperature (39°C to 41°C, or 102°F to 106°F). Where sweating has ceased, the skin becomes flushed and red. Severe, throbbing headaches and lack of coordination will occur. The victim will

become delirious or convulse. Hospitalization is essential, but meanwhile get victims out of the sun, remove their clothing, cover them with a wet sheet or towel and fan them continually.

Infectious Diseases

Diarrhea A change of water, food or climate can all cause the runs, but diarrhea caused by contaminated food or water is more serious. Despite precautions, you may still have a mild bout of traveler's diarrhea – known informally in Mexico as Montezuma's revenge or *turista* – but a few rushed toilet trips with no other symptoms are not indicative of a serious problem.

Moderate diarrhea, involving half a dozen loose movements in a day, is more of a nuisance. Dehydration is the main danger with any diarrhea, particularly for children, in whom it can occur quite quickly, and fluid replacement is the mainstay of management. Soda water, weak black tea with a little sugar, or soft drinks allowed to go flat and diluted 50% with water are all good.

With severe diarrhea a rehydrating solution is necessary to replace lost minerals and salts. Commercially available oral rehydration salts are very useful; add the contents of one packet to a liter of boiled or bottled water. In an emergency, you can make up a solution of six teaspoons of sugar and a half teaspoon of salt to a liter of boiled or bottled water. Stick to a bland diet as you recover.

Lomotil or Imodium can be used to bring relief from the symptoms, though they do not cure the problem. Use these drugs only if absolutely necessary – for example, if you *must* travel. Do not use them if you have a high fever or are severely dehydrated.

In the following situations, antibiotics may be necessary (and gut-paralyzing drugs such as Imodium or Lomotil should be avoided):

- watery diarrhea with blood and mucus
- watery diarrhea with fever and lethargy
- persistent diarrhea for more than five days
- severe diarrhea, if it is logistically difficult to stay in one place

Diarrhea can also be a sign of giardiasis, dysentery, cholera or typhoid – see the following sections on those diseases.

Giardiasis The parasite causing this intestinal disorder is present in contaminated water. The symptoms are stomach cramps, nausea, a bloated stomach, frequent gas and watery, foul-smelling diarrhea. Giardiasis can appear several weeks after you have been exposed to the parasite. The symptoms may disappear for a few days and then return; this can go on for several weeks. Tinidazole, known as Fasigyn, or metronidazole (Flagyl) are the recommended treatments.

Dysentery This serious illness is caused by contaminated food or water and is characterized by severe diarrhea, often with blood or mucus in the stool.

Bacillary dysentery is characterized by a high fever and rapid onset of illness; headache, vomiting and stomach pains are also symptoms. It generally does not last longer than a week, but it is highly contagious.

Amebic dysentery ('amoebas') is often more gradual in onset, with cramping abdominal pain and vomiting less likely; fever may not be present. It will persist until treated and can recur and cause long-term health problems.

A stool test is necessary to diagnose which kind of dysentery you have, so you should seek medical help urgently. In an emergency, norfloxacin 400mg twice daily for three days or ciprofloxacin 500mg twice daily for five days can be used as presumptive treatment for bacillary dysentery.

For amebic dysentery, metronidazole (Flagyl) can be used as presumptive treatment in an emergency. An alternative is Fasigyn. Avoid alcohol during treatment and for 48 hours afterward.

Cholera Cholera vaccination is not very effective. The bacteria responsible for cholera are waterborne, so attention to the rules of eating and drinking should protect you. Parts of Yucatán suffer occasional epidemics of cholera. Cholera spreads quickly where sewage systems and water supplies

are rudimentary. Beware of foods that are partly cooked or uncooked, such as the popular *ceviche*, made from marinated raw fish, as well as salads and raw vegetables.

The disease is characterized by a sudden onset of acute diarrhea with 'rice water' stools, vomiting, muscular cramps and extreme weakness. You'll need medical help – but treat for dehydration, which can be extreme, and if there is an appreciable delay in getting to a hospital, begin taking tetracycline. The adult dose is 250mg four times daily; it is not recommended for children age eight or younger, nor for pregnant women. Fluid replacement is by far the most important aspect of treatment.

Hepatitis Hepatitis is a general term for inflammation of the liver. It has many causes: Drugs, alcohol and contaminated injections are but a few.

The letters A, B, C, D, E and a rumored G identify specific agents that cause viral hepatitis, which is an infection of the liver that can lead to jaundice (yellow skin), fever, lethargy and digestive problems. It can have no symptoms at all, with the infected person not knowing they have the disease. Hepatitis D, E and G are fairly rare (so far), and following the same precautions as for A, B and C should be all that's necessary to avoid them.

Hepatitis A is common in countries with poor sanitation. It's transmitted by contaminated water or food, including shellfish contaminated by sewage. Taking care with what you eat and drink can go a long way toward preventing hepatitis A, but it's a very infectious virus, so additional precautions are recommended. Protection can be provided in two ways – either with the antibody gamma globulin, or with the vaccine Havrix 1440, which provides long-term immunity (possibly longer than 10 years) after an initial injection and boosters at six and 12 months. Gamma globulin should not be given until at least 10 days after administration of the last vaccine needed; it is at its most effective in the first few weeks after administration. Havrix takes about three weeks to provide satisfactory protection.

The symptoms of hepatitis A are fever, chills, headache, fatigue, aches and pains, followed by loss of appetite, nausea, vomiting, abdominal pain, dark urine, light-colored feces and jaundiced skin. The whites of the eyes may turn yellow. You should seek medical advice, but in general there is not much you can do apart from rest, drink lots of fluids, eat lightly and avoid fatty foods. People who have had hepatitis must forgo alcohol for six months after the illness.

Incidence hepatitis B of is low in Mexico, and vaccination is not considered necessary. It's spread through contact with infected blood, blood products or bodily fluids – for example through sexual contact, unsterilized needles or blood transfusions. Other risk situations include getting a shave or tattoo or getting your ears pierced.

The symptoms are much the same as for hepatitis A, except that they are more severe and may lead to irreparable liver damage or even liver cancer.

Hepatitis C is a concern because it seems to lead to liver disease more rapidly than does hepatitis B. The virus is spread by contact with blood, usually via contaminated transfusions or shared needles. Avoiding both is the only means of prevention, as there is no available vaccine.

Typhoid Typhoid fever is a gut infection spread by contaminated water and food. Vaccination is not totally effective, and typhoid is one of the most dangerous infections, so medical help must be sought.

Early symptoms are headache, sore throat and a fever that rises a little each day until it is around 40°C (104°F) or higher. The victim's pulse often gets slower as the fever rises – unlike a normal fever, with which the pulse increases. There may be vomiting, diarrhea or constipation.

In the second week, the high fever and slow pulse continue and a few pink spots may appear on the body; trembling, delirium, weakness, weight loss and dehydration are other symptoms. If there are no further complications, the fever and other symptoms will slowly diminish during the third week. However, you must get medical help before

then, because pneumonia or peritonitis (perforated bowel) are common complications and because typhoid is very infectious.

The victim should be kept cool; watch for dehydration. The drug of choice is ciprofloxacin at 750mg twice a day for 10 days, but it's quite expensive and may not be available. Alternatives are chloramphenicol and Ampicillin. Ampicillin has fewer side effects, but people who are allergic to penicillin should not be given it.

Tetanus This potentially fatal disease is found in undeveloped tropical areas. It is difficult to treat, but preventable with immunization. Tetanus occurs when a wound becomes infected by a germ that lives in the feces of animals or people, so clean all cuts, punctures and animal bites well. Tetanus is also known as lockjaw, and its first symptom may be discomfort in swallowing, or stiffening of the jaw and neck; this is followed by painful convulsions of the jaw and whole body.

Rabies Rabies is caused by a bite or scratch from an infected animal. Dogs are noted carriers, as are monkeys and cats. Any bite, scratch or even lick from a warm-blooded furry animal should be cleaned immediately and thoroughly. Scrub with soap and running water, then clean with an alcohol solution. If there is any possibility that the animal is infected, medical help should be sought immediately. Even if the animal is not rabid, bites should be treated seriously, as they can become infected or result in tetanus. A rabies vaccination is available and should be considered if you are in a high-risk category – for example, if you intend to explore caves (bat bites can be dangerous) or work with animals.

Sexually Transmitted Diseases Sexual contact with an infected partner spreads these diseases. While abstinence is the only sure-fire preventive, using condoms is also effective. (Only latex condoms have proved effective in preventing the transmission of HIV; see the following section for more information.)

Gonorrhea and syphilis are the most common sexually transmitted diseases; their usual symptoms are sores, blisters or rashes around the genitals, discharges, or pain when urinating. Symptoms may be less marked or not observed at all in women. Syphilis symptoms eventually disappear, but the disease continues and can cause severe problems in later years. The treatment for gonorrhea and syphilis is with antibiotics, but this will only work if the disease is detected early enough. There is currently no cure for AIDS.

HIV/AIDS HIV, the Human Immunodeficiency Virus, may develop into AIDS, Acquired Immune Deficiency Syndrome. Any exposure to blood, blood products or bodily fluids may put the individual at risk. Transmission can be by sexual activity or via contaminated needles shared by intravenous drug users. Blood transfusions, vaccinations, acupuncture, tattooing and ear or nose piercing are also potentially dangerous if the equipment is not clean. If you need an injection, ask to see the syringe unwrapped in front of you, or better still, take a needle and syringe pack with you.

Without a blood test it is impossible to detect if an individual, however healthy looking, is HIV-positive.

Nearly 40,000 AIDS cases had been reported in Mexico by 1999, with the highest rates being in the center of the country. An estimated 220,000 people in Mexico are HIV-positive. Foreigners applying for permanent residence in Mexico need to present an HIV-negative certificate.

Insect-Borne Diseases
Malaria This serious disease is spread by mosquito bites; you can greatly reduce your risk by following the antimosquito measures outlined in the earlier Protection against Mosquitoes section. Most visitors to Mexico do not take antimalarial medicine, and do not get malaria, but there's a small risk of contracting the disease in rural areas of Campeche and Quintana Roo.

If you are traveling in areas where malaria is endemic, it is advisable to take malarial prophylactics – none are 100% effective, but

the appropriate drug significantly reduces the risk of contracting the disease. Consult a doctor or one of the medical information services mentioned earlier in this section.

Chloroquine (under various brand names) is the most commonly used antimalarial drug for Yucatán. Chiapas is the only Mexican state where chloroquine-resistant strains of malaria are suspected. You will usually be told to start taking the medicine one or two weeks *before* you arrive in a malarial area and continue taking it while you're there and for a month after you've left.

Symptoms of malaria range from fever, chills and sweating, headache and abdominal pains to a vague feeling of ill-health, so seek examination immediately if there is any suggestion of the disease. It can be diagnosed by a simple blood test and is curable, as long as you seek medical help when symptoms occur. Without treatment malaria can develop more serious, potentially fatal effects.

Dengue Fever There is no prophylactic for this mosquito-spread disease; the main preventive measure is to avoid mosquito bites. A sudden onset of fever, headaches and severe joint and muscle pains are the first signs before a rash starts on the trunk of the body and spreads to the limbs and face. After another few days, the fever will subside and recovery will begin. Serious complications are not common, but full recovery can take up to a month or more.

Cuts, Bites & Stings

Skin punctures can easily become infected in hot climates. Treat any cut with an antiseptic such as Betadine. Avoid bandages and Band-Aids, which can keep wounds wet. An effective folk remedy for jellyfish stings is immediate application of fresh urine.

Scorpion stings are notoriously painful and can even be fatal. Scorpions may hide in shoes or clothing, so in rural areas shake these out before you put them on. When walking through undergrowth where snakes may be present, wear boots, socks and long trousers. Snake bites do not cause instantaneous death, and antivenins are usually available.

Women's Health

Gynecological Problems Poor diet, antibiotics for stomach upsets and even contraceptive pills can lead to vaginal infections in hot climates. Wearing skirts or loose-fitting trousers and cotton underwear will help to prevent them.

Yeast infections, characterized by a rash, itch and discharge, can be treated with a vinegar or lemon-juice douche, or with yogurt. Nystatin suppositories are the usual medical prescription. Trichomoniasis is a more serious infection; symptoms are a discharge and a burning sensation when urinating. Male sexual partners must also be treated, and if a vinegar-water douche is not effective medical attention should be sought. Metronidazole (Flagyl) is the prescribed drug.

Pregnancy Most miscarriages occur during the first three months of pregnancy, so that is the most risky time to travel. Miscarriage is not uncommon and can occasionally lead to severe bleeding. Pregnant women should avoid all unnecessary medication, but needed vaccinations and malarial prophylactics should still be taken when possible. Extra care should be taken to prevent illness, and particular attention should be paid to diet and nutrition.

WOMEN TRAVELERS
Attitudes toward Women

Machismo is a Mexican invention that can be defined as a form of Latin male stupidity. With regard to women, it translates to aggressive social behavior and an inability to 'take a hint.' Attractive lone women should expect frequent efforts by local men to chat them up, and these efforts can get tiresome. If you don't want to talk with a stranger, tell the stranger in a friendly but firm voice that you don't talk to strangers, don't say another word to him and avoid eye contact.

Many Yucatecans view foreign women as promiscuous. Any day of the week, on beaches from Cancún to Playa del Carmen, foreign women can be seen wearing only a bikini bottom. Many foreign women wander the streets in little more than beachwear.

Mexican men equate near-nakedness with sexual easiness; it's something to keep in mind if you don't want to be continuously bothered by sex-starved men during your Yucatán stay.

Safety Precautions

Rape is a very real threat to women in Mexico, which is notorious for low apprehension and conviction rates of criminals. In Playa del Carmen, for example, local businesspeople can't agree: Is a foreign woman raped there once a week, or is it more frequent than that? One well-connected restaurant owner told Lonely Planet that the violent rape of three foreign women each week is probably an accurate figure. This man and other longtime Playa residents said federal police have been suspected in many of the assaults but none – surprise! – has been charged with a crime.

According to many Yucatecans, careless foreign women and lonely local construction workers are equally to blame for rape on the peninsula. The women set themselves up for attack, locals say, because they dress promiscuously, they often wander into secluded areas looking for remote beaches and they often walk alone at night. The rapists are mostly thought to be construction workers from neighboring states, who miss their wives and girlfriends and are only in touristy areas because of the construction opportunities there.

Women should avoid secluded areas and should never walk alone at night. They also should be very careful in what their clothes might say to a Mexican man, and should avoid giving the impression that they 'want it.'

GAY & LESBIAN TRAVELERS

Homosexuality is a subject most Mexicans are extremely uncomfortable with, to put it mildly. The Yucatán Peninsula will likely experience another ice age before it sees its first gay pride parade. Well, OK, that's possibly an overstatement; there are at least two gay clubs in Cancún, up from none a decade ago. But gay bashing isn't unknown to Yucatán, even attacks on homosexuals by federal police, so gay couples would be wise to keep displays of affection behind closed doors.

DISABLED TRAVELERS

Yucatán hasn't made many concessions to the disabled, though a few new public buildings are starting to provide wheelchair access. Mobility is easiest in the major tourist resorts and the more expensive hotels. Still, public transportation for people who use wheelchairs can be quite inconvenient.

SENIOR TRAVELERS

The American Association of Retired Persons (AARP, ☎ 800-424-3410), 601 E St NW, Washington, DC 20049 USA, is an advocacy group for Americans 50 years and older and a good resource for travel bargains. Membership for one/three years costs US$8/20.

Membership in the National Council of Senior Citizens (☎ 301-578-8800), 8403 Colesville Rd, Silver Spring, MD 20910 USA, gives access to discount information and travel-related advice.

Grand Circle Travel (☎ 617-350-7500, fax 617-350-6206), 347 Congress St, Boston, MA 02210 USA, offers escorted tours and travel information in a variety of formats and distributes a useful free booklet, *Going Abroad: 101 Tips for Mature Travelers*.

TRAVEL WITH CHILDREN

Mexicans as a rule like children. Any child whose hair is lighter than jet black will get called *güera* (blond) if she's a girl, *güero* if he's a boy. Children are welcome at all kinds of hotels and in virtually every café and restaurant.

Most children are excited and stimulated by the colors, sights and sounds of Mexico, but younger children especially don't like traveling all the time – they're happier if they can settle in to places and find other children to make friends with.

Children are likely to be more affected than adults by heat or disrupted sleeping patterns. They need time to acclimatize and need extra care to avoid sunburn. Take care to replace fluids if a child gets diarrhea (see the Health section, earlier in this chapter).

Bring some of the kids' own toys and books, and give them time to get on with some of the activities they are used to back home. Otherwise, apart from the obvious attractions of beaches, coasts and swimming pools, in some places you can find excellent special attractions, such as amusement parks, zoos, aquariums and boat rides. A boat ride to the flamingo colonies near the Yucatecan towns of Río Lagartos and Celestún is an adventure people of all ages can enjoy. Archaeological sites can be fun if the kids are into climbing pyramids and exploring tunnels.

Diapers (nappies) are widely available, but you may not easily find creams, lotions, baby foods or familiar medicines outside larger cities and tourist towns. Bring at least some of any of those that you need.

It's usually not hard to find an inexpensive baby-sitter if the grown-ups want to go out on their own; just ask at your hotel.

On flights to and within Mexico, children under two generally travel for 10% of the adult fare, and those between two and 12 normally pay 67%. Children pay full fare on Mexican long-distance buses unless they're small enough to sit on your lap.

Lonely Planet's *Travel with Children*, by Maureen Wheeler, has lots of practical advice on the subject, as well as firsthand stories from many Lonely Planet authors, and others, who have done it.

DANGERS & ANNOYANCES

There has been a big increase in crime throughout Mexico in recent years. With a few precautions you can minimize any danger to your physical safety. More at risk are your possessions, particularly those you carry around with you – but again, a few sensible steps reduce the risk.

For information on the potential risks of travel in Mexico, you can contact your country's foreign affairs department, including: Australia (☎ 02-6261-3305, www.dfat .gov.au/consular/advice/advices_mnu.html); Canada (☎ 613-944-6788, 800-267-6788, www.dfait-maeci.gc.ca/travel/menu-e.asp); UK (☎ 020-7238-4503, http://193.114.50.10/ travel/); USA (☎ 202-647-5225, www.travel .state.gov/travel_warnings.html).

Theft & Robbery

Theft, particularly pocket-picking and pilfering unsecured items left in hotel rooms, is common in Mexico. Tourists are singled out, as they are presumed to be wealthy and carrying valuables. Crowded buses, bus stops, bus stations, airports, markets, thronged streets and plazas, remote beach spots and anywhere frequented by large numbers of tourists are all prime locations for theft.

One fairly common trick played on women bathing on a secluded stretch of beach: While laying there, soaking up the sun, an assailant comes up behind her and steals her belongings. The woman is left having to make her way back to her hotel room wearing only her bathing suit (sometimes only a bikini bottom) and, if she was using one, a towel.

Precautions To avoid being robbed, do not go where there are few other people. Do not camp in a secluded place: It is as good a place as any to be robbed and murdered. Why tempt the Fates?

The following suggestions might prevent you from becoming a victim of theft or robbery:

- Leave valuable items at home. That includes all jewelry and watches that sparkle (real gold, real silver or otherwise). Photographers: a cheap or well-worn camera bag is a whole lot less eye-catching than a fancy one.

- Wear a money belt, shoulder wallet or a pouch on a string around your neck, *underneath your clothing, not where everyone can see it.* Fanny packs are an invitation for thieves.

- Don't keep money, credit or debit cards, purses or bags in open view any longer than you have to. At ticket counters, keep a hand or foot on your bag at all times.

- On trains and buses, keep your baggage with you if you can. Also, it's always safer to use an overhead bin that's near and in front of you than one directly overhead or behind you.

- Do not leave anything that might interest a thief in your vehicle unless you're inside the vehicle or watching it. Trunk theft is common in Mérida, Valladolid and Campeche.

Highway Robbery Bandits sometimes hold up buses and other vehicles on intercity routes, especially at night, taking luggage or

valuables. Sometimes buses are robbed by people who board as passengers. The best way to avoid highway robbery is not to travel at night, which is when highway robbery usually takes place. The state of Campeche is notorious throughout Mexico for highway bandits, as is the highway linking Campeche and Chetumal.

Bad Cops Corrupt police are a big problem on the Yucatán Peninsula, with officers frequently stopping rental vehicles (virtually every bumper of a rental vehicle on the peninsula bears a large, bright sticker with the name of the rental firm on it) on trumped-up charges. This is particularly true in Campeche state, where it's not uncommon for a tourist to be accosted by more than one bad cop in a single day.

Generally what happens is this: You're pulled over and asked for your driver's license. Once you hand it over you're told you were speeding or went through a stop sign and that you have to pay a fine or you won't get your license back. The cost of the ransom varies widely. The author writing the words you are now reading, for example, was stopped three times in a single day in Campeche state, each time allegedly for speeding when in fact yours truly was driving under the speed limit. The ransoms: US$80, US$60 and US$120. That's US$260 in undeserved fines in a single day!

What can you do about it? Well, you can say that you want to pay the fine at the police station or the headquarters of the federal police, depending on who stopped you. Of course, antagonizing bad cops is, say, only slightly more stupid than yanking the whiskers of a wild cat. Before you know it, for example, the bad cop might just happen to find some marijuana in your rental vehicle. The average wait to 'have your day in court' on drug matters in Mexico is three years.

Reporting a Theft Do not report a crime unless you need a police report for insurance reasons (for example, if your rental vehicle was stolen). The police in Yucatán have a reputation for corruption, inefficiency, discretionary abuse of power and involvement

in criminal activity. In the event of theft, consider whether it is worth contacting the police. Mexican police rarely clear up crimes, investigations will be time-consuming and they risk exposing you to corrupt police. If you do report a crime, ensure that the police spend as little time as possible in your hotel room.

If all this corrupt-cops stuff sounds a bit scary, it should. It's a real and present danger. And the Yucatán, like everywhere else on our planet, can be hazardous to your health. But if you're aware of the dangers and are proactive, you can leave the Yucatán as the vast majority of visitors do: a lot more relaxed than when you arrived, a lot more tan, and very glad you chose Yucatán as your destination.

Discrimination

Generally speaking, people of African descent are looked down upon by Yucatecans, but the reasons aren't clear. When asked if there's a racial group they don't really like, many Yucatecans say they don't care much for black people. When asked why, they usually don't seem to know. There's generally a shrug of the shoulders, followed by a long silence, followed by a guess, as in, 'I guess I don't like their music' (which is odd, because hip-hop, reggae and rap – all black creations – are popular among locals who listen to anything other than Spanish-language music).

Another common response is, 'I don't understand them.' Many black people use slang that's alien to Yucatecans, or speak with an urban sound that many people with a fragile grip on English simply don't comprehend. A third (and possibly the main) reason blacks are disliked by many Yucatecans is their size. Many of the blacks who visit Yucatán are from the US, and next to a typical Yucatecan, the typical American black man or woman is enormous. Most prejudices are borne out of fear, and anti-black sentiment on the peninsula is no exception. As one local put it: 'They're just so big. They scare me.'

Most blacks in Yucatán are on vacation, and as free-spending tourists they generally aren't discriminated against. The Maya,

however, often are discriminated against by people who are fairer-skinned Spanish descendants or who've come to the peninsula from Mexico City and view everyone else as simple country folk. As is common throughout Latin America, the lighter your skin color, the greater the number of opportunities available to you. And way down on the social totem pole in the land of the Maya are the Maya.

EMERGENCY

In the event of a police, fire or medical emergency, dial ☎ 060 and you will immediately be connected to an emergency operator. Most of the operators speak English as well as Spanish. If the one who happens to answer your call doesn't speak English, he or she will momentarily connect you to emergency personnel who does speak the language.

LEGAL MATTERS

The most important thing to remember about the criminal justice system in Mexico is that it's corrupt from top to bottom. That fact has been well documented in the press, as has been the fact that Mexico's five police forces (three federal, one municipal and one highway) are swollen with corrupt officers. So, you simply do not want to place yourself in the position where you are likely to have an encounter with Mexican police.

In other words, don't touch drugs, don't drink and drive, don't litter – don't do anything that could bring the wrath of a bad cop upon you. Stay where the people are, blend in. Do not camp outside of commercial camping areas (locals never do because it's downright unsafe) and don't hitchhike (locals do, but standing by the side of a road is a good way to attract the attention of a police cruiser, and that's something you don't want to do).

Finally, no matter what you're accustomed to carrying on you in your home country, do not possess any weapons in Mexico. Drug and weapon charges are extremely serious in Mexico. If you're caught with either, you will do jail or prison time. There are many foreigners rotting in Mexican prisons because they were caught with a couple of marijuana cigarettes. Many locals, especially those offering to sell you grass, will say it's not true. But US State Department officials have told Lonely Planet that there are Americans serving 10-year sentences in Mexican prisons because they were caught with small amounts of marijuana or cocaine.

If you are apprehended for any reason – trumped up or otherwise – try to bribe your way out of the situation as quickly as possible, because more people will get involved the longer you wait, and more people involved means you'll have to pay more in bribes. If you don't pay the police, you'll end up paying a judge – and judges demand much higher bribes. That's just how it is in Mexico. So play it safe and maintain a low profile during your stay in Yucatán.

BUSINESS HOURS

Stores are generally open 9 am to 2 pm, close for siesta, then reopen from 4 to 7 pm Monday to Saturday. In particularly hot locales such as Mérida and Chetumal, stores sometimes take a longer siesta but stay open later in the evening. Some may not be open Saturday afternoon.

Offices have similar Monday to Friday hours; those with tourist-related business might be open for a few hours on Saturday as well.

Some Mexican churches, particularly those that contain valuable works of art, are locked when not in use, but most churches are in frequent use. Be careful not to disturb services when you visit them.

Archaeological sites are usually open 8 am to 5 pm daily. This is unfortunate, because the hours before 8 am and after 5 pm, especially in summer, are cooler and much more pleasant. Most museums have one closing day a week, typically Monday. On Sunday, nearly all archaeological sites and museums are free, and the major ones can get very crowded.

PUBLIC HOLIDAYS & SPECIAL EVENTS

Mexico's frequent fiestas are highly colorful affairs that often go on for several days and add a great deal of spice to life. There's a

major national holiday or celebration almost every month, to which each town adds nearly as many local saints' days, fairs, arts festivals and so on. Christmas through New Year's Day and Semana Santa – the week leading up to Easter – are the chief Mexican holiday periods. If you're traveling at either time, try to book transport and accommodations well in advance.

National Holidays

Banks, post offices, government offices and many shops throughout Mexico are closed on the following days:

Año Nuevo – January 1; New Year's Day

Día de la Constitución – February 5; Constitution Day

Día de Nacimiento de Benito Juárez – March 21; anniversary of Benito Juárez's Birth

Día de Pascua – March or April (date varies); Easter Sunday

Día del Trabajo – May 1; Labor Day

Cinco de Mayo – May 5; anniversary of Mexico's 1862 victory over the French at Puebla

Día de la Independencia – September 16; commemoration of the start of Mexico's war for independence from Spain

Día de la Raza – October 12; Day of the Race; commemorating Columbus' discovery of the New World and the founding of the Mexican *(mestizo)* people

Día de la Revolución – November 20; anniversary of the Mexican Revolution of 1910

Día de Navidad – Christmas Day; the Christmas feast traditionally takes place in the early hours of December 25, after midnight mass

Other National Celebrations

Though not official holidays, some of these are among the most important festivals on the Mexican calendar. Many offices and businesses close.

Día de los Reyes Magos – January 6. Three Kings' Day (Epiphany); Mexican children traditionally receive gifts this day, rather than at Christmas (but some get two loads of presents!).

Día de la Candelaría – February 2. Candlemas; processions, bullfights and dancing in many towns commemorate the presentation of Jesus in the temple 40 days after his birth.

Carnaval – Late February or early March. Carnival; taking place the week or so before Ash Wednesday (which falls 46 days before Easter Sunday), this is the big bash prior to the 40-day penance of Lent; it's celebrated with parades, music, food, drink, dancing, fireworks and fun.

Semana Santa – March or April. Holy Week, starting on Palm Sunday (Domingo de Ramos); closures are usually from Good Friday (Viernes Santo) to Easter Sunday (Día de Pascua or Domingo de Resurrección); most of Mexico seems to be on the move the week leading up to Easter Sunday.

Informe Presidencial – September 1. The president gives the state of the nation address to the legislature.

Día de Todos los Santos – November 1. When the souls of dead children, called *angelitos* because they are believed to have automatically become angels, are celebrated.

Día de los Muertos – November 2. Day of the Dead, Mexico's most characteristic fiesta; the souls of the dead are believed to return to earth this day. Families build altars in their homes and visit graveyards to commune with their dead on the preceding night and the day itself, taking garlands and gifts of, for example, the dead one's favorite foods. A happy atmosphere prevails. Like many Mexican rituals, these events have pre-Hispanic roots. Every cemetery in the country comes alive this day.

Día de Nuestra Señora de Guadalupe – December 12. Day of Our Lady of Guadalupe, Mexico's national patron, the manifestation of the Virgin Mary who appeared to a Mexican Indian, Juan Diego, in 1531; a week or more of celebrations leads up to the big day, with children taken to church dressed as little Juan Diegos or Indian girls; festivities take place nationwide, but the biggest are at the Basílica de Guadalupe in Mexico City.

Posadas – December 16-24. Candlelit parades of children and adults, reenacting the journey of Mary and Joseph to Bethlehem, are held for nine nights (the tradition is more alive in small towns than in cities); the ninth procession, on Christmas Eve, goes to the church. Also around Christmas, *pastorelas* – dramas enacting the journey of the shepherds to see the infant Jesus – are staged.

Yucatecan Celebrations

In addition to the national holidays and celebrations mentioned above, every town and city on the peninsula has its own fiestas,

often in honor of its patron saint. Street parades of holy images, special costumes, fireworks, dancing, lots of music, plenty of drinking – even bloodless bullfights in some places – are all part of the scene. The liveliest patron saint festivals and other town- or Yucatán-specific celebrations are mentioned in the destination chapters.

ACTIVITIES

There's absolutely no shortage of things to do in Yucatán: Some of the best scuba diving and snorkeling in the world is available here, beach lovers will find plenty of powdery particles of rock on which to sunbathe and the ancient Mayan cities that dot the landscape of Yucatán are a thrill to explore. And, of course,

Considerations for Responsible Diving

The popularity of diving is placing immense pressure on many sites. Please consider the following tips when diving, and help to preserve the ecology and beauty of reefs:

Do not use anchors on the reef, and take care not to ground boats on coral. Encourage dive operators and regulatory bodies to establish permanent moorings at popular dive sites.

Avoid touching living marine organisms with your body or dragging equipment across the reef. Polyps can be damaged by even the gentlest contact. Never stand on corals, even if they look solid and robust. If you must hold onto the reef, only touch exposed rock or dead coral.

Be conscious of your fins. Even without contact, the surge from heavy fin strokes near the reef can damage delicate organisms. When treading water in shallow reef areas, take care not to kick up clouds of sand. Settling sand can easily smother the delicate organisms of the reef.

Practice and maintain proper buoyancy control. Major damage can be done by divers descending too fast and colliding with the reef. Make sure you are correctly weighted and that your weight belt is positioned so that you stay horizontal. If you have not dived for a while, have a practice dive in a pool before taking to the reef. Be aware that buoyancy can change over the period of an extended trip. Initially you may breathe harder and need more weight; a few days later you may breathe more easily and need less weight.

Take great care in underwater caves. Spend as little time as possible within them, as your air bubbles may be caught within the roof and thereby leave previously submerged organisms high and dry. Taking turns to inspect the interior of a small cave will lessen the chances of damaging contact.

Resist the temptation to collect or buy corals or shells. Aside from the ecological damage, taking home marine souvenirs depletes the beauty of a site and spoils others' enjoyment. The same goes for marine archaeological sites (mainly shipwrecks). Respect their integrity; some sites are even protected from looting by law.

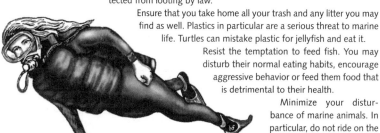

Ensure that you take home all your trash and any litter you may find as well. Plastics in particular are a serious threat to marine life. Turtles can mistake plastic for jellyfish and eat it.

Resist the temptation to feed fish. You may disturb their normal eating habits, encourage aggressive behavior or feed them food that is detrimental to their health.

Minimize your disturbance of marine animals. In particular, do not ride on the backs of turtles, as this causes them great anxiety.

there's Cancún – the nightlife epicenter for all of Mexico – and the similar but quieter Playa del Carmen, Isla Mujeres and Cozumel.

The activities available to you on the peninsula are discussed in detail in the destination chapters. Here is a sampling of the popular options.

Diving & Snorkeling

If God had an aquarium, it would surely resemble the snorkeler's view of Cozumel. There are scores of fine dive and snorkel spots off the coast of Quintana Roo, but few are as awesome as those that hug the west side of the island of Cozumel. In a 1999 reader survey, *Rodale's Scuba Diving* magazine found Cozumel to be the most popular diving destination in the world, edging out by a whisker Egypt's Red Sea for the crystal clarity of its water. The color and variety of marine life along much of the Riviera Maya, but especially off the coast of Cozumel, is absolutely astounding.

Most of the dive operators on the peninsula – and there are literally hundreds of them – offer instruction on how to scuba dive. Some offer a one-day 'resort dive,' in which students are taught the fundamentals and are then taken to a reef where they make one or two shallow dives. These can either be very dangerous, because the amount of instruction before entering the open sea is usually very superficial, or they can be quite safe. It all depends on the level of instruction. Only reputable dive operators are mentioned in this guide.

The value of a resort dive is not questionable. These dives are generally inexpensive, costing US$65 or less for two dives and some degree of instruction, and they're an excellent means by which to determine if you like scuba diving. The alternatives are to dive with a very irresponsible operator, who allows you to use the equipment without any instruction; or to obtain open-water certification, which typically costs US$350 or more and takes several days. If you've not scuba dived before and want to 'test the waters,' consider a resort dive with a reputable dive outfit before spending six times as much money getting certified.

See the Top Dive Sites map, as well as the maps for each destination, for specific diving and snorkeling spots.

Other Water Sports

Cancún is the place to stay if you are looking for a rich blend of water-related activities. Among the more popular of the topside water-sports options are parasailing up and down the beach, jet-skiing your way through a mangrove forest, and cruising between Cancún and nearby Isla Mujeres in style – aboard one of the many party boats that ply the blue water between the two islands.

Big-game fishing is another option, as are swimming with trained dolphins, surfing and bodysurfing.

Hiking the Ruins

The ruins of a great civilization always make for fascinating exploring. And in Yucatán, exploring the ruins means getting in a little exercise. Because most of the old Mayan centers are ringed by forest, a visit to any of them is also a stroll in the woods, and that's a healthy and exciting thing. What better way to glimpse the stone remnants of a lost civilization than to come upon them as Indiana Jones would – emerging from the bush only to find yourself at the foot of a towering rock temple built in honor of the mightiest gods. Remember to bring water with you.

COURSES

Taking classes can be a great way to meet people and get an inside angle on local life, as well as learn the language or history of the country. New programs open and old ones fold frequently, so be sure to contact those mentioned here to check their status and to obtain current rates.

Language

There's a plethora of Spanish-language schools on the Yucatán Peninsula. The ones mentioned here enjoy healthy reputations. All will provide current prices if contacted, and all can arrange for housing if requested. Prices vary substantially, depending on the number of lessons taken, whether the lessons are private or group, include housing arrangements, etc.

In Ciudad Cancún, Berlitz and the Suites El Patio (☎ 9-884-3500, fax 9-884-3540, cancun@cancun-suites.com, www.cancun-suites.com), Av Bonampak at Calle Cereza, have teemed up to offer classes in the ground floor conference room of the hotel. These courses are taught by professional teachers, as opposed to people who teach on the side and make most of their income doing something else. At the time of writing, 30 45-minute lessons over a two-week period, including lodging (double occupancy), cost US$550. Many options were available.

Mérida boasts three reputable Spanish-language schools. The K'u-Kuul-Kaan Academy (☎/fax 9-924-4474, mlocke@bigfoot.com, www.1spirit.com/kukuulkaan/), Calle 53 No 521, between Calles 64 and 66, also offers a variety of instruction and lodging options. Like the Berlitz classes in Ciudad Cancún and Mérida's other language program, the academy offers cultural excursions and homestays as well.

Also in Mérida is the Institute of Modern Spanish (☎/fax 9-927-1683, 4merida@modernspanish.com, www.modernspanish.com), Calle 29 No 128, between Calles 26 and 28, which like the two schools mentioned above offers year-round instruction and a host of instruction and housing options. At the time this book went to press, IMS was offering 20 hours of instruction per week for two weeks with shared-family homestay housing for US$612.

The Insituto Tecnológico de Hostelería (☎ 9-924-0387, fax 9-920-1460, itech@finred.com.mx, www.itech.edu.mx), Calle 57 No 492, between Calles 56 and 58, rounds out Mérida's better-known Spanish-language schools. Classes are offered all year and are limited to five students. The cost of instruction and lodging of all these schools is comparable.

Cooking

Yucatecan cuisine, though not as famous as the cuisine of Oaxaca, is well known throughout North America. Many of the dishes served on the peninsula today have been prepared by the Maya for many generations, using methods as varied as the taste is unique to the region.

In Mérida, the Insituto Tecnológico de Hostelería (☎ 9-924-0387, fax 9-920-1460, itech@finred.com.mx, www.itech.edu.mx), Calle 57 No 492, between Calles 56 and 58, offers a course in Yucatecan culinary art that includes information on the origins and history of each dish as well as hands-on training in its preparation. Tuition for two hours of instruction, five days a week for two weeks, costs US$273.

In Ciudad Cancún, the Suites El Patio (☎ 9-884-3500, fax 9-884-3540, cancun@

cancun-suites.com, www.cancun-suites.com), Av Bonampak at Calle Cereza, also offers classes in Yucatecan cooking. However, instruction is available for groups only, minimum eight students per course. The course includes five lessons spread over one week. The price of US$450 includes lodging at the hotel (double occupancy), a day trip to a Mayan ruin, transfers to and from the airport, and all taxes and tips.

WORK

In 1999, Yucatecans suffered high rates of unemployment and underemployment. To prevent jobs on the peninsula that would otherwise be filled by locals from going to foreigners, the government has created a lot of bureaucratic red tape intended to discourage foreigners from seeking employment in Mexico. But be advised, it *is* possible to work there legally. You only need a permit – and a bit of patience.

Work Permit Requirements

The Mexican Immigrations Office issues the all-important work permit, or FM-3 visa as it's formally known. One of the frustrations in obtaining an FM-3 visa is the seemingly fluid nature of the application requirements. Though the information provided here was totally correct at the time this book went to press, expect to be told of new changes and expect to have to make several trips to the immigrations office. That said, here follows the documents and items you must submit to Immigrations to obtain an FM-3 (office locations follow the list of requirements). Some of these items must be obtained in your home country.

Tourist Card Yes, the process begins with a tourist card – the brief slip of paper issued to you on the airplane (or at the border) and stamped by an immigrations agent. The tourist card tells authorities that you have permission to be in Mexico. When you hand it to the agent, request that you be given the maximum number of days allowed on a tourist card – 180 – because it takes that long to complete the application for a work permit.

Birth Certificate Not only do you need to present a copy of your birth certificate, but it must bear the stamp of the Mexican consulate nearest your place of birth. To obtain the stamp, you'll need to send the original birth certificate to the consulate along with a copy and a cover letter explaining your request for the copy to be stamped, and a self-addressed stamped envelope for the return of the birth certificate and its duplicate. Of course, before sending the certificate, the copy, cover letter and a return envelope, call ahead to learn if there's a fee involved. Most consulates charge a fee for the stamp, but some don't.

Professional Certificate Because Mexico doesn't want you to fill a job that could easily be filled by a local, the government requires that you present it with a stamped copy of a professional certificate or academic degree that would be appropriate for the kind of work you intend to do in Mexico. For example, if you intend to teach scuba diving in Cancún, Isla Mujeres or Cozumel, you'll want to present a dive master's certificate from PADI or one of the other leading scuba institutions. Like the birth certificate, a copy of this document must bear the stamp of the Mexican consulate nearest the place where you obtained your professional certificate or degree.

Passport If you've been putting off getting a passport, it's time to get one. If you want a work permit, you'll need to present it to the almighty powers at the Mexican Immigrations Office.

Job Offer You must have a written job offer to receive a work permit. The job offer must appear on the company's letterhead, it must include your name as it appears on your passport, it must specify the position you'll hold, the date you will start and the salary you'll be paid. The job offer must be signed by a representative of the institution whose name appears on the Acta Constitutiva de la Institución (see below), and you must include a photocopy of the representative's identification.

Acta Constitutiva de la Institución This document, issued to the company that you'll be working for, is the company's permit to do business in Mexico. Of course, if the company you intend to work for doesn't possess such a document, you won't be able to work for them. Not every company working in Mexico is doing so legally; if you have any doubts about the company you expect to work for, be sure to ask them about their Acta Constitutiva de la Institución at the outset. You'll need to present a notarized copy of this document at the time you apply for an FM-3.

Ultima Declaración de Impuestos de la Institución This document shows the company's most recent quarterly tax declaration. Because this is proprietary information, some businesses prefer to make a copy of the document and submit it directly to the immigrations office so that you won't know the amount the company declared in quarterly taxes.

Eight Photographs Yes, eight passport-size photographs of you: four of you facing the camera, and four of your profile. Remember how they photographed you that time you went to jail? Same deal, except that these can't be Polaroids, your hair cannot hide your forehead and your ears must be clearly visible in the profile shots.

Immigration Offices

Once you've obtained all the items above, present them to a Mexican Immigrations Office – any one will do. On the Yucatán Peninsula, there are immigration offices at the following locations:

Campeche (☎ 9-816-2868) Palacio Federal, Av 15 de Septiembre

Cancún Airport (☎ 9-886-0092) Aeropuerto Internaciónal de Cancún

Chetumal (☎ 9-832-8326) Av Tecnológico de Chetumal No 17

Ciudad Cancún (☎ 9-854-1404) Av Nader No 1 at Av Uxmal

Ciudad del Carmen (☎ 9-382-1330) Calle 31 No 144

Cozumel (☎ 9-872-0071) Palacio Municipal

Mérida (☎ 9-926-6141) Calle 60 No 445, near the cathedral

Playa del Carmen (☎ 9-733-1685) Plaza Antigua, Av Sur No 17

Teaching English

English-speakers may find teaching work in language schools, *preparatorias* (high schools), or universities, or can offer personal tutoring. The pay is invariably low, but you can live on it in Mexico.

The News and the telephone directory's yellow pages in large towns are good sources of job opportunities. Positions in high schools or universities are more likely to become available with the beginning of each new term – contact institutions that offer bilingual programs or classes in English; for universities, arrange an appointment with the director of the language department. Language schools tend to offer short courses, so teaching opportunities with them come up more often, and your commitment is for a shorter time, but they pay less than high schools and universities.

Although a foreigner working in Mexico must have a work permit (see the Work Permit section, above), a school will often pay a foreign teacher in the form of a *beca* (scholarship), and thus circumvent the law, or the school's administration will procure the appropriate papers without the teacher having to go through all of the rigmarole described above.

It's helpful to know at least a little Spanish, even though some institutes insist that only English be spoken in class.

Volunteer Work

The Council on International Educational Exchange (☎ 888-268-6245, info@ciee.org), 205 East 42nd St, New York, NY 10017 USA, has information on volunteer programs in Mexico. *Volunteer Vacations*, by Bill McMillon (Chicago Review Press, 1995), lists lots of volunteer work organizations and other information sources.

For work focused on the environment, Earthwatch Institute (www.earthwatch.org) typically runs several projects in Mexico that you pay to take part in. As these projects

vary year to year, it's best to contact them directly for information on their upcoming projects. Among the group's worldwide offices are:

Australia (☎ 03-9600-9100, fax 03-9600-9066, earth@earthwatch.org) Level One, 457 Elizabeth St, Melbourne 3000 Australia

UK (☎ 01865-311600, fax 01865-311383, info@uk.earthwatch.org) 57 Woodstock Rd, Oxford, OX2 6HJ UK

USA (☎ 800-776-0188, fax 617-926-8532, info@earthwatch.org) 680 Mount Auburn St, PO Box 9104, Watertown, MA 02272 USA

One World Workforce (☎/fax 520-779-3639), Rte 4, Box 963A, Flagstaff, AZ 86001 USA, sends paying volunteers to Mexico to work on environmental conservation projects such as protecting sea-turtle nests.

Amigos de las Americas (☎ 800-231-7796, fax 713-782-9267), 5618 Star Lane, Houston, TX 77057 USA, sends volunteers to work on public health projects in Latin America. Volunteers are normally involved in fundraising to defray project costs.

ACCOMMODATIONS
Accommodations in Yucatán range from beachside cabañas just south of the Tulum ruins to five-star resorts in Cancún's hotel zone.

Reservations
It's often advisable to reserve a room in advance at particularly popular hotels or if you plan to visit busy areas during the Christmas-New Year holidays, Semana Santa or during July and August. You should request a reservation by telephone or fax, asking whether a deposit is required and how to send it, and requesting confirmation in writing.

Camping
All Mexican beaches are public property. You can camp for nothing on most of them, but any beach can be a risky place for you and your belongings. Given the high level of crime in Mexico today, it just doesn't make any sense to sleep in a secluded area, separated from possible assailants by nothing more the nylon siding of a tent.

Hammocks & Cabañas
Hammocks are a very cheap way of sleeping. You can rent one and a place to hang it – usually under a palm roof outside a small *casa de huéspedes* (guesthouse; see Casas de Huéspedes & Posadas, below) or beach restaurant – for US$5 on some parts of the peninsula. If you have your own hammock the cost comes down a bit. It's easy enough to buy hammocks in Yucatán; Mérida specializes in them, and you'll find hammocks offered for sale in beach spots all along the Maya Riviera.

Cabañas are palm-thatched huts – some have dirt floors and nothing inside but a bed; others are deluxe, with electric light, mosquito nets, fans, fridge, bar and tasteful decor. Generally, prices for simple cabañas range from US$8 to US$20, though some of the fancy ones along the Caribbean go for far more.

Hostels
Villas juveniles or *albergues de juventud* (youth hostels) exist in only a few places in Yucatán: in Chetumal near Mexico's border with Belize, on Playa del Carmen and near the northern end of Cancún's hotel zone. None of these are very nice, but they are inexpensive.

Casas de Huéspedes & Posadas
The cheapest and most congenial lodging is often a casa de huéspedes, a home converted into simple guest lodgings. Good casas de huéspedes are usually family-run and have a relaxed, friendly atmosphere. Rooms may or may not have a private bathroom. A double typically costs US$10 to US$15, though a few places are more comfy and more expensive. Some *posadas* (inns) are like casas de huéspedes; others are small hotels.

Hotels
Budget Cheap hotels exist in every Mexican town, though on the Yucatán Peninsula there are substantially fewer than most other regions of Mexico. Expect to pay between US$15 and US$25 for a decent double room with private shower and hot water, more if you arrive during a popular time or an event.

Many hotels have rooms for three, four or five people that cost little more than a double.

Note that *cuarto sencillo* usually means a room with one bed, which is often a *cama matrimonial* (double bed). One person can usually occupy such a room for a lower price than two people. A *cuarto doble* is usually a room with two beds, often both 'matrimonial.'

Mid-Range & Top-End Even in relatively pricey Ciudad Cancún and other touristy Yucatecan cities you can usually find a good mid-range hotel, where two people can usually get a room with a private bathroom, TV and perhaps air-con for US$30 to US$60. The hotel will likely have an elevator, and often a restaurant and bar. These places are generally pleasant, respectable, safe and comfortable without being luxurious.

The peninsula is home to many large, modern resort hotels. They offer the expected levels of luxury at expectedly lofty prices. Be advised that nearly all resort guests reserved their rooms while in their home country. By doing this, they were able to save a lot of pesos – because guests who arrive unexpectedly are quoted a rate that's generally much higher than the discounted rates travel agents are allowed to offer.

FOOD

It's tantalizing to consider that some of the dishes prepared in Yucatán's kitchens today may be very similar to ones served in ancient times to Mayan royalty. Many often-used ingredients such as *pavo* (turkey), *venado* (venison) and *pescado* (fish) were available in ancient times, as they are today. At the back of the Glossary of this book, there is a Menu Guide that is specifically devoted to food, beverages and food-related words.

Staples

Mexicans eat three meals a day: *desayuno* (breakfast), *comida* (lunch) and *cena* (supper). Each includes one or more of three national staples: *tortillas*, *frijoles* and *chiles*.

Tortillas are thin round patties of pressed corn *(maíz)* or wheat-flour *(harina)* dough cooked on griddles. Both can be wrapped around or served under any type of food.

Frijoles are beans, eaten boiled, fried or refried in soups, on tortillas, or with just about anything.

Yucatán's renown resident chile is the habanero, quite honestly one of the world's hottest chiles. The author's anthropological theory holds that in the old days the victims of human sacrifice were given a choice: munch a habanero or have your heart carved out. Most thought the heart-ripping option offered a less painful end. If you go after a habanero chile, you had better be equipped with a steel tongue.

Despite its reputation as a fissionable material in vegetable form, the habanero is an important ingredient in *achiote*, the popular Yucatecan sauce, which also includes chopped onions, the juice of sour Seville oranges, cilantro and salt. You'll see a bowl of achiote on most restaurant tables in Yucatán. Put it on your food – or ignore it – as you like.

Also frequently served on the peninsula is the Xcat-ic chile, a tasty chile pepper found only in the Yucatán. It's not very hot, and it typically appears in Yucatecan salsas.

Street & Market Meals

The cheapest food is served up by the thousands of street stands selling all manner of hot and cold food and drinks. At these places you can often get a taco or a glass of orange juice for less than US$0.50. Many are very popular and well patronized, but hygiene can be a risk.

A step up from street fare are the *comedores* found in many markets. They offer Mexico's cheapest sit-down meals – you sit on benches at long tables and the food is prepared in front of you. It's usually typical local fare, and at good comedores it's like home cooking. It's best to go at lunchtime, when ingredients are fresher, and pick a comedor that's busy – which means it's good.

At the open-air markets and cookshops you'll need to know some Spanish to read the menus:

bistec a la Mexicana – bits of beef sautéed with chopped tomatoes and hot peppers
bistec de res/puerco – beef or pork steak

higado encebollado – liver and onions

longaniza – spicy sausage

pollo asado o frito – roasted or fried chicken

puerco empanizado – breaded pork chop

For more help with deciphering menu items, turn to the Menu Guide at the end of the Glossary at the back of this book. It is specifically devoted to food.

Breakfast

The simplest breakfast is coffee or tea and *pan dulce* (sweet rolls), a basket of which is set on the table; you pay for the number consumed. Many restaurants offer combination breakfasts for about US$1.50 to US$2.50, typically composed of *jugo de fruta* (fruit juice), *café* (coffee), *bolillo* or *pan tostado* with *mantequilla* and *mermelada* (roll or toast with butter and jam), and *huevos* (eggs), which are served in a variety of ways. In many places frequented by travelers, granola, *ensalada de frutas* (fruit salad), *avena* (porridge) and even Corn Flakes are available.

A local hearty breakfast favorite is *huevos motuleños*, or eggs in the style of the town of Motúl, east of Mérida. Fresh tortillas are spread with refried beans, then topped with an egg or two, then garnished with chopped ham, green peas and shredded cheese, with a few slices of fried banana on the side. It can be slightly *picante* (spicy) or *muy picante* (very spicy), depending on the cook. Other popular egg dishes include:

huevos pasados por agua – lightly boiled eggs (too lightly for many visitors' tastes)

huevos cocidos – harder-boiled eggs (specify the number of minutes if you're in doubt)

huevos estrellados – fried eggs

huevos fritos (con jamón/tocino) – fried eggs (with ham/bacon)

huevos mexicanos – eggs scrambled with tomatoes, chilies and onions (representing the red, green and white of the Mexican flag)

huevos rancheros – fried eggs on tortillas, covered in salsa

huevos poches – poached eggs

Lunch

La comida, the biggest meal of the day, is usually served between 1 and 3 or 4 pm. Most restaurants offer not only à la carte fare but also special fixed-price menus called *comida corrida*, *cubierto* or *menú del día*. These menus constitute the best food bargains, because you get several courses (often with some choice) for much less than such a meal would cost à la carte.

Prices typically range from US$1.50 or less at a market comedor for a simple meal of soup, a meat dish, rice and coffee to US$8 or more for elaborate repasts beginning with oyster stew and finishing with profiteroles – but typically you'll get four or five courses for US$2.50 or so. Drinks usually cost extra.

Dinner/Supper

La cena, the evening meal, is usually lighter than the comida. Fixed-price meals are rarely offered, so plan to eat your main meal at lunchtime.

For a main course you might order *pollo pibil*, chicken marinated in achiote sauce, sour Seville-orange juice, garlic, black pepper, cumin and salt, then wrapped in banana leaves and baked. There are no nuclear chiles to blow your head off. A variant is *cochinita pibil*, made with suckling pig instead of chicken.

The restaurant named Los Almendros in Ticul, Yucatán, claims to have created *poc-chuc*, slices of pork marinated in sour orange juice, cooked and served with a tangy sauce and pickled onions. A more traditional pork dish is *frijol con puerco*, the Mayan version of pork-and-beans, with black beans, tomato sauce and rice.

Another hearty dish is *puchero*, a stew made with chicken, pork, carrots, cabbage, squash and sweet potato.

The turkey is native to Yucatán and has been used as food for millennia. *Pavo relleno negro*, or dark stuffed turkey, is slices of turkey over a 'filling' made with pork and beef, all topped by a rich dark sauce.

Venison, also native to Yucatán, is perhaps best as a *pipián de venado*, steamed in banana leaves à la pibil and topped with a sauce made with ground squash (marrow, or zucchini) seeds.

Lighter traditional dishes include *papadzules*, tortillas sprinkled with chopped hard-boiled eggs, rolled up and topped with a sauce made with squash or pumpkin seeds. *Salbutes* are the native tacos: fried corn tortillas topped with shredded turkey meat, avocado, jalapeño peppers, pickled onions and lettuce. *Panuchos* resemble salbutes but usually include chicken instead of turkey and refried beans instead of lettuce.

As for seafood, the all-time favorite is *pescado frito*, simple fried fish, but there's also *langosta* (lobster), usually just the tail. The most interesting seafood concoctions are the *ceviches*, cocktails made of raw or parboiled seafood in a marinade of lime juice, tomato sauce, chopped onion and cilantro. *Ceviche de pescado* is the cheapest, made with whatever fish is in season and whatever fish is cheap at the markets. Other choices include *ceviche de camarones* (with shrimp) and *ceviche de ostiones* (with oysters).

Snacks

Antojitos, or 'little whims,' are traditional Mexican snacks or light dishes. Some are actually small meals in themselves. They can be eaten at any time, on their own or as part of a larger meal. There are many, many varieties, some peculiar to local areas. See the Antojitos section the Menu Guide at the back of the Glossary for a detailed list of these tasty treats.

DRINKS

A variety of *bebidas* (drinks), both alcoholic and nonalcoholic, is available in the Yucatán – as befits a region with such a warm climate. Don't drink any water unless you know it has been purified or boiled (see the Health section earlier this chapter). You can buy bottles of inexpensive purified or mineral water everywhere on the peninsula, and they are must-carry items on day trips to the Mayan ruins.

Coffee & Tea

Ordinary Mexican *café*, grown mostly near Córdoba and Orizaba and in Chiapas, is flavorful but often served weak. Those addicted to stronger caffeine shots should ask for 'Nescafé' – unless they're lucky enough to come upon one of the few real coffeehouses that have emerged in recent years. A few of these even serve Mexican organic coffee, from Oaxaca or Chiapas. Tea, invariably in bags, is a profound disappointment to any real tea drinker. Some terms you will want to know if you're a coffee or tea drinker can be found in the Menu section of the Glossary at the back of this book.

Fruit & Vegetable Drinks

Jugos (pure fresh juices) are popular in Mexico and readily available from streetside stalls and juice bars, where the fruit normally is squeezed before your eyes. Every fruit and a few of the squeezable vegetables are used. Ever tried pure beet juice?

Licuados are blends of fruit or juice with water and sugar. *Licuados con leche* use milk instead of water. Possible additions include raw egg, ice and flavorings such as vanilla or nutmeg. The delicious combinations are practically limitless. In Mexico's many juice bars, you can expect the water that is used to be purified – but don't assume the same for streetside juice stalls.

Aguas frescas or *aguas de fruta* are made by mixing fruit juice or a syrup made from mashed grains or seeds with sugar and water. You will usually see them in big glass jars on the counters of juice stands. *Agua fresca de arroz* (literally, 'rice water') has a sweet, nutty taste.

Refrescos

Refrescos are bottled or canned soft drinks, and there are some interesting and tasty local varieties. Sidral and Manzanita are two reasonable apple-flavored fizzy drinks. There's also a nonalcoholic variety of sangría.

There are many brands of *agua mineral* (mineral water) from Mexican springs – Tehuacán and Garci Crespo are two of the best and can sometimes be obtained with refreshing flavors, as well as plain.

Alcoholic Drinks

Breweries were established in Mexico by German immigrants in the late 19th century.

Mexico's several large brewing companies now produce more than 25 brands of *cerveza* (beer), many of which are excellent. Each major company has a premium beer, such as Bohemia and Corona de Barril (usually served in bottles); several standard beers, such as Carta Blanca, Superior and Dos Equis; and 'popular' brands, such as Corona, Tecate and Modelo. All are blond lagers meant to be served chilled – it's a good idea to ask for *una cerveza fría* (a cold beer). Each of the large companies also produces an *oscura* (dark) beer, such as Modelo Negro and Tres Equis. There are also some regional beers, brewed to similar tastes.

Mexico also produces a fascinating variety of intoxicating drinks made from grapes, grains and cacti. Foreign liquors are widely available, too.

ENTERTAINMENT

There are more entertainment options on the Yucatán Peninsula than you can shake a stick at. Nearly every week there's a major fiesta somewhere on the peninsula. This can take the form of a local patron saint

---

Green Is Good

Many of Yucatán's beaches are lined with coconut trees, and their fruit is delicious to eat and drink. The coconut has a thick husk, beneath which is a hard shell. Lining the interior of the shell is the fruit's white meat, which may be soft or hard depending on the coconut's age. Filling most of the shell is the fruit's sweet juice, which chiefly consists of mineral-rich, naturally filtered water that's said to be very good for the kidneys. Coconut juice and coconut meat are best consumed when the fruit is green; when the fruit is brown, the meat has hardened and the juice has begun to sour. Naturally fallen coconuts are decomposing and should not be eaten.

Tapping the juice and exposing the meat is a tricky matter best attempted with a machete. Machetes can be found throughout the peninsula and usually cost under US$10; a small machete is a wise buy if you intend to spend a lot of time at secluded beaches, where purified water won't be readily available to you.

To get to the juice, stand the coconut on end so that its stem faces the ground. Hack the pointy top of the coconut at a 45° angle, rotate the fruit one-fifth and repeat. Do this until a portion of the shell about the length of your thumb is exposed; the husk will peel out and away from the exposed shell as you hack.

Next, carefully strike the bared shell until you've made a hole in it. Tilt your head back and enjoy the refreshing juice. Once it's gone, place the coconut on the ground and split it in two to get at the meat. The meat is best scooped out of the shell with a spoon, but fingers work fine too.

Getting your hands on a coconut can be a problem. The easiest way is to pay someone to climb a tree and pick a few nuts; where there are coconut trees, there is usually a kid around who'll happily liberate a few nuts for US$1 or so. If you're on your own, pick up a fallen coconut and heave it, bowling-ball style, at the lowest bunch on the tree. You can drop several coconuts with a well-aimed throw.

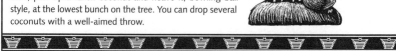

Mexican Cantinas

Everyone knows about Mexican cantinas, those men-only pits of excessive drinking, where most of the patrons deal with a drinking problem immediately after work every day. If there's any art on the wall, it's generally a calendar of a scantily clad woman bending over a car. For the most part, Mexican cantinas are barren, save for a dozen or so tables, 50 or chairs, and a bar at one end of the room.

Cantinas are not usually marked as cantinas, but can be identified by Wild West-type swinging half-doors, signs prohibiting minors and the generally raucous atmosphere. Those who enter must be prepared to drink hard, because alcoholism is one thing the patrons share – and drinkers don't much care to be around sippers. Newcomers might be challenged by a local to go one-for-one at a bottle of tequila, mezcal or brandy.

Cantinas are as popular as they are because they serve cheap booze – low in quality and low in price. If you've got a drinking habit and little disposable income, as many people in the Yucatán do, they're the place to go to tie one on in the company of others. Because gringos are assumed to be rich, if you're a gringo and decide to do some drinking in a cantina, don't be surprised if you suddenly acquire new amigos who eventually ask you to buy them drinks.

Besides cantinas, there are lot of bars, lounges and cafés on the peninsula. The more touristy the area, the more likely the bars are to be American-style versions of Mexican bars; they'll feature a powerful sound system blasting English rock 'n' roll, and the walls and ceiling will be festooned with sombreros, piñatas, bullfight posters and the like. The farther you go from the touristy areas, the more the bars will resemble traditional cantinas.

celebration or the form of a celebrated official holiday such as Christmas or Easter, or as a traditional day of celebration such as All Saints' Day, Day of the Dead or Day of Our Lady of Guadalupe.

In the larger cities and resort towns, the range of entertainment is broad, with music clubs (jazz, salsa, reggae, mariachi, rock), discos, bars and lounges abounding. In Cancún, you'll also find the Ballet Folklórico, and in Mérida every Monday there's a free *vaquería* – an outdoor concert in front of the Palacio Municipal featuring traditional Yucatecan dancing and dress. Every large city also has at least one cinema, where you'll usually find first-run Hollywood films in English with Spanish subtitles (occasionally they're dubbed into Spanish, but that's not usually the case).

Small-town Yucatán is a fairly early-to-bed zone: The best you can expect is a primitive cinema and a bar, possibly with entertainment, in the best local hotel.

If you're like 99.9% of the foreigners in Yucatán, you're there on vacation. This is a time to unwind, have some fun and enjoy some of the simple things in life. In the Tropics, it's best to take it easy, lest you like to sweat, and sweat a lot. At night it cools a little bit, but because the breeze drops then, the humidity increases. This is the time, after a day of activity under the strong sun, to do one of a couple of things: either mellow out, perhaps by enjoying an ice-cold fruit drink in a tranquil bar or café; or dance the night away, whether in an air-conditioned disco, in a beachside bar or even on a party boat, where food and an open bar are included in the price.

SPECTATOR SPORTS

If, as a child, you enjoyed pulling the wings off flies and, as an adult, you take pleasure in the misfortunes of others, you might enjoy a bullfight ('bull execution' is a more appropriate term). The only place on the peninsula where a bull is killed on a routine basis for the sadistic enjoyment of people is the bullring in Cancún. The killing of one large, confused and exhausted bull occurs there every Wednesday. For more on the weekly bullfight, turn to Things to See & Do in the

Ciudad Cancún section of the Quintana Roo chapter, and to the Treatment of Animals section of the Facts about Yucatán chapter.

SHOPPING

Yucatán is famous for its lost cities and for the fabulous snorkeling and scuba diving along its Caribbean coast. But the peninsula is also a gold mine for souvenir shoppers. Fashion know-it-alls will be familiar with the *guayabera*, a light, elegant linen shirt with four square pockets that's standard business wear in southeast Mexico. These shirts were popular with hipsters in Miami and Hollywood in the late 1990s, although few knew much about the shirts.

Guayaberas originally hail from Yucatán, where they are the uniform of local politicians. Indeed, a Yucatecan politician wearing any other kind of shirt would be scandalous. Luckily for them, the best guayaberas are made in Yucatán, and they are still affordable there. While their prices have soared in recent years, high-quality, reasonably priced guayaberas can still be found in Mérida and elsewhere in Yucatán.

Another clothing item that originated in Yucatán and continues to be worn with great pride there is the *huipil*, an always spotless white dress with a wide band of brightly colored flower embroidery around the yoke and another one near the bottom of the dress. Huipiles, which are light, loose fitting and traditionally made of cotton (synthetics are occasionally used today), are ideally suited for the Tropics and are worn by women of all ages. For more information about huipiles, see the Arts section of the Facts about Yucatán chapter.

The Arts section of the Facts about Yucatán chapter also describes many other handicrafts that are available on the peninsula, including high-quality Panama hats, lovely carved-wood objects, and jewelry adorned with silver filigree. In addition, earthenware pots of widely varying quality can be found across the peninsula (potheads will want to visit Ticul, where shops near the city center sell the most interesting ceramics available in Yucatán; the techniques used in Ticul predate the Conquest by hundreds of years).

Also available across the peninsula are handmade blankets, leather goods, decorative cloth, wicker baskets, brilliantly painted gourds and lots of amber jewelry. Yucatecan hammocks are renowned for their quality and durability, so visit one of the hammock stores in Mérida if you are looking to buy one; in fact, shops all along the Mayan Riviera (Tulum Corridor) sell hammocks. For fine jewelry sold by Van Cleef & Arpels and other big-name jewelers, look to the tourist haunts of Cozumel, Isla Mujeres and Cancún. Smart shoppers visiting the upscale jewelers will want to focus on silver goods and works featuring Colombian emeralds and Mexican opals, as both stones are often bargain-priced in Mexico.

Getting There & Away

The vast majority of visitors to Yucatán arrive by air, and greater than 90% of those people touch down at the Aeropuerto Internacional de Cancún. More than a dozen major airlines and a small number of charters provide service to Cancún, which handles a lofty 2350 passengers per hour on average.

In addition to Cancún's airport, there is international service to and from Mérida, Campeche, Chetumal and Cozumel, although the combined number of international flights to these four cities pales in comparison to the amount of air traffic that moves through Cancún. Of Mexico's many airports, only the one serving the country's capital sees more foreign visitors than Cancún's.

Relatively few visitors to Yucatán arrive by land routes. Those persons entering Yucatán by land from elsewhere in Mexico arrive from Tabasco (which borders Campeche state), usually after seeing the Mayan ruins there and in nearby Chiapas. Although Campeche and Quintana Roo share a long border with Guatemala, there are no crossing points between the Yucatecan states and Guatemala. However, Quintana Roo and Belize abut one another, and it is possible to travel between the two, and many people do.

Of course, arrival by sea is another possibility, what with the Yucatán Peninsula being surrounded on three sides by water (the Gulf of Mexico is to the west and north, and the Caribbean is to the east). Cruise ships make regular stops at Cozumel and Cancún.

Other Yucatecan seaports include Chetumal, San Felipe and Ciudad del Carmen.

Visitor Tax

Starting in 1999, visitors traveling to most parts of Mexico are required to pay a visitor tax of about US$15 (the official amount in pesos is N$150). The tax targets all foreign visitors who plan to venture more than 25km beyond the border and plan to stay longer than three days. Tourists staying within the 25km border zone or less than three days are exempt. If you are arriving by air, the tax will be included in the price of your ticket. If not, the tax will be levied at your port of entry.

AIR
Airports & Airlines

Despite the number of people who make Yucatán their final destination, most visitors must first pass through one of five 'hub' airports. These are: Dallas/Fort Worth, Miami, Mexico City, Houston and New York. Due to some inconvenient air-route structuring, few international flights fly direct from anywhere else to Cancún.

More than a dozen international airlines serve Yucatán, including Aeroméxico, American Airlines, British Airways, Continental Airlines, Iberia, Lacsa, Martinair Holland, Mexicana, Northwest Airlines and United Airlines.

Because airlines are constantly adding and dropping routes of service, it's a good idea to contact a travel agent from the outset to obtain the most current information on the airlines linking your hometown to your destination in Yucatán. The airline and airfare information contained in this chapter is extremely susceptible to change and should only be viewed as a guide.

The five international airports (and their airport call signs) on the Yucatán Peninsula are: Aeropuerto Internacional de Cancún (CUN); Aeropuerto Internacional de Cozumel (CZM); Aeropuerto Internacional de

Chetumal (CTM); Aeropuerto Internacional Manuel Crescencio Rejon (MID), in Mérida; and Aeropuerto Internacional Alberto Acuña Ongay (CPE), in Campeche.

Airline Toll-Free Numbers Many airlines have toll-free telephone numbers you can call from anywhere in Mexico. They include:

Aerolitoral	☎ 01-800-36202
Aeroméxico	☎ 01-800-90999
American Airlines	☎ 01-800-90460
Aviacsa/Aeroexo	☎ 01-800-00672
Continental Airlines	☎ 01-800-90050
Delta Air Lines	☎ 01-800-90221
Mexicana	☎ 01-800-21654
Northwest Airlines	☎ 01-800-90008
United Airlines	☎ 01-800-00307

Buying Tickets

There are dozens of airfares that apply to any given route. They vary with each company, class of service, season of the year, length of stay, dates of travel, and date of purchase and reservation. Your ticket may cost more or less depending upon the flexibility you are allowed in changing your plans. The price of the ticket is even affected by how and from whom you buy it.

Independent travel agents and airline ticketing agents should be the first people to consult about fares and routes, because they may be aware of specials that Internet ticketing services and ticket consolidators are unaware of. Once you've got a good idea about the routes and fares that are available from the traditional sources, you can consult ticket consolidators and/or charter airlines to see if their fares are lower. Check the travel sections of major newspapers for their listings.

Tour packages are well worth looking into, and there are quite a number of them to Cancún. They typically include roundtrip airfare, airport transfers and hotel accommodations ranging from a few days in country to a week or more. Tour packages are by far the most economical way to visit Yucatán, unless you'll be traveling on a shoestring. If you'll be counting every peso you spend or if you'd prefer not to stay in one of

Award Yourself Some Space

Gone are the days when you could receive a free trip to an exotic locale as a valued frequent flyer after flying to only few, albeit distant, destinations. That's because many airlines realized several years ago that the generous frequent-flyer programs created during the booming '80s were costing them a fortune. Today, you've practically got to fly to another solar system to accrue enough kilometers to qualify for one free airline ticket.

Regardless of the award requirements, there's a very good reason for you to enroll in the frequent-flyer program offered by the airline (or airlines) you'll use for your upcoming trip to Yucatán: Most carriers allow their frequent-flyer members to board early. Disabled people, 1st-class passengers and families with small children are always allowed to board first, but increasingly, frequent flyers are called immediately afterward, before row-by-row announcements begin.

Boarding early is helpful because it virtually assures you plenty of overhead cargo space for your carry-on baggage. This may not seem important when you're at home selecting your luggage and packing with utmost efficiency. But you'll want to be in front of the herd when you return from Yucatán with newly bought goodies that you'd rather not place in the care of airport luggage handlers.

Joining a frequent-flyer program is easy. You can do it at the time you purchase your ticket, if you obtain the ticket directly from an airline. If you purchased a ticket from a ticket consolidator or travel agent, call the airline and ask to join its program. There's never any charge to join, and most applications can be made simply by calling the carrier's toll-free reservations number. Once the application is completed, you'll be mailed a membership card to present at the time you check in. *Bon voyage!*

the resorts despite all of their amenities, don't bother looking into tour packages.

Of course, every fare mentioned in these pages was only current at the time it was quoted. The fare you are quoted could be substantially higher or lower. Be sure to see what the bucket shops are offering before buying any tickets. Ticket consolidators (also known as 'bucket shops') are organizations that buy thousands of tickets from airlines at considerable discounts and then resell them to the public with a slight markup, often through travel agents but mostly through newspaper ads. Consolidator ads typically include tables of destinations, accompanying fares and a toll-free number to call. They're a good place to turn to for inexpensive airfares.

Air Travel Glossary

Baggage Allowance – This will be written on your ticket and usually includes one 20kg item to go in the hold, plus one item of carry-on luggage.

Bucket Shops – These are unbonded travel agencies specializing in discounted airline tickets.

Bumped – Just because you have a confirmed seat doesn't mean you're going to get on the plane (see Overbooking).

Cancellation Penalties – If you have to cancel or change a discount ticket, there are often heavy penalties involved; insurance can sometimes be taken out against these penalties. Some airlines impose penalties on regular tickets as well, particularly against 'no-show' passengers.

Check In – Airlines ask you to check in a certain time ahead of the flight's departure (usually one to two hours on international flights). If you fail to check in on time and the flight is overbooked, the airline can cancel your booking and give your seat to somebody else.

Confirmation – Having a ticket with the flight and date you want doesn't mean you have a seat until the agent has checked with the airline that your status is confirmed. Meanwhile you could be just 'on request.'

Courier Fares – Businesses often need to send urgent documents or freight securely and quickly. Courier companies hire people to accompany the baggage through customs and, in return, offer a discount ticket that is sometimes a phenomenal bargain. In effect, what the companies do is ship their freight as your luggage on regular commercial flights. This is a legitimate operation, but there are two shortcomings: the short turnaround time of the ticket (usually not longer than a month) and the limitation on your luggage allowance. You may have to surrender all of your allowance and take only carry-on luggage.

ITX – An ITX, or 'independent inclusive tour excursion,' is often available on tickets to popular holiday destinations. Officially, it's a package deal combined with hotel accommodations, but many agents will sell you one of these for the flight only and give you phony hotel vouchers in the unlikely event that you're challenged at the airport.

Lost Tickets – If you lose your airline ticket, an airline will usually treat it like a traveler's check and, after inquiries, issue you another one. Legally, however, an airline is entitled to treat it like cash – if you lose it, it's gone forever. Take good care of your tickets.

MCO – An MCO, or 'miscellaneous charge order,' is a voucher that looks like an airline ticket but carries no destination or date. It can be exchanged through any International Association of Travel Agents (IATA) airline for a ticket on a specific flight. It's a useful alternative to an onward ticket in those countries that demand one, and is more flexible than an ordinary ticket if you're unsure of your route.

Travelers with Special Needs

If you have special needs of any sort – you have a broken leg, you're a vegetarian, you're traveling in a wheelchair, you're traveling with a baby, you're terrified of flying, etc – you should let the airline know as soon as possible so that it can make arrangements accordingly. You should remind the airline when you reconfirm your booking (at least

72 hours before departure) and again when you check in at the airport.

Airports and airlines can be surprisingly helpful, but they do need advance warning. Most international airports will provide escorts from the check-in desk to the plane when needed. Deaf travelers can ask that airport and in-flight announcements be written down for them. Passengers with a weak

Air Travel Glossary

No Shows – No shows are passengers who fail to show up for their flight, whether due to unexpected delays, disasters, forgetfulness or, sometimes, because they made more than one booking and didn't bother to cancel the one they didn't want. Full-fare passengers who fail to turn up are sometimes entitled to travel on a later flight. The rest are penalized (see Cancellation Penalties).

On Request – This is an unconfirmed booking for a flight.

Onward Tickets – An entry requirement for many countries is that you have an onward or return ticket; in other words, a ticket out of the country. If you're not sure what you intend to do next, the easiest solution is to buy the cheapest onward ticket to a neighboring country or a ticket from a reliable airline that can later be refunded if you do not use it.

Open-Jaw Tickets – A return ticket on which you fly to one place but return from another. If available, this can save you backtracking to your arrival point.

Overbooking – Airlines hate to fly with empty seats, and since every flight has some passengers who fail to show up (see No Shows), airlines often book more passengers than they have seats available. Usually the excess passengers balance those who fail to show up, but occasionally somebody gets 'bumped.' If this happens, guess who it is most likely to be? The passengers who check in late.

Point-to-Point Tickets – These are discount tickets that can be bought on some routes in return for passengers waiving their rights to a stopover.

Reconfirmation – At least 72 hours prior to departure time, you must contact the airline and 'reconfirm' that you intend to be on the flight. If you don't do this, the airline can delete your name from the passenger list and you could lose your seat. You don't have to reconfirm the first flight on your itinerary or if your stopover is less than 72 hours. It doesn't hurt to reconfirm more than once.

Restrictions – Discount tickets often have various restrictions on them – advance purchase is the most common. Others are restrictions on the minimum or maximum period you must be away, such as a minimum of 14 days or a maximum of one year (see Cancellation Penalties).

Round-the-World Tickets – RTW tickets give you a limited period (usually a year) in which to circumvent the globe. You can go anywhere the carrying airlines go, as long as you don't backtrack. The number of stopovers or total number of separate flights is decided before you set off, and they usually cost a bit more than a basic return flight.

Standby – This is a discount ticket on which you only fly if there is a seat free at the last moment. Standby fares are usually only available on domestic routes.

Travel Periods – Ticket prices vary with the time of year. There is a low (off-peak) season and a high (peak) season, and often a low-shoulder season and a high-shoulder season as well. Usually the fare depends on your outward flight – if you depart in the high season and return in the low season, you pay the high-season fare.

shoulder or back shouldn't hesitate to ask a flight attendant for a helpful hand when using an overhead bin.

Children two years and younger typically travel for 10% of the standard fare (free on some airlines), as long as they don't occupy a seat; if you'll be traveling with a toddler, be sure to say so when you request tickets and at check-in. 'Skycots' should be provided by the airline if they're requested in advance; these will hold a child weighing up to 10kg. Children between two and 12 years of age can usually occupy a seat for one-half to two-thirds of the full fare.

Departure Tax

A departure tax of US$12, payable in US dollars or Mexican pesos, is collected for all international flights. Generally, the tax is paid at the time you purchase your ticket and no money is requested at the time you check in for your return flight – unless you're purchasing your return ticket at that time.

The USA & Canada

At the time of writing, Aeroméxico, Air Canada, America West, American Airlines, Canadian Airlines, Continental Airlines, Mexicana, Northwest Airlines and United Airlines served Cancún and Cozumel from the US and/or Canada, with most of the airlines making at least one stop prior to arriving in Yucatán.

The cost of roundtrip coach tickets from either country to Cancún or Cozumel generally ranged from US$450 to US$850, depending on the dates of travel, the point of departure and the time between purchase and travel. Roundtrip tickets from most US cities to Cancún could be obtained for less than US$650 if a little effort was made to locate them and if they were purchased at least three weeks before departure.

However, the Air Canada flights orignating in Toronto typically ranged from US$1000 to US$1700, and a few of the Canadian Airlines and America West flights out of Vancouver topped US$1800. Worse still, from a bargain hunter's perspective: Several of the Northwest, United and American roundtrip tickets topped US$2100! Once again, it pays to shop around. A few phone calls can save you a lot of money if you'll be reaching Yucatán from Mexico's neighbors to the north.

At the time of writing, there were no direct flights from the USA or Canada to any airport in the Yucatán besides the ones at Cancún and Cozumel.

Continental Europe

There are many flights each day from Europe to the US and Mexico City, with connections to Yucatán. Among the airlines offering the greatest number of flights to the USA and Mexico City at the time of writing were British Airways, Iberia and Lufthansa. Air France, Delta Air Lines, KLM and Martinair Holland were also providing service between Europe and the USA and Mexico City, with connections south.

The range of roundtrip airfares from Europe is nearly as wide as the continent itself, and not simply due to distances traveled. At the time of writing, Lufthansa was flying from Frankfurt to Mexico City to Cancún and back for US$1126 – as long as the ticket was purchased three weeks or more ahead of departure. However, that very same ticket cost US$3719 when it was purchased just three days ahead of departure.

Meanwhile, a roundtrip ticket from Paris to Mexico City to Cancún and back aboard an Air France airliner cost US$2488 with 30-day advance purchase, and US$3552 with only three days' advance purchase. An alternative at the time placed the connection in Miami instead of Mexico City, but for the Miami connection passengers paid a minimum additional cost of US$694 (if anyone ever asks you what the difference between

---

Remember, Before You Fly...

- Always reconfirm airline reservations, even for short flights.
- Arrive at the airport an hour before departure for domestic flights.
- Arrive at the airport two hours before departure for international flights.

Miami and Mexico City is, now you know). However, yet another alternative was to fly Continental from Paris to Houston to Cancún, returning from Cancún to Miami to Paris. The cost of this coach ticket purchased three days before traveling? A very sizable US$5029.

Low-end Europe-to-Cancún airfares at the time of writing included: Barcelona to Madrid to Cancún and back aboard Iberia, US$1031; Amsterdam to Madrid to Cancún and back aboard Iberia, US$1261; Zurich to Madrid to Cancún and back aboard Iberia, US$1775; Moscow to Frankfurt to Miami to Cancún and back via Lufthansa, United, Iberia and American, US$1555; Milan to Madrid to Cancún aboard Iberia and back, US$1019; Munich to Madrid to New Jersey to Cancún and back aboard Lufthansa, Iberia, Continental, United and Lufthansa, US$1033.

If you've been wondering what a nonstop Iberia flight from Madrid to Cancún cost in late 1999, here's your answer: US$782, roundtrip. From Lisbon to Madrid to Cancún and back, also aboard an Iberia jetliner, you'd have paid an additional US$190.

The UK

For cheap (ie, bucket-shop) tickets from London, pick up a copy of *City Limits*, *Time Out*, *TNT* or any of the other magazines that advertise discount flights. The magazine *Business Traveller* also has a great deal of good advice on airfare bargains. Most bucket shops are trustworthy and reliable, but the occasional sharp operator appears; *Time Out* and *Business Traveller* typically give some useful advice on precautions to take.

If you simply called a travel agent in late 1999 and asked the cost of a roundtrip Glasgow-London-Miami-Cancún ticket, you'd have been told US$1295 to US$3156, depending on the airlines flown and the number of days separating ticket purchase and ticket use. At the same time, a roundtrip London-Houston-Cancún ticket aboard a Continental aircraft cost US$913.

Meanwhile, the cost of flying from Belfast to Manchester to Atlanta to Cancún and back aboard British Airways, Delta, Continental and Aeroméxico was US$1384.

Central & South America

Most flights originating in Latin America in late 1999 and destined for Yucatán generally stopped in Miami or Mexico City first. United Airlines flew from Rio de Janeiro to Miami then back down to Cancún, with the cost of the roundtrip ticket set at US$1065 with 30-day advance purchase. American Airlines also flew that route but generally charged more.

However, American offered the lowest roundtrip airfare from Buenos Aires to Cancún via Miami (US$1210). Mexicana offered a very convenient nonstop flight between the Argentine capital and Cancún, but it cost passengers US$2210.

United offered a Caracas-Miami-Cancún ticket for as little as US$833 roundtrip, and American pretty much cornered the Bogota-Miami-Cancún market, offering a roundtrip fare of US$742. From Santiago to Mexico City to Cancún and back with Aeroméxico, a prospective passenger could expect to pay no less than US$2001, even with a month's advance purchase.

Roundtrip airfare from any of the Central American countries to Cancún rarely cost more than US$600 with advance purchase, but they also rarely cost less than US$400. In late 1999, an Aviateca flight in a rattling ATR Turboprop from Guatemala City to Cancún cost a fairly steep US$221 each way.

Australia

At the time of writing Qantas was flying Down Under folks from Sydney to Auckland to Los Angeles, where they boarded a Mexicana flight for the home stretch to their final destination, Cancún. Taking the same carriers back to Sydney, with 30 days' advance purchase, the total cost of the air travel was US$2009.

Australians departing from Melbourne to Los Angeles to Cancún and back via Qantas and Mexicana paid US$1977 in late 1999 if they paid 30 days or more ahead of departure. Persons flying from Auckland to Los Angeles to Cancún aboard Qantas and Mexicana planes paid US$2012 roundtrip (or US$3697 if they waited until the last minute to buy their tickets).

Asia

Just like the many Australians that transit Los Angeles en route to the southeastern tip of Mexico, so too do many Japanese and Chinese citizens. Among the more popular flights from Japan and China to the Yucatán are the United Airlines flights that originate in Hong Kong, pick up passengers in Tokyo, fly to Los Angeles and proceed nonstop from Los Angeles to Cancún. The cost of this ticket in late 1999, including the return flight, was US$2207. Most flights originating in Beijing also flew to Tokyo before proceeding on to the USA, refueling and then continuing on to Cancún.

Some flights from Japan stopped in Texas instead of California. Typical of those was American Airlines' Osaka-Dallas/Fort Worth-Cancún flight, which costs US$1800 roundtrip with 30-day advance purchase. A Continental Tokyo-Houston-Cancún roundtrip ticket in late 1999 could be purchased for US$1357 with a month's notice.

Africa & the Middle East

South African Airways and American Airlines teamed up in late 1999 to offer a Johannesburg-Miami-Cancún roundtrip ticket for US$1891. Although quotes from Nairobi are usually available, civil unrest in late 1999 prevented carriers from provided anything other than temporary sky-high quotes from Kenya to most any destination outside of Africa.

There were no nonstops from the African continent to Mexico at the time of writing, but a long-distance jetliner under production by Boeing suggested nonstop flights between Africa and Mexico would be available within a year or so. The new jetliner features 28 hours of travel on a single super-large tank of aviation fuel.

Persons flying from Abu Dhabi to Cancún would have found the best airfare by flying first to Paris and then to Miami en route to southeast Mexico and Cancún. If they chose this route, flying Gulf Air, Air France, Iberia and Continental, those persons would have paid US$2670 for a coach seat if purchased from a travel agent a month in advance.

LAND

The few tourists who reach the Yucatán Peninsula by land do so either by entering Campeche state from Tabasco or by entering Quintana Roo from Belize. Short of crossing illegally from Guatemala into Campeche or Quintana Roo – an effort that would require transiting many kilometers of roadless jungle – there's simply no other way to reach Yucatán by land.

Crossing the Mexico-Belize border at the southern tip of Quintana Roo is a rather easy affair for most tourists. An old iron drawbridge on the Río Hondo at the town of Subteniente López, 8km southwest of Chetumal, marks the official Mexico-Belize crossing point.

Persons leaving Belize for Mexico will need to pay an exit tax of US$11.25 at the border; this must be paid in cash (in Belizean or US currency) or in widely accepted traveler's checks such as American Express (credit cards are not accepted). US dollars are accepted everywhere in Belize. At the time of writing, US$1 was equal to BZ$2. For Mexican entry requirements, see the Visa section in the Facts for the Visitor chapter.

Persons leaving Mexico need only turn in their tourist cards and get their passports stamped at the Mexican Immigration Office a stone's throw from the bridge. Once they cross the bridge (either on foot or in a private vehicle; rental vehicles are not permitted to pass), they need only present their passport if they are citizens of the USA, Belgium, British Commonwealth nations, Denmark, Finland, Greece, Iceland, Italy, Liechtenstein, Luxembourg, Mexico, Spain, Switzerland, Tunisia, Turkey or Uruguay. All other visitors need to obtain a visa, which can be obtained from the Belizean Consulate in Chetumal (☎ 9-832-2871, 9-882-2100, fax 9-882-0100), Avenida Álvaro Obregon No 226A.

Bus

There's bus service to Chetumal from the Belizean cities of Corozal, Orange Walk and Belize City. Buses leaving Chetumal bound for those cities depart from two places: from the city bus terminal (Terminal de Autobuses

de Chetumal), and from the bus stop beside the New Market of Lázaro Cárdenas (Nuevo Mercado Lázaro Cárdenas). The bus terminal is located at the intersection of Av de los Insurgentes and Av Belice, 3km north of the Museo de la Cultura Maya and two blocks to the west. The market is located on Calzada Veracruz at Regundo, 1.5km northeast of the museum. See the Chetumal section in the Quintana Roo chapter for details.

Car & Motorcycle

Driving in Mexico is not for everyone – you should know some Spanish and have basic mechanical aptitude, large reserves of patience and access to some extra cash for emergencies. You should also note that the highways between Chetumal and Sabancuy, and Ciudad del Carmen and Campeche, have reputations for crime. Specifically, the police who patrol these stretches of road are renown for citing motorists for bogus moving violations, and highway robbers armed with assault rifles frequently stop motorists at night and rob them at gunpoint. Motorists planning on using either highway should limit their driving to daylight hours and should obey the speed-limit signs.

Cars are most useful for travelers who:

- have plenty of time
- plan to go to remote places
- have surfboards, dive equipment or other cumbersome luggage
- will be traveling with a group or family of four or more
- want to buy lots of bulky handicrafts

Don't take a car if you:

- have a low budget
- plan to spend most of your time in urban areas
- will be traveling alone
- want a relaxing trip with minimum risks

Cars are generally expensive to buy or rent in Mexico, although it's usually possible to rent a vehicle at a reasonable price is you reserve one well ahead of your trip; see the Getting Around chapter for details on renting a car in Yucatán.

Be advised that while there are Volkswagen, Nissan/Datsun, Chrysler, General Motors and Ford manufacturing or assembly plants in Mexico, the parts used in these vehicles adhere to the metric system. Therefore, parts for US-made Volkswagens, Chryslers, etc, which follow the imperial system, are hard if not impossible to acquire in Mexico. For this reason, it's best not to take a vehicle into Mexico. Also, it's not possible to take a rental car into or out of Mexico.

Motorcycling in Mexico is not for the fainthearted. Chickens, turkeys, iguanas, even rattlesnakes commonly appear on roads in the Yucatán. Many pedestrians cross highways without first looking for oncoming cars. Roads and traffic can be rough, and parts and mechanics are generally hard to come by. The only parts you'll find at all will be for Kawasaki, Honda and Suzuki bikes.

The rules for taking a vehicle into Mexico, described in the sections that follow, have in the past changed from time to time. You can check with the American Automobile Association (AAA), a Mexican consulate, a Mexican government tourist office or the US toll-free information number ☎ 800-446-3942 for general Mexico travel info.

See also the Getting Around chapter for more information on driving and motorcycling in Mexico.

Car Insurance It is foolish to drive in Mexico without Mexican liability insurance. If you are involved in an accident, you can be jailed or forbidden to leave the immediate area until all claims are settled, which could take weeks or months. A valid Mexican insurance policy is regarded as a guarantee that restitution will be paid, and it will expedite release of the driver. Mexican law recognizes only Mexican *seguro* (car insurance), so a US or Canadian policy won't help. The cost of insurance varies with the value of the vehicle. It's possible to save money if you rent the vehicle using an American Express card. See the Getting Around chapter for details.

Driver's License To drive a motor vehicle – car, camper van, motorcycle or truck – in

Mexico, you need a valid driver's license from your home country. Mexican police are familiar with US and Canadian licenses; those from other countries may be scrutinized more closely, but they are still legal. International Driver's Licenses, provided by auto clubs, generally are not considered valid driver's licenses by Mexican authorities.

Vehicle Permit You will need a *permiso de importación temporal de vehículos* (a temporary import permit for vehicles) if you want to take a vehicle more than 25km into Mexico. The permits are available at the *aduana* (customs) office near border crossings.

In addition to a passport – or proof of US or Canadian citizenship if you hail from one of those countries – the person importing the vehicle will need originals of the following documents, which must all be in his/her own name: a tourist card (go to *migración* before you go to the aduana); a certificate of title or ownership for the vehicle; a current registration card or notice; a driver's license; and either an international credit card (Visa, MasterCard, American Express or Diner's Club) issued by a non-Mexican bank or cash to pay a very large bond (see below). You need at least one photocopy of each of these documents as well as the original, but people at the office may make photocopies for a small fee.

If the vehicle is not fully paid for, you need a letter from the lender authorizing its use in Mexico for a specified period. If it's a company car and you do not have a certificate of ownership in your own name, bring a notarized affidavit certifying that you work for the company and are allowed to take the car into Mexico. If the vehicle is leased or rented, bring the original contract (plus a copy), which must be in the name of the person importing the car, and a notarized affidavit from the rental firm authorizing the driver to take it into Mexico.

One person cannot bring in two vehicles. If, for example, you have a motorcycle attached to your car, you'll need another adult traveling with you to obtain a permit for the motorcycle, and he/she will need to have all the right papers for it. If the motorcycle is

registered in your name, you'll need a notarized affidavit authorizing the other person to take it into Mexico. A special permit is needed for vehicles weighing more than about 3.3 US tons (3 British tonnes).

At the border there will be a building with a parking area for vehicles awaiting permits. Go inside and find the right counter at which to present your papers. After some signing and stamping of papers, you sign a promise to take the car out of the country, the Banco del Ejército (also called Banjército; it's the army bank) charges US$11 to your credit card, and you are sent out to wait with your vehicle. Make sure you get back the originals of all documents. Eventually someone will come out, check the details of your vehicle, put a hologram sticker on the top corner of the windshield, and give you a permit (with another hologram sticker) and your tourist card, stamped *'con automóvil'* (with vehicle).

If you don't have an international credit card, you will have to deposit a cash bond (not a check) with the Banco del Ejército or an authorized Mexican *afianzadora* (bonding company). The required bond amounts for medium or small cars are US$6000 for a vehicle up to two years old, US$3000 (three or four years old), US$1000 (five or six years old), US$750 (seven to 14 years old), and US$500 (15 years or older). There may be taxes and processing fees to pay, too. The bond should be refunded, plus any interest, when the vehicle finally leaves Mexico and the temporary import permit is canceled. If you plan to leave Mexico at a different border crossing, make sure that the bonding company will give you a refund there.

There are offices for Banco del Ejército and authorized Mexican bonding companies at or near all the major border points. Banco del Ejército offices at major crossings are always open, except at Tijuana (it is open 8 am to 10 pm Monday to Friday, 8 am to 6 pm Saturday, noon to 4 pm Sunday), and at Tecate (open it's open 8 am to 4 pm daily).

The permit entitles you to take the vehicle in and out of Mexico for the period shown on your tourist card. If the car is still in Mexico after that time, aduana will start

charging fines to your credit card. Cars in Mexico without a current permit can be confiscated. The permit allows the vehicle to be driven by the owner's spouse or adult children or by other people if the owner is in the vehicle.

When you leave Mexico for the last time you must have the permit canceled by the Mexican authorities, no later than the day before it expires. An official may cancel the permit as you enter the border zone, usually about 25km before the border itself. If not, you will have to find the right official from aduana and/or Banco del Ejército at the border crossing. If you leave Mexico without having the permit canceled, once the permit expires the authorities will assume that you've left the vehicle in the country illegally and will start charging fines to your credit card.

Only the owner can take the vehicle out of Mexico – and as a rule, the owner cannot leave Mexico without it. If it's wrecked completely, you must obtain permission to leave it in the country from either the Registro Federal de Vehículos (Federal Registry of Vehicles) in Mexico City, or a Hacienda (Treasury Department) office in another city or town; your insurance company can help with this. If you have to leave the country in an emergency, the vehicle can be left in temporary storage at an airport or seaport or with an aduana or Hacienda office.

SEA
Virtually all of the big-name cruise lines that plied the sea from Florida to Venezuela in 1999 included Cozumel in at least one of their Caribbean island-hopping packages. If visiting Cozumel (or to a lesser extent, Cancún) as part of a cruise appeals to you, be sure to contact the Carnival (www.carnival .com/), Princess (www.princesscruises.com) and Holland America (www.hollandamerica .com) cruise lines.

The vast majority of Cozumel-bound cruises originate in Miami, as do a much smaller number of cruises that call upon Cancún. Contact a travel agent or do an Internet search for 'Cozumel and cruises' or 'Cancún and cruises' for prices and departure dates. An Internet search will likely show all of the cruises that call on Cozumel and Cancún.

ORGANIZED TOURS
If you just want a short holiday in Yucatán, consider signing up for one of the many package deals offered by travel agents and in newspaper travel sections. Mexican government tourist offices can give you armfuls of brochures about these trips; see the Tourist Offices Abroad section in the Facts for the Visitor chapter. Costs depend, among other things, on where and when you go (peak time is usually December to February), but some packages give you flights and accommodations for little more than the cost of an individually bought discount airfare. Some packages also include a rental car and airport transportation.

If you are looking for an adventure- or activity-focused group trip to Mexico you'll find a wide selection, especially from the USA. Below are reputable foreign-based outfits that offer tours to or on the peninsula. Because these tours often change, with new tours being added all the time, you're encouraged to contact them before making any decisions.

Backroads (☎ 510-527-1555, 800-462-2848, fax 510-527-1444, goactive@backroads.com, www .backroads.com), 801 Cedar St, Berkeley, CA 94710-1800, USA, offers a bike-walk-snorkel trip each winter in Yucatán that's generated strong reviews.

Caravan Tours Yucatán (☎ 312-321-9800, 800-227-2826), 401 N Michigan Ave, Chicago, IL 60611, USA, typically offers nine-day tours of the peninsula, with emphasis on Mérida, Cancún and the Maya Riviera. Visits to Uxmal, a flamingo colony, even the Sian Ka'an reserve are generally included.

Dive Tours (☎ 800-433-0885, fax 281-257-1783, info@divetours.org, www.divetours.org), 18219 Strack Drive, Spring, TX 77379, USA, is a wholesale tour operator offering snorkel and dive trips to Cozumel that feature a reputable local tour operator, Go Playa.

Far Horizons (☎ 505-343-9400, 800-552-4575, fax 505-343-8076, journey@farhorizon.com, www .farhorizon.com), PO Box 91900, Albuquerque, NM 87199-1900, USA, usually offers several

expert-led tours of Mayan ruins in Yucatán and Central America.

Journey Latin America (☎ 020-8747-8315, fax 020-8742-1312, tours@journeylatinamerica.co.uk, www.journeylatinamerica.co.uk), 12 & 13 Heathfield Terrace, Chiswick London W4 4JE, England, and (☎ 161-832-1441, fax 161-832-1551, man@journeylatinamerica.co.uk) 51-63 Deansgate, Manchester M3 2BH, England, offers regular three-country trips to Yucatán, Guatemala and Belize that emphasize the region's Mayan and colonial past.

Roads Less Traveled (☎ 800-488-8483, fax 303-413-0926, fun@roadslesstraveled.com, www .roadslesstraveled.com), 2840 Wilderness Place, No F, Boulder, CO 80301, USA, regularly offers a weeklong biking, hiking, sea kayaking, snorkeling and horseback riding 'adventure extravaganza' in the Yucatán.

Wild Women Adventures (☎ 800-992-1322, fax 707-829-1999, travel@wildwomenadv.com, www .wildwomenadv.com), 152 Bloomfield Rd, Sebastopol, CA 95472, USA, offers an annual upscale trip for gal pals to Mayan ruins in Belize and Quintana Roo. WWA's motto, 'Insanity with dignity,' hints at the personalities behind this organization, two women who see themselves as 'Thelma and Louise meet Lucy and Ethel.'

Getting Around

Travel within Yucatán is fairly agreeable with most tourists. The bus service linking the major cities on the peninsula is good, and buses are generally clean and comfortable. Moreover, there's ample public and private transportation to many of the region's top attractions, including the Mayan ruins at Chichén Itzá, Uxmal and Tulum, as well as Cancún and the popular islands of Cozumel and Isla Mujeres. Taxis are plentiful and fill the gaps in bus service quite well.

However, if you're short on time and/or anxious to visit areas not frequented by tourists, you'd be wise to rent a car. Renting a car on the peninsula is easy and can be inexpensive if you shop around and reserve a car well in advance of your visit. If you don't have your own wheels and are trying to visit off-the-beaten path places, expect to spend an inordinate amount of time waiting for local buses. Hitchhiking is not a smart option due to the crime level in Mexico today.

According to an August 1999 article in the respected newspaper *Reforma*, a full 30% of all airplanes owned by Mexican airlines are unsafe 'junk' prohibited from landing in airports in the USA, where safety standards are higher than they are in Mexico. The article, which cited a report by the research arm of the Mexican Airline Pilots Union, singled out the small Mexican airlines Taesa, Aviacsa and Aero Cozumel, saying that most of the airplanes owned by these three companies were more than two decades old, with quite a few going on 30 years or more. Moreover, on November 24, 1999, Mexican authorities grounded Taesa, two weeks after one of their DC-9s crashed, killing 18. At press time, the airline was still not in service.

Given the convenience and comfort of 1st-class Mexican buses (all of which are equipped with regulators that prevent the driver from operating the vehicle over 95km/h), there's little reason to board a domestic airline if your travel is limited to the peninsula. Add to that the reported danger of using these airlines, and it really doesn't make sense to board a Taesa, Aviacsa or Aero Cozumel plane unless you'll be flying a great distance (from Mérida to Mexico City, for example).

AIR
Domestic Air Services

All of the large cities on the peninsula have passenger airports. Aeroméxico and Mexicana are the country's two largest airlines. There are also numerous smaller ones, often flying useful routes between provincial Yucatecan cities that the big two don't bother with. These airlines include Aerocaribe, Aero Cozumel and Aviacsa.

These four smaller airlines are generally included in travel agents' computerized reservation systems in Mexico and abroad, but you may find it impossible to get information on smaller ones until you reach a city served by them. At the time of writing, none of the four had helpful Internet sites.

Aerocaribe and Aero Cozumel are feeder airlines for Mexicana and normally share its ticket offices. At several Yucatecan airports, in the absence of Aerocaribe and Aero Cozumel representatives, questions about Aerocaribe and Aero Cozumel services can usually be answered by Mexicana agents.

Fares

Information on specific flights is given in the city sections of this book. Fares can vary a lot depending on airline, whether you fly at a busy or quiet time of the day or week, and how far ahead you book and pay. For low domestic fares you may have to buy the ticket seven days ahead of departure and be prepared to fly late in the evening.

Aeroméxico and Mexicana work in tandem, with identical fare structures, but other airlines usually offer cheaper fares. Though some roundtrip excursion fares exist, they're usually twice the price of one-way tickets.

For a list of some airline toll-free numbers in Mexico, see the Getting There & Away chapter.

Taxes
There are two taxes on domestic flights: IVA, the consumer tax (15%), and TUA, an airport tax of about US$8.50. In Mexico, the taxes are normally included in quoted fares and paid when you buy the ticket. If you bought the ticket outside of Mexico, TUA will not have been included – you will have to pay it when you check in.

BUS
The bus system on the peninsula is generally user-friendly, especially in Cancún and Ciudad Cancún. Interstate buses are fairly frequent and go most everywhere, typically for US$3 or US$4 an hour (60km to 80km) on 1st-class buses. For trips of up to three or four hours on busy routes, you can usually just go to the bus terminal, buy a ticket and head out within a couple of hours. For longer trips, or trips on routes with infrequent service, it's best to book a ticket at least a day in advance.

Immediate cash refunds of 80% to 100% are often available if you cancel your ticket more than three hours before the listed departure time. To check whether refunds apply, ask '*¿Hay cancelaciones?*' (Are there any cancellations?).

Most 1st-class buses are air-conditioned, and most 1st-class bus companies have computerized ticket systems that allow you to select your seat from an on-screen diagram. Avoid sitting in the back of the bus, which is where the toilets are. For a long journey, it helps to work out which side the sun will be on and sit on the other side. If the bus is not air conditioned, it's a particularly good idea to get a window seat so that you have some control over the window – Mexicans often have different ideas from yours about what's too warm or too cool.

Conventional wisdom on luggage is of two minds. One says you should keep your luggage with you in the passenger compartment, where, under your watchful eye, it will be safer. The other says you should have it safely locked in the luggage compartment below the bus. In practice, many bus companies don't allow big baggage, such as backpacks, to be carried into the cabin. We suggest that you carry your valuables on your person in a money belt or pouch and store most of your stuff in the luggage compartment on 1st-class buses. Don't allow it to be hoisted onto the open luggage rack atop a 2nd-class bus unless you feel you can keep an eye on it.

Terminals & Schedules
Most cities and towns have a main bus station where all long-distance buses arrive and depart. It's variously called *Central Camionera*, *Central de Autobuses*, *Terminal de Autobuses*, *Central de Camiones* or simply *El Central*, and it's usually at least five blocks from the center of town. Frequent local buses link bus stations with town centers.

Note the crucial difference between the *Central* (bus station) and the *Centro* (city center); if you tell a taxi driver to take you to Central, don't be surprised if you end up at a bus station at the edge of town. If there is no single main terminal, different bus companies will have their own terminals scattered around town.

Most bus lines have schedules posted at their ticket desks in the bus station, but they aren't always comprehensive. If your destination isn't listed, ask: It may be en route to one that is. From big towns, many different bus companies may run on the same routes, so compare fares and classes of service.

Classes
Long-distance buses range in quality from comfortable, nonstop air-con vehicles to decaying, suspensionless ex-city buses grinding out their dying years on dirt roads to remote settlements. The differences between the deluxe and 1st-class bus lines are not clearcut. All of these bus lines offer a combination of features, such as extra legroom, reclining seats, drinks, snacks or videos. But broadly, buses fall into three categories:

De lujo – Deluxe services run mainly on the busy routes. They bear names such as 'Plus,' 'GL' or 'Ejecutivo.' The buses are swift, new, comfortable and air conditioned; they may cost just 10% or 20% more than 1st-class, or double for the most luxurious lines, such as ETN and UNO, which have few or no stops and offer reclining seats.

plenty of legroom, snacks, hot and cold drinks, videos and toilets on board.

Primera (1a) clase – 1st-class buses have a comfortable *numerado* (numbered) seat for each passenger and often show videos. Their standards of comfort are usually perfectly adequate. They usually have air-con and a toilet. They stop infrequently and serve all the sizable towns. As with deluxe buses, you must buy your ticket in the bus station before boarding.

Segunda (2a) clase – 2nd-class buses serve small towns and villages, and also offer cheaper, slower travel on some intercity routes. A few are almost as quick and comfortable as 1st-class buses and may even have videos; others are old, tatty, uncomfortable, liable to break down, and will stop anywhere for someone to get on or off. Except on some major runs, there's usually no set limit on capacity, which means that if you board midroute you might make the trip *parado* (standing) rather than *sentado* (seated).

Types of Service

It is also important to know the types of service offered. It's a good idea to become acquainted with the following terms if you will be using buses to get around the peninsula.

Sin escalas – nonstop

Directo – very few stops

Semi-directo – a few more stops than directo

Ordinario – stops wherever passengers want to get on or off; deluxe and 1st-class buses are never ordinario

Express – nonstop on short to medium trips, very few stops on long trips

Local – bus that starts its journey at the bus station you're in and usually leaves on time; preferable to *de paso*

De paso – bus that started its journey somewhere else but is stopping to let off and take on passengers. A de paso bus may be late and may or may not have seats available; you also may have to wait until it arrives before any tickets are sold; if the bus is full, you may have to wait for the next one

CAR & MOTORCYCLE

Driving anywhere in Mexico can be risky, but you can minimize those risks a great deal by driving only during daylight hours and by driving on paved roads only. That said, having your own wheels is often the only way to reach many destinations in a timely and convenient manner.

Unfortunately, all rental vehicles on the peninsula come equipped with wide stickers on their bumpers identifying them as rental vehicles and, therefore, likely driven by a tourist. As a result, corrupt traffic police tend to target them for alleged violations and 'fines' payable on the spot.

If you're driving a rental vehicle, be sure to obey the posted speed limits closely. You'll notice that few local drivers obey the speed laws, but that excuse won't help you at all if you're stopped by a police officer in Mexico and you really were speeding. All the officer wants is your money, not some sermon on justice.

At the time of writing, rental motorcycles were not available on the peninsula. Mopeds are available for rent in Cancún and other touristed spots, but due to the number of people who crashed theirs at night after drinking too much it is no longer possible to rent a moped in Yucatán past 8 pm. Mexico has a helmet law, which the police strictly enforce. If you rent a moped, be sure to request a helmet.

Fuel & Service

All *gasolina* (gasoline) and diesel fuel in Mexico is sold by the government's monopoly, Pemex (Petróleos Mexicanos), for cash (no credit cards). Most towns, even small ones, have a Pemex station, and the stations are pretty common on most major roads. Nevertheless, in remote areas it's better to fill up when you can.

Unleaded gas is available at just about every Pemex station. It's called Magna Sin and is sold from green pumps. It's 92 octane by Mexican standards but 87 octane by US standards (equivalent to US regular unleaded). Mexico has plans to eliminate leaded fuel, but at the time of writing Nova leaded fuel was still available, from blue pumps. It's 82 octane by Mexican standards, 80 by US standards. Diesel fuel, in red or purple pumps, is also widely available.

At 1999 rates, Magna Sin and Nova both cost a little under US$0.40 a liter (US$1.50 a

DRIVING DISTANCES

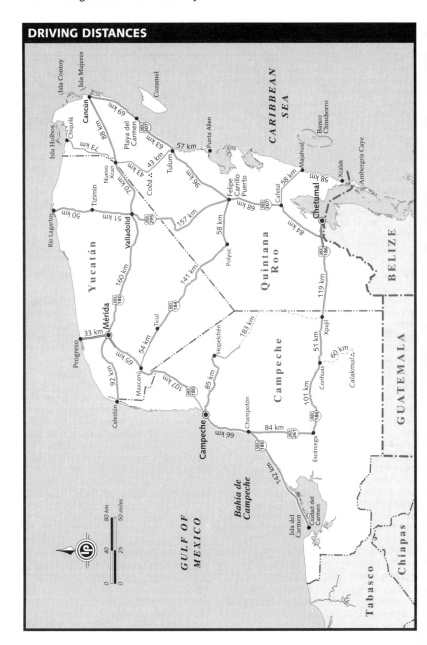

US gallon), with Nova marginally cheaper; those prices were a bit higher than the typical US prices. Mexican fuel prices are low compared with European, Asian or Australian prices.

All stations have pump attendants (who expect tips), but they are not always trustworthy. Check that the pump registers zero pesos to start with, and be quick to check afterward that you have been given the amount you requested – the attendants often reset the pump immediately and start to serve another customer. Don't have the attendants do your gas, oil and water all at once, or you may not get what you paid for.

Road Conditions

Highways in Yucatán are generally up to European and North American standards, although secondary highways (those serving remote communities) occasionally have many potholes. Driving at night is especially dangerous – unlit vehicles, rocks and livestock on the roads are common – and hijacks and robberies do occur. Also, expect fairly frequent drug and weapon searches by the army and police, especially at night.

In towns and cities you must be especially wary of *alto* (stop) signs, *topes* (speed bumps) and potholes. They are often not where you'd expect, and missing one can cost you in traffic fines or car damage. Topes, especially, are the worst: The signs are literally right at the tope, with no advance warning at all. Before you know it, your VW Beetle is traveling over the speed bump way too fast – not a comfortable feeling, that's for sure.

One-way streets are the rule in towns: Usually alternating streets run in opposite directions, so if you cross one that's westbound only, the next one will probably go east.

Toll Roads There are several toll roads on the peninsula, and they are very convenient because: They are generally straight, plowing through land features rather than circumventing them; they are never broken by speed bumps, which are a total nuisance if you're trying to make good time; and the speed limit placed on toll roads is typically

20km/h to 30km/h higher than the speed limits set on free roads.

That's the good. The bad: Toll roads are expensive. Use of the toll road that runs from Cancún nearly to Mérida costs US$14 each direction. Still, if you're in a hurry or are concerned about safety, the toll roads are vastly superior to free roads. Because the toll roads always consist of at least two lanes in each direction, motorists using them also needn't be concerned with slow-moving traffic.

Motorcycle Hazards Certain aspects of Mexican roads make them more hazardous for bikers than for drivers. They include:

- poor signage of road or lane closures
- lots of dogs on the roads
- lack of hotels/motels on some stretches of highway
- debris and deep potholes
- vehicles without taillights
- lack of highway lighting

In addition, it rains a lot on the peninsula, and riding in the rain isn't fun – it's practically suicidal. Also – and bikers overlook this fact all the time – you've got no protection from the burning tropical sun when you're on the back of a motorcycle.

Maps

Town and country roads are often poorly or idiosyncratically signposted. It pays to get the best road maps you can if you'll be driving. Two high-quality maps are Guia Roji's national road atlas called *Carreteras de México*, and ITMB Publishing's *Yucatán Peninsula*, an easy-to-read and detailed map. See the Planning section in the Facts for the Visitor chapter for a detailed discussion on these maps and more.

Parking

It's inadvisable to park on the street overnight, and most cheap city hotels don't provide parking. Sometimes you can leave a car out front and the night porter will keep an eye on it. Usually you have to use a commercial *estacionamiento* (parking lot), which

might cost US$2.50 overnight and US$0.50 per hour during the day. Hotels with parking tend to be the more expensive ones. Be advised: The cost of replacing a set of hubcaps (thieves in Valladolid and Mérida seem to target hubcaps at night) typically runs US$300. It pays to pay for parking.

Breakdown Assistance

The Mexican tourism ministry, SECTUR, maintains a network of *Ángeles Verdes* (Green Angels) – bilingual mechanics in green trucks who patrol each major stretch of highway in Mexico at least twice daily during daylight hours searching for stranded motorists. They make minor repairs, replace small parts, provide fuel and oil, and arrange towing and other assistance by radio if necessary. Service is free; parts, gasoline and oil are provided at cost.

Most mechanical problems can be fixed efficiently and inexpensively by mechanics in towns and cities as long as the parts are available. Volkswagen, Ford, Nissan/Datsun, Chrysler and General Motors parts are the easiest to obtain; others may have to be ordered from the USA. For parts suppliers, consult the telephone directory's yellow pages under *Refacciones y Acesorios para Automóviles y Camiones*. For authorized dealer service, look under *Automóviles – Agencias*.

Accidents

Under Mexico's legal system, people involved in an incident are assumed to be guilty until proven innocent. They can be incarcerated until the matter is resolved, perhaps weeks or months later. For minor accidents, drivers will likely be released if they have insurance to cover any property damage they may have caused. If it's a serious accident, involving injury or death, the drivers may be held until the authorities determine who is responsible (ie, the drivers can expect to spend weeks or months in prison).

The guilty party will not be released until he/she guarantees restitution to the victims and payment of any fines. Your embassy can help only by recommending a lawyer and contacting friends or family at home. Adequate insurance coverage is the only real protection, and defensive driving (including driving only during daylight hours and obeying all traffic laws) is the best way to minimize your risks of being in an accident. Whatever you do, *never* get behind the wheel of a vehicle in Mexico if you've been drinking.

Rental

Car rental in Mexico generally is expensive by North American or European standards, but the cost of renting a vehicle can be reasonable if you're willing to call around for the best rates and reserve a vehicle well in advance of your visit. This means contacting Avis, Budget, Hertz or one of the many other international car-rental services that have counters at the Cancún airport at least a month before you travel and request an economy car. Indeed, a rental vehicle is the best way to go if you want to visit several places in a short period of time and have two or three people to share the cost. It can also be useful for getting off the beaten track, where public transport is slow or scarce.

It's very easy to rent a vehicle in Yucatán if you meet certain requirements. In fact, there are rental agencies at the Cancún airport as well as in Ciudad Cancún, downtown Mérida, Playa del Carmen, Cozumel – anywhere you'd likely want to rent one. Renters must have a valid driver's license from their home country and a passport, and are usually required to be at least 25 years old. Sometimes age 21 is acceptable, but you may have to pay more. A major credit card or a huge cash deposit is needed.

In addition to the basic daily or weekly rental rate, you must pay for insurance, tax and fuel. You can expect to pay an additional US$5 to US$15 a day for insurance. However, many agencies will pass on the insurance if you place the cost of the rental on an American Express card; call AmEx in your home country to see if your AmEx card allows you to do this (cards issued in some countries do not provide this cost-saving feature). Also, ask about the insurance coverage; it's generally very limited.

Most agencies offer a choice between a per-kilometer deal or unlimited kilometers.

Reduced Rental Rates

It really pays to call around and to call ahead when lining up a rental vehicle for your Yucatán stay. Here are some things to keep in mind to obtain low rental rates:

Book a rental vehicle as soon as you know your vacation dates. Why? Because rental agencies don't make any money if their vehicles aren't being used, so they are usually willing to offer very attractive rates if you reserve a vehicle at a time when they are nervous about their ability to rent their entire inventory. Also, the sooner you call, the greater the selection of vehicles available to you.

Contact numerous rental agencies. Representatives of big-name agencies such as Avis, Budget and Hertz can glance at a computer screen while you're on the phone with them and tell you exactly what's available and what it would cost, and they will reserve the vehicle for you as soon as you provide a credit card number. You can also contact these agencies and smaller ones via the Internet (do a keyword search for an agency's name or try 'Cancún and car rental').

Call the same rental agency several times for a quote. This writer called Avis' toll-free number in the USA three times within an hour asking about the rental cost of a VW Beetle from Avis' Cancún airport office. The quote differed each time. Naturally, the writer opted for the lowest quote – and saved US$5 a day on his rental rate. By putting the rental on his American Express card, he saved another US$7 a day by not having to pay for insurance.

The latter is usually preferable if you intend to do some hard driving. Local firms are often cheaper than the international ones. During the low tourist season, you can usually find a Volkswagen Beetle – often the cheapest car available – for US$25 to US$35 a day with unlimited kilometers and insurance and tax included; add US$15 to US$20 if renting the vehicle during high tourist season, and even then you must book ahead to reserve one. The weekly rate is often equivalent to six single days. The charge for drop-off in another city is usually about US$0.30 per kilometer.

You can book vehicles (cars, trucks and SUVs) in Mexico through the foreign offices of the big-name international agencies. Doing this generally gets you lower rates. Here are toll-free telephone numbers for some of the international firms that have offices in Yucatán:

company	in the USA	in Mexico
Avis	☎ 800-331-2112	☎ 01-800-70777
Budget	☎ 800-527-0700	☎ 01-800-70017
Dollar	☎ 800-800-4000	☎ 01-800-90010
Hertz	☎ 800-654-3131	☎ 01-800-70016
National	☎ 800-328-4567	☎ 01-800-00395
Thrifty	☎ 800-367-2277	☎ 01-800-01859

BICYCLE

Only hard-core bicyclists ought to consider getting around the peninsula on bike. The tropical sun is brutal; people who are unaccustomed to it tend to underestimate its strength. Also, Mexican highways do not have bike lanes or shoulders and nine times out of 10 the highway is only two lanes wide, which means that if you and two vehicles are abreast of one another, you will likely be hit or at least driven off the road.

Of course, you could easily be hit even without the presence of a second motor vehicle. Mexican motorists tend to not give wide clearance to bicyclists. In the country that invented machismo, there seems to be a feeling among drivers that, 'I'm in a car. You're on a bicycle. *You* move over for *me*.' That's not only an unhealthy mind-set, but a potentially lethal one for bicyclists.

Rental

You can rent bicycles in Cancún and Valladolid, and not simply the cheap ones. There

are plenty of 10-, 12- and 15-speed bikes available for rent in Cancún, as well as a few equipped with motors. It also may be possible to rent bikes on Isla Mujeres and Cozumel.

Purchase

Of course it's possible to purchase a bicycle in Yucatán. Indeed, if you plan on staying on the peninsula for months and want to get around by bike or at least exercise on one, purchasing isn't a bad option, as there are many inexpensive models available in the big cities. Just check the Paginas Amarillas (yellow pages) phone directories for 'Bicicletas' for the location of the nearest bike store. Often it's possible to buy worn bikes at rental shops. It never hurts to inquire, but don't expect a particularly reliable vehicle if its owner is happy to part with it.

HITCHHIKING

Hitchhiking is dangerous anywhere in Mexico these days. The notoriously low apprehension and conviction rates of criminals in Mexico basically gives criminals confidence that they can pretty much do to a hitchhiker what they please and get away with it. Combine this confidence with the belief that most tourists are carrying a lot of money on them and you've got a potentially bad situation.

A woman alone certainly should not hitchhike in Mexico, and two women without at least one male companion are not advised to either. If you decide to ignore this advice and hitchhike anyway, be advised that motorists who provide rides expect a tip in return. In Mexico, it's customary for the hitchhiker to offer to pay this tip, rather than wait for the driver to ask for one. As a general rule, expect to tip US$1 per person for every 30 minutes of the ride but never less than US$2 and never more than US$10 for a ride.

LOCAL TRANSPORT
Bus

Generally known as *camiones*, local buses are the cheapest way of getting around cities and to nearby villages. They run everywhere, frequently, and are dirt cheap (fares in cities

are rarely more than US$0.40); in Cancún and Ciudad Cancún, they cost US$0.50 a ride, a bargain at that.

Older buses are often noisy, dirty and crowded, but in some cities there are fleets of small, modern microbuses, which are more pleasant. In cities, buses halt only at specific *paradas* (bus stops), which may or may not be marked. Look for people standing at road's edge for an indication of a bus stop.

Colectivo & Combi

Colectivos are minibuses or big cars that function as something between a taxi and a bus. A *combi* is a VW minibus. Colectivos and combis are cheaper than taxis, quicker and less crowded than buses. They run along set routes, which are usually displayed on the windshield, and will pick you up or drop you off on any corner along that route.

If you're not at the start of a colectivo's route, go to the curb and wave your hand when you see one. The driver may indicate how many places are free by holding up the appropriate number of fingers. Tell the driver where you want to go; you normally pay at the end of the trip, and the fare usually depends on how far you go.

Taxi

Taxis are common in towns and cities. They're often surprisingly economical, and they're useful if you have a lot of baggage, need to get from point A to point B quickly, or are worried about theft on public transport. If a taxi has a meter, ask the driver, '¿*Funciona el taxímetro?*' (Is the meter working?). If it's not, or if the taxi doesn't have a meter, establish the price of the ride *before* getting in.

The Cancún airport has taxi *taquillas* (kiosks) where you buy a fixed-price ticket to your destination, then hand it to the driver instead of paying cash. This can save haggling and major rip-offs, but fares are usually higher than you could get outside on the street. If you're reaching Yucatán by way of the Cancún airport, be sure to take one of the shuttles to your hotel or into Ciudad Cancún; the airport shuttles are much cheaper than taxis.

Finding Your Way in Cities

Mexican street naming and numbering can be confusing. When asking directions, it's better to ask for a specific place, such as the Hotel Central or the Museo Regional, than for the street it's on. To achieve a degree of certainty, ask three people.

ORGANIZED TOURS

If you're looking for an activity-focused group trip, you might want to call upon the companies mentioned in the Organized Tours section in the Getting There & Away chapter before you leave for Yucatán.

Once you've arrived, you'll discover a plethora of free publications packed with ads promoting scores of organized tours. Most of those tours are day trips that leave from Cancún, visit Chichén Itzá, Tulum, Mérida, Xelha, Xcaret or the flamingo sanctuary at Río Lagartos, and return to Cancún before sunset.

If you reach Yucatán via the Cancún airport, you'll be handed lots of free literature as you pass through the airport, much of it containing information on the organized activities available to you. Many local operators are discussed in depth in the Quintana Roo chapter.

Quintana Roo

Quintana Roo is Mexico's most enticing state. It is home to all of the country's Caribbean beaches, to numerous impressive Mayan ruins and to a nightlife that's as steamy as any in Latin America. But that's not all. Quintana Roo also hosts some of the finest scuba diving and snorkeling in the world. Indeed, for water visibility and biodiversity, there are few dive and snorkel spots in the same league as Quintana Roo's.

What's more, Quintana Roo's fantastic dive opportunities are not limited to the sea. The peninsula is riddled with underground rivers and subterranean caves which make for incredible journeys for qualified divers. These sites are as intriguing as their names, among them Hidden World, Palace of Ornaments and Temple of Doom. Best of all is Nohoch Nah Chich (Mayan for 'Giant Birdhouse'), the world's longest underwater cave system; it consists of colossal connecting hallways filled with speleological wonders and water as clear as thin air.

Amazingly, the state was little more than a forgotten backwater for most of the 20th century, which is partially due to the fact that Quintana Roo's only Spanish ruins – at the edge of Laguna Bacalar, 20km or so north of the Mexico-Belize border – aren't nearly as impressive as those in Mérida,

Campeche and elsewhere. And even before the arrival of the Spanish, Cobá, Tulum and countless smaller Mayan cities had seen their heyday and been abandoned.

So insignificant was Quintana Roo in the minds of Mexican authorities that the region didn't even have an official name prior to the start of the 20th century. The jungly, sparsely inhabited region simply didn't warrant one, such was the sentiment in Mexico City anyway. But in 1902 it was decided that the region should be given territory status, and like many other Mexican territories it was named after an army general – in this case Andrés Quintana Roo, despite the fact that he never served in the territory.

Remarkably, Quintana Roo didn't become a state until 1974. And it likely wouldn't have received statehood even then except that the government and influential developers had ambitious plans for Cancún, and it was agreed that Cancún would be difficult to promote as a world-class getaway if it was located in a region the government apparently viewed as unworthy of statehood.

Cancún

☎ 9 • pop 57,221

According to local officials, during the late 1960s a handful of analysts in Mexico's tourism department rated all of the country's natural attractions, placed that data into a computer and, after doing some intense number crunching, the fabulous machine spit out Cancún. While this popular tale sounds good, it's not very likely since computers weren't nearly as prevalent back then as they are today, and Mexican tourism authorities weren't nearly as resourceful back then, either.

But, indeed, a decision *was* made to develop Isla Cancún (Cancun Island), which three decades ago was merely a sliver of sand nearly 18km long, visited only by local fishermen and a few gringo adventurers.

Highlights

- Cancún, Mexico's premier tourist destination and chief party scene
- Cozumel, often ranked No 1 by scuba divers the world over
- Playa del Carmen, a burgeoning beach resort with many European touches
- Tulum, stunning Mayan ruins and scores of cheap waterfront cabañas
- Banco Chinchorro off the Costa Maya, graveyard of storm-tossed ships and haven for wreck divers

Shaped like a wobbly Lucky 7, the island was separated from the coast by two narrow channels, which were bridged early in the resort's development (in or about 1970, no one seems certain anymore).

Next, a town sprung up where Ciudad Cancún (Cancun City) now stands, occupied by Isla Cancún's construction workers and the workers' families. Despite some reports, Ciudad Cancún never was a sleepy fishing village. It feels 'authentic' Mexican, much more so than Isla Cancún, because unlike the island it didn't receive careful planning. Indeed, most of the city's streets, when viewed on a map, reflect the scant attention that was given to their location – the road layout resembles spaghetti.

Out on the island, which is generally referred to as Cancún or Zona Hotelera, a well-paved street bordered by wide sidewalks was run down the center of the island. Many hectares of mangrove and scrub brush were ripped out and scores of gardens planted. Then, 'a very towered land,' as one 16th-century Spanish historian wrote when describing the Mayan-temple-strewn coast of southeast Mexico, acquired even more towers as multistory resorts went up.

When Cancún opened in 1974 – the same year Quintana Roo became a state – the carefully developed island was promoted as a tropical paradise. In short time, Mexico's newest sun-and-fun destination attracted snowbirds from Canada and wealthy beach bums from the USA, Europe and elsewhere. Today, more than 2 million visitors descend on Cancún each year, with the number of visitors increasing 3% annually.

Can 2 million people be wrong about Cancún? Sure. More than that many people pick the wrong team to win the World Cup or the Super Bowl. But few of those 2 million people seem to leave Cancún dissatisfied, and many of the globetrotters you'll meet on the sandy Lucky 7 will be repeat visitors, and that says a lot.

ORIENTATION

Cancún is often viewed as one city, with a downtown area and a hotel zone, but that's not an accurate description. It's more correct to say that there are two Cancúns – the island and the city – which share a name and a history. On the mainland lies Ciudad Cancún, which is home to the thousands of people who make their living in the *other* Cancún – Isla Cancún, which is also commonly called the Zona Hotelera (Hotel Zone) or, simply, Cancún. In this book, therefore, the city is always referred to as Ciudad Cancún (and is covered separately in the next section), while the island is variously referred to by its three common names – Isla Cancún, Zona Hotelera or just plain Cancún.

In the minds of most people, however, the only Cancún is the one of the sea. This is the Cancún of world fame, and it is this Cancún that for all practical purposes put Quintana Roo on the global map.

Familiarizing yourself with Isla Cancún is easy. It contains fewer than 10 roads in all, only one of which – Blvd Kukulcán – is more than a few kilometers long. The four-lane boulevard starts in Ciudad Cancún and goes eastward for 4.2km before crossing a bridge and entering Isla Cancún. From the bridge, the boulevard continues east on the island for 4.8km – past condominium developments, a youth hostel, several moderately priced hotels and some expensive larger ones, and several shopping complexes – to Punta Cancún (Cancún Point) and the Centro de Convenciones (Convention Center).

From Punta Cancún, the boulevard turns south for 13km, flanked on both sides for much of the way by mammoth hotels, shopping centers, dance clubs and many restaurants and bars, to Punta Nizuc (Nizuc Point), where it turns eastward and rejoins the mainland. From there, the boulevard cuts through light tropical forest for several more kilometers to its southern terminus at Cancun's international airport.

To simplify matters, few of the buildings on Isla Cancún have numbered addresses. Instead, because the vast majority of the structures are located along Blvd Kukulcán, their location is described in relation to their distance from the boulevard's northern terminus. That terminus, on the eastern edge of Ciudad Cancún, is identified with a roadside

QUINTANA ROO

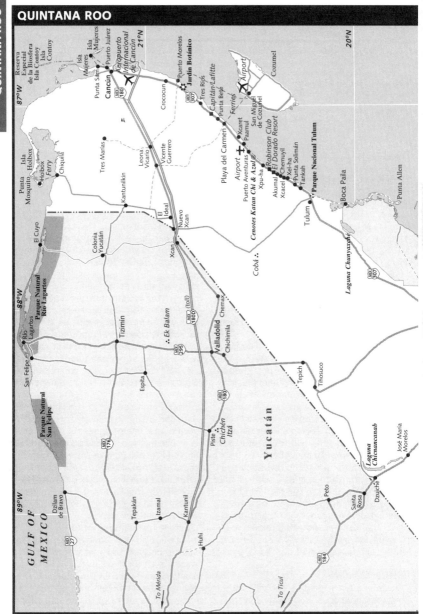

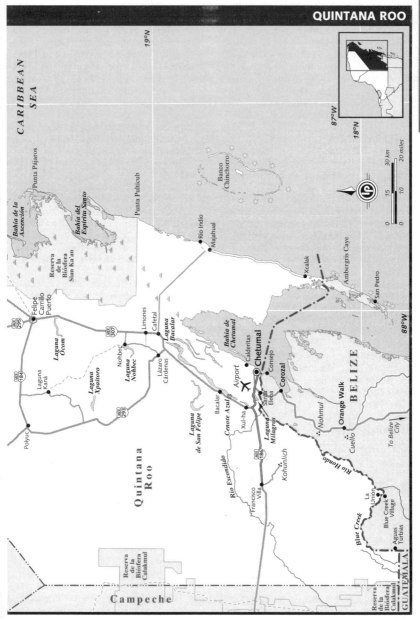

'Km 0' marker. After traveling east on Blvd Kukulcán for 1km, a Km 1 marker appears at roadside. After another kilometer a 'Km 2' marker appears, and so forth all the way to the airport, some 30 or so markers away. The Km 22 marker is located near the bridge linking the southern tip of the island and the mainland. For example, the address for Club Mediterranée, which is 0.5km from the bridge, is given as Blvd Kukulcán Km 21.

INFORMATION
Tourist Offices
Remarkably, there are no tourist offices on Isla Cancún. Instead, there's a tourist counter at the Cancún airport that's generally staffed with friendly, helpful and bilingual receptionists. It is located near Immigration and quite apparent to inbound travelers. There is a government-sponsored tourist office in Ciudad Cancún as well; see the Ciudad Cancún section for details.

On the island you'll come across 'Information' signs in front of many businesses, and tourists are certainly welcome to come inside and pose questions. Of course, if you enter one of these establishments, expect a sales pitch for time-share units, leather goods, etc, to accompany the response to your questions.

Also, please be sensitive in your questioning. With most of the area's locals making under US$10 a day, asking them which steak house is the island's best or which of the dive operators is most safety conscious is somewhat callous. It's a bit like asking a poverty stricken taxi driver for a resort recommendation. You'll get an answer, but don't expect anything more than a guess.

Money
There are no banks on Isla Cancún, but there are plenty of *casas de cambio* (exchange houses) at which to swap currency. Also, virtually all of the resorts on the island will change money, although they generally offer poor exchange rates and occasionally won't change money for nonguests.

There's a casa de cambio inside every one of Cancún's malls, and there are several facing Blvd Kukulcán at the ever-popular Punta Cancún. These booths are usually open from sunrise until well after midnight every day. The exchange rates on the island are generally less favorable than those found in Ciudad Cancún, but usually not so different as to warrant a special trip inland, unless you'll be changing more than US$100 or so.

For your convenience, there are ATMs at Punta Cancún and inside each of the malls. They generally give very competitive exchange rates, but remember: There's usually a transaction fee accompanying every cash withdrawal.

Post
There is no post office in the Zona Hotelera. However, all but the few moderately priced hotels sell stamps at their reception desks, provide complimentary stationery and will accept mail for sending. For parcels, you must go to the post office in Ciudad Cancún; see the Ciudad Cancún section for details.

Be forewarned: A package sent from a Mexican post office can take months to reach its destination. If you must send a parcel from Mexico and its contents are valuable, use a private service such as UPS or Federal Express; their locations can be found in the Cancún phone directory.

Telephone
There are Telmex Ladatel phones on practically every corner in Cancún, and numerous other pay phones are springing up all the time. The Telmex phones use phone cards that can be purchased in any store that has a blue-and-yellow Ladatel sign out front; just look for the word 'Ladatel' and inquire inside. The others permit users to insert credit cards or place collect calls. Before you call, be sure to check the rates with the operator as they can be outrageously high to some countries – in excess of US$10 a minute with a three-minute minimum.

Email & Internet Access
At the speed with which Internet services change, it's unlikely anything written here will be very accurate by the time you read this. That said, in late 1999 there were no Internet cafés on Isla Cancún, although two

Internet service booths had recently opened. One was located at the entryway of The Forum mall at Punta Cancún, and the other was located on the second floor of Plaza Kukulcán mall. Both were in operation only about 50% of the time, due to bad telephone connections. For reliable and comfortable Internet service at the end of the 20th century, a tourist visitor had to leave the island and venture to one of the Internet cafés in Ciudad Cancún (for details, see that section later in this chapter).

Travel Agencies

Most of the big hotels have travel agencies, any one of which can book airline reservations. Three of the most reputable independent travel agencies on the island are: Royal Holiday Travel (☎ 885-1467), Plaza Flamingo mall, Blvd Kukulcán Km 11; Mayaland Tours (☎ 883-0679), Party Center, Blvd Kukulcán Km 9; and Thomas Moore Travel Agency (☎ 883-4938), Playa Langosta, Blvd Kukulcán Km 5.

Bookstores

The one main bookstore on Isla Cancún is Librería Dali (☎ 885-1404), 2nd floor, Plaza Kukulcán mall, Blvd Kukulcán Km 13. Here, you will find thousands of books in Spanish and/or English, with a very impressive selection of books about the Yucatán. Likewise, there also is an extensive offering of maps and magazines, and newspapers from Mexico and the US. It's a very nice find, with a very helpful sales staff.

Inside the Plaza Flamingo mall there is a small general store selling an assortment of snack foods, T-shirts and souvenirs, but it also has a couple of racks containing locally published guidebooks to Cancún and at least one guidebook on Mexican dive sites. Magazines and local newspapers are also on sale at this store, the name of which is not displayed. However, the store is located just inside the western entrance of the popular mall.

Laundry

All of the resorts on the island offer laundry service, but if you're not staying at one and you want to save some money there are two laundries on Isla Cancún. Happy Wash Laundry, on Paseo Pok-ta-Pok near the Hotel Suites Laguna Verde, is open 9 am to 9 pm daily. No Name Laundry, located on Blvd Kukulcán Km 7.5, is open 8 am to 9 pm Monday to Friday, 9 am to 5 pm Saturday, 8 am to 6 pm Sunday. Laundry costs US$1 per kilogram for bulk service. Same-day service is usually available when the clothes are dropped off in the morning.

Medical Services

Most of the area's medical facilities are located in Ciudad Cancún; see that section later in this chapter for details. However, Isla Cancún does have some medical facility, and it is the American Medical Care Center (☎ 883-1001, 883-0113 after-hours), beside Plaza Quetzal, Blvd Kukulcán Km 8. As its name suggests, it is American owned and operated, and it is the first place you should turn if you have a serious malady while in the Cancún area.

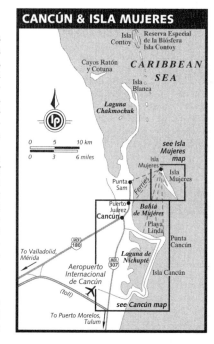

CANCÚN & ISLA MUJERES

QUINTANA ROO

CANCÚN

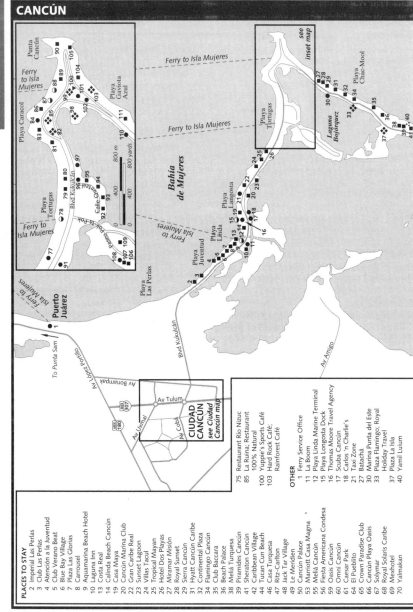

PLACES TO STAY
2 Imperial Las Perlas
3 Club Las Perlas
4 Atención a la Juventud
5 Club Verano Beat
6 Blue Bay Village
7 Plaza Las Glorias
8 Carrousel
9 Aquamarina Beach Hotel
10 Laguna Inn
13 Costa Real
14 Calinda Beach Cancún
19 Casa Maya
20 Cancún Marina Club
22 Gran Caribe Real
23 Sunset Lagoon
24 Villas Tacul
25 Tropical Mayan
26 Hotel Dos Playas
27 Miramar Misión
28 Royal Sunset
29 Sierra Cancún
31 Hyatt Cancún Caribe
32 Continental Plaza
34 Flamingo Cancún
35 Club Baccara
36 Beach Palace
38 Meliá Turquesa
39 Piramides Cancún
41 Sheraton Cancún
42 Caribbean Village
44 Tucan Cun Beach
46 Casa Turquesa
47 Ritz-Carlton
48 Jack Tar Village
49 Le Meridien
50 Cancún Palace
53 Marriott Casa Magna
55 Meliá Cancún
56 Fiesta Americana Condesa
59 Oasis Cancún
60 Omni Cancún
61 Caesar Park
64 El Pueblito
65 Crown Paradise Club
66 Cancún Playa Oasis
67 Solymar
68 Royal Solaris Caribe
69 Mexhotel
70 Yalmakan

75 Restaurant Río Nizuc
85 La Ruina; Restaurant
100 100% Natural
103 Yuppie's Sports Café
     Hard Rock Café;
     Rainforest Café

OTHER
1 Ferry Service Office
11 La Boom
12 Playa Linda Marine Terminal
15 Playa Longosta Dock
16 Thomas Moore Travel Agency
17 Scuba Cancún
18 Carlos 'n Charlie's
21 Taxi Zone
27 Batachá
30 Marina Punta del Este
33 Plaza Flamingo; Royal
     Holiday Travel
37 Plaza La Isla
40 Yamil Luium

CANCÚN

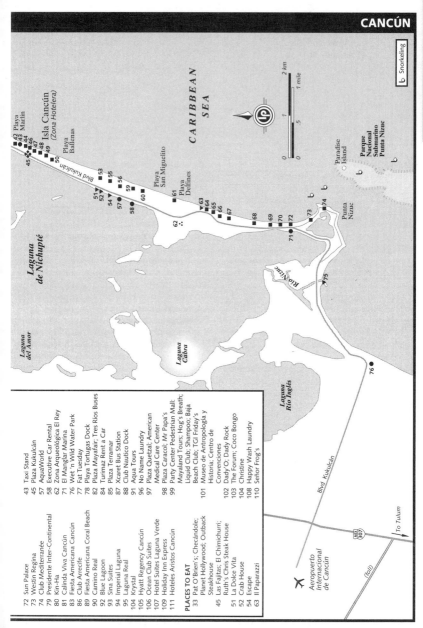

b Snorkeling

CARIBBEAN SEA

Laguna de Nichupté
Laguna del Amor
Laguna Cabra
Laguna Río Inglés

Playa Marlín
Playa Cancún
(Zona Hotelera)
Playa Ballenas
Isla Cancún
Playa San Miguelito
Playa Delfines

Blvd Kukulcán

Paradise Island
Parque Nacional Submarino Punta Nizuc
Punta Nizuc

Río Nizuc

Blvd Kukulcán

MEX 307
To Tulum
(toll)
Aeropuerto Internacional de Cancún

72   Sun Palace
73   Westin Regina
74   Club Mediterranée
79   Presidente Inter-Continental
80   Kin-Ha
81   Calinda Viva Cancún
83   Fiesta Americana Cancún
86   Club Arrecife
89   Fiesta Americana Coral Beach
90   Camino Real
92   Blue Lagoon
93   Sina Suites
94   Imperial Laguna
95   Laguna Real
104 Krystal
105 Hyatt Regency Cancún
106 Ocean Club Suites
107 Hotel Suites Laguna Verde
109 Holiday Inn Express
111 Hoteles Aristos Cancún

PLACES TO EAT
33   Pat O'Brien's; Checándole;
     Planet Hollywood; Outback
     Steakhouse
45   Las Fajitas; El Chimichurri;
     Ruth's Chris Steak House
51   La Dolce Vita
52   Crab House
54   Escape
63   Il Paparazzi

43   Taxi Stand
45   Plaza Kukulcán
57   AquaWorld
58   Executive Car Rental
62   Zona Arqueológica El Rey
71   El Manglar Marina
76   Wet 'n Wild Water Park
77   Fat Tuesday
78   Playa Tortugas Dock
82   Plaza Mayafair; Tres Ríos Buses
84   Turimax Rent a Car
85   Plaza Terramar
87   Xcaret Bus Station
88   Club Nautico Dock
91   Aqua Tours
96   No Name Laundry
97   Plaza Quetzal; American
     Medical Care Center
98   Plaza Caracol; Mr Papa's
99   Party Center Pedestrian Mall;
     Mayaland Tours; Hog's Breath;
     Liquid Club; Shampoo; Baja
     Beach Club; TGI Friday's
101 Museo de Antropología y
     Historia; Centro de
     Convenciones
102 Dady'O; Dady Rock
103 The Forum; Coco Bongo
104 Christine
108 Happy Wash Laundry
110 Señor Frog's

Hotels on the island are accustomed to tourists requesting medical aid for upset stomachs, sunburns and the like. If you're staying at a Cancún resort and would like a physician to visit you, contact the concierge and request a house call. Several bilingual doctors perform this service and the concierges know who they are and will contact one for you. However, if you are able, make your way to the American Medical Care Center, which has a sterling reputation.

Emergency

The two most helpful emergency numbers on the island are the Hotel Zone Police (☎ 885-0569) and the Tourist Assistance Office (☎ 884-8073). However, if you have hurt yourself at a resort or believe you are having a heart attack or otherwise need emergency response, you should notify the front desk immediately and have them place the proper calls. That's because, among other things, phone numbers change often in Mexico and the person answering the emergency call might have trouble with English; for a host of reasons, it's prudent to convey your urgent situation to hotel staff and get them working on your behalf. As stated in the Medical Services section, above, your best option is to go to the American Medical Care Center, if you can.

Dangers & Annoyances

Cancún has a reputation as being a safe place. Neither the news media nor area residents nor private intelligence services report a violent-crime problem on the island, but as is the case everywhere in the world these days visitors are advised to not leave valuables unattended in their hotel rooms or beside their towels at the beach. And when at the beach, if you've been drinking, don't go in the water. Cancún's currents are usually mild, but mild currents have drowned many a drunken fool.

A danger that's often overlooked but very real on Isla Cancún is the vehicular traffic on Blvd Kukulcán, particularly as it passes between the malls, bars and dance clubs at Punta Cancún. At least once a week a drunken visitor stumbles into a moving vehicle.

To keep the number of these accidents down, there are traffic cops seemingly every 20m on the island. These police do a superlative job of enforcing traffic laws and curbing the number of tragedies on Blvd Kukulcán.

By far the greatest danger in Cancún is overexposure to the sun. Every single day of the year, except during hurricanes, at least one poor soul allows him- or herself to receive second-degree burns from Mr Sun. Don't join that painful crowd. Unless you're accustomed to the blistering tropical sun, play it safe and apply sunscreen *liberally*. If you don't, you'll wish you did.

MUSEO DE ANTROPOLOGÍA Y HISTORIA

The Archaeological Museum of Cancún (which uses a different Spanish name, as you see) is located on the south side of the Centro de Convenciones in the Zona Hotelera. It contains a limited collection of Mayan artifacts, among them a ceramic incense burner and many vases, pots and plates.

Although most of the items are from the Late Postclassic period (1200-1524 AD) – including jewelry, masks and intentionally deformed skulls – there is a Classic-period hieroglyphic staircase inscribed with dates from the 6th century, as well as the stucco head that gave the local archaeological zone its name of El Rey (the King; despite the name, there is no evidence that a king ever ruled the island).

While the museum contains some interesting exhibits, be advised that only a few are accompanied by informative signs, and most of the signs are in Spanish only. However, if you ask for an English information sheet at the ticket counter, you will be given a three-page handout that describes in fairly good detail the museum's 47 showcases. Museum hours are 9 am to 8 pm daily. Admission costs US$2, free on Sunday and holidays.

MAYAN RUINS

There are two sets of Mayan ruins on Isla Cancún, and though neither is particularly impressive, both are worth a look if time permits. The most extensive of the two are

the ruins in the **Zona Arqueológica El Rey**, on the west side of Blvd Kukulcán between Km 17 and Km 18. The ruins, which consist of a small temple and several ceremonial platforms, are open 8 am to 5 pm daily; admission costs US$2. Depending on whoever's on duty, visitors are occasionally 'required' to be accompanied by a guide, no doubt a friend or relative of the ticket seller.

The much smaller of the two sites is **Yamil Lu'um**, and it's located atop a beachside knoll on the parklike grounds separating the Sheraton Cancún and Piramides Cancún towers. The site consists primarily of a very weathered temple, the knowledge of the god to whom it was built long since lost to time. Also lost to time is the temple's roof and whatever stone carvings that might once have been found on the knoll. Only the outward-sloping remains of the temple's walls still stand. Still, the ruin makes for a pleasant venture, as much for its lovely setting as anything else. There is no charge to see Yamil Lu'um, but to reach the site visitors must pass through either of the hotels flanking it or approach it from the beach; there is no direct access from the boulevard.

WET 'N WILD WATER PARK

Located at Blvd Kukulcán Km 25.5, Wet 'n Wild is a water theme park for kids. There's a wave pool and several enormous water slides, but the highlight of this expensive (and somewhat silly) place, given that the Caribbean is only 100m or so away, is a large pool where snorkelers can spend up to an hour with dolphins, stingrays and even sharks. The pool offers users a tiny taste of the Caribbean with a reduced risk of drowning. The park is open 10 am to 6 pm Monday to Saturday and 10 am to 7 pm Sunday. Admission costs US$25 for persons age 10 and older, US$19 for kids 3 to 9, and free for kids under 3.

BEACHES

Under Mexican law you have the right to walk and swim on every beach in the country except those within military compounds. In practice, however, it is difficult to approach many stretches of beach without

---

Physical Features of the Maya

In case you've ever wondered what the physical features of the Maya were, the following passages, which appear verbatim on a sign at the Museo de Antropología y Historia in Cancún, answer the question.

'Although there is not a unique physical constitution for the inhabitants of the Mayan area, there are certain shared features such as: aquiline nose, epicanthic eyefold, mongolic spot in the base of the spine, and they are brachycefalous.

'Almond-shaped eyes are common and according to the relative length between arms and the total stature, they have longer arms than those of the Mesoamerican group.

'The other physical features of this group are the same as those observed in the other Mesoamerican groups: low stature, dark skin, dark brown or black eyes, broad shoulders, developed thorax and strong muscled legs.'

And there you have it – the physical features of the Maya, according to the museum. In the unlikely event you've forgotten the meaning of *brachycefalous* (today spelled 'brachycephalous'), it simply means that Mayan people have big heads.

---

walking through the lobby of a hotel; that's particularly true on Isla Cancún, where several kilometers of beach at a stretch are bordered by numerous resort properties without so much as a 1m-wide public path separating any of them. However, unless you look suspicious or unless you look like a local (the hotels tend to discriminate against locals, particularly Mayans), you'll usually be permitted to cross the lobby and proceed to the beach.

Starting at Ciudad Cancún and heading out to Isla Cancún, all of the beaches will be on the left-hand side of Blvd Kukulcán and beachless Laguna de Nichupté will be on the right-hand side of the road. The beaches, from north to south, are: Playa Las Perlas, Playa Juventud, Playa Linda, Playa Langosta, Playa Tortugas, Playa Caracol, Playa Gaviota Azul, Playa Chac-Mool, Playa

Marlin, Playa Ballenas, Playa San Miguelito and Playa Delfines.

Which of these beaches is best is, of course, a matter of personal opinion. The sand varies little from one beach to another, but the personalities of the crowds who use them vary greatly from site to site. If you want a party atmosphere, you'll want to head to the north end of Playa Gaviota Azul, directly behind The Forum mall at Punta Cancún. There, you'll often find a surfer band belting out Eagles tunes, and there's usually at least one game of pick-up volleyball in progress. There are bars nearby, and having drinks brought to you while you lounge on the white sand is *no problema*.

Playa San Miguelito and neighboring Playa Delfines are bordered by public parking spaces. Because locals don't need to pass through hotels to use these beaches, they tend to be used mainly by area residents. Also, the surf out in front of these beaches occasionally permits surfing; nowhere else along Isla Cancún are the waves big enough. If you're looking for a 'local scene' with local families and local surfers, this is a good place to find it.

Another fine place to find locals enjoying life at seaside is the Restaurant Río Nizuc located at the end of a short, nameless road near Blvd Kukulcán Km 22. Overlooking the mouth of the southern river that links Laguna de Nichupté and the Caribbean Sea, this humble restaurant is a good place to sit under a *palapa* with a friend and sip drinks, chat and just let the world revolve for awhile without you. It's open from 11 am to 6 pm daily. If this scene appeals to you, be sure to see Restaurant Río Nizuc in the Places to Eat section for further details.

To reach the beaches from Ciudad Cancún, catch any bus with 'Hoteles' or 'Zona Hotelera' on its windshield as it travels south along Av Tulum or east along Av Cobá; the bus will soon be on Blvd Kukulcán and rolling onto the island. The cost of the ride each way is a mere US$0.45 – a bargain if ever there was one. To catch a ride back into town, simply go to one of the bus stops along Blvd Kukulcán and board any of the buses headed toward Ciudad Cancún (ie, away from the airport). If there isn't a bus stop near you, just wave at the driver of an approaching bus and the driver will stop for you. It's easy, convenient and cheap.

You can also reach the beaches by taxi. The cost of a taxi depends on how far you travel, but throughout Mexico taxis are always more expensive than buses. For taxi information, see Getting Around at the end of the Cancún section.

SNORKELING

Most snorkelers who wish to explore the area's superb reefs visit nearby Isla Mujeres, or they head farther south to Cozumel (see those sections for details). Other than a few scattered coral heads, there is little marine life to see in the water within wading distance of Isla Cancún – with one exception: There's some very good snorkeling to be found within swimming distance of the Club Mediterranée (☎ 885-2900), at Punta Nizuc. That's because a finger of the Great Maya Barrier Reef reaches up from the south and nearly touches the point.

Day passes to Club Med are available for US$30. They are good from 10 am to 5:30 pm daily. With the pass, visitors can participate in all of the activities available to Club Med guests except waterskiing, and they have access to the resort's bars and restaurants. Nonguests can also purchase a night pass. If

---

Beach Safety

Cancún's Rescate 911 ambulance crews respond to as many as a dozen near-drownings each week. Though surf along the Hotel Zone is usually gentle, undertow is possible, and storms can arrive with little warning. Local authorities have devised a system of colored pennants to alert beachgoers of potential dangers. Look for the pennants on the beaches where you swim:

Blue	Normal, safe conditions
Yellow	Use caution, changeable conditions
Red	Unsafe conditions; use a swimming pool instead

you reach the guarded entrance to the club by bus or taxi, be forewarned that it's a very long walk from the entry gate to the reception desk. (For more information on Club Med's daytime and nighttime activities and facilities, see Club Méditerranée under Places to Stay, later this chapter.)

Alternatively, the resort hotels, travel agencies and the various tour operators in the area can also book you on day-cruise boats that take snorkelers to the reef, as well as others within 100km of Cancún, but going to the distant reefs (such as those near Isla Holbox) isn't necessary to see a fantastic array of marine life.

Among the tour operators offering snorkel trips in the area is Aqua Tours (☎ 883-0400, fax 883-0403, info@aquatours.net, www.aquatours.net), Blvd Kukulcán Km 6.25. Aqua Tours offers two 3½-hour snorkel trips to Punta Nizuc daily, with departures at 9:30 am and 1:30 pm. The cost of US$40 includes continental breakfast, snorkel instruction and gear, life jackets, soft drinks and beer, and a light lunch after snorkeling.

An even better option if time and money permit is the Cozumel day trip offered by AquaWorld (☎ 885-2288, fax 885-2299, www.aquaworld.com.mx), Blvd Kukulcán Km 15.2. Your US$72 ticket includes roundtrip private transportation, snorkel gear, guided snorkel tour, beach buffet, shopping time and refreshments.

If you're satisfied seeing the sparser aquatic life off Cancún's beaches and you haven't brought any equipment, you can generally rent snorkel equipment for about US$10 a day from most of the luxury hotels.

SCUBA DIVING

Cancún offers scuba divers superb value. Why? Because with a little effort a budget-conscious diver can usually find an appealing Cancún airfare-and-hotel package, and from Isla Cancún that diver can take day trips to Quintana Roo's best dive sites. From Cancún, that visitor can also take day trips to Chichén Itzá, Tulum, Mérida and other fine land-based attractions. Making Cancún a base of operations is a great idea for people who want the variety of entertainment and

dining options available in Cancún *and* easy access to the spectacular diving at Cozumel.

The area's premiere dive operator, Aqua-World (see Snorkeling, above), offers numerous dive tours from its primary center at Blvd Kukulcán Km 15.2. The PADI-certified center offers a variety of reef and freshwater cavern dives, as well as a resort course (US$88, including a one-tank ocean dive) and a PADI open-water certification course (US$385, including four ocean dives) that can be completed in as little as four days. PADI specialty certification programs are also available, and all necessary equipment is available for rent.

Dive choices originating from Aqua-World's Cancún center include a two-tank reef dive (US$60/55 with/without equipment); a two-tank dive at Cozumel (US$110/100); a two-tank cavern dive for qualified divers (US$130/120); and a combination two-tank reef dive and two-tank twilight dive and your choice of a two-tank Cozumel dive or two-tank cavern dive (US$200, includes all equipment).

Other reputable dive centers that operate from Isla Cancún include Aqua Tours (see Snorkeling, above) and Scuba Cancún (☎ 883-5846, 883-1011, fax 884-2336, scuba@cancun.com.mx, www.scubacancun.com.mx), Blvd Kukulcán Km 5. Like AquaWorld, Aqua Tours and Scuba Cancún employ only PADI-certified dive masters and provide visitors with a wide range of dive options at reasonable prices.

FISHING

Deep-sea fishing excursions can be booked through a travel agent or one of the large hotels. They are also available from Aqua Tours (see Snorkeling, above) for as little as US$70 for four hours of fishing, US$100 for six hours; price includes captain, mate, soft drinks, beer, bait and tackle. Those prices are for a shared boat. Prices for a private charter service with Aqua Tours start at US$320 for four hours and US$400 for a bigger boat. The crews at Aqua Tours boast decades' of fishing experience, and by the looks of them, they're telling the truth. AquaWorld offers comparable fishing tours at competitive prices.

A less-expensive (but not necessarily better) way to go is to head over to the Puerto Juárez ferry dock just north of Ciudad Cancún and negotiate a deal with the fishers who offer their services there. Typically, if you show up at the dock in the morning you'll be approached by numerous fishers offering three- and four-hour fishing trips for US$100 per person. These prices are subject to negotiation, with fishers expecting prospective clients to bargain.

It might interest you to know that grouper, sea bass, mackerel, barracuda and snapper are available in the area all year, while the fishing season for marlin, sail fish, amberjacks, tuna, wahoo and mahi-mahi is April to August.

BOAT EXCURSIONS

Many companies offer short cruises that begin and end at one of the piers along Isla Cancún. Some of the boats carry passengers to one of the reefs just off the coast of Isla Mujeres, where guests are encouraged to snorkel for an hour or so, and then the boats make their way back to Cancún. Others actually dock at Isla Mujeres and guests enter the sea from the beach. Some of the boats don't stop at all, but instead serve as floating dance halls.

Among the popular cruise options available is the *Isla Mujeres Dolphin Express* (☎ 883-1488, 883-3283), which departs at 10 am daily from the Playa Langosta Dock near the Casa Maya hotel and returns at 4:30 pm. Included in the US$35 price is continental breakfast aboard the yacht, open bar all trip long, snorkeling and shopping at the Pirate's Village activities center on Isla Mujeres, and an opportunity to watch people interact with pet dolphins. Yes, for additional money you, too, can swim with the dolphins.

Equally popular is the *Dolphin Discovery* cruise (☎ 883-0777, 883-0780), which leaves from the Playa Langosta Dock for an activities center on Isla Mujeres at 8 am and returns at 8 pm. Like Pirate's Village, the Dolphin Discovery facility features – one guess only – dolphins. But here, you not only get to swim with the small toothed whales, but you also get to play games with them. There are two prices: US$119 for a 45-minute frolic with the dolphins, during which you actually ride a pair of dolphins, and US$65 for a half-hour encounter in which you 'receive a kiss' from a dolphin and are allowed to pet and tread water with them.

Don't like dolphins? Paddle wheelers more your speed? You're in luck. The *Cancún Queen* is the only paddle wheeler in Mexico, and it pushes off from the AquaWorld center, at Blvd Kukulcán Km 15.2, daily at 6 pm and returns around 9 pm. The rather handsome vessel cruises through the mangroves of Laguna de Nichupté, while passengers dance the evening away to live music and feast on lobster and steak (US$60) or fish and chicken (US$40). The bar is open.

Or, perhaps you'd prefer to spend the evening aboard a pirate ship. *Capitan Hook* (☎ 883-3736, 883-3738) is a replica of a Spanish galleon that departs from a pier near Blvd Kukulcán Km 4.5 daily at 7 pm and returns around 10:30 pm. In between, athletic men in pirate garb swing down from the masts and engage in mock sword fights while the ship cruises the Caribbean. The booze flows freely and the price of the evening varies with entrée – US$65 for lobster, US$55 for steak.

Yet another cruise option involves a boat that thinks it is a submarine. AquaWorld's *Sub See Explorer* resembles a submarine, but it never dives. It has an underwater level with lots of windows and seats. Passengers simply take a seat and watch the sea go by. With the *Sub See Explorer*, you have two options: You can simply go for a ride and eat lunch on the move (US$35; hourly departures from 9 am to 3 pm from the AquaWorld center at Blvd Kukulcán Km 15.2), or you can take it to AquaWorld's Paradise Island, which is a nearby man-made island in an otherwise protected area (US$45; hourly departures from 9 am to 2 pm from the AquaWorld center). At tiny Paradise Island, passengers are invited to snorkel, dine and sunbathe. Children 11 and under pay half-price.

OTHER WATER SPORTS

Most of the major resorts now offer kayaks for rent. A few make them available to guests free of charge. If you're not a guest at any of the resorts, you can still rent a kayak from some of them when supply permits. You'll see signs beside Cancún's main beaches indicating kayaks for rent. If kayaking Cancún is important to you, be sure to check on their availability at your prospective hotel before reserving a room.

AquaWorld, at Blvd Kukulcán Km 15.2, rents Wave Runners for US$77 an hour and private mini-speedboats for US$85 an hour. AquaWorld also rents boogie boards (US$11 a day), inflatables (US$11 a day) and snorkel gear (US$11 a day).

Water-skiers will want to head to Aqua Tours, at Blvd Kukulcán Km 6.25, which will provide you with a speedboat, an instructor and water skis for US$1 per minute with a 15-minute minimum. Service is available from 8 am to 5 pm daily.

PARASAILING

For those of you unfamiliar with this lawsuit-waiting-to-happen activity, it's a cross between skydiving and waterskiing. Parasailers/riders are hooked up to a parachute, which is spread out on the beach. A rope connected to a speedboat 75m or so away is attached to the parasailer's harness. When the boat pulls away from the beach, the parasailer is yanked forward, the chute fills with air and the rider is raised off the ground. Depending on the speed of the boat, the weight of the parasailer and the prevailing winds, the suspended rider can be lifted 100m or more as the speedboat cruises parallel to beach for several kilometers.

In Cancún, wanna-be parasailers need only go to one of the more popular beaches along the Zona Hotelera and look for a parachute spread out on the sand. Nearby there will be several people willing to separate you from US$40 or US$50 for a 15-minute ride. There are a half dozen or so of these operators on Cancún's beaches, none any safer than another. The people promoting parasailing behind The Forum mall probably have as much experience doing it

as anybody, so if you're going to parasail you might want to do it with them.

Prospective parasailers will want to remember two things: First, to lower yourself at the end of the ride, it's necessary for you to pull hard on the control ropes dangling from the parachute. If you've got a weak grip, weak arms or a bad shoulder, you'd be foolish to parasail as problems usually arise during landing, not takeoff. Second, if you panic and freeze up, or you learn the hard way that you're not strong enough to lower yourself, the operators sometimes opt to land you in the sea or in a nearby swimming pool.

It should go without saying that landing in a swimming pool while simultaneously roped to a speedboat and to a parachute is a dangerous thing to do. If you have a fear of heights, if you're at all nervous about parasailing, if you aren't as strong as you once were or if you've been drinking alcohol, leave this activity to others. If the root of your interest in parasailing is like most people's – you're hoping to draw attention to yourself – you'd likely make more friends buying a round of beers for everyone at the bar.

ORGANIZED TOURS
'Jungle Tours'

There aren't any jungle tours offered by Cancún's various tour operators, despite what they say. Rather, the so-called jungle tours are either Wave Runners or mini-speedboat tours mostly of the Laguna de Nichupté. They usually last two hours and involve an hour or so snorkeling in the Caribbean in a protected area near the mouth of the Río Nizuc, which is the short river ('channel' is more accurate) that runs through Punta Nizuc.

For US$35 on up, one or two guests are given the keys to a Wave Runner (or small, sporty boat, depending on which company is used). Typically, a single 'tour' will include a dozen or so people on a half dozen or so watercraft following a leader through a maze of mangrove in the lagoon that separates Isla Cancún from the mainland. Is jungle involved? No. Really, the tour is just a great excuse to zip around, make a splash and do some high-quality snorkeling.

AquaWorld offers these tours (US$35, Wave Runners), as does Aqua Tours (US$40, small speedboats); see the Snorkeling section for contact information. Smaller operators, such as El Manglar Marina (☎ 885-0196, 885-0179), Blvd Kukulcán Km 19, offer 'jungle tours' as well. All are comparably priced. El Manglar Marina uses small speedboats instead of Wave Runners.

Package Tours
Extremists will want to check out Aqua Tours' combination deals. These include: a jungle tour, a snorkel tour and an Isla Mujeres tour for US$90. Or, you might want to consider a combination snorkel, Isla Mujeres and fishing tour, also offered by Aqua Tours and costing US$120.

AquaWorld offers an even greater variety of discount packages. Among them: a jungle tour, Paradise Island snorkeling and an Isla Mujeres trip (US$90); Paradise Island snorkeling, Isla Mujeres tour and Wave Runner riding or waterskiing (US$110); Cozumel day trip, Isla Mujeres snorkeling, and Wave Runner riding or waterskiing (US$140); a resort course and one-tank dive in Cancún plus a two-tank dive in Cozumel (US$200).

For Aqua Tours and AquaWorld contact information, see the Snorkeling section earlier this chapter.

Land Tours
Every hotel on Isla Cancún and every area travel agency works with companies that offer tours to the following sights for approximately the amount of money indicated: Chichén Itzá (US$60, includes admission); Tulum ruins and Xel-ha private marine park (US$60, includes admission); and Xcaret private park (US$90, includes admission). Budget-conscious travelers: If you go to the public bus station in Ciudad Cancún you can join a guided tour of the sights for a lot less money; see Ciudad Cancún's Getting There & Away section for station information.

Xcaret, which is described in detail later in this chapter, has become so popular that it has its own bus station on Isla Cancún; it's on the north side of Blvd Kukulcán at Km 8.5, just west of the Fiesta Americana Coral Beach resort. Buses leave Cancún for Xcaret at 9, 10 and 11 am daily, and leave Xcaret at 5:30 and 9:30 pm (on Sunday, all buses exit the park at 5:30 pm). The round-trip transportation costs US$69 for adults, US$45 for kids ages 5 to 11. Admission to the park is an additional US$39, US$24 for kids ages 5 to 11.

PLACES TO STAY
With the exception of one inexpensive hostel and a handful of moderately priced hotels, all of the accommodations in the Zona Hotelera are pricey compared to other Mexican vacation retreats. However, they are also excellent values, generally, considering their location, services and amenities. Their value is even greater when rooms are reserved from abroad. That's because hotel clerks in Cancún have been trained to charge surprise arrivals the maximum room rate, as this practice encourages visitors to make reservations (which makes it easier for hotel administrators to fill rooms). The bottom line: If you're considering a Cancún vacation, one of your first moves should be to a travel agency, the Internet or both to learn of the hotel deals available to you.

On Isla Cancún and at other popular Yucatán destinations, seasons also influence hotel rates. Room 100 at Resort X can cost twice as much per night during the high tourist season (mid-December through March); the week between Christmas and New Year's Day, in particular, is always a period of steep price gouging. If you choose to arrive in Cancún when seemingly everyone does, expect high room rates. But again, you can usually lower your costs (even during high season) by simply doing a little research. Oftentimes, the travel sections of major newspapers contain advertisements promoting enormously enticing hotel-and-airfare packages.

If you're traveling on a shoestring but want to take advantage of Isla Cancún's many offerings, your best bet might be to stay in Ciudad Cancún, where the hotel rates are much lower than they are on the island. Only a brief and inexpensive bus ride separates the Hotel Zone from the city. For

detailed options, see the Ciudad Cancún section, later in this chapter.

The room rates quoted here, as well as the rest of the book, are off-season rates – the rates that apply more than eight months of the year. If you'll be visiting during the high tourist season, expect the rates to be at least 30% to 50% higher (much higher around Christmas and New Year's Day). Your rates, however, could be significantly lower *if* you shop around.

Places to Stay – Budget

Four kilometers from the bus station, the area's one budget accommodation and only hostel is the ***Atención a la Juventud*** (*☎ 883-1337, fax 883-0484, Blvd Kukulcán Km 3.2*), on the left-hand side of the road just past the Km 3 marker as you come from Ciudad Cancún. Built decades ago as a modern 600-bed complex in honor of youth, it is now

sadly dilapidated, though functioning with 300 beds still in use. The staff is friendly and the place reasonably priced for what you get: a single-sex dorm bed for US$8 (plus a US$6 deposit for a sheet and pillow). Camping on the lawn out back costs US$4 per person, including a locker and use of the hostel's shower and bathroom facilities. The beach there is silty and shallow, but all of Cancún's beaches are but a brisk bus ride away. There is no age limit and space is usually available.

Places to Stay – Mid-Range

In choosing a moderately priced hotel on Isla Cancún (that is, one that's under US$100 for two people most of the year), it's good to keep in mind that the closer you are to Blvd Kukulcán, the closer you are to cheap and convenient transportation. That said, there really aren't any stinkers in this category

---

Research Those Room Rates

Room rates in Cancún can vary considerably depending on where they are purchased. In general, the worst are 'rack rates' – the rates charged to people who simply walk in and ask for a room. The best rates, in general, are found on the Internet.

The 800 numbers provided by hotels are helpful in locating promotional deals, which provide the most significant savings, but the numbers can only be used in North America. The hotels' reservations clerks, who may be reached using the local numbers provided, can often offer rates better than those offered by the operators tending the toll-free lines.

Really price-sensitive people will want to start their research online. The biggest and best of the Web's virtual travel agents is Travelocity (www.travelocity.com). Travelocity typically offers a wide range of special deals for a specified resort, from AAA discounts to seasonal promotions to American Express rates. What's more, the site is user-friendly.

Travel agents are a mixed lot. Many belong to a consortium or subscribe to a service that gets them hotel rates guaranteed to be the lowest available. However, most of those rates are usually no better than the standard corporate rates offered by the hotels. If you have an American Express card, it is worthwhile to call AmEx to see what deals they've got going with Cancún resorts. Some AmEx programs offer superlative value. It's strictly hit or miss.

Faxing the hotels is usually a waste of time. Expect to wait weeks for a reply to a fax sent to the land of *mañana*. If and when it does arrive, expect the response to show only a list of rack rates. If, for example, the resort is offering a special rate for guests who pay for their stay with an American Express card, you can be sure the faxed reply would make no mention of it.

Another thing to keep in mind: Discount travel clubs generally provide rates that are higher than you can find on your own, and the low rates they occasionally advertise are typically unavailable for the dates you request (because the rooms eligible for the discount have already been sold). These clubs (among them Travelers Advantage, Encore and Quest) charge an annual fee.

and, with few exceptions, most offer excellent value.

The **Hotel Dos Playas** (☎ 883-0500, fax 883-2037, Blvd Kukulcán Km 6.2) offers 108 air-con (but otherwise forgettable) rooms, and the beach here isn't too lovely. But its location right on the main drag is excellent, and you don't hear its mostly German clientele complaining about the room rates, which typically range from US$60 to US$100.

The **Laguna Real** (☎ 883-2899, fax 883-0003, 0.1km off Blvd Kukulcán Km 7.7, Calle Quetzal 8) is an excellent find. Its 36 air-con rooms feature two double beds and cable TV, and guests have use of all of the facilities at its swankier sister resorts – the seaside Gran Caribe Real and Costa Real. What's more, there's free shuttle service between Laguna Real and the resorts. There's also a pool on the premises. Room rates range from US$65 to US$95, depending on the dates visited.

A stone's throw from the Laguna Real is the budget-pleasing **Imperial Laguna** (☎ 883-0070, fax 883-0106, in the USA ☎ 407-331-7355, fax 407-834-3337, Calle Quetzal 13), which offers 30 standard guest rooms, 10 one-bedroom suites, 10 two-bedroom suites and two three-bedroom suites. All of the suites contain at least two double beds and a sofa bed, kitchenette with utensils, satellite TV, marble floors and a balcony. This is a super value at only US$65 a room.

Just down the street a little from the Imperial Laguna is **Sina Suites** (☎ 883-1017, 883-1018, fax 883-2458, in the USA ☎ 877-666-9837, Calle Quetzal 33). It's yet another great find. Sina offers 33 spacious suites, each with kitchen, 1½ bathrooms, separate living room with sofa bed, bedroom with two double beds, satellite TV, air/con, a pleasing view of the lagoon, great cross ventilation, a pool, bar and restaurant. The room rate is US$70 except during the month of December, when it's US$106 or US$117. Each room can accommodate up to four people. Add US$20 for a master suite that's perfect for two couples (there's a separate bedroom and bathroom for each couple).

The last of four hotels on Calle Quetzal, all of which abut the Laguna de Nichupté,

is the **Blue Lagoon** (☎ /fax 883-1215, Calle Quetzal 39), which offers 24 one-bedroom suites with private balcony, air-con and cable TV. Each suite is quite roomy and comfortable and there's a swimming pool on the grounds. This place is a great find for US$60 per room most of the year.

In the same price category and facing the lagoon is the aptly named **Laguna Inn** (☎ 883-2055, fax 883-2061, in the USA ☎ 407-331-7355, fax 407-834-3337, Calle del Pescador, Lote D-8-3). The Inn features 90 air-con rooms, each containing either two double beds or one queen-size bed. There's a swimming pool, a tree-shaded courtyard and an inviting palapa bar-restaurant. Rooms typically rent for US$70 a night for one person or two.

Hotel Suites Laguna Verde (☎ 883-3414, 883-4014, fax 883-4897, bambutravel@caribe .net), on Paseo Pok-ta-Pok 1km off Blvd Kukulcán Km 7, while not at lagoon's edge or even the Caribbean side (it's separated from the lagoon by a golf course), is a terrific find all the same for couples and small families. The rates are per room and range from US$56 from April 10 to December 20 to US$135 from December 21 to January 2. All 48 poolside rooms are kitchen-equipped air-con suites with private phone, safety deposit box, cable TV, and two side-by-side queen-size beds. Shuttle service to the Xcaret bus station is provided free of charge at 9, 10 and 11 am, with pickup at 3 and 5 pm. There's a travel agency and a gift shop on the premises, taxis are nearby and a doctor is available for house calls 24 hours. There's also a laundry and restaurant nearby.

Next door is the **Ocean Club Suites** (☎ 883-3300, 883-3773, chboyce@mpsnet .mx), which at US$95 per room for most of the year is getting very close to competing with some of the top-end places but without the benefit of a Caribbean beach out back. However, when you consider what it offers it's hard not to view the Ocean Club as moderately priced: spacious air-con suites overlooking a golf course and the lagoon, private phone, cable TV, use of a nearby swimming pool, a tennis court, a squash court, a video-game room, a billiard table

and a beach club. Greens fees are additional. There's also a restaurant and a bar on the premises.

The **Club Verano Beat** (☎ 883-0781, fax 883-0173, verbeat@cancun.com.mx, Blvd Kukulcán Km 3) caters mostly to French and German tourists and is none too fancy. It lost much of its beach to erosion during a mid-1990s hurricane. However, it's actually on the Caribbean (as opposed to the lagoon) and all 93 rooms have air-con and cable TV, and there's a pool. Rates for one or two people start at US$70 much of the year. Not a bad deal at all.

One of the better finds for sure is the **Holiday Inn Express** (☎ 883-2200, fax 883-2532, in the USA ☎ 800-465-4329), on Paseo Pok-ta-Pok. The 119 rooms are located in two-story buildings that ring two swimming pools. Every cookie-cutter room comes with air-con and satellite TV. A private shuttle whisks guests to and from the airport. Most likable about this hotel is the price: US$65 per room most of the year.

The Best Western **Aquamarina Beach Hotel** (☎ 883-1425, fax 883-1751, in the USA ☎ 800-780-7234, aquavent@cancun.com.mx, www.bestwestern.com, Blvd Kukulcán Km 4.5) was built with tour groups of young-adult sun lovers in mind. Rooms, single or double, go for US$85 most of the year, nearly twice that during the high tourist season. Some rooms have kitchenettes and refrigerators. If you call the 800 number or the hotel directly, be sure to inquire about specials.

Another good find is the **Imperial Las Perlas** (☎ 883-1428, fax 883-0106, Blvd Kukulcán Km 2.5), which offers 118 air-con studio rooms with kitchenettes, double beds, satellite TV, marble floors and balconies in three-story buildings flanking a swimming pool. This place is a little too stark ('institutional' comes to mind) for some people's liking, but for US$80 per room most of the time it's a good deal. It faces the Caribbean but the water out front isn't very nice. Most of its beach-loving guests head east on a bus rather than sunbathe at Las Perlas.

The **Cancún Marina Club** (☎ 883-1561, 883-1409, in the USA ☎ 800-448-8355, Blvd Kukulcán Km 5.5), although on the lagoon side of the road, is very popular, and for good reason. The modern complex has one of the most inviting pools in Cancún and a very pleasant restaurant-bar that overlooks the lagoon. There's a travel agency on the premises as well as a water-sports center. Among the 75 rooms are 10 penthouses with Jacuzzi tubs. Expect to pay US$85 per room most of the time.

Considering its location and amenities, the **Hoteles Aristos Cancún** (☎ 883-0011, fax 883-00-78, in the USA ☎ 800-527-4786, aristoshotels@worldnet.att.net, www.aristoshotels .com, Blvd Kukulcán Km 9.6) offers the best value of Cancún's moderately priced digs. Its 250 balconied guest rooms come with satellite TV, air-con, and your choice of two double beds or one king-size bed. All rooms face the sea or the lagoon. Facilities include two pools (one for kids), two tennis courts, billiards and pool tables, two restaurants and three bars. Rooms rates generally range from US$80 to US$100.

Places to Stay – Top End

Cancún's premiere accommodations are full-service resorts. Room rates in this category range from US$100 to US$500, and all but one of these places borders the Caribbean. Many feature vast grounds with rolling lawns of manicured grass, tropical gardens, swimming pools with swim-up bars, and recreational facilities and equipment. Some resemble Mayan pyramids, others would look at home in Spain or Italy.

Additionally, the vast majority of the top-end hotels have at least one restaurant and a separate bar, all have at least a sliver of beach, and all are staffed with English-speaking individuals. All guest rooms in this price category have air-con and satellite TV, and many have balconies with a sea view.

To obtain the best rate at any of these luxury hotels, shop around (see the 'Research Those Room Rates' boxed text). Be sure to check both airline and travel websites, and if you have an American Express card be sure to contact American Express Travel Services to inquire about special deals. Often the best room rates available are contained in hotel-and-airfare packages.

If time permits, request brochures from the resorts that interest you, as they contain facility photos and a full list of their amenities and services – valuable information when weighing accommodations options.

Because the rates offered by each resort vary greatly depending on when and where guests book reservations, and because all of the resorts are conveniently located along Blvd Kukulcán, the top-end hotels are arranged by their location along the boulevard rather than by cost.

Club Las Perlas (☎ 883-2022, fax 883-0830, clperlas@cancun.rce.com.mx, Blvd Kukulcán Km 2.5) is part of the Spanish Barceló Hotels chain and boasts 194 rooms in a close grouping of three- and four-story buildings that are moderately attractive. The resort's location, at the top end of the Hotel Zone, means its beach is considerably quieter than those farther east and to the south. Rates typically start at US$100 per double occupancy.

Blue Bay Village (☎ 880-1063, fax 883-0904, cancun@bluebayresorts.com, Blvd Kukulcán Km 3.4) is an adults-only all-inclusive resort that offers garden-view standard rooms and ocean-view junior suites. Complimentary snorkel and scuba lessons in the pool, nightly shows and a full range of non-motorized water sports are featured. Rates typically start at US$120 per person.

Plaza Las Glorias (☎ 883-0811, fax 883-0901, Blvd Kukulcán Km 3.5) offers 128 standard rooms and 12 suites (all rooms have private terraces) and features a travel agency and car, bike and moped rental. Room rates typically start around US$140. Because the hotel is U-shaped (with a pool and gardens at the center), most of the rooms face other rooms instead of the sea.

Carrousel (☎ 883-0778, 883-0513, fax 883-2312, Blvd Kukulcán Km 3.7) is, like Plaza Las Glorias, U-shaped, but all of its small but appealing rooms are angled so their they and their terraces face the sea. There's a small marina out in front of the resort's expansive beach, and a single tennis court. Rates are all-inclusive and reasonable starting at US$100 per person much of the year.

Costa Real (☎ 881-7300, fax 881-7399, in the USA ☎ 800-543-7556, real@bestday.com, www.real.com.mx, Blvd Kukulcán Km 4) is a very large, all-inclusive resort with very attractive grounds and a shared-facilities agreement with the much more spectacular Gran Caribe Real to the east. With per-person double-occupancy rates as low as US$100 (yes, including food), this place offers great value most of the year.

Calinda Beach Cancún (☎ 883-1600, fax 883-1857, in the USA ☎ 800-221-2222, Blvd Kukulcán Km 4.25), facing the Playa Linda Marine Terminal, has a decor of red tiles, white stucco and modern muted colors. All 470 rooms, most of which face the sea, have a cheerful, airy feel. Rooms at this popular resort typically start at US$125.

Casa Maya (☎ 883-0555, fax 883-1188, in the USA ☎ 800-207-9280, pablolar@cancun.rce.com.mx, Blvd Kukulcán Km 5.25) features 352 pleasant-but-small and terrace-less rooms and an unknown number of suites contained in two monoliths. The lovely grounds include two pools, two Jacuzzis, two restaurants, two tennis courts and, yes, two conference rooms. Room rates are reasonable when they're around US$140.

Gran Caribe Real (☎ 881-7300, fax 881-7399, in the USA ☎ 800-543-7556, real@bestday.com, Blvd Kukulcán Km 5.7) is, as its brochures say, a 'spectacularly elegant' resort. Its 466 deluxe rooms (all with ocean views), 32 junior suites and two three-story, three-bedroom penthouse suites all come with private terraces that overlook a dazzling swimming pool and 200m of beach. Room rates start at US$275. An all-inclusive plan is also offered and usually runs US$150 per person, double occupancy.

Sunset Lagoon (☎ 881-4500, fax 881-4696, www.sunsetworld.com, Blvd Kukulcán Km 5.75) is the only top-end resort in the Hotel Zone that faces the crocodile-inhabited lagoon instead of the sea, and yet it's an excellent place to stay – because a beautiful stretch of Caribbean beach is only a brief bus ride away. A host of nonmotorized water toys (kayaks, pedal boats, Windsurfers, Sunfish sailboats, etc) are free to use. Including all meals, rates generally start at a very reasonable US$112 per person.

Villas Tacul (☎ 883-0000, fax 883-0349, in the USA ☎ 800-221-5333, Blvd Kukulcán Km 5.8) consists of 23 separate villas nestled on 12 lush acres and connected by a stone walkway. Fourteen of the tastefully appointed villas are steps from the surf. Facilities include two tennis courts, a playground for kids and 300m of beach. The entire resort is gated and private. Room rates usually start at US$145. Weekly rates are available.

Tropical Mayan (☎ 883-2554, fax 883-0605, troplus@oasishotels.com.mx, Blvd Kukulcán Km 6) features simple, utilitarian swimming pools, 40 forgettable rooms and a sad garden. Its mostly European clientele generally pays between US$150 and US$180 per person to stay here, meals included. Not a horrible value, but not a good one either.

Presidente Inter-Continental (☎ 883-0200, fax 883-2515, in the USA ☎ 800-327-0200, cancun@interconti.com, Blvd Kukulcán Km 8) is an semi-elegant affair consisting of an L-shaped tower containing 300 rooms, including a presidential suite, each with private balcony, and a pleasant dining room on the beach. Room rates start at US$200.

An often-overlooked bargain is the *Kin-Ha* (☎ 883-2377, fax 883-2147, kinha3@mail.caribe.net.mx, Blvd Kukulcán Km 8.1), which consists of 166 suites in four buildings. The property, one of the oldest in Cancún, was entirely renovated in 1993. All rooms feature air-con, a balcony and two double beds or one king-size bed. A travel agency, car rental, mini-market, bars and a gym are on premises. Room rates start at US$140 much of the year.

Calinda Viva Cancún (☎ 883-0800, fax 883-2087, Blvd Kukulcán Km 8.25) has 210 standard rooms in two large towers, two tennis courts, a swimming pool and three bars. A variety of motorized and nonmotorized sports are available. Room rates typically start around US$175.

Fiesta Americana Cancún (☎ 883-1400, in the USA ☎ 800-343-7821, Blvd Kukulcán Km 8.45) is an oddity, resembling nothing so much as an old-city streetscape: it's an appealing jumble of windows, balconies, roofs and other features. Rooms often cost US$165

to US$225; add 20% or more during the high tourist season.

Club Arrecife (☎ 883-1005, fax 883-1881, armmoli@total.net, www.all-inclusive-resorts.com, Blvd Kukulcán Km 8.5) is an all-inclusive resort with lovely views of the Caribbean and the beaches from most of its 121 air-con rooms in several seven-story buildings. Included in the per-person rate that usually starts around US$90 double occupancy are three daily meals, local drinks, water sports, Spanish lessons, volleyball, pool games and basketball. This is a very fun place with a very enticing swimming pool.

Fiesta Americana Coral Beach (☎ 883-2900, fax 883-3173, in the USA ☎ 800-343-7821, reserv@fiestaamericana.com, www.fiestaamericana.com, Blvd Kukulcán Km 8.7) is one of the most luxurious resorts on the Yucatán Peninsula, offering only suites (602 of them, all with balconies and marble floors) in tiered towers overlooking spectacular grounds. Rack rates start at US$325 a room, but much lower rates are available with a little research (start by doing an Internet search using the hotel's name).

Camino Real (☎ 883-0100, fax 883-1730, in the USA ☎ 800-722-6466, cun@caminoreal.com, www.caminoreal.com, Blvd Kukulcán Km 8.8) consists of 294 spacious rooms inside a very modern six-story structure and a 16-story tower. Everything about this resort is tastefully done. Rack rates start at US$200 per room.

The *Hyatt Regency Cancún* (☎ 883-1234, fax 883-1694, in the USA ☎ 800-233-1234, hyattreg@cancun.rce.com.mx, Blvd Kukulcán Km 8.85) is a 15-story cylinder with a lofty open court at its core and 300 smartly decorated guest rooms arranged around it. Situated right on Punta Cancún, virtually all of its balconied rooms have excellent views. There is little beach beside the Hyatt, but guests find a pier built just for sunbathers to be an excellent alternative. Room rates start at US$180.

Krystal (☎ 883-1133, fax 883-1790, in the USA ☎ 800-231-9860, Blvd Kukulcán Km 8.9) offers 314 utilitarian guest rooms and so-so suites. Its enormous 'plus' is its location – just several minutes' walk to The

Forum mall and surrounding shops, restaurants and dance clubs. Rack rates start at US$165 per room.

Miramar Misión (☎ *883-1755, fax 883-1136, miramar@sybcom.com, Blvd Kukulcán Km 9.75)* offers guests a lot for the money, including: a rooftop swimming pool, several ground-floor pools, a bar with live salsa most nights, 300 fully equipped guest rooms with private balconies, and an excellent location. Room rates typically run US$150 to US$200.

Royal Sunset (☎ *881-4500, fax 881-4694, in the USA* ☎ *800-221-5333, Blvd Kukulcán Km 9.85)* is mostly a time-share deal, with 80% of the rooms set aside for 'members.' None of the remaining rooms features a view of the sea, and the push to become a member is rather unappealing. Its beachside bar and restaurant are among its highlights. Rates generally begin at US$215 per person, meals included.

Sierra Cancún (☎ *883-2444, fax 883-3486, in the USA* ☎ *800-448-5028, Blvd Kukulcán Km 10)* features 123 standard rooms (most with lagoon view), 124 mini-suites (all with ocean view), and a variety of larger suites – done up in Caribbean colors. This Mexican-owned and -operated resort offers all the usual amenities for a reasonable price of US$90 and up per person, meals included.

Hyatt Cancún Caribe (☎ *883-0044, fax 883-1514, in the USA* ☎ *800-233-1234, www.hyatt.com, Blvd Kukulcán Km 10.3)* has a terrific variety of accommodations. Its 198 lovely guest rooms and suites include ground-level rooms with private terraces, upper-level rooms with fine sea views, and Regency Club villas surrounding their own clubhouse with private pool and Jacuzzi. Rooms start around US$180 and villas around US$230.

Continental Plaza (☎ *881-5500, fax 880-5695, in the USA* ☎ *800-882-6684, Blvd Kukulcán Km 10.5)* is an all-inclusive Mediterranean-style resort with 626 balconied guest rooms, each equippedwwith all the usual modern amenities. Facilities include three swimming pools. Per-person rates typically start around US$100. Not a bad value at all.

Flamingo Cancún (☎ *883-1544, fax 883-1029, in the USA* ☎ *800-544-3005, Blvd Kukulcán Km 11)* is an attractive, modern resort with a long, wide swath of beach and 220 guest rooms and suites, all with private terraces and most with sea views. Its location across from popular Plaza Flamingo is a big plus. Room rates can occasionally be found for US$125.

Club Baccara (☎ *883-2077, in the USA* ☎ *219-784-7911, baccara@starmedia.com, Blvd Kukulcán Km 11.1)* is a colorful resort – some would say too colorful. But while the painter may have gone too far, the resort's architect presents a thoroughly Spanish product with beautiful use of Mexican tiles and tropical gardens. Room rates typically start at US$145.

Beach Palace (☎ *885-0533, fax 885-1244, in the USA* ☎ *800-346-8225, palacemx@ ix.netcom.com, www.palaceresorts.com, Blvd Kukulcán Km 11.45)*, one of the many popular Palace resorts, offers 200 rooms, 156 of which are junior suites with massage baths and 44 of which are luxury suites with Jacuzzi tubs. Guests of this all-inclusive resort can use the facilities of sister resorts during their stay. Per-person rates typically start at US$190.

Meliá Turquesa (☎ *883-2544, fax 885-1241, in the USA* ☎ *800-336-3542, www .solmelia.es, Blvd Kukulcán Km 11.55)*, one of the Spanish-owned Meliá chain resorts, is an enormous, modern and luxurious affair with 450 balconied guest rooms, all facing either the sea or lagoon. The resort is known for superior service and food. Room rates generally start around US$225.

Piramides Cancún (☎ *885-1333, fax 885-0113, Blvd Kukulcán Km 11.75)* consists of two identical side-by-side towers containing a total of 286 charming and balconied rooms and suites. The grounds are idyllic and the beach particularly deep here. The resort 'shares' a real Mayan ruin (see the Mayan Ruins section earlier this chapter) with its neighbor, the Sheraton, to the south. Room rates often start at a very reasonable US$140; add US$60 for high season.

Sheraton Cancún (☎ *883-1988, fax 885-0204, in the USA* ☎ *800-325-3535, www*

RICHARD I'ANSON

One creative outfitter vies for tourist dollars.

RICHARD I'ANSON

A wide variety of beverage options.

SCOTT DOGGETT

Pursue your pleasure in Cancún, where the nightclubs rival those in Río.

The bull's wounded, but he's not down yet.

The view of Cancún's Zona Hotelera from the beach.

Sandy, palm-shaded beaches are a top attraction for many.

.sheraton.com, Blvd Kukulcán Km 12) is a resort with tremendous appeal, from the elegant lobby to the immaculate gardens to the gorgeous tiled art in the restaurant. This is a real treat that, at times, goes for as little as US$130 a room. An excellent value at that.

Caribbean Village *(☎ 885-0112, fax 885-0999, in the USA ☎ 800-858-2258, www .allegroresorts.com, Blvd Kukulcán Km 12.25)* features 283 guest rooms and 17 suites, four restaurants, four bars and a discotheque, all in a modern, six-story building. Tennis courts, a tours desk and nightly entertainment are also provided. Room rates typically run US$190 and up.

Tucan Cun Beach *(☎ 885-0814, fax 885-1850, ventasj@cancun.com.mx, Blvd Kukulcán Km 12.9)* is a fun, value-minded all-inclusive resort with 260 guest rooms, decent food and a very inviting pool with a swim-up bar. Per-person rates most of the year hover around US$130.

Casa Turquesa *(☎ 885-2924, fax 885-2922, in the USA ☎ 888-528-8300, www .casaturquesa.com, Blvd Kukulcán Km 13)* is a small resort (only 32 rooms) catering to rich jet-setters and secondary celebrities. An elevated pool provides guests with privacy from passing riffraff, and service and cuisine in the restaurants Celebrity and Belle Vue are usually first-rate. Room rates generally range from US$300 to US$450.

Ritz-Carlton *(☎ 885-0808, fax 885-1015, in the USA ☎ 800-241-3333, Blvd Kukulcán Km 13.9)* is an expansive resort with 369 ocean-view rooms, kilometers of marble, 400m of sugary beach, three lighted tennis courts, an oceanfront whirlpool, a fitness center and a large variety of water sports options. This resort has won top hotel honors, among them inclusion on *Condé Nast Traveler*'s Gold List for highest-rated hotel in Latin America. A very elegant to-do, with standard room rates ranging from US$200 to US$600, depending on time of visit.

Jack Tar Village *(☎ 885-1366, fax 885-1363, in the USA ☎ 800-858-2258, www .allegroresorts.com, Blvd Kukulcán Km 14)* is one of the few adults-only resorts on the peninsula. It generally caters to romantic couples, although singles are welcome. The

resort's 175 guest rooms are set in a five-story, pyramid-style building complimented by private balconies. Per-person rates at this popular all-inclusive often start at US$190.

Le Meridien *(☎ 881-2200, fax 881-2201, in the USA ☎ 800-225-5843, meridiencancun@ acnet.net, Blvd Kukulcán Km 14.1)* opened in 1999 to many ohs and ahs. Its graceful French exterior and stylish French decor throughout is a fine detour from the reds, pinks and oranges so often found in Mexican resorts. The luxury and elegance don't come cheap: room rates start at US$350 and go up to US$3000 for the Presidential Suite.

Cancún Palace *(☎ 885-0533, fax 885-1244, in the USA ☎ 800-346-8225, palacemx@ix .netcom.com, www.palaceresorts.com, Blvd Kukulcán Km 14.25)*, works extra hard to offer a good value to guests. The 421 rooms and suites have all the amenities and services you'd expect, plus balconies with water views. Per-person rates typically start around US$175 double occupancy, meals included.

Marriott Casa Magna *(☎ 881-2000, fax 881-2085, in the USA ☎ 800-228-9290, www .marriott.com, Blvd Kukulcán Km 14.8)* consists of 452 tastefully appointed guest rooms and 38 suites in six-story towers. Facilities include tennis, a full range of water sports and golf nearby. Rates start at a very reasonable US$130, including buffet breakfast.

Meliá Cancún *(☎ 885-1160, fax 885-1263, in the USA ☎ 800-336-3542, www.somelia .es, Blvd Kukulcán Km 15.1)* is an elegant pyramid-resembling resort with a breathtaking, glasshouse-like lobby filled with tropical plants. Every guest room and suite comes with private balcony with a lovely ocean or lagoon view, and facilities include an 18-hole golf course, a stunning swimming pool, lighted tennis courts and 400m of magazine-ready beach. Rack rates start at US$200, but steep discounts are often available from Internet brokers.

Fiesta Americana Condesa *(☎ 885-1000, fax 885-1800, in the USA ☎ 800-343-7821, www.fiestaamericana.com, Blvd Kukulcán Km 15.3)* offers 502 balconied, cheerful and marble-floored guest rooms in two new-Spanish-style buildings that flank a lovely, island-containing swimming pool and a

seaside restaurant-bar. Rates are generally US$130 to US$160 per room, twice that during the year-end holidays.

Oasis Cancún *(☎ 883-1741, fax 883-0867, in the USA ☎ 404-240-5500, Blvd Kukulcán Km 15.6)* consists of a pyramidesque central building flanked by four wings filled with balconied guest quarters totaling a whopping 1554 suites and standard rooms. The Oasis is not only one of the largest resorts in the Yucatán, but it also offers excellent value most of the time with room rates generally well under US$200. Facilities include a sports bar, tennis and volleyball courts, and numerous restaurants.

Omni Cancún *(☎ 885-0714, fax 885-0059, in the USA ☎ 800-643-6664, omnicancun@cancun.rce.com.mx, Blvd Kukulcán Km 16)* features 346 guest rooms, suites and villas on beautifully maintained grounds. The Omni Cancún features a popular swim-up bar, a Mediterranean bistro, seemingly *acres* of swimming pools, a fitness center and sauna, and two lighted tennis courts. Rates tend to run slightly higher here than at comparable resorts, starting at US$220 a room.

Caesar Park *(☎ 881-8000, fax 881-8082, in the USA ☎ 800-228-3000, www.caesarpark.com, Blvd Kukulcán Km 17)* is a former Hilton and certainly one of the most elegant resorts in southeast Mexico. Built to resemble the pyramid at Chichén Itzá, the 426-room resort features a par-72 18-hole golf course, two lighted tennis courts, a fully equipped fitness center, a magnificent pool with a swim-up bar, and 600m of spectacular beach. Rack rates start at US$240.

El Pueblito *(☎ 881-8800, fax 885-0731, pueblito@mail.infosel.net.mx, Blvd Kukulcán Km 18.1)* is an all-inclusive resort with 227 guest rooms, each with a private balcony or terrace, and five cascading swimming pools. The hotel, which is Mexican owned and operated, isn't nearly as attractive or intelligently designed as other area resorts (many of the rooms face one another, for example). Per-person rates generally start at US$100.

Crown Paradise Club *(☎ 885-1022, fax 885-1707, in the USA ☎ 800-544-3005, www.crownparadise.com.mx, Blvd Kukulcán Km 18.3)* is an all-inclusive resort featuring a curving tower that offers soothing sea views from every one of the 364 balconied and marble-floored guest rooms. Facilities include four restaurants, four bars and four pools, as well as the only water park for children available at a Cancún resort. Rack rates typically start at US$155 per person.

Cancún Playa Oasis *(☎ 883-1741, fax 883-0867, in the USA ☎ 404-240-5500, Blvd Kukulcán Km 18.6)* originally consisted of two towers joined by a central lobby. It has since expanded two or three times and from most angles looks like a major add-on job. If you can look beyond the architectural mayhem, you'll see newly renovated and balconied rooms, inviting pools and a gorgeous beach. Rack rates typically start at US$140 per room.

Solymar *(☎ 885-1811, fax 885-1689, solyres@mail.caribe.net.mx, Blvd Kukulcán Km 18.75)* is one of Cancún's few 'condominium hotels' – its units look like condos inside and out. There are 245 rooms in all, most with kitchens. Although none of the buildings on the property is more than five stories, it seems every square meter has been developed. Facilities include two pools, two restaurants and three bars. Rack rates start at US$140 a room; check the Internet for steep discounts.

Royal Solaris Caribe *(☎ 885-0100, fax 885-0354, in the USA ☎ 800-368-9779, Blvd Kukulcán Km 19.2)* is an all-inclusive resort with 500 rooms in a single pyramid-shaped building. The guest rooms are small, cheaply furnished and lack balconies, and the facilities (mini-golf course, basketball court, pool tables) are geared for a younger crowd. Rates runs US$120 to US$190 per person, meals included.

Mexhotel *(☎ 885-0361, fax 885-0236, in the USA ☎ 800-216-8800, mexhotel@qr001.telmex.net.mx, Blvd Kukulcán Km 19.45)* offers 200 guest rooms (many with balconies) in a massive pseudo-Mediterranean-style building that overlooks two pools and swim-up bars. The grounds are otherwise austere and nothing about the Mexhotel could be described as 'elegant.' Room rates are usually kind on the wallet, rarely exceeding US$125.

Yalmakan (☎ 885-2222, fax 885-0168, in the USA ☎ 800-221-5333, rufus@ihml.demon .co.uk, Blvd Kukulcán Km 19.6) consists of three 9-story structures built in 1989 and renovated in 1996. All three buildings are square towers, none too appealing, but all of the guest rooms are comfortable and have balconies. The grounds are nothing special, but there is a marina and many water sports are available on-site. Per-person rates typically run US$140 to US$180 with meals.

Sun Palace (☎ 885-0533, fax 885-1244, in the USA ☎ 800-346-8225, palacemx@ix .netcom.com, www.palaceresorts.com, Blvd Kukulcán Km 19.75) is one those resorts that ought to have 'fun' in its name. Its 227 junior suites and 78 luxury rooms with double Jacuzzi tubs overlook an inviting pool with a sunbathing island in the center. There's an indoor pool as well, which offers relief for guests who've taken a little too much sun for comfort. Facilities are stylish and smart. Rates typically run about US$170 per person, including meals.

Westin Regina (☎ 885-0086, fax 885-0779, in the USA ☎ 800-228-3000, westin@sybcom .com, Blvd Kukulcán Km 20) features 293 roomy guest rooms, but only those on the top floor of the six-story resort have balconies – and you have to be a Royal Beach Club member to use one of those rooms. Still, guests are treated to elegance at every turn, including use of Caesar Park's golf course for US$78 a day. Many tours, even scuba instruction and certification, are available at the Westin Regina. Rack rates start at US$165 per room.

Club Mediterranée (☎ 885-2900, fax 885-2290, in the USA ☎ 305-716-9280, Blvd Kukulcán Km 21) is the oldest of the resorts on Isla Cancún and has a feel that's unique to the area. For one thing, not one of the 429 guest rooms is in a structure more than three stories tall. Another reason is that no one under 18 years old is allowed. The architecture is Mexican, and most of the guests' quarters have balconies facing the sea. All of the guest rooms were renovated in 1999, so despite their age, they look new. Rates start around US$200 a person. Superb snorkeling is within wading distance of the club (see the

Snorkeling section earlier this chapter), and the staff offers daytime group activities, which typically include aerobics, tennis lessons, kayaking lessons, windsurfing lessons, volleyball, a water-ski show and 'splash parties' in the pool. Dancing and other options, such as buffet dinner, group dance lessons, karaoke at the main bar and tequila shooters at the beach, rule the night. A variety of excursions is available as well. Nonguests can purchase a day pass (good from 10 am to 5:30 pm daily) to Club Med for US$30; a night pass (good from 6:30 pm until the dance club closes at 2:30 am) costs another US$30.

PLACES TO EAT
Cancún exists to cater to globetrotters. So all of the restaurants on the resort island are predictably upscale and pricey, right? Wrong. In fact, in and between every shopping mall along Blvd Kukulcán you'll find a wide variety of inexpensive and moderately priced restaurants.

So, while it is possible to enjoy fine cuisine in Cancún as well as fun food at lively places such as the Hard Rock Café and Pat O'Brien's – as you'd expect – tasty local food that's soft on the pocketbook is also available. If you've just got to scarf down a Big Mac or Whopper, you'll be glad to know there's no shortage of McDonald's and Burger Kings on the island.

Budget
Inside Plaza Flamingo, Blvd Kukulcán Km 11, is arguably the island's top budget restaurant, *Checándole*, which specializes in Yucatecan food. Popular items here include *tampiqueña*, which is a thin, plate-covering marinated beef steak, served with guacamole and beans; *checánpollo*, chicken breast smothered in onion, chili and melted cheese; *costilla queso*, a taco made with beef sliced off the rib; and *milaneza de res o pollo*, breaded beef or chicken, served with a salad, mashed potatoes and guacamole. No items at Checándole cost more than US$5. It's open noon to 10 pm Monday to Saturday, 1 to 9:30 pm Sunday.

At the west end of Plaza Kukulcán, Blvd Kukulcán Km 13, on the 2nd floor, there are

two inexpensive Yucatecan restaurants to keep in mind. *Las Fajitas* serves a variety of combination plates such as tampiqueña, which they serve enchilada-style with rice, beans and a soft drink for US$6.20. *El Chimichurri* specializes in grilled meats prepared Mexican style; most dishes feature top sirloin yet cost under US$7 with side dishes.

Facing Blvd Kukulcán near Km 8.5 and comprising part of the Plaza Terramar is *La Ruina*, which specializes in undeniably unhealthy and delicious Mexican traditions. If you've been really good and feel like being really bad, consider ordering a burrito here. They come stuffed with chunks of chicken or beef, fresh guacamole, black beans and salsa, and added last and glopped over everything is a heated white cheese that brings out the trucker in you. Burritos are best when consumed with one of La Ruina's potent margaritas. It's open late, with live music on occasion.

The *Restaurant Río Nizuc*, located at the end of a short, nameless road near Blvd Kukulcán Km 22, is a very simple place that's got 'mellow' written all over it. In fact, despite its name it's more of a glorified taco stand than a restaurant. Popular items include five different ceviches (fish, conch, octopus, shrimp and mixed), several shrimp dishes and lobster. Nothing's priced over US$7 except the lobster, but this is not the place to order it. Here, patrons settle into a chair under a palapa and watch caravans of snorkelers in sporty little boats or Wave Runners pass by en route to a nearby reef. This is a great place to chat, sip drinks and relax. Life's a breeze at the Río Nizuc. It's open 11 am to 6 pm daily.

Mid-Range

One of the island's most popular bars/restaurants/discos is *Pat O'Brien's*, at the north end of Plaza Flamingo, Blvd Kukulcán Km 11. This place is synonymous with fun when the sun goes down and hard-bodied types circle the copper-plated tables. This is the kind of place where cute barmaids pour blue liquor down customers' throats and bardudes carry drinks on their heads. There are lots of munchies here, including burgers

(US$7.50), nachos (US$6.50), sandwiches (US$8) and filet mignon (US$17.50). Thirsty? How 'bout a Big Hurricane – five gallons of Jamaican rum and fruit juices topped with an orange slice. It only costs US$170. The music is always rock 'n' roll.

Despite all the hype its celebrity owners gave it, the *Planet Hollywood* chain slipped into bankruptcy in 1999. However, some of its restaurants were expected to remain open, and the one at the south end of Plaza Flamingo was still alive at the start of 2000. Its walls are covered with Hollywood memorabilia, and TV monitors throughout show clips from popular films. The food's quite OK though American priced: burgers around US$6.50, sandwiches US$8 to US$9, pizzas US$8, grilled sirloin strip US$13.50, BBQ ribs US$13.50 and grilled ranch chicken US$9. Specialty drinks are large but pricey (US$7 and up).

Like Planet Hollywood only successful, the *Rainforest Café*, at The Forum mall, Blvd Kukulcán Km 9, 2nd floor, is a popular American chain. As its name suggests, the café is decked out in jungle fatigues – the walls are lined with fanciful faux rain forest scenes including a short waterfall, and amid the tables there are several beautiful and enormous aquariums. There's faux lightning, faux thunder and faux rain, and somehow it's all more amusing than tacky. The food's good though resort priced. Among the choices: a chicken sandwich, a Caesar salad, chicken pasta – all for around US$8.

Also at The Forum mall, the *Hard Rock Café* is a big hit despite the fact that its prices are a bit outrageous: a cheeseburger with bacon and BBQ sauce for US$9.50, a pork sandwich for US$10, even some of the salads are around US$10. If you order a margarita here, be sure to specify that you want it with or without the souvenir glass. If it arrives in the souvenir glass, expect another weighty charge on your bill. For the same kind of upscale American fast food with some Mexican options but at lower cost, try *Señor Frog's (Blvd Kukulcán Km 9.8)*, or *Carlos 'n Charlie's (Blvd Kukulcán Km 5.25)*.

Inside the Plaza Flamingo and also at the Plaza Mayafair (Blvd Kukulcán Km 8.5)

you'll find a **Sanborns Café**, which is a popular, clean and air-con Mexican restaurant chain with reasonably priced soups (all under US$2.50), fruit plates and salads (US$3.50 to US$4.50) and Mexican entrées and burgers (US$3.50 to US$5). It's open 24 hours.

The **Restaurant 100% Natural**, on the north side of Plaza Terramar (Blvd Kukulcán Km 8.65), is one of a chain of 24-hour restaurants specializing in healthy food, including low-fat sandwiches, burgers and pasta dishes, numerous chicken and fish dishes, and a wide selection of yogurt/fruit/vegetable combinations. Few items cost over US$9.

For a little athletics with your food try **Yuppie's Sports Café**, which is opposite The Forum mall and 100m to the west. Here, you'll find the usual American sports-bar food: burgers, onion rings, nachos, etc. Most items cost under US$8. The English-pub decor is enlivened by dozens of blaring TVs, all switched to one sports program or another.

Pizza fans will want to make a note of **Escape** (Blvd Kukulcán Km 15.4). Open 24 hours, Escape offers small two-item pizzas for US$5.50 and large four-cheese pizzas for US$9.50. Other items include pasta dishes from US$4 to US$7 and seafood entrées (most expensive) from US$9 to US$20.

Top End

Open noon to 11:30 pm daily, the **Crab House** (Blvd Kukulcán Km 14.8) is a draw as much for its lovely view of the lagoon from its second-story location as for its seafood. The long menu at the new-in-'99 restaurant includes a hearty selection of appetizers (most in the US$6-to-US$10 range), five seafood pasta choices (all US$12.50), a variety of seafood specials (from US$11.50 to US$22.50), and many shrimp and filet of fish dishes (around US$15). And, of course, there's crab – lots of it – priced by the pound. If you're coming for the crab, expect to pay between US$20 and US$30 for your meal, drink excluded.

Twenty-five meters north of the Crab House is **La Dolce Vita**, one of Cancún's two fancy Italian restaurants; the other is **Il Paparazzi** (Blvd Kukulcán Km 18). Both establishments enjoy healthy reputations, and patrons can expect to pay around US$20 for a meal with beverage at either. La Dolce Vita has been a local favorite since it opened in the mid-1990s. Il Paparazzi came along in 1999. The Sweet Life faces the lagoon and has a pleasant view, while the Paparazzi overlooks Playa Delfines and offers a gorgeous view.

For beef steaks, there are two names to remember in Cancún: **Ruth's Chris Steak House**, at Plaza Kukulcán, Blvd Kukulcán Km 13, and **Outback Steakhouse**, which is inside Plaza Flamingo, Blvd Kukulcán Km 11. Which of the two chains serves the better cuts of meat is a no-brainer. Ruth's Chris is known internationally for its never-frozen, always US corn-fed beef. It's an upscale restaurant with upscale prices (none of the meat dishes costs under US$20, and most are substantially more). Outback Steakhouse is known as a fun Aussie-themed restaurant, and prices are considerably less, though still expensive.

ENTERTAINMENT

Most of Cancún's nightlife is loud and booze oriented, as befits a supercharged beach resort that predominantly caters to people in their 20s and 30s. If the boisterous and often outrageous scenes at the various theme restaurants, bars and dance halls don't appeal to you, consider taking a dinner cruise (see Boat Excursions, earlier this chapter).

Folkloric Ballet

An excellent alternative to the party scene is an evening with the **Folkloric Ballet of Cancún** (☎ 881-0400 ext 193, fax 881-04020, inside the Centro de Convenciones, Blvd Kukulcán Km 8.8. The show is first-rate, featuring music by talented mariachis. Performances include the 'fire dance,' a ritualized dance with ancient-Mayan ceremonial themes, and folkloric dances from various Mexican regions. Some of the music and dances are absolutely exhilarating, while others are profoundly soothing. A testament to the quality of the performances is the fact that, on most nights, most of the audience is Mexican. The Folkloric Ballet performs

nightly at 8 pm; arrive no later than 7:15 pm for good seats. Preceding the show is a welcome cocktail and/or buffet dinner. Cost is US$28 for show and drink only, US$46 for buffet dinner, drink and show (the food is delicious, and second and – oink, oink – third helpings are permitted).

Dance Clubs & Bars

The dance clubs in Cancún are as wild as any you'll find anywhere except in Rio on a Carnaval night. Most charge US$10 admission and offer an entry-plus-all-you-can-drink special of US$20. Some don't open their doors before 10 pm, but none is hopping much before midnight; plan accordingly. The following is a partial list of the dance clubs, or discos ('DEES-cos'), that were pulsating the night away when this book went to press.

Dady'O, opposite The Forum mall, Blvd Kukulcán Km 9, is one of Cancún's three hottest dance clubs (hereafter, the 'Big Three'; the others immediately follow). The setting is a five-level black-walled faux cave stuffed with black-clothed tables semi-circling a two-level dance floor. Every song is pure disco beat that's never live, but that's just fine with this crowd. A zillion green laser beams, flashes of red and blue light and lots of strobe add to the palpable energy here. There's usually a US$10 cover, and bikini contests are regular events here.

Dady Rock, adjacent to Dady'O, is a steamy rock 'n' roll club where female patrons routinely take to dancing on the bar and scenes on the dance floor frequently deserve an NC-17 rating. The decor in this two-level joint facing the bandstand is, appropriately, industrial warehouse, and the bands never disappoint. If there's a 'Wet T-Shirt Contest Tonight' sign out front, be advised that these contests never start before 1 am. Admission usually costs US$10.

Like Dady'O, ***Coco Bongo***, in The Forum mall, is a dance club with a driving disco beat. Only here, the dance floor is located at the center of the club and ringed on all sides by bleachers. Beside the dance floor is a rectangular bar, upon which women are allowed to dance and usually do. Cameras are welcome and frequently used to capture the hot

action, but unless they're loaded with 1000 or 1600 ASA film, the captured images will be blurry. Cover is usually US$10.

Not as hot as the Big Three, ***Christine*** *(Blvd Kukulcán Km 8.85)* is still a happening place, featuring a synchronized light, sound and video system as well as English rock from the 1970s and '80s. Whereas Dady'O, Dady Rock and Coco Bongo draw a mostly twentysomething crowd, Christine attracts a fair number of thirtysomethings and even older people (including the author). Generally there's no cover before 10:30 pm and thereafter it's US$10. Live music is on Saturday only.

Carlos 'n Charlie's *(Blvd Kukulcán Km 5.25)* is a restaurant with a bar, not a dance club per se, but every night of the week you'll find people dancing up a storm to DJ-spun chart toppers. The bar is situated on the water, beside a marina, with most tables open-air and the bar under a broad palapa. A state-of-the-art sound system, a wide variety of exotic drinks and a low cover charge (usually US$2) help make this place super popular with people 20 to 40 years of age.

The aptly named ***La Boom*** *(Blvd Kukulcán Km 3.8)* is mostly a dance club featuring Top 40 tunes (few live bands) played at many decibels. The two-level London-themed club is most popular with folks under 30, who express their deep appreciation for the establishment by dancing around and sometimes upon a central S-shaped bar while watching themselves and the occasional paid performers on a cinema-size screen.

Situated on the lagoon side of Blvd Kukulcán at about Km 9.8 is ***Señor Frog's***, an undeniably hokey joint that's packed nightly even during the low season. The music's generally canned, but that doesn't seem to matter here; by midnight, the dance floor is always wall-to-wall with sweaty souls having a great time. It's usually US$2 at the door, more if there's a band.

Due to the usually fun atmosphere of ***Pat O'Brien's***, a bar-restaurant at the north end of Plaza Flamingo, Blvd Kukulcán Km 11, it's often hard to find a free table long before anyone starts dancing. There's live entertainment (variously rock or Top 40) most

nights, and there's rarely a cover charge. The establishment is open-sided with a waterfront patio (ergo, no air-con); if the heat's bothersome, you'll find the Big Three more to your liking.

Fat Tuesday, Blvd Kukulcán Km 6.2, an open-sided daiquiri bar and dance club, is packed on Tuesday nights, and during Spring Break and around the year-end holidays, but otherwise it's generally not the hip-to-hip scene found at the Big Three or even at Carlos 'n Charlie's. For excitement, head to one of those hedonistic zones or to Señor Frog's or Pat O'Brien's.

Most of the clubs and bar-restaurants mentioned here are geared for gringos. *Batachá*, next to the entrance of the Miramar Misión resort, Blvd Kukulcán Km 9.75, is an exception. This club features salsa bands that attract tourists and locals alike. There's rarely a cover; when there is, it's generally US$10 and it's used to pay the truly talented talent inside.

If you read about *La Ruina* in the Places to Eat section, you'll recall that this bar-restaurant is basically a good place to get tasty artery-clogging food. But starting around 11 pm most nights a rock band named Nexos sets up in the back and plays a mix of classic and contemporary rock – Zeppelin, Doors, Clapton, U2 – and they do a good job of it. If good rock 'n roll strikes a chord with you, stop by and ask if the band will be playing later. There's never a cover and, unfortunately for the band, rarely a crowd.

Unlike many of the restaurant-bar-clubs, which are clearly American takes on a Mexican theme, *Mr Papa's*, Plaza Caracol, Blvd Kukulcán Km 8.5, has a distinctly Mexican flavor to it. To be sure, whistle-blowing barmaids do come around and pour liquor down customers' throats for a couple bucks a shot. But *cerveza* is the primary drink at this open-sided restaurant-bar, and the music is performed by mariachis who play Mexican classics. There's never a cover charge.

There's one true reggae club in Cancún, and it's *Cat's*. Located on the south side of Plaza La Parilla, Blvd Kukulcán Km 8.75, this second-story club features a Jamaican

reggae band nightly except Monday and Wednesday in a venue that's heavily decorated in black and blue (wear white if you want to be seen). There's no cover charge from 9 pm till midnight, when a US$10 admission fee kicks in. Music never commences before midnight. A hip-hop band usually plays on nights the house band is off.

No soft rock here, señor. It's only hard rock live from about 11 pm till 1 am nightly at the *Hard Rock Café*, an ever-popular two-story restaurant and bar that's laid out in a semicircle facing a bandstand. There's rarely a cover charge or a drink minimum, and the bands are usually on par with the got-potential bands you'd find in Los Angeles and New York City.

Hog's Breath, above a Hooter's restaurant in the Party Center, Blvd Kukulcán Km 9, is an open-sided bar-restaurant featuring rock 'n roll bands nightly except Monday. The music's generally from the 1960s and '70s, there's rarely a cover charge and 2-for-1 beers are standard issue here. (The establishment next door, *Shampoo*, is a female strip club.)

Fifty meters south of Hog's Breath is the *Liquid Club*. This fully enclosed club boasts a formal dress code and milling doormen who intimidate prospective patrons. Around the corner is the *Baja Beach Club*, an open-sided affair that usually drives people away with excessively loud US inner-city music. Opposite the BBC is a *TGI Friday's*, one in a chain of generally popular meat racks, with candy-striped bar decor and piped music.

SHOPPING

Isla Cancún is a shopper's delight. There are lots of free-standing shops as well as ones nestled in small clusters and wedged between restaurants, bars and dance clubs. Moreover, there are also four very large shopping malls and several smaller ones. All are located along Blvd Kukulcán, and all are filled with boutiques selling items of varying quality and restaurants ranging from inexpensive food stands to very pricey steak houses.

The largest of the malls is Plaza Kukulcán, at Blvd Kukulcán Km 13, which in addition to many stores is home to a bowling

alley, a movie theater that shows first-run Hollywood films in English, a video arcade and a huge food court with lots of cheap and tasty meal options. You'll find the following stores here: one specializing in film, including some high-quality slide film (but for Fuji Velvia, see Shopping in the Ciudad Cancún section); one specializing in 'braid wrap' (think of Bo Derek's hairstyle in the movie *10*); another specializing in Harley-Davidson goods; a bookstore with many English- and Spanish-language books and magazines; and La Ruta de las Indias, a shop on the second floor featuring wooden models of Spanish galleons and replicas of conquistadors' weaponry and body armor.

The next-largest mall is the Plaza Flamingo, at Blvd Kukulcán Km 11, which includes numerous souvenir shops; a sporting-goods store; a convenience store with sunscreen, naughty postcards and some nonprescription medicines for belly aches; the very popular Pat O'Brien's restaurant; an Outback Steakhouse; and a slew of fast-food places, including McDonald's, Domino's Pizza and Dunkin' Donuts. Also here is a Checándole, a fast-food joint where the food is Yucatecan and very, very tasty; if you're hungry, feel like trying some authentic local food and are in the area, give this place a look-see. There's also a Sanborns Café, which is a popular Mexican chain restaurant that's open 24 hours; it's a good place to remember for those elegant moments after the nightclubs have all closed and you find yourself thinking, 'I'd better eat something and drink lots of water or I'm gonna feel like hell tomorrow.' See also the Places to Eat section, earlier this chapter, for restaurant details.

The Plaza La Isla shopping complex, at Blvd Kukulcán Km 12, opened in late 1999 and is the newest of the island's malls. Among the wide variety of dining choices available here are a Fashion Café, a Super Deli and a Modern Art Café. There's also a McDonald's, a Hooter's, a Häagen-Dazs ice-cream parlor, a kids' play area and scores of shops.

The three malls mentioned above are located within walking distance of each other.

The fourth major mall, the Plaza Caracol, at Blvd Kukulcán Km 8.5, is a good distance away but shoppers won't want to miss it. This three-story mall features lots of boutiques with recognizable names such as Fila and Nautica. Also found here are many shops selling quality Mexican handicrafts, the usual mall fixtures, including a McDonald's, and plenty of shops offering T-shirts, swimsuits and silver (and imitation silver) jewelry.

At Punta Cancún near Blvd Kukulcán Km 9, on the south side of the Convention Center, there's also Plaza La Fiesta, which is one huge store filled with leather goods, jewelry, bottles of tequila, sundresses, T-shirts, handicrafts, etc.

The Forum mall, Blvd Kukulcán Km 9, south of the Convention Center, contains souvenir and jewelry shops, but it's known mostly for its restaurants (a Rainforest Café and a Hard Rock Café among them) and live entertainment (at the Hard Rock and Coco Bongo nightly and behind the Zanduga Grill most afternoons).

Biker dudes and dudettes will want to check out Mordo Boots & Leather, a stone's throw from Plaza La Fiesta. At Mordo, you'll find leather motorcycle jackets with Mexican accents, such as designs of bulls and snakes stitched on the back. All prices are subject to negotiation, with very deep discounts available to smooth talkers. This store, as well as all of the mall shops, keep long hours and are open daily.

GETTING THERE & AWAY
Air
Cancún's international airport, Aeropuerto Internacional de Cancún, is also its domestic airport, which means you won't have to leave the airport if you're merely passing through Cancún (en route, for example, from your country to Cozumel). For information on international air travel to and from Cancún, see the Getting There & Away chapter.

Domestically, the major carriers are Aerocaribe and Aero Cozumel, both of which are owned by Mexicana. From Cancún, between the two carriers there is one flight daily to: Campeche (US$85), Ciudad del Carmen (US$85), Mexico City (US$130), Oaxaca

(US$115), Tuxtla Gutiérrez (US$115) and Veracruz (US$145). The airlines have a total of two flights daily to Chetumal (US$70), Chichén Itzá (US$50) and Palenque (US$115), three flights daily to Villahermosa (US$115) and four flights daily to Mérida (US$70). These are one-way prices.

In addition, together Aerocaribe and Aero Cozumel also provide 15 flights daily from Cancún to Cozumel (US$50 one way) and service to: Belize City (one flight daily, US$115); Flores, Guatemala (one flight daily except Thursday and Saturday, US$115); and Havana, Cuba (two flights daily, US$115). US citizens traveling to Cuba should ask authorities there to not stamp their passports, lest they want to incur a fine upon their return to the USA.

Aviacsa, a regional carrier based in Tuxtla Gutiérrez, has flights from Cancún to Mérida, Mexico City, Oaxaca, Tapachula, Tuxtla Gutiérrez, Villahermosa and points in Guatemala. Aviateca, Guatemala's national airline, runs flights from Cancún to Flores and onward to Guatemala City several times a week. Several major international carriers also offer domestic flights from Cancún.

In general, if you intend to fly from Cancún to other parts of Mexico, you are well advised to reserve your airline seat ahead of time to avoid any unpleasant surprises. If you decide to do this, you might wish to contact a travel agent or book your reservation through an airline's website (all of the websites mentioned in the following list offer convenient online reservation services).

Aerocaribe/Aero Cozumel (☎ 884-2000, ☎ 886-0162 at the airport, www.aerocaribe.com), Av Cobá No 5, Plaza América, Ciudad Cancún

Aeroméxico (☎ 884-1097, ☎ 886-0003 at the airport, www.aeromexico.com), Av Cobá No 80, between Avs Tulum and Bonampak, Ciudad Cancún

American Airlines (☎ 884-1057, ☎ 886-0055 at the airport, www.aa.com), Av Yaxchilán at Calle Jazmines, Ciudad Cancún

Aviacsa (☎ 887-4211, fax 884-6599, www.aviacsa .com), Av Cobá No 37, Plaza América, Ciudad Cancún

Aviateca (☎ 884-3938, fax 884-3328, www.grupotaca .com), Av Cobá No 37, Plaza América, Ciudad Cancún

Continental (☎ 886-0006, fax 886-0007, www.continental.com), Av Yaxchilán at Calle Jazmines, Ciudad Cancún

LACSA (☎ 887-3101, ☎ 887-4101 at the airport, www.grupotaca.com), Av Cobá No 5, Plaza América, Ciudad Cancún

Mexicana (☎ 887-4444, ☎ 883-4881 at the Centro de Convenciones, www.mexicana.com), Av Cobá No 39, Ciudad Cancún

Northwest (☎ 886-0046, 886-0044, www.nwa.com)

Cancún airport
The general information number at the airport is ☎ 886-0049.

Bus

There is no bus station linking Isla Cancún with other major cities on the Yucatán Peninsula. Rather, the nearest bus station is located in Ciudad Cancún. That bus station and Isla Cancún are connected by frequent buses. To get from the bus station in Ciudad Cancún to the Hotel Zone, simply step outside the terminal and catch any bus on Av Tulum that has 'Zona Hotelera' scrawled across its windshield. To get to the bus station from the Hotel Zone, simply catch any bus with 'Av Tulum' on its windshield, and hop out when the bus nears Av Uxmal (the bus station is located at the intersection, but the bus won't pull into the terminal).

For information on the major routes served by the bus station, see the Getting There & Away section for Ciudad Cancún, later in this chapter.

Ferry

There are frequent ferries from Isla Cancún to Isla Mujeres. See the Getting There & Away section of Isla Mujeres, later in this chapter, for detailed information.

GETTING AROUND
To/From the Airport

Orange-and-beige airport vans (Transporte Terrestre, US$7.50) monopolize the trade, charging taxi fare for a van ride with other travelers. If you want taxi service (that is, if you want the van or car to yourself, direct to your hotel), the cost is an outrageous US$41 (just a bit less than airfare to Cozumel).

The van route is invariably via Punta Nizuc and north up Isla Cancún along Blvd Kukulcán, passing all of the luxury beachfront hotels before reaching the youth hostel and Ciudad Cancún. If your hotel is in Ciudad Cancún, the ride may take as long as 45 minutes.

If you walk out of the airport and follow the access road, you can often flag down a taxi that will take you for less, as the driver is no longer subject to the expensive regulated airport fares. Or, if you're willing to walk the 2km to the highway, you can flag down a passing bus, which is very cheap (US$0.45).

To return to the airport you must take a taxi (from Punta Cancún it costs US$12), or hop off a southbound bus at the airport junction and walk the 2km to the terminal.

Bus

To get to the Zona Hotelera from Ciudad Cancún, catch a Ruta 1 'Hoteles-Downtown' or 'Zona Hotelera' local bus heading southward along Av Tulum. The fare is a flat US$0.45.

To reach Puerto Juárez to the north, and the Isla Mujeres ferries that embark from there, take a Ruta 13 ('Pto Juárez' or 'Punta Sam') bus.

Car & Moped

Renting a car in Cancún is a snap. Alamo (☎ 883-0666), Avis (☎ 886-0147), Dollar (☎ 886-0179), Executive (☎ 846-1387), Hertz (☎ 886-0150) and Mónaco (☎ 886-0239) have counters at the airport. Bear in mind that you may receive better rates and have a better selection of vehicles if you make your reservation ahead of time. Most of these companies have toll-free local numbers worldwide; see the Getting Around chapter for more details.

Additionally, Executive Car Rental (☎ 885-0372, 885-0373, fax 884-2699, www .executive.com.mx), Blvd Kukulcán Km 15.5, occasionally has vehicles long after the airport offices have rented out all of theirs. The following are typical of their low-season daily rates with unlimited mileage: VW sedan (US$45), Nissan Tsuru (US$68), Jeep Tracker (US$75), Ford Escort (US$75), Ford

Windstar minivan (US$150), Ford Lobo pickup truck (US$150) and GM Malibu (US$150). Sorry, no Winnebagos.

Weekly rates are available. For further information about car rentals, see the Getting Around chapter.

Turimaz Rent a Car (☎ 841-3470), Blvd Kukulcán Km 8.25, rents dune buggies for US$50 an hour most of the year and US$65 an hour during high tourist season. Be advised there are no sand dunes in the area. Turimaz also rents Honda Elite scooters for US$10 an hour, 18-speed bikes for US$2 an hour and electric bikes for US$6 an hour (electric bikes have a top speed of 20km/h – whoa!).

Marina Punta del Este (☎ 883-1210), Blvd Kukulcán Km 10.3, rents Yamaha BWS 100cc scooters (mopeds) for US$10 an hour and US$50 for the day (9 am to 5 pm). Included in the cost are: gas, oil and use of helmet (police do fine cyclists who are not wearing a helmet). The scooters have a top speed of 60km/h, their transmission is automatic and maximum load is two riders.

No motorcycles were available for rent at the time this was digitally recorded, and mopeds must be returned by sunset (no overnight use) due to the propensity of past partiers to crash the vehicles after tipping back too many cervezas.

Taxi

Cancún's taxis do not have meters, so you must haggle over fares. Generally, the fare between Punta Cancún (where the Hyatt, Camino Real and Krystal hotels and the Centro de Convenciones are) and Ciudad Cancún starts at US$5. To Puerto Juárez from Punta Cancún you'll pay about US$13. Taxis can usually be found parked in designated taxi zones on Blvd Kukulcán at Km 4.8 and Km 13.

Ciudad Cancún

☎ 9 • pop 297,183

Tourists often comment that Ciudad Cancún is much more authentic than Isla Cancún. While it might seem more authentic, the city owes its existence entirely to developers

and tourism authorities, the same as the resort island. The city is in no way, shape or form the offspring of a fishing and/or farming community.

Before work began on Isla Cancún, there were only a few scattered homes where the city now stands. A town developed as construction started on Isla Cancún in the late 1960s, and its early residents were the workers who'd come from all parts of the peninsula to make money building the island resorts.

When the construction boom ended, many of the workers remained in town, and joining them were thousands of other people who'd arrived to investigate employment opportunities on Isla Cancún. Today, morning buses leaving Cuidad Cancún for the Zona Hotelera are packed with people heading off to work.

However, the city has become a tourist attraction in its own right. There are many restaurants in town, plenty of bars and music venues, numerous boutiques, a theater and a cinema, even a bullring (it's true, no bull). What's more, Ciudad Cancún offers area visitors a greater variety of budget accommodations than can be found on Isla Cancún, and only a brief bus ride separates the two.

Most people who stay in Ciudad Cancún do so to save money. But if you're one of those tourists who fly thousands of kilometers to Cancún only to complain that the planned resort is very commercial, you might want to hop on a bus to Cuidad Cancún. It's no more authentic than the Cancún of Wave Runners and beach bunnies, but it certainly seems like it is.

ORIENTATION

Most visitors to Ciudad Cancún arrive via Isla Cancún. One minute they are on Blvd Kukulcán, the next they find themselves on Av Cobá, which is what the thoroughfare Blvd Kukulcán becomes at Av Bonampak, on the eastern edge of town.

Most of the city's major streets cross Av Cobá, starting with Av Bonampak, which is home to Cancún's Plaza de Toros, or bullfighting ring. The next major street as you proceed west is Av Nader, on which you'll

find the Immigration Office (for visa extensions, work permits, etc). Two short blocks farther is Av Tulum, home to tourist-oriented businesses. The bus station serving both Cancúns is located at the intersection of Avs Tulum and Uxmal. The next (and last) major street crossing Av Cobá is Av Yaxchilán, which is also a tourist haven.

Most tourists who visit Ciudad Cancún hang out on Av Tulum or Av Yaxchilán. Av Tulum has more restaurants, shops and banks, and probably receives three times as many tourists as Av Yaxchilán. So if you're in town to shop, dine or exchange currency, you'll likely spend time on Av Tulum, the busiest section of which is bookended by monuments at Av Cobá and Av Uxmal. However, Av Yaxchilán also offers attractions and is a lot less touristy than Av Tulum.

INFORMATION
Tourist Offices

The Quintana Roo Tourism Office (☎ 884-8073), Av Tulum No 26, is in front of City Hall in an office beside the Banco Inverlat. It's open 9 am to 9 pm daily and is usually staffed with helpful, English-speaking people.

Immigration Offices

For visa and tourist-card extensions, visit the Insituto Nacional de Migracion (☎ 854-1404), Av Nader No 1, at Av Uxmal. The office handles extension requests from 9 am to noon, Monday to Friday. For further details, see the Visas & Documents section in the Facts for the Visitor chapter.

Money

There are several banks on Av Tulum between Avs Cobá and Uxmal, including a Bancomer and a Banamex. There's also a Bananorte on Av Yaxchilán at Av Sunyaxchén. The banks are open 9 am to 5:30 pm Monday to Friday, but they occasionally limit foreign exchange transactions to 10 am to noon. Regardless, for better exchange rates, use one of the currency-exchange booths on the east side of Av Tulum about 150m north of Av Cobá. They are open 8 am to 8 pm daily. ATMs are common in Ciudad Cancún.

QUINTANA ROO

CIUDAD CANCÚN

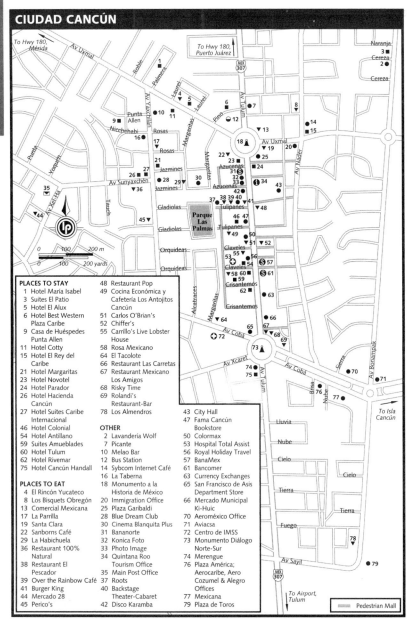

PLACES TO STAY
1 Hotel María Isabel
3 Suites El Patio
5 Hotel El Alux
6 Hotel Best Western Plaza Caribe
9 Casa de Huéspedes Punta Allen
11 Hotel Cotty
15 Hotel El Rey del Caribe
21 Hotel Margaritas
23 Hotel Novotel
24 Hotel Parador
26 Hotel Hacienda Cancún
27 Hotel Suites Caribe Internacional
46 Hotel Colonial
54 Hotel Antillano
59 Suites Amueblades
60 Hotel Tulum
62 Hotel Rivemar
75 Hotel Cancún Handall

PLACES TO EAT
4 El Rincón Yucateco
8 Los Bisquets Obregón
13 Comercial Mexicana
17 La Parrilla
19 Santa Clara
29 Sanborns Café
29 La Habichuela
36 Restaurant 100% Natural
38 Restaurant El Pescador
39 Over the Rainbow Café
41 Burger King
44 Mercado 28
45 Perico's

48 Restaurant Pop
49 Cocina Económica y Cafetería Los Antojitos Cancún
51 Carlos O'Brian's
52 Chiffer's
55 Carrillo's Live Lobster House
58 Rosa Mexicano
64 El Tacolote
66 Restaurant Las Carretas
67 Restaurant Mexicano Los Amigos
68 Risky Time
69 Rolandi's Restaurant-Bar
78 Los Almendros

OTHER
2 Lavandería Wolf
7 Picante
10 Melao Bar
12 Bus Station
14 Sybcom Internet Café
16 La Taberna
18 Monumento a la Historia de México
20 Immigration Office
25 Plaza Garibaldi
28 Blue Dream Club
30 Cinema Blanquita Plus
31 Bananorte
32 Konica Foto
33 Photo Image
34 Quintana Roo Tourism Office
35 Main Post Office
37 Roots
40 Backstage Theater-Cabaret
42 Disco Karamba

43 City Hall
47 Fama Cancún Bookstore
50 Colormax
53 Hospital Total Assist
56 Royal Holiday Travel
57 BanaMex
61 Bancomer
63 Currency Exchanges
65 San Francisco de Asis Department Store
66 Mercado Municipal Ki-Huic
70 Aeroméxico Office
71 Aviacsa
72 Centro de IMSS
73 Monumento Diálogo Norte-Sur
74 Merengue
76 Plaza América; Aerocaribe, Aero Cozumel & Alegro Offices
77 Mexicana
79 Plaza de Toros

Post

The main post office (Oficina de Correos, Cancún, Quintana Roo 77500) is at the west end of Av Sunyaxchén. Hours for buying stamps and picking up poste restante mail are 8 am to 7 pm Monday to Friday, 9 am to 1 pm Saturday and holidays, closed Sunday. For international money orders and registered mail, hours are 8 am to 6 pm Monday to Friday, 9 am to noon Saturday and holidays, closed Sunday.

Telephone

Telmex-owned 'Ladatel' pay phones can be found on street corners and in large public buildings in Ciudad Cancún. Ladatel calling cards can be purchased at any store that has a yellow-and-blue 'Ladatel' sign out front. From these phones and other pay phones found in Mexico's cities, it is possible to place collect calls. However, before placing a collect call, ask the operator for rates. They can be very outrageously high – in excess of US$10 per minute to some countries.

Fax

Most hotels will send faxes for you, especially if you insist that you have a document that must be faxed right away, and many businesses in town offer fax service; just look for 'Fax' signs in the windows of businesses along the main drags (Av Tulum, Av Cobá and Av Yaxchilán). Additionally, both of the Internet facilities listed below can send faxes.

Email & Internet Access

There are two public Internet facilities in Ciudad Cancún. The better of the two is La Taberna (☎ 887-7300), Av Yaxchilán No 23, which is a primarily a popular neighborhood bar with a couple of pool tables, a dart board and canned rock 'n' roll from the 1960s, '70s and '80s. However, in a room off the spacious tavern there are a half-dozen computers for public use managed by friendly English-speaking people. Rates are US$4 an hour. It's open 10 am to 5 am (yes, 5 am) daily.

Whereas La Taberna is a cozy place, the Sybcom Internet Café (☎ 885-0055), Av Náder No 42, is rather utilitarian and cold. Situated under bright fluorescent lighting in

a room that smacks of cheap office space are a handful of computers. Coffee and sodas are available. Rates are US$1 for 15 minutes or less, US$2 for 15 to 30 minutes, and US$3 for 30 to 60 minutes. Prices are roughly half as much if you show student identification. It's open 10 am to 10 pm daily.

Travel Agencies

There are numerous businesses in the area that call themselves travel agencies, but many seem more interested in selling time-share deals than helping visitors with their travel needs. If you want the service of a full-fledged travel agency that can book tours to area attractions in addition to handling domestic and international airline tickets, visit the centrally located Royal Holiday Travel (☎ 887-3400, fax 884-5892, royalh@telmex .com.mx), Av Tulum No 33. Royal Holiday has a professional, English-speaking staff that provides a wide range of assistance. It's open 9 am to 8 pm Monday to Friday, 9 am to 7 pm Saturday, closed Sunday.

If you only want to purchase an airline ticket or need to make changes to an existing one, you can do this by phone, at the airport, or, in some instances, you can visit an airline's downtown sales office and save yourself a trip to the airport. The following airlines have local sales offices in Ciudad Cancún: Aerocaribe and Aero Cozumel share an office and a telephone number (☎ 884-2000), Plaza América, Av Cobá between Calles Brisa and Nube; Alegro (☎ 884-3459), also in Plaza América; Aeroméxico (☎ 884-1097), Av Cobá No 80; Aviacsa (☎ 887-4211), Av Cobá No 37 (shared with Aviateca); and Mexicana (☎ 887-4444), Av Cobá No 39. For more detailed information, turn to the Getting There & Away section of Cancún, earlier in this chapter.

Bookstores

Fama Cancún Bookstore, Av Tulum No 105, at Calle Tulipanes, offers a fair number of books, most on Cancún, the Yucatán Peninsula and the ancient Mayan civilizations, and it has the largest variety of domestic and international magazines in Ciudad Cancún. This is also a good place to obtain road

atlases for Mexico. It's open 9 am to 6 pm Monday to Saturday, closed Sunday.

Laundry

While there are numerous laundries in the residential neighborhoods away from Av Tulum and Av Yaxchilán, there are none on these major streets. If your hotel doesn't offer laundry service (few of the city's hotels do), consider hauling your soiled and stinking clothes off to Lavandería Wolf (☎ 880-7723), Av Bonampak at Calle Cereza. There, laundry costs a very reasonable US$1.50 per kilogram for bulk service. To have a pair of trousers washed and ironed costs US$4, or $6.50 for dry cleaning. Generally, if you leave your clothes by 11 am, you can pick them up at 5 pm the same day. It's open 8 am to 6 pm Monday to Saturday, closed Sunday.

Medical Services

If you need a doctor and you're ambulatory, get yourself to the American Medical Care Center (☎ 883-1001, 883-0113 after-hours), beside Plaza Quetzal, Blvd Kukulcán Km 8, on Isla Cancún. From downtown, it's a 15-minute bus ride to the center. For further information on the center, see Medical Services under Cancún, earlier in this chapter.

If you don't want to leave town, your best options are the Hospital Total Assist (☎ 884-1092, 884-8116), Calle Claveles 22, next to the Hotel Antillano, just off Av Tulum, and the Centro de IMSS (Social Security Center, ☎ 884-2342), Av Cobá at Av Tulum. If you believe you're having heart trouble or are being afflicted by another medical emergency, call for an ambulance (☎ 883-1010, 883-1000) or take a taxi to the American Medical Care Center.

THINGS TO SEE & DO

Ciudad Cancún makes little effort to compete against the daytime activities and attractions available on Isla Cancún. There is a cinema, but even it is generally closed till sundown. Aside from watching the bullfights, daytime doings in Ciudad Cancún are limited to shopping, dining and people-watching, but downtown nights come alive with dancing, live performances and even

theater. For details, see the Entertainment and Shopping sections immediately following the Places to Stay and Places to Eat sections, below.

Bullfights

If you're just *dying* to watch a man in a body-hugging outfit and stockinged legs slowly stab a bull to death in a so-called sport where the outcome is virtually assured, you'll be glad to know there's a *Plaza de Toros* in Ciudad Cancún, where these acts of sadism take place on a weekly basis. Every Wednesday at 3:30 pm at the bullfighting ring, where Av Bonampak meets Av Sayil, you can fork over US$35 – yes US$35, not US$3.50 – to watch animal cruelty. If you can't think of a better use of your money, consider buying a hat to keep the debilitating tropical sun off your head.

PLACES TO STAY

Ciudad Cancún doesn't offer the kind of super-value accommodations you can find most anywhere else in Mexico, but given the city's proximity to world-class snorkel and dive sites, the hotel rates here are reasonable most of the year. Expect to pay more than the rates shown during the peak travel period of late December through March.

Places to Stay – Budget

The *Hotel El Alux* (☎ 884-6613, fax 884-0556, Av Uxmal No 21) is only a block from the bus station. The hotel's 35 air-con rooms with hot-water shower, telephone and TV go for US$22 to US$25 a single and US$26 to US$30 a double. An *alux*, if you didn't know, is the Mayan version of a leprechaun.

Across Av Uxmal on the south side is the 38-room *Hotel Cotty* (☎ 884-1319, fax 884-0550, Av Uxmal No 44), a motel-style place that's more or less quiet. Rooms with shower, air-con, cable TV and two double beds cost US$25/27/30 single/double/triple. Off-street parking is available.

A few steps farther west along Av Uxmal is Calle Palmera and the *Hotel María Isabel* (☎ 884-9015, Calle Palmera No 59), a clean, nine-room place in a quieter location. Rooms with private shower, air-con and cable TV

cost US$23/27 single/double. This is perhaps the best value close to the bus station.

From Av Uxmal, walk south along Av Yaxchilán and turn right after one block at Calle Punta Allen to find the quiet *Casa de Huéspedes Punta Allen* (☎ 884-0225, 884-1001, Calle Punta Allen No 8). This family-run guesthouse has several double rooms with bath and air-con for US$23 to US$27, light breakfast included.

The *Hotel Colonial* (☎/fax 884-1535, Calle Tulipanes No 22) has 50 rooms facing a court-yard and offers very good value at US$26 per room without air-con and US$31 with air-con. This hotel is a favorite with Mexico City-based businesspeople who frequent Cancún.

Another fine hotel is the *Suites El Patio* (☎ 884-3500, fax 884-3540, www.cancun-suites .com), on Av Bonampak, which features 13 charming rooms, ranging from US$27 to US$55, depending on size, air-con and other amenities. There's a communal refrigerator, a communal TV room and a restaurant on the premises, and a laundry across the street (see the Laundry section, above). The friendly owner speaks English, French and Spanish. Spanish language and Mexican cooking classes are offered here (see Courses in the Facts for the Visitor chapter for details).

Not nearly as nice as the Suites El Patio but a good place to keep in mind if hotel rooms are hard to come by is the *Hotel Rivemar* (☎ 884-1708, fax 884-1996, Av Tulum 49). All 36 rooms are located upstairs and have TV and telephone. Those with fan only are US$27 single or double and those with air-con US$30 single or double.

Just off Av Yaxchilán stands the *Hotel Hacienda Cancún* (☎ 884-3672, fax 884-1208, Av Sunyaxchén 39-40), on the north side. Its 25 rooms are popular with Mexican tour groups. For US$30 to US$38 (single or double) you get an air-con room with color TV and private bath and use of the hotel's swimming pool and patio. It's quite OK.

Offering air-con rooms with cable TV for US$38 most of the year is the *Hotel Cancún Handall* (☎ 884-1122, fax 884-1976), on Av Tulum 50m south of Av Cobá. There's no pool on the premises, and noise can be a problem at the Handall, with all rooms stemming from two wide hallways, but the hotel is perfectly comfortable and the rooms are cleaned daily.

The *Hotel Tulum* (☎ 884-1890), at the corner of Av Tulum and Calle Claveles, offers 22 rooms with two twin-size beds, air-con, cable TV, telephone and minibar for US$39 per room. This is a good deal for the price. (The appealing, nearby Suites Amuebladas is a condo complex.)

Not as centrally situated as the Hotel Tulum but a better value room for room is the *Hotel El Rey del Caribe* (☎ 884-2028, fax 884-9857, reycarib@cancun.rce.com.mx), at the corner of Avs Uxmal and Nader. All 23 guest rooms are air-con suites with fully equipped kitchenettes, and there's a pool, a Jacuzzi and private parking on the grounds. Room rates are US$39 single or double most of the year.

Places to Stay – Mid-Range

Directly across from the bus station is the *Hotel Best Western Plaza Caribe* (☎ 884-1377, fax 884-6352, in the USA ☎ 800-528-1234, www.bestwestern.com), on Calle Pino between Avs Tulum and Uxmal, offering 140 very comfortable air-con rooms and all the amenities for US$60 a double. A pool, a restaurant and two meeting rooms are on the premises.

Around the corner from the bus station is the *Hotel Novotel* (☎ 884-2999, fax 884-3162, Av Tulum No 75). Rooms in the main building have air-con and cost US$38 single or double; front rooms can be noisy. TV-less rooms in cabañas behind the main building around the pool have fans only, are quiet and cost US$27 to US$32.

Across Av Tulum from the Novotel is the *Hotel Parador* (☎ 884-1043, fax 884-9712, Av Tulum No 26), a modern building with 66 guest rooms, each with two double beds, air-con, satellite TV and telephone, and costing US$42 per room. There's a bar, a travel agency and a pool on the premises.

The very pleasant *Hotel Antillano* (☎ 884-1532, fax 884-1878), Calle Claveles just off Av Tulum, has 48 guest rooms with air-con and cable TV for US$45/52/58 single/double/triple. There's a pool as well.

Certainly the nicest place to stay along popular Av Yaxchilán is the **Hotel Margaritas** (☎ 884-9333, fax 884-1324, Av Yaxchilán No 22). This hotel features 100 guest rooms with air-con, cable TV and bathtub, plus a pool, a restaurant and a bar on the premises. The hotel is cheerful and a bargain at US$60 per room.

The **Hotel Suites Caribe Internacional** (☎ 884-3999, fax 884-1993, Av Sunyaxchén No 36) has 80 standard rooms with air-con and cable TV for US$70 and numerous junior suites with two beds, sofa, kitchenette and living room for US$85.

PLACES TO EAT

Isla Cancún put 'Cancún' on the map, but Ciudad Cancún offers globetrotters plenty to talk about. That's particularly true with regard to restaurants. There are plenty of restaurants serving tasty inexpensive food, and there are quite a few restaurants in town serving delicious meals at reasonable prices. There's no reason to suffer through bland cuisine or pay more than you ought to in Ciudad Cancún.

Budget

As usual, market eateries provide the biggest portions at the lowest prices. Ciudad Cancún's market, near the main post office, is a building set back from the street and emblazoned with the name Mercado Municipal Artículo 115 Constitucional. Called simply **Mercado 28** (that's 'mercado veintiocho') by the locals, it has shops selling fresh vegetables, fruits and prepared meals.

In the second courtyard in from the street are **Restaurant Margely**, **Cocina Familiar Económica Chulum**, **Cocina La Chaya** and others. These are pleasant, simple eateries with tables beneath awnings and industrious señoras cooking away behind the counters. Most are open for breakfast, lunch and dinner, and all offer *comidas corridas* (full meals) for as little as US$3, and sandwiches for less.

Nearly as cheap as the market eateries and probably freer of bacteria is the **Cocina Económica y Cafetería Los Antojitos Cancún**, Calle Tulipanes near Parque Las Palmas. This place presents a long list of fruit juices, lots of egg dishes, salads, nine kinds of tacos, five vegetable dishes – the whole nine yards, as Americans like to say – with most dishes under US$5. It's open for breakfast, lunch and dinner.

The **Over the Rainbow Café** (Calle Tulipanes No 30) is a charming air-con café specializing in crêpes for under US$3 (the *crepa nutella*, or chocolate crêpe, is divine). There's also a fine variety of sandwiches, salads and pastries (most items under US$4), and a good selection of coffee drinks. The canned music is generally jazz or opera. This is a very pleasant and civilized place to start your day. It's open early until very late.

If nothing about Over the Rainbow Café appeals to you, you'll probably like **Risky Time**, Av Cobá at Av Tulum. This is a small and usually smoky black-walled bar-restaurant that never closes. It specializes in cheeseburgers and other high-fat food. All the menu items here are cheap and delicious and, yes, artery clogging. There's a solitary pool table to help you work off your burger.

El Rincón Yucateco (Av Uxmal 24), across from the Hotel Cotty, serves excellent yet inexpensive Yucatecan food. Among the house specialties are: tampiqueña, which is marinated beefsteak, accompanied by enchiladas, tacos, beans, rice and lettuce (US$4); and *poc-chuc* (charbroiled pork), also served with side dishes (US$3.25). It's open 7 am to 10 pm.

Whereas the atmosphere at El Rincón is traditional Mexican (small and fan-cooled, nothing fancy), **Los Bisquets Obregón**, Av Nader near Av Uxmal, is a big, modern, air-con place that would be at home in an American city, only cheaper. Breakfasts (such as yogurt and fruit) and sandwiches typically cost US$4 or less, and many of the Mexican plates cost less than US$6. Los Bisquets Obregón is a bit out of the way but worth the trek. It's open 7 am to 1 am daily.

El Tacolote, on Av Cobá west of Av Tulum, is brightly lit and attractive, with dark wood benches, earth tones, lots of potted plants, and photos of revolutionaries and Old Mexico on the walls. Meals consist of a large offering of tacos, house specials, steaks

served Mexican style (thinly cut, overcooked and tasty), and a half-dozen seafood items. Most dishes cost under US$7. El Tacolote (the name is a pun on a combination of the words 'taco' and *'tecolote'*, owl) is open noon to 2 am daily.

Often overlooked but an excellent bargain is the *Restaurant Pop*, Av Tulum, three blocks south of Av Uxmal. There's outdoor seating as well as seating in an air-con dining room, and breakfast options such as granola with milk and banana (US$2) and a variety of egg dishes (most under US$3.50) are available after 8 am. A variety of salads, soups, pastas, fish, chicken and beef dishes are available for lunch and dinner. Few items cost over US$6. It's open until midnight daily.

The *Restaurant Mexicano Los Amigos* (*Av Tulum No 10*) is a fairly popular open-air restaurant that serves decent food at reasonable prices. Menu items include burgers (US$4), spaghetti (US$8), three burritos with ham and cheese (US$4.50), filet of grouper (US$8.50) and grilled squid (US$8). It's open late daily.

Next to Los Amigos and very similar is the *Restaurant Las Carretas*, which offers a combination plate of beef tips, chicken tacos, cheese fondue, beans and guacamole for US$9.50, and a combination of steak, chicken and fish filet for US$11.50. Most other items are considerably less expensive. It's open late.

Chiffer's, on the east side of Av Tulum, has welcome air-conditioning and specializes in red meat. You can spend as much as US$15 for a full, heavy meal with dessert and drink, but most people can keep their bill under US$9. It's open 7 am to 11 pm daily.

There's a *Sanborns Café* across the intersection from the bus depot. This is a popular, air-con chain featuring reasonably priced soups (all under US$2.50), fruit plates and salads (US$3.50 to US$4.50) and Mexican entrées and burgers (US$3.50 to US$5). It's open 24 hours.

If you're in Ciudad Cancún, it's hot as Hades and all you really want is ice cream, you're in luck. *Santa Clara*, Av Tulum at Av Uxmal, specializes in ice cream and other dairy products. With a few tables outside and a few in the air-con dining room, this is as good a place as any to take some weight off your feet and enjoy some tasty ice cream. It's open late daily.

Do-it-yourselfers will want to check out the *Comercial Mexicana*, at the corner of Avs Tulum and Uxmal. There are several supermarkets in the area, but this one has the freshest produce and the best selection of meats and cheeses. It's open 7 am to midnight daily.

Mid-Range

Most of the moderately priced restaurants are located in the city center. If you're willing to spend between US$12 and US$20 for dinner, you can eat very well in Ciudad Cancún.

The *Restaurant El Pescador* (*Calle Tulipanes No 28*), has been serving dependably good meals since the early days of the two Cancúns. The menu lists *sopa de lima* (chicken broth with lime and tortillas) and fish ceviche for starters, then charcoal-grilled fish, red snapper in garlic sauce and beef shish kebab. As its name suggests, El Pescador (the Fisherman) specializes in seafood, and most of the specialties will set you back US$14 or more. It's open for lunch and dinner. There's no air-con.

Rolandi's Restaurant-Bar (*Av Cobá No 12*), between Avs Tulum and Nader just off the southern roundabout, is an attractive Italian eatery open daily. It serves elaborate one-person pizzas (US$7 to US$11), spaghetti plates and more substantial dishes of veal and chicken. Watch out for the high drink prices. Its hours are 1 pm to midnight Monday to Saturday, 4 pm to midnight Sunday.

Los Almendros, Av Bonampak near Av Sayil, is the local incarnation of Yucatán's most famous restaurant. Started in Ticul in 1962, Los Almendros set out to serve country food for the bourgeoisie. The chefs at Los Almendros (the Almond Trees) claim to have created poc-chuc, a dish of succulent pork cooked with onion and served in a tomato sauce made tangy with bitter

oranges. If you're famished, try the *combinado yucateco*, which includes a sampling of poc-chuc, barbecued pork sausage, and turkey seasoned with pepper, cinnamon, garlic, bay leaves and Xcat-ic chili (a tasty chili found only in the Yucatán). A full meal costs around US$15 per person. It's open daily for lunch and dinner.

Restaurant 100% Natural, Av Sunyaxchén near Av Yaxchilán, is an airy café specializing in mostly healthy food. Although the menu lists several natural food items, such as fruit salads and juices, green salads and yogurt, it also includes hamburgers, enchiladas, and wine and beer at moderate prices. Most dishes cost less than US$9.

La Parrilla (Av Yaxchilán No 51) is an upscale traditional Mexican restaurant that's very popular with the city's wealthier residents (upscale in atmosphere, not in prices). The air is fan-cooled, large Spanish tiles cover the floor and pillars, an orange-brown paint coats the walls wrought iron abounds. Mariachis make their rounds here between the tables and waiters carry plates filled with grilled steak wrapped in cactus leaves (US$7.50), sautéed grouper in tomato sauce with olives and sweet pepper (US$7.50) and mole enchiladas (US$4.50). It's open noon to 4 am.

Though the name is oddly Spanish and Irish, the food at *Carlos O'Brian's*, on Av Tulum near Calle Claveles, is 100% Mexican and the atmosphere similar to a sports bar (the TV monitors here are abundant and usually set to a match of some sort). Menu items include beef fajitas (US$7.50), Mexican combination plates (US$7 to US$9), fish (US$7.50) and chicken (US$6 to US$8). It's open late.

Top End

Perico's (Av Yaxchilán No 71) is a huge thatched structure stuffed with stereotypical Mexican icons: saddles, enormous sombreros, baskets, bullwhips and so forth. An army of señors and señoritas dressed in Hollywood-Mexican costumes doesn't serve so much as they 'dramatize your dining experience.' If you're in the mood for dinner à la Disney, Perico's is the place for you. The menu is heavy with the macho fare most popular with group tourists: filet mignon, jumbo shrimp, lobster, barbecued spareribs. After semi-spontaneous outbursts of song and dance by the waitstaff, expect to fork over US$25 or more for food and drinks. It's open 1 pm to 2 am, but best visited after 7 pm, when the heat diminishes and the staff livens up.

A long-standing favorite is *Rosa Mexicano (Calle Claveles No 4)*, the place to go for unusual Mexican dishes in a pleasant hacienda decor. There are some concessions to Cancún, such as tortilla soup and filete tampiqueña, but also squid sautéed with three chilies, garlic and scallions, and shrimp in a *pipían* sauce (made of ground pumpkin seeds and spices). Dinner, served 5 to 11 pm daily, goes for US$10 to US$30 (for lobster).

Another dependable favorite (since 1977) is *La Habichuela (Calle Margaritas No 25)*, just off Parque Las Palmas in a residential neighborhood. The menu tends toward dishes easily comprehended and easily perceived as elegant: shish kebab flambé, lobster in champagne sauce, jumbo shrimp and beef tampiqueña. Dinner costs US$20 to US$25 per person. Service is excellent and the decor elegant. Hours are 1 pm to about 11 pm, every day of the year. La Habichuela means the String Bean.

If you love lobster, the place for it in Ciudad Cancún is *Carrillo's Live Lobster House (Calle Claveles No 35)*. The lobster dishes at this somewhat formal restaurant typically cost US$30. A combination plate of grilled lobster, grilled fish and filet mignon is US$40. There are also numerous shrimp and fish dishes for around US$10. The restaurant has air-con indoors and is fan-cooled outdoors, and entertainment is provided by mariachis. It's open 1 pm to 10:30 pm daily.

ENTERTAINMENT
Music

For wild disco scenes, Ciudad Cancún can't hold its own against the *other* Cancún. However, the city isn't without music venues.

For live music, *Roots*, on Av Tulipanes, features a jazz, reggae or rock band most nights

that it's open (Tuesday through Saturday). Even flamenco guitarists play here on occasion. There's rarely a cover and Roots is a full-menu restaurant as well as a club, serving pasta, salads, seafood and meat dishes, with few entrées over US$10.

Rockers will want to check out **Blue Dream Club**, on Av Yaxchilán at Av Sunyaxchén. The Blue Dream is a hole in the wall, but the best rock bands in southern Mexico frequently play the club. There's only a cover fee when a popular band plays. When the music isn't live it's typically US rock from the late 1960s and early '70s.

For live Cuban music, try **Melao Bar**, on Av Yaxchilán at Calle Punta Allen. This is an intimate, open-sided upstairs club that's easy to overlook, but some fine Cuban musicians play here on a regular basis, and the atmosphere can be magical. There's no cover, but be forewarned that the performers often don't take the stage until 11 pm or later.

Located next to the Hotel Cancún Handall on Av Tulum, **Merengue** features music by Cuban singers with buttery voices and fine backup bands. There are three shows nightly, at 9:30 and 11 pm and 1 am. This is a dressy, local affair (ie, few tourists). There's no cover, you just pay for drinks or you pay US$5 for buffet dinner and entertainment. A great deal, but don't come casually dressed.

If you're looking for a popular locals' bar whose owners have a healthy appreciation for American and British rock music of the 1960s, '70s and '80s, look no farther than **La Taberna** *(Av Yaxchilán No 23)*. It's where macho men (and a few macho women) smoke and talk for hours on end – the modern equivalent of the *cantina*, only nicer and with a couple of pool tables.

Gay Clubs

There's a fairly significant gay scene in Ciudad Cancún, but it's not apparent until well after sunset – when men can slip in and out of gay clubs with greater confidence that one of their coworkers won't witness it. There are no lesbian clubs in town, but lesbian couples can often be seen at the predominantly male clubs mentioned here.

¿Habla Mariachi?

Spanish-speaking mariachi fans might want to drop by the Jardín del Trovador, a small fenced-off sitting area beside La Taberna bar-restaurant on Av Yaxchilán in Ciudad Cancún. This is where the city's mariachis hang out when they're not wandering the streets. They don't perform here, instead they watch TV or chat it up. If you're interested in speaking with a mariachi and you speak Spanish, this is as good a place as any to say hello and get acquainted with one.

The most popular of the city's three predominantly gay clubs is the **Backstage Theater-Cabaret** *(☎ 887-9106, Calle Tulipanes No 30)*. New in 1999, Backstage is a lovely theater that features transvestite shows, strippers (male and female), fashion shows and musicals. This is a very cool place, with terrific ambiance fueled by a joyful crowd. Fun-loving straights as well as gays really have a good time here. Cost of admission is usually US$3. This cabaret is highly recommended.

The city's other gay-oriented clubs are the **Disco Karamba**, above the Ristorante

Casa Italiana, at the corner of Calle Azucenas and Av Tulum; and *Picante*, on Av Tulum 100m north of Av Uxmal. Disco Karamba is open 10 pm till the wee hours Tuesday through Sunday and is famous for its frequent drink specials. Picante isn't as hot as its name suggests, but rather it's the long-time neighborhood gay bar (it's mainly for talkers, not dancers).

Cinema

Opposite the Parque Las Palmas in the center of town is the *Cinema Blanquita Plus*, which usually shows first-run Hollywood movies in English with Spanish subtitles. The cinema is generally closed till sundown.

SHOPPING

Neither Isla Cancún or Ciudad Cancún fits the bill as a bargain-hunter's paradise, but if you've been hankering for a bullwhip or a machete – or other objects you possibly don't come across all that often back home – there's a chance you'll find what you're looking for at a price you could live with at either an Isla Cancún mall or a Ciudad Cancún boutique. For the lowdown on the island's huge air-con malls, see the Isla Cancún Shopping section. For Ciudad Cancún shop talk, read on.

The Mercado Municipal Ki-Huic, on Av Tulum near Av Cobá, consists of dozens of shops under one roof selling jewelry, handicrafts and a variety of clothing items with 'Cancún' boldly emblazoned on them. Discerning shoppers will also find cheap leather goods, straw hats, switchblade knives and faux Rolexes. It's open daily.

If you don't find what you're looking for at Ki-Huic, head north to the Plaza Garibaldi, at Avs Tulum and Uxmal. There are yet more crafts shops here, and because they entertain as many tourists as the larger market, there seems to be a bit more room to bargain down prices at Plaza Garibaldi.

Professional photographers and serious amateurs will be glad to know that it's possible to buy high-quality film in the Cancún area. For a wide assortment of Fuji film including Velvia, Provia and Reala, try Colormax, on Av Tulum just north of Calle Claveles. For yet more Fuji film and Kodak and Konica film, try Photo Image, on Av Tulipanes at Calle Azucenas, or Konica Foto, a couple doors down.

If you're in need of groceries and/or household items, the big San Francisco de Asis department store, at the corner of Avs Cobá and Tulum, will likely contain what you're looking for. If you don't find what you're looking for there, try the Comercial Mexicana, at the corner of Avs Uxmal and Tulum.

GETTING THERE & AWAY
Air

Both Ciudad Cancún and Isla Cancún are served by the Aeropuerto Internacional de Cancún. See Getting There & Away in the Cancún section, earlier this chapter, for airport and airline information.

Bus

The bus station, at the intersection of Avs Uxmal and Tulum, has two separate parts under the same roof; look in both. Companies include Autobuses de Oriente (ADO), Autotransportes de Oriente (Oriente), Transportes de Lujo Línea Dorada (Línea Dorada, a 2nd-class line despite its pompous name), Autotransportes del Sur (ATS), Autotransportes del Noroeste and Autobuses del Centro. Services are 2nd-class, 1st-class or any of several luxury flavors.

Across from the bus station entrance is the ticket office of Playa Express, which runs shuttle buses down the Caribbean coast to Tulum and Felipe Carrillo Puerto at least every 30 minutes all day, stopping at major towns and points of interest along the way.

Here are some major routes from Ciudad Cancún (daily):

Chetumal – 382km, six hours, US$10 to US$14; 12 buses

Chichén Itzá – 205km, two to 3½ hours, US$5 to US$9; 10 buses

Mérida – 320km, three to five hours, US$7 to US$12; buses at least every half hour; Super Expresso buses make the run in under three hours

Mexico City – 1772km, 20 hours, US$63; six buses

Playa del Carmen – 65km, 40 minutes, US$2.50; Playa Express buses every 30 minutes; others 12 times daily

Puerto Morelos – 36km, 40 minutes, US$2; Playa Express buses every 30 minutes; others 12 times daily

Ticul – 395km, four to six hours, US$13; five buses by Línea Dorada

Tizimín – 212km, three hours, US$5; six buses via Valladolid

Tulum – 132km, one hour, US$3.50 to US$5; Playa Express buses every 30 minutes; other buses about every two hours

Valladolid – 160km, 1$^{1}/_{2}$ to two hours, US$8; buses at least every half hour

Villahermosa – 915km, nine hours, US$38; three by ADO

Also available at the bus station are the following guided bus tours:

Chichén Itzá – air-con bus, buffet lunch, entrance fee included, departs 9 am, returns 5 pm; US$40

Tulum & Xel-ha – air-con bus, entrance fee included, two departures daily (9 and 10 am), buses return at 6 pm; US$38

Xcaret – air-con bus, entrance fee included, maps and information sheet, two departures daily (9 and 10 am), return at 6 pm; US$50

Ferry
There are frequent ferries that take both passengers and cars from Ciudad Cancún to Isla Mujeres. See the Getting There & Away section of Isla Mujeres, later in this chapter, for detailed information for the ferries from Punta Sam and Puerto Juárez.

GETTING AROUND
To/From the Airport
For details on getting to/from the Cancún airport, see Cancun's Getting Around section earlier in this chapter. Basically, you want to take one of the orange-and-beige shuttle vans into town. It will first pass through the Hotel Zone, providing you with a free tour (that's a positive way to look at it). The cost is US$7.50. If you're in a hurry, catch a taxi. The taxi will travel straight up the coast from the airport, saving you 20 minutes' travel time. The cost is US$10.

Bus
Although it is possible to walk most everywhere in Ciudad Cancún, to get to the Zona Hotelera from the city, catch a Ruta 1 'Hoteles-Downtown' local bus heading southward along Av Tulum. The cost is a bargain at US$0.45. To reach Puerto Juárez and the Isla Mujeres ferries, take a Ruta 13 ('Pto Juárez' or 'Punta Sam') bus. The cost is US$0.50. To get back to the city, take any bus with 'Downtown' appearing on the windshield.

Taxi
Ciudad Cancún's taxis do not have meters, so you must haggle over fares. Generally, the fare between Ciudad Cancún and Punta Cancún (where the Hyatt, Camino Real and Krystal hotels and the Centro de Convenciones are) is US$5 to US$8. To Puerto Juárez you'll pay about US$3.

North of Ciudad Cancún

Most of the land north and northwest of Ciudad Cancún up to the mouth of the Gulf of Mexico is entirely uninhabited. Indeed, not a single road connects the city to the mouth of the gulf, and only one road in all of Quintana Roo even reaches the Gulf Coast, the road connecting El Ideal to Chiquilá. Neither El Ideal nor Chiquilá, nor any of the other mainland communities in northern Quintana Roo, offer the tourist anything of particular interest.

That's not to say the land north of Ciudad Cancún is void of attractions. Rather, they all just happen to be on or around islands, namely, Isla Mujeres, Isla Contoy and Isla Holbox. Better still, each of these islands offers the visitor something different: Isla Mujeres is popular for its lovely beaches and its bustling tourist town; Isla Contoy is a bird sanctuary; and Isla Holbox is known for its sea shells, and it's often possible to see red flamingos strutting about the island.

Isla Contoy can be reached by private boat from Isla Mujeres (several tour companies

facilitate the trip), and inexpensive ferries service Islas Holbox and Mujeres. What's more, each of these islands can be made into a day trip from either Ciudad Cancún or Isla Cancún.

ISLA MUJERES
☎ 9 • pop 8322

Isla Mujeres (Island of Women) has a reputation as a backpacker's Cancún – a quieter island where many of the same amenities and attractions can be found but for a whole lot less money. Though that's less true today, Isla Mujeres continues to offer excellent value, a popular sunbathing beach, a beautiful marine park, and plenty of dive and snorkel sites.

However, the island's chief attribute is that it offers a relaxed social life in a tropical setting, with surrounding waters that are turquoise blue and bathtub warm. Unlike Cancún, there are no megaresorts here, and noise bombardment from inconsiderate motorists, partiers and shop owners is much less common. Fishing remains a big way of life here, just as it has been for years.

The principal beach is rather small, however, and the island as a whole is not all that

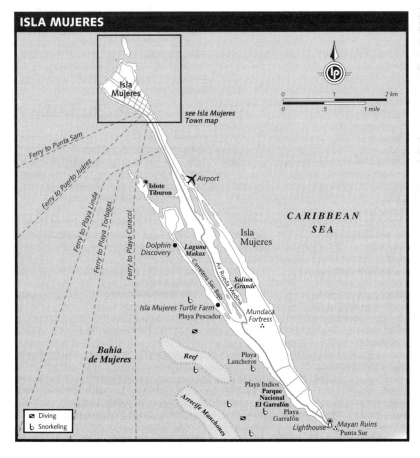

ISLA MUJERES

Isla Mujeres

see Isla Mujeres Town map

Ferry to Punta Sam
Ferry to Puerto Juárez
Ferry to Playa Linda
Ferry to Playa Tortugas
Ferry to Playa Caracol

Islote Tiburon

Airport

CARIBBEAN SEA

Isla Mujeres

Dolphin Discovery ● **Laguna Makax**

Salina Grande

Carretera Sac Balo

Av. Rueda Medina

Isla Mujeres Turtle Farm ●
Playa Pescador

Mundaca Fortress

Bahía de Mujeres

Reef

Playa Lancheros

Playa Indios
Parque Nacional El Garrafón

Playa Garrafón

Arrecife Manchones

Lighthouse △ Mayan Ruins
Punta Sur

0   1   2 km
0   .5   1 mile

◣ Diving
ᕃ Snorkeling

attractive by the high standards set by Cancún and the Riviera Maya (Tulum Corridor) farther south. Most of the island's palm trees were killed by a blight during the 1970s or knocked down by Hurricane Gilbert in 1988, and the undeveloped parts of the island consist of scrub bush. The ballyhooed snorkeling at Garrafón National Park is a bit overrated due to overcrowding, but it's still pretty remarkable.

To the dismay of many Isla Mujeres visitors, Cancún makes itself felt each morning as boatload after boatload of package tourists arrives for a day's excursion. Every year, ever more restaurants and nightclubs close and T-shirt shops and moped-rental agencies open, highlighting the shift from local tourism to that supplied in bulk from Cancún. Though changing, the island continues to retain much of its mellow, fishing-village character.

History
Although many locals believe Isla Mujeres got its name because Spanish buccaneers kept their lovers there while they plundered galleons and pillaged ports, a less romantic but still intriguing explanation is probably more accurate.

According to the writings of Friar Diego de Landa, during 1517 Francisco Hernández de Córdoba sailed from Cuba with three ships to procure slaves for the mines there. The expedition came upon Isla Mujeres and in the course of searching it the conquistadors located a stone temple containing clay figurines of Mayan goddesses. Córdoba named the island after the icons.

Today, all that remains of the ceremonial site are some very weather-worn ruins.

Orientation
The island is 8km long and from 300m to 800m wide. The town of Isla Mujeres is located at the northern tip of the island, and the ruins of the Mayan temple are at the southern tip. The two are linked by Av Rueda Medina, which is a loop road that hugs the coast of the island. Between the two tips there are a handful of small fishing villages, several saltwater lakes, the

---

Down Went the Cross

Isla Mujeres was founded on August 17, 1854, and every year the islanders mark that date with celebrations. In 1984, they went one step farther, erecting a 12m-tall concrete cross in the middle of Arrecife Manchones (Manchones Reef) to the south of the island. The bronze-painted one-ton cross rose out of the water and looked ever so Biblical for 11 years – until Hurricane Roxanne knocked it down in October 1995. Although you can still find photographs of it in brochures, the cross now lies on the bottom of the sea and is gradually being overtaken by coral.

---

remains of a pirate's home known as the Mundaca Fortress, a turtle hatchery, a string of west-facing beaches, a large lagoon and a small airport.

The best snorkel sites and some of the better swimming beaches are on the southern part of the island along the western shore; the eastern shore is washed by the open sea, and the surf there is dangerous. The ferry docks, the town and the most popular sand beach (Playa Norte) are at the northern tip of the island.

Information
Tourist Offices There is an island-sponsored Tourist Information office (☎ 877-0767, ☎/fax 877-0307, infoisla@qroo1.telmex .net.mex), on Av Rueda Medina between Calles Madero and Morelos. One member of its friendly staff speaks English, the rest Spanish only. Brochures, maps and information are available. It's open 8 am to 9 pm Monday to Friday, 9 am to 2 pm Saturday and Sunday.

For information, also contact the Café Internet (☎/fax 877-0461), on Calle Hidalgo near Calle Abasolo, whose English- and Spanish-speaking owner-manager knows the island as well as anyone and is receptive to inquiries from friendly visitors. It's open 10 am to 2 pm and 5 pm to 8 pm Monday to Friday, 10 am to 7 pm Saturday, 10 am to noon and 6 to 8 pm Sunday.

Money There are several banks on Isla Mujeres, all located within a couple of blocks of the ferry docks. Among them is Banco del Atlántico, Av Rueda Medina at Calle Morelos. All of the banks exchange currency and have ATMs. The banks are open 8:30 am to 5 pm Monday to Friday, 9 am to 2 pm Saturday.

Post The post office, on Calle Guerrero at Calle López Mateos, is open 8 am to 7 pm Monday to Friday, 9 am to 1 pm Saturday and Sunday.

Telephone Telmex pay phones are in abundant supply and operated least expensively by using a Ladatel debit card, available in all shops that post a blue-and-yellow sign out front with 'Ladatel' boldly stenciled across it.

Email & Internet Access There were several Net-access facilities on the island at the time this was penned, and there will likely be others by the time you read this. At the time of writing, all charged 1 peso per minute and had 15-minute (US$1.50) minimums. Given the proximity of the facilities, if you intend to spend a significant amount of time online you'd be wise to visit all and compare prices.

The Café Internet, on Calle Hidalgo near Calle Abasolo, offers image scanning and Spanish-English translation services in addition to Internet access and email services. As the name suggests, food and beverages are available. The owner-manager has been on the island a long time and has a wealth of information. It's open 10 am to 2 pm and 5 pm to 8 pm Monday to Friday, 10 am to 7 pm Saturday, 10 am to noon and 6 to 8 pm Sunday.

La Casita Bakery, on Calle Madero between Calles Hidalgo and Guerrero, is a great place to nibble on danishes while sending sorry-you're-home-working emails to friends – a delightful combination if ever there was one. It's open 7:30 am to 9:30 pm daily.

CompuIsla, on Calle Abasolo just south of Calle Juárez, provides Internet and email services from 8 am to 10 pm daily. Food and beverages were not available at the time of writing.

Bookstores There's a nifty bookstore on Isla Mujeres that's worth your while if you're hoping to do a little pleasure reading on the beach and forgot to pack reading material. The store is called Cosmic Cosas and it's located on Calle Matamoros No 82, just north of Calle Hidalgo. Cosmic Cosas primarily buys, sells and trades English-language books and magazines, but you'll find literature in a number of languages here.

Also on the premises are numerous new titles on ancient Mayan life, contemporary local cooking and the history of the region. The store has a comfortable living room and guests are welcome to 'just come and hang out,' so says its friendly owner-manager Geneviere Pritchard. If you've just arrived and have questions about Isla Mujeres, you'll find Geneviere enjoys offering tourist information. It's open 9 am to 2 pm and 4 to 9 pm daily.

Laundry There is no shortage of laundries on Isla Mujeres, all of which are located in town and will wash, dry and fold 4 kilos of clothes for US$3.50. All are open 7 am to 9 pm Monday to Friday, 9 am to 1 pm Saturday and Sunday.

The Lavandería Automática Tim Phó is located on Calle Juárez at Calle Abasolo. Lavandería Angel is located on Calle Matamoros between Calles Hidalgo and Guerrero. Lavandería JR is located on Calle Abasolo between Av Rueda Medina and Calle Juárez.

Playa Norte
Walk west along Calles Hidalgo or Guerrero to reach Playa Norte, sometimes called Playa Los Cocos or Cocoteros, the town's principal beach. The slope of the beach off shore is gradual, and the transparent and calm waters are only chest-high, even far from shore. However, the arcing beach – which runs the length of the northwest shore of the island – is relatively small for the number of sun seekers who flock to it.

Isla Mujeres Turtle Farm
Long before a human being first set eyes on Isla Mujeres, numerous species of sea turtle

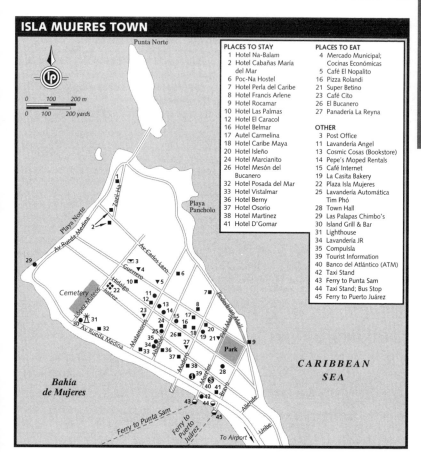

ISLA MUJERES TOWN

PLACES TO STAY
1 Hotel Na-Balam
2 Hotel Cabañas María del Mar
6 Poc-Na Hostel
7 Hotel Perla del Caribe
8 Hotel Francis Arlene
9 Hotel Rocamar
10 Hotel Las Palmas
12 Hotel El Caracol
16 Hotel Belmar
17 Autel Carmelina
18 Hotel Caribe Maya
20 Hotel Isleño
24 Hotel Marcianito
26 Hotel Mesón del Bucanero
32 Hotel Posada del Mar
33 Hotel Vistalmar
36 Hotel Berny
37 Hotel Osorio
38 Hotel Martinez
41 Hotel D'Gomar

PLACES TO EAT
4 Mercado Municipal; Cocinas Económicas
5 Café El Nopalito
16 Pizza Rolandi
21 Super Betino
23 Café Cito
26 El Bucanero
27 Panadería La Reyna

OTHER
3 Post Office
11 Lavandería Angel
13 Cosmic Cosas (Bookstore)
14 Pepe's Moped Rentals
15 Café Internet
19 La Casita Bakery
22 Plaza Isla Mujeres
25 Lavandería Automática Tim Phó
28 Town Hall
29 Las Palapas Chimbo's
30 Island Grill & Bar
31 Lighthouse
34 Lavandería JR
35 Compulsla
39 Tourist Information
40 Banco del Atlántico (ATM)
42 Taxi Stand
43 Ferry to Punta Sam
44 Taxi Stand; Bus Stop
45 Ferry to Puerto Juárez

were using its beaches as nesting grounds. Today, six species of sea turtle continue to lay eggs in the sand along the island's calm western shore, from Playa Garrafón to the mouth of Laguna Makax.

Turtle eggs and turtle meat are a delicacy throughout Latin America, and Isla Mujeres is no exception. Residents continue to kill pregnant mothers who emerge from the sea to nest, as much for their meat and valuable shells as for their cue ball-resembling eggs. In a battle to save the turtles, a local fisherman named Gonzalez Cahle Maldonado began a crusade to encourage other area fishers to

spare at least some of the turtle eggs they were removing from nests.

Maldonado's efforts during the 1980s led to the founding a dozen years ago of the Centro de Investigaciones, a group of marine biologists who created and now manage the Isla Mujeres Turtle Farm (☎ 877-0595), Carretera Sac Bajo Km 5, which receives it funding from private and governmental interests.

The Turtle Farm helps the species by protecting their breeding grounds and by rounding up eggs and placing them in incubators, out of harm's way. When the eggs hatch, the hatchlings are placed in three

large pools for up to a year, at which time they are free to head out to sea. Because most turtles in the wild die within their first few months, the practice of guarding them until they are a year old greatly increases their chances of survival.

Moreover, the turtles that leave this protected beach have the uncanny ability to remember to return to this exact beach a year later, which means that their offspring will also receive the special treatment they were given when they were terribly vulnerable to seagulls, frigate birds, sharks, dogs, raccoons and man.

The Turtle Farm is a scientific facility (every turtle that's released is tagged and monitored), not an amusement center, so it's not for every Isla Mujeres visitor. But if you'd like to see several hundred sea turtles, ranging in weight from a mere 150g to more than 300k, this is a place for you. Tours are available in Spanish and English, and admission costs a mere US$2. From town, the facility is best reached by taxi (US$2 more).

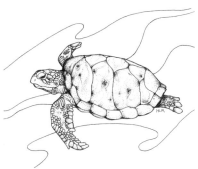

Mundaca Fortress

The story behind the ruins of this house and fort are more intriguing than what remains of them. A 19th-century slave trader and reputed pirate, Fermin Antonio Mundaca de Marechaja, fell in love with a local woman known only as La Trigueña (the Brunette). To win her, Mundaca built a two-story mansion complete with gardens and graceful archways, as well as a small fortress.

But as Mundaca built the house, La Trigueña married another islander. Broken-hearted, Mundaca died, and his house, fortress and garden fell into disrepair. Today, all that remain of the structures are a stone gate and some stone walls. If you look closely, you can still make out the name *La Trigueña* etched into the impressive stone archway.

Some documents indicate that Mundaca died during a visit to Mérida and was buried there. Others say he died on the island, and indeed there's a grave in the town cemetery that supposedly contains his remains. The grave is notable for the skull and crossbones chiseled into it and an inscription, in Spanish, that reads, 'As you are, I was. As I am, you will be.'

Despite the skull and crossbones, there's no evidence in history books that Mundaca was ever a pirate. Instead, they tell that Mundaca accumulated his wealth by transporting slaves from Africa to Cuba, where they were forced to work mines and sugarcane fields.

The Mundaca Fortress is east of the main road near Playa Lancheros, about 6km south of the town. A taxi ride from town will set you back about US$3.

Playa Lancheros

Five kilometers south of the town and 1.5km north of Garrafón is Playa Lancheros, the southernmost point served by local buses. The beach is less attractive than Playa Norte, at the northern end of the island, but it generally has free festivities on Sundays and you might want to go to enjoy the music.

Parque Nacional El Garrafón

Although the waters are translucent and the fish abundant, Garrafón National Park is perhaps a bit overrated. Hordes of day-trippers from Cancún fill the water during the middle of the day, so you are more often ogling fellow snorkelers than you are aquatic life. Furthermore, the reef has been heavily damaged by hurricanes and careless visitors, which makes it less likely to inflict cuts but also reduces its color and the intricacy of its formations. Average visibility is 10m.

The water can be very choppy, sweeping you into jagged areas. When the water is

running fast – not an unusual occurrence – snorkeling is a hassle and can even be dangerous. Those without strong swimming skills should be advised that although much of the marine park contains shallow reef, the bottom falls off steeply quite close to shore. If you are having trouble, you might not be noticed amid all those bobbing heads, so play it safe and don't venture too far.

Garrafón is open 8 am to 5 pm daily, and the earlier you get there, the more time you will have free of the milling mobs from Cancún. Admission to the park costs US$4. There are lockers for your valuables – recommended as a safeguard. You can rent snorkel equipment for the day for US$8. Garrafón also has a small aquarium and museum, but it's the thousands of colorful fish in the open water that make this park regionally famous.

A taxi to Garrafón costs US$4 from town. Or, you can take a bus to Playa Lancheros (see Getting Around) and walk from there.

Mayan Ruins

At the southern tip of the island, just past Garrafón, are the severely worn remains of a **temple to Ixchel**, Mayan goddess of the moon and fertility, and possibly lesser goddesses (clay idols of several women were found at the site when the crew of Francisco Hernández de Córdoba came upon them in 1517 while looking for slaves; whether the idols were all likenesses of Ixchel or represented several goddesses has not been determined).

The temple was fairly deteriorated when the conquistadors came across it, and it's been crumbling ever since. Hurricane Gilbert in 1988 nearly finished it off. Except for a still-distinguishable stairway and scattered remnants of the site's once-impressive stone structures, there's really little left to see other than a fine sea view and, in the distance, Cancún. The clay female figurines were pilfered long ago, and so powerful was Gilbert that it washed several of the temple's walls into the Caribbean.

You can walk to the ruins, beyond the lighthouse at the south end of the island, from Garrafón. From downtown, a taxi ride would cost you US$4.

Snorkeling & Scuba Diving

Diving to see sunken ships and beautiful reefs in the crystalline waters of the Caribbean is a great way to make the most of your Isla Mujeres stay. All of the dive and snorkel sites mentioned here, as well as others that are continually being discovered, are served by tour operators based on the island. Some of the operators are mentioned below.

Within a short boat ride of the island are a handful of lovely reef dives, including Arrecife Barracuda, an excellent shallow dive 1km northeast of Isla Mujeres that features a plethora of barracuda, grunts, snappers and sponges; La Bandera, a shallow dive in the Bahía de Mujeres that's famous for grunts and snappers; Arrecife Manchones (Manchones Reef), a shallow dive and snorkel site with awesome coral heads and a plethora of fish; Manchones Xico, a shallow dive and snorkel site south of Arrecife Manchones known for red-spotted hawkfish; and El Jigueo, a shallow dive and snorkel site southeast of Punta Sur that's locally famous for its spotfin butterflyfish and French angelfish.

In addition to the sleeping sharks (see the 'Sleeping Sharks Cave' boxed text), another popular non-reef dive is that of a cargo ship that rests in 30m of water 90 minutes by boat northeast of Isla Mujeres. Known as El Frío (the Deep Freeze) due to its depth and the unusually cool water found there, the dive site contains the intact hull of a 60m-long cargo ship that is thought to have been deliberately sunk, although no one seems to know much else about the ship. Among the fish that can usually be found at the wreck are sergeant majors, large jewfish and dog snapper.

At all of the reputable dive centers, divers will be asked to show their certification cards and will be expected to have their own personal gear, although any piece of scuba equipment you might need is generally available for rent.

Some of the better dive and snorkel trip prices found on Isla Mujeres are from Coral Scuba Dive Center (☎ 877-0763, fax 877-0371, coral@coralscubadivecenter.com,

www.coralscubadivecenter.com), Calle Matamoros at Av Rueda Medina. Coral Scuba offers two-tank reef dives starting at US$39; Sleeping Shark Cave and a shipwreck dive for US$59 each; and El Frío wreck dive for US$98 (advanced divers only). Night dives start at US$45 (one tank only).

Coral Scuba also offers a resort course with two shallow dives for people who aren't certified but would like to try scuba diving (US$65). Actual PADI open-water certification typically costs US$350. Snorkel trips are offered for US$14.

Delfin Diving (☎/fax 877-0374, cindi@ qroo1.telmex.net.mx) has dive shops at the Hotel Na-Balam and in the Plaza Isla Mujeres, which is located on Calle Lopéz Mateos between Calles Juárez and Hidalgo. Delfin offers reef dives (starting at US$39), Sleeping Sharks Cave (US$59), El Frío wreck dive (US$98, advanced divers only), and a resort course that includes two dives (US$65).

Sea Hawk Divers (☎/fax 877-0296), on Calle Zazil-Ha behind the Hotel Na-Balam, offers one-tank reef dives for US$40, two-tank reef dives for US$50 and a resort course that includes a shallow dive for US$75. Snorkel tours are also offered beginning at US$20.

Swimming with Dolphins

Dolphin Discovery (☎ 883-0779, 883-0780, www.dolphindiscovery.com), located beside the Carretera Sac Bajo, approaching the mouth of Laguna Makax, is a large sea enclosure that contains several dolphins so that tourists can swim with them. The cost? US$119 for a one-hour frolic with the dolphins during which you ride a pair of dolphins, and US$65 for a half-hour encounter in which you 'receive a kiss' from them and are allowed to pet and tread water with them. Despite the high prices, reservations are recommended.

There's no question about it: Frolicking with dolphins is fun, and it's fun to watch (spectators pay US$3 for the privilege). The dolphins seem happy enough with the arrangement, but it would be interesting to see if they'd return to the enclosure if a hole opened up in the barrier and they managed to escape. Swims are available daily, usually at 10 am, noon, 2 pm and 4 pm. Call for possible schedule changes.

Dolphin Discovery is best reached from town by taxi for about US$5.

Places to Stay

During the busy seasons (mid-December to March and Easter week), many island hotels are booked solid by midday; at these times prices can double. The prices shown here reflect those you can expect to find during the remaining eight months of the year.

Budget *Poc-Na Hostel (☎ 877-0090, fax 877-0059)*, on Calle Matamoros at Calle Carlos Lazo, is a privately run youth hostel with camping sites (US$2.50 per person). The fan-cooled dormitories take both men and women together. The charge for a bunk and bedding is US$4; you must put down a deposit on the bedding. The Poc-Na is a bit worn, but for the price it can't be beat, and lockers provided free of charge offer security for valuables.

Sleeping Sharks Cave

Five kilometers northeast of Isla Mujeres and between 15m to 25m underwater exists a large jumble of rocks and coral that is world famous for its sleeping sharks. Discovered several decades ago by a lobster fisherman and eventually featured in a Jacques Cousteau documentary, the Sleeping Sharks Cave dispelled the notion that sharks must always be swimming lest they stop breathing and die.

Until recently, any visitor to the rocks and overhangs could expect to find several or more nurse sharks lying in the sand, their eyes shut and apparently asleep. Some scientists prefer to believe that the sharks are in a state of hypnosis rather than sleep, but just what is it about the cave that so deeply relaxes them remains a mystery. Today, due to the number of divers who visit the cave, your chances of seeing a sleeping shark are less than one in three.

The **Hotel Marcianito** (☎ 877-0111), on Calle Abasolo between Calles Juárez and Hidalgo, offers excellent value with eight clean and fan-cooled rooms, each containing two beds and a hammock for US$14 per room.

The **Hotel Vistalmar** (☎ 877-0209, fax 877-0096), on Av Rueda Medina between Calles Matamoros and Abasolo, offers 30 very acceptable rooms for US$14/20 single/double with fan, US$18/24 with air-con.

Hotel Las Palmas (☎ 877-0416, Calle Guerrero No 20), across from the Mercado Municipal, offers basic but cheap and clean rooms with fan and bath for US$13 for one or two persons.

The friendly **Hotel Caribe Maya** (☎ 877-0684), on Calle Madero between Calles Guerrero and Hidalgo, charges US$17 a double with fan, US$21 with air-con. It's a bargain at these prices.

Hotel El Caracol (☎ 877-0150), on Calle Matamoros between Calles Hidalgo and Guerrero, offers 19 rooms with insect screens, ceiling fans and clean tiled bathrooms, and many have two double beds. You pay US$15/24 a double with fan/air-con.

Hotel Osorio (☎ 877-0294), on Calle Madero at Calle Juárez, is a basic place with fans only for US$18 a double. It may be closed in summer. If so and you like the rate, try the nearby and equally priced **Hotel Martinez**, on Calle Madero, which is basic and fairly worn but OK for the cost.

The **Autel Carmelina** (☎ 877-0006, Calle Guerrero No 4) also has mediocre-but-cheap rooms for US$15 single or double with fan and US$20 with air-con, but its management has been known to treat visitors disrespectfully.

Hotel Isleño (☎ 877-0302), on Calle Madero at Calle Guerrero, has rooms with ceiling fans, with shared bathroom for US$12 or with private bathroom for US$17 a double. Get a room on the upper floor if you can. The Isleño's manager can be quite unpleasant.

Hotel D'Gomar (☎ 877-0541), on Av Rueda Medina between Calles Morelos and Bravo, above a boutique and facing the ferry dock, has four floors of double-bedded, clean and air-con rooms that rent for a very appealing US$25 a double.

The **Hotel Berny** (☎ 877-0132, fax 877-0859), on Calle Abasolo between Av Rueda Medina and Calle Juárez, offers 36 rooms, nine with air-con for US$35/38 single/double and 27 with fan only for US$23/27. The rooms are not pridefully maintained. There's a pool.

Mid-Range Moderately priced rooms have private baths and usually (but not always) air-con, a balcony and/or a nice sea view with on-premises restaurant, bar and swimming pool.

Hotel Francis Arlene (☎/fax 877-0310), on Calle Guerrero between Calles Abasolo and Madero, offers comfortable rooms (many with balconies and sea views) for a very reasonable US$35/40 with fan/air-con.

Hotel Mesón del Bucanero (☎ 877-0126, fax 877-0210), on Calle Hidalgo between Calles Abasolo and Madero, is located above the restaurant of the same name. Its air-con rooms are charming and come with your choice of two double beds or one queen-size bed for a very reasonable US$36 for one person, US$41 for two.

Hotel Belmar (☎ 877-0430, fax 877-0429), on Calle Hidalgo between Calles Abasolo and Madero, is located above the Pizza Rolandi restaurant and is run by the same friendly family. All rooms are comfy, well kept and well priced and are a bargain at US$40 a double with air-con. There's also a suite with a Jacuzzi for US$85.

The **Hotel Rocamar** (☎ /fax 877-0101), at the eastern end of Calle Guerrero, was the town's first real hotel, built decades ago. The 24-room, one-suite hotel has been updated and charges US$40/50/60 single/double/triple for its rooms, most with fine sea views and balconies. There's a pool on the premises. Rooms come with fan only.

Top End The **Hotel Perla del Caribe** (☎ 877-0444, fax 877-0011, in the USA ☎ 800-258-6454), on Calle Madero a block north of Calle Guerrero, right on the eastern beach, has 91 very nice rooms on three floors, all with balconies and air-con, most

with wonderful sea views and good cross-ventilation, for US$67 to US$79 a double, depending on the view. There's a pool.

The *Hotel Posada del Mar* (☎ *877-0044, fax 877-0266, in the USA* ☎ *800-544-3005, www.mexhotels.com)*, on Av Rueda Medina between Calles López Mateos and Matamoros, is a lovely, newer place with 30 rooms in a three-story building (most with sea views) and 12 one-story bungalows ringing a swimming pool. All of the guest quarters have air-con. Rates typically run US$40 for a bungalow and US$50 for a room.

The *Hotel Cabañas María del Mar* (☎ *877-0179, fax 877-0213, in the USA* ☎ *800-223-5695)*, on both sides of Av Carlos Lazo near Playa Norte, offers 29 cabañas and 44 hotel rooms priced from US$50 to US$80 a double in low season, US$100 to US$120 in the winter season, light breakfast included. All rooms have air-con. The hotel offers many other services, such as a restaurant and swimming pool.

Hotel Na-Balam (☎ *877-0279, fax 877-0446, www.nabalam.com)*, on Calle Zazil-Ha, faces Playa Norte on the northern tip of the island. Most of the 31 spacious, air-con junior suites have fabulous sea views. There are numerous nice touches, such as bathroom vanities made of colorful travertine. Prices range from US$120 to US$170. There is a pool on the grounds as well. This is the finest hotel on the island.

Places to Eat

Beside the market, on Av Guerrero, are several *cocinas económicas* (economical kitchens) serving simple but tasty and filling meals at the best prices on the island. Breakfasts are rarely more than US$3, and for the other meals, there's a good variety of shrimp dishes and few items are more than US$4. Hours are usually (and approximately) 7 am to 6 pm.

If you're simply looking for a danish, an apple turnover or a sandwich, check out the very pleasant *La Casita Bakery*, on Calle Madero between Calles Guerrero and Hidalgo. Here, you can read your email while you nibble if you wish. It's open 7:30 am to 9:30 pm daily.

Super Betino, the food store on the plaza, has a little cafetería serving tacos and fruit plates for US$1 and change, and sometimes cheap breakfasts.

Panadería La Reyna, on Calle Madero at Calle Juárez, is *the* place for breakfast buns, picnic breads and snacks.

Most of the island's restaurants fall into the mid-range category. Depending on what you order, breakfast goes for US$3 to US$5, lunch or dinner for US$7 to US$12 per person, unless you order lobster.

Café Cito, a small place at the corner of Calles Juárez and Matamoros, has a New Age menu printed in English and German offering croissants, fruit, 10 varieties of crêpes and good coffee. Come for breakfast (8 am to 2 pm, about US$5), or supper (5:30 to 10:30 pm, about US$10); closed Thursday night.

Café El Nopalito, on Calle Guerrero near Calle Matamoros, serves delicious set breakfasts from 8 am to 1 pm and daily special plates for US$5 to US$7. It specializes in healthful but fancy food.

El Bucanero, on Calle Hidalgo between Calles Abasolo and Madero, is a fan-cooled restaurant with a pleasing ambiance and a wide variety of nonalcoholic tropical drinks such as watermelon, banana and papaya shakes, and jamaica, a semi-sweet drink made with boiled hibiscus flowers. Entrées, most priced around US$7, include Mexican-style beef tips, bell peppers stuffed with meat, cheese or tuna, and fish filet prepared as you wish. All entrées arrive with soup, beans, rice and coffee.

Pizza Rolandi, across the street from El Bucanero, serves pizzas and calzones cooked in a wood-fired oven and pastas with various sauces for US$6 to US$10 per person. The menu includes fresh salads, fish and some Italian specialties. Hours are 1 pm to midnight daily, except 6 pm to midnight on Sunday.

Entertainment

The nightlife on Isla Mujeres is fairly nonexistent Sunday through Thursday. Hardcore partiers would fare better – much better – in Cancún. In general, a quieter crowd is

attracted to Isla Mujeres and that becomes apparent at night.

If you're looking for a crowd, head to the beach – specifically the beach bar of the *Hotel Na-Balam*, which offers live music every Friday and Saturday night. Here, people tend to dance until they begin to perspire and then they stop. That's generally the case, although Na-Balam's bar scene does have its moments.

And then there's *Las Palapas Chimbo's*, located on Playa Norte, behind the cemetery. Every Friday and Saturday night a band converts the restaurant into a public jam session where the foreign youth on the island dance, sweat or no sweat. At the time of writing, it was definitely the place to be after dark on the weekend.

The *Island Grill & Bar*, beside the lighthouse on Av Rueda Medina at Calle López Mateos, occasionally hosts a rock 'n' roll band; it depends, as the owner says, 'if the guys show up.' Regardless, the Grill (there's actually no grill or food service whatsoever) is a fine place to have a drink and kick back. There's a 2-for-1 on national drinks and beer from 5 pm till midnight daily.

Getting There & Away

There are five main points of embarkation by ferry from the Cancún area to Isla Mujeres, which is 11km off the coast. Starting from the northernmost port, they are:

Punta Sam Car ferries, which also take passengers, depart from Punta Sam, about 5km north of the city center and 3.5km north of Puerto Juárez. The car ferry is more stable but less frequent and slower than the other ferries, taking no less than an hour to reach the island.

Ferries leave Punta Sam at 8 and 11 am and 2:45, 5:30 and 8:15 pm. Departures from Isla Mujeres are at 6:30 and 9:30 am and 12:45, 4:15 and 7:15 pm. Passengers pay US$1.50; a car costs US$11, a van US$13, and a bike or motorcycle US$4. If you're taking a car, be sure to get to the dock an hour or so before departure time. Put your car in line and buy your ticket early.

Puerto Juárez In Ciudad Cancún, take a Ruta 13 bus heading north on Av Tulum (US$0.45) or a taxi (US$4) to Puerto Juárez, about 3km north of the city center.

Transportes Marítimos Magaña operates boats every 30 minutes from 6:30 to 8:30 pm, for a fare of US$2.25 per person one way. It's a 20-minute ride to the island from Puerto Juárez using one of these boats.

The boats *Sultana del Mar*, *Blanca Beatriz* and others run about every hour from 7 am to 5:30 pm, taking 45 minutes to reach Isla Mujeres, for US$1 per person. Unless you're counting your pennies, these slower boats are a frustrating option.

Playa Linda Marine Terminal Four times daily, *The Shuttle* departs from Playa Linda on Isla Cancún for Isla Mujeres. Voyages are at 9 and 11:15 am and 4 and 7 pm from Playa Linda; return voyages depart Isla Mujeres at 10 am and 12:30, 5 and 8 pm. The shuttle takes 45 minutes. The roundtrip fare is US$14, but it includes free beer and soft drinks on board.

Show up at the Playa Linda Marine Terminal – Blvd Kukulcán Km 5 on Isla Cancún, just west of the bridge, between the Aquamarina Beach and Calinda Beach Cancún hotels – at least 20 minutes before departure so you'll have time to buy your ticket and get a good seat on the boat.

Playa Tortugas Dock The Isla Mujeres Shuttle departs Isla Cancún near Fat Tuesday on Playa Tortugas beach at 9:15 and 11:30 am and 1:45 and 3:45 pm, returning from Isla Mujeres at 10 am and 12:30, 2:30 and 5 pm, for US$10 per person each way.

Club Nautico Dock Sharing a parking lot with the Xcaret bus station, and located next to the Fiesta Americana Coral Beach, is this new-in-1999 dock. A water taxi whisks people to Isla Mujeres at 9 and 11 am and 1 and 3 pm, and back to Isla Cancún at 10 am, noon, 2 and 5 pm. The trip takes 35 minutes. It costs US$10 each way, or about four times what you'd pay if you took the Puerto Juárez ferry. As they say here: When in the tourist zone, expect to pay tourist prices.

QUINTANA ROO

Getting Around

Bus & Taxi By local (and infrequent) bus from the market or dock, you can get within 1.5km of Parque Nacional El Garrafón; the terminus is Playa Lancheros. The personnel at the Poc-Na Hostel can give you an idea of the bus' erratic schedule. Locals in league with taxi drivers may tell you the bus doesn't exist.

Regardless, unless you're pinching pennies, you'd be better off making the most of your limited time by taking a taxi (the most expensive one-way trip on the island is US$5). Or consider renting a vehicle; see below.

Taxi rates are set by the municipal government and are posted at the ferry dock, though the sign is frequently defaced by the taxi drivers.

If you elect to walk to Garrafón from town, take some water with you – it's a hot, two-hour, 6km walk.

Bicycle, Moped & Golf Cart Bicycles can be rented from a number of shops on the island, including Sport Bike, on the corner of Calles Juárez and Morelos, a block from the ferry docks. Before you rent, compare prices and the condition of the bikes in a few shops, then arrive early in the day to get one of the better bikes. Costs are generally about US$5 for four hours, only a bit more for a full day; you'll be asked to plunk down a deposit of US$10 or so.

Everybody and his/her grandmother is prepared to rent you a moped on Isla Mujeres. Shop around, compare prices and look for these things: new or newer machines in good condition, full gas tanks and reasonable deposits. Cost per hour is usually US$5 or US$6 with a two-hour minimum, US$25 all day, or even cheaper by the week. Shops away from the busiest streets tend to have better prices, but not necessarily better equipment. Pepe's Moped Rentals, on Calle Hidalgo between Calles Matamoros and Abasolo, offers mopeds for a very reasonable US$16 for the day.

When driving, remember that far more people are seriously injured on mopeds than in cars. Your enemies are inexperience, speed, sand, wet or oily roads and other people on mopeds. Don't forget to slather yourself with sunblock before you take off. Be sure to do your hands, feet, face and neck thoroughly.

Yet another popular option on this island with few cars is a motorized golf cart. Pepe's and a handful of other shops rent them. Pepe's competitive prices for golf-cart rentals are US$10 an hour, US$40 for a day and US$55 for a 24-hour period. Pepe's is open 8 am to 6 pm daily.

ISLA CONTOY

From Isla Mujeres it's possible to take an excursion by boat to tiny, uninhabited Isla Contoy, a national bird sanctuary 25km north of Isla Mujeres. It's a treasure trove for bird-watchers, with more than 100 species, particularly brown pelicans, olive cormorants, turkey birds, brown boobies and red-pouched frigates, as well as frequent visits by red flamingos, snowy egrets and white herons.

There is good snorkeling both en route to and just off Contoy, which sees about 1500 visitors a month. Be advised: Those visitors who arrive without mosquito repellent often wish they had. Although you're unlikely to swim in some of the enclosed brackish ponds that can be found on the densely foliaged island – foliage that includes two types of mangrove – you want to be aware of the boa constrictors and small crocodiles that live in them. Although neither critter would attack an adult, they might take interest in your baby. All things considered, teaching a toddler to swim in brackish water that snakes and crocs call home isn't a wise move.

Getting There & Away

Numerous tour operators on Isla Mujeres offer day trips to Isla Contoy, including Coral Scuba Dive Center (☎ 877-0763, fax 877-0371), on Calle Matamoros at Av Rueda Medina. The Coral Scuba's Isla Contoy trip (US$35) includes lunch and opportunities to snorkel and bird-watch.

Located at the dock that extends from the western end of Calle Madero are several boats that are owned and operated by

The diving off Quintana Roo is world-class.

Olmec head at Parque Chankanab, Cozumel.

The famous underwater wonders of Cozumel.

SCOTT DOGGETT

Day's end at the port in San Miguel de Cozumel.

RICHARD NEBESKY

Ruin remnant in Puerto Morelos.

SCOTT DOGGETT

Pet the dolphins at Parque Chankanab.

Captain Ricardo Gaitan, who makes daily trips to Isla Contoy for US$38 per person. Gaitan's tour includes a hearty lunch, free use of snorkeling gear, fishing en route, scientific information on the island, and your choice of purified water or soft drinks.

ISLA HOLBOX

Fed up with the tourist hordes of Cancún, Isla Mujeres and Cozumel? Want to find a beach site virtually devoid of gringos? If that's the case, Isla Holbox might appeal to you. But before you leave for the peninsula (it's not really an island, despite its name), note that there are only very basic hotels in the area and the beaches are not Cancún-perfect strips of clean, conditioned sand. To enjoy Isla Holbox, you must be willing to rough it.

The peninsula, which is 25km long and 3km wide, has seemingly endless beaches, as well as tranquil waters where you can wade out quite a distance before the sea reaches shoulder level. Moreover, Isla Holbox is a paradise for shell collectors, with a galaxy of shells of various shapes and colors. The peninsula's fishing families are friendly, and there are even red flamingos and the occasional roseate spoonbill.

As to drawbacks, the water is not the translucent turquoise so common to Quintana Roo beach sites, because here the Caribbean waters mingle with those of the darker Gulf of Mexico. Seaweed can create silty waters near shore at some parts of the beach. And, there is no shortage of mosquitoes during the rainy season (the entire western end of the peninsula isn't called Punta Mosquito for nothing!).

While there are big plans to develop Isla Holbox, at the time of this writing there were only three modest hotels in town – the *Hotel Flamingo*, the *Hotel Holbox* and the *Posada Amapola*. All were priced at US$15 a night. The few simple restaurants on Isla Holbox specialize in fish.

Getting There & Away

To reach Isla Holbox, take the ferry from the port village of Chiquilá. If you are going from Isla Mujeres or Cancún to Isla Holbox,

catch a direct bus from Puerto Juárez or Cancún to Chiquilá. There are also buses three times a day from Valladolid to Chiquilá (155km, two hours, US$6), and in theory the ferry is supposed to wait for them. However, it may not wait for a delayed bus or may even leave early should the captain feel so inclined.

It is therefore recommended that you reach Chiquilá as early as possible. The ferry is supposed to depart for the island at 8 am and 3 pm and make the trip in about an hour. Ferries return to Chiquilá at 2 and 5 pm. The cost is US$2.50.

Tulum Corridor

The Tulum Corridor is the 135km stretch of Hwy 307 that runs from Ciudad Cancún to the town of Tulum. It is flanked to the west by light forest and to the east by turnoffs to beachside communities, Mayan ruins and ecoparks. The corridor, which promoters often refer to as the Riviera Maya, is the fastest-growing area of southeast Mexico, with new hotels and restaurants opening every month.

The three top tourist destinations along the corridor are Tulum, which is famous for its seaside Mayan ruins; Playa del Carmen, which is connected to ever-popular Cozumel by ferry but which in recent years has overtaken the island resort as the corridor's chief party town; and Cozumel, which is world famous for its snorkeling and dive sites.

Secondary destinations include the private ecoparks of Xcaret, Xel-ha, Xpu-ha and Tres Ríos. All offer a variety of activities, such as snorkeling nearby reefs, swimming with dolphins and paddling a canoe inside a mangrove. Secondary only in popularity but first-rate in adventure are the cavern-diving opportunities made available to qualified divers by area dive operators. And if you just *love* crocodiles, there's even a croc farm to visit.

Because most people who visit the Riviera Maya approach it from Cancún, the sights are presented in the order you'd see them (or their turnoffs) if you were coming from

QUINTANA ROO

Cancún. Public buses travel along Hwy 307, and many of the larger communities are served by bus lines that have downtown stations, but not every sight in the pages that follow can be reached by public transportation.

If you're short on time and plan on making many stops, consider renting a car. Otherwise, the white, local buses that travel Hwy 307 can be hailed at roadside anywhere along the highway from sunrise to sunset. Cost varies with distance but the fare is never more than US$0.60 within the Tulum Corridor.

CROCOCUN

Thirty-two kilometers south of central Ciudad Cancún, and located on the west side of Hwy 307, is the Zoológico Regional Crococun (☎ 9-880-1645), which is both a regional zoo and a croc farm. The zoo portion consists of a number of compounds containing parrots, wild pigs, deer and other species that are native to the area. Yes, there *are* a lot of dangerous snakes and spiders in the area, aren't there? That's certainly the feeling many people have after seeing the snake and spider exhibits.

All of the other pens, and there are quite a lot of them, are set aside for crocodiles. Not all that long ago crocs could be seen with little effort in the many lagoons that ring the Yucatán Peninsula. Today, the largest of the species appear here at Crococun, the big crocs having been severely poached everywhere else on the peninsula. You'll see all sizes, from cute babies to bone-crushing behemoths.

Crococun is open 8:30 am to 5:30 pm daily. Admission costs US$10. Guided tours are available. There's no signage describing the creatures.

Places to Stay

Crococun is only a kilometer or so from the turnoff to Puerto Morelos, where there are several places to stay, but if you're looking for a place you might be able to have all to yourself, travel down the dirt road that has its entrance beside Crococun. After 2km you'll come to the *Acamaya Reef Motel* (☎ /fax 9-887-1032), a small seaside property

with a small patch of beach. The Acamaya Reef offers camping with use of facilities (US$6 per person), full RV hookups (US$25, no vehicles over 14m), and pleasant rooms for US$42/47 fan only/air-con. Not a bad deal, but Paamul, farther south, offers a better one; see the Paamul section for details.

PUERTO MORELOS
☎ 9 • pop 829

Puerto Morelos, 33km south of Cancún, is a quiet fishing village known principally for its car ferry to Cozumel. There are several good hotels here and travelers who have reason to spend the night in Puerto Morelos generally find it refreshingly free of tourists. A handful of scuba divers come here to explore the splendid reef 600m offshore, reachable by boat.

Puerto Morelos is 2km from the highway. Several taxis can usually be found by the turnoff to shuttle people into town, and there's usually a taxi or two near the town square to shuttle them back to the highway (the cost is US$2 each ride).

A battle over the mangrove flanking both sides of the connecting road is the reason Puerto Morelos has changed little in recent years, while towns up and down Mexico's Caribbean coast have changed dramatically. At the heart of the matter is the reef out front of Puerto Morelos. It's a very healthy reef, and like most along the coast its vitality is directly effected by the supply of nutrients from mangrove nearby. As of mid-1999, the residents of Puerto Morelos had successfully steered away every developer who'd proposed to replace their mangrove with a megaresort.

However, by late 1999 a developer was poised to construct a megaresort *and* a marina. At the time of writing it was unclear whether the developer's plans would be realized. One need only look at the dying reef at Akumal, where all of the mangrove has been replaced with hotels and condos, to see what the future holds for Puerto Morelos' reef if the developer did get his way.

Services beside the can't-miss town square include a money exchange, a travel agency, an Internet café, a dive shop, a car-rental

agency, two snorkeling operators, a couple of restaurants and a juice bar.

Places to Stay & Eat

The ***Posada Amor*** (☎ 871-0033, fax 871-0178, Apdo Postal 806, 77580 Cancún), 100m southwest of the town square, is the long-time lodging here. Rooms with fan, shared bathroom and a double bed are on the high side at US$22, or US$28 with two beds, single or double. This place is quite acceptable if you don't mind the heat. Meals are available.

Hotel Hacienda Morelos (☎/fax 871-0015), 150m south of the plaza on the water-front, has appealing, breezy rooms with sea views for US$62, single or double, and a decent restaurant called ***El Mesón***. There's an often-littered white-sand beach, a swimming pool, and Johnny Cairo's beach bar and grill.

Farther to the south, beyond the ferry terminal, is the best place in town, the ***Rancho Libertad*** (☎ 871-0181, in the USA ☎ 888-305-5225, fax 719-685-2332, www.rancholibertad .com), which features 15 charming guest rooms in one- and two-story thatched bungalows. Every room is unique, and most have a theme (Guatemala, Maya, ocean, etc). All rooms have good ventilation, some even air-con. There's a pleasing beach on the premises, massage and congo drum lessons are available. Upstairs rooms are priced at US$55 April to December double occupancy (add US$20 during the high season). Downstairs go for US$45/65 during low/high seasons, double occupancy. All rooms have private bath, an a buffet breakfast is included in the rates. Dive and snorkel gear is available for rent, as are bicycles. The hotel is managed by a very pleasant and informative American woman.

The ***Caribbean Reef Club*** (☎ 871-0191, fax 871-0190, in the USA ☎ 800-322-6286, fax 714-374-5797), next to the aforementioned Rancho Libertad, is a beautiful, comfortable, quiet, all-inclusive hotel right on the beach that caters mostly to married couples but is clothing optional at the pool, beach and Jacuzzi. The club is extremely private; only registered guests are allowed onto the property. Room rates start at US$275 most of the year.

Next door to Hacienda Morelos is ***Las Palmeras***, a good restaurant, though the best is ***Los Pelícanos***, just off the southeast corner of the plaza.

Getting There & Away

Playa Express buses running between Ciudad Cancún and Playa del Carmen drop you on the highway, 2km west of the center of Puerto Morelos. All 2nd-class and many 1st-class buses stop at Puerto Morelos coming from, or en route to, Ciudad Cancún. See Ciudad Cancún's Getting There & Away section for specifics.

The car ferry, or *transbordador*, to Cozumel leaves Puerto Morelos at 5 am, 10 am and noon daily. Departure times are subject to change from season to season, and according to the weather; during high seas, the ferry won't leave at all. Call ☎ 872-0950 (in Cozumel) for information.

Unless you plan to stay for awhile on Cozumel, it's hardly worth shipping your vehicle. You must get in line at least 30 minutes before departure time and hope there's enough space on the ferry for you. Fare for the $2^1/2$- to four-hour voyage is US$55 per car, US$4.50 per person.

Departure from Cozumel to Puerto Morelos is from the dock in front of the Hotel Sol Caribe, south of town along the shore road.

JARDÍN BOTÁNICO

Two kilometers south of the turnoff for Puerto Morelos, and also on the east side of Hwy 307, is the 60-hectare (150-acre) Jardín Botánico Dr Alfredo Barrera. Named in honor of a biologist who spent years studying the ecology of the area, the garden is a wonderful place to take a quiet stroll on well-maintained trails that meander for 3km through several habitats.

Many of the plants at trail's edge bear identifying labels in English, Spanish and Latin. Here, you can expect to see a plethora of orchids and bromeliads, and it's often possible to walk within a few meters of a big iguana before it seeks safety by climbing a tree. The iguanas are seemingly everywhere.

The garden is open 9 am to 5 pm daily. Admission costs US$2. There is a restroom and an information center on the premises. The local buses ceaselessly plying Hwy 307 may be hailed directly in front of the garden. If you're staying in Puerto Morelos and have the legs for it, you could walk to the highway turnoff from Puerto Morelos and then take a taxi to the gardens. Expect to spend US$10 for the roundtrip and the driver's 45-minute wait. Or, simply hike the 4km from Puerto Morelos to the garden.

If you choose to visit the garden, bring insect repellent. There usually aren't many mosquitoes there, but it never hurts to be protected.

TRES RÍOS

Tres Ríos (☎ 9-887-4977) is the first of the four ecoparks you'll encounter if you travel Hwy 307 from Cancún to Tulum. Like the others, it's a private reserve that attempts to strike a balance between nature's needs and its entertainment value. It's actually a fairly magical place, a 150-hectare (370-acre) swath of coastal forest where, despite its name, four underground rivers surface a kilometer or so from the sea and visitors have the marvelous option of exploring the freshwater, jungle-flanked rivers in canoes or kayaks.

But, folks, that's not all. Visitors also have the choice of riding mountain bikes along jungle paths and galloping (yes, on horseback) down the beach. Sound like too much work? Then consider sunbathing on the lovely white-sand beach and taking a dip in the sea when the tropical heat causes you to perspire. If the water feels refreshing, don a mask and snorkel (they are available to rent for US$7) and you'll see some *very* refreshing sights in the sea, as there's a lovely reef out front. Sure, there's a restaurant. Sure, there's a bar. It's even possible to scuba dive here.

Tres Ríos, which opened in 1999, is open 8:30 am to 5:30 pm daily. The US$20 admission includes use of canoe, kayak and bike. Be advised that only biodegradable sunscreen is allowed here. Any kind that's not good for the environment is not tolerated.

A special Tres Ríos bus leaves Cancún's Plaza Mayafair, at Blvd Kukulcán Km 8.5, at 8:30 am and returns at 5 pm daily. Another Tres Ríos bus is said to leave Playa del Carmen at 10 am and return at 4 pm daily. Remember, taxis from the nearest town are always an option, as are local buses that can drop you near the entrance.

CAPITÁN LAFITTE

No, the pirate Jean Lafitte, who plied the Caribbean and the Gulf of Mexico during the early 19th century, isn't clinging to life and managing a bar in the Yucatán. That wild man was buried long ago, but his spirit lives on at the ***Posada del Capitán Lafitte*** (☎ 9-873-0212, fax 9-873-0214, in the USA ☎ 800-538-6802, fax 303-674-8735, lafitte@ qroo1.telmex.net.mx), 62km south of Ciudad Cancún and about 1km east of Hwy 307.

Capitán Lafitte is a seaside inn with 62 comfortable rooms on a beautiful beach with gorgeous water out in front. There's also a splendid poolside bar, and breakfast and dinner are served at an oceanfront restaurant. Dive, snorkel and fishing trips can be arranged here. Rates run US$120 single or US$65 per person double occupancy and include full breakfast, full dinner, tip and tax. Optional air-con is US$10 more. An excellent find, this is the kind of place people return to year after year.

PUNTA BETE

Punta Bete, a reef-hugged point 65km south of Ciudad Cancún, is reached by a dirt road that weaves 1km or more from Hwy 307 through scrub forest before reaching the sea. North and south of the stubby point there are beautiful and occasionally wide stretches of beach upon which sit a total of six small, low-profile hotels (most offering cozy bungalows at budget prices) and two so-mellow restaurants.

The intimate hotels are easy to overlook from the highway due to poor signage and because of the meandering road from the highway that leads to them. But if you travel the unpaved coastal road you can expect to find a simple but pleasing guest room at each hotel for US$25 to US$60,

with a fine beach nearby for lounging in the sand and coves for safe snorkeling. If you're looking for a private beach, a relaxing environment and accommodations that are easy on the wallet, you ought to consider staying here.

Los Piños *(☎ 9-873-1506)* is a rustic but clean hotel with four spacious guest rooms with hot-water private baths, and a simple but likeable restaurant with a fine sea view. The rooms rent for a very appealing US$30 a day – a bargain considering that the ocean is practically at Los Piños' front door. Camping is available on the premises for a bargain US$4, the use of clean bathroom facilities included.

Paradise Point Resort Cabañas *(in the USA fax 651-762-8282)* is also located on the beach and features nine basic cabañas with private hot-water bathrooms and one or two beds per cabaña. The beach out front is wide and lovely, but the surf can be rough at times. A very good value at US$35 a night.

Just before you reach Los Piños is ***Coco's Cabañas*** *(☎ 9-884-8493, fax 9-884-3129, cchr@caribe.net.mx, www.mayan-riviera.com, www.yucatanweb.com)*, which consists of five charming cabañas with fan, hot-water private bath, good beds (one king- or queen-size per room) and electricity. There's a bar, a pool and a restaurant. This place is very nice, as is its English-speaking German owner. Room rates generally run US$60 for one or two persons and are a good deal at that. Pickup from Cancún can be arranged for an additional US$35. Coco's Cabañas is 75m from the beach. Next to it is ***Richard's Sports Bar***, which is a pleasant place to have a drink or grab a bite to eat.

Also reached by the coastal road are the ***Ocean Park***, ***Playa X'Calacoco*** and ***Bahía X'Calacoco*** hotels, and ***Frederico's***, an open-sided, thatch-roofed, inexpensive seaside restaurant where German, English and Spanish are spoken. All of the hotels and restaurants in Punta Bete are within walking distance of each other. If you've got good legs and aren't carrying too much, you could take a bus to the Punta Bete turnoff and walk in. This is not advisable if you're unaccustomed to the heat of the Tropics.

PLAYA DEL CARMEN
☎ 9 • pop 17,621

For decades Playa del Carmen was a simple fishing village that foreigners only passed through on their way to a ferry that would take them to Cozumel and the reefs that Jacques Cousteau made famous with a documentary. But with the construction of Cancún, the number of travelers roaming this part of Yucatán increased exponentially, as did the number of hotels and restaurants to serve them.

Most of Playa's foreign visitors during the 1980s and '90s were Europeans who found Cancún a bit too commercial. In Playa, they discovered a small town with a lovely stretch of beach and a beautiful reef out front, a few small hotels, and restaurants that served fresh seafood. Some of these visitors stayed and opened businesses. Today, most of the town's accommodations are stylish European-owned and -managed inns, and several of Playa's restaurants serve delicious French and Italian cuisine.

Today, Playa del Carmen has overtaken Cozumel as the preferred resort town in the area. Playa's beaches are better and nightlife groovier than Cozumel's, and the reef diving is just as good. On the beaches, no one will hassle you if you prefer to sunbathe topless, and the police permit total nudity about a kilometer north of Playa (although it isn't recommended; see Playa del Carmen's Dangers & Annoyances section, below).

What's there to do in Playa? Hang out. Swim. Dive. Shop. Eat. Drink. Stroll the beach. Get some sun. Listen to beach bands. Dance in clubs. Catch the Playa Express shuttle to other points along the coast. In the evening, Playa's pedestrian mall, on Av Quinta, is a popular place to sit and have a meal or a drink, or stroll and watch others having meals and drinks.

Playa del Carmen's central location (halfway between Tulum and Cancún, an hour's ferry ride to Cozumel, a day trip to the ruins of Cobá, within striking distance of beaches, cenotes and ecoparks up and down the Tulum Corridor) and its supply of inexpensive hotels and restaurants make it an excellent base from which to explore Quintana Roo

PLAYA DEL CARMEN

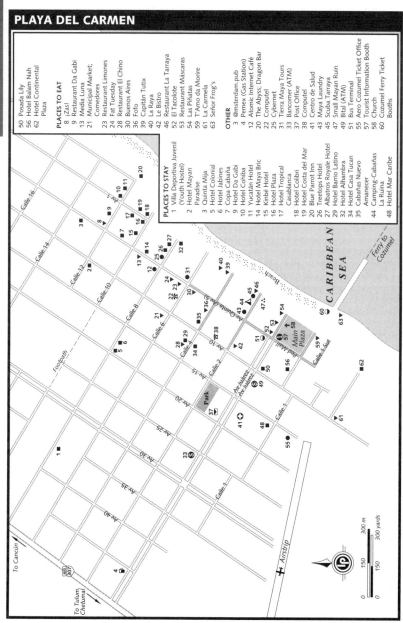

PLACES TO STAY
1 Villa Deportiva Juvenil (Youth Hostel)
2 Hotel Mayan Paradise
3 Quinta Mija
5 Hotel Colonial
6 Hotel Jabines
9 Hotel Da Gabi
10 Hotel Cohiba
11 Yucatán Hotel
14 Hotel Maya Bric
15 Kinbé Hotel
16 Hotel Plaza
17 Hotel Tropical
    Casablanca
18 Hotel Colibrí
19 Hotel Costa del Mar
26 Blue Parrot Inn
26 Treetops Hotel
27 Albatros Royale Hotel
29 Hotel Barrio Latino
32 Hotel Alhambra
34 Hotel Casa Tucan
35 Cabañas Nuevo Amanecer
44 Camping-Cabañas La Ruina
48 Hotel Mar Caribe

50 Posada Lily
56 Hotel Balam Nah
62 Hotel Continental Plaza

PLACES TO EAT
8 ¡Zas!
9 Restaurant Da Gabi
13 Media Luna
21 Municipal Market; Comedores
23 Restaurant Limones
24 Fat Tuesday
28 Restaurant El Chino
30 Buenos Aires
36 Fofo
39 Capitán Tutix
40 La Raya
42 Le Bistro
46 Restaurant La Tarraya
52 El Tacolote
53 Restaurant Máscaras
54 Las Piñatas
59 T'Amo da Morire
61 La Carmela
63 Señor Frog's

OTHER
3 @msterdam.pub
4 Pemex (Gas Station)
12 Atomic Internet Café
20 The Abyss; Dragon Bar
22 Computel
25 Cybernet
31 Tierra Maya Tours
33 Bancomer (ATM)
37 Post Office
38 Computel
41 Centro de Salud
43 Maya Laundry
45 Scuba Tarraya
47 Small Mayan Ruin
49 Bital (ATM)
51 Bus Terminal
55 Aero Cozumel Ticket Office
57 Tourist Information Booth
58 Church
60 Cozumel Ferry Ticket Booths

(it offers much better values than Cancún). Most of the sites in Playa can be reached easily enough by bus, and taxis abound.

Orientation
Playa del Carmen follows a grid pattern, with numbered avenues running in one direction and numbered streets running in the other. The layout couldn't be simpler, and the section of Playa of interest to tourists is contained in an easily walked 20-square-block area near the beach.

The main road into town is Av Juárez, which follows a straight line from Hwy 307 to the beach and Playa's beachside plaza. A block before reaching the beach, Av Juárez meets Av Quinta, which is closed to vehicular traffic for several blocks on both sides of Av Juárez. This pedestrian street, which is flanked by hotels, restaurants, bars, travel agencies, water sports centers and handicrafts shops, is Playa's main drag. The city bus station is conveniently located at the corner of Avs Juárez and Quinta.

Information
Playa doesn't have a formal tourist office. Instead, it has an information booth in the northwest corner of the main plaza. The booth is staffed from 8 am to 6 pm daily.

Money There's a Bital bank on Av Juárez between Avs 10 and 15, and a Bancomer at Avs Juárez and 25. Both will exchange major currencies for pesos, have ATMs and are open 8 am to 5 pm Monday to Friday, 9 am to 1 pm Saturday. There are money-exchange booths along Av Quinta as well, which keep later hours than the banks and are open daily.

Post & Communications The post office is located at the intersection of Avs Juárez and 20. It's open 8 am to 4:30 pm Monday to Friday.

There is no shortage of Telmex pay phones in Playa del Carmen and they offer the traveler the least-expensive option if used with a Ladatel calling card. Long-distance calls can also be placed at the Computel offices on Av 10 between Calles 2 and 4, and on Calle 6 between Avs 5 and 10.

Email & Internet Access The Atomic Internet Café, on Calle 8 near Av Quinta, is American owned and operated and the most efficiently run of the city's several Internet access businesses. At the time of writing it charged US$0.15 per minute, but those rates are likely to drop. The café features eight speedy computers, air-con, a bar and a variety of coffee drinks. It's open 9 am to 11 pm Monday to Saturday, noon to 8 pm Sunday.

If there's a line at that Internet café, try Cybernet, on Calle 8 on the beach side of Av Quinta. It's not quite as pleasant as the Atomic Internet Café, but it offers the same rates and its nine computers are operational most of the time. It's open 7:15 am to 10:30 pm daily.

Another Internet access point is the @msterdam.pub (yes, that's @msterdam.pub), located in the courtyard of the Quinta Mija hotel on Av Quinta between Calles 12 and 14. The prices are competitive and the atmosphere tropical, pleasant and friendly, just like the hotel. It's open 8 am to 10 pm daily.

Travel Agencies A host of travel agencies and tour operators and can be found along Av Quinta. Among the better ones is Tierra Maya Tours (☎ 873-1385, fax 873-1386, tmt@expo-yucatan.com), Av Quinta at Calle 6, where English, German, French and Spanish are spoken. Tierra Maya staff can issue national and international airline tickets; arrange package deals to Uxmal, Palenque, Tikal and Cuba; provide day tours to Chichén Itzá, Tulum and Cobá; and hook you up with a private guide and driver, if you so desire.

Bookstores La Librería, on Calle 8 between Avs 5 and 10, carries a good selection of books, including Lonely Planet travel guides.

Laundry Maya Laundry, on Calle 2 at Av Quinta, operates in a pretty straightforward way: Drop off your clothing in the morning and come back for it around 5 pm. If all goes well, it will have been washed, dried and neatly folded when you return. Cost is US$4 for a heaping load of laundry.

Dangers & Annoyances Playa isn't as safe as it seems. The city is in the midst of a construction boom, and construction jobs have attracted male workers from far away. These workers live alone in a shantytown north of Playa. Their loneliness and excessive drinking and the appearance of near-naked women on the beaches and, occasionally, in town have resulted in an outrageous rape problem in Playa, with townsfolk saying that no less than one rape and as many as three rapes occur each week.

Another fairly common occurrence here is theft and robbery on remote patches of beach north of Playa. If you go walking along the beach until you find an isolated spot, bear in mind that you are now close to the shantytown and, unfortunately, some of its residents like to target sunbathers. One minute your purse or your pack is beside you while you lay on a towel, the next it's been grabbed and your assailant is running back into the brush from which he emerged.

Play it safe. Don't take valuables to the beach. Don't wear jewelry that's going to attract the attention of robbers. Don't isolate yourself and increase your odds of being raped and/or robbed. And, don't walk the streets alone late at night. Recent crimes include the gang rape and murder of a Canadian woman who wandered into the shantytown, and the stabbing to death of a 70-year-old Italian man whose attacker wanted the man's silver bracelet and no witnesses.

Be advised that federal police have been implicated in rapes and murders in Playa, so don't turn to them for help if you've been assaulted. Obviously, if you survive an attack and do go to the police, only to recognize an officer as one of your assailants, he won't be likely give you the chance to identify him in a court of law (or anywhere else for that matter). Life's precious; don't jeopardize it over the perfect tan or a fancy watch that only impresses thieves and airheads.

Snorkeling & Scuba Diving

Playa and Cozumel are famous for their reefs, and there are many local operators who can take you to them. Perhaps the most

reputable of the bunch is Scuba Tarraya (☎ 873-2040, fax 873-2060, g_millet@hotmail .com, gmillet@yuc1.telmex.net.mx), at the east end of Calle 2. Services include: two-tank reef dive, US$65; one-tank night reef dive, US$65; two-tank cenote dive, US$100; three-hour snorkel trip, US$25; fishing, maximum four persons per boat, US$150; boat rides, US$10 per person per hour. Snorkel and scuba equipment are available for rent. Introductory scuba classes and certification are also available. Scuba Tarraya also rents kayaks and can arrange for horseback rides.

Other dive centers include: Aqua Venturas (☎/fax 873-0969), Av Quinta between Calles 2 and 4; The Abyss (☎ 873-2164, abyss@playadelcarmen.com), at the Blue Parrot Inn, east end of Calle 12; and Phocea Caribe (☎/fax 873-1024), Av Quinta between Calles 12 and 14.

Places to Stay

Playa del Carmen is developing and changing so fast that almost anything written about it is obsolete by the time it's printed. Expect many new hotels by the time you arrive, and many changes in the old ones. The room prices appearing below are for the off-season, which represents eight months of the year (mid-April through mid-December). Prices are generally 25% (or more) higher from mid-December to mid-April.

Budget The youth hostel, or *Villa Deportiva Juvenil (no phone)*, on Calle 8 at Av 35, is a modern establishment offering the cheapest clean lodging in town, but it's quite a walk to the beach and guests sleep in worn single-sex dorm bunks. It's cheap at US$4 per bunk, but a much better bet, unless you're counting every peso, is Camping-Cabañas La Ruina.

Camping-Cabañas La Ruina (☎ 873-0405, fax 872-1598), on Calle 2 just off the beach, offers several cheap ways to sleep: pitch your own tent for US$3 per person; hang your hammock beneath their palapa for US$5; rent a hammock from them (US$6); or stay in a simple cabaña with two cots and ceiling fan for US$8 to US$11. A more comfortable cabaña with private bath can be

had for US$25 to US$35. Be sure to secure your stuff from roaming thieves. La Ruina rents lockers, but it's best to have your own sturdy lock.

At **Cabañas Nuevo Amanecer** (☎ 873-0030), Calle 4 between Avs 5 and 10, each cabaña has a shady little porch complete with hammock. These cabañas are a good value at US$15 with a private bathroom and US$20 for a cabaña with a private bathroom and fridge.

Tour groups sometimes fill the nine-room **Hotel Mar Caribe** (☎ 873-0207), Av 15 at Calle 1, but if you can get a room it'll be clean, if simple, and cost US$16 (fan only) to US$30 (with air-con) with private bath. The Mar Caribe offers very good value.

The **Posada Lily** (no phone), on Av Juárez just a block inland from the main square, offers clean rooms with private shower and fan for US$17 a double.

The **Hotel Casa Tucan** (☎/fax 873-0282), on Calle 4 between Avs 10 and 15, features 20 rooms on two levels (the upstairs rooms catch a welcome breeze), a swimming pool and a lovely, jungly tropical garden. All rooms are fan-only, and mosquito nets keep you bite free. The Casa Tucan provides excellent value at US$20 a room.

The **Hotel Barrio Latino** (☎/fax 873-2384, posadabarriolatino@yahoo.com), on Calle 4 between Avs 10 and 15, offers 14 very clean, stylish rooms, all with tiled floors, ceiling fan and hammocks. The Italian owners and managers are enormously friendly, speak Italian, English and Spanish, and maintain strict security. With low-season rates of US$20 a room, it's very easy to see why this hotel is often full. Off-street parking is available.

The **Yucatán Hotel** (☎ 876-3799, no fax), on Calle 12, is an appropriately priced budget hotel with five no-frills rooms with fan only and hot water, two twin beds per room, for US$20 a room. Its strong suits are its price and its proximity to the beach scene at the Blue Parrot Inn.

Mid-Range Hotel Da Gabi (☎ 873-0048, fax 873-0198, www.dagabi.com), Av 1 near Calle 12, is much less fancy than its adjoining restaurant, Restaurant Da Gabi (see Places

to Eat, below). Serviceable (though far from fancy) rooms with private shower and ceiling fan cost US$20 to US$35.

Hotel Maya Bric (☎ 873-2041, fax 873-2206, mayabric@playa.com.mx), on Av Quinta between Calles 8 and 10, is a small hotel with big rooms, set around a swimming pool amid flowering shrubs and coconut trees. Rates vary with the seasons, but range from US$30 in summer to US$45 in winter for a double with bath.

The **Hotel Jabines** (☎ 873-0861, fax 873-0352), on Calle 8 between Avs 15 and 20, features 16 rooms, all on the ground level, with secure parking, cable TV and two or three beds per room. These often-overlooked rooms are a good bargain at US$26/31 fan only/air-con for a single or double.

Hotel Balam Nah (☎ 873-2117, fax 873-2116, www.xaac.com/playacar), on Calle 1 between Avs 5 and 10, was remodeled in 1999 and offers 20 nicely decorated rooms (11 with air-con) in a three-story building. The rooms offer no views to speak of, but they're comfortable, each has cable TV and a fridge, and the hotel is near the ferry. Rooms run US$35 for a double with fan, US$43 for a double with air-con, and US$48 for a double with air-con and balcony.

Hotel Costa del Mar (☎ 873-0058, fax 873-0850), on Av 1 near Calle 10, has 38 pleasing rooms overlooking the beach for US$55/65 a double with fan/air-con. The hotel also has simpler cabañas that are considerably cheaper (US$40) but have no air-con.

Across the street, the **Hotel Tropical Casablanca** (☎/fax 873-0057), Av 1 between Calles 10 and 12, is nice, clean and neat, with a palapa restaurant-bar perched above the street and both a swimming pool *and* a cenote (a natural pool) on the premises. Double rooms cost US$40 with fan only and US$50 with air-con.

Copa Cabaña (☎ 873-0218), Av 5 between Calles 10 and 12, boasts 30 comfortable, fan-cooled rooms with private showers arranged around a particularly lush courtyard. A Jacuzzi, a gym and hammocks are offered for guests' use. You pay US$35 for a double with one or two beds. Rooms on the third story provide sea views.

Even more posh and atmospheric is the *Quinta Mija* (☎/fax 873-0111), Av Quinta between Calles 12 and 14, where the lush tropical courtyard features a quiet bar. Rooms with kitchenettes and double beds go for US$40, or US$50 with two beds. There's a pool and an Internet café on the premises. This place is very nice and sees a lot of return visitors.

Treetops Hotel (☎ 873-0351, fax 873-1493, treetops@playadelcarmen.com), on Calle 8 near the beach, offers 16 air-con guest rooms and several bungalows, all with mosquito nets and most with private patios. There's a pool and a bar on the premises. Rates aren't unreasonable at US$35 and up, but there are better bargains around.

The *Hotel Colonial* (☎ /fax 873-0456), Av 20 at Calle 8, offers 18 rooms in two stories with cable TV, balcony and two double beds. Rooms with fan only run US$40, those with air-con go for US$45. There's a restaurant on the premises.

The *Hotel Cohiba* (☎ 873-2080, fax 873-2090, www.xaac.com/playacar), on Calle 12 at Av 1, offers 19 appealing rooms, all with air-con, balcony and a security box for US$40 for a standard ground-floor room, US$50 for a superior 2nd-floor room, US$60 for a 3rd-floor ocean-view room, and US$85 for the breezy, romantic top-floor junior suite. There's a restaurant on the premises and, what's more, this European-run hotel is only a brief walk from the hip beach scene at the Blue Parrot Inn. An excellent value.

The new, German-owned and -managed *Hotel Colibri* (☎/fax 873-1833), Av 1 at Calle 10, offers five thatch-roof cabañas with one bed in each and fan only (US$50) and 28 lovely guest rooms with a tropical motif and a choice of fan or air-con starting at US$40 for fan only and US$60 with air-con. There's a restaurant and bar on the beach and fine dining specializing in seafood and German cuisine. All guest quarters face a lovely courtyard, not the ocean. A good value considering the beachside location.

The new-in-1999 *Hotel Plaza* (☎ 873-2193, fax 873-2196, www.xaac.com/playacar), Av 1 at Calle 10, has 34 air-con rooms with cable TV and two double beds. Ten of the rooms have ocean views. All go for US$50

single or double. A restaurant and bar are also on the premises.

The Italian-owned and -operated *Kinbé Hotel* (☎ 873-0441, fax 873-2215, hotelkinbe@ playadelcarmen.com), on Calle 10 between Avs 1 and 5, has 19 rooms, each of which has a clean, modern look and varies in size and decor. The only drawback to this hotel, which opened in 1998, is that the newer Hotel Plaza blocks most of the ocean views its rooms would have had. Nevertheless, the rooms are a bargain starting at US$35.

The *Hotel Alhambra* (☎ 873-0735, fax 873-0699, olas@cancun.com.mx), at the beach end of Calle 8, opened in 1999 and has lots of pluses. Its 25 rooms offer a variety of options, from fan-only to ones with balcony and a beach view. There's a private deck for sunbathing on the roof and the English-, Spanish- and French-speaking owner offers instruction in kundalini yoga. Given its location, the room rates of US$40 to US$80 are very reasonable. There's a restaurant on the beach.

The *Albatros Royale Hotel* (☎ 873-0001, fax 873-0002, in the USA ☎ 800-538-6802), at the east end of Calle 8, has 31 lovely air-con rooms with cable TV, telephone and ceiling fan. There's a bar on the premises and breakfast at a nearby restaurant is included. Rates at this well-situated hotel are a very reasonable US$60 single or double.

Top End The *Blue Parrot Inn* (☎ 873-0083, fax 873-0049, in the USA ☎ 800-634-3547), on the beach end of Calle 12, is the hippest hotel in Playa del Carmen. Many of the inn's 45 rooms have terraces or balconies and sea views, and 31 of the rooms have air-con. There are also a number of beachside bungalows and villas. All of the rooms are charming, and the management couldn't be friendlier. The inn's beachfront bar often features surfer bands. This is the place most people wish they were staying when they wander up the beach and discover it. Room rates range from US$55 to US$105, bungalows from US$90 to US$135 and the even fancier villas from US$135 to US$275. Beachside palapa rooms (Nos 31-39) offer the best value at US$65 to US$100.

The *Hotel Mayan Paradise* (☎ 873-0933, fax 873-2015, in the USA ☎ 800-217-2192), Av 10 at Calle 12, is a lovely, secure place. Beautifully kept two- and three-story wooden thatch-roofed bungalows house 40 large, comfortable, modern rooms with bath, kitchenette, cable TV, fans and air-con. The pool is ringed on three sides by tropical gardens; there's a bar to one side. With a light breakfast, you pay US$125 for one or two persons and US$145 for three.

Those of you seeking international-class luxury lodging will like the large *Hotel Continental Plaza* (☎ 873-0100, fax 873-0105, in the USA ☎ 800-882-6684), on the beach south of the ferry docks. Rooms cost US$150 to US$280, and tourists generally arrive by the busload.

Places to Eat

It's possible to consume some excellent food in Playa del Carmen at very reasonable prices, particularly in the mid-range category.

Budget The cheapest meals can be found at the *comedores* (eateries) near the Municipal Market, at the intersection of Calle 6 and Av 10, but those are also the very best places in town to ingest a bellyful of parasites. Do yourself a favor: Don't patronize the cheapo food stands.

The *Restaurant La Tarraya*, at the southern end of Calle 2, is one of the few eateries in town that dates from the 1960s, yet it continues to offer good food at low prices, including guacamole for US$1.50, fried fish for US$2.50 and *pulpo* (octopus) for US$3.25. Good, clean food cheap – and it's right on the beach!

Capitán Tutix, at the beach end of Calle 4, is a superior choice for fast Mexican food, decent pasta, acceptable seafood and a half-dozen vegetable items (mostly combinations of fruit, yogurt and honey) – all within sight of scantily-clad dudes and dudettes. Many of the items are under US$5. *La Raya*, also on the beach and next door to the good Capitán, serves the same purpose: decent food you can gobble while you ogle people in swimwear.

Mid-Range Most tourists don't venture south of Av Juárez, and that's a pity because some of the best Mexican cuisine on the entire Yucatán Peninsula is served there. *La Carmela*, on Av 10, three blocks south of Av Juárez, is known for its succulent chicken smothered in dark mole, its white pork slow-cooked in a green tomatillo sauce, and its *ropa vieja* ('old clothes,' shredded beef served in a tomato sauce seasoned with guajilo chilies). For seafood, the shrimp flown in from Veracruz and served in a delicious vanilla sauce is excellent. Most of the specialties cost under US$10. It's open daily for lunch and dinner. Dress nicely.

The best Italian food in town is served at *T'Amo da Morire*, which overlooks the main plaza. This upstairs restaurant is at its best in the evening, when the day's heat has passed and you can sit beside one of the romantic restaurant's big open windows while you feast. Entrées include spinach ricotta ravioli au gratin (US$5), fettuccine with shrimp and mushrooms (US$5.50), and fried shrimp and squid (US$7). The seafood salad appetizer (US$4) is delicious, and for dessert the chocolate ice cream is absolutely dreamy. Like the name says, the food here is to die for.

For French cuisine, turn to *Le Bistro*, on Calle 2 between Avs Quinta and 10. Le Bistro specializes in French home cooking, as does another restaurant in town that's formal, pricey and inferior. This simple, open-sided, fan-cooled restaurant with 10 little wooden tables and excellent service offers homemade cognac pâté served with salad and a warm baguette (US$4.50) for a starter, and entrées include red snapper with a mango-chili sauce served with fried plantains and white rice (US$6.50) and a chicken dish that's simmered with fresh mushrooms in a creamy white wine sauce, served in a crock, gratinéed with mozzarella for US$6.50. It's open 8 am to 11 pm Tuesday through Sunday. This restaurant is divine.

The name in Playa for pizza is *Fofo*, on Calle 4 near Av Quinta. Fofo makes pizzas only, and it makes really good ones. Most cost well under US$10 and the ingredients vary a lot. Among them: garlic, black olives,

tuna, bacon, smoked salmon, brandy, lobster, capers, squid, artichoke, oregano and salami. It's open daily for lunch and dinner.

If you *love* beef you'll love ***Buenos Aires***, on Av Quinta between Calles 4 and 6, tucked away behind two very mediocre restaurants. Buenos Aires serves grilled fish and tacos and even crêpes, but the restaurant is famous in Quintana Roo for its rib eye (US$12.50), top sirloin (US$6), flank steak (US$8.50), short ribs (US$7.50) and other meaty items. The meaty meals are accompanied by slices of grilled vegetables and arrive on butcher blocks. Only Angus beef is used here – none of the chewy range-fed beef so common in Mexico. Buenas Aires opens at 6 pm daily. A wine list is provided upon request, and burgers are available for us barbarians.

Media Luna, on Av Quinta, takes top honors in the veggie category. A quick run-down includes crêpes with fruit, granola with yogurt and/or fruit plates for breakfast; an eggplant and mushroom sandwich, grilled fish on a baguette, and/or a quesadilla with salsa and cilantro cream for lunch; for dinner, your choice from a wide selection of salads, pastas and seafood. All meals are priced for the budget-minded. It's open 8 am to 11:30 pm daily.

¡Zas!, on Av Quinta at Calle 12, is owned by the same people who own Media Luna, and it's very good for international food. The cuisine here is interesting and delicious. A typical entrée consists of five-spice crusted pork tenderloins with charred Asian greens, rice and a zesty fruit salad for US$8. It opens at 5 pm daily.

Restaurant Da Gabi, on Calle 12 near Av Quinta, is fancier than the adjoining hotel of the same name, but prices are moderate and the quiet atmosphere soothed by jazz is more refined than that of Av Quinta. Pasta plates and huge pizzas sell for US$6 to US$8, grilled meat and fish for US$7 to US$12. They even have a few imported wines.

Because it's farther from the beach and Av Quinta, ***Restaurant El Chino***, Calle 4 between Avs 10 and 15, has lower prices and better food, but also a pleasant setting and decent service. A full meal of soup, ceviche

or grilled fish and dessert might cost US$10 or US$12, beverage and tip included.

El Tacolote, on Av Juárez near Av Quinta, is open-sided and faces the plaza, and its meals consist of a large offering of tacos, house specials, steaks served Mexican style (thinly cut, overcooked and tasty), and a half-dozen seafood items. Most dishes cost under US$7. El Tacolote (the name is a pun on taco and *tecolote*, owl) is open noon to 2 am daily. The food's no joke; it's very tasty and reasonably priced.

Top End Of the more expensive places, the ***Restaurant Máscaras***, on the main plaza, is the most famous and long-lived. The pizzas (US$5 to US$9) are dependably good, the more complex dishes less so, but it's the company you come for. Drinks are expensive. ***Las Piñatas***, downhill from Máscaras, has decent food and the best sea view.

A better choice as far as the food is concerned is the ***Restaurant Limones***, Av Quinta at Calle 6, where the atmosphere is more sedate than jolly. Though you can pay up to US$19 for their 'Symphony of Seafood' with lobster, shrimp and conch, most fish dishes cost around US$10, and filet mignon costs US$12.

For Mexican restaurants that resemble bad American knockoffs on festive Mexican themes, try ***Fat Tuesday***, on Av Quinta between Calles 6 and 8, and/or ***Señor Frog's***, beside the dock that serves the pier that serves the ferry that goes to Cozumel. If you're dying for a break from intelligent talk and just want to meet someone with a firm body and uncomplicated perspectives, these restaurant-bars are recommended.

Entertainment

When the sun goes down in Playa, the sound of beer bottles being opened is louder than the crash of surf. That's especially the case at the ***Dragon Bar***, at the Blue Parrot Inn, where Calle 12 meets the sand. Surfer bands generally play at the open-sided palapa bar during the day and at night a reggae band usually comes on. There's never a cover nor do you have to be a guest of the Blue Parrot to get in. You only need to wear a big smile – that's the house rule.

If you're unable to muster a smile, head to *Capitán Tutix*, at the beach end of Calle 12. No one leaves the Capitán with a frown. This restaurant-bar is another palapa-roofed joint within a crazy bull's charge of the surf, and inside there's a bar built to resemble a galleon, replete with sails and a bartender who looks like he's spent the better part of his life on deck. Most nights a band starts up about 10 pm, playing reggae, rock, calypso or salsa. You'll want to dust off your blue suede shoes if you packed any.

If you're at the Capitán and none of your one-liners goes over very well there, try *La Raya*, next door. You wouldn't be the first person to wander from one of these classy establishments to the other (the 'you puke, you clean' rule applies at both). There's occasional live music (usually salsa) at La Raya, generally starting after 8 pm. There's never a cover here, same deal at Capitán Tutix.

Secondary music scenes but not necessarily secondary party scenes can be found along Av Quinta most nights. One of the niceties of Playa del Carmen is that it's still small enough that you can check out the scene at one end of town, then scope the scene on Av Quinta, then drop down to the beach and investigate the happenings there. And after doing *all* that legwork, which takes 30 minutes tops, you can return to the scene that did the most for you.

Shopping

Playa del Carmen is not the place to shop for fine jewelry, but it does offer the consummate shopper lots of quality browsing material. Av Quinta is lined with shops featuring handicrafts from throughout Mexico – and offering them at reasonable prices. Beachwear and T-shirt shops abound. If you haven't got a hat and your face is sunburnt or getting there, consider picking up a hat here. There are plenty from which to choose and a hat can make a fine momento.

Getting There & Away

Air Playa's little airstrip handles mostly small charter, tour and air-taxi flights. Aero Cozumel (☎ 873-0350), part of Mexicana, has an office next to Playa's airstrip. The airline will fly you to Cozumel for US$26, or round-trip to Chichén Itzá for US$139 per person.

Bus ADO, Autotransportes del Sur (ATS), Cristóbal Colón, Mayab, Autotransportes de Oriente (Oriente), TRP, Premier, Maya de Oro and Altos serve Playa's bus terminal at the corner of Avs Juárez and Quinta. Playa Express buses run up and down the coast every 20 minutes, charging US$1.75 from Playa to either Tulum or Cancún.

Chetumal – 315km, five hours; eight by ADO (US$10), one by ADO GL (US$12), one by Cristóbal Colón (US$11), one by Mayab (US$12) and one by Altos (US$8)

Chichén Itzá – 272km, three hours; one by TRP (US$7); it's best to take an early bus to Ciudad Cancún, then transfer

Ciudad Cancún – 65km, 40 minutes; frequent buses by ADO, Playa Express and Oriente for US$2.50

Cobá – 113km, 1½ hours; one by Premier (US$3.50)

Mérida – 385km, five hours; one by ADO (US$12.50), four by TRP (US$11), 12 by Premier (US$12.50), one by ADO GL (US$15)

Palenque – 800km, 10 hours; one each by Cristóbal Colón (US$26) and Altos (US$23)

San Cristóbal de las Casas – 990km, 16 hours; one each by Maya de Oro (US$36), Cristóbal Colón (US$32) and Altos (US$30)

Tulum – 63km, one hour; Playa Express (US$2.50) every 20 minutes, five by ADO (US$2), and three by TRP (US$1.70)

Valladolid – 213km, three hours; two by TRP (US$6); many buses going to Mérida via Cancún stop at Valladolid, but it's faster to go on the *ruta corta* (short route) via Tulum and Cobá (see Cobá)

Ferry to Cozumel Approach the dock and you can't miss the ticket booths for the ferries to Cozumel, which run every hour on the hour from 5 am to 10 pm. The ride takes 45 minutes to an hour and costs US$7 each direction. When boarding you'll usually have the choice of an exposed top deck or an enclosed lower deck (some of the newer ferries have three decks). A lot of people get vicious sunburns riding on the exposed deck. People on the lower deck are subjected to nonstop MTV music videos. Take your pick.

QUINTANA ROO

Getting Around

Although mopeds weren't available at the time of writing, there was talk in late 1999 of a moped-rental business 'opening soon.' All of the sites in Playa del Carmen could easily be reached by moped, and adventurous spirits would find the rides great fun. Cars can be rented at Julia Car Rentals (☎ 873-0556, fax 873-1211), on Calle 6 between Avs 20 and 25.

COZUMEL

☎ 9 • pop 47,841

Cozumel is a teardrop-shaped coral island ringed by crystalline waters 71km south of Cancún. It is Mexico's only Caribbean island and, measuring 53km by 14km, it is also the country's largest island.

Called Ah-Cuzamil-Peten (Island of Swallows) by its earliest inhabitants, Cozumel has been a favorite destination for divers since 1961, when a Jacques Cousteau documentary on the island's glorious reefs appeared on TV. Today, no fewer than 100 world-class dive sites have been identified within 5km of Cozumel, and no fewer than a dozen of these sites are shallow enough for snorkelers to enjoy.

Except for the superb dive and snorkel opportunities the island offers, there's really very little reason for anyone to visit Cozumel specifically. There are no rivers to run, no mountains to climb, few birds to admire, and the few Mayan ruins are nothing special. Fortunately, a very good museum, a terrific national park on Chankanab Bay, and a picturesque lighthouse round out the island's attractions, offering visitors some alternatives to the gorgeous underwater scenes.

As a party destination, Cozumel has been eclipsed by Playa del Carmen, which offers visitors more for their money in terms of accommodations, restaurants and nighttime activities. The best reason to come to Cozumel remains its nearby reefs – and that's an excellent reason to visit – but they can be reached nearly as quickly from Playa.

History

Mayan settlement here dates from 300 AD. During the Postclassic period, Cozumel flourished as a trade center and as a ceremonial site – principally as the latter. Every Mayan woman on the Yucatán Peninsula and beyond was expected to make at least one pilgrimage to the island to pay tribute to Ixchel, the goddess of fertility and the moon, at a temple erected in her honor at what's now San Gervasio, in the northeast quadrant of the island.

At the time of the first Spanish contact with Cozumel (in 1518, by Juan de Grijalva and his men), there were at least 32 Mayan building sites on the island. Grijalva came and left in peace, and a year later Cortés and his force of 11 ships and 500 men arrived. According to respected Spanish chronicler Friar Diego de Landa, Cortés sacked one of the Mayan centers but left the others intact.

Describing Cortés, Landa wrote: 'On the admiral's ship he set a banner of white and blue in honor of Our Lady, and whose image, together with the cross, he always placed wherever he destroyed idols.' Through an Indian interpreter, Cortés reportedly persuaded the Maya on Cozumel 'to adore the cross; this he placed in their temples with an image of Our Lady, and therewith public idolatry ceased,' Landa wrote.

Soon after, Cortés left the island for the mainland, where he began his conquest of Mexico. The destruction of the Maya on Cozumel began not with Cortés, but, according to Landa, with smallpox brought in 1520 by one African slave on a Spanish ship. The Maya, who had no immunity to the disease, fell like sheep. Within a year, half of the 8000 Maya on the island had died. Of the survivors, only about 200 survived genocidal attacks by conquistadors during the late 1540s.

While the island remained virtually deserted into the late 17th century, its coves provided sanctuary and headquarters for several notorious pirates, including Jean Lafitte and Henry Morgan. Pirate brutality led the remaining populace to move to the mainland. It wasn't until 1848 that Cozumel began to be resettled by Indians fleeing the War of the Castes.

At the beginning of the 20th century, the island's now mostly mestizo population grew, thanks to the craze for chewing gum.

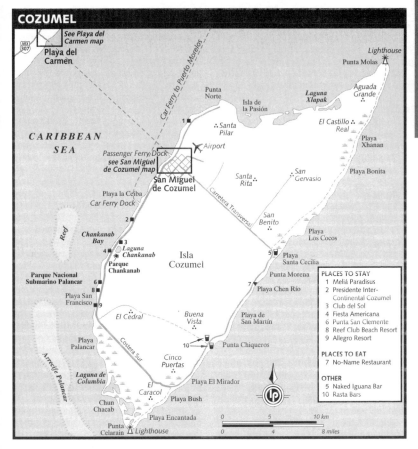

COZUMEL

See Playa del
Carmen map
Playa del
Carmen

Car ferry to Puerto Morelos

Lighthouse
Punta Molas

*CARIBBEAN
SEA*

Punta
Norte
Isla de
la Pasión

*Santa
Pilar*

*Laguna
Xlapak*

Aguada
Grande

El Castillo
Real

Playa
Xhanan

Playa
Bonita

Airport
Passenger Ferry Dock
see San Miguel
de Cozumel map

*Santa
Rita*

*San
Gervasio*

San Miguel
de Cozumel

Carretera Transversal

Playa la Ceiba
Car Ferry Dock

*San
Benito*

Playa
Los Cocos

Reef

Chankanab
Bay

*Laguna
Chankanab*
Parque
Chankanab

Isla
Cozumel

Playa
Santa Cecilia

Punta Morena

Playa Chen Río

*Parque Nacional
Submarino Palancar*

Playa San
Francisco

El Cedral

*Buena
Vista*

Playa de
San Martín

Punta Chiqueros

Playa
Palancar

Costera Sur

*Cinco
Puertas*

*Laguna de
Columbia*

*El
Caracol*

Playa El Mirador

Chun
Chacab

Playa Bush

Punta
Celarain Lighthouse

Playa Encantada

0   5   10 km
0   4   8 miles

PLACES TO STAY
1 Meliá Paradisus
2 Presidente Inter-
   Continental Cozumel
3 Club del Sol
4 Fiesta Americana
6 Punta San Clemente
8 Reef Club Beach Resort
9 Allegro Resort

PLACES TO EAT
7 No-Name Restaurant

OTHER
5 Naked Iguana Bar
10 Rasta Bars

Cozumel was a port of call on the chicle export route and locals harvested chicle on the island. Although chicle was later replaced by synthetic gum, Cozumel's economy remained strong with the building of a US air base during WWII.

When the US military departed, the island fell into an economic slump and many of its people moved away. All those who stayed fished for a livelihood until 1961, when Cousteau introduced Cozumel's glorious sea life to the world in one of his terrific documentaries and tourists began arriving almost overnight.

Orientation

It's easy to make your way on foot around the island's only town, San Miguel de Cozumel. The airport, 2km north of town, is accessible only by taxi or on foot (ie, there is no bus or shuttle service to the airport).

The waterfront boulevard is Av Melgar; along Av Melgar south of the main ferry dock (the 'Muelle Fiscal') there is a narrow but usable sand beach. The main plaza is just opposite the ferry dock.

Lockers can be rented at the landward end of the Muelle Fiscal for US$2 per day, but they're not big enough for a full backpack.

In order to see most of the island outside of San Miguel (except for Chankanab Bay), you will have to rent a moped or car, or take a taxi (see Getting Around, at the end of this section). A pleasant sightseeing route takes you south from the town of San Miguel, then counterclockwise around the island.

Information

Tourist Offices The local tourist office (☎ 872-0972) is conveniently located a short distance from the main dock, facing the main plaza, at the corner of Av Juárez at Av 5 Norte. It's open 8 am to 5 pm Monday to Friday.

Money For currency exchange, try any one of the five banks near the main plaza (see the map). All of the banks are open 8 am to 4:30 pm Monday to Friday, and on Saturday morning. Banamex, Bancomer and Banca Serfin have ATMs.

The casas de cambio around town are your best bets for long hours and fast service, though they may charge as much as 3.5% commission (versus the bank rate of 1%) to cash a traveler's check. Most of the major hotels, restaurants and stores will also change money.

Post & Communications The post office (☎ 872-0106) is south of Calle 7 Sur on the waterfront just off Av Melgar. It's open 9 am to 1 pm and 3 to 6 pm Monday to Friday, 9 am to noon Saturday.

Telmex Ladatel phones abound on Isla Cancún and represent the least-expensive way to place long-distance calls.

The Internet Cozumel, on Calle 1 Sur at Av 10 Norte, offers eight computers in an air-con environment and has coffee most of the time. Internet access cost US$0.10 per minute at the time this was written. It's open 9 am to 10:30 pm daily.

The Coffee Net, on Av Melgar at Calle 11 Sur, is an Internet café serving coffee and other libations and providing Internet access for US$9 an hour with a US$5 minimum. It's open 9 am to 10 pm daily.

Bookstores The Gracia Agencia de Publicaciones, on the southeast side of the plaza, is open seven days a week selling English, French, German and Spanish books, and English and Spanish magazines and newspapers. Fama Bookstore, one block north along Av 5 Norte, also carries a fairly good selection of books and periodicals in English and Spanish.

Laundry Margarita Laundromat, on Av 20 Sur near Calle 3 Sur, is open 7 am to 9 pm Monday to Saturday, 9 am to 5 pm Sunday, and charges US$1.50 to wash a load (US$0.40 extra if you don't bring your own detergent), US$0.70 for 10 minutes in the dryer. Ironing and folding cost extra.

There's also the Express Lavandería, on Calle Salas just south of Av 5 Sur. It opens at 8 am and closes at 9 pm daily.

Museo de la Isla de Cozumel

This museum, on Av Melgar between Calles 4 Norte and 6 Norte, is very worthwhile. Together with thoughtful and complete signage in English and Spanish, the exhibits – which were intelligently created and are pridefully maintained – present a clear and detailed picture of the island's plants and animals, of its geography and geology, and of the ancient Maya who once inhabited the island.

Also at the museum are exhibits that describe the conquistadors' history in the region and illustrate the navigation routes they used as they plundered the New World; a wonderful exhibit devoted to the region's pirates and their weapons, including original flintlock pistols and muskets; and an exhibit devoted to Caribbean shipwrecks of the 16th, 17th and 18th centuries.

Moreover, there are also beautiful exhibits that tell you everything you could possibly want to know about coral. Visit these exhibits before you go snorkeling or diving so you can fully appreciate what you're seeing when you're in the water.

One of the most interesting rooms features a terrific collection of photos of Cozumel and its inhabitants taken during the 20th century up to and including scenes of widespread destruction dealt by Hurricane Gilbert in 1988.

Before leaving, be sure to enter the traditional Mayan home that's been constructed

at the back of the museum. Here, an older Mayan couple introduces visitors to traditional Mayan ways of life – the medicines they use, their sleeping arrangements, their cooking practices, and so forth. It's an educational and personal exhibit that will increase your appreciation of the Maya.

This fine museum is open 9 am to 8 pm daily. Admission costs US$3.

Parque Chankanab

This national park on Chankanab Bay is famous for its clear water and fabulously colored fish. Lots of people come here to soak up the sun and to snorkel – so many people, in fact, that they often to reduce visibility to just 15m due to the amount of sediment they kick up. (For spectacular snorkeling and diving, you really have to visit a reef by boat.)

That said, most people are very pleased with the marine life here, and there's a small archaeological park on the grounds containing Olmec heads and Mayan artifacts that is enjoyable to stroll through. There is also a small museum containing objects imported from Chichén Itzá. The cost of admission to both is included in the national park's entrance fee (US$7).

Fifty meters from the beach you'll see a lovely lagoon. The lagoon is connected to the sea by a natural tunnel, which visitors used to be permitted to pass through until it partially collapsed during the early 1990s. Today, no one is allowed to enter the lagoon out of concern someone will enter the tunnel, get stuck and drown.

The beach is a beauty, and it's lined with palapas for shade and fiberglass lounge chairs, which any park guest can use. The chairs allow users to kick back and watch the snorkelers, look out across the gorgeous green-blue sea and admire the cumulus clouds that are always overhead. Topless sunbathing is permitted here.

If you didn't bring any water-sports equipment, don't fret. The following snorkel and dive equipment is available for rent: mask (US$3), fins (US$3), tank (US$6), regulator (US$7), BC (US$7), octopus regulator (US$10), underwater camera (US$25) and snorkel vest (US$3). You can rent a towel for US$2, and basic dive instruction is available for US$50. This is a great place to try scuba diving.

Swimming with dolphins is also available at the national park, though the cost of flipping around with Flipper is additional. The dolphins are kept in a penned area along the shore about the size of a football field, and a maximum of two groups of six people are allowed in the pen at one time. For about US$65, one group is allowed to swim to the center of the pen and tread water, while the dolphins swim among them. Individuals in the other group pay US$119 for the privilege of riding a pair of dolphins and performing with them in other ways. The less expensive of the two programs lasts 30 minutes, while the other lasts an hour. Swims are scheduled for 10 am, noon and 2 and 4 pm. The dolphin encounters are organized by Dolphin Discovery (☎ 872-6604, fax 872-2660, www.dolphindiscovery.com). Reservations are recommended.

There's a seaside restaurant with a bar on the grounds, plus several snack shops. The beach has dressing rooms, lockers and showers, which are included in the US$7 admission price to the national park. The park, which is open 9 am to 5 pm daily, also has a botanical garden with 400 species of tropical plants.

Playa San Francisco & Playa Palancar

Playa San Francisco and Playa Palancar are the loveliest of the island's beaches. San Francisco's white sands run for more than 3km, and rather expensive food is served at its restaurant. If you want to scuba dive or snorkel at nearby Arrecife Palancar, you will have to sign on for a day cruise or charter a boat.

El Cedral

To see this Mayan ruin the size of a small house – the oldest of the 32 known archaeological sites on the island – go 3.5km down a paved road a short distance south of Playa San Francisco (there's a sign for the turnoff). Although El Cedral might once have been an important ceremonial site (no one really knows), its minor remnants have been poorly preserved.

Most visitors likely react to the site much the way this writer did, with a heartfelt *That's it?* There's no signage at the much-littered site, which perhaps is most impressive these days for the massive roots that grip it – roots from a tree that grew on the structure's roof for quite a long time, apparently. Mercifully, there is no cost to see the site. In fact, there's no gate at the site and no attendant, so feel free to visit it at anytime.

Punta Celarain

The southern tip of the island has a picturesque lighthouse, accessible via a dirt track, 4km from the highway. To enjoy truly isolated beaches en route, climb over the sand dunes. There's a fine view of the island from the top of the lighthouse.

East Coast Drive

The eastern shoreline is the wildest part of the island and highly recommended for beautiful seascapes of rocky coast. Unfortunately, except for Punta Chiqueros, Playa Chen Río and Punta Morena, swimming is dangerous on Cozumel's east coast due to riptides and undertows. Also, because the beaches are rarely swept for litter, you'll find more seaweed and refuse on them than you'd care for.

Of all of the eastern beaches, by far the least touristy and yet the most festive is the one at Playa Chen Río. There's a simple restaurant at the beach that's wildly popular with local families but, at the time of writing, was being passed up by tourists. Perhaps the place strikes most gringo visitors as too authentic, but the nameless restaurant is a terrific find. Every morning fishers bring their catches to the restaurant, where they're tossed on ice and cooked by nightfall. Lobster, conch, octopus, snapper, grouper – it's all served here, accompanied by large slices of avocado, heaps of rice and chunks of tomato.

The cost of a seafood feast at Playa Chen Río runs about US$8 to US$13, if you spruce up your meal with a delicious margarita. The margaritas are very popular here, possibly because they arrive in glasses the size of small swimming pools and quite possibly because

they are delicious. Because they are so large, most people have trouble finishing theirs and the ones that do then have trouble walking! Exercise restraint if you're driving. The restaurant, with its chairs and tables on the beach under palapas, is open 10 am to 5 pm.

Before reaching the nameless but unforgettable restaurant at Playa Chen Río, you'll pass two rasta/reggae bar-restaurants at Punta Chiqueros. Unlike the nameless restaurant, which is authentic Caribbean Mexico, these places were built for gringos and it's gringos who patronize them. That's not a put-down; they are surfside fun centers with beautiful Caribbean views, no question about it. But if you're looking for something really special, keep on driving and don't stop till you reach Playa Chen Río.

Elsewhere along the mostly undeveloped coast you'll come across some bars owned and run by gringos for gringos. There's one at Playa Santa Cecilia named Naked Iguana Bar. They're fine places if you're looking to mingle with gringos in a bar that could be dropped beside any beach in 100 countries and not look out of place. Each is the cultural equivalent of a McDonald's.

San Gervasio, Aguada Grande & El Castillo Real

Surveys and excavations undertaken during the past three decades indicate that there were at least 32 Mayan centers on Cozumel at the time of the conquistadors' arrival. Nearly all of the centers were located along the coast, and 16th-century Spanish documents tell us that the island had been a trading hub.

All of the Mayan centers on Cozumel were linked by roads, and archaeologists believe the centers were widely separated to minimize losses in the event of attack. The largest center appears to have been San Gervasio, which was the site of a shrine at which women – particularly prospective mothers – worshiped Ixchel, goddess of fertility, medicine, the moon and pilgrims, among a host of other things.

Beyond where the east coast highway meets the Carretera Transversal (ie, the cross-island road) that runs to San Miguel,

intrepid travelers may take the partially paved road about 17km from the junction to the Mayan ruins known as El Castillo Real, and a few kilometers farther to the Aguada Grande. Both sites are very far gone and their significance has been lost to time.

The small ruins at San Gervasio are Cozumel's only preserved ruins, and yet there's very little to them. The structures are small and crude, and the clay idols of Ixchel were long ago destroyed by Spaniards. In his book *A Guide to Ancient Mayan Ruins*, Bruce Hunter writes that priests, hidden behind the shrine, answered the petitions to the large pottery image of the goddess. Who can say? Some visitors to the unimpressive ruins find the jungle en route more interesting.

Playa Bonita & Playa Xhanan

There are some fairly good beaches and some very minor, unmapped Mayan ruins in the vicinity of the northeast point of Cozumel, accessible only by 4WD vehicle or foot. Because the road to Punta Molas is so bad, police never drive to it. If you get stranded, you could find yourself in big trouble because few people travel the road and there are no facilities along it. If you decide to make the trip, be sure to carry lots of water with you. The best camping spot along the entire road is Playa Bonita. Playa Xhanan isn't nearly as pretty, and there are no sandy beaches north of it.

Diving & Snorkeling

Cozumel is a world-class destination for snorkelers and scuba divers, and that's not only our opinion. In a recent reader survey, *Rodale's Scuba Diving* magazine found Cozumel to be the most popular dive destination in the world, all things considered. It ranked second by a whisker to Egypt's Red Sea for the crystal clarity of its water, and second to Cay Sal Bank in the Bahamas in dollar value.

There are many reasons Cozumel's diving is unsurpassed, and chief among them is some of the best year-round visibility anywhere. Visibility of 50m and greater is common here. And the attractions – ballets of eagle rays, gulping moray eels, scowling groupers, metallic barracuda with razor-sharp teeth,

brain corals and sponges as big as garbage cans – are jaw-dropping awesome.

To facilitate your underwater adventures, there are no fewer than 100 dive centers on Cozumel and dozens more in Playa del Carmen. Due to the stiff competition, there is little disparity in prices and services among the operators. In general, you can expect to pay US$60 for a two-tank dive (less if you bring your own BC and regulator), US$75 for an introductory 'resort' course and US$350 for PADI open-water-diver certification.

For equipment rental, instruction and/or boat reservations, there are numerous dive shops on Av Melgar along San Miguel's waterfront.

Here are a few of the reputable dive shops on Cozumel:

Blue Bubble Divers (☎ 872-4483, ☎/fax 872-1865, in the USA ☎ 800-878-8853, www.cozumel-diving .net/blue_bubble), at the corner of Av 5 Sur and Calle 3 Sur

Caribbean Divers (☎ 872-1080, 872-1145, www .cozumel-diving.net/caribbean_divers), Calle 3 Sur between Avs Melgar and 5 Sur

Diving Adventures (☎ 872-3009, in the USA ☎ 888-338-0388, www.cozumel-diving.net/diving _adventures), Calle 5 Sur near Av Melgar

Scuba Du (☎/fax 872-1994, www.cozumel-diving .net/scubadu), Calle 3 Sur between Avs Melgar and 5 Sur 01 98 724130

Yucatech Expeditions (☎ 872-5659, fax 872-1417, www.cozumel-diving.net/yucatech), Av 15 Norte between Calle Salas and Calle 1 Sur; this outfit specializes in diving caves and caverns

There are two hyperbaric chambers in San Miguel: Buceo Medico Mexicano (☎ 872-2387, 872-1430, fax 872-1848), on Calle 5 Sur between Avs Melgar and 5 Sur; and Cozumel Hyperbaric Research (☎ 872-3070, CHF Radio on Channel 65), in the Medica San Miguel clinic on Calle 6 Norte between Avs 5 Norte and 10 Norte.

Snorkelers: All of the best snorkel sites are reached by boat. It makes little sense to spend the money to travel all the way to Cozumel and then short-change yourself by passing on the boat option. A half-day boat tour will set you back US$20 to US$35, but you'll do some world-class snorkeling. If you

Cozumel's Top Dive Sites

Ask any dive operator in Cozumel to name the best dive sites in the area, and the following names will come up time and again:

Santa Rosa Wall This is the biggest name of the name sites. The wall is so large most people are able to see only a third of it on one tank. Regardless of where you're dropped, expect to find enormous overhangs and tunnels covered with corals and sponges. Stoplight parrotfish, black grouper and barracuda hang out here. Average visibility is 30m and minimum depth 10m, with an average closer to 25m. Carry a flashlight with you, even if you're diving at noon. A flashlight really helps bring out the color of coral at depth and illuminate the critters hiding in crevices.

Punta Sur Reef This is also a deep wall dive, with a minimum depth of 20m, but it's unforgettable for its coral caverns, each of which is named. Before you dive be sure to ask your dive master to point out The Devil's Throat. This cave opens into a cathedral room with four tunnels, all of which make for some pretty hairy exploring. Only cave-certified divers should consider entering The Devil's Throat, but anyone who visits Punta Sur Reef will be impressed by the cave system and the butterflyfish, the angelfish and the whip corals that abound there.

Colombia Shallows Also known as Colombia Gardens, Colombia Shallows lends itself equally well to snorkeling and scuba diving. Because it's a shallow dive (maximum depth 10m, average 2m to 4m), its massive coral buttresses covered with sponges and other resplendent lifeforms are well illuminated. The current at Colombia Gardens is generally light to moderate; the combination of shallow water and light current allows you to spend hours at the site if you want, and you'll never get bored spying all the elkhorn coral, pillar coral and anemones that live there.

Palancar Gardens Also known as Palancar Shallows, this dive can also be appreciated by snorkelers due to the slight current usually found there and the low maximum depth of the site (20m). The Gardens consists of a strip reef about 25m wide and very long, riddled with fissures and tunnels. The major features here are enormous stove-pipe sponges and vivid yellow tube sponges, and you can always find damselfish, parrotfish and angelfish around you. In the deeper parts of the reef, divers will want to keep an eye out for the lovely black corals.

International Pier This pier, located near Playa la Ceiba and used by cruise ships and the car ferry, was built on a sandy bottom in 1978. The concrete rubble at the foot of the pier is so dense that lots of critters are now calling it home, and it makes for some terrific exploring. Just beyond the pier is the first of several small walls that offer spectacular beauty. Of particular note are the red sponges and fire coral found there. The pier can only be dived on weekends and only with the permission of the harbor master; if you want to dive it, plan accordingly.

want to be pound-foolish and penny-wise, you can do that by saving on the boat fare and walking into the usually gentle surf at Chankanab Bay, Playa San Francisco, Playa La Ceiba and elsewhere. Unfortunately, the best snorkel sites simply aren't that convenient.

Glass-Bottom Boat Rides
You can enjoy the coral formations and aquatic life by taking a tour on a glass-bottom boat, the *Palapa Marina* (☎ 872-0539), on

Calle 1 Sur, between Avs 5 Norte and 10 Norte. The boat departs the Sol Caribe pier, south of San Miguel near the car ferry dock, daily at 9 am and 1 pm. The fare is US$15 per person.

Places to Stay
Budget To camp anywhere on the island, you'll need a permit from the island's naval authorities, which you can obtain 24 hours a day, for free, from the naval head-

quarters south of the post office on Av Melgar. The best camping places are along the relatively unpopulated eastern shore of the island.

All rooms described below come with private bath and fan, unless otherwise noted.

Hotel Cozumel Inn (☎ 872-0314, fax 872-3156), on Calle 4 Norte between Avs Melgar and 5 Norte, has 20 rooms for only US$20/25 a double with fan/air-con in summer. There's a pool on the premises. This is an excellent value.

Also an excellent value, *Hotel Saolima* (☎ 872-0886), on Calle Salas between Avs 10 Sur and 15 Sur, has clean, pleasant rooms in a quiet locale for US$21 with fan only and US$23 with air-con.

Hotel Posada Edém (☎ 872-1166), on Calle 2 Norte between Avs 5 Norte and 10 Norte, is uninspiring but cheap at US$15/20 single/double with fan and US$25/30 with air-con.

Hotel Marruang (☎ 872-1678), on Calle Salas between Avs 20 Sur and 25 Sur, is entered from a passageway across from the municipal market. A clean room with one double and one single bed costs US$18 to US$24. Add US$5 for air-con.

Posada Letty (☎ 872-0257), on Av 15 Sur at Calle 1 Sur, offers inexpensive no-frills rooms for US$20 in the summer, US$22 in the winter. The Hotel Pepita, nearby, offers better value.

Hotel Kary (☎ 872-2011), on Calle Salas at Av 25 Sur, is five blocks east of the plaza and a bit out of the way, but it has a pool and reasonably priced rooms: US$25 for a double with fan and US$28 with air-con.

Hotel El Pirata (☎ 872-0051), centrally-located on Av 5 Sur between Calles 1 Sur and Salas, offers decent rooms with private bath and fan for US$23 a double in summer, US$32 with air-con.

Hotel Pepita (☎ 872-0098, fax 872-0201), on Av 15 Sur at Calle 1 Sur, has well-maintained rooms around a delightful garden for US$25 in summer, US$30 in winter. All of the rooms have two double beds, insect screens, fans and little refrigerators as well as the air-con, and there's free morning coffee. This is a very good deal!

Mid-Range Most mid-range hostelries offer air-conditioning and swimming pools. All have private bathrooms.

Hotel Flamingo (☎ 872-1264), on Calle 6 Norte near Av Melgar, was remodeled in 1999. Each guest room now has air-con, and a new bar and small dining area were added. With the changes, the island's best budget hotel jumped substantially in price. The 22 rooms now go for US$35 to US$50 a double, depending upon the season.

Hotel Vista del Mar (☎ 872-0545, fax 872-0445), Av Melgar between Calles 5 Sur and 7 Sur, has 26 air-con rooms, a small swimming pool, restaurant, liquor store and rental car and travel agency. Some rooms have balconies with sea views. The price in summer is US$40 a double, rising to US$45 in winter.

Tried and true, clean, comfortable lodgings are yours at the *Hotel Mary-Carmen* (☎ 872-0581), on Av 5 Sur, half a block south of the plaza. The 27 tidy, air-con rooms cost US$28 a double in summer, US$40 in winter.

The *Hotel Safari Inn* (☎ 872-0101, fax 872-0661, div@aquasafari.com), on Av Melgar at Calle 5 Sur, features 12 rooms with air-con and fans for a reasonable US$40 a double. Rooms Nos 1 and 7 face the beach.

Colonial Hotel & Suites (☎ 872-4034, fax 872-1387), on Av 5 Sur near Calle Salas, has studios and one-bedroom suites (some of which can sleep up to four people) with kitchenette, air-con and pretensions to decor for US$45 for a studio and US$55 for a one bedroom during summer.

The similar *Hotel Bahía* (☎ 872-0209, fax 872-1387), facing the sea on Av Melgar at Calle 3 Sur, is under the same management and charges slightly more.

Hotel Maya Cozumel (☎ 872-0011, fax 872-0781), on Calle 5 Sur between Avs Melgar and 5 Sur, has good, air-con, TV-equipped rooms and a very inviting swimming pool surrounded by grass and bougainvillea for US$40/45/50 a single/double/triple in winter, about US$5 less per room in summer. This is a very good value.

Sun Village San Miguel (☎ 872-0323, fax 872-1820, in the USA ☎ 800-221-5833), on Av Juárez between Avs Melgar and 5 Norte, has a little pool, blissful air-con, a restaurant and

QUINTANA ROO

SAN MIGUEL DE COZUMEL

PLACES TO STAY
5 Hotel Flamingo
7 Hotel Cozumel Inn
12 Sun Village San Miguel
14 Hotel Posada Edém
15 Hotel Bahia
18 Hotel Mary-Carmen
25 Colonial Hotel & Suites
26 Hotel El Pirata
33 Hotel Vista del Mar
34 Hotel Safari Inn
35 Hotel Maya Cozumel
40 Hotel Pepita
41 Posada Letty
47 Hotel Saolima
56 Hotel Marruang
57 Hotel Kary

PLACES TO EAT
1 Pizza Rolandi
6 Carlos 'n Charlie's
8 Pasteleria y Panaderia
   Zermatt
11 Hard Rock Café
16 Pepe's Grill
19 Restaurant Plaza Leza
24 Pizza Prima
31 Restaurant El Abuelo
   Gerardo
32 Hog's Breath Saloon
36 Coffee Bean
37 Restaurant La Choza
39 Cocina Económica
   Mi Chabelita
45 Restaurant Costa Brava

49 Mercado Municipal;
   Loncherías
52 Acuario
55 Miss Dollar

OTHER
2 Central de Artesanías
3 Three Shop Emporium
4 Museo de la Isla
   de Cozumel
9 Medica San Miguel
10 Banorte
13 Fama Bookstore
17 Banamex (ATM)
20 Gracia Agencia de
   Publicaciones
21 Bancomer (ATM)
22 Tourist Office
23 Express Lavandería
27 Bital
28 Banca Serfin (ATM)
29 Internet Cozumel
30 Parroquia de San
   Miguel Arcángel
42 Naval Headquarters
43 Lighthouse
44 Post Office
46 Hyperbaric Chamber
   (24 Hours)
48 Joe's Restaurant &
   Reggae Bar
50 Cruz Roja
51 Pemex (Gas Station)
53 Neptuno's;
   Coffee Net
54 Margarita Laundromat

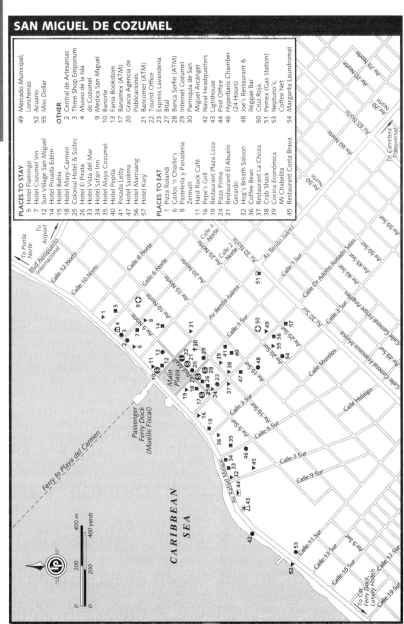

100 rooms with balconies. There's also a separate beach club with water-sports facilities seven blocks from the hotel on the water. Rates are US$35/75 a double in summer/winter.

The **Club del Sol** (☎ 872-3777, fax 872-5877, clubdelsol@cozunet.finred.com.mx), Carretera a Chankanab Km 6.8, has a mere 41 air-con rooms with an oversize whirlpool tub and pool tables on the premises. Kitchenettes are available. This hotel charges a very reasonable US$60 for one person or two most of the year.

Top End Beginning several kilometers south of town (see the Cozumel map, earlier) are the big, all-inclusive, luxury resort hotels, which typically charge between US$125 and US$150 per person most of the year, double occupancy. Prices vary significantly with season and promotional deals.

North of town along the western shore of the island are numerous smaller, more modest resort hotels, usually cheaper than the big places, but catering mostly to package tour groups. The one exception is the **Meliá Paradisus** (☎ 872-0411, 872-1599, in the USA ☎ 800-336-3542), north of town, which is very upscale with prices to match; all-inclusive rates typically run US$125 to US$190 per person double occupancy. Again, prices vary considerably based on demand. Most of the air-con rooms at the multilevel Meliá Paradisus offer sea views, and all come with either a balcony or terrace.

South of town, the **Presidente Inter-Continental Cozumel** (☎ 872-0322, fax 872-3120, www.interconti.com), Carretera a Chankanab Km 6.5, is hard to miss with its 253 guest rooms, many with sea views, set amidst tropical gardens and swimming pools. Rates are all-inclusive and range from US$110 to US$150 per person most of the year, with price varying with sea view and other features.

One of the finest hotels on the island is certainly the **Fiesta Americana** (in the USA ☎ 800-343-7821, fiesta@gate.net), Carretera a Chankanab Km 10, which features 172 oceanfront and balconied rooms and 56 suites, plenty of gardens and a spectacular swimming pool. Rates are all-inclusive and

typically run US$140 per person double occupancy, lower during the summer.

Next up on the road south is the **Punta San Clemente** (☎ 874-3625), Carretera a Chankanab Km 12.9, which features 240 very stacked-up guest rooms beside the sea. Rates typically run US$100 per person double occupancy and aren't a deal at that.

The **Reef Club Beach Resort** (☎ 874-3626, fax 876-0733, hotelreefclub@infosel.net.mx), Carretera a Chankanab Km 14, isn't quite as nice as the Fiesta Americana or the Allegro, but it's in the same price range.

The **Allegro Resort** (☎ 872-3443, fax 872-4508, in the USA ☎ 800-858-2258), Carretera a Chankanab Km 16.5, has 300 rooms contained in two-story, Polynesian-style thatch-roofed villas. There are three restaurants on the grounds and a pool with a swim-up bar. Rates are US$150 per person, all-inclusive, double occupancy.

Places to Eat

Budget Cheapest of all eating places, with fairly tasty food, are the market loncherías located next to the Mercado Municipal on Calle Salas between Avs 20 Sur and 25 Sur. All of these little señora-run eateries offer soup and a main course for less than US$3, with a large selection of dishes available. Hours are 6:30 am to 6:30 pm daily.

Restaurant Costa Brava, on Av Melgar just south of the post office, is among the more funky places to dine on the island. Cheap breakfasts (US$2 to US$3), and such filling dishes as chicken tacos, grilled steak and fried fish or chicken for US$4 to US$7, are served daily from 6:30 am to 11:30 pm.

The **Cocina Económica Mi Chabelita**, Av 10 Sur between Calles 1 Sur and Salas, is a tiny, inexpensive eatery run by a señora who serves up decent portions of decent food for US$3 or less. It opens for breakfast at 7 am and closes at 7 pm.

The forthrightly named **Miss Dollar**, on Av 20 Sur near Calle Salas, earns its money by providing inexpensive meals to take out.

The **Coffee Bean**, on Calle 3 Sur just off Av Melgar, serves up the latest trendy java recipes. It's enormously popular and open 7 am to 11 pm daily.

For pastries, try the **Pastelería y Panadería Zermatt**, Av 5 Norte at Calle 4 Norte.

Mid-Range *Pizza Prima*, on Calle Salas between Avs 5 Sur and 10 Sur, is open 1 to 11 pm daily except Wednesday. The American owners produce homemade pasta and fresh pizza (US$6 to US$12) as well as excellent Italian specialties (US$8 to US$15). Dine streetside, or upstairs on the patio.

Pizza Rolandi, on Av Melgar between Calles 6 Norte and 8 Norte, serves good one-person (20cm diameter) pizzas cooked in a wood-fire oven for US$7.50 to US$9.50. Homemade pasta is also available here. The Rolandi is open 11:30 am to 11:30 pm; closed Sunday.

The *Crab Shack*, on Av 10 Sur at Calle Salas, is a casual corner joint that whips up some excellent seafood at reasonable prices. Specialties include: breaded scallops (US$9.50), crab cakes (US$6), Cajun crawfish (US$9.50) and snow crab clusters (US$25 per kilo). If you appreciate crabs, you'll love this place.

Restaurant El Abuelo Gerardo, on Av 10 Norte at Av Juárez, is attractive, with locally made crafts for decoration and lively salsa music. The menu is extensive and prices reasonable (though only three years ago they were half what they are now): beef fajitas (US$7), chicken fajitas (US$7) and fried fish, typically snapper or grouper (US$8). Guacamole and chips are on the house.

Restaurant La Choza, on Calle Salas at Av 10 Sur, is an excellent and popular restaurant specializing in authentic regional cuisine. Typical dishes include: pork in tomato sauce (US$7), garlic fish filet (US$9), shrimp

chiles rellenos (US$8.50) and beef fajitas (US$9.50). All entrées include soup.

Cozumel's *Hard Rock Café*, on Av Melgar near the main ferry dock, features walls covered with rock 'n' roll memorabilia and serves lots of American food, such as a hickory BBQ bacon cheeseburger (US$7.50), a 'Pig Sandwich' that contains 'select pork shoulder, hickory smoked for 10 hours, then hand-pulled so it is tender and juicy' (US$8.50), and lots of appetizers. It's a good place to watch a sunset.

Carlos 'n Charlie's, on Av Melgar between Calles 2 Norte and 4 Norte, is like a low-class Hard Rock, emphasis on low class. Sea water tastes better than the establishment's margaritas. People with discerning tastes don't frequent the place. It's mentioned here because a lot of folks wander in and find themselves planted and ordering food before realizing they should have gone elsewhere. Specialties include lobster chowder (US$5.50), chicken (US$7) and chicken soup (US$3.75).

Hog's Breath Saloon, on Calle 7 Sur at Av Melgar, is a popular rock club at night and restaurant-bar during the day. Breakfast items include yogurt, omelets and a fruit bowl (around US$4); lunch and dinner items include a fish sandwich (US$7), a grilled chicken sandwich (US$7) and chicken fajitas (US$8).

Restaurant Plaza Leza, on the main plaza, is a fan-cooled, sedate, indoor-outdoor restaurant specializing in fajitas and massive Mexican combination plates for around US$8, but the food is absolutely mediocre. Plaza Leza is mentioned because it happens to be the best of the few restaurants

Big-Name Art at the Hard Rock

Cozumel's Hard Rock Café is, like all of the Hard Rocks on this planet, a shrine to rock 'n' rollers. The walls are covered with rock memorabilia, as you might suspect. But the quality of the memorabilia at Cozumel's Hard Rock will impress even the most critical rock fanatics. The wall art, if you will, includes an 'LA Woman' album cover signed by every member of The Doors; the black-and-white vest worn by Prince during his 1988 'Love Sexy' tour; and a poster advertising the Jimi Hendrix concert at Stuttgart on January 15, 1969.

on the plaza, and because it's high profile and looks promising.

Top End Cozumel's traditional place to dine richly is **Pepe's Grill**, Av Melgar at Calle Salas. Entrées include New York steak, pepper steak or prime rib (US$19), Chateaubriand for two (US$30) and charcoal-broiled lobster served with garlic (market price, typically around US$35).

Acuario, on Av Melgar at Calle 11 Sur, is a popular, upscale seaside restaurant featuring excellent seafood that's really overpriced. The fish of the day runs US$14, grilled Caribbean lobster (these aren't the huge Maine lobsters you might be accustomed to seeing) is priced at US$30, red snapper stuffed with shrimp costs US$20 and a filet mignon and lobster plate goes for US$28.

Entertainment

Most of the year, Cozumel can't keep up with Playa del Carmen as a nightlife destination. Indeed, some nights Cozumel is downright sleepy. But if you're in Cozumel a couple hours after sunset and looking for a happening scene, there are a few places that warrant investigation.

The **Hard Rock Café**, near the main ferry dock, features live rock 'n' roll most nights of the week. Same goes for the **Hog's Breath Saloon**, on Calle 7 Sur at Av Melgar, four blocks south of the main plaza. For reggae, head to **Joe's Restaurant & Reggae Bar**, on Av 15 Sur between Calles Salas and 3 Sur. For disco, there's only one name in town, and it's **Neptuno's**, Av Melgar at Calle 11 Sur; open Thursday, Friday and Saturday nights.

Shopping

There are souvenir shops up and down Av Melgar that cater mostly to the cruise-line crowds who flood the town for a day and generally don't stray from the frontage road. Most of these stores sell low-quality handicrafts at so-so prices. The two places mentioned here pretty much fit that description, but people (the writer included) like them anyway. If you're looking for a 'gift from Cozumel' for a friend, these places have lots to offer that won't leave you broke.

The Central de Artesanías, on Av Melgar near Calle 4 Norte, offers lots of carved wooden handicrafts, heads carved from coconuts, coffee mugs with 'Cozumel' on them, ceramic dolls, faux-silver jewelry, bullwhips, belts, colorful ceramic figurines of toucans, fish, cats and whatnot, and T-shirts by the closetful.

Next door, the Three Shop Emporium features many of the same items, as well as many objects made of cut onyx – onyx chess sets, onyx figurines, onyx pencil holders, colorful onyx fruit. If you arrived in Cozumel without beachwear, or if you're looking to upgrade your current surf wardrobe, the Three Shop Emporium can help you.

Getting There & Away

Air Cozumel has a surprisingly busy international airport (Aeropuerto Internacional de Cozumel), with numerous direct flights from other parts of Mexico and the USA. Flights from Europe are usually routed via the USA or Mexico City. There are direct flights on Continental (☎ 872-0251) and American (☎ 872-0899) from Dallas, Houston, and Raleigh-Durham, NC, with many flights from other US cities via these hubs. Mexicana (☎ 872-0263) has nonstops from Miami and direct flights from Mérida and Mexico City. See the Getting There & Away chapter for details on international flights to Cozumel.

Aero Cozumel (☎ 872-0928, 872-0503), with offices at the Cozumel airport, operates daily flights between Cancún and Cozumel for US$50 one way. The airline also has daily flights between Cozumel and Belize City (US$165 one way). Reserve in advance.

Ferry Passenger ferries to Cozumel run from Playa del Carmen, car ferries run from Puerto Morelos. See those sections for details.

Getting Around

To/From the Airport The airport is about 2km north of town. You can take a minibus from the airport into town for less than US$2, slightly more to the hotels south of town, but you'll have to take a taxi (US$4) to return to the airport.

Bus & Taxi Cozumel's taxi drivers have a lock on the local transport market, defeating any proposal for a convenient bus service. Fares in and around town are US$4 per ride. From the town to Laguna Chankanab is US$10.

Car & Moped Rates for rental cars run US$40 to $55 per day, all-inclusive, more during late December and January. You could probably haggle with a taxi driver to take you on a tour of the island, drop you at a beach, come back and pick you up, and still save money. If you do rent, observe the law on vehicle occupancy. Usually only five people are allowed in a vehicle (say, a Jeep). If you carry more, the police will fine you.

The island has few fuel stations. You'll find one location on Av Juárez five blocks east of the main square.

Rented mopeds represent the best way to tour the island on your own, and it seems every citizen and business in San Miguel – hotels, restaurants, gift shops, morticians – rents mopeds, generally for as little as US$10 to US$15 per day (24 hours), gas included. Insurance and tax are also included in these prices. Remember: All prices are negotiable. If someone approaches you as you're getting off the ferry offering mopeds for rent for US$25 a day, reply 'US$10 a day.' Oftentimes the response is a quick, 'OK.'

You must have a valid driver's license, and you must use a credit card to rent, or put down a deposit (usually US$100). Also, there is a helmet law and it is enforced, although most moped rental people won't mention it. Before you sign a rental agreement, be sure to request a helmet. If you don't ride with one, expect to pay at least one police officer US$25 in fines.

The best time to rent is first thing in the morning, when all the machines are there. Choose a good one, with a working horn, brakes, lights, starter, rearview mirrors, and a full tank of fuel; remember that the price asked will be the same whether you rent the newest, pristine machine or the oldest, most beat-up rattletrap. (If you want to trust yourself with a second-rate moped, at least haggle the price down significantly.)

Don't plan to circumnavigate the island with two people on one moped. The much-used and ill-maintained machine may well break down under the load, stranding you a long way from civilization with no way to get help.

When riding, keep in mind that you will be as exposed to sunshine on a moped as if you were roasting on a beach. Slather yourself with sun block (especially the backs of your hands, feet and neck, and your face) or cover up – or suffer the consequences. Another thing: The seats on mopeds are always made of black plastic, which heats to burning-skin temperatures under the tropical sun. When you ride, always travel with a towel you can toss on your seat when the vehicle's parked.

Be aware of the dangers involved. Of all motor vehicle operators, the inexperienced moped driver on unfamiliar roads in a foreign country has the highest statistical chance of having an accident, especially when faced by lots of other inexperienced moped drivers. If you're a bit clumsy or are easily distracted or just can't operate a moped well, stay away from them.

XCARET

Once a communal turkey farm, Xcaret ('ISHKAR-et,' ☎ 9-883-3143, fax 9-883-3324), 'Nature's Sacred Paradise,' 10km south of Playa del Carmen, has been heavily Disneyfied. The beautiful inlet filled with tropical marine life is ringed by several minor Mayan ruins and has a cenote for swimming, a restaurant, and an 'ancient Mayan ceremonies' evening show worthy of Las Vegas. Also on the premises are a butterfly pavilion, a botanical garden and nursery, an orchid farm and a mushroom farm, a museum containing models of the most significant Mayan ruins, and a wild-bird breeding area.

Package tourists from Cancún fill the place every day, arriving in a caravan of special Xcaret buses (Xcaret even has its own bus station on Isla Cancún) and happily paying the US$39 admission fee, plus additional fees for many attractions and activities such as swimming with dolphins (US$30

for 15 minutes, US$55 for 30 minutes, US$80 for an hour); a snorkeling tour of underground caverns (US$23); and a one-tank reef dive (US$39). Xcaret is open 8:30 am to 10 pm Monday to Saturday, 8:30 am to 6 pm Sunday, April to October, and 8:30 am to 9 pm Monday to Saturday, 8:30 am to 5 pm Sunday, November to March. Radios and other noisy items, nonbiodegradable suntan lotions and sunscreens, and outside food and drinks are prohibited.

PAAMUL

Paamul, located 87km south of Ciudad Cancún and 5km north of Puerto Aventuras, is both the name of a beach and the name of a hotel (☎/fax 9-876-2691) with beachfront cabañas and full RV hookups. This is an excellent find. The cabañas consist of duplexes that are a bit worn but spacious and all face a protected bay with fine coral heads. Each cabaña has a private bathroom with hot water, a ceiling fan and two beds. Cost for one or two persons is US$41, a third person is US$4 more. The RV park offers electricity, water, and toilet and shower use. Cost is US$17 a day, US$105 a week, US$395 a month. Camping is offered at US$8 for two people per site. There are two communal telephones.

Paamul's beach is lovely and fringed with palms, but as there are lots of small rocks and shells in the sand as you enter the water, you'll want to make sure to bring a pair of scuba booties or other appropriate footwear with you. They don't have to be fancy, they just need to offer the bottom of your feet some protection.

If you walk only about 2km north of Paamul you will find an alabaster sand beach to call your own, but then you wouldn't be able to order drinks and food from Paamul's pleasant restaurant-bar. What a dilemma! The least rocky section of Paamul's beach is the southern end, but watch out for spiked sea urchins in the shallows offshore. Again, bring appropriate footwear so you don't have to worry about your feet.

Divers: Paamul is a terrific find. On the premises is Scuba-Mex (☎ 9-874-1729, fax 9-873-0667, www.scubamex.com), which has been offering dive trips to area sites since

1983 and boasts not a single accident in all those years. Run by a couple of friendly Texans who've been diving in the area since 1967, Scuba-Mex takes divers to 30 superb sites – of which two are truly spectacular. Perhaps the better of the two is The Canyons, which consists of many mountains of coral that range in depth from 10m to 30m. The coral is in great condition and divers can expect to see at least one sea turtle per dive (there are four species in the area). Nowhere else along the coasts of Mexico can that be said.

The other awesome site is The Wall, although in reality it consists of three walls laid out like a series of giant steps. Sand is on the horizontal surfaces and coral on the vertical, and you swim from the top of the first step, down the first wall (12m to 20m) to the sandy top of the second step, then down the second wall (28m to 40m) to the sandy top of the third step, and from there you can only look at the top of the third wall (50m to a head-crushing depth). Within and around the three walls expect to see moray eels, lobsters and lots of sharks (lemon, nurse, reef and bull ply these waters).

Scuba-Mex charges a very reasonable US$35 for the first dive, US$30 for a second dive on the same day (US$5 less if you provide your own equipment). Night dives (highly recommended) cost US$45 (US$35 with your equipment). Also offered are cenote dives (US$65) and a slew of packages, including seven dives for US$210 with equipment (US$140 without). If you pay before you arrive, the package rates are even lower. Resort courses (instruction and one dive) are offered for US$65. Open-water certification (available from PADI, NAUI, CMAS, SSI, YMCA and IDEA) takes four days and costs a reasonable US$350.

Moreover, nearly every dive is led by a dive instructor, not simply a dive master (which is one reason they've never had a serious injury or fatality). Snorkel gear and booties in a limited number of sizes are available. You're best off bringing your own mask and booties to ensure a good fit.

Scuba-Mex has regularly scheduled dives at 9:30 am and at 2:30 pm, weather permitting.

Divers should arrive at least 30 minutes ahead of time. Resort courses are taught at 11 am.

Giant sea turtles come ashore here at night in July and August to lay their eggs. If you run across a turtle during your evening stroll along the beach, please keep a good distance from it, and don't shine a flashlight at the turtle, as this will scare it off. Instead, if you let your eyes adjust to the darkness you'll be able to see well enough and not interfere with nature.

Be advised that if you intend to reach Paamul by bus, you'll still have a 400m walk from the highway to the hotel/beach.

PUERTO AVENTURAS
☎ 9 • pop 900

This resort community 92km south of Ciudad Cancún and 40km north of Tulum was, like Cancún, a planned development from the get-go. Puerto Aventuras never was a fishing village or a seaside farming community. Prior to 1990, there was scarcely a structure where today condos and hotels crowd the shoreline. Instead, there was mangrove teeming with wildlife and there were beaches where sea turtles had returned year after year for 50 millennia to lay eggs.

Today, the mangrove is mostly gone and the rest soon will be. In its wake there's a golf course, several thousand rooms for rent, and a marina that can accommodate 300 boats. Though some turtles continue to nest on the beaches of Puerto Aventuras, their numbers diminish yearly. The untreated waste from the marina, the hotels and the condos is destroying the reef out front. And, at the time of writing, two huge resorts were nearing completion at the

north end of the community. Puerto Aventuras is an environmentalist's nightmare.

If your primary reason for staying in the area is its awesome marine life, you'd be much better off staying at Paamul and snorkeling and diving there, or staying in Playa del Carmen where you can have your marine life and your nightlife (not to mention a wide selection of accommodations and dining options). If you do opt to stay in Puerto Aventuras, your choices of activities include reef diving, cenote diving, visiting a small maritime museum and frolicking with dolphins.

Activities

CEDAM Dive Center (☎ 873-5147, fax 873-5129, www.cedamdive.com), at the north end of the first cluster of buildings you come to after you've turned off the highway, offers reef dives starting from US$50 with equipment, and a discount is offered if you provide your own equipment. CEDAM also offers cenote diving within the incomparable Nohoch Nah Chich cave system (see Nohoch Nah Chich, later this chapter), which starts at US$60 per dive; and an Indiana Jones Jungle Adventure that includes a jungle trek, a visit to a Mayan ranch and snorkeling in a stalactite- and stalagmite-rich cenote.

CEDAM's Puerto Aventuras location contains a small and worthwhile museum featuring artifacts salvaged from a Spanish galleon found just offshore. There's no cost to enter.

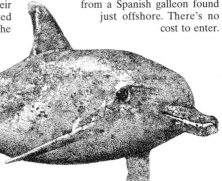

Many places in Yucatán offer the chance to swim with dolphins.

Dolphin Discovery (☎ 873-5216, www .dolphindiscovery.com), which has its large dolphin enclosure behind the first long cluster of buildings you come to, offers visitors the chance to frolic with several very well-trained dolphins. The staff and their dolphins also put on a humorous performance for visitors. The cost is US$119 and reservations are a must.

Places to Stay & Eat

From Hwy 307, the road into Puerto Aventuras winds several hundred meters. If you turn right (south) at the first opportunity to do so, you'll soon come to the beachfront *Papaya Republic (☎ 873-5170, 873-5191).* Unlike most of the area's structures, which are concrete-block-and-stucco buildings with tile roofs, the Papaya Republic is made of thatch and bamboo, and a strong Caribbean ambiance pervades the place. Whereas most of the other buildings started on lots that had been bulldozed clean, the Papaya Republic was built on a large piece of property among existing palm trees and scrub brush. The result: The restaurant and the 10 cabañas on the property have loads of tropical character. Taking the bite out of the day's heat is a lovely swimming pool from which guests can watch the surf break. The cabañas rent for US$90 a night, which is higher than it should be. The Papaya Republic is locally famous for is delicious food, which includes: Galician octopus (US$7), crab Tampico style (US$7), fish filet in mustard sauce (US$10), beef tenderloin in a pepper sauce (US$10) and shrimp in a curry sauce (US$16).

The newest and nicest of the waterfront resorts is the fairly intimate *Omni Puerto Aventuras (☎ 873-5101, fax 873-5102, www .omnihotels.com),* which features 30 elegant guest rooms, two connecting swimming pools and a children's pool, and three restaurants (one serving regional and international fare, another featuring seafood and a third providing Italian cuisine). Room rates start at US$140 for one or two persons.

CENOTES KANTUN CHI & AZUL

Five kilometers south of the turnoff for Playa Aventuras are two sets of cenotes within a kilometer of each other. Cenotes Kantun Chi consist of a series of four natural pools situated in light jungle. They are more pleasant than the people who run them, who won't let you see the cenotes (let alone test the temperature of the water to see if it's too cool for your liking) until you've paid US$3.

An even nicer series of natural freshwater pools can be found at Cenote Azul, which is more open-air than those at Kantun Chi. The sunlight hitting the cenotes here increases the proliferation of algae, and so these cenotes tend to have much more algae than their shadier cenotes down the road. However, every day a man with a scrub brush goes at the rocks, somewhat successfully keeping the slippery foliage under control. The edge of the cenote is ringed by light jungle and there's no shortage of playful lizards. Cost of admission is US$2.

There are snack bars at both cenotes. Both are a short distance from the highway and open during daylight hours. Signs indicating their presence are visible from the road.

XPU-HA

Xpu-ha ('IShpoo-HA,' ☎ 9-843-3306, fax 9-887-2870, xpuhavta@cancun.com.mx), a private ecopark 97km south of Ciudad Cancún, offers most or all of the things the other three ecoparks along the Riviera Maya (Tulum Corridor) offer, but the US$29 entrance fee charged here is all-inclusive. Visitors don't have to pay more to use a kayak to meander the park's cenotes, they don't need to pay more to take a catamaran ride, nor do they need to go on a guided ecological tour. Boogie boards and bicycles are, likewise, free to use. In addition to a restaurant and a gift shop, visitors will find a snake house, pens containing deer, crocodiles and turtles, and an aviary. Xpu-ha is open 9 am to 5 pm daily.

VILLAS DEL CARIBE

One kilometer south of the turnoff to Xpu-ha is the lengthy turnoff to this fairly remote, generally overlooked beachside hotel. The *Villas del Caribe (☎ 9-872-1429, fax 9-872-2475, tqroo@cozumel.com.mx)* offers 30 basic but spacious rooms with a single light and a single fan per room. What guests are really paying for is the tranquillity that can

be found here and on the beach. This is a good place to 'get away from it all' for awhile. Rates are US$45 a room.

ROBINSON CLUB

The *Robinson Club* (☎ 9-881-1010, fax 9-881-1004), located 98km south of Ciudad Cancún, is a megaresort with all the amenities on a beautiful stretch of beach with coral heads out front. The hotel, which caters almost exclusively to Germans, offers all of the water sports, as well as lovely gardens for strolling, eight tennis courts, several large swimming pools, and a gift shop, a silver shop and a theater. Rates tend to run US$150 a room, less if you prepay.

EL DORADO RESORT

A couple of kilometers farther south along Hwy 307 is the turnoff for *El Dorado Resort* (☎ 9-884-8341, fax 9-884-8342, in the USA ☎ 800-334-1197, eldorado@mail.caribe.net .mx), which is much more subdued than the Robinson Club. Whereas the Robinson Club has the look and somewhat impersonal feel of a megaresort, this all-inclusive resort is low profile, with just one line of two-story buildings set back from the surf 75m and nestled in among palm trees. The beach out front is wide, deep and lovely, and there are some scattered coral heads within swimming distance. There are several restaurants, four bars and two swimming pools on the premises. Every room is a junior suite. Those with ocean view generally rent for US$210, and those without US$200.

AKUMAL

Famous for its beautiful beach, Akumal (Place of the Turtles) does indeed see some giant turtles (greens and loggerheads) come ashore to lay their eggs during the summer, although fewer and fewer do so each year due to the development taking place there and the insensitivity of the property owners and hotel managers to the turtles' needs. Akumal is one of the Yucatán's oldest resort areas, and consists primarily of dozens of pricey hotels and condominiums situated on nearly 5km of wide beach that border four consecutive bays.

Because of its length, Akumal is often referred to by the names given to stretches of the coast or features of the coast within its boundaries. The northernmost area of Akumal, for example, is called the Yal-Ku Lagoon, after the name of a beautiful lagoon there that can be accessed for US$5 a day. Heading south, but still within the area generally referred to as Akumal, are Half Moon Bay, Akumal, South Akumal and Aventuras Akumal. If you are traveling south on Hwy 307, you will see signs for most of these turnoffs (there is no sign for Half Moon Bay) starting 105km south of Ciudad Cancún, or 5km south of El Dorado Resort.

Although population is taking a heavy toll on the reefs that parallel Akumal, diving remains the area's primary attraction, and visitors are served by three dive operators: Akumal Dive Shop (☎ 9-872-2453, in the USA ☎ 800-777-8294); Akumal Dive Center (in the USA ☎ 915-584-3552, 800-351-1622, in Canada ☎ 800-343-1440); and CEDAM Dive Center (☎ 9-873-5147, fax 9-873-5129, www.cedamdive.com).

A particularly popular dive is the wreck of the Spanish galleon *Mantancero*, which went down in 1741. You can see artifacts from the galleon at the CEDAM museum in Puerto Aventuras. The dive shops can arrange all your scuba excursion needs. Beginners' scuba instruction can be provided for less than US$120; if you want certification, the dive shops offer three-day courses. They will also arrange deep-sea fishing excursions.

Places to Stay & Eat

For a low-down on most of the lodgings available in Akumal and to make a reservation or get more information, call Akumal Vacations (in the USA ☎ 800-448-7137). You'll quickly realize that there are few rooms in Akumal under US$100 a day. For value, there are many better options along the coast.

One of Akumal's better deals is the *Villa Las Brisas* (☎ 9-876-2110, fax 9-876-2245), located in Aventuras Akumal. It's a small place consisting of only two one-bedroom condos, two two-bedroom condos and one studio apartment – all under one roof. Villa

Las Brisas is located on the beach and it's quite lovely and modern inside and out. Rates run from US$55 for the studio to US$95 for a one-bedroom to US$125 for a two-bedroom condo during the low season, add US$25 during the high season. The owners speak English, Spanish, German, Italian and some Portuguese.

The **Hotel Club Akumal Caribe/Hotel Villas Maya** (☎ 9-875-9012, in the USA ☎ 800-351-1622, fax 915-581-6709, www .hotelakumalcaribe.com) offers bungalows starting at US$80 and villas starting at US$120 most of the year. All have air-con, and amenities include tennis and basketball courts.

Las Casitas Akumal (☎ 9-875-9071, fax 9-875-9072) has cabañas containing a kitchen, a living room, two bedrooms and two bathrooms – good accommodations for a family. Rates run US$140 to US$160.

Even the shade huts near the beach are expensive for light lunches and snacks, considering what you get. Just outside the walled entrance of Akumal is a **grocery store** patronized largely by the resort workers; if you are day-tripping here, this is your sole inexpensive source of food. The store also sells tacos.

CHEMUYIL

Here there's a beautiful sand beach shaded by coconut palms, and good snorkeling in the calm waters with exceptional visibility. However, the site was sold to a developer in 1999 and access to the beach was being denied to the public at year's end.

XCACEL

Xcacel ('ishkah-CELL') is the name of an area with a beach on a somewhat turbulent bay. As of late 1999, it had yet to be sold to the highest-bidding developer. The only structure in the area then was a beat-up building occasionally used by biologists who were studying the sea turtles who lay eggs in the sand here. Because of the turtles, no camping is permitted; indeed, no one except the biologists are allowed into Xcacel after sunset (a guard posted at the end of the long dirt road that links Xcacel to Hwy 307 turns

unauthorized people away after 5 pm). During the day, he charges some visitors US$2 to enter the area. Who he hits up seems to depend on his mood.

In addition to the beach, which is rockier and trashier than most along the coast, there's a fairly inviting cenote nestled in the scrub brush about 150m away from the surf. To reach it, walk south about 100m on the dirt trail that leaves the dirt parking area and borders the edge of the beach. When you come to a trail that runs away from the beach and into the scrub bush, take it. After another 75m or so you'll come to the cenote. It isn't nearly as nice as the cenotes at the ecoparks along the Tulum Corridor, but then access to it doesn't cost at least US$25, either.

XEL-HA

Once a pristine natural lagoon brimming with iridescent tropical fish and ringed on three sides by untouched mangrove, Xel-ha ('SHELL-hah') is now a private park with landscaped grounds, a dolphin enclosure (yes, you can frolic with them for a price), changing rooms, numerous restaurant-bars and a gift shop. The fish are regularly driven off by the dozens of busloads of sun-oiled day-trippers who come to enjoy the beautiful site and to swim in the pretty lagoon.

Should you visit Xel-ha? Sure, so long as you come off-season (in summer), or in winter either very early or very late in the day to avoid the tour buses. Admission costs US$39. The park is open 8:30 am to 5:30 pm daily. You can rent snorkeling gear for US$8.

On the west side of the highway, 500m south of the park's turnoff, you'll come across **Ruinas del Xel-ha**, a small archaeological site. The ruins, which are not all that impressive, date from Classic and Postclassic periods, and include El Palacio and the Templo de los Pájaros. The site is open 8 am to 5 pm daily and admission costs US$2.50.

NOHOCH NAH CHICH

The Nohoch Nah Chich cave system, which is situated below ground from at least Akumal to the north to Tulum to the south and mostly on the west side of Hwy 307, is the largest underwater cave system in the

world, according to *The Guinness Book of Records*. Discovered by CEDAM Dive Center director Mike Madden in 1987, Nohoch Nah Chich contains an identified 50km of passageways. This is the amount Madden and his team have surveyed, but it's possible the full extent of the system is considerably larger.

The surveying work continues, with Madden now offering certified cave divers the opportunity of assisting with the work. This is high adventure – indeed, National Geographic's *Adventure* magazine has rated it as one of the top adventures on Earth – and to date it's been reasonably priced. Because Madden schedules expeditions generally only three months ahead of launch time, you'll need to contact him for costs and start dates. See the Puerto Aventuras section for CEDAM contact information, or email Madden directly (mmadden@cancun.com.mx).

A variety of snorkel and dive options are also available, from CEDAM as well as from the Dos Ojos Dive Center (☎ 9-876-0987, www.xaac.com/dosojos), which has its office alongside Hwy 307, on the west side of the road, 3km south of the turnoff for Xel-ha and 3km north of the turnoff for Punta Solimán. Run by master cave diver Buddy Quattlebaum, Dos Ojos offers divers and snorkelers a host of adventures and services.

Like CEDAM, Dos Ojos offers certified open-water divers the chance to cavern dive – ie, divers are never out of sight of a ray of sunlight. Snorkelers are also allowed to ply the crystal-clear water in a cavern. Certified cave divers are permitted to venture into the blackness illuminated only by their flashlights. Either type of dive gives visitors an opportunity to see an ethereal array of stalactites and stalagmites, most of which are submerged. Rates start at US$60 per cavern dive, considerably less to snorkel, and generally around US$80 for an unforgettable two-tank cave dive.

Another (nearly forgotten but very dependable) dive center providing highly recommended service is located along Hwy 307 in Tulum. The Aktún Dive Center (☎ 9-871-3348, fax 9-871-3349, www.aktundive .com) offers reef dives (US$35), cavern

dives (US$50), cave dives (US$80) and night reef dives (US$45). Prices include tank, weights and guide. PADI open-water and advanced-open-water certification is available, as is NACD-IANTD cave and technical instruction.

PUNTA SOLIMÁN

One hundred and twenty-three kilometers south of Ciudad Cancún and 11km north of Tulum, travelers will see a large sign on the east side of Hwy 307 that reads 'Bahías de Punta Solimán'; if it also said, 'A wonderful secret,' it wouldn't be misleading. Beside the sign there's a road that bisects mangrove for several hundred meters before it reaches a fork. The left (north) fork winds to Punta Solimán, a point that separates two beautiful, protected bays that offer excellent snorkel and dive opportunities. To protect the level of marine life visible in both bays, the area's landowners prohibit anyone from fishing in them.

The bay to the north is Bahía de Punta Solimán; the one to the south is Bahía de San Francisco. Overlooking Bahía de Punta Solimán is ***Restaurant-Bar Oscar y Lalo*** (☎ 9-871-2209), a wonderful, simple, friendly restaurant that has the entire picturesque bay to itself. Camping is available on the restaurant's grounds (US$2.50 per person), and the owner (Oscar) was in the process of purchasing tents and kayaks for rent when Lonely Planet dropped in on him in 1999. Oscar requested that drug users, partiers and people with noisy music machines stay elsewhere.

Whether you intend to camp at Restaurant-Bar Oscar y Lalo or not, you should try to work it into your meal plans. The house specialty is the 'supercombinación grouper,' which consists of a full grouper topped with filets of barracuda and snapper, chunks of conch, a liberal portion of shrimp and lobster, all garnished with tomato, onion and limes and accompanied with guacamole, french fries, fried platano, rice and beans. A plate of tortillas with green and red salsas comes on the side. This feast isn't cheap at US$35 for two persons, but it is unforgettable. Other dishes include a whole grilled fish (the catch of the day, US$7) and chicken

MICHAEL LAWRENCE

RICHARD NEBESKY

Hats of all sorts are popular and useful souvenirs.

A typical example of Mexican folk art.

SCOTT DOGGETT

Playa del Carmen is a good place to shop for handicrafts from all over Mexico.

JOHN NEUBAUER

Their setting is what makes Tulum's ruins so memorable.

RICHARD NEBESKY

Caimans are often seen in the lakes near the Cobá ruins.

fajitas (US$6). Tourists tend to photograph the food here, which gives you an idea of the presentation.

If you turn south at the fork, you'll come to a small number of intimate, lovely fan-cooled hotels and beach houses on the Bahía de San Francisco. None of these places is more than a few years old, all have lots of character, all are situated on the beach and all overlook a gorgeous bay with terrific coral heads, zillions of colorful fish, plenty of grouper and reef sharks, and the occasional sea turtle and even tuna.

The least expensive and the least fancy of the bunch is *The Last Resort* (☎ 9-875-9111, fax 9-875-9108, www.tulum.org), which is ideal for people looking for a great snorkel site but don't want to spend a lot of money. The resort consists of a single cabaña (or *palapa*, as they prefer to call cabins here), with two beautiful rooms (one upstairs and one downstairs). This is a no-frills place as amenities go, but it's very comfortable with superior cross ventilation and mosquito nets to keep any bugs off you at night. Room rates are a bargain at US$75 (low season) and US$95 (high season), including breakfast for two.

Playa Naturel (☎ 9-877-8571, www.playanaturel.com) is a very private, very appealing clothing-optional place featuring an inviting swimming pool (Punta Solimán's only one), several lovely thatch-roofed cabañas and the gracious hospitality of the friendly American couple who own and run it. The owners are excellent cooks and their margaritas are not to be believed. Rates are per room, and start at US$200 per couple. The rate includes breakfast, dinner and pickup from the Cancún airport. This is an excellent place to unwind. No one under 18 is permitted.

Casa Playa Maya (☎ 9-877-8560, www.tulum-mexico.com, www.locogringo.com) is an environmentally friendly beach house that is solar and natural gas-powered but has all of the amenities (including satellite TV). Even the toilet is self-treating. The house is designed in such a way that you can rent the entire thing, or just the first floor. The weekly rate for the home is US$940

most of the year. Included in the price is a cook who prepares delicious Yucatecan food and doesn't mind if you want to watch her shop and cook. This is a great find.

The *Casa del Corazon* (☎ 9-875-9052, www.locogringo.com) is also an environmentally friendly beach house with a fully equipped kitchen, a master bedroom with a king-size bed, a spacious bathroom and a loft with a king-size futon. There's very good cross ventilation and, like all the other places on the kilometer-wide bay, guests have a patch of beach all to themselves. The Casa's quite comfortable but a bit less polished than all of the other places mentioned here, except The Last Resort, which is budget-minded. The weekly rate is US$950 (May 15 to November 19) and US$1300 the rest of the year. There's also a *casita* (little house) on the property that rents for US$750 and US$950 a week.

Groups or large families won't want to overlook the pridefully designed and maintained *Casa Solimán* (☎ 9-875-9052, www.locogringo.com), which has five bedroom suites with private baths, each suite decorated in a different theme. Four have king-size beds and one has two twin beds. The kitchen is done up in tropical Mexican style and is a joy to be in. There are also two full-size living rooms in the lovely house, which rents for US$2200 and US$2900 a week most of the year, considerably more around Christmas and New Year's. There's also a two-bedroom casita that's very nice and rents for US$1500 a week during the low season.

Incidentally, avid birders say the birding in the perennially dry mangrove at Punta Solimán is terrific, and hotel owners report they've seen a puma and her cubs in the area upon occasion. Birds of interest here are said to include the Yucatán vireo, Yucatán woodpecker, rose-throated tanager, black catbird and orange oriole.

Most people get to Punta Solimán by taking a bus to Tulum and a taxi from there.

TANKAH

A few kilometers south of the Hwy 307 turnoff for Punta Solimán is the turnoff for Tankah, which is very similar to Punta Solimán. It, too, consists chiefly of a picturesque

QUINTANA ROO

stretch of beach lined with intimate rental properties that have a sea for a front yard and mangrove out back. And it, too, is a quiet neighborhood where one can escape the pressures of life back home for awhile.

One of the more popular of the places here is the **Tankah Inn** (☎ 9-874-2188, fax 9-871-2092, in the USA ☎ 800-878-3703 ext 1937, tankah_inn@yahoo.com), owned and run by Americans Jimmy and Shaleh Clark. The inn is both a PADI-certified dive operation and a hotel with five basic but comfortable rooms with good cross ventilation and hot-water private bathrooms. Rates, which include room, meals and beverages, are US$95 (May through December 15) to US$125 (December 16 through April) per person, double occupancy. Rates are half as much without the food (the food here is good and the portions are generous). Services offered include: snorkel tour by boat to the reef (US$20), cenote snorkel tour (US$40), two-tank reef dive (US$50), cavern dive (US$80), and Cozumel diving starting at US$90.

Down the coastal road 200m farther is the **Casa Cenote** (☎ 9-874-5170, fax 9-871-2092, www.casacenote.com), which is both a very pleasant palapa-style restaurant featuring fresh seafood and burgers at reasonable prices and a hotel with eight very appealing standard rooms and four suites, all done up with Mayan touches and plenty of detailing. Suite rates are US$125 per couple, room rates weren't set in late 1999. Casa Cenote struck the writer as a great place for a romantic interlude.

Two houses are also available for rent in Tankah, both new, both two-story with gorgeous sea views, both modern and stylish with three bedrooms and three bathrooms. The slightly less expensive of the two is the American-owned **Villa Zama** (in the USA ☎ 612-758-4161, fax 612-758-4085, dwornson@aol.com); it rents for US$1600 and US$1800 a week most of the year. The **Villa de Paz** (☎ 9-875-9052, www.locogringo.com) is more luxurious, and included in the cost are maid service, a cook, outdoor grill and sea kayaks. Rates vary five times a year and increase annually; contact Villa de Paz directly for current rates.

TULUM
☎ 9 • pop 3603

There are actually several Tulums: Tulum Crucero is the junction with Hwy 307 and the old access road to the ruins (the new entrance to the Zona Arqueológica is 400m south of Tulum Crucero); Tulum Ruinas are the ruins, 800m southeast of Tulum Crucero; Tulum Pueblo (in the following text, referred to as the town) is the modern settlement 3.5km south of Tulum Crucero; and Tulum Zona Hotelera is the assortment of waterfront cabañas 1km to 7km south of the ruins. The Zona Hotelera is reached by an access road 2km south of Tulum Crucero (1.5km north of Tulum Pueblo), opposite the road to Cobá.

South of the Zona Hotelera, the road enters the Reserva de la Biósfera Sian Ka'an, and continues for some 50km past Boca Paila to Punta Allen.

Information

Money There are numerous currency-exchange booths but no banks in town. The booths with the best exchange rates are located opposite the bus station (Terminal de Autobuses). Look for a two-story building with 'ADO' painted on it in large letters – this is the bus station and it's visible from far away.

Telephone There are Telmex Ladatel phones in town, but few along the coastal road, although there was talk of more pay phones going in along the road in 2000.

Email & Internet Access There were three businesses in town offering Internet access in late 1999, but all were unreliable at the time and quite expensive (US$0.30 and up per minute). All three are on the east side of the highway and north of the bus terminal. The least expensive of the three is the Internet Club, which is open 9 am to 9 pm daily.

Tulum Ruins

The ruins of Tulum (Mayan for 'Wall'), though very well preserved, would hardly merit rave notices if it weren't for their setting. And

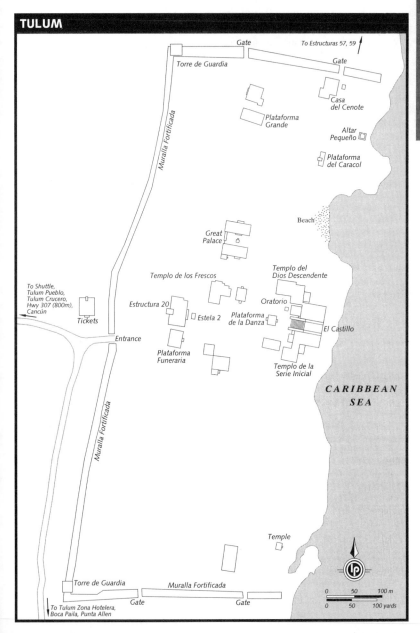

TULUM

Gate

To Estructuras 57, 59

Torre de Guardia

Gate

Casa del Cenote

Plataforma Grande

Altar Pequeño

Plataforma del Caracol

Muralla Fortificada

Beach

Great Palace

Templo del Dios Descendente

Templo de los Frescos

To Shuttle, Tulum Pueblo, Tulum Crucero, Hwy 307 (800m), Cancún

Estructura 20

Oratorio

Tickets

Estela 2

Plataforma de la Danza

El Castillo

Entrance

Plataforma Funeraria

Templo de la Serie Inicial

Muralla Fortificada

CARIBBEAN SEA

Temple

Torre de Guardia

Muralla Fortificada

To Tulum Zona Hotelera, Boca Paila, Punta Allen

Gate

Gate

0   50   100 m

0   50   100 yards

what a setting it is: The grayish-tan buildings of the past dominate a palm-fringed beach, lapped by the turquoise waters of the Caribbean. Even on dark and stormy days, the majestic cliff-top ruins overlooking vast stretches of pristine beach in both directions look fit for the cover of a magazine.

Don't come to Tulum expecting majestic pyramids or anything comparable to the architecture of Chichén Itzá or Uxmal. The buildings here, decidedly Toltec in influence, were the product of a Mayan civilization in decline.

Tulum's proximity to the tourist centers of Cancún and Isla Mujeres makes it a prime target of tour buses. The press of crowds can be aggravating, especially to photographers. To best enjoy the ruins, visit them either early in the morning or late in the day – when the tour groups aren't there. The ruins are open 8 am to 5 pm daily. The costs involved are for parking (US$1.50), the mini-train shuttle to the site (US$1.30), and the entrance fee (US$3).

The name 'Tulum,' though Mayan, was not the name its residents knew it by. Rather, they called it Zama, or 'Dawn.' The site's current name was apparently coined by explorers during the early 20th century.

History Most archaeologists believe that Tulum was occupied during the Late Post-classic period (1200-1524), and that it served as an important port town during its heyday. When Juan de Grijalva's expedition sailed past Tulum in 1518, he was amazed by the sight of this walled city, with its buildings painted a gleaming red, blue and yellow, and a ceremonial fire flaming atop its seaside watchtower.

The ramparts that surround three sides of Tulum (the fourth side being the sea) leave little question as to its strategic function as a fortress. Averaging nearly 7m in thickness and standing 3m to 5m high, the walls protected the city during a period of considerable strife between Mayan city-states.

The city was abandoned about three-quarters of a century after the Spanish conquest. Indeed, it was one of the last ancient cities to be abandoned; most had been given

back to nature long before the arrival of the Spanish. Mayan pilgrims continued to visit over the years and Indian refugees from the War of the Castes took shelter here from time to time.

The Wall An enormous wall *muralla fortificada*, many sections of which can still be seen, measures approximately 380m north to south and 170m on its sides. The seaside cliff protected the site from an invasion from the east.

Not all of Tulum was situated within the walls. Indeed, the vast majority of the city's residents lived outside the walls, while the civic-ceremonial buildings and palaces likely housed Tulum's ruling class.

El Castillo Tulum's tallest building is a watchtower fortress overlooking the Caribbean, appropriately named El Castillo (the Castle) by the Spaniards. Note the Toltec-style serpent columns at the temple's entrance, echoing those at Chichén Itzá.

Templo del Dios Descendente The Temple of the Descending God is named for the relief figure above the door, a diving figure, partly human, which may be related to the Mayas' reverence for bees. This figure appears at several other east coast sites, as well as at Cobá.

Templo de los Frescos This two-story building (Temple of the Frescoes) was constructed in several stages sometime around 1400 to 1450. Its decoration was among the more elaborate examples at Tulum, including the diving god, relief masks and colored murals on an inner wall. The murals, painted in three levels, show the three realms of the Mayan universe: the dark underworld of the deceased, the middle order of the living and the heavenly home of the creator and rain gods. This monument might have been the last built by the Maya before the Spanish conquest.

Great Palace Smaller than El Castillo, this largely deteriorated site contains a fine stucco carving of a diving god.

Templo de la Serie Inicial The restored Temple of the Initial Series is named for Stela 1, now in the British Museum, which was inscribed with the Mayan date corresponding to 564 AD (the 'initial series' of Mayan hieroglyphs in an inscription gives its date). At first this confused archaeologists, who believed Tulum to have been settled several hundred years later than this date. It's now believed that Stela 1 was brought to Tulum from Tankah, 4km to the north, a settlement dating from the Classic period.

Estructuras 57 & 59 These two small temples are north of the city wall. Estructura 57, about 500m north of the wall, is a one-room shrine in good condition. Estructura 59, another 500m to the north, is another one-room temple with remains of a roofcomb, the only one found at Tulum.

Places to Stay & Eat
Along Hwy 307 Right at the junction of Hwy 307 and the old Tulum ruins access road are several hotels and restaurants that offer the convenience of not requiring you to take a taxi or to hike to them, as do those near the sea. However, none of the places in town or down the highway a little has anywhere near the character or charm of those by the sea. (See the next section for those options.)

At the junction you'll find the well-used *Motel El Crucero*, expensive at US$10 to US$15 a double with shower and fan. The restaurant and shop selling ice, meals, drinks and souvenirs are more useful. A chicken dinner costs US$6.

Facing the Motel El Crucero across the access road are the *Hotel Acuario* (☎ 871-2195, fax 871-2194, www.hotelacuario.com), with air-con rooms for US$35 to US$50 double most of the year, and its *Restaurant El Faisan y El Venado*.

In Tulum town, the *Hotel El Meson* (☎/fax 871-2311, www.aktundive.com) is primarily used by divers employing the services of the adjacent Aktún Dive Center, which owns and operates the hotel. This newer, pleasant hotel offers four standard rooms with air-con (US$37) and four without (US$33). The attached restaurant offers

tasty breakfasts, lunches and dinners at reasonable prices.

Also in town is the *L'Hotelito* (☎/fax 871-2092) and the attached Italian restaurant (good food, and cheap!). The Italian-owned and -managed hotel offers 10 basic rooms for US$20 (low season) or US$30 (high season). The rooms could use mosquito nets over the beds.

The best restaurant in town is *Charlie's*, opposite the bus station. The garden-ringed fan-cooled restaurant specializes in *comida Mexícana* and serves food from 8 am to 10 pm daily. Typical offerings include hotcakes with your choice of fruit (US$2.50), black bean soup served with onion, chile and cilantro on the side (US$1.20), four tacos prepared with strips of beef, grilled onion, avocado, lettuce and fried beans (US$4) and filet of fish (US$5).

Just north of the bus station, the *Café Frances* serves breakfast, lunch and dinner. The café specializes in French salads, crêpes and beef dishes. Except for the meat dishes, most of the entrées cost under US$5. The café offers some delicious desserts, and the fruit with yogurt and honey is a fine way to start the day.

Along the Boca Paila-Punta Allen Rd
Along this coastal road south of the archaeological zone, starting less than 1km from the ruins, is a string of cabaña hotels that cater primarily to budget travelers. Most have simple restaurants serving fresh seafood and beef and chicken dishes. Most do not have electricity or telephones, or they have electricity only to 9 or 10 pm, and then it's lights out (bring a flashlight or, better still, a battery-powered lantern).

The cheapest way to sleep here is to have your own hammock and a tube-like mosquito net to cover it; if you don't carry your own, several of the cheaper places will rent you what you need. At the cheapest places, you'll have to supply your own towel and soap. See the 'Tips on Tulum Cabañas' boxed text for helpful hints on selecting a cabaña.

These places appear in the order you'd find them if you were to travel south on the coastal road from the ruins.

Closest to the ruins is **Cabañas El Mirador**, which features 28 on-the-sand cabins with beds, but no fans or anything else. Cost is US$10 per room. There's a wide swimmable beach out front and a decent restaurant perched on a bluff with lovely views and a breeze. The restaurant's open 9 am to 9 pm. Breakfasts go for US$2, lunch and dinner twice that. El Mirador is located 600m from the ruins.

Tips on Tulum's Cabañas

The waterfront cabañas south of the Tulum ruins are world famous with backpackers. The first four are side-by-side and within 1km of the ruins. Thereafter, the cabañas are mixed in with more expensive places and spread out over the next 9km. Here are a few tips to keep in mind if you intend to stay at one of them:

Those cabañas closest to the ruins are usually occupied by 10 or 11 am every day from mid-December through March and in July and August. You must get here early to get one, or make a reservation the night before.

Taxis are recommended to cover the 2km to 3km separating Tulum's bus station or the bus stops at the Tulum Crucero and the Zona Arqueológica entrance from the cabañas. The fare is US$3 one way.

The cheapest of the cabañas are very rustic – made of sticks and built on sand (some have concrete floors, but are most just sand). Either way, you'd be wise to bring a mosquito net with you to hang over you at night.

Security is a big problem. Few of the flimsy, primitive cabañas can be reliably secured. Thieves lift the poles in the walls to gain entrance, or burrow beneath through the sand, or jimmy the locks. Never leave valuables unattended in a cabaña.

Sandals, thongs, flip-flops: Whatever you chose to call them, you'll be glad to have a pair with you. Most of the cabañas, even at the pricier places, have shared bathrooms. Thongs help you keep sand out of your bed and reduce the chance of catching athlete's foot.

Next door is **Cabañas Santa Fe**, which also features mostly thatch-roofed cabins with sides made of wooden poles and sandy floors. A few of the newer cabañas have concrete floors and are made of cinder block. There are 45 cabañas in all, ranging in price from US$11 to US$25. The fancier cabañas have electricity, beds and private bathrooms. Camping is permitted for US$2.

Cabañas Don Armando, just south of Santa Fe, offers cabañas on concrete slabs (instead of sand) for US$14 to US$18 (single or double). The poles have been filled in with concrete, which make them more secure, but prevents ventilation. Rates range with features such as lockable doors, hammocks and beds (you pay a deposit for sheets and pillows), and mosquito netting. Lighting in the rooms is by candles. This place is still only a 10-minute walk from the ruins.

Beside the Don Armando is **Cabañas Mar Caribe**, with 28 thatch-and-slats cabañas, no electricity, communal bathrooms – the usual – for US$12 for two beds and US$8 for one.

Cabañas Playa Conjesa is 500m farther south and offers 15 cabañas, all of which are more comfortable than those found closer to the ruins. Each cabaña features a bed that is suspended by rope from the ceiling, mosquito netting to keep the bugs off you while you sleep, a concrete floor and slat/pole siding with enough space in between to permit good ventilation. Guests can use the restaurant at the Hotel Diamante K, two doors to the south. Rates are US$12 to US$15. There's no beach here, only a rocky shore, but there's beach only 100m away.

Next south is the **Ranchito Dzi-Baan-Actun**, which is another thatch-and-slat deal. No one was around when Lonely Planet paid a visit, but it appeared that a restaurant was under construction. If the other places are full, you might want to inquire here.

Next to the Ranchito Dzi-Baan-Actun is the very popular but pricey **Hotel Diamante K** (☎ 871-2376, fax 871-2283), which offers a variety of rooms, all with wooden pole or bamboo siding, suspended beds and a table for a candle (the lights go off at 10 pm). Rooms with communal bathrooms

start at US$30, while those with private bathrooms start at US$70. There are two communal rooms with beds for US$10 each; a much better deal than the comparably priced first four places mentioned in this section. The Diamante K has a small beach and a fine restaurant-bar, and fills up even during the low tourist season.

About 700m south of the Diamante K, just south of the road that links the coastal road and Tulum town, is the *Papaya Playa* (☎ 871-2091, fax 871-2092, s_trapote@ hotmail.com). The Papaya Playa has 15 rooms, four very comfortable with private bathroom, furniture and beds, the rest with sandy floors but otherwise fine. All have screened windows and ocean views. There's a very cozy bar and restaurant, a communal BBQ area and a clothing-optional beach (actually, clothing is optional on all the area beaches, but the two good-looking Latin men who own and run the Papaya Playa like to emphasize it). Be advised that the owners check their email only once every two weeks, and that reservations are recommended due to the popularity of the place. Rooms range from US$40 to US$60. There are also teepees available and hammocks swung between trees (both US$5). This is a very good find.

Cabañas Copal is the next place to the south and consists of three very comfortable cabañas with concrete floors, private bathrooms and ocean view for US$50. These rooms aren't quite as lovely as the four best rooms at the Papaya Playa, but they cost US$10 less. There are also 12 budget cabañas with sandy floors, mosquito nets, firm mattresses and good ventilation. Not bad at all, but there's no beach here, and there's little space between the cabañas.

Next to the south, and by now 4km to 5km south of the ruins, is *Cabañas La Conchita (no phone, fax 871-2092 – put 'attn La Conchita')*, with eight rooms in all. These are a major step up from all the rooms/cabañas described thus far. The rooms vary substantially, but most have cool, concrete walls and standard windows and lockable doors (good security). Most have some degree of sea view, and the beach here is lovely. The rooms closest to the sea are especially at-

tractive, with many architectural details. Rates at this family-run hotel are very reasonable at US$60 for most of the rooms, breakfast included.

Next door to La Conchita is *Cabañas Punta Piedra*, which offers eight cabañas, only one of which faces the sea. Five contain one bed, three contain two beds. Even at US$18 (single) and US$20 (double), it's not much of a bargain. However, it's possible to rent bikes (US$6 a day) and snorkel gear (US$5) here.

A stone's throw away is the *Restaurant y Cabañas Nohoch Tunich* (☎ 876-9407, fax 871-2092, www.secom.net/nohochtunich), which offers both appealing hotel rooms with porches and electricity until 11 pm, and breezeless, thatch-and-board cabañas. The rates are US$60 for the hotel rooms, US$20 for most of the cabañas. Two of the cabañas have private bathrooms and rent for US$35; they are the only good-value cabañas here. Breakfast is included in the prices.

Next door is the *Piedra Escondida Hotel y Restaurant* (☎/fax 871-2217, www.secom .net/piedraescondida), which offers eight hotel rooms in all (four upstairs and four at ground level). All have private bathrooms and balconies/porches, and all are nicely decorated and have good ventilation. There's a pleasing palapa-style restaurant-bar. Rates are very reasonable at US$65 much of the year, up to US$85 during the high season.

Cabañas La Perla is the next place to the south, and it offers six rooms and two cabañas. The rooms have private bathrooms and rent for US$40 (one bed) and US$50 (two beds). The cabañas have shared bathroom and are rustic – nothing special but inexpensive (US$20). La Perla shares a small beach with Nohoch Tunich and Punta Piedra.

Five hundred meters south is the *very* lovely and upscale *Maya Tulum (in the USA ☎ 888-515-4580, www.mayatulum.com)*, which is in a different league from all the other places mentioned here. There are 34 deluxe cabañas and two houses with lots of architectural details and comfort (no aircon, however). There's a gorgeous, arcing beach nearby and the facility features a yoga room, a vegetarian restaurant and massage.

This place was pridefully designed and constructed, and it's pridefully maintained. Some people know it as Oshotulum, it's previous name. Rates run US$60 to US$70 for a shared-bathroom cabaña, US$70 to US$80 for a cabaña with private bathroom, and US$120 to US$140 for a larger beach house with private bathroom.

The ***Rancho Hemingway***, 150m to the south, is a place Ernest Hemingway might have liked. It was under construction at the time Lonely Planet passed by. It appeared to be another rustic-cabañas deal, but the beach over a dune out front of the cabañas is beautiful. It warrants a look, unless a sea view is essential; the sand dune blocks the view and makes getting to the beach a little chore.

Yet another 100m south is ***Cabañas La Flor***, which consists of a dozen or so very rustic cabañas on a very lovely stretch of beach. It was being updated at the time Lonely Planet stopped by. If you've got your own wheels, it deserves a look. Some of the cabañas had concrete floors. Rates were US$20 to US$40.

Lots of other hotels and cabañas were under construction to the south of Cabañas La Flor en route to Punta Allen. Amid the development is ***Ana y José*** (☎ 887-5470, fax 887-5469, www.tulumresorts.com), which is approximately 10km south of the Tulum ruins on a gorgeous swimmable beach lined with palapas. Ana y José is locally famous for its superb food but now also offers very comfortable accommodations with a swimming pool. This is a great find. There are 15 rooms in all, ranging from US$70 (no sea view, so-so room) to US$120 (with sea view). There's electricity 24 hours and international calls can be made from here. Food includes: mixed ceviche with red snapper base for US$4, filet of fish (usually snapper) served with chaya (a Mexican spinach) for US$7, and the *camarones al gusto*, which is grilled or breaded shrimp in a buttery garlic sauce and served with chaya for US$11. If you prefer your shrimp doused with tequila, you can have it that way, too, for US$13.

Just south is the ***Cabañas Tulum*** (☎ 825-8295), where older concrete bungalows look out through palms to the beach. The rate of US$50 is reasonable.

Continuing south you'll come to ***Cabañas Tropical Padus*** (☎ 876-2088, 871-2092, www .secom.net/tropicalpadus), which consists of 12 extremely fine cabañas built on stilts to keep them cooler and to keep insects out. Ten of the upscale cabañas face the ocean, while two are suites but don't offer sea view. The restaurant is open-sided and lovely, with a huge palapa roof and candle-lit wooden tables on a sprawling hardwood floor. It's simple yet elegant, and the cuisine is Italian and Mediterranean, with most entrées around US$10. The Italian owner took care not to cut down any trees when he built, but instead constructed his place around them. And he installed a sewage plant – a rarity in these parts. There is also a dive center on the premises.

Getting There & Around

You can walk from Tulum Crucero to the ruins (800m), or take the mini-train shuttle for a fee (US$1.30).

Reaching the various cabañas is more difficult. The closest ones are 600m south of the ruins, but to get to them by taxi you have to take a circuitous route because the road to the ruins is closed to private vehicles when the ruins are open. In addition, no buses serve the cabañas.

The good news is that taxis in Tulum are cheap and they are fixed-rate. At the center of small, roadside Tulum town you'll see the large sign of the Sindicato de Taxistas, on which are posted the following taxi rates: to ruins (US$1.60), to most of the cabañas (US$2.60 to US$3), to Ana y José (US$5.60), to Playa del Carmen (US$30), Puerto Morelos (US$45), Cancún airport (US$57), Ciudad Cancún (US$62), Cancún (US$67), Cobá (US$22, US$45 roundtrip), Valladolid (US$48), Chichén Itzá (US$62), Chetumal (US$92) and Mérida (US$137).

There's a bus station at the southern end of Tulum town (look for the two-story building with 'ADO' painted on it in huge letters; that's the building). When leaving Tulum, you can also wait at Tulum Crucero for a Playa Express or regular intercity bus.

Here are some distances and travel times for buses leaving Tulum:

Cancún – 132km, one hour, US$3 to US$5

Chetumal – 251km, 4 hours, US$5 to US$7

Chichén Itzá – 402km, five hours, US$5

Cobá – 45km, 30 minutes, US$1.20

Felipe Carrillo Puerto – 98km, 1¾ hours, US$3.50

Mérida – 320km, five hours via Cobá; or 450km, six hours via Cancún, US$10

Playa del Carmen – 63km, 1 hour, US$2

Punta Allen – 57km, one hour, US$1.60 (at 11 am and noon, only)

COBÁ

Perhaps the largest of all Mayan cities, Cobá, 50km northwest of Tulum, offers the chance to explore mostly unrestored antiquities set deep in tropical jungles.

History

Cobá was settled earlier than Chichén Itzá or Tulum, its heyday dating from 600 AD until the site was mysteriously abandoned, about 900 AD. Archaeologists believe that this city once covered 50 sq km and held 40,000 Maya.

Cobá's architecture is a mystery; its towering pyramids and stelae resemble the architecture of Tikal, several hundred kilometers away, rather than the much nearer sites of Chichén Itzá and the northern Yucatán Peninsula.

Some archaeologists theorize that an alliance with Tikal was made through marriage to facilitate trade between the Guatemalan and Yucatecan Maya. Stelae appear to depict female rulers from Tikal holding ceremonial bars and flaunting their power by standing on captives. These Tikal royal females, when married to Cobá's royalty, may have brought architects and artisans with them.

Archaeologists are also baffled by the network of extensive sacbeob (stone-paved avenues) in this region, with Cobá as the hub. The longest runs nearly 100km from the base of Cobá's great pyramid Nohoch Mul to the Mayan settlement of Yaxuna. In all, some 40 sacbeob passed through Cobá. The

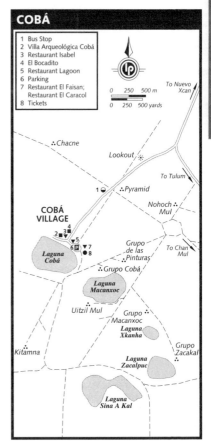

COBÁ

1 Bus Stop
2 Villa Arqueológica Cobá
3 Restaurant Isabel
4 El Bocadito
5 Restaurant Lagoon
6 Parking
7 Restaurant El Faisan;
   Restaurant El Caracol
8 Tickets

sacbeob were part of the huge astronomical 'time machine' that was evident in every Mayan city.

The first excavation was by the Austrian archaeologist Teobert Maler. Hearing rumors of a fabled lost city, he came to Cobá alone in 1891. There was little subsequent investigation until 1926, when the Carnegie Institute financed the first of two expeditions led by J Eric S Thompson and Harry Pollock. After their 1930 expedition not much happened until 1973, when the Mexican government began to finance excavation. Archaeologists now estimate that Cobá contains some 6500

QUINTANA ROO

structures, of which just a few have been excavated and restored.

Orientation

The small village of Cobá, 2.5km west of the Tulum-Nuevo Xcan road, has several small, simple and cheap eating places. At the lake, turn left for the ruins, right for the upscale Villa Arqueológica Cobá hotel.

Cobá archaeological site is open 8 am to 5 pm daily; admission costs US$3, free on Sunday.

Be prepared to walk at least 5km to 7km on paths. Dress for heat and humidity, and bring insect repellent. It's a good idea to bring a canteen of water; it's hot and there are no drinks stands within the site, only at the entrance (bug spray can also be bought here). Avoid the midday heat if possible. Most people spend two hours at the site.

Grupo Cobá

Just under 100m along the main path from the entrance brings you to the Templo de las Iglesias (Temple of the Churches), on your right, the most prominent structure in the Cobá Group. It's an enormous pyramid, and from the top you can get a fine view of the Nohoch Mul pyramid to the north and shimmering lakes to the east and southwest.

Back on the main path, you pass through the Juego de Pelota (ball court), 30m farther along. It's now badly ruined.

Grupo Macanxoc

About 500m beyond the Juego de Pelota is the turning (right) for the Grupo Macanxoc, a group of stelae which bore reliefs of royal women thought to have come from Tikal.

Conjunto de las Pinturas

One hundred meters beyond the Macanxoc turning, a sign points left toward the Conjunto de las Pinturas, or the Temple of Paintings. It bears easily recognizable traces of glyphs and frescoes above the door, and traces of richly colored plaster inside.

You approached the Temple of Paintings from the southwest. Leave by the trail at the northwest (opposite the temple steps) to see several stelae. The first of these is 20m along,

beneath a palapa. A regal figure stands over two others, one of them kneeling with his hands bound behind him. Sacrificial captives lie beneath the feet of a ruler at the base. Continue along the path past another badly weathered stela to the Nohoch Mul path, and turn right.

Nohoch Mul – The Great Pyramid

A further walk of 800m brings you to Nohoch Mul. Along the way, just before the track bends sharply to the left, a narrow path on the right leads to a group of badly weathered stelae. Farther along, the track bends between piles of stones – obviously a ruined temple – before passing Temple 10 and Stela 20. The exquisitely carved stela bears a picture of a ruler standing imperiously over two captives. Eighty meters beyond the stela stands the Great Pyramid.

At 42m high, the huge Great Pyramid is the tallest of all Mayan structures in the Yucatán Peninsula. Climb the 120 steps, observing that the Maya carved shell-like forms where you put your feet.

There are two diving gods carved over the doorway of the Nohoch Mul temple at the top, similar to the sculptures at Tulum. The view is spectacular.

From Nohoch Mul, it's a 1.4-km, 30-minute walk back to the site entrance. Be advised that at least one person a year loses his or her footing on the pyramid and dies somewhere along the way down. Wear appropriate shoes here – shoes with traction and that stay snug on the feet. Most sandals are not recommended.

Places to Stay & Eat

As for camping, there's no organized spot, though you can try finding a place along the shore of the lake. No person is likely to bother you there. Be advised that there are some crocodiles and caimans in the lake, and while they are said to be small, their powerful parents lurk nearby.

For upscale lodging and dining the choice is easy: Club Med's *Villa Arqueológica Cobá* (in Cancún ☎ 9-884-2574, in the USA ☎ 800-528-3100). The pleasant hotel has a

swimming pool and a good restaurant. Air-conditioned rooms cost US$65/75/90 single/double/triple.

El Bocadito *(9-876-3738, www.cancunsouth .com/bocadito)*, in Cobá Village, is a restaurant that rents inexpensive rooms with two beds, ceiling fan and bath for about US$10.

There are several small restaurants among the souvenir shops at the ruins by the parking lot. The staff at the drinks stand right by the entrance tends to be surly, so buy your drinks at either the **Restaurant El Faisan** or the **Restaurant El Caracol**, both of which serve cheap meals.

In the village of Cobá, **Restaurant Lagoon** is nearest the lake, with good views and friendly service. The **Restaurant Isabel** and **Restaurant Bocadito** are also popular.

Getting There & Away
There are several buses daily from Tulum to Cobá and four buses daily from Cobá to Tulum. The fare is US$1.20. There are also buses from Cobá to Valladolid. However, actually leaving Cobá by bus is problematic, because most of the buses are full when they pass here.

A more comfortable, dependable, but expensive way to reach Cobá is by taxi from Tulum Crucero. Find some other travelers interested in the trip and split the cost, US$45 roundtrip, including two hours at the site.

By the way, many maps show a road from Cobá to Chemax, but this road is in bad shape.

The South

The southern half of Quintana Roo, from approximately Tulum to the Belizean border, is very different than the state's northern half. Although the state capital (Chetumal) is here, the south is much less developed than the north. The highway linking Tulum and Chetumal passes through tropical forest most of the way, with few breaks in the scenery. Felipe Carrillo Puerto, the main city between Tulum and Chetumal, offers the tourist little in the way of attractions, although it does offer the traveler good and inexpensive accommodations.

There are some pleasant and tranquil seaside destinations along the coast at Punta Allen, Majahual and Xcalak, and several good-value places overlooking the beautiful Laguna Bacalar, offering fine escapes for people who are really looking to get away from it all. The Reserva de la Biósfera Sian Ka'an, while an impressive sight on a map, hasn't yet been exploited by tour operators. To take advantage of it, you must have your own vehicle. Then, when you're within the reserve, you'd want to make forays down the few roads that run west from the Tulum-Punta Allen road. Still, there are few roads within the reserve; much of it is basically off-limits.

The southern half of Quintana Roo will mostly appeal to people who want to see a section of Caribbean Mexico before it gets developed. As for the capital city, it offers tourists a fine museum featuring the ancient Maya, but little else. The ruins of Kohunlich are definitely worth a stop if you happen to be in their vicinity, but only avid ruins fans would find them worthy of a special trip.

TULUM TO PUNTA ALLEN
The scenery on the 50km stretch from the Tulum ruins past Boca Paila to Punta Allen is the mostly monotonous flat Yucatecan terrain, but the land, rich with wildlife, is protected as the Reserva de la Biósfera Sian Ka'an. The surfy beaches aren't spectacular, but there's plenty of privacy.

A white minivan makes the trip from Tulum Pueblo to Punta Allen daily, taking about two hours for the trip. Times vary frequently; check at the bus station for current times. Motorists: It's important to have plenty of fuel before heading south from Tulum as there is no fuel available on the Tulum-Punta Allen road.

Reserva de la Biósfera Sian Ka'an
Over 5000 sq km of tropical jungle, marsh, mangrove and islands on Quintana Roo's coast have been set aside by the Mexican government as a large biosphere reserve. In 1987, the United Nations appointed it a World Heritage Site – an irreplaceable natural treasure – and UN money has been set aside

QUINTANA ROO

to pay for rangers. However, you're only likely to encounter one ranger, an elderly fellow who solicits donations from tourists – and pockets them.

It's been reported that Sian Ka'an (Where the Sky Begins) is home to howler monkeys, foxes, ocelots, pumas, vultures, crocodiles, eagles, raccoons, giant land crabs and jaguars. They may be there, but you're not likely to see any during a hike. Unfortunately, the rangers don't make trails, so hiking is inadvisable anyway. This means there are only two ways to get much out of this reserve. The first is to drive down one of the few roads that intersect the Tulum-Punta Allen road, pull to the side at a promising stretch and walk the road a ways. Do not enter the forest – there's a good chance you'll become lost.

The other way is to enter the reserve with a professional guide who can lead you to interesting parts of the forest – and can lead you back out. At the time of writing, only one group – Aventuras Tropicales de Sian Ka'an (November to April ☎ 9-871-2092, April to November in the USA ☎/fax 218-388-9455, ☎ 800-649-4166, www.boreal.org/yucatan) – had permission to lead tourists in the reserve. Run by Florida residents Jim Holzman and Margy Nelson, Aventuras Tropicales offers outings that combine sea kayaking and/or mountain biking, snorkeling, luxury camping, gourmet dining, quality hammock time and total immersion in a truly remote tropical wilderness.

Holzman and Nelson have been spending their winters in the Sian Ka'an area since the late 1980s and probably know it as well as anyone. Most of their trips last four to eight days and are centered around kayaking and camping. They also offer trips centered around birding, ecosystem study and kayak certification/specialization.

Aventuras Tropicales' base camp is in Punta Allen.

Punta Allen

Once a pocket of wealthy lobster fishers in a vast wilderness, Punta Allen suffered considerable damage from the ferocious winds of Hurricane Gilbert in 1988. The hurricane and overfishing have depleted lobster stocks,

but a laid-back ambiance reminiscent of the Belizean cayes gives hope for a touristic future. The area is known primarily for its bonefishing, and for that, many people come a long way.

However, there's also a healthy reef 400m from shore that offers snorkelers and divers wonderful sights. Between the reef and the beach there's lots of sea grass, and that's a turn-off to a lot of people, but the sea grass provides food and shelter to lots of sea critters and is one of the reasons the snorkeling and diving is so good. Same goes for Xcalak, farther down the coast. (But Xcalak is also within easy striking distance of the Banco Chinchorro, a gorgeous and little-visited atoll that contains reefs festooned in marine life, and Xcalak has a dive center while Punta Allen does not; see the Xcalak & Costa Maya section for details.)

The Bonefishing Club of Ascension Bay (www.joefish.com) specializes in guided fishing expeditions, offering packages that include six full days of guided fishing, including boat transportation, pickup from Cancún, and all meals and taxes, for US$2000 to US$2300 (depending on the time of year).

The ***Cruzan Inn*** (☎ 9-834-0383, fax 9-834-0292, fishcruzan@aol.com) has eight cabañas on stilts with private bathrooms and two beds in each, mosquito netting over the beds and 24-hour lighting for US$50 a double low season, US$75 high season. The couple who run it offer breakfast, lunch and dinner. They also offer snorkel excursions, gear included, for US$25 per person, and they can arrange fishing and birding expeditions.

Let It Be Inn (www.letitbeinn.com) has several thatched cabañas with tiled floors and comforts such as private bath with hot water and sea-view porches hung with hammocks. Most visitors stay for the fishing and to relax. The rate of US$55 a double includes a hearty breakfast.

FELIPE CARRILLO PUERTO
☎ 9 • pop 16,427

Now named for a progressive governor of Yucatán, this town 95km south of Tulum was once known as Chan Santa Cruz, the dreaded rebel headquarters during the War

of the Castes. It offers the visitor little in the way of attractions, but there's a gas station on the highway and inexpensive, air-con accommodations in town.

History

In 1849, the War of the Castes turned against the Maya of the northern Yucatán Peninsula, who made their way to this town seeking refuge. Regrouping their forces, they were ready to sally forth again in 1850, just when a 'miracle' occurred. A wooden cross erected at a cenote on the western edge of the town began to 'talk,' telling the Maya they were the chosen people, exhorting them to continue the struggle against the whites, and promising eventual victory. The talking was actually done by a ventriloquist who used sound chambers, but the people nonetheless looked upon it as the authentic voice of their aspirations.

The oracular cross guided the Maya in battle for more than eight years, until their great victory in conquering the fortress at Bacalar. For the latter part of the 19th century, the Maya in and around Chan Santa Cruz were virtually independent of governments in Mexico City and Mérida. In the 1920s, a boom in the chicle market brought prosperity to the region, and the Maya decided to come to terms with Mexico City, which they did in 1929.

Some of the Maya, unwilling to give up the cult of the talking cross, left Chan Santa Cruz to take up residence in small villages deep in the jungle, where they still revere the talking cross to this day. You may see some of them visiting the site where the cross spoke, especially on May 3, the day of the Holy Cross.

You can visit the **Santuario del Cruz Parlante** (Sanctuary of the Talking Cross), six blocks west of the Pemex fuel station on the main street (Hwy 307), in the commercial center of town, though the cenote is dry now and the stone shelter isn't really much to look at. Also, be advised that the town's residents do not like strangers in the sanctuary, and they will try to take your camera if they see you using it there.

Places to Stay & Eat

El Faisán y El Venado (☎ 834-0702, Av Juárez No 781) is a great find for the weary

---

Time Among the Maya

The history of the Talking Cross is not over. Every year on May 3, the Feast of the Holy Cross, Mayas gather in Felipe Carrillo Puerto – known as Noh Cah Santa Cruz Balam Na to them – to celebrate the cross as the symbol of ancient Mayan traditions, and specifically the Talking Cross as the last great symbol of Mayan independence.

Just a short drive inland from Felipe Carrillo Puerto, Mayan villagers observe many aspects of traditional life, including even the use of the ancient Mayan calendar.

In the mid-1980s, English writer Ronald Wright came here in search of Mayas who still understood the Long Count and lived by the dictates of the *tzolkin*, the ancient Mayan almanac. Wright wrote about his experiences in a fascinating book, *Time Among the Maya*, in 1989.

Wright found what he was seeking in X-Cacal Guardia and nearby villages, where descendants of the survivors of the 19th-century War of the Castes settled. Enveloped in the Yucatecan jungle, away from the wealth and centers of power which the government in Mexico City sought to control, they guard their ancient crosses and religious beliefs while accepting innovations like electric light, automobiles and Coca-Cola.

The 25m-long church at X-Cacal Guardia is guarded by men with rifles, its inner sanctum to be entered only by the Nohoch Tata (Great Father of the Holy Cross) himself. It may be that Chan Santa Cruz's famous Talking Cross, spirited away from the doomed city by the Mayas retreating from the last battle of the War of the Castes, has come to rest here. This is Ronald Wright's guess.

QUINTANA ROO

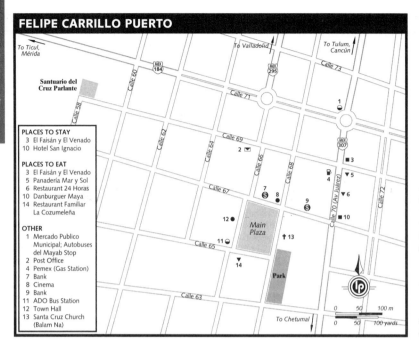

FELIPE CARRILLO PUERTO

PLACES TO STAY
3 El Faisán y El Venado
10 Hotel San Ignacio

PLACES TO EAT
3 El Faisán y El Venado
5 Panadería Mar y Sol
6 Restaurant 24 Horas
10 Danburguer Maya
14 Restaurant Familiar
   La Cozumeleña

OTHER
1 Mercado Publico
  Municipal; Autobuses
  del Mayab Stop
2 Post Office
4 Pemex (Gas Station)
7 Bank
8 Cinema
9 Bank
11 ADO Bus Station
12 Town Hall
13 Santa Cruz Church
   (Balam Na)

traveler. It has 13 air-con rooms with private showers, firm mattresses and ceiling fans for US$15 a double. They have a restaurant with surprisingly good food and service; try the shrimp ceviche, which costs US$6 and consists of an entire plate filled with shrimp. Just a few dozen meters to the south is the *Restaurant 24 Horas*, which is a bit cheaper.

South of the 24 Horas, on Av Juárez, is the *Hotel San Ignacio*, with 12 air-con rooms for US$16 for one or two persons, and an air-con restaurant with the odd name of *Danburguer Maya*.

Restaurant Familiar La Cozumeleña, on Calle 65, is a tidy family-run place, cheaper than the others, in front of the bus station.

For breads and pastries, try the *Panadería Mar y Sol*, on Av Juárez.

Getting There & Away

Buses running between Cancún (230km, 3½ hours, US$8) and Chetumal (155km, 3 hours, US$4 to US$6) stop here, as do buses traveling from Chetumal to Valladolid (160km, three hours, US$5) and Mérida (310km, five hours, US$9.50). There are also a few buses between Felipe Carrillo Puerto and Ticul (200km, four hours, US$8); change at Ticul or Muna for Uxmal. Bus fare between Felipe Carrillo Puerto and Tulum is US$3.50, and to Playa del Carmen it's US$5.25. There are also numerous buses from Felipe Carrillo Puerto to Cancún, Chetumal and Mérida, but only two to Tizimín.

Note that there are very few services such as hotels, restaurants or fuel stations between Felipe Carrillo Puerto and Ticul.

MAJAHUAL

Majahual (also often Mahahual) is a fishing village with a small navy base that's visited almost exclusively by people wanting to fish, snorkel or scuba dive. It is one of two springboards to the glorious reefs within the Banco Chinchorro, 20km to the east. Though little known and rarely visited, the

Banco Chinchorro is the largest coral atoll in the Northern Hemisphere and the site of many wrecks.

Orientation & Information

Majahual is a one-road town with 200 to 300 inhabitants who live in a mix of modern cinder-block and traditional Caribbean-style wooden houses facing the sea. Most of the people live off the sea, including the contingent of navy personnel who live in a small base at the entrance of town.

When you reach the coast, turn right (south) and within the next 500m you'll come to a couple of hotels and several simple restaurants. Opposite them lies a fair beach, then a grassy sea, and then, several hundred meters from shore, a reef. There are no banks, no laundry and certainly no Internet services in this sleepy seaside town.

Be advised that everyone visiting Majahual by car will be searched twice – once by army personnel on the Hwy 307-Majahual road, and again at the entrance of town. The troops don't do body searches, but they are usually thorough in searching vehicles. They are looking for drugs and guns. In Mexico, possession of a joint or a gun is punishable by 20 years in prison; see Legal Matters in the Facts for the Visitor section.

Places to Stay

The first hotel you'll come to is *Hotel Mahahual Caribe* *(in Chetumal ☎ 9-832-8111)*, which is a modern 20-room, two-story hotel that seems very out of place, given the primitive look of most everything else in Majahual. The rooms are standard, with ceiling fan, hot-water private bathroom and two beds per room. There's electricity from 6 pm till midnight. The cost is US$30 per room. The owner promotes fishing, which costs US$12.50 per hour to trawl. Or, for US$180, you can trawl all day. Barracuda, marlin, dorado, sailfish and small tuna are found in these waters.

One hundred meters south (and just beyond the pier) is *Cabañas de Fernando* *(no phone)*, which offers three cabañas with concrete floors, with one bed with mosquito net and one inferior hammock and shower in each. The toilets are communal. The cost is a reasonable US$10.

Continuing south another 150m you'll come to *Chinchorro Bungalows* *(no phone)*, which had a large sign out front advertising that it was 'run by divers,' presumably for divers. However, the owner wasn't around at the time Lonely Planet stopped by and the caretaker didn't have any information about the apparent dive operation there (there was a dive boat out front). There are two very comfortable cabañas on the premises with private bathroom for US$20 a night.

Getting There & Around

It's possible to get to Majahual by bus, but it's not easy. From Chetumal or Felipe Carrillo Puerto, take a bus that passes through Limones, which is near the Hwy 307 turnoff for Majahual. In Limones, there are somewhat regular but infrequent buses to Majahual.

The other option is to hire a taxi, but taxis aren't always available in Limones. With some negotiating, it should be possible to take a cab to Majahual for US$45 now that the road's in good shape. The vast majority of tourists who reach Majahual do so in a rental car; from Hwy 307, turn east at Cafetal and follow the road 58km to Majahual.

There are no taxis in Majahual, but the town is very small and can be easily walked.

XCALAK & COSTA MAYA

The coast south of the Reserva de la Biósfera Sian Ka'an to the small fishing village of Xcalak ('shka-LAK') is often referred to as the Costa Maya. Unknown and difficult to access until 1981, it is now drawing increasing numbers of adventurous travelers in search of that fast-disappearing natural asset – the undeveloped stretch of coastline.

Today, despite the recent paving of the road linking Xcalak and Hwy 307 – a road that reduced travel time on the 116-km stretch of road by 80% – Xcalak remains a fairly primitive part of Mexico. There are several fine places to stay and several decent restaurants, but you won't find a bank, a gas station, a laundry or a tourist office here. Credit cards? Forget it. Most residents have

electricity only six hours a day. With its older, Caribbean-style wooden homes, its swaying palm trees and quiet streets, 'Internet Age' is about the last thing you'd associate with Xcalak.

Xcalak's appeal lies in its laid-back atmosphere and its natural beauty. It's Playa del Carmen 25 years ago. There are lovely beaches – and mangrove as well; developers have yet to chop it down and put in a Señor Frog's. There's no discotheque to go to at night. Here, you might admire the stars while chatting with a new friend. If you did any snorkeling or diving earlier in the day, your conversation would likely revolve around that – especially if you made it out to the little-explored **Banco Chinchorro**, a lovely atoll 40km away. Not only lovely, it's also the largest coral atoll in the Northern Hemisphere.

In addition to its many natural beauties, the atoll is a wreck diver's paradise. So many ships have crashed into the ring of islands during adverse weather that parts of it resemble a ship graveyard. There are no scuttlings here, only the aftermath of ships' violent encounters with reefs during hurricanes or poor judgment exercised by pilots who should have navigated these waters with greater care. Xcalak offers good bonefishing, but the sportfishing along the Costa Maya is nothing to write home about.

Aventuras Chinchorro (☎ 9-838-7824, in the USA ☎ 941-488-4505, 800-480-4505, www.xcalak.com) offers dive and snorkel trips to the Banco Chinchorro, rents equipment and offers certification for scuba divers. It also offers local dive and snorkel trips as well as day trips to Belize. Among the offerings: local diving, two tanks, US$50; local night dive, US$50; Banco Chinchorro, four to six divers/snorkelers, US$125 per diver or US$65 per snorkeler (includes three tanks, weights, captain, dive master, lunch, snacks, beverages); and snorkeling up a river and to Bird Island (US$25 and up).

Orientation

The only road into town runs into the coastal road at about the center of town, which is generally regarded as the town's soccer field.

Most of the tourist facilities are reached by taking the coast road north, so take a left turn when the Hwy 307-Xcalak road reaches the coast. A stone's throw away you'll come to Hotel Caracol. After 250m you'll see a sign to Costa de Cocos (a hotel), which asks you to turn left. If, instead, you continue straight for another 100m, you'll come to Marina Mike's (a hotel).

If you turn left at the Costa de Cocos sign and follow the road, after 500m you'll come to Aventuras Chinchorro (the dive shop). About 600m farther along the same road you'll come to Costa de Cocos. After another 300m you'll come to Hotel Tierra Maya. If you continue on 2.5km farther, you'll come to the Villa Caracol, then after another 500m the Sand Wood Villas, and 200m farther, the Sin Duda Villas. Between Hotel Tierra Maya and Villa Caracol, the Casa Carolina was scheduled to open in late 2000.

There is no reliable local transportation.

Places to Stay & Eat

The six-room *Hotel Caracol (no phone)* is the town's only cheap place to stay, offering decent rooms with fans and cold-water-only private bathrooms for US$9. Electricity is available from 7 to 11 pm. Look for the owner next door to the hotel. For the money, this place is a good find.

Costa de Cocos (in the USA ☎ 888-968-6181, www.costadecocos.com), 1.5km north of Xcalak, has 14 very appealing thatched cabañas with private baths, solar hot water, screened windows all around and 24-hour electricity. There's an attractive restaurant-bar, and breakfast and dinner are included in the price (US$65 to US$75, depending on the time of year). Kayak tours are available here, as well.

The *Hotel Tierra Maya (in the USA ☎ 800-480-4505, 941-627-3888, fax 941-627-0089, www.xcalak.com)* is a modern beachfront hotel featuring six rooms (three quite large), each tastefully appointed and boasting lots of architectural details. All of the rooms have a balcony facing the sea, hot-water private bathrooms, mahogany furniture – the bigger rooms even have small refrigerators. There's electricity 24 hours,

and a mangrove to wander through nearby. Rates are a bargain at US$55 double occupancy for the smaller rooms, and US$65 for the larger rooms. Add US$10 from December 21 to April 14.

Marina Mike's (☎ 9-831-0063, www .xcalak.com) features five well-constructed, oceanside cabañas, all of which are quite nice and three of which are wheelchair-accessible (something you rarely find in Mexico). Marina Mike's is perhaps the most centrally located of the hotels, and its owners, Mike and Lili Braddock of Florida, are very friendly.

The *Villa Caracol* (☎ 9-838-1872) features two second-floor double rooms plus four individual beach cabañas, each with two queen-size beds, purified water, private baths and 24-hour electricity. All of the rooms have air-con *and* cellular phone service is available. Rates are a bargain at US$83 double occupancy, including breakfast and dinner and unlimited use of snorkel equipment, bicycles, paddleboats, fishing tackle and more. Scuba, fishing and snorkeling expeditions can be arranged from here.

The *Sand Wood Villas* (☎ 9-877-0025, in the USA ☎/fax 305-418-7478, ☎ 888-420-3613, www.mundacatravel.com) offers beautiful two-bedroom, two-bathroom villas on the beach with hot water, a fully equipped kitchen, fans in every room, even maid service upon request. Rates are very attractive at US$67 (July 1 through December 14) and US$89 (December 15 through June 30) for one or two persons.

The pridefully crafted *Sin Duda Villas* (☎/fax 9-831-0006, in the USA ☎ 888-881-4774, www.sindudavillas.com) features four modern and elegant beachfront villas with a total of seven guest quarters, each of which contains a handsome sleeping room with a double bed, trundle, desk, wardrobe, and private hot-water bathroom. Four of the rooms have lovely terraces that face the resort's sugary beach and a gorgeous sea studded with coral heads. One of the two fully contained guest quarters offers a 360° view, ocean to lagoon, the other is a step from the beach. The jungle-flanked Sin Duda, from its overhead shelves for books and art

in the bedrooms to the Mayan patterns of its stone and clay tile floors to the communal kitchen/social area with its vaulted concrete ceiling and carved-wood beams, was designed with thoughtfulness at every turn and Without a Doubt aptly named by architect/owner/manager Robert Schneider and his partner Margo Reheis. Sea kayaks, snorkel gear and seaside palapas are available for guests' use, as is a romantic rooftop deck that's perfect for stargazing and all-over tans. Solar-generated power is available 24 hours. Rates start at a very reasonable US$72, single or double, most of the year.

There are several small and decent restaurants near the center of town, including *Capitan Caribe*, *Brisas del Mar* and *Lonchería Silvia*. Of these, the best of these is Lonchería Silvia, although all offer seafood, chicken and beef dishes for US$3.50 to US$7.

Getting There & Away

It's possible to get to Xcalak by bus, but it's tricky. From Chetumal or Felipe Carrillo Puerto, you want to take a bus that would pass through Limones, which is near the Hwy 307 turnoff for Xcalak. In Limones, there are somewhat regular but infrequent buses to Xcalak. The other option is to hire a taxi, but it's an expensive option and taxis aren't always available in Limones. With some negotiating, it should be possible to take a cab to Xcalak for US$90 now that the road's in good shape. The vast majority of tourists who reach Xcalak do so in a rental car.

Getting Around

There are no taxis in Xcalak, so even if you do take a bus to town you'll still have to do some walking. Fortunately, with the exception of a couple of the hotels, everything in Xcalak is within easy walking distance.

LAGUNA BACALAR

Nature has set a turquoise jewel in the midst of the scrubby Yucatecan jungle – Laguna Bacalar. A large, clear, freshwater lake with a bottom of gleaming white sand, Bacalar comes as a surprise in this region of tortured limestone.

QUINTANA ROO

The small, sleepy town of Bacalar, just east of the highway some 125km south of Felipe Carrillo Puerto, is the only settlement of any size on the lake. It's noted mostly for its old Spanish fortress and its swimming facilities.

The **Spanish fortress** was built over the lagoon to protect citizens from raids by pirates and Indians. It served as an important outpost for the whites in the War of the Castes. In 1859, the fortress was seized by Mayan rebels who held the fort until Quintana Roo was finally conquered by Mexican troops in 1901. Today, with formidable cannon still on its ramparts, the fortress remains an imposing sight. It houses a museum exhibiting colonial armaments and uniforms from the 17th and 18th centuries. The museum is open 8 am to 1 pm daily; admission costs US$1.

A divided avenue runs between the fortress and the lakeshore northward a few hundred meters to the *balneario* (public swimming area – in this case both a pool and a shallow, safe part of the lake). Small restaurants line the avenue and overlook the balneario, which is very busy on weekends.

Costera Bacalar & Cenote Azul

The road that winds southward along the lakeshore from Bacalar town to Hwy 307 at Cenote Azul is called the Costera Bacalar. It passes a few lodging and camping places along the way.

Hotel Laguna (☎ 9-834-2206, in Chetumal ☎/fax 9-832-3517), 3.3km south of Bacalar town along the Costera Bacalar, is only 150m east of Hwy 307, so you can ask a bus driver to stop there for you. Clean, cool and hospitable, it boasts a wonderful view of the lake, a swimming pool, and a breezy terrace restaurant and bar. Its weakness: mattresses that are in need of replacing. Rooms cost US$27 single or double.

On the shore, only 700m south of the Hotel Laguna along the Costera Bacalar, is *Los Coquitos* camping area, which is run by a family who lives in a shack on the premises. You can camp in the dense shade of the palm trees, enjoy the view of the lake from the palapas and swim from the grassy banks,

all for US$5 per couple. Bring your own food and drinking water, as the nearest supplier is the restaurant at the Hotel Laguna.

Cenote Azul is a 90m-deep natural pool on the southwestern shore of Laguna Bacalar, 200m east of Hwy 307. (If you're approaching from the north by bus, get the driver to stop and let you off here.) Since this is a cenote there's no beach, just a few steps leading down to the water from the vast palapa which shelters the restaurant. You might pay US$8 to US$12 for the average meal here. A small sign purveys Mayan wisdom: 'Don't go in the cenote if you can't swim.'

Getting There & Away

Coming from the north, have the bus drop you in Bacalar town, at the Hotel Laguna, or at Cenote Azul, as you wish; check before you buy your ticket to see if the driver will stop.

Heading west out of Chetumal, you turn north onto Hwy 307; 15.5km north of this highway junction is a turn on the right marked for the Cenote Azul and Costera Bacalar.

Catch a minibus from Chetumal's minibus terminal on Av Primo de Verdad at Av Hidalgo. Departures are about every 20 minutes from 5 am to 7 pm for the 39km (45 minutes, US$2) run to the town of Bacalar; some northbound buses (US$2.50) departing from the bus terminal will also drop you near the town of Bacalar. Along the way they pass Laguna Milagros (14km), Xul-ha (22km) and Cenote Azul (33km), and all four of these places afford chances to swim in fresh water. The lakes are beautiful, framed by palm trees, with crystal clear water and soft white limestone-sand bottoms.

AROUND BACALAR

Just north of Bacalar town and with a driveway extending east from Hwy 307 is the lovely, American-owned *Rancho Encantado* (☎ 9-831-0037, in the USA ☎ 800-505-6292, www.encantado.com). Rancho Encantado features 12 beautiful, handcrafted casitas on parklike grounds beside Laguna Bacalar. The casitas are spread out enough to provide privacy, yet near enough so no one has to walk too far to get to the restaurant, the dock or the parking lot. At the center of

things is a lakeside palapa-roofed, open-sided restaurant (and gift shop!) that serves breakfasts and gourmet dinners. Rates vary with casita but typically start at US$104 double occupancy (low season) and US$140 double occupancy (high season). Lake-view casitas generally cost US$15 or US$20 more. Rates include breakfast and dinner; be sure to order the fish ceviche (US$7 for nonguests). Canoe and kayak are available for rent, and tours to Mayan ruins can be arranged.

Also just a few kilometers north of Bacalar town is ***Puerto del Cielo Hotel y Restaurante*** (☎ 9-837-0414), which offers 12 air-con rooms with TV and hot-water private bathroom, and there's a swimming pool on the grounds overlooking Laguna Bacalar. For US$25 per room, this place is a great find. There's also a restaurant here specializing in chicken and fish dishes, few costing more than US$7.

CHETUMAL
☎ 9 • pop 115,152
Before the Spanish Conquest, Chetumal was a Mayan port for shipping gold, feathers, cacao and copper from this region and Guatemala to the northern Yucatán Peninsula. After the conquest, the town was not actually settled until 1898, when it was founded to put a stop to the illegal trade in arms and lumber carried on by the descendants of the War of the Castes rebels. Dubbed Payo Obispo, the town's name was changed to Chetumal in 1936. In 1955, Hurricane Janet virtually obliterated Chetumal.

During the rebuilding, the city planners laid out the new town on a grand plan with a grid of wide boulevards. In times BC (Before Cancún), the sparsely populated territory of Quintana Roo could not support such a grand city, even though Quintana Roo was upgraded from a territory to a state in 1974. But the tourist boom at Cancún brought prosperity to all, and Chetumal is finally fulfilling its destiny as an important capital city.

Chetumal is also the gateway to Belize. With the peso so low and Belize so expensive, Belize nearly empties out on weekends with shoppers coming to Chetumal's markets.

Orientation
Despite Chetumal's sprawling layout, the city center is easily manageable on foot. Once you find the all-important intersection of Av de los Héroes and Av Alvaro Obregón, you're within 50m of several cheap hotels and restaurants. The best hotels are only four or five blocks from this intersection.

Information
Tourist Offices A tourist information kiosk (☎ 832-3663), on Av de los Héroes at the eastern end of Calle Efrain Aguilar, can answer questions. Hours are 8 am to 1 pm and 5 to 8 pm daily.

Money See the map for locations of currency-exchange offices and banks with ATMs.

Post & Communications The post office (☎ 832-0057) is at Av Plutarco Elías Calles No 2A. There is no shortage of public telephones around town from which to place international calls. However, it's possible to place long-distance calls and send faxes from the Telmex on Calle Cárdenas between Avs Independencia and Juárez. It's open 8 am to 6 pm Monday to Friday.

Museo de la Cultura Maya
This dramatic museum is the city's claim to cultural fame, a bold blocklong air-con showpiece designed to draw visitors from as far away as Cancún. Indeed, this superb museum represents the only significant attraction in the capital city – and it's a great place to escape the heat!

The exhibits cover all of the Mayab (lands of the Maya), not just Quintana Roo or Mexico, and seek to explain the Mayan way of life, thought and belief. There are beautiful scale models of the great Mayan buildings as they may have appeared; replicas of stelae from Copán, Honduras; and reproductions of the murals found in Room 1 at Bonampak, as well as artifacts discovered at sites in Quintana Roo.

The museum is organized into three levels, as was Mayan cosmogony based on the 'World-Tree': the main floor represents this

CHETUMAL

PLACES TO STAY
2 Hotel Cristal
5 Hotel Ucum
9 Holiday Inn Chetumal
   Puerta Maya
13 Hotel Brasilia
16 Hotel Los Cocos
20 Hotel El Cedro
29 Hotel María Dolores
32 Hotel Caribe Princess
33 Instituto Quintanarroense
   de la Juventud y El Deporte
   (Youth Hostel)

PLACES TO EAT
5 Restaurant Ucum
6 Restaurant Pantoja
8 Mercado Ignacio Manuel Altamirano
16 Hotel Los Cocos Sidewalk Café
17 Restaurant Vegetariano La Fuente
18 Hawaiian Paradise
22 Restaurant Típico El Taquito
24 Café-Restaurant Los Milagros
27 Pollo Brujo
29 Restaurant Sosilmar;
   Panadería La Muralla
31 María's; Sergio's Pizzas
37 Panadería y Pastelería La Invencible

OTHER
1 Minibus Terminal
3 ADO Bus Ticket Office
4 Museo de la Cultura Maya
7 Clinica de Chetumal
10 Tourist Information Kiosk
11 Cruz Roja
12 Hospital Morelos
14 Telmex
15 Banco Santander Mexicano
19 Banorte (ATM);
   BanCrecer (ATM)
21 Post Office

23 Chetumal Express
   Casa de Cambio
25 Bancomer (ATM)
26 Banamex
28 Banca Serfin (ATM)
30 Easy Money Casa
   de Cambio
34 Pemex (Gas Station)
35 El Palamar
36 Scorpion's
38 Bital
39 Parque Renacimiento
40 Palacio de Gobierno

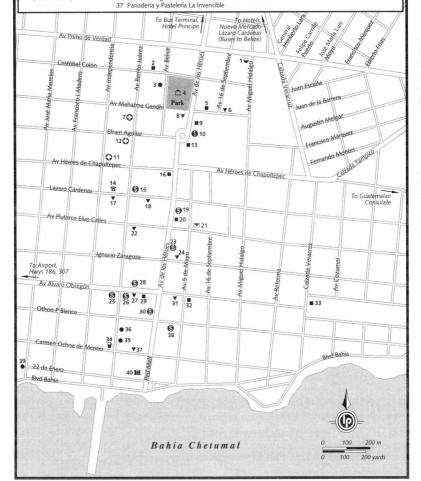

world, the upper floor the heavens and the lower floor Xibalba, the underworld. All exhibits are labeled in Spanish and English. It's open 9 am to 7 pm Tuesday through Thursday, 9 am to 8 pm Friday and Saturday, 9 am to 2 pm Sunday, closed Monday. Admission costs US$2.50, half-price for children.

Places to Stay

Budget *Instituto Quintanarroense de la Juventud y El Deporte* (☎ 832-0525), the youth hostel, on Calle Calzada Veracruz near the corner with Av Obregón, is the cheapest place in town. It has a few drawbacks: single-sex dorms, 11 pm curfew, and a location five blocks east of the intersection of Avs de los Héroes and Obregón. The cost is US$4 for a bunk in a room with four or six beds and shared bath. Meals are not available here.

Hotel María Dolores (☎ 832-0508, Av Obregón No 206), west of Av de los Héroes above the Restaurant Sosilmar, is the best for the price, with tiny, stuffy rooms for US$9/11/13/15 a single/double/triple/quad with fans and private bath. Some rooms sleep up to six.

Hotel Ucum (☎ 832-0711, 832-6186, Av Gandhi No 167) is a large place with lots of rooms around a bare central courtyard and a good cheap little restaurant. Plain rooms with fan, TV and shower cost US$12 single or double, or US$22 a double with air-con.

Hotel Cristal (☎ 832-3878, Calle Colón No 207), between Avs Juárez and Belice, is run by an energetic señora who offers clean rooms for US$9/11/14 single/double/triple with fan, US$23 a double with air-con and TV.

Hotel El Cedro (☎ 832-6878), on Av de los Héroes between Av Plutarco Elías Calles and Calle Cárdenas, has slightly worn but OK rooms for US$22 double with air-con, TV and private baths. This is a good find.

The quiet *Hotel Caribe Princess* (☎/fax 832-0900, Av Obregón No 168) has lots of marble and good air-con rooms for US$21/26/30.

Two blocks south of the Nuevo Mercado and the stop for buses to Belize, the *Hotel Nachancan* (☎ 832-3232, Calle Calzada Veracruz No 379) offers decent, more-or-less quiet rooms with air-con and TV for

US$21/24/27. The *Hotel Posada Rosas del Mar* (Calle Calzada Veracruz No 407) is directly across from the market, and is cheap at US$11 double, but is nothing special.

One kilometer north of the Museo Maya on the way to the bus terminal, the *Hotel Principe* (☎ 832-4799, fax 832-5191, Av de los Héroes No 326) has decent rooms, a restaurant and even a small swimming pool. Rooms cost US$27 double with air-con.

Mid-Range *Hotel Los Cocos* (☎ 832-0544, fax 832-0920), Av de los Héroes at Av Héroes de Chapultepec, has a nice swimming pool set in grassy lawns, a guarded parking lot and a popular sidewalk restaurant. Air-con rooms with TV, rich in nubby white stucco, cost US$40 to US$50, single or double.

Hotel Brasilia, on Av de los Héroes half a block down from the Holiday Inn Chetumal Puerta Maya, was under construction at the time of writing. Slots for air-con units were in place, and by all outward appearances the hotel looked promising.

Top End Two blocks north of Los Cocos along Av de los Héroes, near the tourist information kiosk, is the *Holiday Inn Chetumal Puerta Maya* (☎ 832-1100, 832-1080, fax 832-1676, in the USA ☎ 800-465-4329, Av de los Héroes No 171). Its comfortable rooms overlook a small courtyard with a swimming pool set amid tropical gardens; there's a restaurant and bar. Rooms cost US$95 single or double. This is the best place in town.

Places to Eat

Across from the Holiday Inn and the tourist information kiosk is the *Mercado Ignacio Manuel Altamirano* and its row of small, simple market eateries purveying full meals for US$2 or US$3.

Restaurant Sosilmar, on Av Obregón below the Hotel María Dolores, is bright and simple, with prices listed prominently. Filling platters of fish or meat go for US$5 to US$7.

Next door is the *Panadería La Muralla*, providing fresh baked goods for bus trips, picnics and make-your-own breakfasts. An even grander pastry shop is the *Panadería y*

Pastelería La Invencible on Calle Carmen Ochoa de Merino, west of Av de los Héroes.

West of the Sosilmar is **Pollo Brujo**, where a roasted half chicken is yours for US$3.50. Take it with you, or dine in their air-con salon. Be sure to sample their secret sauce.

Restaurant Vegetariano La Fuente (Calle Cárdenas No 222), between Avs Independencia and Juárez, is a tidy meatless restaurant next to a homeopathic pharmacy. Healthy meals cost US$6 or less.

Café-Restaurant Los Milagros, on Calle Zaragoza between Avs de los Héroes and 5 de Mayo, serves meals for US$4 to US$7 indoors or outdoors, and there's a book exchange with numerous English titles. It's a favorite place for Chetumal's student and intellectual set.

The family-owned **Restaurant Pantoja**, Av Gandhi at Av 16 de Septiembre, is a neighborhood favorite that opens for breakfast early, and later provides a comida corrida for US$2.50, enchiladas for US$2 and meat plates such as bistec a la tampiqueña, which is a generous portion of thinly sliced beef served with onions, fries, tomatoes, rice, beans and lettuce. Few items cost over US$3.

The nearby **Restaurant Ucum** (Av Gandhi No 167), in the Hotel Ucum, also provides good cheap meals.

To sample the typical traditional food of Quintana Roo, head for the **Restaurant Típico El Taquito** (Av Plutarco Elías Calles No 220), at Av Juárez. You enter past the cooks, hard at work, to an airy, simple dining room where good, cheap food is served. Tacos cost US$1 each, slightly more with cheese. There's a daily comida corrida for US$2.75. This is a good place to go with a jolly group of friends.

Maria's and **Sergio's Pizzas** (Av Obregón No 182), a block east of Av de los Héroes, are actually the same full-service restaurant with two wood-paneled, air-con dining rooms open 1 pm to midnight daily. Look for the stained-glass windows, and enter to low lights and soft classical music. In Maria's, order one of the many wines offered, then any of the Mexican or continental dishes, such as seafood, or beef cordon bleu (US$7), finishing up with sweet dessert. In Sergio's,

order a cold beer in a frosted mug and select a pizza priced from US$4 (small, plain) to US$16 (large, fancy).

If all you really want is something cool, head to **Hawaiian Paradise**, on Calle Cárdenas a half block west of Av de los Héroes, which is the modern alternative to the traditional Mexican juice stand. Here, available in small (US$0.60), medium (US$0.80) and large (US$1) sizes, is a variety of natural and artificial beverages, most containing ice. The sweet drinks, or slushies (concentrados), consist of crushed ice and syrup (in cherry, lime, pineapple and other flavors). The leches (milk-based drinks) likewise come in a wide variety of flavors and contain real fruit. The naturales contain juice and nothing but juice (and ice). It's open 11 am to 10 pm daily.

Entertainment

For entertainment, there are two major places in town and they happen to be next door to one another near the south end of Av Juárez. Every day, starting at 1:30 pm and going till 10 pm, there's live music at **El Palamar**. This place is often packed with attendees ranging in age from 18 to 60 as the vocalists belt out traditional Mexican songs. This is Corona time, big time, under a palapa.

Next door is **Scorpion's**, which is a blackwall, heavy-disco-sound club popular with Chetumal's 18 to 25 crowd. Few tourists ever enter. There's no cover charge. It's open every evening.

Getting There & Away

Air Chetumal's small airport is less than 2km northwest of the city center along Avs Obregón and Revolución.

Mexicana's regional carrier Aerocaribe (☎/fax 832-6675), Av Héroes No 125, Plaza Baroudi Local 13, operates flights between Chetumal and Cancún, Cozumel, Flores (Petén, Guatemala) and Palenque.

Aviacsa (☎ 832-7676, fax 832-7654; at the airport ☎ 832-7787, fax 832-7698) flies nonstop to Villahermosa and direct to Mexico City.

For flights to Belize City (and on to Tikal) or to Belize's cayes, cross the border into Belize and fly from Corozal.

Bus The bus terminal (Terminal de Autobuses de Chetumal) is 3km north of the center (Museo de la Cultura Maya), at the intersection of Avs de los Insurgentes and Belice. ADO, Autotransportes del Sur, Cristóbal Colón, Omnitur del Caribe, Línea Dorada, Unimaya and other carriers provide service. The terminal has lockers, a tourism information kiosk, bookstore, newsstand, post office, international phone and fax services, and shops. Next to the terminal is a huge San Francisco de Asis department store.

You can buy ADO tickets in the city center on Av Belice just west of the Museo de la Cultura Maya.

Many local buses, and those bound for Belize, depart from the Nuevo Mercado Lázaro Cárdenas, on Calle Calzada Veracruz at Regundo, 10 blocks (1.5km) north of the Museo de la Cultura Maya along Av de los Héroes; turn at the Jeep dealership and go three blocks east.

The Minibus Terminal, at the corner of Avs Primo de Verdad and Hidalgo, has minibuses to Bacalar and other nearby destinations.

Here are some distances and travel times for buses leaving Chetumal:

Bacalar – 39km, 45 minutes; frequent minibuses from the Minibus Terminal for US$2; hourly 2nd-class buses from the bus terminal for US$2.50

Belize City – 160km, four hours, US$5; express three hours, US$7; Batty's runs six northbound buses from Belize City via Orange Walk and Corozal to Chetumal's Nuevo Mercado from 5:30 am to 6 pm; six southbound buses from Chetumal's Nuevo Mercado run from 10:30 am and 6:30 pm. Venus Bus Lines has buses departing from Belize City every hour on the hour from noon to 7 pm; departures from Chetumal are hourly from 4 to 10 am

Campeche – 422km, seven hours, US$11 to US$14; three buses

Cancún – 382km, five to six hours, US$10 to US$14; 28 buses

Corozal (Belize) – 30km, one hour with border formalities, US$1.75; see Belize City schedule, above

Felipe Carrillo Puerto – 155km, three hours, US$4 to US$6; 28 buses

Flores (Guatemala) – 350km, nine hours, US$35; Servicio San Juan operates a bus at 2:30 pm daily from Chetumal's main bus terminal to Flores and Tikal

Kohunlich – 67km, one hour; take a bus heading west to Xpujil or Escárcega, get off just before the village of Francisco Villa and walk 5km to the Villas Ecológicas hotel, then take a taxi to the site

Mérida – 456km, eight hours, US$9 to US$13; 12 buses

Orange Walk (Belize) – 91km, 2¼ hours; Urbina's and Chell's each run one bus daily (US$4), departing Chetumal's Nuevo Mercado around lunchtime; see also Belize City, above

Playa del Carmen – 315km, five hours; seven buses by ADO (US$10 to US$12), one by Colón (US$11), three by Mayab (US$6.50)

Ticul – 352km, six hours, US$9; nine buses

Tulum – 251km, four hours, US$5 to US$7; many buses

Xcalak – 200km, 4½ hours, US$3; Sociedad Cooperativa del Caribe runs buses at 6 am and 3:30 pm from the Minibus Terminal

Xpujil – 120km, 1½ hours, US$3 to US$4; eight buses

Getting Around

Official taxis from the bus terminal to the center overcharge. Instead, you should walk out of the terminal to the main road, turn left, walk to the traffic circle and catch a regular cab for about US$3.

AROUND CHETUMAL

West of Chetumal along Hwy 186 is rich sugarcane and cattle country; logging is still important here, as it was during the 17th and 18th centuries.

Kohunlich Ruins

The archaeological site of Kohunlich is being aggressively excavated, though most of its nearly 200 mounds are still covered in vegetation. The surrounding jungle is thick, but the archaeological site itself has been cleared selectively and is now a delightful forest park. Admission to the site costs US$2.50, and it is open 8 am to 5 pm daily. Drinks are sometimes sold at the site. The toilets are usually locked and 'under repair.'

These ruins, dating from the Late Preclassic (300 BC to 250 AD) and Early Classic (250 to 600 AD) periods, are famous for the great Pirámide de los Mascarones (Pyramid of the Masks): A central stairway is flanked by huge, 3m-high stucco masks of the sun

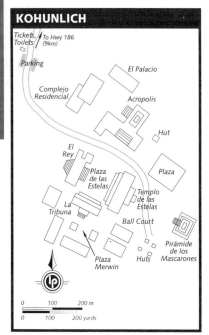

KOHUNLICH

Tickets, / To Hwy 186
Toilets / (9km)

Parking

El Palacio

Complejo
Residencial

Acropolis

Hut

El
Rey

Plaza
de las
Estelas

Plaza

La
Tribuna

Templo
de las
Estelas

Ball Court

Plaza
Merwin

Huts

Pirámide
de los
Mascarones

0   100   200 m
0   100   200 yards

god. The thick lips and prominent features are reminiscent of Olmec sculpture. Though there were once eight masks, only two remain after the ravages of archaeology looters.

The masks themselves are impressive, but the large thatch coverings that have been erected to protect them from further weathering also obscure the view; you can see the masks only from close up. Try to imagine what the pyramid and its masks must have looked like in the old days as the Maya approached it across the sunken courtyard at the front.

The hydraulic engineering used at the site was a great achievement; nine of the site's 21 hectares were cut to channel rainwater into Kohunlich's once-enormous reservoir.

Getting There & Away At the time of writing, there was no public transport running directly to Kohunlich. To visit the ruins without your own vehicle, you need to start early, taking a bus to the village of Francisco Villa near the turnoff to the ruins, and from there you can either walk 5km to the Villas Ecológicas hotel and take a taxi the remaining 4km, or walk the entire 9km.

Better still, take a taxi from Chetumal to the ruins, have the driver wait for you, and then return. Roundtrip taxi fare, with the wait, will cost about US$60 per party.

To return to Chetumal or to head westward to Xpujil or Escárcega, you must hope to flag down a bus on the highway; not all buses will stop.

SOUTH TO BELIZE & GUATEMALA

Corozal, 18km south of the Mexican-Belizean border, is a pleasant, sleepy, laid-back farming and fishing town, and an appropriate introduction to Belize. There are several decent hotels that will appeal to a full range of budgets, and there are restaurants to match.

Buses run directly from Chetumal's market to Belize City via Corozal and Orange Walk. From Belize City you can catch westward buses to Belmopan, San Ignacio, and the Guatemalan border at Benque Viejo, then onward to Flores, Tikal and other points in Guatemala.

A special 1st-class bus service operated by Servicio San Juan goes directly between Chetumal's bus terminal and Flores (near Tikal in Guatemala) once daily (350km, nine hours, US$35).

Yucatán State

The state of Yucatán is a pie slice at the top of the Yucatán Peninsula. Until the development of Cancún in neighboring Quintana Roo, it was the economic engine of the peninsula. It was in Yucatán state, beginning in the mid-19th century, that fiber derived from agave plants was made into twine. The twine from the region was shipped worldwide, and it wasn't until the advent of synthetic fibers a century later that twine from Yucatán state fell out of favor on the world market.

While Quintana Roo's tourist-driven economy has surpassed Yucatán's in recent years, historically and culturally Yucatán remains the peninsula's primary state. Within the state you'll find the peninsula's most impressive Mayan ruins (Chichén Itzá and Uxmal), its finest colonial cities (Mérida and Valladolid) and two coastal communities nationally famous for their wild red flamingos (Río Lagartos and Celestún). It is also in this often-sweltering state of 1.5 million people that visitors will find many majestic missions and, in the Grutas de Loltún, grandiose caves that make for memorable exploring.

As a tourist destination, traditional Yucatán complements increasingly commercial Quintana Roo extremely well, and travel between the two states is convenient and affordable. A high-speed highway, served by numerous first-class buses, links Cancún and Mérida, and a visit to Mexico's 'White City,' as Mérida is locally known, is highly recommended. A visit to one of Mexico's oldest cities following a visit to one of the country's most modern resorts has the feel of a journey backward in time.

MÉRIDA
☎ 9 • pop 612,261

The capital of the state of Yucatán is a prosperous, charming city of narrow streets, colonial buildings and shady parks. Known throughout Mexico as the 'White City' due to the preponderance of quarried limestone and white paint used there, Mérida was a

Highlights

- Mérida, a prosperous city boasting many fine colonial buildings
- Chichén Itzá, the great Maya-Toltec ceremonial center
- Río Lagartos, home to Mexico's largest flamingo colony
- Uxmal, the graceful chief city of the Puuc region
- Izamal, the 'Yellow City,' site of an awesome Franciscan monastery

center of Mayan culture in Yucatán long before the conquistadors arrived.

Today, Mérida is the peninsula's center of commerce as well, a bustling city that has benefited greatly from *maquiladoras* (foreign-operated companies) that opened in the 1980s and '90s and tourism that picked up during those decades. There are lots of hotels and restaurants of every class and price range in Mérida and good transportation services to any part of the peninsula and the rest of the country.

Mérida is busiest with tourists from mid-December through March and in July and August. You'd be wise to reserve a hotel room if you intend to visit the city during these times, and expect the hotel rates to be 20% or higher than the low-season rates quoted here; like most everywhere else on the peninsula, hotel rates in Mérida fluctuate with demand.

History

Francisco de Montejo the Younger founded a Spanish colony at Campeche, about 160km to the south, in 1540. From this base he was able to take advantage of political dissension among the Maya, conquering Tihó (now Mérida) in 1542. By the end of the decade, Yucatán was mostly under Spanish colonial rule.

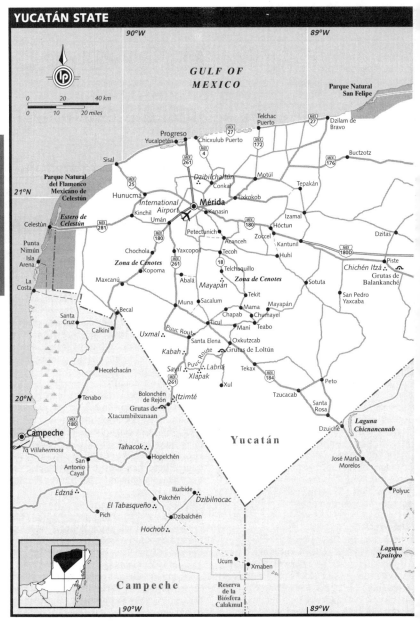

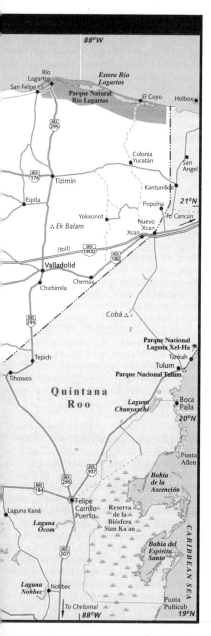

When Montejo's conquistadors entered defeated Tihó, they found a major Mayan settlement of lime-mortared stone that reminded them of Roman architectural legacies in Mérida, Spain. They promptly renamed the city and proceeded to build it into the colonial capital, dismantling the Mayan structures and using the materials to construct a cathedral and other stately buildings. Mérida took its colonial orders directly from Spain, not from Mexico City, and Yucatán has had a distinct cultural and political identity ever since.

During the War of the Castes (1847-55), only Mérida and Campeche were able to hold out against the rebel forces; the rest of the Yucatán Peninsula came under Indian control. On the brink of surrender, the ruling class in Mérida was saved by reinforcements sent from central Mexico in exchange for Mérida agreeing to take orders from Mexico City. Although Yucatán is certainly part of Mexico, there is still a strong feeling in Mérida and other parts of the state that the local people stand a breed apart.

Orientation

The Plaza Mayor, or main square, has been the center of Mérida since Mayan times. Most of the services you want are within five blocks of the square; the rest are on the broad, tree-lined boulevard Paseo de Montejo.

Be advised that house numbers may progress unevenly from street to street: you cannot know whether Calle 57 No 481 and Calle 56 No 544 are one block or 10 blocks apart. Perhaps for this reason, addresses are usually given in this form: Calle 57 No 481 X 56 y 58 (between Calles 56 and 58).

Information

Tourist Offices There are information booths of minimal usefulness at the airport and the main bus station, Terminal CAME, but there are two very helpful tourist offices downtown.

Your best bet for reliable information is the Tourist Information Center (☎ 924-9290, 924-9389), at the corner of Calles 60 and 57A, in the southwest corner of the huge Teatro

Peón Contreras, less than two blocks north of the Plaza Mayor. The office is managed by José Acosta Varquez, who is extremely knowledgeable about Mérida and speaks both English and Spanish.

Those Historic Signs

Observant visitors to Mérida will notice small, artistic plaques on the corners of some buildings beside major intersections. The ceramic plaques are located about 3m above the sidewalk – about where you'd expect to see a street sign if sign posts weren't used.

Indeed, the plaques, which feature paintings of people, animals and other subjects with their Spanish names underneath, *are* oldfashioned Mérida street signs. For example, on the building housing a Burger King (Calle 59 at Calle 60), you'll see a painted figure of a dog and, just below it, the words *el perro* (the dog).

Signs like this one were placed on corner buildings during colonial days by conquistadors trying to teach the native populace some Spanish. The signs reflected the streets' local names. Unfortunately, all of the original plaques disappeared over time; the several dozen you see today were affixed to buildings in 1994 by city officials hoping to increase tourism and maintain a piece of history. Although new, the plaques are said to closely resemble the originals, and their locations are supposedly historically accurate.

A sign on the corner of Calle 65 and Calle 60, for example, shows an old lady. The sign was posted at that particular location because local people knew the street as 'the old lady's street' on account of an elderly woman who had once worked in a bakery near the corner.

Likewise, the 'two faces' sign found at the intersection of Calles 65 and 58 has its origin in a liar who lived nearby. The 'headless man' street (look for the sign on Calle 67 at Calle 60) took its name from a man who had the misfortune of being under a window when it broke and was beheaded by a falling piece of glass.

The City Tourist Office (☎ 923-0883), at the corner of Calles 59 and 62, is generally staffed with helpful, bilingual people and, like the Tourist Information Center, is generally open 8 am to 8 pm daily. Both tourist offices provide brochures and maps and can offer the most current information on the city's Internet cafés, hotels, restaurants and local events.

Money There are lots of banks along Calle 65 between Calles 60 and 62, one block behind Banamex/Casa de Montejo (that is, one block south of the Plaza Mayor). Banking hours are 9 am to 5 pm Monday to Friday, and 9 am to 1 pm Saturday. Most of the banks have ATMs outside.

Post & Communications The main post office (☎ 921-2561) is in the market area on Calle 65 between Calles 56 and 56A, open 8 am to 7 pm Monday to Friday and 9 am to 1 pm Saturday. There are postal service booths at the airport and the bus station, open Monday to Friday.

Pay phones are found on the Plaza Mayor, in Parque Hidalgo, at the airport, the CAME bus station, the corner of Calles 59 and 62 or Calles 64 and 57, and on Calle 60 between Calles 53 and 55.

CDC, a private telephone company, has phones in many transport termini, hotels and pensions. Before you make a call, find out what it will cost.

Email & Internet Access At the time of writing there were four public Internet-access service providers in Mérida and more on the way.

The centrally located Cybernet, on Calle 57A between Calles 58 and 60, makes available a half-dozen or so computers in an air-con environment 10 am to 8 pm Monday to Saturday, closed Sunday. Computer time costs US$0.10 per minute with a 15-minute (US$1.50) minimum. Be advised that its employees tend to take their lunch together, shutting down the Cybernet from about 2 to 4 pm (the time fluctuates).

Near the Mercado Municipal you'll find the Multi Servicios Rada, on Calle 58 between

Calles 65 and 67. This open-sided (ie, not air-conditioned) business charges US$1.50 for a half-hour and US$2.50 for an hour surfing the Net or reading/sending email. The Rada catches a lot of street noise and is made even louder by a radio (the owner *loves* whatever happens to be on), but it is the only Net service open on Sunday. Hours are 9 am to 8 pm Monday to Saturday, 9 am to 7 pm Sunday.

Internet access is also available at the Instituto Tecnológico de Hotelería, on Calle 57 between Calles 56 and 58, and the 2nd-floor ICM Internet Club, on Calle 59 at Calle 58.

Bookstores Librería Dante Peón, in the Teatro Peón Contreras, on the corner of Calles 60 and 57, has some English, French and German books as well as Spanish ones. It's open seven days a week. There are also several bookstores on Calle 62 between Calles 57 and 59.

Laundry Lavandería La Fe, Calle 61 No 520, at Calle 64, will gladly wash and dry your clothing for US$1 per kilo (no other laundry in town is as inexpensive). La Fe offers same-day service, providing you drop your clothes off in the morning. It's open 8 am to 7 pm Monday to Friday, 8 am to 5 pm Saturday.

The Lavandería Flamingo, on Calle 57 between Calles 56 and 58, is also a drop-off, pick-up establishment. Leave your clothes in the morning and come back for them in the late afternoon. Costs: US$0.20 per shirt, pants, shorts or blouse, and US$0.05 for each undergarment (yes, it's US$0.10 for a pair of socks). It's open 9 am to 6 pm daily.

A third laundry is located above the National Car Rental office on Calle 60 between Calles 55 and 57. Also, most of the better hotels, including the Gran Hotel, offer overnight laundry service.

Medical Services Hospital O'Horan (☎ 924-4100), the best hospital in Mérida, is near the Parque Centenario, on Av de los Itzaes. For the Red Cross, call ☎ 924-9813.

Dangers & Annoyances Guard against pickpockets, bag-snatchers and bag-slashers in the market district and in any crowd, such as at a performance. They see you, but you won't see them.

Plaza Mayor

The most logical place to start a tour of Mérida is in Plaza Mayor, a large yet lovely and at times surprising, intimate square containing lots of shade trees and benches and ringed by impressive colonial buildings. Also frequently call 'El Centro' (as in the center of town), the Plaza Mayor was the religious and social center of ancient Tihó; under the Spanish it was the Plaza de Armas, or parade ground, laid out by Francisco de Montejo the Younger.

The plaza is surrounded by some of the city's most impressive and harmonious colonial buildings, and its carefully pruned laurel trees provide welcome shade for the romantic young couples and chatty retired folk who mostly use the benches beneath them. On Sunday, the adjoining roadways are off-limits to vehicular traffic.

Cathedral On the east side of the plaza, on the site of a Mayan temple, is Mérida's huge, hulking, severe cathedral, begun in 1561 and completed in 1598. Some of the stone from the Mayan temple was used in the cathedral's construction.

Walk through one of the three doors in the baroque façade and into the sanctuary. The great crucifix at the east end of the nave is Cristo de la Unidad (Christ of Unity), a symbol of reconciliation between those of Spanish and Mayan stock. To your right, over the south door, is a painting of Tutul Xiú, cacique of the town of Maní, paying his respects to his ally Francisco de Montejo at Tihó (Montejo and Xiú jointly defeated the Cocoms; Xiú converted to Christianity and his descendants still live in Mérida).

Look in the small chapel to the left of the principal altar for Mérida's most famous religious artifact, a statue of Jesus called *Cristo de las Ampollas* (Christ of the Blisters). Local legend has it that this statue was carved from a tree in the town of Ichmul after the tree was hit by lightning and supposedly burned for an entire night without

YUCATÁN STATE

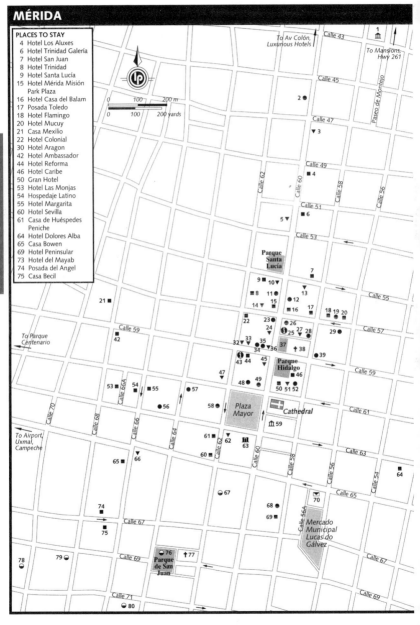

MÉRIDA

PLACES TO STAY
4 Hotel Los Aluxes
6 Hotel Trinidad Galería
7 Hotel San Juan
8 Hotel Trinidad
9 Hotel Santa Lucía
15 Hotel Mérida Misión
   Park Plaza
16 Hotel Casa del Balam
17 Posada Toledo
18 Hotel Flamingo
20 Hotel Mucuy
21 Casa Mexilio
22 Hotel Colonial
30 Hotel Aragon
42 Hotel Ambassador
44 Hotel Reforma
46 Hotel Caribe
50 Gran Hotel
53 Hotel Las Monjas
54 Hospedaje Latino
55 Hotel Margarita
60 Hotel Sevilla
61 Casa de Huéspedes
   Peniche
64 Hotel Dolores Alba
65 Casa Bowen
69 Hotel Peninsular
73 Hotel del Mayab
74 Posada del Angel
75 Casa Becil

charring. The statue was originally placed in the local church, where it alone is said to have survived the fiery destruction of the church some years later, though it was blackened and blistered from the heat. It was moved to the Mérida cathedral in 1645.

The rest of the church's interior is plain, its rich decoration having been stripped by angry peasants at the height of anticlerical feeling during the Mexican Revolution. You won't find any stained-glass windows here, and there's only a modest display of religious art and artifacts. Sections of the cathedral's marble floor bear the names of the formerly influential people buried beneath it.

If you forgot to pack your rosary, don't worry; plenty of them, and innumerable Christian crosses and glow-in-the-dark crucifixes, are always for sale beside the entrance to the cathedral.

MACAY On the south side of the cathedral, housed in the former archbishop's palace, is the Museo de Arte Contemporáneo Ateneo de Yucatán (Yucatán Contemporary Art Museum and Athenaeum, ☎ 928-3258), at Pasaje de la Revolución No 1907. More commonly known as MACAY, this attractive museum holds permanent exhibits of Yucatán's most famous painters and sculptors, as well as changing exhibits of local arts and artisans.

MACAY is open 10 am to 6 pm daily except Tuesday, when it is closed. Admission costs US$2.50; students, teachers, workers, campesinos and seniors may enter for free. Admission is free to all on Sunday. There's a *cafetería* inside.

Palacio de Gobierno On the north side of the plaza, the Palacio de Gobierno houses the state of Yucatán's executive government offices. It was built in 1892 on the site of the palace of the colonial governors. The palace is open 8 am to 8 pm daily. There is no cost to enter.

Inside, you'll find murals painted by local artist Fernando Castro Pacheco. The murals, which were completed in 1978, were 25 years in the making. They portray a symbolic

history of the Maya and their interaction with the Spaniards. The largest of the murals depicts corn, which the Maya held as sacred – the 'ray of sun from the gods.' On Sunday at 11 am, there's usually a concert (jazz, classical, pop, Yucatecan) in the Salón de la Historia of the Palacio de Gobierno.

Palacio Municipal Facing the cathedral across the square, the Palacio Municipal is topped by a clock tower. Originally built in 1542, the Palacio Municipal has twice been refurbished, in the 1730s and the 1850s. It continues to serve as Mérida's city hall.

Today, the building also serves as the venue for traditional Yucatecan dances. These free performances take place in the street out front of the Palacio Municipal every Monday starting around 9 pm (arrive early to get a good seat). The dances and accompanying music, which reflect a mixture of Spanish and Mayan cultures, date from the earliest days of the Vaquería Regional, a local festival that celebrated the branding of the cattle on neighboring haciendas.

Every Sunday at 1 and 6 pm, the city also sponsors a reenactment of a colorful mestizo wedding at the Palacio Municipal. The earlier show features child performers and the 6 pm show features professional entertainers. There's no cost to watch, and both shows are highly recommended.

Casa de Montejo The House of Montejo, on the south side of the Plaza Mayor, dates from 1549. The structure originally housed soldiers, but soon after it was converted into a mansion which served members of the Montejo family until 1970. Sometimes called the Palacio de Montejo, the building is named after the conqueror of Mérida, Francisco de Montejo the Younger. These days the great house shelters a bank branch, and you can enter the building and look around whenever the bank is open (9 am to 5 pm Monday to Friday, 9 am to 1 pm Saturday).

If the bank is closed, content yourself with a close look at the plateresque façade, where triumphant conquistadors with halberds hold their feet on the necks of generic barbarians (who are not Maya, but the association is inescapable). Also gazing across the plaza from the façade are busts of Montejo the Elder, his wife and his daughter. The armorial shields are those of the Montejo family.

Walking up Calle 60

A block north of the Plaza Mayor is the shady refuge of **Parque Hidalgo**. The park's benches always hold a variety of conversationalists, lovers, taxi drivers, hammock peddlers and tourists.

At the far end of the park, several restaurants offer alfresco dining. The city sponsors free marimba concerts here on Sunday at noon.

Just to the north of the park rises the 17th-century **Iglesia de Jesús**, also called the Iglesia La Tercer Orden. Built by the Jesuits in 1618, it is the sole surviving edifice in a complex of Jesuit buildings that once filled the entire city block. Always interested in education, the Jesuits founded schools that later gave birth to the Universidad de Yucatán nearby. The 19th-century General Manuel Cepeda Peraza collected a library of 15,000 volumes, which is housed in a building behind the church.

Directly in front of the church is the little **Parque de la Madre**, sometimes called Parque Morelos. The modern Madonna-and-child statue, which is a common fixture of town squares in Mexico, is a copy of a Renoir statue that stands in the Jardin du Luxembourg in Paris.

Just north of Parque de la Madre you confront the enormous bulk of the great **Teatro Peón Contreras**, built from 1900 to 1908 during Mérida's henequen heyday. (For more about henequen, see the boxed text, 'Yucatán's Past Tied to Natural Rope.') Designed by Italian architect Luis Roncoroni, it boasts a main staircase of Carrara marble, a dome with imported frescoes by Italian artists and, in its southwest corner, the Tourist Information Center.

The main entrance to the theater is on the corner of Calles 60 and 57. A gallery inside the entrance often holds exhibits by local painters and photographers; usual hours are 9 am to 2 pm and 5 to 9 pm Monday to

The Group of the Thousand Columns and the Temple of the Warriors, Chichén Itzá.

Closer view of the Thousand Columns.

A cenote in the Ik Kil Parque Ecoarqueologico.

RICHARD I'ANSON

Tourists rest after the long climb up.

RICHARD I'ANSON

Carving at the Ball Court at Chichén Itzá.

RICHARD I'ANSON

Chac-Mool statue inside El Castillo, Chichén Itzá.

Yucatán's Past Tied to Natural Rope

Henequen *(Agave fourcroydes)*, also called sisal, is a common plant in Yucatán and indeed in most of Mexico. Its stalk grows almost two meters high in the wild, about one meter high in cultivation, and has lance-shaped leaves up to two meters long and 10 to 15 cm wide, edged with thorns. The plant's evil-smelling flowers are borne on a central stalk, which grows straight up to heights of six meters. Agaves flower periodically but infrequently, some species only once in a century.

A cultivated henequen plant yields about 25 leaves annually from the fifth to the sixteenth year after planting. The leaves are cut off by a worker with a machete, taken to a factory, and crushed between heavy rollers. The pulpy vegetable matter is scraped away to reveal fiber strands up to 1.5 meters in length, which are slightly stretchable and resistant to marine organisms.

Around Izamal and en route from Chichén Itzá to Mérida you pass through the henequen fields that gave rise to Yucatán's affluence in the 19th century. Prosperity in these parts reached its high point during WWI, when the demand for rope was great and synthetic fibers had not yet been invented.

Sometimes you can smell the grayish, spike-leafed henequen plants before you can see them, as they emit a putrid, excremental odor. Once planted, henequen can grow virtually untended for seven years. Thereafter, the plants are annually stripped for fiber. A plant may be productive for upwards of two decades.

Although growing henequen for rope is still economically viable, synthetic fibers have significantly diminished the profits. This decline has not been all that devastating for Mayan farm workers, as the crop never employed a great many laborers to begin with, and those who worked during henequen's heyday on the haciendas were badly exploited.

Spiky, smelly henequen can be made into rope.

Friday, and 9 am to 2 pm Saturday and Sunday. To see the grand theater itself, you'll have to attend a performance.

Across Calle 60 from the theater is the entrance to the main building of the **Universidad de Yucatán**. Though the Jesuits provided education to Yucatán's youth for centuries, the modern university was only established in the 19th century by Governor Felipe Carrillo Puerto and General Cepeda Peraza. The story of the university's founding is rendered graphically in a mural by Manuel Lizama. Ask for directions to the mural, which was done in 1961.

The central courtyard of the university building is the scene of concerts and folk performances every Friday at 9 pm (check with the Tourist Information Center for possible schedule changes).

A block north of the university, at the intersection of Calles 60 and 55, is the pretty little **Parque Santa Lucía**, with arcades on the north and west sides. When Mérida was a lot smaller, this was where travelers would get into or out of the stagecoaches that bumped over the rough roads of the peninsula, linking towns and villages with the provincial capital.

Today, the park is the venue for orchestral performances of Yucatecan music on Thursday at 9 pm and Sunday at 11 am. Also here on Sunday at 11 am is the **Bazar de Artesanías**, the local handicrafts market.

To reach the Paseo de Montejo, walk 3¹/₂ blocks north along Calle 60 from the Parque Santa Lucía to Calle 47. Turn right on Calle 47 and walk two blocks to the Paseo de Montejo, on your left.

Paseo de Montejo

The Paseo de Montejo was an attempt by Mérida's 19th-century city planners to create a wide European-style grand boulevard, similar to Mexico City's Paseo de la Reforma or Paris' Champs-Élysées. Though more modest than its predecessors, the Paseo de Montejo is still a beautiful swath of green and open space in an urban conglomeration of stone and concrete.

As the Yucatán Peninsula has always looked upon itself as distinct from the rest of Mexico, its powerful *hacendados* (landowners) and commercial barons maintained good business and social contacts with Europe. Europe's architectural and social influence can be seen along the Paseo de Montejo in the surviving fine mansions built by wealthy families around a century ago. Many other mansions have been torn down to make way for the banks, hotels and other establishments. Most of the remaining mansions are north of Calle 37, which is three blocks north of the Museo Regional de Antropología.

Every Saturday, from 9 pm to midnight, at the southern end of Paseo de Montejo (where it meets Calle 47), the city celebrates 'Mexican Night' with mariachis and other traditional Mexican musicians. If you're in town on a Saturday night, the festivities are well worth the effort to reach them.

Museo Regional de Antropología The great white palace on the corner of Paseo de Montejo and Calle 43 is the Museo Regional de Antropología de Yucatán, housed in the Palacio Cantón. The great mansion was designed by Enrico Deserti. Construction took place from 1909 to 1911. The mansion's owner, General Francisco Cantón Rosado (1833-1917), lived here for only six years before his death. No building in Mérida exceeds it in splendor or pretension. It's a fitting symbol of the grand aspirations of Mérida's elite during the last years of the materialistic Porfiriato.

Admission to the museum costs US$2; free Sunday. It's open 9 am to 8 pm Tuesday to Saturday, 9 am to 2 pm Sunday, closed Monday. The museum shop is open 9 am to 3 pm (9 am to 2 pm Sunday). Labels on the museum's exhibits are in Spanish only.

The museum covers the peninsula's history since the age of mastodons. Exhibits on Mayan culture include explanations of forehead-flattening, which was done to beautify babies, and other practices such as sharpening teeth and implanting them with tiny jewels. If you plan to visit archaeological sites near Mérida, you can study the many exhibits here – which are lavishly illustrated with plans and photographs. The exhibits cover the great Mayan cities of Mayapán, Uxmal and Chichén Itzá, as well as lesser sites.

Av Colón For more mansion-viewing, turn left (west) onto Av Colón. The first block west of Paseo de Montejo is Mérida's posh entertainment and shopping district serving the big hotels: Holiday Inn, Fiesta Americana and Hyatt. Beyond the hotels are several splendid mansions dating from around a century ago.

Parque Centenario

About 12 blocks west of the Plaza Mayor lies the large, verdant Parque Centenario, bordered by Av de los Itzaes, the highway to the airport and Campeche. There's a zoo in the park that specializes in exhibiting the fauna of Yucatán. To get there, take a bus westward along Calle 61 or 65. The park is open 6 am to 6 pm daily except Monday; the zoo is open 8 am to 5 pm. Admission is free.

Centro Cultural de los Pueblos Mayas

The Centro Cultural de los Pueblos Mayas (Mayan Cultural Center), on Calle 59 between

Calles 48 and 50, six blocks northeast of the Plaza Mayor, holds displays of the best of indigenous arts and crafts. Located behind the ancient ex-Convento de la Mejorada, it will satisfy your curiosity about the weaving of colorful *huipiles*, the carving of ceremonial masks, the weaving of hammocks and hats and the turning of pottery. It's open 8 am to 8 pm Tuesday through Saturday, 9 am to 2 pm Sunday, closed Monday. Admission costs US$1.

Organized Tours

Guided two-hour bus tours of Mérida are offered by Paseo Turístico (☎ 927-6119). The bus departs from the Parque Santa Lucía, Calle 55 at Calle 60, at 10 am and 1, 4 and 7 pm Monday to Saturday, and at 10 am and 1 pm Sunday. Tours cost US$7. Seating capacity is 30 people. You can buy your tickets ahead of time at the nearby Hotel Santa Lucía. The tour is given in English.

You can choose from many group tours to sites around Mérida. Ask at your hotel reception desk for brochures, or consult any of the various travel agencies along Calle 60. Typical prices are: Chichén Itzá (US$17), Chichén Itzá with drop-off in Cancún (US$29), Uxmal and Kabah (US$17), Uxmal light-and-sound show (US$17), Ruta Puuc (Puuc Route, US$32), Izamal (US$23). All prices are per person and include transportation, guided tour and lunch.

One of the city's top travel agencies is Turismo Bolontikú (☎/fax 924-7285), Calle 60 No 486, between Calles 55 and 57. Turismo Bolontikú offers guided tours to Celestún, leaving at 9 am and returning to Mérida at 5 pm, Tuesday through Sunday; Ruta Puuc and Grutas de Loltún (Loltún Caves), leaving at 9 am and returning at 7 pm, on demand; Uxmal light-and-sound show, leaving at 5 pm and returning at 10:30 pm, daily; Uxmal light-and-sound show and dinner, leaving at 1 pm and returning at 10 pm, daily; Uxmal-Kabah, leaving at 9 am and returning at 5 pm, daily; and Chichén Itzá, leaving at 9 am and returning at 5 pm, daily. The agency can also arrange transportation to Cuba.

Special Events

Prior to Lent in February or March, Carnaval features colorful costumes and nonstop festivities. It is celebrated with greater vigor in Mérida than anywhere else in Yucatán.

Also during the last days of February or the beginning of March (the dates vary) is Kihuic, which is the Mayan name for a market that attracts handicrafts makers from all parts of Mexico. During this period, artisans fill the Plaza Mayor and make crafts, all of which are for sale.

From September 15 to October 15, the Cristo de las Ampollas (Christ of the Blisters) statue in the cathedral is venerated with processions.

Another big religious tradition is the Exposición de Altares, held at night every November 1. On this night, the Maya welcome the spirits of their ancestors with elaborate dinners outside their homes. Although this custom is more apparent in the countryside, Mérida observes it from 11 am November 1 to 11 am November 2 with extravagant festivities in the center of town.

Places to Stay

Budget Prices for basic but suitable rooms in Mérida just a short walk from the plaza range from US$7 to US$20 for a small but clean double with fan and private shower. All hotels should provide purified drinking water, usually at no extra charge. (Sometimes the water bottles are not readily evident, so ask for *agua purificada*.)

Hotel Las Monjas (☎/fax 928-6632, Calle 66A No 509), between Calles 61 and 63, is the best deal in town. All 31 rooms in this cozy place have ceiling fans and sinks or private baths with hot and cold water. Doubles with one bed cost US$10, with two beds US$12. One room has air-con and goes for US$12. Rooms are generally tiny and most are dark, but they're clean. Room Nos 30 and 12 are best due to their superior ventilation.

The *Hospedaje Latino* (☎ 923-5087, Calle 66 No 505), between Calles 61 and 63, offers 29 fan-cooled rooms with good mattresses and private hot-water bathrooms for US$6/7 single/double and three air-con rooms for US$11 per room. This is an excellent value,

second to Las Monjas only due to a higher noise factor (a problem easily solved with earplugs).

Hotel Margarita (☎ *923-7236, Calle 66 No 506*), between Calles 61 and 63, offers low standards for low prices, but is in a convenient location. Its small, fairly grubby rooms with fans and running water cost US$7/9/11/13 single/double/triple/quad. Aircon is in some rooms for a few dollars more.

Casa de Huéspedes Peniche (☎ *928-5518, Calle 62 No 507*), between Calles 63 and 65, is in terrible condition, but right off the Plaza Mayor, and singles/doubles without running water cost as little as US$5/6, or US$7 for a double with shower. If you're really broke, look at this place.

Hotel Mucuy (☎ *928-5193, fax 923-7801, Calle 57 No 481*), between Calles 56 and 58, has been serving thrifty travelers for more than a decade. It's a family-run place with 22 tidy rooms on two floors facing a long, narrow garden courtyard. Señora Ofelia Comin and her daughter Ofelia speak English; Señor Alfredo Comin understands it. Singles/doubles/triples with ceiling fans and private showers cost US$14/16/19.

Casa Bowen (☎ *928-6109, Calle 66 No 521B*), near Calle 65, is a large old Mérida house converted to a hotel. The narrow courtyard has a welcome swath of green grass. Rooms are simple, even bare, and some are dark and soiled, but all have fans and showers for US$10/13 single/double, US$20 with air-con. Staff tends to be sullen. The Café Terraza across the street provides quick, cheap meals.

Casa Becil (☎ *924-6764, Calle 67 No 550C*), between Calles 66 and 68 near the bus station, is a 13-room house with a high-ceilinged sitting room/lobby and small, sometimes hot, guest rooms at the back. With private shower and fan, the price is US$13 to US$16 a double.

Hotel Sevilla (☎ *923-8360, Calle 62 No 511*), at the corner of Calle 65, offers a whisper of faded elegance, but most rooms are musty and dark. The price is not too bad: US$10/12/14 single/double/triple.

The *Hotel Flamingo* (☎ *924-7755, fax 924-7070, Calle 57 No 485*), near Calle 58,

offers 39 worn rooms, but each contains air-con, TV, telephone and a private hot-water bathroom for just US$15 per room. There's a laundry service, a restaurant, a swimming pool and a travel agency on the premises.

If you don't mind walking or busing a few extra blocks and you really want to save money, try the *Hotel del Mayab* (☎ *928-5174, fax 928-6047, Calle 50 No 536A*), between Calles 65 and 67. Streetside rooms can be noisy, but interior rooms with showers are quiet, and there's a swimming pool, all for US$11 a double with fan, US$17 with air-con.

Hotel Santa Lucía (☎ *928-2662, ☎/fax 928-2672, Calle 55 No 508*), between Calles 60 and 62, facing the Parque Santa Lucía, has 51 decent, well-located double rooms with air-con for US$19/22 single/double. There's a swimming pool on the premises and every room has a TV and telephone. This place is clean, secure and very popular. It's an excellent value.

The colonial *Hotel Trinidad* (☎ *923-2033, fax 924-1122, ohm@sureste.com, Calle 62 No 464*), between Calles 55 and 57, is run by artists and looks it (this is a compliment). Modern Mexican paintings draw your eye from the peeling paint on the walls. The 19 fan-cooled guest rooms, priced from US$13 double with shared bathroom and US$19 double with private bathroom, are all different and exhibit both charm and squalor. Continental breakfast is included in the price. Guests are welcome to use the pool at the Hotel Trinidad Galería.

The Trinidad's sister hotel, *Hotel Trinidad Galería* (☎ *923-2463, fax 924-2319, Calle 60 No 456*), at Calle 51, was once an appliance showroom. There's a swimming pool, a bar, art gallery and antique shop as well as presentable rooms with fans and private showers for US$20/25. This place is very funky and most appreciated by artists.

The 45-room *Hotel Peninsular* (☎ *923-6996, fax 923-6902, Calle 58 No 519*), between Calles 65 and 67, is in the heart of the market district. You pass through a long corridor to find a neat restaurant and a maze of rooms, most with windows opening onto the interior spaces. It costs US$12

single or double with private bath and fan; add US$4 for air-con. There's a pool on the premises.

The neocolonial 30-room *Posada del Angel* (☎ 923-2754, Calle 67 No 535), between Calles 66 and 68, is three blocks northeast of Terminal CAME and is quieter than most other hotels in this neighborhood. It's convenient, and rooms are priced at US$13 to US$18 a double, US$18/22 single/double with air-con.

The *Hotel Reforma* (☎ 924-7922, fax 928-3278, hreforma@yuc1.telmex.net.mx, Calle 59 No 508), between Calles 60 and 62, is a two-story colonial hotel with 50 rooms ringing a courtyard with a swimming pool at its center. Every room contains a TV, telephone and ceiling fan. Laundry service is available. Rooms with fan only run US$16/20 single/double, or US$18/22 with air-con. This is a very good value.

The *Hotel San Juan* (☎/fax 924-1742, Calle 55 No 497), Calle 55 near Calle 58, offers 60 air-con rooms each with phone, TV and private hot-water bathroom. There's a pool on the premises and at US$20/24 single/double, the San Juan offers excellent value. In this price range, the San Juan and the Hotel Santa Lucía are tops.

The *Hotel Aragon* (☎ 924-0242, fax 924-1122, www.hotelaragon.com, Calle 57 No 474), between Calles 52 and 54, offers 17 very clean air-con rooms for US$24 per room. An 18th room (Room No 12) is larger than the rest, has a king-size bed and terrace, and costs a little more. The rooms are located on three floors overlooking a charming little courtyard. Purified water, tea and coffee are available for free 24 hours.

Mid-Range Mérida's mid-range places provide surprising levels of comfort for what you pay. Most charge between US$35 and US$60 for a double room with air-conditioning, ceiling fan and private shower; most have restaurants, bars and little swimming pools.

Gran Hotel (☎ 924-7730, fax 924-7622, granh@sureste.com, Calle 60 No 496), between Calles 59 and 61, is on the southern side of the Parque Hidalgo and couldn't be better situated. Corinthian columns support terraces on three levels around the verdant central courtyard, and fancy wrought-iron and carved wood decoration evoke a past age. All 28 rooms have air-con and cost a very reasonable US$35/40 single/double most of the year.

The *Hotel Colonial* (☎ 923-6444, fax 928-3961, in the USA ☎ 888-886-2982, hcolonial@finred.com.mx, Calle 62 No 476), at the corner of Calle 57, features 73 comfortable air-con rooms in a colonial building with lots of pleasing arches and a swimming pool for a reasonable US$35 single or double.

Hotel Dolores Alba (☎ 921-3745, Calle 63 No 464), between Calles 52 and 54, 3½ blocks east of the plaza, was undergoing major renovations in late 1999 and was expected to offer handsome rooms on four levels around two courtyards and a swimming pool for US$35 a single or double with shower, fan and air-con. There's private parking on the premises.

Hotel Caribe (☎ 924-9022, 800-712-0003, fax 924-8733, in the USA ☎ 888-822-6431, Calle 59 No 500), on the Parque Hidalgo, is a favorite with visiting foreigners because of its central location, rooftop pool and two restaurants. Most rooms have air-con and range in price from US$30 for a small single with fan to US$42 for a large double with air-con.

The very romantic *Casa Mexilio* (☎/fax 928-2505, in the USA ☎ 800-538-6802, info@turqreef.com, Calle 68 No 495), between Calles 59 and 57, is Mérida's most charming pension – a well-preserved and decorated house with a pool and 10 quiet, beautifully appointed rooms for US$40 to US$58 a double, breakfast included. Some of the rooms have air-con. This is highly recommended.

Posada Toledo (☎ 923-1690, 923-5735, ☎/fax 923-2256, Calle 58 No 487), at Calle 57, three blocks northeast of the main plaza, is a colonial mansion with rooms arranged on two floors around the classic courtyard, a dining room straight out of the 19th century, and small, modernized double rooms with air-con for US$30 per room. The newer, upstairs rooms are larger than the ground-floor rooms.

The new-in-1999 *Hotel Ambassador* (☎ 924-2100, fax 924-2701, www.ambassadormerida .com, Calle 59 No 546), at Calle 68, offers 100 comfortable, modern rooms with satellite TV for a very reasonable US$62 per room. There's a pool, a travel agency, a car rental outfit and a conference room on the premises, and laundry service is available.

Top End Top-end hotels charge between US$70 and US$150 for a double room with air-con. Each hotel has a restaurant, bar, swimming pool and other services such as a newsstand, hairdresser, travel agency and nightclub.

If you reserve your top-end room through your travel agent at home, you're likely to pay typical international-class rates. But if you walk in and ask about *promociones* (promotional rates), or – even better – look through local newspapers and handouts for special rates aimed at a local clientele, you can lower your lodging bill substantially.

Hotel Casa del Balam (☎ 924-2150, fax 924-5011, in the USA ☎ 800-624-8451, www .yucatanadventure.com.mx, Calle 60 No 488), at Calle 57, has numerous advantages: agreeable colonial decor, modern rooms and services, a central location and a price of US$85 per room, with discounts offered when not busy.

For all-round quality, convenience and price, try the *Hotel Los Aluxes* (☎ 924-2199, fax 923-3858, in the USA ☎ 800-782-8395, Calle 60 No 444), at Calle 49. This 109-room hotel, popular with tour groups, has all the services, plus modern architecture and an intriguing name – *aluxes* are the Mayan equivalent of leprechauns. Rates are US$70 a single or double.

The *Hotel Mérida Misión Park Plaza* (☎ 923-9500, fax 923-7665, in the USA ☎ 800-224-8837, www.misionpark.com.mx, Calle 60 No 491), at Calle 57, is half modern and half colonial in decor, comfortable without being particularly charming. Rates for the 150 air-con rooms are US$100 for a single or double.

Mérida's most luxurious hotel is the 17-story, 300-room *Hyatt Regency Mérida* (☎ 942-1234, fax 925-7002), Av Colón at Calle 60, 100m west of Paseo de Montejo

and about 2km north of the Plaza Mayor. Rooms with all the comforts cost US$95 to US$135, but promotional deals can bring those prices down.

Holiday Inn Mérida (☎ 925-6877, fax 925-7755, in the USA ☎ 800-465-4329, Av Colón 498), at Calle 60, half a block off the Paseo de Montejo, behind the US Consulate General, is one of Mérida's most luxurious establishments. Its 213 air-con rooms cost US$75 to US$95.

Across Av Colón from the Hyatt and Holiday Inn is a large multipurpose building within which you'll find the *Fiesta Americana Mérida* (☎ 942-1111, fax 942-1112, in the USA ☎ 800-343-7821), a new neocolonial luxury hotel charging US$115 to US$140 for its very comfortable rooms and junior suites.

Places to Eat

Budget Mérida's least-expensive eateries are located on Calle 67 near the Mercado Municipal. Here, you'll find the family-run *El Chimecito*, *La Temaxeña*, *Saby*, *Mimi*, *Saby y El Palon*, *La Socorrito*, *Reina Beatriz* and others. *Comidas corridas* (full meals) here are priced from US$1.50. Main-course platters of beef, fish or chicken with vegetables and rice or potatoes go for as little as US$2.50. The market eateries are open from early morning until early evening.

El Louvre, on Calle 62 at Calle 61, is grubby, but has a loyal local clientele who come for the daily US$2 *comida corrida*, though it's hardly a gourmet treat. Breakfast costs the same.

The best cheap breakfasts can be had by picking up a selection of *pan dulces* (sweet rolls and breads) from one of Mérida's several *panificadoras* (bakeries). A convenient one is the *Panificadora Montejo*, at the corner of Calles 62 and 63, at the southwest corner of the main plaza. Pick up a metal tray and tongs, select the pastries you want and hand the tray to a clerk who will bag them and quote a price, usually US$2 or so for a full bag.

The air-con *Café y Restaurante WAO*, on Calle 57A near Calle 58, offers lots of delicious food at very reasonable prices. Among the better choices here are the *poc-chuc*

(slices of pork marinated in sour orange juice, cooked and served with a tangy sauce and pickled onions; US$3.50), the chicken mole (US$3.50) and the *pollo pibil* (chicken marinated in achiote sauce, orange juice, garlic, black pepper, cumin and salt, then wrapped in banana leaves and baked; US$4). Yogurt (US$1), fresh fruit (US$1.20) and hotcakes (US$1.30) are also available. It's open 7 am to 10:30 pm daily.

Another good place to get a quick, inexpensive meal is at the *Café Terraza*, Calle 66 at Calle 65, across the street from Casa Bowen.

For American-style fast food, the *Burger King*, on the corner of Calles 59 and 60, is hard to beat.

Mid-Range Those willing to spend a bit more money can enjoy the pleasant restaurants on the Parque Hidalgo at the corner of Calles 59 and 60.

The least expensive of these, yet one of the most pleasant restaurants in Mérida, is the *Cafetería El Rincón* (the stained-glass sign above the door reads El Mesón), in the Hotel Caribe. Meat, fish and chicken dishes are priced from US$4 to US$7, but sandwiches and burgers are less. El Rincón opens early and stays open until 10 pm or so.

The 24-hour, air-con *Café La Habana*, at the corner of Calles 59 and 62, is one of the most popular restaurants in town, but tourists tend to overlook it. Too bad, because there's good food at low prices at the stylish

Food of the Yucatán

Called by its Maya inhabitants 'the Land of the Pheasant and the Deer,' Yucatán has always had a distinctive cuisine. Here are some of the Yucatecan dishes you might want to try:

Frijol con puerco – Yucatecan-style pork and beans, topped with a sauce made with grilled tomatoes, and decorated with bits of radish, slices of onion and leaves of fresh cilantro; served with rice

Huevos Motuleños – 'Eggs in the style of Motul'; fried eggs atop a tortilla, garnished with beans, peas, chopped ham, sausage, grated cheese and a certain amount of spicy chile – high in cholesterol, fat and flavor

Papadzules – Tortillas stuffed with chopped hard-boiled eggs and topped with a sauce of marrow squash (zucchini) or cucumber seeds

Pavo relleno – Slabs of turkey meat layered with chopped, spiced beef and pork and served in a rich, dark sauce; the Yucatecan *faisán* (pheasant) is actually the *pavo* (ocellated turkey)

Pibil – Meat wrapped in banana leaves, flavored with achiote, garlic, sour orange, salt and pepper, and baked in a barbecue pit called a *pib*; the two main varieties are *cochinita pibil* (suckling pig) and *pollo pibil* (chicken)

Poc-chuc – Tender pork strips marinated in sour orange juice, grilled and served topped with a spicy onion relish

Puchero – A stew of pork, chicken, carrots, marrow squash (zucchini), potatoes, plantains and *chayote* (vegetable pear), spiced with radish, fresh cilantro and sour orange

Salbutes – Yucatán's favorite snack: a handmade tortilla, fried, then topped with shredded turkey, onion and slices of avocado

Sopa de lima – 'Lime soup'; chicken broth with bits of shredded chicken, tortilla strips, lime juice and chopped lime

Venado – Venison, a popular traditional dish, might be served as a *pipián*, flavored with a sauce of ground marrow squash (zucchini) seeds, wrapped in banana leaves and steamed

La Habana, including: egg dishes (US$1 to US$3), cereals and fruit (US$1 to US$1.50), soups (US$1 to US$3), chicken (US$3 to US$4), seafood (US$5 to US$6) and sandwiches (US$2 to US$4). There's also a full bar on the premises and plenty of desserts.

The ***Restaurant-Bar Tiano's***, on Calle 60 between Calles 51 and 53, is a long and deep restaurant with piñatas hanging from the ceiling, childish jungle scenes painted on the walls and a festive atmosphere. It's often recommended by locals guessing what tourists like, but the food is thoroughly mediocre. If an award for Greasiest Chips in Mérida existed, only then would Tiano's come out a winner. It's best avoided, despite what you might hear.

The ***Café-Restaurant Express***, on Calle 60 near Calle 59, is a popular, noisy meeting place, with prices a little on the high side, but the food is OK and service is generally good. It's also one of the few places in town where you can get a cappuccino. Also available are juices and shakes that go down easily in the heat of the day. Hours are 7 am to midnight daily.

A few steps north along Calle 60 from the Parque Hidalgo is the ***Cafe Peón Contreras***, which is attractive for its outdoor sidewalk tables. The menu is long, varied and moderately priced, with breakfasts for US$2.50 to US$4, pizzas for around US$6 and a combination plate of Yucatecan specialties for around US$10.

Restaurant Santa Lucía (☎ 928-5957, *Calle 60 No 479*), at Calle 55, is cozy and atmospheric, with low lights and a strolling guitarist. The Yucatecan combination plate, including *sopa de lima* (chicken broth with lime and tortillas), costs US$5, though other main courses may go as high as US$13. Service is slow, and some dishes are bland.

Pop Cafetería, on Calle 57 between Calles 60 and 62, is plain, modern and cool, and for what it's worth it's named for the first month of the 18-month Mayan calendar. The menu includes hamburgers and spaghetti, but smart diners will choose the chicken mole (US$4) and order some delicious guacamole. Breakfast is offered as well. It's open 7 am to 11 pm daily.

The best pizza in town is served at ***Giorgio's Pizza & Pasta***, located next to the Gran Hotel and facing the Parque Hidalgo. The pizzas are reasonably priced (US$3 to US$7) and the portions generous, and the outdoor tables present prime people-watching opportunities. This is a great place for a rendezvous. It's open 11 am to 11 pm daily.

Pizza aficionados also might want to check out the ***Café Pizza Club***, on Calle 55 between Calles 58 and 60, for comparison purposes. Many people like the Club's pizza pies, which come in 11 combinations of toppings and range from US$2 to US$6. It's also open for breakfast, but closes at 5 pm.

Pancho's, on Calle 59 between Calles 60 and 62, tends to bring out the party animal in people. The inset entryway is lined with historic Mexican artifacts and photos that make for fun viewing, and through the door there are three spacious dining areas and two full bars served by bandoleer-toting, sombrero-wearing waiters. There's live music most nights starting about 11 pm, and the happy hour (6 to 8 pm) is always festive. The food is only fair (pasta, fish, burgers and local specialties are US$6 to US$15), but the atmosphere makes up for it. Pancho's is open 6 pm to 3 am daily.

Top End   The secret to enjoying a dinner at ***La Bella Epoca***, on Calle 60 between Calles 57 and 59, opposite the Parque de la Madre, is to get there early enough to get one of the five little tables set out on the second-floor balconies. Have an appetizer, pollo pibil, dessert and a beer for US$12 per person. It's open for dinner only, 5 to 11:30 pm daily.

Restaurante Portico del Peregrino, on Calle 57 between Calles 60 and 62, is a 'Pilgrim's Refuge' of several pleasant, almost elegant traditional dining rooms (some are air-conditioned) around a small courtyard replete with colonial artifacts. Yucatecan dishes are the forte, but you'll find many continental dishes as well. Lunch (noon to 3 pm) and dinner (6 to 11 pm) are served daily, and your bill for a full meal might be US$12 to US$20 per person.

La Casona, on Calle 60 between Calles 47 and 49, is a fine old city house with tables set out on a portico next to a small but lush garden; dim lighting lends an air of romance. Italian dishes crowd the menu, with a few concessions to local cuisine. Plan to spend US$10 to US$20 per person. La Casona is open for dinner only.

Los Almendros, on Calle 50A between Calles 57 and 59, specializes in authentic Yucatecan country cuisine such as *pavo relleno negro* (grilled turkey with hot peppered pork stuffing), *papadzul* (tacos filled with egg smothered in a fiery sauce), sopa de lima and Los Almendros' most famous dish – poc-chuc – the zingy onion-and-tomato pork dish. Full meals cost US$9 to US$15.

Entertainment

Proud of its cultural legacy and attuned to the benefits of tourism, the city of Mérida offers nightly *folkloric events* by local performers of considerable skill. Admission is free to city-sponsored events. Check with the tourist offices for a schedule of events; see Tourist Offices earlier in this chapter for contact information.

Many English-language films, some of fairly recent release, are screened in Mérida with Spanish subtitles. Buy your tickets (usually about US$2) before show time and well in advance on weekends. There's the popular *Cine Fantasio*, Calle 59 at Calle 60, facing the Parque Hidalgo between the Gran Hotel and Hotel Caribe; the *Cinema 59*, Calle 59 between Calles 68 and 70; and the *Plaza Cine Internacional*, Calle 58 between Calles 57 and 59.

For dancing to live salsa, head to *Pancho's*, on Calle 59 between Calles 60 and 62 (see the entry under Places to Eat – Mid-Range, above).

Shopping

From standard shirts and blouses to Mayan exotica, Mérida is *the* place on the peninsula to shop. Purchases you might want to consider include traditional Mayan clothing such as the colorful women's embroidered tunic called a huipil; a Panama hat woven from palm fibers; local craft items; and of course the wonderfully comfortable Yucatecan hammock, which holds you gently in a comfortable cotton web.

Guard your valuables extra carefully in the market area. Watch for pickpockets, purse-snatchers and slash-and-grab thieves.

Mérida's main market, the Mercado Municipal Lucas do Gálvez, is bound by Calles 56 and 56A, at Calle 67, four blocks southeast of the Plaza Mayor. The market building is more or less next door to the city's main post office and telegraph office, on the corner of Calles 65 and 56. The surrounding streets are all part of the large market district, lined with shops selling everything one might need.

Handicrafts There are three places to go for high-quality craft and art items: the Casa de los Artesanías, on Calle 63 between Calles 64 and 66; Popol-Na, on Calle 59 between Calles 60 and 62; and Miniaturas Arte Popular Mexicano, on Calle 59 between Calles 60 and 62.

The Casa is a government-supported market for local artisans. Here you'll find earthenware, textiles, wicker baskets, sandals, wind chimes, ceramic dolls, vases, colorful purses, pouches, figurines of Mayan deities – the 'whole enchilada,' as they say in the USA. Also found here are bottles of locally made liquor such as *licor de guanábana*, *licor de anis* and *licor de manta*. The market is open 8 am to 8 pm Monday to Saturday, 9 am to 1:30 pm Sunday.

Popol-Na sells high-quality hammocks and high-quality guayaberas (same quality as

Intricately embroidered *huipil*

those found at Jack's, a Yucatecan-clothing shop adjacent to the Gran Hotel, only much cheaper), as well as carved Mayan calendars, carved masks of Mayan gods, lovely quilts, tablecloths, ponchos, sundresses, jewelry, Panama hats, lots of bags and plenty of earthenware. It's open 9 am to 6 pm daily.

At Miniaturas, you'll find *lots* of miniature figurines of varying quality (they all have one thing in common: they are easy to pack!). Here, you'll find palm-size miniatures of Day-of-the-Dead figures, Mexican mamas, naked ladies in boots, topless women in dancing poses, and so forth. The store is definitely fun to browse. It's open 10 am to 2 pm and 4 to 8 pm, *'más o menos,'* according to the sign.

You can also check out locally made crafts at the Museo Regional de Artesanías, on Calle 59 between Calles 48 and 50. The work on display is superb, but the items for sale here are not as good as the three stores mentioned above. Admission is free and it's open 8 am to 8 pm Tuesday to Saturday, 9 am to 2 pm Sunday.

Panama Hats Locally made Panama hats are woven from jipijapa palm leaves in caves, as humid conditions keep the fibers pliable when the hat is being made. Once exposed to the relatively dry air outside, the Panama hat is surprisingly resilient and resistant to crushing. The Campeche town of Becal is the center of the hat-weaving trade, but you can buy good examples of the hat maker's art in Mérida.

The best-quality hats have a very fine, close weave of slender fibers. The coarser the weave, the lower the price should be. Prices range from a few dollars for a hat of basic quality to US$50 or more for top quality. Panama hats can be found at the Casa de los Artesanías and Popol-Na (see Handicrafts, above, for addresses).

Hammocks You will be approached by peddlers on the street wanting to sell you hammocks about every hour throughout your stay in Mérida (every five minutes in the Parque Hidalgo). Check the quality of the hammocks carefully. You can save your-

self a lot of trouble by shopping at a hammock store with a good reputation; see the accompanying boxed text on hammocks for details.

Getting There & Away

Air Mérida's modern international airport is a 10km, 20-minute ride southwest of the Plaza Mayor off Hwy 180 (Av de los Itzaes). The airport has car-rental desks and a tourist office that can help with hotel reservations.

Most international flights to Mérida are connections through Mexico City or Cancún. The only nonstop international services are Aeroméxico's daily flights from Miami and Aviateca's flights to Guatemala City. Domestic flights are operated mostly by smaller regional airlines, with a few flights by Aeroméxico and Mexicana.

Aerocaribe (☎ 924-9500, 923-0002), Paseo de Montejo 476A; flies between Mérida and Cancún, Havana (Cuba), Chetumal, Ciudad del Carmen, Mexico City, Oaxaca, Tuxtla Gutiérrez (for San Cristóbal de las Casas), Veracruz and Villahermosa

Aerolíneas (☎ 926-0609, fax 927-7999), Calle 56A No 579 between Calles 67 and 69; flies round-trips daily from Mérida to Cancún, Chetumal and Palenque

AeroLitoral (☎ 800-29020, 8-156-1600), based in Veracruz; flies to Ciudad del Carmen, Veracruz and Monterrey

Aeroméxico (☎ 927-9566, 927-9277), Paseo de Montejo 460; has a few flights

Aviacsa (☎ 926-3253, 926-3954, fax 926-9087), at the airport; flies nonstop to Cancún, Villahermosa and Mexico City

Aviateca (☎ 924-4354), at the airport; flies to Tikal and Guatemala City several times a week

Mexicana (☎ 924-6633), Calle 58 No 500; has nonstop flights to and from Cancún and Mexico City

Bus Mérida is the bus transport hub of the Yucatán peninsula. If you take an all-night bus, don't put anything valuable in the overhead racks, as gear being stolen at night has been a problem.

Bus Stations Mérida has several bus stations. Here's a rundown of stations and com-

For Some, Yucatecan Hammocks Are the Only Way to Sleep

The fine strings of Yucatecan hammocks make them supremely comfortable. In the sticky heat of a Yucatán summer, most locals prefer sleeping in a hammock, where the air can circulate around them, rather than in a bed. Many inexpensive hotels used to have hammock hooks in the walls of all guest rooms, though the hooks are not so much in evidence today.

Yucatecan hammocks are normally woven from strong nylon or cotton string and dyed in various colors; there are also natural, undyed versions. In the old days, the finest, strongest, most expensive hammocks were woven from silk.

Hammocks come in several widths. From smallest to largest, the names generally used are: *sencillo* (about 50 pairs of end strings, US$8 to US$10); *doble* (100 pairs, US$10 to US$15); *matrimonial* (150 pairs, US$12 to US$20); and *matrimonial especial* or *cuatro cajas* (175 pairs or more, US$18 to US$30).

When selecting a hammock, you must check to be sure that you're really getting the width you're paying for. Because hammocks fold up small and the larger hammocks are more comfortable (though more expensive), consider the bigger sizes.

During your first few hours in Mérida you will be approached on the street by hammock peddlers. They may quote very low prices, but a low price is only good if the quality is high, and street-sold hammocks are mediocre at best. Check the hammock very carefully.

You can save yourself a lot of trouble by shopping at a hammock store with a good reputation. La Poblana, Calle 65 No 492, between Calles 58 and 60, is fairly good. Some travelers report slightly cheaper prices for good quality at El Aguacate, Calle 58 No 604, at the corner of Calle 73.

It's interesting to venture out to the nearby village of Tixcocob to watch the hammocks being woven. A bus runs regularly from the Progreso bus station, south of the main plaza, at Calle 62 No 524, between Calles 65 and 67.

YUCATÁN STATE

panies that serve them (see Bus Companies and Bus Routes for points served):

Terminal CAME – Mérida's main bus terminal, seven blocks southwest of the Plaza Mayor at Calle 70 No 555 between Calles 69 and 71, is known as Terminal CAME ('KAH-meh'). It handles ticketing and departures for ADO, one of Mexico's biggest bus companies. Come here if you're headed for Campeche, Palenque, San Cristóbal de Las Casas, Tuxtla Gutiérrez, Villahermosa or points in the rest of Mexico. Buses run by Línea Dorada and UNO depart from CAME, but their ticket counters are in the old Terminal de Autobuses around the corner on Calle 69. CAME has pay phones and a hotel desk.

Terminal de Autobuses – The old bus terminal, around the corner from CAME, has ticket counters for Línea Dorada and UNO, and also for Autotransportes de Oriente, Autotransportes del Sur (ATS), Omnitur del Caribe and Transportes Mayab. Come here for buses to points in the state, Yucatán Peninsula and some beyond.

Parque de San Juan – The Parque de San Juan, on Calle 69 between Calles 62 and 64, is the terminus for Volkswagen minibuses going to Dzibilchaltún Ruinas, Muna, Oxkutzcab, Peto, Sacalum, Tekax and Ticul. Fares from here generally don't exceed US$2.

Oriente & Noreste – Autotransportes de Oriente and Autotransportes del Noreste en Yucatán share a terminal at Calle 50 No 527A between Calles 65 and 67.

Autotransportes del Sur (ATS) – Though most ATS buses depart from the old Terminal de Autobuses, the company also runs buses to Celestún from its new terminal at Calle 71 between Calles 64 and 66.

Progreso – The separate bus terminal for Progreso is at Calle 62 No 524 between Calles 65 and 67.

Bus Companies Here's a quick rundown on the companies and the destinations they serve:

Autobuses de Oriente (ADO) – long-haul 1st-class routes to Campeche, Palenque, Villahermosa, Veracruz, Mexico City and beyond.

Autotransportes de Oriente (Oriente) – frequent buses between Mérida and Cancún, stopping at Chichén Itzá and Valladolid; buses between Mérida and Cobá, Izamal, Playa del Carmen and Tulum.

Autotransportes del Sur (ATS) – hourly buses to Cancún and buses every 20 to 40 minutes to Campeche. They also run buses to Bolonchén de Rejón, Cancún, Celestún, Chiquilá, Ciudad del Carmen, Emiliano Zapata, Hecelchakán, Hopelchén, Izamal, Ocosingo, Palenque, Playa del Carmen, San Cristóbal de Las Casas, Tizimín, Tulum and Valladolid. Special buses serve the Ruta Puuc, and Uxmal for the evening light-and-sound show; see Getting There & Away in the Uxmal section, later, for details.

Expresso – 16 deluxe nonstop buses to Cancún and eight deluxe buses to Valladolid.

Noreste – service to many small towns in the northeastern part of the peninsula, including Río Lagartos and Tizimín.

Omnitur del Caribe (Caribe) – deluxe service between Mérida and Chetumal via Felipe Carrillo Puerto; ticket counter in the old Terminal de Autobuses.

Super Expresso – eight deluxe buses to Cancún, four deluxe buses to Chetumal, one deluxe bus to Ticul.

Transportes de Lujo Línea Dorada (LD) – deluxe service to Felipe Carrillo Puerto and Chetumal; ticket counter in the old Terminal CAME, departures from Terminal CAME.

Transportes Mayab (Mayab) – buses to Cancún, Chetumal, Felipe Carrillo Puerto, Peto and Ticul; ticket counters and departures in the old Terminal de Autobuses.

UNO – super-deluxe service on major routes, such as Mérida to Cancún and Mérida to Villahermosa and Mexico City.

Bus Routes Here's information on daily trips to and from Mérida:

Campeche – 195km (short route via Becal), $2^1/2$ to three hours; 250km (long route via Uxmal), four hours; ATS has buses every 20 to 30 minutes for US$6; 13 buses by ADO (US$7).

Cancún – 320km, four hours; Oriente has buses every 30 minutes for US$9; ATS runs buses hourly for US$7; ADO has 21 deluxe buses daily for US$8.75; UNO has morning and evening super-deluxe buses for US$11; Expresso has 16 deluxe buses for US$11 and Super Expresso has eight more for the same price.

Celestún – 95km, $1^1/2$ to two hours, US$2.30; 12 buses, departing the Unión de Camioneros de Yucatán terminal on Calle 71 between Calles 62 and 64.

Chetumal – 456km, eight hours; several deluxe Caribe buses for US$13; four deluxe buses by Super Expresso for US$11; LD and Mayab have buses for less.

Chichén Itzá – 116km, 2 hours, US$2.75 to US$3.50; 10 buses, most in the morning; those by Oriente stop right at the ruins.

Dzibilchaltún – 15km, 30 minutes, US$0.55; minibuses and colectivo taxis depart when full from the Parque de San Juan, and go all the way to the ruins; the alternative is a bus from the Progreso terminal, which drops you on the highway at the Dzibilchaltún access road, 5km west of the ruins.

Felipe Carrillo Puerto – 310km, five hours; Caribe, LD and Mayab run for US$6.50 to US$8.

Izamal – 72km, $1^1/2$ hours, US$1; 20 buses by Oriente from its terminal at Calle 50 between Calles 65 and 67.

Kabah – 101km, two hours, US$2; buses on the *'chenes'* or inland route between Mérida and Campeche may stop at Kabah on request.

Mexico City (TAPO) – 1550km, 20 hours; five buses by ADO (US$52).

Palenque – 556km, nine hours; two each (morning and evening) by ATS (US$15) and ADO (US$17) go directly to Palenque; many more drop you at Catazajá, the main highway junction 27km north of Palenque Town. From Catazajá you can hitchhike or catch a bus or colectivo to Palenque.

Playa del Carmen – 385km, seven hours; nine by ADO (US$10 to US$12), several others by ATS (US$8) and Mayab (US$10).

Progreso – 33km, 45 minutes, US$0.90; Autoprogreso buses depart every 12 minutes from 5 am to 9 pm from the Progreso bus terminal (see Bus Stations, above).

Río Lagartos – 261km, $3^1/2$ hours; service provided by Noreste.

Ticul – 85km, $1^1/2$ hours, US$3; Mayab runs frequent buses, or you can take a minibus from the Parque de San Juan; one deluxe Super Expresso bus from CAME (7:30 am).

Tizimín – 210km, four hours, US$3.75; Noreste, Oriente and ATS have a few buses daily, or take a bus to Valladolid and change there for Tizimín.

Tulum – 320km, five hours via Cobá, or 450km, six hours via Cancún; Oriente (US$7) and ADO (US$8.25) have a few buses.

Tuxtla Gutiérrez – 995km, 14 hours; three by Colón (US$25), or change at Palenque or Villahermosa.

Uxmal – 80km, 1½ hours; six by ATS, including two special excursions. The Ruta Puuc excursion (US$4.50) departs Mérida's old Terminal de Autobuses at 8 am, goes to Uxmal, Kabah and several other sites, departing Uxmal on the return journey to Mérida at 2:30 pm. The light-and-sound excursion (US$3.75) departs Mérida at 6 pm, and Uxmal at 10 pm.

Valladolid – 160km, three hours, US$5; many buses, especially ADO, Oriente and ATS; eight deluxe buses by Expresso, US$6.

Villahermosa – 700km, nine hours; ADO (US$20) runs 10 buses, UNO (US$32) one, and ATS (US$16) has several buses as well.

Car Rental car is the optimal way to tour the many archaeological sites south of Mérida, especially if you have two or more people to share costs.

Assume you will pay a total of US$40 to US$60 per day (tax, insurance and gas included) for the cheapest car offered, usually a bottom-of-the-line Volkswagen or Nissan.

Tourist Car Rental (☎ 924-9471, 924-6255, harrycaam@hotmail.com), Calle 60 between Calles 45 and 47, offer rates the big-name agencies often can't touch – especially if you offer to pay in cash. It's occasionally possible to get a VW for as little as US$25 a day; it all depends on demand, form of payment and length of rental (weekly rates, for example, are available).

Other car-rental agencies in Mérida include:

Dollar (☎ 928-6759, fax 925-0155), Calle 60 No 491 between Calles 55 and 57

Hertz (☎ 924-2834, fax 984-0114), Calle 60 No 486D between Calles 55 and 57

National (☎ 923-2493), Calle 60 No 486F between Calles 55 and 57

Getting Around

To/From the Airport Bus 79 ('Aviación') travels infrequently between the airport and the city center for US$0.50. Most arriving travelers use the Transporte Terrestre minibuses (US$10) to go from the airport to the center; to return to the airport you must take a taxi (US$8.50).

To/From CAME Bus Station To walk from CAME to the Plaza Mayor, exit the terminal, turn left, then right onto Calle 69; the old Terminal de Autobuses will be on your right. Walk straight along Calle 69 for four blocks, passing the Iglesia de San Juan and a park (Parque de San Juan), to Calle 62. Turn left on Calle 62 and walk the remaining three blocks north to the plaza.

Bus Most parts of Mérida that you'll want to visit are within five or six blocks of the Plaza Mayor and are thus accessible on foot. Given the slow speed of city traffic, particularly in the market areas, travel on foot is also the fastest way to get around.

City buses are cheap at US$0.20 per ride (US$0.30 in a minibus), but routes are confusing. Most routes start in suburban neighborhoods, meander through the city center and terminate in another distant suburban neighborhood.

To travel between the Plaza Mayor and the upscale neighborhoods to the north along Paseo de Montejo, catch a 'Tecnológico' bus or minibus on Calle 60 and get out at Av Colón; to return to the city center, catch almost any bus – López Mateos, Chedraui, etc – along Paseo de Montejo.

The bus system is supplemented by colectivo minibuses, which are easier to use as they run shorter and more comprehensible routes. The one you're liable to find most useful is the Ruta 10 (US$0.20), which departs from the corner of Calles 58 and 59, half a block east of the Parque Hidalgo, and travels along the Paseo de Montejo to Itzamná.

Taxi Taxis in Mérida are not metered. However, to prevent price abuse, Mérida's taxi drivers belong to a union, the members of which have agreed on rates to various destinations. A broad sampling of those fixed rates are posted beside the taxi stand at the corner of Calles 60 and 57A (across from the Tourist Information Center). At the time of writing, no ride within city limits exceeded US$3.50. To call a taxi, dial ☎ 928-5322 or 923-1221; service is available 24 hours.

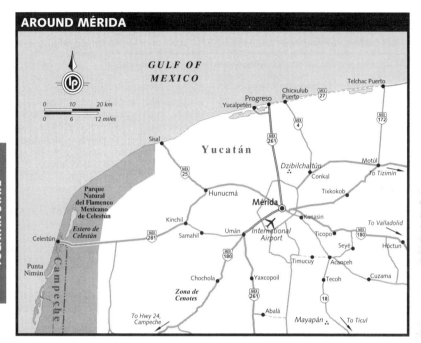

AROUND MÉRIDA

GULF OF MEXICO

DZIBILCHALTÚN

Dzibilchaltún (Place of Inscribed Flat Stones) is a large, very worn site. It was the longest continuously utilized Mayan administrative and ceremonial city, serving the Maya from 1500 BC or earlier until the European conquest in the 1540s. At the height of its greatness, Dzibilchaltún covered 80 sq km. Archaeological research in the 1960s mapped 31 sq km of the city, revealing some 8500 structures.

Though the site itself is far less exciting today than Chichén Itzá or Uxmal, you'll find a fine museum, the interesting little Temple of the Seven Dolls and a cenote swimming pool.

Dzibilchaltún is open 8 am to 5 pm Tuesday through Sunday. Admission is US$2.50 most days, free on Sunday. Parking costs US$0.50; there's a US$4 fee for use of a video camera.

You enter the site along a nature trail that terminates at the modern, air-conditioned

Museo del Pueblo Maya, featuring artifacts from throughout the Mexican-Mayan region. Exhibits explaining Mayan daily life and beliefs, from ancient times until the present, are in Spanish and English.

Beyond the museum, a path leads to the central plaza, with an open chapel dating from early Spanish times (1590-1600).

The **Templo de las Siete Muñecas** (Temple of the Seven Dolls), which got its name from seven grotesque dolls discovered here during excavations, is a 1km walk from the central plaza. While still a good distance away from the temple, note that you can see right through the building's doors and windows on the east-west axis, but when you approach, this view is lost. The temple's construction is such that you can't see through from north to south at all. The rising and setting sun of the equinoxes 'lit up' the temple's windows and doors, making them blaze like beacons and signaling this important turning point in the year. Thus the

temple is impressive not for its size or beauty, but for its precise astronomical orientation and its function in the Great Mayan Time Machine.

The **Cenote Xlacah**, now a public swimming pool, is more than 40m deep. In 1958, an expedition sponsored by the US National Geographic Society sent divers down and recovered 30,000 Mayan artifacts, many of ritual significance. The most interesting of these are now on display in the site's small but good museum.

Getting There & Away

Minibuses and colectivo taxis depart frequently from Mérida's Parque de San Juan, on Calle 69 between Calles 62 and 64, for the village of Dzibilchaltún Ruinas (15km, 30 minutes, US$0.55). If you're driving from Mérida, head north on the Paseo de Montejo, which turns into Hwy 261. Look for signs for the Dzibilchaltún turnoff. But enough history – plunge in and cool off!

PROGRESO

☎ 9 • pop 40,005

This is a seafarer's town, the port for Mérida and northwestern Yucatán. The Yucatecan limestone shelf declines so gradually into the sea that a *muelle* (pier) 6.5km long had to be built to reach the deep water. It is Mexico's longest pier, and from the popular beach immediately to the east the pier seems endless.

This same gradual slope of land into water affects Progreso's long beach: The waters are shallow, warm and safe from such dangers as riptide and undertow, though usually murky with seaweed and swirling sand. The beach is nearly shadeless, having lost its palm trees to hurricanes. The few small shelters are inadequate for the crowds, so you bake and burn. The beach at Yucalpeten, a 10-minute bus ride west, is much better.

Progreso is normally a sleepy little town, but on weekends, especially in summer, it seems as if all of Mérida is here. Despite the town's popularity, don't expect to find a Cancúnlike beach here. The beach faces the Gulf of Mexico, not the Caribbean; you

won't find any spectacular coral heads near the beach and water visibility even on calm days rarely exceeds 5m. From a tourist's perspective, there's really little reason to visit Progreso.

Orientation

Progreso is long and narrow, stretched out along the seashore. Though it has an apparently logical street grid, it is illogically subject to two numbering systems fifty numbers apart. One system has the city center's streets numbered in the 60s, 70s and 80s, another has them in the 10s, 20s and 30s. Thus you might see a street sign on Calle 30 calling it Calle 80, or on a map Calle 10 might also be referred to as Calle 60. We've included both systems on our map.

The bus stations are near the main square. It's six short blocks from the main square to the Malecón and the pier.

Places to Stay

Progreso is looked upon as a resort, if a modest one, so rooms here tend to be a bit more expensive than in other Yucatecan towns. On Sundays in July and August, the cheapest hotels fill up.

New in 1999, the **Hotel Don José** (no phone), on the corner of Calle 78 and Calle 71, offers 17 rooms, 12 with fan only for US$13 and five with air-con for US$15. There's a pool on the premises.

Hotel Miralmar (☎ 935-0552, Calle 77 No 124), at the corner of Calle 76, offers rooms with private shower, fan and one double bed for US$11, with two beds for US$14. Rooms on the upper floor are preferable – they're not as dungeonlike as the ground-floor rooms. In addition, three bubble-shaped rooms were added in 1999; though they look a tad bizarre, they offer the best ventilation of all of the rooms in this small hotel.

At the corner of the Malecón and Calle 70 is the seaside **Tropical Suites** (☎ 935-1263, fax 935-3093). Its 21 tidy rooms with shower go for US$28 a double fan only, US$30 with air-con. Be sure to request a room with sea view.

Hotel Real del Mar (☎ 935-0798), on Calle 70 at Calle 71, behind the Restaurant

Los Pelícanos, is an older hostelry that looks its age, but is still a good deal as it's just a stone's throw from the beach. Its 15 rooms with shower and fan cost US$11 single, US$14 double with one bed, US$15 double with two beds, and US$24 double with sea view.

Hotel Carismar *(☎ 935-2907, Calle 71 No 151)*, at Calle 80, has cheap, uninspiring rooms with bath for US$12 one or two persons.

Places to Eat

Seafood is the strong point on the menus of Progreso's restaurants. Note that if you come on a day trip to Progreso, you can often change clothes at the *vestidores* (changing cubicles) attached to most beachfront restaurants.

An all-purpose inexpensive eatery on the north side of the main square is ***Restaurant El Cordóbes***, at the corner of Calles 81 and 80, open from early morning until late

at night. Standard fare – tacos, enchiladas, sandwiches, chicken, etc – is served cheap.

For cheap seafood, you must avoid the Malecón and seek out the ***Restaurant Mary Doly***, on Calle 75 between Calles 74 and 76, a homey place with no sea view, but with good food and low prices.

About the best prices you can find in an eatery on the Malecón are at ***Las Rocas***, at the corner of Calle 78, a homey eatery where you can get a full fish dinner for about US$5, everything included. The popular, bright and concrete-walled ***Sol y Mar*** and the *palapa*-topped ***Le Saint Bonnet*** are more upscale.

The California-surfer-bar-resembling ***Restaurant Carabela***, on the Malecón between Calles 68 and 70, is so casual its management doesn't even mind if you write on its walls. With a full bar and a lovely perch overlooking the beach, the Carabela is a fine place to pass time, and it won't cost you much if you decide to dine there. Particularly

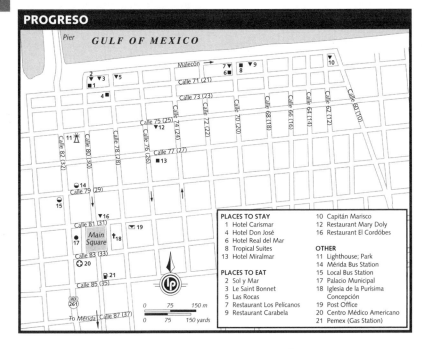

PROGRESO

Pier **GULF OF MEXICO**

PLACES TO STAY
1 Hotel Carismar
4 Hotel Don José
6 Hotel Real del Mar
8 Tropical Suites
13 Hotel Miralmar

PLACES TO EAT
2 Sol y Mar
3 Le Saint Bonnet
5 Las Rocas
7 Restaurant Los Pelicanos
9 Restaurant Carabela

10 Capitán Marisco
12 Restaurant Mary Doly
16 Restaurant El Cordóbes

OTHER
11 Lighthouse; Park
14 Mérida Bus Station
15 Local Bus Station
17 Palacio Municipal
18 Iglesia de la Purísima
   Concepción
19 Post Office
20 Centro Médico Americano
21 Pemex (Gas Station)

inexpensive dishes include spaghetti with butter and cheese (US$2), a hearty lime soup (US$2) and filet of grouper (US$4).

The **Restaurant Los Pelícanos**, on the Malecón at Calle 70, by the Hotel Real del Mar, is appealing with its shady terrace, sea views, good menu and moderate prices.

At the eastern end of the Malecón between Calles 60 and 62, almost a kilometer from the pier, stands **Capitán Marisco**, perhaps Progreso's fanciest seafood restaurant and certainly one of its most pleasant. Very few items here are priced over US$7, and there's a wide selection of dishes from which to choose.

Getting There & Away
Both Dzibilchaltún and Progreso are due north of Mérida along a fast four-lane highway (Hwy 261) that's basically a continuation of the Paseo de Montejo. If you're driving, head north on the Paseo and follow signs for Progreso.

Progreso is 18km (20 minutes) beyond the Dzibilchaltún turnoff. Autoprogreso buses depart the Progreso bus terminal, 1 1/2 blocks south of the main plaza in Mérida, at Calle 62 No 524 between Calles 65 and 67, every 12 minutes from 5 am to 9 pm. The fare is US$0.90 one way. Travel time is 45 minutes.

Progreso's local bus station is on Calle 82 and Calle 79. The Mérida bus station is nearby, on Calle 79 between Calles 80 and 82.

IZAMAL
☎ 9 • pop 14,548
In ancient times, Izamal was a center for the worship of the supreme Mayan god Itzamná and the sun god Kinich-Kakmó. A dozen temple pyramids in the town were devoted to these or other gods. Perhaps these bold expressions of Mayan religiosity are why the Spanish colonists chose Izamal as the site for an enormous and very impressive Franciscan monastery, which today stands at the heart of this small city.

Izamal of the 21st century is a quiet provincial town with an atmosphere of life from decades past. Here, many people still rely on horse-drawn carriages to get around, and the Internet Age seems as distant as Mars. Of the city's 12 pyramids, only one, Kinich-Kakmó, three blocks directly north of the monastery and very visible from it, has been restored. The pyramid, some 207m long and 190m wide, was rebuilt during the early 1990s and provides fine city views. There's no cost to climb it.

Izamal's two principal squares face the monastery and are surrounded by impressive arcades painted in the town's signature yellow, and dominated by the gargantuan bulk of the Convento de San Antonio de Padua. This *Ciudad Amarilla* (Yellow City), as it's known throughout the peninsula, has a few budget hotels, one very good restaurant and many eateries. Izamal, a colonial gem that's easily explored on foot, makes for a great day trip from Mérida.

Convento de San Antonio de Padua
When the Spaniards conquered Izamal, they destroyed the major Mayan temple, the Popul-Chac pyramid, and in 1533 began to build from its stones one of the first monasteries in the Western Hemisphere. The work was finished in 1561. While walking under the monastery's arcades, keep an eye out for building stones with an unmistakable maze-like design; these were clearly taken from the earlier Mayan temple.

The monastery's principal church is the **Santuario de la Virgen de Izamal**, approached by a ramp from the main square. Walk up the ramp and through an arcaded gallery to the Atrium, a spacious arcaded courtyard in which the fiesta of the Virgin of Izamal takes place each August 15. Indeed, it is the largest enclosed atrium in Mexico, approximating the dimensions of those of St Paul in Rome.

The frescoes beside the entrance of the sanctuary were painted during the 16th century, but at some point they were completely whitewashed. For years – no one knows how many – they remained concealed under a thin layer of white paint, completely hidden from view. A few years ago they were discovered by a maintenance worker who was giving the walls of the sanctuary a good cleaning.

In a courtyard beside the church you'll see a carved-stone sundial. It is not original, despite what most of the local guides believe. However, if while you're in the courtyard you look up toward the sky you will see the original sundial, which is located at roof's edge.

Likewise, most local guides tell visitors the church's altar is original. It is not. A fire, believed to have been started by a fallen candle, consumed the original altar. The one you see now – which, like perishable goods in an American supermarket, is protected from the elements by sheets of clear plastic – was built during the 1940s.

While in the small courtyard adjacent to the church (the one where the sundial is located), notice the small window with wooden bars on it. In the distant past, the bars were made of metal and the tiny room behind them served as a jail.

Entry to the church is free. The best time to visit is in the morning, as it is occasionally closed during the afternoon siesta. The monastery and church were restored and spruced up for the papal visit of John Paul II in 1993.

Places to Stay & Eat

In front of the monastery there are two budget hotels – *Hotel Kabul* and *Hotel Canto* – and numerous inexpensive eateries. Of the two hotels, the Kabul is more attractive, offering worn but clean basic rooms for US$4 with shared bathroom, US$8 with one bed and private bathroom, and US$9 with two beds and private bathroom.

About eight blocks southwest of the monastery is the much nicer *Hotel Green River* (*☎/fax 954-0337, Av Zamna No 342*), on the tree-lined Av Zamna between Calles 39 and 41. Here you'll find 14 air-con rooms with cable TV, minibar, purified water, telephone and private parking in a residential neighborhood only a 10 minutes' walk from the center of town. Rates fluctuate with demand, but are typically about US$20 per room.

The *Restaurant Kinich-Kakmó* is Izamal's best restaurant, and it compares very favorably to the best Mérida has to offer.

Located on Calle 27 between Calles 28 and 30 (one block west of the towering Kinich-Kakmó pyramid), this casual and cozy restaurant offers fan-cooled dining on a back patio beside a charming garden. The Kinich-Kakmó specializes in traditional Yucatecan food, and you can have an absolute feast here for less than US$10.

Getting There & Away

Oriente runs frequent buses between Mérida and Izamal (75km, 1$1/2$ hours, US$1) from its terminal in Mérida, on Calle 50 between Calles 65 and 67; there are buses from Valladolid as well. Coming from Chichén Itzá, you must change buses at Hóctun. If you're driving from the east, turn north at Kantunil. Izamal's bus station is conveniently located just one block west of the monastery.

From Izamal it's possible to take buses to Cancún, Valladolid and Dzitas (the same bus goes to all three places, leaving at 5, 6:30 and 9 am, and 1 and 5 pm). Auto Centro has medium-class buses to Mérida, Cancún, Dzitas and elsewhere.

CHICHÉN ITZÁ
☎ 9

The most famous and best restored of the Yucatán Peninsula's Mayan sites, Chichén Itzá will awe even the most jaded of visitors. Many mysteries of the Mayan astronomical calendar are made clear when one understands the design of the 'time temples' at this archaeological site.

But one astronomical mystery remains: Why do most people come here from Mérida and Cancún on day trips, arriving at 11 am, when the blazing sun is getting to its hottest point, and departing around 3 pm when the heat finally begins to abate? You'd do better to stay the night nearby and do your exploration of the site either early in the morning or late in the afternoon.

Should you have the good fortune to visit Chichén Itzá on the vernal equinox (March 20 to 21) or autumnal equinox (September 22 to 23), you can witness the light-and-shadow illusion of the serpent ascending or descending the side of the staircase of El Castillo. The illusion is almost as good in

the week preceding and the week following the equinoxes.

History

Most archaeologists agree that Chichén Itzá's first major settlement, during the Late Classic period, was pure Mayan. In about the 9th century, the city was largely abandoned for unknown reasons.

The city was resettled around the late 10th century, and shortly thereafter, Chichén appears to have been invaded by Toltecs who had moved down from their central highlands capital of Tula, north of Mexico City. Toltec culture was fused with that of the Maya, incorporating the cult of Quetzalcóatl (Kukulcán in Maya); see the History section in the Facts About Yucatán chapter for more on this. You will see images of both Chac, the Mayan rain god, and Quetzalcóatl, the plumed serpent, throughout the city.

The substantial fusion of highland central Mexican and Puuc architectural styles make Chichén unique among the Yucatán Peninsula's ruins. The fabulous El Castillo, the Temple of Panels and the Platform of Venus are all outstanding architectural works built during the height of Toltec cultural input.

After a Mayan leader moved his political capital to Mayapán while keeping Chichén as his religious capital, Chichén Itzá fell into decline. Why it was subsequently abandoned in the 14th century is a mystery, but the once-great city remained the site of Mayan pilgrimages for many years.

Orientation

Most of Chichén's lodgings, restaurants and services are ranged along 1km of highway in the village of Piste ('PEESS-teh'), to the west (Mérida) side of the ruins. It's 1.5km from the ruins' main (west) entrance to the first hotel (Pirámide Inn) in Piste, or 2.5km from the ruins to Piste village square (actually a triangle), which is shaded by a huge tree. Buses generally stop at the square; you can make the hot walk to/from the ruins in 20 to 30 minutes.

On the eastern (Cancún) side, it's 1.5km from the highway along the access road to the eastern entrance to the ruins. On the way

Chichén's Sacred Cenote

Around 1900, Edward Thompson, a Harvard professor and US Consul to Yucatán, bought the hacienda that included Chichén Itzá for US$75. No doubt intrigued by local stories of female virgins being sacrificed to the Mayan deities by being thrown into the cenote, Thompson resolved to have the cenote dredged.

He imported dredging equipment and set to work. Gold and jade jewelry from all parts of Mexico and as far away as Colombia was recovered, along with many other artifacts and a variety of human bones. Many of the artifacts were shipped to Harvard's Peabody Museum, but many have since been returned to Mexico.

Subsequent diving expeditions in the 1920s and '60s turned up hundreds more valuable artifacts, as well as more skeletons. It appears that all sorts of people, including children and old people, the diseased and the injured, as well as the young and the vigorous, were forcibly obliged to take an eternal swim in Chichén's Sacred Cenote.

you pass the Villa Arqueológica, Hacienda Chichén and Mayaland luxury hotels.

Chichén's little airstrip is north of the ruins, on the north side of the highway, 3km from Piste's main square.

Information

You can change money in the Unidad de Servicios (see Zona Arqueológica, below) at the western entrance to the ruins, or at your hotel. There are several telephone casetas in Piste. Look for the signs.

Zona Arqueológica

Chichén Itzá is open 8 am to 6 pm daily; the interior passageway in El Castillo is open only from 11 am to 1 pm and from 4 to 5 pm. Admission to the site costs US$7.50 (except free on Sunday and holidays); US$10 extra for your video camera and US$5 extra if you use a tripod with your camera. Admission is free to children under 12 years of age.

Parking costs US$1. Explanatory plaques are in Spanish and English.

The main entrance is the western one, which has a large parking lot and a big, modern entrance building called the Unidad de Servicios, open 8 am to 10 pm. The Unidad has a small but worthwhile museum (open 8 am to 5 pm) with sculptures, reliefs, artifacts and explanations of these in Spanish, English and French.

The Chilam Balam Auditorio next to the museum has audiovisual shows about Chichén in English at noon and 4 pm. In the central space of the Unidad stands a scale model of the archaeological site, and off toward the toilets is an exhibit on Thompson's excavations of the sacred cenote in 1923. There are two bookstores with a good assortment of guides and maps; a currency-exchange desk (open 9 am to 1 pm); and a *guardarropa* at the main ticket desk where you can leave your belongings (US$0.35) while you explore the site.

A light-and-sound show lasting 45 minutes begins each evening in Spanish at 7 pm in summer and 8 pm in winter for US$3.75. The English version (US$5) starts at 9 pm year-round.

El Castillo As you pass through the turnstiles from the Unidad de Servicios into the archaeological zone, El Castillo rises before you in all its grandeur. Standing nearly 25m tall, the 'castle' was originally built before 800 AD, prior to the Toltec invasion. Nonetheless, the plumed serpent was sculpted along the stairways and Toltec warriors are represented in the doorway carvings at the top of the temple. No doubt this is grist to the mill of those inconvenient historians who believe that the Toltec capital Tula, near Mexico City, was influenced from Chichén Itzá, rather than vice versa as conventional wisdom has it.

Climb the steep steps to the top for a view of the entire site. This is best done early in the morning or late in the afternoon, both to avoid the heat and to see Chichén without the crowds.

The pyramid is actually the Mayan calendar formed in stone. Each of El Castillo's nine levels is divided in two by a staircase, making 18 separate terraces which commemorate the 18 20-day months of the Vague Year. The four stairways have 91 steps each; add the top platform and the total is 365, the number of days in the year. On each façade of the pyramid are 52 flat panels, symbolizing the 52 years in the Calendar Round.

Most amazing of all, during the spring and fall equinoxes (around March 21 and September 23), light and shadow form a series of triangles on the side of the north staircase that mimic the creep of a serpent. The illusion lasts three hours and 22 minutes.

This pyramid holds more surprises: There's another pyramid *inside* El Castillo. When archaeologists opened it, they found the brilliant red jaguar throne with inlaid eyes and spots of shimmering jade which still lies within. The inner sanctum also holds a Toltec chac-mool figure.

The inner pyramid is only open from 11 am to 1 pm and 4 to 5 pm. Entry is not a good idea for claustrophobes or those who dislike close, fetid air.

Principal Ball Court The principal ball court (Juego de Pelota Principal), the largest and most impressive in Mexico, is only one of the city's eight courts, indicative of the importance of the games held here. The court is flanked by temples at either end and bound by towering parallel walls with stone rings cemented up high.

There is evidence that the ball game may have changed over the years. Some carvings show players with padding on their elbows and knees and it is thought that they played a soccerlike game with a hard rubber ball, forbidding the use of hands. Other carvings show players wielding bats; it appears that if a player hit the ball through one of the stone hoops, his team was declared the winner. It may be that during the Toltec period the losing captain, and perhaps his teammates as well, were sacrificed.

Along the walls of the ball court are some fine stone reliefs, including scenes of decapitations of players. Acoustically the court is amazing – a conversation at one end can be heard 135m away at the other end, and if you clap, you hear a resounding echo.

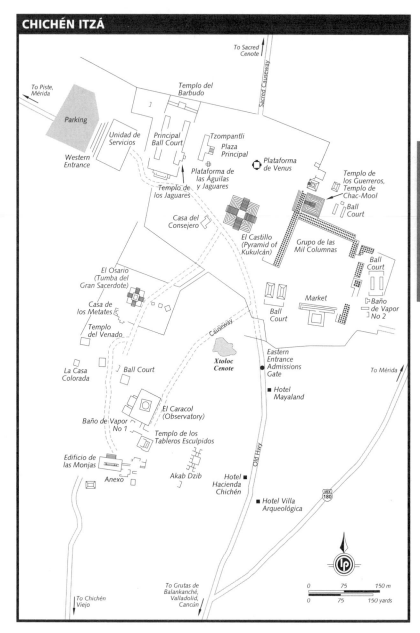

CHICHÉN ITZÁ

To Piste,
Mérida

Parking

Unidad de
Servicios

Western
Entrance

Templo del
Barbudo

To Sacred
Cenote

Principal
Ball Court

Tzompantli

Plaza
Principal

Plataforma
de Venus

Templo de
los Guerreros,
Templo de
Chac-Mool

Ball
Court

Plataforma de
las Águilas
y Jaguares

Templo de
los Jaguares

Casa del
Consejero

El Castillo
(Pyramid of
Kukulcán)

Grupo de las
Mil Columnas

Ball
Court

El Osario
(Tumba del
Gran Sacerdote)

Casa de
los Metates

Market

Baño
de Vapor
No 2

Ball
Court

Templo
del Venado

La Casa
Colorada

Ball Court

Causeway

Xtoloc
Cenote

Eastern
Entrance
Admissions
Gate

To Mérida

Hotel
Mayaland

El Caracol
(Observatory)

Baño de Vapor
No 1

Templo de los
Tableros Esculpidos

Edificio de
las Monjas

Anexo

Akab Dzib

Hotel
Hacienda
Chichén

HEX
180

Hotel Villa
Arqueológica

To Chichén
Viejo

To Grutas de
Balankanché,
Valladolid,
Cancún

0   75   150 m

0   75   150 yards

YUCATÁN STATE

To Sacred
Cenote

Sacred Causeway

Old Hwy

Templo del Barbudo & Templo de los Jaguares The structure at the northern end of the ball court, called the Templo del Barbudo (Temple of the Bearded Man) after a carving inside it, has some finely sculpted pillars and reliefs of flowers, birds and trees. The Templo de los Jaguares (Temple of the Jaguars), to the southeast, has some rattlesnake-carved columns and jaguar-etched tablets. Inside are faded mural fragments depicting a battle.

Tzompantli The Tzompantli, a Toltec term for 'Temple of Skulls,' is between the Templo de los Jaguares and El Castillo. You can't mistake it because the T-shaped platform is festooned with carved skulls and eagles tearing open the chests of men to eat their hearts. In ancient days this platform held the heads of sacrificial victims.

Plataforma de las Águilas y Jaguares Adjacent to the Tzompantli is the Plataforma de las Águilas y Jaguares (Platform of the Eagles & Jaguars). The platform's carvings depict jaguars and eagles gruesomely grabbing human hearts in their claws. It is thought that this platform was part of a temple dedicated to the military legions responsible for capturing sacrificial victims.

Jaguar Eating Heart carving

Plataforma de Venus Rather than a beautiful woman, the Toltec symbol for the planet Venus is a feathered serpent bearing a human head between its jaws, and you can see many examples of this image on this structure, the Plataforma de Venus (Platform of Venus), just north of El Castillo.

Sacred Cenote A 300m rough stone road runs north (a five-minute walk) to the huge sunken well that gave this city its name (*chi* = mouth, *chen* = cenote or well, so: Mouth of the Well). The Sacred Cenote is an awesome natural well, some 60m in diameter and 35m deep. The walls between the summit and the water's surface are ensnared in tangled vines and other vegetation. There are ruins of a small steam bath next to the cenote, as well as a modern drinks stand with toilets.

Although some of the guides enjoy telling visitors that female virgins were sacrificed by being thrown into the cenote to drown, divers in 1923 brought up the remains of men, women and children. Skeletons were not all that was found in the Sacred Cenote. Artifacts and gold and jade jewelry from all parts of Mexico were recovered.

The artifacts' origins show the far-flung contacts the Maya had (there are some items from as far away as Colombia). It is believed that offerings of all kinds, human and otherwise, were thrown into the Sacred Cenote to please the gods.

Grupo de las Mil Columnas Comprising the Templo de los Guerreros (Temple of the Warriors), Templo de Chac-Mool (Temple of Chac-Mool) and Baño de Vapor No 2 (Sweat House or Steam Bath), this group takes its name Grupo de las Mil Columnas (Group of the Thousand Columns) from the forest of pillars in front.

The platformed temple greets you with a statue of the reclining god, Chac, as well as stucco and stone-carved animal deities. The temple's roof, once supported by columns entwined with serpents, disappeared long ago.

Archaeological work in 1926 revealed a Temple of Chac-Mool beneath the Temple of the Warriors. You may enter via a stairway

on the north side. The walls inside have badly deteriorated murals that are thought to portray the Toltecs' defeat of the Maya.

Just east of the Temple of the Warriors lies the rubble of a Mayan sweat house, with an underground oven and drains for the water. The sweat houses were regularly used for ritual purification.

El Osario El Osario (the Ossuary), otherwise known as the Bonehouse or High Priest's Grave, is a ruined pyramid. As with most of the buildings in this southern section, the architecture is more Puuc than Toltec.

La Casa Colorada Spaniards named this building La Casa Colorada (the Red House) for the red paint of the mural on its doorway. This building has little Toltec influence, and its design shows largely a pure Puuc Maya style. Referring to the stone latticework on the roof façade, the Maya named this building Chichán-Chob, or House of Small Holes.

El Caracol Called El Caracol (the Giant Conch Snail) by the Spaniards for its interior spiral staircase, this observatory is one of the most fascinating and important of all of Chichén Itzá's buildings. Its circular design resembles some central highlands structures, although, surprisingly, not those of Toltec Tula. In a fusion of architectural styles and religious imagery, there are Mayan Chac rain god masks over four external doors facing the cardinal directions.

The windows in the observatory's dome are aligned with the appearance of certain stars at specific dates. From the dome, the priests decreed the times for rituals, celebrations, corn planting and harvests.

Edificio de las Monjas & El Anexo Thought by archaeologists to have been a palace for Mayan royalty, the Edificio de las Monjas (Nunnery), with its myriad rooms, resembled a European convent to the conquistadors, hence their name for the building. The Nunnery's dimensions are imposing: its base is 60m long, 30m wide and 20m high. The construction is Mayan rather than Toltec,

Chac mask at Chichén Itzá

although a Toltec sacrificial stone stands in front. A small building added onto the west side is known as El Anexo (the Annex). These buildings are in the Puuc-Chenes style, particularly evident in the lower jaw of the Chac mask at the opening of the Annex.

Akab Dzib On the path east of the Nunnery, the Akab Dzib is thought by some archaeologists to be the most ancient structure excavated here. The central chambers date from the 2nd century. Akab Dzib means Obscure Writing in Mayan and refers to the south-side Annex door whose lintel depicts a priest with a vase etched with hieroglyphics. The writing has never been translated, hence the name. Note the red fingerprints on the ceiling, thought to symbolize the deity Itzamná, the sun god from whom the Maya sought wisdom.

Chichén Viejo Chichén Viejo (Old Chichén) comprises largely unrestored ruins, scattered about and hidden in the bush south of the Nunnery. The predominant architecture is Mayan, with Toltec additions and modifications. Though trails lead to the most prominent buildings, you may want to hire a guide.

Grutas de Balankanché

In 1959, a guide to the Chichén ruins was exploring a cave on his day off when he came upon a narrow passageway. The guide, whose name history records only as Gómez, followed the passageway for 300m, meandering through a series of caverns as he went. In each of those caverns, perched on mounds amid scores of glistening stalactites, were hundreds of ceremonial treasures the Maya had placed there 800 years earlier.

The guide brought his discovery to the attention of Dr Wyllys Andrews of the National Geographic Society, who was directing an excavation in the area. In the years that followed Gómez's discovery, the ancient ceremonial objects were removed and studied. Eventually most of the objects were returned to the caves, placed exactly where they were found – cleaned up and no doubt looking much as they did when they'd been offered to gods eight centuries earlier.

Today, it's hard not to roam the underground passageway, gazing upon the Mayan offerings, without being swept away by the mystery of it all, and it's interesting to imagine how many similar sites have yet to be discovered in the land of the Maya.

The Grutas de Balankanché (Balankanché Caves) are 6km east of the ruins of Chichén Itzá, and 2km east of the Hotel Dolores Alba on the highway to Cancún. Second-class buses heading east from Piste toward Valladolid and Cancún will drop you at the Balankanché road. You'll find the entrance to the caves 350m north of the highway.

As you approach the caves, you'll enter a botanical garden displaying many of Yucatán's native flora. In the entrance building is a little museum, a shop selling cold drinks and souvenirs, and a ticket booth. The museum mostly features large photographs taken during the exploration of the caves

and descriptions (in English, Spanish and French) of the Mayan religion and the offerings found in the caves (mostly earthenware).

Also on display at the open-air museum are photographs of modern-day Mayan ceremonies called Ch'a Chac that continue to be held in all the villages in the Yucatán during times of drought, with the aim of winning a god's favor and receiving the longed-for rain. The ceremonies mostly consist of much praying and numerous offerings of food to Chac.

Plan your visit for an hour when the compulsory tour and light-and-color show will be given in a language you can understand: The 40-minute show (minimum six people, maximum 30) is given in the cave at 11 am and 1 and 3 pm in English, at 9 am, noon and 2 and 4 pm in Spanish, and at 10 am in French. Tickets are available between 9 am and 4 pm (last show) daily. Admission costs US$3.75.

Places to Stay

Most of the lodgings convenient to Chichén Itzá and the caves are in the mid-range and top-end price brackets, but there are budget options. No matter what you plan to spend on a bed, don't hesitate to haggle in the off season (May, June, September and October), when prices should be lower.

Budget

Camping There's camping at the very likable ***Pirámide Inn***. For US$4 per person you can pitch a tent or hang a hammock under a palapa (a lot of young people do!), enjoy the Pirámide Inn's pool and watch satellite TV in the lobby. There are hot showers and clean, shared toilet facilities. Those in campers pay US$12 for two for full hookups. See the hotel's entry in the Mid-Range section for further details.

Hotels Two blocks south of the highway by Artesanías Guayacan, ***Posada Olalde*** is the best of Piste's several small pensions. The Olalde offers seven clean, quiet and attractive rooms for US$13/17 double/triple. There are also four even-cheaper bungalows on the premises.

Posada Chac-Mool, just east of the Hotel Misión Chichén-Itzá on the opposite (south) side of the highway in Piste, charges US$17 for a double with shower and fan. *Posada Novelo*, on the west side of the Pirámide Inn, charges the same for similar basic accommodations, but you can use the Pirámide's pool.

Hotel Posada Maya (☎ 851-0211), a few dozen meters north of the highway (look for the sign), charges US$14 for clean double rooms with shower, fan and good beds. You can also hang a hammock here for a mere US$4 a night. It's fairly quiet but drab. *Posada Poxil*, at the western end of town, charges the same for relatively clean, quiet rooms.

Mid-Range *Hotel Dolores Alba* (in Mérida ☎ 928-5650, fax 928-3163, www.doloresalba .com), on Hwy 180, at Km 122, is just over 3km east of the eastern entrance to the ruins and 2km west of the road to Balankanché, on the free highway to Cancún. Here, you'll find 40 modern, air-con rooms facing two very inviting swimming pools and an air-con restaurant (poolside dining is also offered). The hotel will transport you to and from the ruins. Singles/doubles cost US$25/39.

The *Pirámide Inn* (☎ 851-0115, fax 851-0114, www.piramideinn.com), in Piste, less than 2km from Chichén, has been here for years and keeps getting better (the entire place was renovated in 1999). Its gardens have had time to mature, and its swimming pool is a blessing on a hot day. All 42 rooms have air-con, and there's a spiritually cleansing Mayan-style sauna on the parklike grounds. The restaurant serves international and vegetarian cuisine. Here, you're as close as you can stay to the archaeological zone's western entrance. The rate of US$44 per room is reasonable, all things considered. There's also camping on the premises; see the Budget section for more details.

Stardust Inn (☎/fax 851-0122), next to the Pirámide Inn in Piste, and less than 2km west of the ruins, is an attractive place with two tiers of rooms surrounding a palm-shaded swimming pool and restaurant. The 57 air-con rooms with TV cost US$48 single or double.

Top End All of these hotels have swimming pools, restaurants, bars, well-kept tropical gardens, comfortable guest rooms and tour groups coming and going. Several are very close to the ruins.

The *Hotel Mayaland* (☎ 851-0128, fax 851-0077, in the USA ☎ 800-235-4079, www .mayaland.com), a mere 200m from the eastern entrance to the archaeological zone, is the oldest and most gracious hotel in Chichén's vicinity. From the lobby of the circa 1923 hotel you look through the main portal to see El Caracol framed as in a photograph. Rooms are priced at US$114/126 single/ double.

Hotel Hacienda Chichén (in Mérida ☎ 924-2150, fax 924-5011, in the USA ☎ 800-624-8451, www.yucatanadventures.com.mx), a few hundred meters farther from the ruins on the same eastern access road, is an elegant converted hacienda that dates from the 16th century. It was here, on this pridefully maintained colonial estate, that the archaeologists who excavated Chichén during the 1920s lived. Their bungalows have been refurbished, new ones have been built and a swimming pool added. Rooms in the garden bungalows, priced at US$70 single or double, US$80 triple, have ceiling fans, air-con and private baths, but no TV or phone. The dining room serves simple meals at moderate prices.

The Club Med-run *Hotel Villa Arqueológica* (☎ 851-0018, fax 851-0034, in the USA ☎ 800-258-2633, in France ☎ 801-802-803) is a few hundred meters south of the Mayaland and Hacienda Chichén, on the eastern access road to the ruins. As you'd expect from Club Med, the hotel is modern with a good restaurant, tennis courts and swimming pool. The 40 air-con rooms are fairly small but comfortable and are priced at about US$65 most of the year.

On the western side of Chichén, in the village of Piste, the *Hotel Misión Chichén-Itzá* (☎ 851-0022, fax 851-0023, misionchichen@ finred.com.mx) is comfortable without being distinguished, to be generous. Its pool is refreshing and its vast restaurant is often filled with bus tours. The 42 air-con, cable-TV rooms cost US$75 single or double. The

Misión Chichén-Itzá would offer good value if it slashed its rate in half.

Places to Eat

The cafetería in the *Unidad de Servicios*, at the western entrance to the archaeological zone, serves mediocre food at high prices in pleasant surroundings. Although there's a restaurant at the site, you'd be wise to plan your midday meal elsewhere.

The highway through Piste is lined with more than 20 small restaurants. The cheapest places are the entirely unatmospheric little market eateries on the main square opposite the huge tree. The others, ranged along the highway from the town square to the Pirámide Inn, are fairly well tarted up in a Mayan villager's conception of what foreign tourists expect to see.

Los Pajaros and *Cocina Económica Chichén Itzá* are among the cheapest ones, serving sandwiches, omelets, enchiladas and quesadillas for around US$3. *Restaurant Sayil*, facing the Hotel Misión Chichén-Itzá, offers good value: *bistec* (beefsteak), *cochinita* (suckling pig) or pollo pibil for US$2.50. Another simple little eatery with wooden benches and tables is the *Restaurant Parador*.

Prices are higher at the larger, more atmospheric restaurants such as the *Pueblo Maya*, *Carrousel* and *Fiesta*. *Restaurant Ruinas* serves big plates of fruit for US$2, tuna salad with mango for US$4, and hamburgers, sandwiches, fried chicken and spaghetti plates for around US$4.

The restaurant at the *Hotel Dolores Alba* specializes in Yucatecan food, and they do a good job of it. Try the pollo pibil for US$4.50 or boneless red snapper for US$6.50. Burgers, sandwiches, vegetarian plates and breakfast are also available.

Across the street from the Hotel Dolores Alba is the *Ik Kil Parque Ecoarqueológico*, a so-called eco-archaeological park. Basically, it's a woody area with a beautiful cenote in the middle of it and a restaurant a short walk away. The cenote offers an absolutely divine plunge after a day of ruin roaming; the cost to use the cenote is US$3, half that for kids. A buffet breakfast is served from 9 am to noon (US$4), and a buffet lunch from noon to 5 pm (US$9). The food is very good and a bargain for big eaters. Be advised that the restaurant and cenote are about 400m from the roadside entrance. Plans were in the works to add a hotel to the 'park.'

The big *Restaurant Xaybe*, opposite the Hotel Misión Chichén-Itzá, has decent food and reasonable prices, about US$10 per person. Customers of the restaurant get to use its swimming pool for free, but even if you don't eat here, you can still swim for about US$2.

The luxury hotels all have restaurants, with the Club Med-run *Villa Arqueológica* serving particularly distinguished cuisine. If you try its French-inspired Mexican-Mayan restaurant, it'll cost you about US$15 per person for a four-course comida corrida, and almost twice that much if you order à la carte – but the food is good.

Getting There & Away

Air Aerocaribe runs same-day roundtrip excursions by air from Cancún to Chichén Itzá in little planes, charging US$109 for the flight. Aero Cozumel runs a similar service from Chichén Itzá to Cozumel for US$118.

Bus The fastest buses between Mérida, Valladolid and Cancún travel by the Cuota (toll highway), and do not stop at Chichén Itzá.

Autotransportes de Oriente has a ticket desk right in the souvenir shop in Chichén's Unidad de Servicios. Oriente's 2nd-class buses leave the ruins to: Mérida at 9 and 10 am, noon and 2, 2:30 and 5 pm (US$3.50); Cancún and Valladolid at 9:30, 10:30 and 11:30 am and 12:30, 2:30, 3:30 and 4:30 pm (US$5.40 and US$1.50, respectively); Playa del Carmen at 8:30 am and 1:30 pm (US$7.20); Tulum at 8:30 am and 1:30 pm (US$5.40); and Cobá at 8:30 am and 1:30 pm (US$4.30).

Additionally, 1st-class buses leave the ruins to: Mérida at 1 and 5 pm (US$3.90); Playa del Carmen at 2:45 pm (US$9.20); Cobá at 8 am (US$3.20); Tulum at 8 am (US$4.70); Valladolid at 11:15 am and 2:45 pm (US$1.30); and Cancún at 3:30 pm (US$5.70).

Getting Around

Be prepared to walk at Chichén: from your hotel to the ruins, around the ruins, and back to your hotel, all under a broiling sun. For the Grutas de Balankanché, you can set out to walk early in the morning when it's cooler (it's 8km from Piste, less if you're staying on the eastern side of the ruins) and then hope to hitch a ride or catch a bus for the return.

A few taxis are available in Piste and sometimes at the Unidad de Servicios parking lot at Chichén Itzá, but you cannot depend on finding one unless you've made arrangements in advance. Despite a demand for them, taxis are fairly uncommon in these parts.

VALLADOLID

☎ 9 • pop 34,857

Valladolid is only 40km east of Chichén Itzá and 160km west of Cancún, but as it has no sites of stop-the-car immediacy, few tourists do stop here; those with wheels typically prefer to hurtle on through to the next major site, or they arrive by tourist bus from Cancún, stroll the town square for 20 minutes, and then head to Mérida or Chichén Itzá. It's just as well that their visits are brief, for this preserves Valladolid for those of us who want a deeper encounter with this colonial town.

In addition to glossing over its historic sites, most visitors to Valladolid miss an interesting daily ritual many of the city's residents take part in: Every night at sunset, the main square – the Parque Francisco Cantón Rosado – fills with townspeople who've left the heat of their homes for a hoped-for evening breeze under a sunless sky. The people fill the benches in the park and gossip, and overhead the shade trees fill with black birds that seem equally ecstatic that the outside temperature is falling. The buzz of the people is often drowned out by the cackle of the birds, but no one seems to mind; both species have been enjoying this ritual for a long time.

History

The Mayan ceremonial center of Zací was here long before the Spaniards arrived. The initial attempt at conquest in 1543 by Francisco de Montejo, nephew of Montejo the Elder, was thwarted by fierce Mayan resistance, but the Elder's son Montejo the Younger ultimately conquered the Maya and took the town. The Spanish laid out a new city on the classic colonial plan.

During much of the colonial era, Valladolid's distance from Mérida, its humidity and the surrounding forests kept it isolated from royal rule and thus relatively autonomous. Banned from even entering this town of pure-blooded Spaniards, the Maya rebelled, and in the War of the Castes of 1847 they made Valladolid their first point of attack. Besieged for two months, Valladolid's defenders were finally overcome; many of the citizens fled to the safety of Mérida and the rest were slaughtered by the Mayan forces.

Orientation & Information

The old highway goes right through the center of town, though all signs direct motorists to the toll highway north of town. To follow the old highway eastbound, follow Calle 41; westbound, Calles 39 or 35. The bus terminal is at Calle 39 at Calle 46.

Recommended hotels are on the Parque Francisco Cantón Rosado, or just a block or two away from it. Facing the park is the Ayuntamiento (City Hall), on the first floor of which is a tourist office (☎ 856-2529) that is open 8 am to 9 pm daily except during siesta. English speakers and maps may be found there.

Also on the east side of the plaza is the city's main post office, which is open 8 am to 5 pm Monday to Friday, 9 am to 1 pm Saturday. There are several banks near the center of town, including Bancomer (with ATM), on Calle 40, and Bital, on Calle 41. Banks are generally open 9 am to 5 pm Monday to Friday, 9 am to 1 pm Saturday, closed Sunday.

Templo de San Bernardino & Convento de Sisal

Although Vallàdolid has a number of interesting colonial churches, the Church of San Bernardino de Siena and the Convent of Sisal, 1.5km southwest of the plaza, are said to be the oldest Christian structures in

YUCATÁN STATE

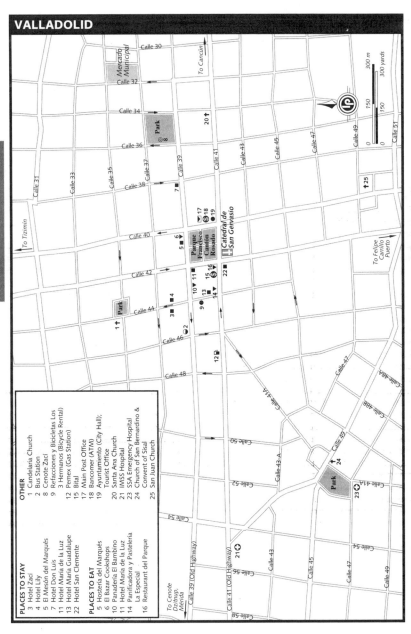

VALLADOLID

PLACES TO STAY
3 Hotel Zací
4 Hotel Lily
5 El Mesón del Marqués
7 Hotel Don Luis
11 Hotel María de la Luz
13 Hotel María Guadalupe
22 Hotel San Clemente

PLACES TO EAT
5 Hostería del Marqués
6 El Bazar Cookshops
10 Panadería El Bambino
11 Hotel María de la Luz
14 Panificadora y Pastelería
   La Especial
16 Restaurant del Parque

OTHER
1 Candelaria Church
2 Bus Station
8 Cenote Zací
9 Refacciones y Bicicletas Los
   3 Hermanos (Bicycle Rental)
12 Pemex (Gas Station)
15 Bital
17 Main Post Office
18 Bancomer (ATM)
19 Ayuntamiento (City Hall);
   Tourist Office
20 Santa Ana Church
21 IMSS Hospital
23 SSA Emergency Hospital
24 Church of San Bernardino &
   Convent of Sisal
25 San Juan Church

Yucatán. Constructed in 1552, the complex was designed to serve a dual function as fortress and church.

If the convent is open, go inside. Apart from the likeness of the miracle-working Virgin of Guadalupe on the altar, the church is relatively bare, having been stripped of its decorations during the uprisings of 1847 and 1910.

To get to the church, walk west on Calle 41 for 1km, then turn left and walk 500m to the convent. If you're riding a bicycle to the Cenote Dzitnup, you can stop at the convent on your way.

Cenotes

Cenotes, those vast underground pools of rain runoff, were the Maya's most dependable source of water. The Spaniards used them also. The Cenote Zací, on Calle 36 between Calles 37 and 39, is Valladolid's most famous.

Set in a pretty park that also holds the town's museum, an open-air amphitheater and traditional stone-walled thatched houses, the cenote is vast, dark, impressive and covered with a layer of algae and bat crap. It's open 8 am to 7 pm daily; admission costs US$0.50 for adults, half that for children. There's also a small zoo on the premises.

Much more enticing, but less easily accessible, is the Cenote Dzitnup (also sometimes called Xkakah), 7km west of Valladolid's main plaza. To reach it from the center of town, follow the main highway (Calle 41) west toward Mérida for 5km. Turn left (south) at the sign for Dzitnup and follow the road for just under 2km to get to the site, which will be on the left. A taxi from Valladolid's main plaza charges US$14 for the excursion there and back, with half an hour's wait. While you're there, notice the blind fish that inhabit the lovely pool.

Another way to reach the cenote is on a bicycle rented from the Refacciones y Bicicletas Los 3 Hermanos, on Calle 44 between Calles 39 and 41. Rental costs US$2 per hour. Check out your bike carefully before putting money down. They rent some wrecks here, and you don't want yours to break down. The first 5km are not particularly pleasant

La Virgen de Guadalupe

because of the traffic, but the last 2km are on a quiet country road. It should take you only 20 minutes to pedal to the cenote.

Yet another way to get there is to hop aboard a westbound bus, ask the driver to let you off at the Dzitnup turnoff, then walk the final 2km (20 minutes) to the site. Cenote Dzitnup is open 7 am to 6 pm daily. Admission costs US$1.50.

As you approach, a horde of village children will likely surround you, each wanting to be your 'guide' to the cenote, 10m away. Even if you don't appoint one, they often will accompany you down into the cave.

There's a restaurant and soft drinks stand at the entrance of the cave. If you've brought a bathing suit and towel you can go for a swim here. If you didn't, you'll wish you had.

Places to Stay

Budget *Hotel María Guadalupe* (☎ 856-2068, Calle 44 No 188), between Calles 39 and 41, is a study in modernity in this colonial town. The eight simple rooms go for US$9 a single or double with private shower and fan.

The *Hotel Lily* (☎ 856-2163, Calle 44 No 190) is cheap and very basic but reasonably

priced, with 20 rooms at US$7/11 single/double with private bathroom and fan. There's also one air-con room with three beds for US$18.

Hotel Don Luis (☎ 856-2008, Calle 39 No 191), at the corner of Calle 38, is a motel-style structure with a palm-shaded patio, murky swimming pool and acceptable rooms priced at US$10 a single or double with fan, or US$12 with air-con.

Mid-Range & Top End Most of Valladolid's better places have swimming pools, restaurants and secure parking facilities.

The best is *El Mesón del Marqués (☎ 856-2073, fax 856-2280, h_marques@chichen.com.mx, Calle 39 No 203)*, on the north side of the main plaza. It has two beautiful colonial courtyards and modernized guest rooms with both air-con and ceiling fans. There's a pool on the premises as well. Rates are US$45 for a suite most of the year.

Next best is the *Hotel María de la Luz (☎ 856-2071, fax 856-1181, maria_luz@chichen.com.mx)*, on Calle 42 at Calle 39, at the northwest corner of the plaza. Boasting one of the more popular restaurants on the square, it also has serviceable air-con rooms on two levels around a pool for US$21 a single or double.

Hotel San Clemente (☎/fax 856-2208, Calle 42 No 206), at the southwest corner of the main plaza, is a very agreeable place. Colonial decor abounds, but the 64 double rooms have private baths and fans for a very competitive US$22 a double, add US$2 for air-con. There's a swimming pool as well.

The well-kept *Hotel Zací (☎ 856-2167, Calle 44 No 191)*, between Calles 37 and 39, has 50 rooms built around a quiet, long and narrow courtyard with a swimming pool. You may choose from rooms with fan (US$15/18) or with air-con (US$17/22).

Places to Eat

El Bazar is a collection of little open-air market-style cookshops at the corner of Calles 39 and 40 (northeast corner of the plaza). This is popular place for a big, cheap breakfast. At lunch and dinnertime, comidas corridas of soup, main course and drink cost

less than US$5 – if you ask prices before you order. There are a dozen eateries here – *Doña Mary*, *El Amigo Panfilo*, *Sergio's Pizza*, *La Rancherita*, *El Amigo Casiano*, etc – open from 6:30 am to 2 pm and from 6 pm to about 9 or 10 pm.

For a bit more, you can dine at the breezy tables in the *Hotel María de la Luz*, on Calle 42, overlooking the plaza. The breakfast buffet costs only US$4, a luncheon comida corrida the same or a little more. There's a wide selection of items and the restaurant generally catches a nice breeze. This place is tops for people-watching. The comida costs even less at the old-fashioned, high-ceilinged *Restaurant del Parque*, at Calles 41 and 42, which offers many natural juices among the typical fare.

Valladolid has several good bakeries, including *Panificadora y Pastelería La Especial*, on Calle 41 less than a block west of the plaza, and *Panadería El Bambino*, on Calle 39 a half block west of the plaza.

The best restaurant in the area is the *Hostería del Marqués*, the dining room of El Mesón del Marqués hotel, on the north side of the main plaza. Half of the restaurant is outside and half is air-con nonsmoking indoors. Suggestion: Start with gazpacho, continue with pork loin Valladolid-style (in a tomato sauce) or grilled pork steak, and finish up with a sliced banana with cream for US$9.50.

Getting There & Away

Bus The bus terminal is on Calle 39 at Calle 46. The main companies are Autotransportes de Oriente Mérida-Puerto Juárez (1st- and 2nd-class) and Expresso de Oriente.

There are 11 1st-class buses from Valladolid to Mérida daily, with the first departures at 6:45 am and the last at 9:45 pm (US$5.50).

There are nine 1st-class buses to Cancún, with the first departure at 7:30 am and the last at 10 pm (US$5.50).

There are two 1st-class buses to Cobá, at 9:15 am and 3:50 pm (US$2). The same buses continue on to Tulum for an additional US$1.50.

There are eight 1st-class buses to Playa del Carmen from Valladolid, with the first

leaving at 7:45 am and the last at 7:15 pm (US$7.50).

There are no fewer than 22 2nd-class buses daily to Mérida, all passing by the turnoff for Chichén Itzá along the way (be sure to tell the driver to let you out there if you're on your way to the ruins). The cost is US$4.30 to Mérida and US$1.20 to Chichén Itzá.

There are also 24 2nd-class buses daily to Cancún from Valladolid (US$4.30); five to Playa del Carmen (US$6.10); two to Chetumal (at 5:30 am and 2:30 pm, US$8.10); 14 to Tizimín (US$1.40); and three to Tulum and Cobá (US$4.30 and US$3.20, respectively). Yes, the 2nd-class ride to Tulum and Cobá is more than the 1st-class, due to the different routes taken.

There are 2nd-class buses to Izamal (at 1:10 am and 7:30 pm, US$2.40), Espita (10:30 am and 3 pm, US$1.30), and Chiquila (2:30 pm, US$4.10).

Taxi A quicker, more comfortable and, yes, more expensive way to Cancún, Mérida or elsewhere is by taking one of the shared taxis parked outside the bus station; they leave as soon as all seats are filled. The trip

costs at least twice the bus fare but – hey! – you're on vacation and your happiness is most important. If you're sick of buses, splurge and enjoy.

TIZIMÍN
☎ 9 • pop 38,328

Many travelers on their way to Río Lagartos have to change buses in Tizimín (Place of Many Horses), the third-largest city in the state of Yucatán (behind Mérida and Progreso). There is little point in arranging for an overnight stay, but the tree-filled central plaza is pleasant, particularly at sundown when birdsong fills the air and children in school uniforms play tag and other games.

Two great colonial structures – the Convento de los Tres Reyes Magos (Monastery of the Three Wise Kings) and the Convento de San Francisco de Asis (Monastery of St Francis of Assisi) – are worth a look. Five lengthy blocks from the plaza, northwest on Calle 51, is a modest zoo, the Parque Zoológico de la Reina.

There are several banks facing the Parque Principal, at least one of which has an ATM.

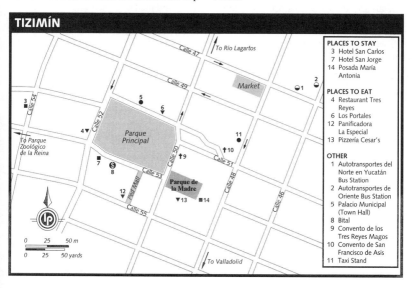

TIZIMÍN

PLACES TO STAY
3   Hotel San Carlos
7   Hotel San Jorge
14 Posada María Antonia

PLACES TO EAT
4   Restaurant Tres Reyes
6   Los Portales
12 Panificadora La Especial
13 Pizzería Cesar's

OTHER
1   Autotransportes del Norte en Yucatán Bus Station
2   Autotransportes de Oriente Bus Station
5   Palacio Municipal (Town Hall)
8   Bital
9   Convento de los Tres Reyes Magos
10 Convento de San Francisco de Asis
11 Taxi Stand

Places to Stay

The **Posada María Antonia** (☎ 863-2384, Calle 50 No 408), on the east side of the Parque de la Madre, is an excellent value with 11 air-con rooms for US$15 a single or double. The reception desk is also a telephone caseta – you can place international calls from it.

The **Hotel San Jorge** (☎ 863-2037, Calle 53 No 411) has basic but serviceable rooms with private bath for US$18 a single or double with air-con. Avoid room No 3, which is particularly loud and has a bad bed. **Hotel San Carlos** (☎ 863-2094, Calle 54 No 407) is built like a motel, and charges identical prices for 25 somewhat worn rooms.

Places to Eat

The **market**, a block west of the bus station, has the usual cheap eateries. The bakery **Panificadora La Especial** is on Calle 55, down a little pedestrian lane from the plaza.

The festive **Restaurant Tres Reyes**, on the corner of Calles 52 and 53, opens early for breakfast and is a favorite with town notables who take their second cup of coffee around 9 am. Lunch or dinner costs US$3.50 to US$7, and is well worth it. The *filete de Tres Reyes* (roast beef, US$6) is the house special, and it's divine, as are the natural juices (particularly the mango juice). It's open early until late.

Facing the plaza are several simple places good for a quick, cheap bite, including the **Los Portales**, which has been around a long time. The popular **Pizzería Cesar's**, at the corner of Calles 50 and 53, serves pizza, pasta, sandwiches and burgers from 4 pm to midnight. Few items are over US$5.

Getting There & Away

Autotransportes de Oriente runs intermediate-class buses to: Cancún at 3:30, 5:15, 7 and 8:30 am and 2:30, 3:30 and 7:30 pm (US$5); Cobá at noon (US$4.60); Playa del Carmen at 8:30 am and noon (US$7.10); Tulum at noon (US$5.70); Mérida at 6 and 11:20 am (US$5); Izamal at 11:20 am (US$3.80); and Valladolid (14 buses daily, the first departing at 4:30 am and the last at 7 pm; US$1.40). The Oriente bus station is on Calle 46 near Calle 47.

Autotransportes del Noreste en Yucatán runs 1st-class buses to Mérida at 5:30, 6:45 and 7:30 am, noon and 2, 5 and 6:30 pm (US$5.50) and to Río Lagartos at 4, 5, 6:30, 9:15, 10, 10:30 and 11:15 am and at 2:15, 4:30, 7:30 and 7:45 pm (US$1.40). This bus station is on Calle 47 between Calles 46 and 48.

A taxi ride to Río Lagartos costs US$15, the same as a taxi ride to San Felipe. There's a taxi stand on Calle 48 between Calles 49 and 51.

RÍO LAGARTOS

☎ 9 • pop 1905

It is worth going out of your way to this little fishing village, 103km north of Valladolid and 52km north of Tizimín, to see the most spectacular flamingo colony in Mexico. The estuaries are also home to snowy egrets, red egrets, great white herons and snowy white ibis. Although Río Lagartos (Lizard River) was named after the once substantial crocodile population, don't expect to see any, as hunting has decimated the local croc population.

The town of Río Lagartos itself, with its narrow streets and multihued houses, has little charm, though the panorama of the boats and the bay is pleasant. Were it not for the flamingos, you would have little reason to come here. Although the state government has been making noise about developing the area for tourism, this has not happened yet. Privately, things are picking up.

Orientation

There's one street into town and it's Calle 10. At the entrance of town, Calle 10 passes the Restaurant Los Negritos, then it crosses Calle 19, then Calle 17 and so on until it reaches water's edge. Where Calle 10 reaches the Río Lagartos there's one white kiosk run by a man who links tourists with boat captains.

Running parallel to Calle 10 and to the west of the main street are Calles 12 and 14 and after that the waterfront road of Av Hol Koben. Most of the town's hotels are located along Calle 14. To the east of Calle 10 are Calles 8 and 6. No one knows what happened to Calles 2 and 4, but they don't seem

Xlapak (Old Walls) is small but ornate.

Corn is ground into *masa* to make tortillas.

The quiet fishing village of San Felipe.

The Palace of Sayil, on the Puuc Route, had sacred and civic functions.

Find your fill of tropical fruit in the markets of Oxkutzcab, in southwest Yucatán.

Statue of a Mayan warrior in the city of Ticul.

A cavern in the Grutas de Loltún cave system.

to exist. The bus depot is located on Calle 19 at Calle 8, one block east of Calle 10.

There are no banks in town, nor is there a tourist office. If you have questions, your best bet is to visit the Hotel Hol Koben, at the corner of Calles 14 and 17, or the Restaurante-Bar Isla Contoy, overlooking the water on Calle 19. You'll find helpful English speakers at both places.

Flamingos

When you approach a horizon of hundreds of these brilliant orange-red birds, you will fully understand why they are called flamingos. The name is derived from the Spanish word *flamenco*, which means 'flaming.' When the flock takes flight, the sight of the suddenly fiery horizon makes all the long hours on the bus to get here worthwhile.

However, in the interests of the flamingos' well-being, ask your boat captain not to frighten the birds into flight. Being frightened away from their habitat several times a day can't be good for them, however good it may be for the captain's business or for photography. (Photographers: Because the birds are skittish, you'll need at least a 200mm lens to get close-ups, and you'll want to use a polarizing filter to minimize the glare off the water.)

There are four primary flamingo haunts in the lagoon near the town of Río Lagartos. In order of distance, with the closest mentioned first, and their cost per boat in parentheses, they are: Punta Garga (US$30), Yoluk (US$35), Necopal (US$35) and Nahochin (US$35). Basically, for US$35 you see all four flamingo haunts. The names refer to the patches of mangrove near the flamingo colonies. The greatest number of flamingos can usually be found at Nahochin.

If you haven't seen mangrove up close, the ride to the flamingos will be a treat. As your long and narrow fiberglass launch winds its way toward the flamingos, you'll pass virgin mangrove that's 25m tall in some places. The water is green-yellow, mostly freshwater, despite the appearance of a huge salt pile visible from Nahochin.

You can generally get to within 100m of flamingos before they start walking away

from you or take to the air. The birds here are the red subspecies, which means they are the color of wild-salmon meat – not pink at all but instead a vibrant orange-red with black along their wingtips and beaks, which resemble tiny bent index fingers. Depending on your luck, you'll see hundreds of flamingos or thousands of them.

Río Lagartos is small. To hire a boat captain, simply head to the kiosk at water's edge. Not one of the captains speaks English, but the gentleman at the kiosk does and he will hook you up with a captain. You negotiate the price and destination with the representative, not the captain. Or, you can visit the Restaurante-Bar Isla Contoy and hire Diego Nuñez Martínez, who speaks fluent English. His family owns the restaurant, and he's a very friendly guy.

If you'll be staying in town a night, consider hiring Diego to take you out looking for crocodiles. There are some in the lagoon (it's really not a river at all, despite being named Río Lagartos), and they are best seen at night in the beam of a flashlight. The cost of a croc adventure runs US$40 per boat, one to four persons per boat. Diego charges US$20 to US$40 for flamingo tours, with price varying with time involved or distance covered.

Diego also offers turtle-watching expeditions from May to September. During those months, no fewer than four species of sea turtle (green, hawksbill, loggerhead and

Virgin mangrove still grows at Río Lagartos.

leatherback) ramble up the beaches on a nearby semi-protected island and lay eggs in the sand. Like the croc adventures, these take place only at night. Suave visitors will negotiate a 2-in-1 croc and turtle night trip. Scooting around the lagoon at night is highly recommended.

Special Events

La Feria de Santiago, the patron saint festival of Río Lagartos, is held about July 18-25 every year, and it's a blast. A bullfight (really bullplay) ring is erected in the middle of town during the weeklong event, and every afternoon anyone who wishes is able to enter it and play matador with a young bull. No, the animal is not killed or even injured, just a little angry at times. Don't turn your back to it or it will knock you down.

Day One of the festival begins with a big dance that lasts all night. Day Two the bullplay sessions start; also on this day there's a procession that winds from the entrance of town and goes to the bullfight ring, where a ceibo tree is planted in the center of the ring. During each of the remaining days the festivities begin with Mass at the town church followed by a procession; each procession is led by a guild (one day it's the ranchers, another it's the fishermen, another it's the farmers, and so on).

The fair begins the Saturday prior to July 25, Patron Saint Day, and lasts at least a week. If the Saturday before July 25 falls on July 23 or July 24, then the celebration actually begins two Saturdays before the 25th. The festival always lasts at least a week, but never more than nine days. Yes, it's confusing, and residents of Río Lagartos don't always follow this rule.

Another big annual event in Río Lagartos is the Día de la Marina (Day of the Marine Force), which is always June 1. On this day, following 9 am Mass, a crown of flowers is dedicated to the Virgin and is carried from the church to a boat, where it is then taken 4km out to sea and placed in the water as an offering to all the fishermen who have perished at sea.

What's remarkable about this is that virtually every boat in this fishing town goes to the sea site, and scores of fishermen sing en route to the honored site and pray there before a selected queen lays the gorgeous wreath in the water. For one minute after the wreath is placed in the water, there is a moment of total silence in honor of the lost fishermen. After the service, everyone heads back to town and celebrates with dancing, drinking and games. The queen dances with every fisherman to bring him good luck.

The boats, not incidentally, are heavily decorated on this day, and tourists are welcome to ride to the site for free. Just ask if you can go, and be friendly and respectful. At the sea service, keep your chatter to a minimum and simply observe. Doing so will encourage the fishermen to welcome tourists to join them year after year. A tip for their kindness, following the service, is always appreciated (US$5 to US$10 per person is very appreciated).

Places to Stay

At the time of writing there were two hotels in town and a third under construction.

The least expensive of the three is the *Posada Leyli* (☎ 862-0106), on Calle 14 at Calle 11. It offers six pleasing, fan-cooled rooms: two singles with shared bathroom for US$9, two singles with private bathroom for US$10 and two doubles with private bathroom for US$15. The Leyli offers excellent value.

Two blocks north of the Leyli, where Calle 14 meets the lagoon, is the new-in-1999 *Hotel Villas de Pescadores* (☎ 862-0048), which offers 12 pleasing rooms with good cross ventilation – three suites for US$35 single or double and nine rooms for US$20 single or double. The suites have air-con, TV, sofa, bed and a minibar. The rooms feature two beds and a fan, and several have lagoon views. This is a very good value.

The multilevel *Hotel Hol Koben* (www.riolagartos.com.mx), on Calle 14 at Calle 17, was near completion in late 1999. The hotel's manager boasted that every room in the establishment will have air-con, a bathtub, a small living room and two double beds. There will be a library with large-screen TV, and an artists' room where paint, clay and

musical instruments will be provided at nominal cost. A swimming pool and a roof-top café with live music most nights are also planned. The proposed rate of US$60 single or double seems reasonable and includes continental breakfast.

Places to Eat

The **Restaurante-Bar Isla Contoy**, on Calle 19 at water's edge, two or three blocks west of Calle 10, is very popular. It serves grouper or sea bass stuffed with shrimp (US$4.20), fried grouper with tomato salsa (US$3.50) and lots of other seafood at reasonable prices. It's open from 8 am to 10 pm daily, and this is a good place to meet other travelers.

At the open-sided, fan-cooled **Restaurant Los Negritos**, on Calle 10 near the entrance of town, the *filete de camarones* is the house specialty. It consists of a white fish (usually grouper) stuffed with shrimp and mayonnaise – lots of mayo (most people prefer much less, so say 'menos mayo' or 'no mayo,' unless you're some kind of mayo freak). Don't want to chance it? Then order the *pescado frito* (fried fish) or the *ceviche de pulpo* (octopus ceviche), both of which are very good and under US$5. The restaurant is generally open from 9 am to 7 pm, later if business is brisk.

Getting There & Away

From Río Lagartos, Autotransportes del Noreste en Yucatán has direct buses to: Mérida (5:30 and 11 am and 12:30 and 4 pm, US$7.40); Tizimín (same hours as Mérida, US$1.70); and Cancún (11 am and 4 and 5 pm daily except Wednesday, when there is no direct bus to Cancún, US$7.20). Noreste also offers semidirect buses to Tizimín (hourly from 5:30 am to 5:30 pm, US$1.40) and San Felipe (6:30, 7:30, 10:15 and 11:30 am and 12:30, 3:50 and 5:30 pm, US$1).

SAN FELIPE
☎ 9 • pop 1516
This tiny, seldom-visited fishing village of painted wooden houses on narrow streets, 12km west of Río Lagartos, makes a nice day trip from Río Lagartos. Other than lying on the so-so beach, bird-watching is the main attraction in San Felipe, as there is abundant bird life just across the estuary at Punta Holochit.

Places to Stay & Eat

There's really only one place to stay in town, and it's the very nice **Hotel San Felipe de Jesús** (☎ 863-3378, fax 862-2036), on Calle 9 between Calles 14 and 16 (where the main street into town meets the sea, turn left (west) and walk or drive 100m or so until you come to the seaside hotel). Six of the hotel's 18 rooms are oversize and have private balconies with lovely sea and sunset views. All of the rooms have good cross ventilation and lots of details and are a super bargain at US$22 for a single or double. Smaller rooms go for US$16. Good wine is available in the restaurant, which offers tasty seafood at low prices. Pizza is available at night. The owner welcomes guests into his clean kitchen to dispel any doubts. And from the hotel it's usually possible to see flamingos wading in shallow water just 300m away.

Getting There & Away

Some buses from Tizimín to Río Lagartos continue to San Felipe and return. The 12km ride takes about 20 minutes. To save time, take a taxi from Tizimín. From San Felipe, buses to Tizimín leave at 5:45, 8:30 and 10 am, noon and 3 and 6 pm (US$1.50). The same buses continue on to Valladolid (US$2.50).

There are no taxis stationed in Río Lagartos or San Felipe.

CELESTÚN
☎ 9 • pop 5201
Famed as a bird sanctuary, Celestún makes a good beach-and-bird day trip from Mérida. Although this region abounds in anhingas and egrets, most bird-watchers come here to see the flamingos.

The town is located on a spit of land between the Río Esperanza and the Gulf of Mexico. Brisk westerly sea breezes cool the town on most days. The white-sand beach is appealing, but on some days fierce afternoon

winds swirl clouds of choking dust through the town. The dust makes the sea silty, and therefore unpleasant for swimming in the afternoon. Row upon row of fishing boats outfitted with twin long poles line the shore. Given the winds, the best time to see birds is in the morning.

There are two places to hire a boat for bird-watching: from the bridge on the highway into town about 1.5km from the beach, or from oceanside. The more attractive of the options is the latter. The 'sea tour' lasts about 2½ hours and initially involves a 10km boat ride parallel to the coast and headed north. During this portion of the tour you can expect to see egrets, herons, cormorants, sandpipers and many other species of bird. The boat then turns inland, passing through a petrified forest where tall coastal trees once belonging to a freshwater ecosystem were killed more than a millennium ago, most likely by a hurricane that polluted the freshwater with seawater. Today, the trees are as hard as rock.

After the forest you'll pass along a river/ lagoon where fishermen catch shrimp and crabs. You'll soon come to a bridge (the highway bridge at the entrance of town), beyond which flamingos can generally be seen doing a little fishing of their own. Depending on the tide, you may see hundreds or thousands of the colorful birds here. After seeing the birds, the sea tour winds through mangrove to a freshwater cenote for a refreshing dip (be sure to wear a bathing suit under your clothes this day). The cost for this tour is US$55 for two persons and US$60 for three or four. You can join this tour at several beachside places, but we recommend the Restaurant Celestún, at the corner of Calles 11 and 12. The people here seem a little more with it than elsewhere. The guide with the best reputation in town is Alberto Rodríguez, who can often be found at the Restaurant Celestún.

The alternative tour begins at the bridge and lasts about an hour. It involves simply getting into a boat and heading over to the flamingos. The cost is US$30 for the boat *and* US$2 per person, up to six persons per boat.

Be advised that there is no bank in town and neither credit cards nor traveler's checks are accepted.

Orientation

You come into town along Calle 11, past the marketplace and church (on your left, or south), to Calle 12, the waterfront street.

Places to Stay

Celestún has several hotels, all of which are located on Calle 12 within a short walk of each other, and new hotels are opening every year. The better places are mentioned here.

The **Hotel María del Carmen** (*☎*/fax 936-2051) offers 14 beachfront rooms: four with air-con for US$20/23 single/double, 36 fan-cooled for US$18/20. Every room here is clean and pleasant and has a private balcony facing the sea.

The next-best hotel in town is the **Hospedaje Sol y Mar** (in Mérida *☎* 9-944-9787), which offers 16 rooms, half with air-con (US$25 single or double) and half without (US$15 single or double).

The **Hospedaje Sofía** (no phone) offers seven fan-cooled rooms for US$10/12. New-in-1999, it's *the* place to stay if you're low on funds.

If you've got your own wheels, consider turning right (north) on Calle 12 and following the signs about 7km to the **Eco Paraíso** resort (*☎* 9-916-2100, fax 9-991-2111, www .mexonline.com). Here you'll find 15 fan-cooled, palapa-roofed cabañas with lovely tiled floors. Seven of the cabañas are on the beach, the rest are set back a little. There's a beautiful elevated pool on the grounds, as well as a fine restaurant and a communal room, and many hectares of natural terrain to explore on foot. This is a good place to escape life's pressures. Rates, which include breakfast and dinner, are very reasonable at US$130/170 single/double.

Places to Eat

Celestún's specialty is crab claws, and of course fresh fish. To keep from pricing themselves out of business, the restaurants have agreed on prices for main items. Service and decor vary from restaurant to restaurant in

Celestún, but the menu for the most part does not.

Expect to pay US$3.50 for the catch of the day, US$5.50 for delicious ceviche and US$3 for a conch cocktail. Irresponsible and mean people will want to consider the *cazon entomado* (baby shark in a tomato sauce); it should be priceless but the union ruled US$3.50 was fair.

The ***Restaurant Celestún***, at the corner of Calles 11 and 12, offers good service, good food and pleasing decor, but several other beachside restaurants are just as decent. Basically, there's no shortage of good, cheap seafood restaurants in Celestún.

Getting There & Away
Buses from Mérida head for Celestún 12 times daily beginning at 5 am from the Unión de Camioneros de Yucatán terminal on Calle 71 between Calles 62 and 64. The last bus leaves at 8 pm. The 95km trip takes about 1½ hours and costs US$2.30.

UXMAL
Set in the Puuc Hills, which lent their name to the architectural patterns in this region, Uxmal ('oosh-MAL') was an important city during the Late Classic period (600-900 AD) in a region that encompassed the satellite towns of Sayil, Kabah, Xlapak and Labná. Although Uxmal means 'thrice built' in Mayan, it was actually reconstructed five times.

That a sizable population ever flourished in this area is a mystery, as there is precious little water in the region. The Mayan cisterns (chultunes) must have been adequate.

History
First occupied in about 600 AD, the town was architecturally influenced by highland Mexico, and features the well-proportioned Puuc style, which is unique to this region.

Given the scarcity of water in the Puuc Hills, Chac the rain god was of great significance. His image is ubiquitous here in monsterlike stucco masks protruding from façades and cornices.

There is much speculation as to why Uxmal was abandoned around 900 AD.

Drought conditions may have reached such proportions that the inhabitants had to relocate. One widely held theory suggests that the rise to greatness of Chichén Itzá drew people away from the Puuc Hills.

Rediscovered by archaeologists in the 19th century, Uxmal was first excavated in 1929 by Frans Blom. Although much has been restored, there is still a good deal to discover.

Orientation & Information
As you come into the site from Hwy 261, the big new Lodge at Uxmal hotel is on the left, with the Hotel Villa Arqueológica beyond it; the parking lot is to the right (US$1 per car).

You enter the site through the modern Unidad Uxmal building, which holds the air-con Yax-Beh restaurant. Also in the Unidad Uxmal are a small museum, shops selling souvenirs and crafts, the auditorium Kit Bolon Tun, and toilets. The Librería Dante has a good selection of travel and archaeological guides in English, Spanish, German and French, though imported books are pricey.

The archaeological site at Uxmal is open 8 am to 5 pm daily; admission costs US$7.50, free on Sunday. The Unidad Uxmal building stays open until 10 pm because of the 45-minute Luz y Sonido (Light and Sound) show, held each evening in English (US$5.50) at 9 pm and in Spanish (US$4) at 8 pm.

If you come for the day and want to stay for the evening light-and-sound show, plan to have dinner and a swim at one of the restaurants; most hotels allow restaurant patrons to use their pools.

As you pass through the turnstile and climb the slope to the ruins, the rear of the Pyramid of the Magician comes into view.

Pirámide del Adivino
The Pirámide del Adivino (Pyramid of the Magician), 39m high, was built on an oval base. The smoothly sloping sides have been restored; they date from the temple's fifth incarnation. The four earlier temples were covered in the rebuilding, except for the high doorway on the west side, which has been retained from the fourth temple. Decorated

UXMAL

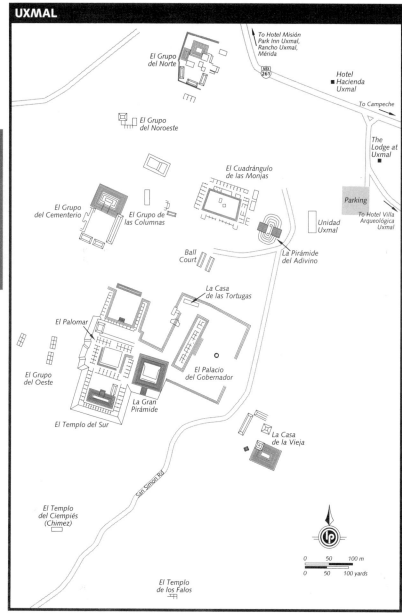

El Grupo del Norte

To Hotel Misión Park Inn Uxmal, Rancho Uxmal, Mérida

MEX 261

Hotel
■ Hacienda Uxmal

To Campeche

El Grupo del Noroeste

The Lodge at Uxmal
■

El Cuadrángulo de las Monjas

Parking

El Grupo del Cementerio

El Grupo de las Columnas

Unidad Uxmal

To Hotel Villa Arqueológica Uxmal

La Pirámide del Adivino

Ball Court

La Casa de las Tortugas

El Palomar

La Casa del Gobernador

El Grupo del Oeste

La Gran Pirámide

El Templo del Sur

La Casa de la Vieja

El Templo del Ciempiés (Chimez)

San Simón Rd

0   50   100 m
0   50   100 yards

El Templo de los Falos

in elaborate Chenes style, the doorway proper takes the form of the mouth of a gigantic Chac mask.

The ascent to the doorway and the top is best done from the west side. Heavy chains serve as handrails to help you up the very steep steps.

From the top of the pyramid, you can survey the rest of the archaeological site. Directly west of the pyramid is the Cuadrángulo de las Monjas (Nunnery Quadrangle). On the south side of the quadrangle, down a short slope, is a ruined ball court. Farther south stands the great artificial terrace holding El Palacio del Gobernador (the Governor's Palace); between the palace and the ball court is the small La Casa de las Tortugas (House of the Turtles). Beyond the Governor's Palace are the remains of La Gran Pirámide (the Great Pyramid), and next to it are the El Palomar (Pigeon House) and the Templo del Sur (South Temple). There once were many other structures at Uxmal, but most have been recaptured by the jungle and are now just verdant mounds.

Cuadrángulo de las Monjas

Archaeologists guess that the 74-room Cuadrángulo de las Monjas (Nunnery Quadrangle) might actually have been a military academy, royal school or palace complex. The long-nosed face of Chac appears everywhere on the façades of the four separate temples that form the quadrangle. The northern temple, grandest of the four, was built first, followed by the south, east and west temples.

Several decorative elements on the façades show signs of Mexican, perhaps Totonac, influence. The feathered serpent (Quetzalcóatl) motif along the top of the west temple's façade is one of these. Note also the stylized depictions of the *na*, or Mayan thatched hut, over some of the doorways in the northern and southern buildings.

Ball Court

Pass through the corbeled arch in the middle of the south building of the quadrangle and continue down the slope to the ball court (juego de pelota), which is much less impressive than the great ball court at Chichén Itzá.

La Casa de las Tortugas

Climb the steep slope up to the artificial terrace on which stands the Governor's Palace. At the top on the right is La Casa de las Tortugas (the House of the Turtles), which takes its name from the turtles carved on the cornice. The frieze of short columns or 'rolled mats' that runs around the top of the temple is characteristic of the Puuc style. Turtles were associated by the Maya with the rain god Chac. According to Mayan myth, when the people suffered from drought, so did the turtles, and both prayed to Chac to send rain.

El Palacio del Gobernador

The magnificent façade of El Palacio del Gobernador (the Governor's Palace), nearly 100m long, has been called 'the finest structure at Uxmal and the culmination of the Puuc style' by Mayanist Michael D Coe. Buildings in the Puuc style have walls filled with rubble, faced with cement and then covered in a thin veneer of limestone squares; the lower part of the façade is plain, the upper part festooned with stylized Chac faces and geometric designs, often lattice-like or fretted. Other elements of Puuc style are decorated cornices, rows of half-columns and round columns in doorways. The stones forming the corbeled vaults are shaped like boots, in the Puuc style.

La Gran Pirámide

Adjacent to the Governor's Palace, the 32m Gran Pirámide (Great Pyramid) has been restored only on the northern side. There is a quadrangle at the top which archaeologists theorize was largely destroyed in order to construct another pyramid above it. This work, for reasons unknown, was never completed. At the top are some stucco carvings of Chac, birds and flowers.

El Palomar

West of the Great Pyramid sits a structure whose roofcomb is latticed with a pigeon-hole pattern – hence the building is called El

Palomar (Pigeon House). The nine honey-combed triangular belfries sit on top of a building that was once part of a quadrangle. The base is so eroded that it is difficult for archaeologists to guess its function.

Places to Stay & Eat

Budget As there is no town at Uxmal – only the archaeological site and several top-end hotels – you cannot depend upon finding cheap lodging or food.

Campers can pitch their tents 5km north of the ruins on Hwy 261, the road to Mérida, at *Rancho Uxmal* (☎ 950-1118) for US$2.50 per person. The *Parador Turístico Cana Nah* next door has a 'trailer park' camping lot as well.

In addition to camping, Rancho Uxmal has 28 basic, serviceable guest rooms with shower and fan for US$25 a double – expensive for what you get, but this is Uxmal. There's a restaurant and a pool (although the pool is usually bone dry for reasons that aren't clear).

Other than Rancho Uxmal, there's no cheap lodging in the area. If you don't want to return to Mérida for the night, make your way to Ticul (turn to that section, later in this chapter).

The *Salon Nicté-Ha*, just across the highway from the road to the ruins, on the grounds of the Hotel Hacienda Uxmal, is an informal air-con restaurant offering sandwiches, fruit salads and similar fare at prices slightly higher than those at the Yax-Beh. There's a swimming pool for restaurant patrons. It's open 1 to 8 pm daily.

Top End Mayaland Resorts' *Hotel Hacienda Uxmal* (☎ 926-2012, fax 926-2011, in the USA ☎ 800-235-4079), 500m from the ruins and across the highway, originally housed the archaeologists who explored and restored Uxmal. High ceilings with fans, good cross ventilation and wide, tiled verandahs set with rocking chairs make this an exceptionally pleasant and comfortable place to stay. The beautiful swimming pool is a dream come true on a sweltering hot day. Simple rooms in the annex cost US$50 a single or double; the nicer rooms in the main building go for US$70. Meals are unremarkable and moderately priced.

Another Mayaland Resort, *The Lodge at Uxmal* (☎ 923-2202, fax 925-0087, in the USA ☎ 800-235-4079), just opposite the entrance to the Unidad Uxmal and the archaeological site, is Uxmal's newest, most luxurious hotel, and the closest to the ruins. Air-con rooms with all the comforts cost US$120 a single or double. If you can live without the air-con, you'll save US$30 a room. There's a pool and a pleasing restaurant-bar on the premises (the service is slow and the food so-so).

Hotel Villa Arqueológica Uxmal (☎/fax 928-0644, in the USA ☎ 800-258-2633, in France ☎ 801-802-803), run by Club Med, is an attractive modern hotel with swimming pool, tennis courts, a French-inspired restaurant and air-con guest rooms for US$60 a single or double.

The *Hotel Misión Park Inn Uxmal* (☎ 924-7308, fax 924-2516, in the USA ☎ 800-448-8355) is set on a hilltop 2km north of the turnoff to the ruins. Many rooms have balcony views of Uxmal, but they are a bit overpriced at US$80 a single or double. There's a lovely pool on the premises.

Getting There & Away

From Mérida's old Terminal de Autobuses, it's 80km (1½ hours) to Uxmal. The inland route between Mérida and Campeche passes Uxmal, and most buses coming from the cities will drop you at Uxmal. However, when you want to leave, buses may be full and not stop.

The daily Ruta Puuc excursion (US$4.50), run by Autotransportes del Sur, departs Mérida's old Terminal de Autobuses at 8 am, goes to Uxmal, Kabah and several other sites, and departs from Uxmal on the return journey to Mérida at 2:30 pm, returning to Mérida by 4 pm. If you're going to Ticul, hop on a bus heading north, get off at Muna and get another bus eastwards to Ticul.

For buses to Kabah, the Ruta Puuc turnoff and points on the road to Campeche, flag down a bus at the turnoff to the ruins.

THE PUUC ROUTE

The Puuc Route, or Ruta Puuc, is the name given to the road that winds through the Puuc Hills from the graceful ancient Mayan city of Uxmal to the Grutas de Loltún (Loltún Caves). Along the route, which bisects vast expanses of dense brush and fields once cleared for crops but long since abandoned, are the other partially restored ruins of Kabah, Sayil, Xlapak and Labná.

Uxmal is the most awesome of the lost cities along this scenic route, which were home to a powerful and artistic civilization from at least 600 to 900 AD. For reasons that

baffle experts, the cities were abandoned long before the Spanish arrived.

Uxmal is a must-see, but the Codz Poop (Palace of Masks) at Kabah and El Palacio at Sayil are also very impressive and well worth visiting. The Grutas de Loltún, a spectacular cave system used by the Maya, make for fun touring.

The best way to see these sites is via rental car or guided tour. Many tours of the region are available in Mérida and Cancún. It is also possible to move from one site to another via local bus, but these buses are infrequent.

YUCATÁN STATE

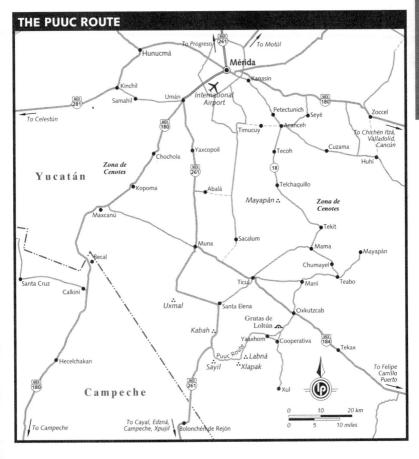

An excellent option is to make your way to Muna in time to catch a tour bus departing for Labná, Sayil, Xlapak, Kabah and Uxmal at 9 am, and returning you to Muna at 2:45 pm. The cost of the tour is US$4. Be advised there are no hotels in Muna, but there are a number of decent places to stay in Ticul, only 22km away.

Kabah

The ruins of Kabah, just over 18km southeast of Uxmal, are right astride Hwy 261. The sign says 'Zona Arqueológica Puuc.' The site is open 8 am to 5 pm daily. Admission costs US$2, free on Sunday.

The guard shack and souvenir shop are on the east side of the highway as you approach. Cold drinks and junky snacks are sold.

Undoubtedly the most impressive building here is the **Codz Poop** (El Palacio de los Mascarones; Palace of Masks), set on its own high terrace on the east side of the highway.

KABAH

To Camping Sacbé, Santa Elena, Uxmal, Mérida

MEX 261

Las Tumbas

Tercera Casa (Templo de las Columnas)

Gran Teocalli

El Arco

Office

El Palacio

To El Cuadrángulo del Oeste

La Pirámide de los Mascarones

La Casa de las Brujas

El Palacio de los Mascarones (Codz Poop)

0   100   200 m
0   100   200 yards

MEX 261

To Campeche

It's an amazing sight, with its façade covered in nearly 300 masks of Chac, the rain god or sky serpent.

To the north of the Palace of Masks is a small **pyramid** (La Pirámide de los Mascarones). Farther north is **El Palacio**, with a broad façade having several doorways; in the center of each doorway is a column, a characteristic of the Puuc architectural style. Walk around the north side of El Palacio and follow a path into the jungle for several hundred meters to the **Tercera Casa**, also called the Temple de las Columnas (Temple of Columns), which is famous for the rows of semi-columns on the upper part of its façade.

Cross the highway to the west of El Palacio, walk up the slope and on your right you'll pass a high mound of stones that was once the **Gran Teocalli**, or Great Temple. Continue straight on to the *sacbé*, or cobbled and elevated ceremonial road, and look right to see a ruined monumental arch with the Mayan corbeled vault (two straight stone surfaces leaning against one another, meeting at the top). It is said that the sacbé here runs past the arch and through the jungle all the way to Uxmal, terminating at a smaller arch; in the other direction it goes to Labná. Once, all of the Yucatán Peninsula was connected by these marvelous sacbeob, or 'white roads' of rough limestone.

Beyond the sacbé, about 600m farther from the road, are several other complexes of buildings, none as impressive as what you've already seen. **El Cuadrángulo del Oeste** (Western Quadrangle) has some decoration of columns and masks. North of the quadrangle are the **Temple of the Key Patterns** and the **Templo de los Dinteles** (Temple of Lintels); the latter once had intricately carved lintels of tough sapodilla wood.

Places to Stay & Eat The quiet, well-kept *Camping Sacbé* (no phone), on the south side of the village of Santa Elena, 7.5km north of Kabah, has two simple but pleasant and clean rooms with spotless shared bathrooms for US$8/10 single/double and two rooms with private bathrooms for US$11/13. Camping in a parklike setting costs US$2.50 per person. There are even spaces for motor

homes (six with electricity, for US$8 per motor home). Good breakfasts and dinners are served at low prices. If you stay here, it is possible to catch a local bus to the Ruta Puuc ruins, and the English-speaking owner even provides bus schedules. This place offers tremendous value. Its only drawback is the lack of telephone, which prohibits reserving one of the four rooms.

Getting There & Away Kabah is 101km from Mérida, a ride of about two hours, and just over 18km south of Uxmal. The inland route between Mérida and Campeche passes Kabah, and most buses coming from the cities will drop you here.

To return to Mérida, stand on the east side of the road at the entrance to the ruins and try to flag down a bus. Buses in both directions are often full, however, and won't stop, so it may be a good idea to try organize a lift back with some other travelers at the site itself. Many visitors come to Kabah by private car and may be willing to give you a lift, either back to Mérida, or southward on the Ruta Puuc. If you're leaving Kabah headed for Sayil, Xlapak and Labná, stand on the west side of the highway.

Sayil

Five kilometers south of Kabah a road turns east off Hwy 261. Signs indicate it only as being part of the Ruta Puuc. Despite the interesting archaeological sites along the route, there is not much traffic, and hitchhiking can be difficult. The ruins of Sayil are 4.5km east of the junction with Hwy 261, on the south side of the road. The site is open 8 am to 5 pm daily; admission costs US$2, free on Sunday.

El Palacio Sayil is best known for El Palacio, the huge three-tiered building with a façade some 85m long, reminiscent of the Minoan palaces on Crete. The distinctive columns of Puuc architecture are used here over and over, as supports for the lintels, as decoration between doorways and as a frieze above the doorways, alternating with huge stylized Chac masks and 'descending gods.'

Climb to the top level of the Palacio and look to the north to see several *chultunes*, stone-lined cisterns in which precious rainwater was collected and stored for use during the dry season. Some of these chultunes can hold more than 30,000 liters.

El Mirador If you take the path southwards from the palace for about 800m you come to the temple named El Mirador, with its interesting roosterlike roofcomb once painted bright red. About 100m beyond El Mirador, by the path to the left, is a stela beneath a protective palapa. It bears a relief of a phallic god, now badly weathered.

Xlapak

From the entrance gate at Sayil, it's 6km east to the entrance gate at Xlapak ('shla-PAK'). The name means Old Walls in Mayan and was a general term among local people for ancient ruins, about which they knew little. The site is open 8 am to 5 pm daily; admission is US$2, free on Sunday.

The ornate palace at Xlapak is smaller than those at Kabah and Sayil, measuring only about 20m in length. It's decorated with the inevitable Chac masks, columns and

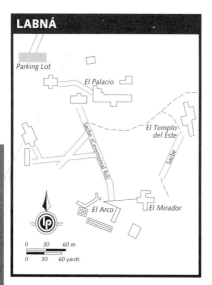

LABNÁ

Parking Lot

El Palacio

El Templo del Este

Sacbé (Ceremonial Rd)

Sacbé

El Arco

El Mirador

0   30   60 m
0   30   60 yards

colonnettes and fretted geometric latticework of the Puuc style. To the right is the rubble of what were once two smaller buildings.

Labná

From the entrance gate at Xlapak, it's 3.5km east to the gate at Labná. The site here is open 8 am to 5 pm daily; admission costs US$2.

El Arco Labná is best known for its magnificent arch, once part of a building that separated two quadrangular courtyards. It now appears to be a gate joining two small plazas. The corbeled structure, 3m wide and 6m high, is well preserved and stands close to the entrance of Labná. The mosaic reliefs decorating the upper façade are exuberantly Puuc in style.

If you look at the ornate work on the northeastern side of the arch, you will make out mosaics of Mayan huts. At the base of either side of the arch are rooms of the adjoining building, now ruined, including upper lattice patterns constructed atop a serpentine design.

El Mirador Standing on the opposite side of the arch, and separated from it by the

limestone-paved sacbé, is a pyramid with a temple atop it called El Mirador. The pyramid itself is poorly preserved, being largely stone rubble. The temple, with its 5m-high roofcomb, true to its name, looks like a watchtower.

El Palacio Archaeologists believe that at one point in the 9th century, some 3000 Maya lived at Labná. To support such numbers in these arid hills, water was collected in chultunes. At Labná's peak there were some 60 chultunes in and around the city; several are still visible.

The palace, the first edifice you come to at Labná, is connected by a sacbé to El Mirador and the arch. One of the longest buildings in the Puuc Hills, its design is not as impressive as its counterpart at Sayil. There's a ghoulish sculpture at the eastern corner of the upper level of a serpent gripping a human head between its jaws. Close to this carving is a well-preserved Chac mask.

GRUTAS DE LOLTÚN

From Labná it's 15km eastward to the village of Yaaxhom, surrounded by lush orchards and palm groves, which are surprising in this generally dry region. From Yaaxhom a road goes another 4km northeast to Loltún.

The Grutas de Loltún (Loltún Caves), the most interesting and largest cave system in Yucatán, provided a treasure trove of data for archaeologists studying the Maya. Carbon dating of artifacts found here reveals that the caves were first used by humans 2500 years ago. Chest-high murals of hands, faces, animals and geometric motifs were apparent as recently as 20 years ago, but so many people have touched them that scarcely a trace of them remains. Today, visitors to the illuminated caves mostly see natural limestone formations, some of which are quite lovely.

Loltún is open 9 am to 5 pm daily; admission is US$4. To explore the labyrinth, you must take a scheduled guided tour at 9:30 or 11 am, or at 12:30, 2, 3 or 4 pm, but these may depart early if enough people are waiting. The English-speaking guides may be willing

to take you through at other hours if you offer a few dollars' tip. The guides, who are not paid by the government, expect a tip at the end of the hourlong tour (US$3 per person is the norm).

For refreshments there's the **Restaurant El Guerrero**, near the exit of the caves, a walk of eight to 10 minutes (600m) along a marked path from the far side of the parking lot near the cave entrance. Once you get to the restaurant you'll find that the comida corrida costs about US$7. Near-ice-cold drinks are served at high prices.

Getting There & Away

Loltún is on a country road that leads to Oxkutzcab ('Osh-kootz-KAHB,' 8km) and there is usually some transport available along the road. Colectivos – often a *camioneta* (pickup truck) or *camión* (truck or lorry) – regularly ply this route, charging just US$0.50 for a ride. A taxi from Oxkutzcab may charge US$6 or so, one way, for the 8km ride.

There are frequent buses daily between Mérida and Oxkutzcab via Ticul.

If you're driving from Loltún to Labná, drive out of the Loltún parking lot, turn right and take the next road on the right, which passes the access road to the restaurant. Do not take the road marked for Xul. After 4km you'll come to the village of Yaaxhom, where you turn right to join the Ruta Puuc westwards.

TICUL

☎ 9 • pop 26,887

Ticul, 30km northeast of Uxmal, is the largest town south of Mérida in this ruin-rich region. It has several agreeable hotels and restaurants, and good transport – although there is no public transportation available to the Ruta Puuc from here. (It is possible to stay the night in Ticul and catch a bus to Muna in time to catch a tour bus that travels from Muna to the Ruta Puuc ruins; see Ticul's Getting There & Away section for details.) Ticul is also a center for fine huipil weaving, and ceramics made here from the local red clay are renowned throughout the Yucatán.

Lush palm groves surround Las Grutas de Loltún.

Due to the number of Mayan ruins in the vicinity from which to steal building blocks, and the number of Mayans in the area converting to Christianity, Franciscan friars built many churches in the region that is now southern Yucatán state. Among these churches is the one at Ticul, construction of which dates from the late 16th century.

Although looted on several occasions, the church is remarkable for its many original touches, including: the choir window which bears a date of 1625, most likely the year the church was commemorated; doorway-flanking stone statues of friars in primitive style; and a Black Christ altarpiece ringed by crude medallions.

Saturday mornings are particularly memorable in Ticul. It's then that Calle 23 in the vicinity of the public market (mercado) is closed to motorized traffic and the street fills with 'rickshaws' (three-wheeled cycles) that are used to transport shoppers between the meat-and-produce market and their homes.

Orientation & Information

Ticul's main street is Calle 23, sometimes called the Calle Principal, going from the highway northeast past the market and the town's best restaurants to the main plaza, or Plaza Mayor.

A post office faces the plaza, as does a Bital bank, and the bus station is less than 100m away. A cultural center was under construction nearby at the time this was written. A tourist office had yet to open. There's a Telmex office on Calle 23 between Calles 26A and 28; long-distance calls can be placed there or from any of the Ladatel pay phones around town.

Places to Stay

New in 1997, the **Hotel Plaza** (☎ 970-1997, fax 972-0026) is the best hotel in town. Located on Calle 23 at Calle 26, the Plaza offers 17 rooms with air-con, telephone and cable TV for US$22. It also offers five rooms with fan instead of air-con for US$18. The rooms ring a lovely courtyard with a huge mango tree in the middle of it.

The **Hotel Sierra Sosa** (☎ 972-0008, fax 972-0282, Calle 26 No 199A), half a block northwest of the plaza, has basic but decent rooms for US$12 with fan, US$18 with air-con. A few rooms at the back have windows, but most are dark. For the money, the Sierra Sosa offers very good value.

The **Hotel San Miguel** (☎ 972-0382, Calle 28 No 195), near Calle 23 and the market, used to be a good deal but its rooms are now very worn. Singles at the San Miguel cost US$5, doubles US$6 to US$7, with fan and bath.

Places to Eat

Ticul's lively **market** provides all the ingredients for picnics and snacks. It also has lots of those wonderful market eateries where the food is good, the portions generous and the prices low. For variety, try out some of the **loncherías** along Calle 23 between Calles 26 and 30.

For bread and sweet rolls, there's **El Buen Samaritano**, on Calle 23 west of Calle 26. For a sit-down meal, there's the cheap **Restaurant El Colorín**, Calle 26 No 199B, half a block northwest of the plaza. Have a look at **La Carmelita**, on the opposite side of the Hotel Sierra Sosa, as well.

The **Jarro Café**, facing the main plaza, is an attractive Mexican-style café with cheap but decent food: burgers (US$1.75), a vegetarian sandwich (US$1), burritos (US$1.50) and tacos (US$2.50). Also served here are numerous nonalcoholic beverages, none more than US$1.50. This is a good place to sip beer or juice in the evening.

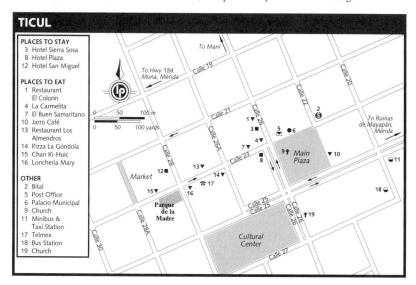

TICUL

PLACES TO STAY
3 Hotel Sierra Sosa
8 Hotel Plaza
12 Hotel San Miguel

PLACES TO EAT
1 Restaurant
   El Colorín
4 La Carmelita
7 El Buen Samaritano
10 Jarro Café
13 Restaurant Los
   Almendros
14 Pizza La Góndola
15 Chan Ki-Huic
16 Lonchería Mary

OTHER
2 Bital
5 Post Office
6 Palacio Municipal
9 Church
11 Minibus &
   Taxi Station
17 Telmex
18 Bus Station
19 Church

Pizza La Góndola, Calle 23 at Calle 26A, serves the best pizza in Ticul, but it isn't really all that good. Prices range from US$4 to US$6. A half-dozen pastas are also available here. *Chan Ki-Huic*, on Calle 23 west of Calle 28, is bright and clean. The *Lonchería Mary*, on Calle 23 east of Calle 28, is a clean, family-run place.

Restaurant Los Almendros (Calle 23 No 207), between Calles 26A and 28, specializes in Yucatecan food. The *combinado yucateco* (Yucatecan combination plate), with a soft drink or beer, costs less than US$7 and offers a fine sampling of local specialties. This is the best restaurant in town.

Shopping
If you are in the market for pottery, shops near the city center sell the most interesting ceramics available in Yucatán; the techniques used in Ticul predate the Conquest by hundreds of years.

Getting There & Away
Bus Ticul's bus station is behind the massive church off the main square. Mayab makes the 85km, 1½-hour run between Mérida and Ticul every 40 minutes during daylight hours for US$3. There are also five buses to Felipe Carrillo Puerto (US$7), frequent ones to Oxkutzcab (US$1), and nine a day to Chetumal (6½ hours, US$9.50). There are also eight buses to Cancún each day (US$13).

It's also possible to take a minibus (combi) from the minibus station and taxi stand, at the corner of Calles 20 and 25, to Oxkutzcab (16km) and the Grutas de Loltún (8km away). If you decide to go to the caves, ask for the camión to Xul ('shool'), but get off at the Grutas de Loltún.

Minibuses to Santa Elena (15km), the village between Uxmal and Kabah, also depart from the intersection of Calles 23 and 28, taking a back road and then leaving you to catch another bus northwest to Uxmal (15km) or south to Kabah (3.5km). You may find it more convenient to take a minibus or bus to Muna (22km) on Hwy 261 and another south to Uxmal (16km).

An excellent option for Ruta Puuc-bound travelers is to catch one of the early-morning buses from Ticul to Muna, where a tour bus departs for Labná, Sayil, Xlapak, Kabah and Uxmal at 9 am and returns you to Muna at 2:45 pm. Any of the 6, 6:30, 7:10 or 8 am buses leaving Ticul for Muna will get you there in time to catch the Ruta Puuc tour bus. Cost of the Ticul-Muna bus is US$0.60. The Ruta Puuc tour bus costs US$4.

Car Those headed eastwards to Quintana Roo and the Caribbean coast by car can go via Hwy 184 from Muna and Ticul via Oxkutzcab to Tekax and Tzucacab. At Polyuc, 130km southeast from Ticul, a road turns left (east), ending after 80km in Felipe Carrillo Puerto, 210km from Ticul, where there are hotels, restaurants, fuel stations, banks and other services. The right fork of the road goes south to the region of Laguna Bacalar.

From Oxkutzcab to Felipe Carrillo Puerto or Bacalar there are few services: very few places to eat (those that exist are rock-bottom basic), no hotels and few fuel stations. Mostly you see small, typical Yucatecan villages with their traditional Mayan na, *topes* (speed bumps) and agricultural activity.

Getting Around
The local method of getting around is to hire a three-wheeled cycle, Ticul's answer to the rickshaw. You'll see them on Calle 23 immediately east of the market, and the fare is less than US$0.50 for a short trip.

TICUL TO VALLADOLID
The 239km route from Ticul to Valladolid via Tihosuco is seldom traveled by tourists. The highways that link the three cities variously pass through farmland and jungle and occasionally offer travelers a glimpse of Mayan life that has changed little in recent centuries. Indeed, the Maya in these parts entered the 21st century continuing to honor the gods of rain, wind and agriculture, and to hold religious ceremonies in their fields presided over by a wise man, just as their ancestors had done before them.

Along this route it's still possible to find hamlets of thatched wooden huts nearly identical to those used by the ancient Maya a millennium ago. The homes of today's rural

Maya are still rectangular-shaped, wood-framed huts with lean-to roofs of palm. The walls are made of bamboo poles or branches, and the spaces between the poles are often filled with mud to keep rats and other pests out.

The typical Mayan home is generally no bigger than a two-car garage, and the dwelling may be divided into two rooms by a curtain or wall, with one room used as a kitchen and the other as a living room and sleeping area. Contemporary Maya prefer hammocks to beds, just like their ancestors.

Never more than a stone's throw from the hut is a *milpa*, or corn field. Corn tortillas remain the staple of the Mayan diet, but the Maya also raise pigs and turkeys and produce honey, squash and other crops, which they sell in town markets.

Except in the towns of Oxkutzcab, Tekax and Tihosuco, which offer budget accommodations, there are no hotels to be found along roads connecting Ticul, Tihosuco and Valladolid. The towns along this route are linked by combis and, less frequently, local buses; they may be hailed from roadside.

Oxkutzcab

Located 16km southeast of Ticul, Oxkutzcab is renowned for its daily produce market and its colonial church. Markets were the principal means of trade for the ancient Maya, and the peninsula's indigenous people continue to travel from the countryside to central communities to exchange produce at stalls beside a main square. Oxkutzcab is such a community.

Here, alongside Hwy 184, which becomes a slow-moving, two-lane road as it passes through central Oxkutzcab, the visitor can't miss seeing the magnificent Franciscan mission at the center of town, out front of which is the sprawling produce market.

One of the interesting features of the open-sided produce market is the similarity between a colorful mural that appears on the church's façade and the scene inside the market. At times the mural, which contains images of Mayan women in traditional dress selling fruit and Mayan men out front of the market unloading trucks, resembles a

snapshot of the scene around it. The church is remarkable mostly for its ornamental façade, at the center of which is a stone statue of St Francis, the mission patron. Pinnacles decorate the two enormous belfries flanking the statue of the saint, and sharp-eyed visitors can make out worn statues of friars between the bell openings. The church, which was constructed at a snail's pace from 1640 to 1693, is also remarkable for its magnificent altarpiece. Indeed, it's one of only a few baroque altarpieces in the Yucatán to survive the revolts that have occurred since its construction. Among the many finely detailed features of the altarpiece are six relief panels that illustrate the main events in the lives of Christ and the Virgin. Images of friars and saints surround the Virgin, and tokens of thanks appear at the foot of the shrine.

Tekax

Unlike the church at Oxkutzcab, the one in Tekax has been looted a couple of times, initially during the War of the Castes and later during the Mexican Revolution. Still, it's worth a visit if you happen to be in the area.

Situated in an increasingly prosperous area, due to a successful crop switch from corn to sugarcane and citrus, Tekax in recent years replaced the church's damaged floor with a beautiful tiled floor and added a lovely new stone altar. The interior was whitewashed and looks probably as good as it ever did.

According to *Maya Missions: Exploring the Spanish Colonial Churches of Yucatán*, a fabulous book by Richard and Rosalind Perry, during construction of the church one of the church's belfries collapsed, burying (and presumably crushing) the many indigenous laborers beneath it under tons of rubble. Miraculously, as local legend has it, no one lost their life in the collapse, and construction thereafter continued uneventfully until completion.

Also noteworthy is the shape of the church, which undoubtedly was constructed of materials taken from nearby Mayan temples. The general form of the church is that of a three-tiered pyramid. Possibly the

architecture took the shape from the Mayan structure from which the building blocks were taken.

Certainly not 'borrowed' from the Maya are the Moorish belfries at the front corners of the building, and a framed relief of the Franciscan coat of arms situated atop an elaborately decorated doorway. Inside, only the simply carved scalloped basins are original; everything else that could have been destroyed or removed with ease is gone.

Tihosuco (Quintana Roo)

Tihosuco, which is located several kilometers inside the state of Quintana Roo, was a major military outpost for the Spanish during the late 16th century and for 300 years thereafter. During this time, the town came under numerous Mayan assaults, and in 1686 it was attacked, though not sacked, by pirates led by legendary Dutch buccaneer Lorencillo.

During many of those attacks, the Spaniards retreated to the heavily fortified 17th-century church at the center of town, which for much of its life served as both a house of God and an arsenal and stronghold. At one time it was quite beautiful, with ornamental details throughout and a colonnaded façade that was pure artwork.

But the town and church fell to rebel hands in 1866 following a long siege, and much of the magnificent building was gutted. Today, a third of the roof is gone, as is more than half of the façade. What remains of the once-great church is still worth investigating if time permits.

Also in Tihosuco, located in an 18th-century building one block straight ahead of the church, is the Museo de la Guerra de Castas (Museum of the War of the Castes). This little-visited and fairly unimpressive museum houses lots of paintings and weapons from the war. Signs are in Spanish only. The museum does not hold regular hours.

TICUL TO MÉRIDA

From Ticul to Mérida you have a choice of routes: The western route is via Muna and Yaxcopoil, while the eastern route is via the Ruinas de Mayapán.

Via Muna & Yaxcopoil

The western route to Muna, then north on Hwy 261 to Mérida via Yaxcopoil, is fastest, with the best bus services.

Muna, an old town 22km northwest of Ticul, has several interesting colonial churches, including the former Convento de la Asunción and the churches of Santa María, San Mateo and San Andrés. It's worth a brief visit. Be advised that there are no hotels in town.

Muna is a major transportation hub for the area. From Muna it's possible to take Mayab buses to: Mérida (18 buses daily, US$1.70); Felipe Carrillo Puerto (six buses daily, US$6.40); Cancún (at 7 and 10:35 am, US$12.50); Playa del Carmen (at 9 and 11 pm, US$10.60); Uxmal (at 7, 9 and 10 am and 1:30 and 6 pm, US$0.50); Ticul and Oxkutzcab (hourly from 5 am to 10 pm, US$0.40 and US$1.10); Campeche (at 7 and 10 am and 1:30 and 6 pm, US$4).

The hacienda of Yaxcopoil, 29km north of Muna on the west side of Hwy 261, has numerous French Renaissance-style buildings that have been restored and turned collectively into a museum of the 17th century (open from 8 am to 5 pm Tuesday through Saturday, 9 am to 1 pm Sunday; US$2.50). This vast estate specialized in the growing and processing of henequen. (Read the boxed text, 'Yucatán's Past Tied to Natural Rope,' earlier in this chapter, for the story of henequen cultivation.)

From Yaxcopoil it's 16km north to Umán, and then another 17km to the center of Mérida.

Via Ruinas de Mayapán

The eastern route north follows Yucatán state Hwy 18 from Ticul via the ruins of Mayapán to Tecoh, Acanceh and Mérida. The Ruinas de Mayapán themselves are coved separately in the next section. Transport on this route is difficult without your own car. Buses and colectivos run fitfully, so you should plan the better part of a day, with stops in Ruinas de Mayapán and Acanceh, to travel the route by public transport.

Those taking this route should be careful to distinguish between Ruinas de Mayapán,

the ruins of the ancient city, and Mayapán, a Mayan village some 40km southeast of the ruins past the town of Teabo.

If you're driving to the ruins, follow the signs from Ticul northeast via Chapab to Mama (25km), which has a peculiarly fortresslike church, then farther northeast to Tekit (7km). At Tekit, turn left (northwest) on Yucatán state Hwy 18 toward Tecoh, Acanceh and Kanasin. The Ruinas de Mayapán are 8km northwest of Tekit on the west side of the road.

RUINAS DE MAYAPÁN

The city of Mayapán, once a major Mayan capital, was huge, with a population estimated at around 12,000. Its ruins cover several sq km, all surrounded by a great defensive wall. More than 3500 buildings, 20 cenotes and traces of the city wall were mapped by archaeologists working in the 1950s and early '60s.

However, the city's workmanship was inferior to the great age of Mayan art; though the Cocom rulers of Mayapán tried to revive the past glories of Mayan civilization, they succeeded only in part. Despite the city's past importance, its architecture is nothing special, and a visit to the partially restored ruins of Mayapán after seeing Uxmal or Chichén Itzá will likely disappoint.

History

Mayapán was supposedly founded by Kukulcán (Quetzalcóatl) in 1007, shortly after the former ruler of Tula arrived in Yucatán. His dynasty, the Cocom, organized a confederation of city-states that included Uxmal, Chichén Itzá and many other notable cities. Despite their alliance, animosity between the Cocoms and the Itzaes during the late 1100s led to the storming of Chichén Itzá by the Cocoms, which forced the Itzá rulers into exile. The Cocom dynasty under Hunac Ceel Canuch emerged supreme in all of the northern Yucatán Peninsula and obliged the other rulers to pay tribute.

Cocom supremacy lasted for almost $2^{1/2}$ centuries, until the ruler of Uxmal, Ah Xupán Xiú, led a rebellion of the oppressed city-states and overthrew Cocom hegemony.

The great capital of Mayapán was utterly destroyed and remained uninhabited ever after.

But there was no peace in Yucatán after the Xiú victory. The Cocom dynasty recovered and frequent struggles for power erupted until 1542, when Francisco de Montejo the Younger founded Mérida. The ruler of the Xiú people, Ah Kukum Xiú, submitted his forces to Montejo's control in exchange for a military alliance against the Cocoms. The Cocoms were defeated, but the Xiú rulers realized – too late – that they had willingly signed the death warrant of Mayan independence.

Ruins

Jungle has returned to cover many of the buildings, but several of the larger ones have been restored and you can visit several cenotes (including Itzmal Chen, a main Mayan religious sanctuary). Though the ruins today are far less impressive than those at other sites, Mayapán has a stillness and a loneliness (usually undisturbed by other tourists) that seems to fit its sorrowful later history.

The site is open 8 am to 5 pm daily; admission costs US$2.

RUINAS DE MAYAPÁN TO MÉRIDA

About 2km north of the Ruinas de Mayapán is **Telchaquillo**. Beneath the village plaza is a vast cenote filled with rainwater, which is still used today as a water source during the dry months.

From Telchaquillo it's 11km north to **Tecoh**, with its church and well-kept Palacio Municipal separated by a green soccer field. From Tecoh it's only 35km to Mérida, but you should plan a short stop in **Acanceh**, where the step-pyramid is a rare example of a surviving Early-Classic pyramid.

The road enters Acanceh and goes to the main plaza, which is flanked by a shady park and the church. To the left of the church is a partially restored pyramid (admission US$1.50), and to the right are market *loncherías* if you're in need of a snack. In the park, note the statue of the smiling deer; the name Acanceh means 'Pond of the

Deer.' Another local sight of interest is the cantina *Aqui Me Queda* (I'm Staying Here), a ready-made answer for husbands whose wives come to urge them homeward.

Continuing northwest you pass through Petectunich, Tepich, San Antonio and Kanasin before coming to Mérida's *periférico* (ring road).

Campeche State

Although it's the least-visited of Yucatán's three states, Campeche has a lot to offer the tourist. Among its top attractions: the uncrowded Mayan archaeological sites of Edzná, Calakmul and Chicanná; the impressive walled city of Campeche, with its ancient fortresses and colonial architecture; and the Reserva de la Biosfera Calakmul, the largest biosphere reserve in Mexico.

Geographically, the state contains much of the flat landscape found elsewhere on the peninsula, but instead of the light forest and brush found in Yucatán state and northern Quintana Roo, one-third of Campeche's 56,000 sq km is covered with jaguar-approved jungle. Likewise, several sizable above-ground rivers and lots of hills are located in the southern part of the state, which borders Guatemala and Tabasco. Marshlands, ponds and inlets are common along the state's coastline, which faces the dark and generally uninviting waters of the Gulf of Mexico (sorry, no Caribbeanlike beaches here).

Historically, the state is renowned more for its marauders than for its Mayans. For more than 200 years, pirates plagued the western coast of the peninsula, pillaging ships and towns alike with all the wanton cruelty men of their ilk could muster. Today,

the state capital of Campeche still boasts many of the fortifications erected during the 17th century to keep pirates out.

But the state also boasts some very impressive Mayan ruins that have been partially restored in recent years. The former independent kingdom of Edzná, for instance, is home to an elegant five-story temple that is simply breathtaking in afternoon sunlight. Edzná's Platform of the Knives and its Temple of the Masks are as intriguing as their names.

Calakmul, located at the heart of the biosphere reserve, was once a great city of the order of Tikal in Guatemala. Covering no less than 100 sq km, today only a fraction of it has been restored, but staring out across the endless jungle that surrounds it from atop one of the site's numerous pyramids leaves a lasting impression.

Chicanná, or 'House of the Snake's Jaws,' is remarkable for a profusely garnished façade that is believed to depict the face of the god Itzamná, Lord of the Heavens, Creator of all things. The low, stone building features a dramatic entrance that is said to resemble the gaping jaws of the chief deity, and when you look upon it you can't help but think it's true.

The great Reserva de la Biosfera Calakmul is so vast and jungly and virtually void of humans that, for all practical purposes, it's best left alone save for the sprawling Mayan ruins of Calakmul. With no trails except those that now wind through the ancient city, it would take very little effort to lose one's way and perish in the sea of rain forest.

However, when you've got jungle trails *and* mighty Mayan ruins together, as you have at the long-ago-abandoned city of Calakmul, there's no reason for anyone to take a 'walk in the woods' anywhere else in the reserve. With only a handful of people visiting the extremely remote site on any given day, a jungle trek at Calakmul is a true adventure.

Highlights

- Campeche, once treasured by pirates, now rich in history
- Calakmul, a vast semi-restored ancient city in a sea of rain forest
- Edzná, remnants of a Mayan city that are strikingly picturesque
- Becán, 'Path of the Snake,' an abandoned city atop a rock outcrop
- Becal, a sleepy town, most of whose residents make hats in caves

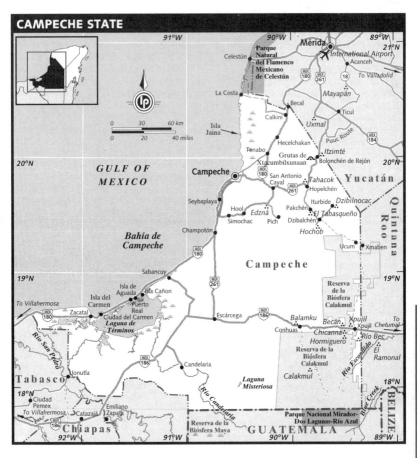

CAMPECHE STATE

CAMPECHE STATE

CAMPECHE

☎ 9 • pop 178,160

With colonial buildings and fortifications, the center of Campeche is quite visually appealing. The local economy is fueled by shrimp fishing and oil mining, and the prosperity brought by those two activities is apparent in the downtown area (unfortunately, the wealth hasn't reached several of Campeche's residential areas). During its heyday, many wealthy Spanish families lived in Campeche, and some built mansions that still stand. No fewer than seven *baluartes* (bastions) have survived the times as well, as

have large segments of Campeche's famous protective wall. Many of the city's downtown streets are paved with cut stone taken from the segments of the wall that were brought down. Of the seven bastions, six survive in their original (slightly dilapidated) state and one has been restored. Today, one of the original 18th-century forts contains a fine museum that houses exhibits of Mayan jade art, while another is home to a lovely botanical garden. Campeche's fortifications and other colonial constructions are the city's chief attractions and can be visited on a walking tour.

Pirates & More Pirates

As early as the mid-16th century, Campeche was flourishing as the Yucatán Peninsula's major port under the careful planning of Viceroy Hernández de Córdoba. Locally grown timber, chicle and dyewoods were major exports to Europe, as were gold and silver mined from other regions and shipped from Campeche.

Such wealth did not escape the notice of pirates, who arrived only six years after the town was founded. For two centuries, the depredations of pirates terrorized Campeche. Not only were ships attacked, but the port itself was invaded, its citizens robbed, its women raped and its buildings burned. In the buccaneers' Hall of Fame were the infamous John Hawkins, Diego the Mulatto, Laurent de Gaff, Barbillas and the notorious 'Pegleg' himself, Pato de Palo. In their most gruesome assault, in early 1663, the various pirate hordes set aside their jealousies to converge as a single flotilla upon the city, where they massacred many of Campeche's citizens.

It took this tragedy to make the Spanish monarchy take preventive action, but not until five years later. Starting in 1668, 3.5m-thick ramparts were built. After 18 years of construction, a 2.5km hexagon incorporating eight strategically placed *baluartes*, or bastions, surrounded the city. A segment of the ramparts extended out to sea so that ships literally had to sail into a fortress, easily defended, to gain access to the city.

With Campeche nearly impregnable, the pirates turned their attention to ships at sea

and other ports. In response, in 1717, the brilliant naval strategist Felipe de Aranda started attacking the buccaneers and in time made the Gulf of Mexico safe from piracy.

History

Once a Mayan trading village called Ah Kim Pech (Lord Sun Sheep-Tick), Campeche was first entered by the Spaniards in 1517. The Maya resisted, and for nearly a quarter of a century the Spaniards were unable to fully conquer the region. Colonial Campeche was founded in 1531, but later abandoned due to Mayan hostility. By 1540 the conquistadors had gained sufficient control, under the leadership of Francisco de Montejo the Younger, to found a settlement here that survived. They named it the Villa de San Francisco de Campeche.

The settlement soon flourished as the major port of the Yucatán Peninsula, but suffered from pirate attacks from an early date. After a particularly appalling attack in 1663 that left the city in ruins, the king of Spain ordered construction of Campeche's famous bastions, which put an end to the periodic carnage.

Orientation

Though the bastions still stand, the city walls themselves have been mostly razed and replaced by Av Circuito Baluartes, or Circular Ave of the Bulwarks, which rings the city center just as the walls once did.

Besides the modern Plaza Moch-Cuouh, Campeche also has its Parque Principal, also called the Plaza de la Independencia, a standard Spanish colonial park with a cathedral on one side and the former Palacio de Gobierno on another.

According to the compass, Campeche is oriented with its waterfront to the northwest, but tradition and convenience hold that the water is to the west, inland is east (we observe that rule in the following text). The street grid is numbered so that streets running north-south have even numbers, while east-west streets have odd numbers; street numbers ascend toward the south and the west.

Information

Tourist Offices A state-run Coordinación General de Turismo (☎ 816-6068, 816-6767) is on Calle 57, opposite the Parque Principal. The staff is very friendly and available 9 am to 1 pm and 5 to 8 pm daily.

The city maintains a Coordinación Municipal de Turismo, on Calle 55 at Calle 8, just west of the cathedral facing the Parque Principal. It does not maintain regular hours.

Money Banks are open 9 am to 4 pm Monday to Friday, 9 am to 1 pm Saturday. Most have ATMs. See the map for locations.

Post & Communications The central post office is at the corner of Av 16 de Septiembre and Calle 53, in the Edificio Federal, or Federal Building. Hours are 8 am to 7 pm Monday to Friday, 8 am to 1 pm Saturday, 8 am to 2 pm Sunday.

There are plenty of pay phones around town that accept Ladatel debit cards, which can be purchased in all stores that have a blue-and-yellow 'Ladatel' sign out front. You can use these cards to place long-distance calls, and you can also call collect using these pay phones.

If, for some reason, you prefer to use a phone at a pricier Telmex office, you can do so at the Telmex office on Calle 8 near Calle 51. It's also possible to send faxes from there.

Email & Internet Access At the time of writing, Campeche had only one Internet café, the En Red Cibercafe, at the corner of Calle 12 and Av Circuito Baluartes Sur. Cost is US$1 for 30 minutes. Coffee and sodas are available and a jukebox offers a host of English- and Spanish-language rock 'n' roll. The air-con café is open 9:30 am to 11:30 pm Monday to Friday, 11:30 am to 9:30 pm Saturday and Sunday.

Laundry There's a Lavandería Campeche on Calle 55 between Calles 12 and 14. You can drop off clothing here in the morning and usually get it back cleaned, dried and folded in the afternoon. Cost is generally about US$4 for a large load. It's open 8 am to 6 pm Monday through Saturday, closed Sunday.

Walking Tour
Seven bulwarks still stand, and four of them are of interest. You can see them all by following Av Circuito Baluartes around the city – it's a 2km walk.

Because of traffic, some of the walk is not very pleasant, so you might want to limit your excursion to the first three or four baluartes described below, which house museums and gardens. If you'd rather have a guided tour, you can sign up for a city tour at the Ramada Hotel Campeche for US$20 (see the Organized Tours section, below). We'll start at the southwestern end of the Plaza Moch-Cuouh.

Half a block from the modern Palacio de Gobierno, at the intersection of Calle 8 and Av Circuito Baluartes Sur, near a ziggurat fountain, is the **Baluarte de San Carlos**. The interior of the bulwark is now arranged as the Sala de las Fortificaciones (Chamber of Fortifications), with some interesting scale models of the city's fortifications as they were in the 18th century. You can also visit the dungeon and look out over the sea from the roof. Baluarte de San Carlos is open 9 am to 1 pm and 5 to 7:30 pm daily. Admission is free.

Next, head back north along Calle 8. At the intersection with Calle 59, notice the **Puerta del Mar** (Sea Gate), which provided access to the city from the sea before the area to the northwest was filled in. The gate was demolished in 1893 but rebuilt in 1957 when its historical value was realized.

The **Baluarte de la Soledad**, on the north side of the Plaza Moch-Cuouh, close to the intersection of Calles 8 and 57, is the setting for the Museo de Estelas Maya. Many of the Mayan artifacts here are badly weathered, but the precise line drawing next to each stone shows you what the designs once looked like. The bulwark also has an interesting exhibition on colonial Campeche. Among the antiquities are 17th- and 18th-century seafaring equipment and armaments used to battle pirate invaders. The museum is open 9 am to 2 pm and 3 to 8 pm Tuesday to Saturday, 9 am to 1 pm Sunday, closed Monday. Admission costs US$1.

Just across the street from the Baluarte de la Soledad is the **Parque Principal**, Campeche's favorite park. Whereas the sterile, modernistic, shadeless Plaza Moch-Cuouh was built to glorify its government builders, the Parque Principal is the pleasant place

CAMPECHE

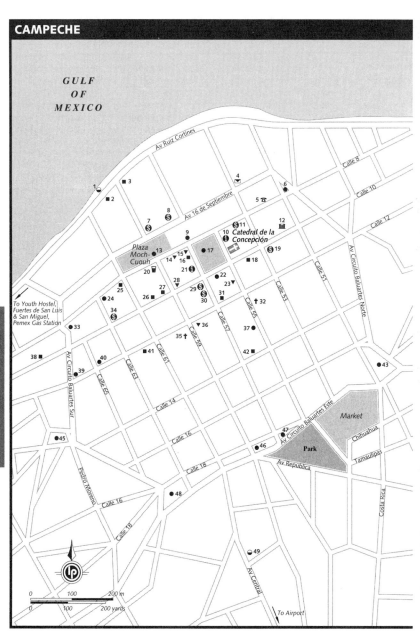

GULF
OF
MEXICO

Av Ruiz Cortines

Calle 8

Calle 10

Calle 12

Av 16 de Septiembre

Plaza
Moch-
Cuouh

Catedral de la
Concepción

Av Circuito Baluartes Norte

Calle 51

Calle 53

Calle 55

Calle 57

Calle 59

Calle 61

Calle 63

Calle 65

Calle 14

Calle 16

Calle 18

Calle 16

Calle 18

Pedro Moreno

To Youth Hostel,
Fuertes de San Luis
& San Miguel,
Pemex Gas Station

Av Circuito Baluartes Sur

Market

Chihuahua

Tamaulipas

Costa Rica

Av Circuito Baluartes Este

Park

Av República

Av Central

To Airport

0   100   200 m
0   100   200 yards

PLACES TO STAY
2 Hotel Baluartes
3 Ramada Hotel Campeche
16 Hotel Campeche
18 Posada San Angel
25 Hotel Castlemar
26 Hotel Roma
27 Hotel América
31 Hotel Regis
38 Hotel del Paseo
41 Hotel López
42 Hotel Colonial

PLACES TO EAT
14 Restaurant Marganzo
15 Restaurant del Parque
16 Café y Restaurant Campeche
23 Restaurant-Bar Familiar
    La Parroquía
28 Panificadora Nueva España
36 Nutri Vida

OTHER
1 Lerma & Playa Bonita
   Bus Stop
4 Post Office; Federal Building
5 Telmex
6 Baluarte de Santiago; Jardín
   Botánico Xmuch Haltun
7 Banco Santander Mexicano
8 Bancomer
9 Baluarte de la Soledad;
   Museo de Estelas Maya
10 Coordinación Municipal de
    Turismo (City Tourist Office)
11 Banorte
12 Mansión Carvajal
13 Puerta del Mar
17 Parque Principal (Plaza
    de la Independencia)
19 Banamex (ATM)
20 Calle 8 Club
21 Centro Cultura; Coordinación
    General de Turismo (State
    Tourist Office)
22 Old Palacio de Gobierno
    (Palacio Municipal)
24 Palacio de Gobierno
29 BanCrecer (ATM)
30 Banca Serfin (ATM)
32 Dulce Nombre de Jesús
    Church
33 Baluarte de San Carlos
34 Banobras
35 San Francisquito Church
37 Lavandería Campeche
39 En Red Cibercafe
40 Instituto de Cultura
    de Campeche
43 Baluarte de San Pedro;
    Exposición Permanente
    de Artesanías
44 ADO (1st-Class) Bus
    Terminal
45 Baluarte de Santa Rosa
46 Puerta de Tierra
47 Baluarte de San Francisco
48 Baluarte de San Juan
49 Sindicato del Campesino
    (Bus to Edzná)

where locals go to sit and think, chat, smooch, plot, snooze, stroll and cool off after the heat of the day, or to have their shoes shined. Come for the concerts on Sunday evenings.

Construction was begun on the **Catedral de la Concepción**, on the north side of the plaza, in the mid-16th century shortly after the conquistadors established the town, but it wasn't finished until 1705. Every Sunday the cathedral overflows with believers. Latecomers can often be seen huddled around the buildings' entrances during mass.

Continue north along Calle 8 several blocks to the **Baluarte de Santiago**, at the intersection of Calles 8 and 51. It houses a minuscule yet lovely tropical garden, the **Jardín Botánico Xmuch Haltun**, with 250 species of tropical plants set around a lovely courtyard of fountains. Tours of the garden are given between 5 and 6 pm Monday to Friday. The garden is open 8 am to 7 pm Tuesday to Sunday. Admission is free.

From the Baluarte de Santiago, walk inland along Calle 51 to Calle 18, where you'll come to the **Baluarte de San Pedro**, in the middle of a complex traffic intersection which marks the beginning of Av Gobernadores. Within the bulwark is the Exposición Permanente de Artesanías, a regional crafts sales center, open 9 am to 2 pm and 5 to 8 pm Monday to Friday. Admission is free.

To make the entire circuit, head south from the Baluarte de San Pedro, along Av Circuito Baluartes to the **Baluarte de San Francisco**, at Calle 57, and, a block farther at Calle 59, the **Puerta de Tierra** (Land Gate). The **Baluarte de San Juan**, at Calles 18 and 65, marks the southernmost point of the old city walls. From here you bear right along Calle 67 (Av Circuito Baluartes) to the intersection of Calles 14 and 67 and the **Baluarte de Santa Rosa**. From here Av Circuito Baluartes leads back to Calle 8 and the Plaza Moch-Cuouh. Admission to these baluartes is free.

Evening Stroll

If you want to see beautiful houses, take a walk through the streets of Campeche, especially Calles 55, 57 and 59. Many of the structures are painted in cheerful pastels with white trim. The walk is best done in the

evening, when the sun is not blasting down and when interior lighting illuminates courtyards, salons and alleys. The city sponsors musical events in the Parque Principal and the Plaza Moch-Cuouh on Saturday and Sunday nights. For more information about these fun, free activities, turn to the Entertainment section later in this chapter.

Centro Cultura

Housed in a building that dates from the 18th century, the Centro Cultura (Cultural Center), beside the Parque Principal, is furnished with pieces of furniture from the 18th and 19th centuries and gives a good idea of how the city's high society lived back then. The center, which houses the state-run tourism office, also contains several computer-interactive exhibits that provide information about the main tourist attractions in the city and state of Campeche. The center is open 9 am to 9 pm daily. Admission is free, as is a guided tour of the building (in Spanish only).

Mansión Carvajal

The Mansión Carvajal, on Calle 10 between Calles 51 and 53, started its eventful story as the city residence of Don Fernando Carvajal Estrada and his wife Señora María Iavalle de Carvajal. Don Fernando was among Campeche's richest *hacendados*, or

landowners. The monogram you see throughout the building, 'RCY,' is that of Rafael Carvajal Ytorralde, Don Fernando's father and founder of the fortune. It's open 8 am to 2 pm Monday to Friday. Admission is free.

Forts

Four kilometers south of the Plaza Moch-Cuouh, along the coastal road, stands the **Fuerte de San Luis**, an 18th-century fortress of which only a few battlements remain. It is open 8 am to 7 pm Tuesday to Sunday. Admission is free.

Near the San Luis, a road off to the left (southeast) climbs the hill 1km to the **Fuerte de San Miguel**, a restored fortress now home to a museum containing exquisite vases, masks and plates that were found at Calakmul, Edzná and Isla Jaina, an island site north of town that wasn't reachable by public transportation at the time this was penned.

The governors of the major Mayan cities were viewed as divine by the population. When buried they were entombed with their personal objects so they could use them in their next life. Many of the objects were stunning pieces of jade jewelry, which are on display at the museum. Also displayed here are arrowheads, weapons, necklaces made of seashells and figurines of various gods made of clay.

Campeche's Rainwater Salesmen

Seventy years ago, the townspeople of Campeche got their drinking water one of two ways: from cisterns they devised that collected rainwater, or from men who collected rainwater and sold it from large barrels they transported through town on horse-drawn carts.

The city's ground water is no good for drinking. It simply has too much of the Gulf in it. In the 1920s a man named Don Anastasio realized he could make money selling water, and he became Campeche's first *aguadore* (water salesman). A year didn't pass before enough aguadores were plying Campeche's streets with horse-drawn barrels to form a union.

For more than four decades, except during times of draught, business was brisk. Then, water trucks arrived on the scene and demand for the sweet, salt- and chlorine-free water has been falling ever since.

Today, most of the city's residents prefer to buy the purified water brought in by tanker trucks, even though it costs US$1 for a 5L bottle compared to just US$0.20 the remaining aguadores charge. Most of the buyers are old folk who credit the rainwater for their longevity.

As for Señor Anastasio, he recently retired at the age of 90.

The fort is itself a thing of beauty, having been restored to mint condition and topped with more than a dozen cannons. Even the drawbridge works. From the hill-top fort you can see all of Campeche, and the powerful breeze coming up off the ocean is a godsend. The fort and museum are open 8 am to 7 pm Tuesday to Sunday. Admission costs US$1, free on Sunday.

To reach the Fuerte de San Luis, take a 'Lerma' or 'Playa Bonita' bus southwest along the coastal highway toward Villahermosa. The bus stop for these buses is located on the west side of Av Ruiz Cortines, opposite the Hotel Baluartes. Tell the driver when you board to take you to the Fuerte de San Luis. If you don't speak Spanish, simply say 'Fuerte de San Luis, por favor.' The driver will let you out at the turnoff for the fort, Av Escenica, which happens to be opposite Fuerte de San Miguel. Be advised that the walk from the coastal road up the hill to the fort, though only 1km long, is quite arduous. The bus ride to the turnoff will set you back a mere US$0.20.

Beaches

If you're really hard up for a swim, head southwest toward the town of Seybaplaya, 33km from Plaza Moch-Cuouh. The highway skirts narrow, pure-white beaches dotted with fishing shacks. The best beach is called Payucan. The beaches don't overlook turquoise waters like those on the eastern coast of the peninsula, but they are pleasant all the same.

Organized Tours

City tours are offered every day from the Puerta de Tierra at 10 am and 4 pm. The cost is US$8. Tours to Edzná also depart from the Puerta de Tierra at 9 am and 2 pm, and cost US$15. You can also sign up for a guided tour of the baluartes at the Ramada Hotel Campeche (☎ 816-2233), Av Ruiz Cortines No 51, for US$20.

Places to Stay

Budget Campeche's youth hostel, *Albergue de la Juventud (☎ 816-1802)*, is in the Centro Cultural y Deportivo Universitario on Av Agustín Melgar, 3.5km southwest of the Plaza Moch-Cuouh, off the shore road. Dormitory beds cost US$4 per night, and a cafetería serves inexpensive meals. The shore road is Av Ruiz Cortines in town, but becomes Av Resurgimiento as it heads toward Villahermosa. Buses marked 'Av Universidad' will take you there. Ask the driver to let you off at the Albergue de la Juventud. Av Agustín Melgar heads inland between a Volkswagen dealership and a Pemex fuel station. The hostel is 150m up on the right.

The cheapest hotels – Reforma, Castlemar, Roma and the like – are fairly dumpy, but they're very cheap – usually around US$5 per room a night. Of these, only the *Hotel Castlemar*, at Calles 8 and 61, and *Hotel Roma*, on Calle 10 between Calles 59 and 61, can be recommended. Expect peeling paint and missing patches of plaster. The *Hotel Campeche (☎ 816-5183, Calle 57 No 2)*, above the Café y Restaurant Campeche, facing the Parque Principal, is cheap and centrally located. Rooms with cold water cost only US$10, those with hot and cold water US$2 more.

Though we've heard a few complaints of noise, beds at the *Hotel Colonial (☎ 816-2222, Calle 14 No 122)* are usually in great demand by budget travelers. Housed in what was once the mansion of Doña Gertrudis Eulalia Torostieta y Zagasti, former Spanish governor of Tabasco and Yucatán, the rooms have good showers with hot water for US$11/13 single/double with fan only; add US$5 for air-con.

Posada San Angel (☎ 816-7718, Calle 10 No 307) is a Swiss-style cell block: Its 14 rooms are Spartan, but modern and clean with private bathroom for US$13/16 with fan only; add US$5 for air-con. Some sheets need replacing, so ask to see several rooms before registering. This inn offers very good value.

Mid-Range The *Hotel América (☎ 816-4588, fax 816-4576, www.campeche.com.mx/hamerica, Calle 10 No 252)* is a converted colonial house with 49 spacious though somewhat Spartan rooms ringing an interior

courtyard. Singles are available with fan only for US$17. Doubles with fans go for US$24; add US$5 for air-con.

The *Hotel López* (☎ *816-3344, fax 816-2488, Calle 12 No 189*) offers slightly less appealing rooms and charges US$17 without air-con single or double, and US$29 single or double with air-con. Some of the rooms have desks, but none have closets. The *Hotel Regis* (☎ *816-3175, Calle 12 No 148*) is conveniently located and serviceable, with adequate air-con rooms for US$24/28.

Top End The best value in town can be found at the *Hotel del Paseo* (☎ *811-0100, 811-0077, fax 811-0097, cslavall@etzna.uacam .mx, Calle 10 No 215*), a new place with 42 air-con standard rooms and six suites. This place is modern in appearance and has a restaurant and bar on the premises, but no pool. Rates are a very reasonable US$35/40 for a single/double, US$60 for a suite.

The *Hotel Baluartes* (☎ *816-3911, fax 816-2410, baluarte@campeche.sureste.com*), on Av Ruiz Cortines near Calle 59, used to be the finest hotel in town, but now it's really showing its age. The Baluartes' well-used rooms have air-con, and half of them have sea views. There is a pool on the grounds. Rates are US$35/40. If you need a swimming pool and don't mind spending the money, the 119-room *Ramada Hotel Campeche* (☎ *816-2233, fax 811-1618, Av Ruiz Cortines No 51*) is the place for you. Prices range from US$90 single or double for a standard room to US$150 for a master suite. There's a restaurant, bar, pool, and even a discotheque on the premises.

Places to Eat

Among the best eateries is the *Restaurant Marganzo*, on Calle 8 between Calles 57 and 59, facing the sea and the Baluarte de la Soledad. Breakfast costs US$3 to US$4, regional specialties US$3 to US$5; the seafood menu, priced up to US$8, includes lots of shrimp. This restaurant is air-conditioned and popular.

The *Café y Restaurant Campeche*, on Calle 57 opposite the Parque Principal, is in the building that saw the birth of Justo Sierra, founder of Mexico's national university, but the restaurant is very simple, bright with fluorescent lightbulbs and loud with a blaring TV set. It's open for breakfast and dinner. Few items cost more than US$3.

In the same block facing the plaza is the *Restaurant del Parque*, a cheerful little place serving fish, meat and shrimp for around US$4 a platter. It opens early for breakfast, and is open on Sunday.

If you'd just like to pick up some sweet rolls, biscuits, bread or cakes, head for the *Panificadora Nueva España*, on Calle 10 at Calle 59, which has a large assortment of fresh baked goods at very low prices.

Every now and then a brave entrepreneur opens a natural foods restaurant in Campeche, only to close soon after. Hopefully the *Nutri Vida* (*Calle 12 No 167*), will still be in business when you visit.

Perhaps the best known restaurant in town is the *Restaurant-Bar Familiar La Parroquía*, on Calle 55 between Calles 10 and 12. The complete family restaurant-café-hangout, La Parroquía serves breakfasts from 7 to 10 am Monday to Friday for US$2.50 to US$4; its substantial lunch and dinner fare – such as *chuleta de cerdo* (pork chop), *filete a la tampiqueña* (marinated beef steak) and shrimp cocktail or shrimp salad – all cost under US$10.

Entertainment

On Saturday at 8 pm (weather permitting) from September to May, the state tourism authorities sponsor *Estampas Turísticas* – performances of folk music and dancing – in the Plaza Moch-Cuouh. Other performances, sponsored by the city government, take place in the Parque Principal Thursday to Sunday evenings around 7 pm.

Also, every Sunday at 7 pm in the Parque Principal you can hear popular Campeche music performed by the Banda del Estado (State Band). There's no cost to attend, and it's a very pleasant way to pass time. Additionally, every Saturday from 7 to 11 pm at the Plaza Moch-Cuouh, near the Puerta del Mar, you can enjoy bands playing the traditional folkloric music of Campeche. It's free and very popular.

CAMPECHE STATE

Getting There & Away
Air The airport is located at the end of Av López Portillo (Av Central), 3.5km from the Plaza Moch-Cuouh. You must take a taxi (US$5) to get to the city center.

Bus Campeche's 1st-class ADO bus terminal is on Av Gobernadores, 1.7km from the Plaza Moch-Cuouh, or about 1.5km from most hotels. The 2nd-class terminal is directly behind it.

Here's information on daily buses from Campeche:

Cancún – 512km, nine hours, US$12 to US$15, change at Mérida; 10 pm and 11:30 pm only (better to catch any bus to Mérida, then catch a Cancún-bound bus)

Chetumal – 422km, seven hours, US$11 to US$14; one bus at noon

Edzná – 66km, 1½ hours; catch bus to Pich or Hool from the Sindicato del Campesino on Av Central, or take a faster bus to San Antonio Cayal (45km) and hitch south from there

Hopelchén – 86km, two hours, US$2; eight 2nd-class buses by Autobuses del Sur

Mérida – 195km (short route via Becal), 2½ to three hours; 250km (long route via Uxmal), four hours; 10 by ADO (US$7) around the clock; every 30 minutes by ATS (US$6)

Mexico City (TAPO) – 1360km, 20 hours, US$57; two by ADO, at 3:30 and 4 pm

Palenque – 362km, five hours; one by ADO (US$13), two by Colón (US$13), two by ATS (US$10); many other buses drop you at Catazajá (Palenque turnoff), 27km north of Palenque village

San Cristóbal de las Casas – 820km, 14 hours; one by Colón at 10:10 pm (US$15 to US$18); one by Maya de Oro (US$24)

Villahermosa – 450km, six hours, US$14 to US$17; 15 buses daily; they'll drop you at Catazajá (Palenque turnoff) if you like

Xpujil – 306km, six hours, US$8; four by ATS, one by ADO at noon

CAMPECHE TO MÉRIDA – SHORT ROUTE (HWY 180)
This is the fastest way to get between the two cities, and if you buy a bus ticket from Campeche to Mérida this is the route your bus will likely follow. If you'd prefer to go the long way via Edzná, Kabah and Uxmal, you should ask for a seat on one of the less frequent long-route buses. If you'd like to stop at one of the towns along the short route, catch a 2nd-class bus.

Hecelchakán
At Hecelchakán, approximately 60km northeast of Campeche, you'll find an archaeology museum and a historic church, both facing the central plaza. The **Museo de Hecelchakán** houses burial artifacts from Isla Jaina as well as ceramics and jewelry from other sites. There are also many artists' renditions of ancient Maya going about their daily lives. It's a fairly impressive museum that's worth a stop if you have your own wheels. The museum, located in a colonial building that was pridefully restored in mid-1999, is open 9 am to 6 pm Tuesday to Saturday. Admission costs US$2. The **Iglesia de San Francisco**, also recently renovated, is said to be built upon the foundation of a Mayan temple. The mission dates from the 16th century, but its dramatic features – a massive octagonal dome and a pair of monumental bell towers – are 18th-century additions. The church is the center of festivities on October 4, the day the townsfolk celebrate their patron saint. From August 9 to 18 (give or take a day or two; exact dates vary annually), a popular festival called the Novenario is held, with bullfights, dancing and refreshments.

Calkiní
After Hecelchakán, it's 24km to Calkiní, site of the 17th-century **Iglesia de San Luis de Tolosa**, with a plateresque portal and lots of baroque decoration. Each year the Festival of San Luis is celebrated on August 19.

Becal
Becal is 8km from Calkiní, just before you enter the state of Yucatán. It is a center of the Yucatán Peninsula's Panama hat trade. The soft, pliable hats, called *jipijapas* by the locals, have been woven by townsfolk from the fibers of the huano palm tree in humid limestone caves since the mid-19th century.

CAMPECHE STATE

The caves – there's at least one on every block, generally reached by a hole in the ground in someone's backyard – provide just the right atmosphere for shaping the fibers, keeping them pliable and minimizing breakage. Each cave is typically no larger than a bedroom. About 1000 of the town's 3000 adult residents make their living making hats. The hats cost US$10 to US$50, depending on quality. If you're in the market, be sure to visit the cooperative located on the main street, a stone's throw from Becal's dominating church.

From Becal it's 85km to Mérida.

CAMPECHE TO MÉRIDA – LONG ROUTE (HWY 261)

Most travelers take the long route (Hwy 261) from Campeche to Mérida, in order to visit the various architectural sites on the way.

Edzná

The closest ruins to Campeche are 61km to the southeast, at Edzná. Edzná means 'House of Grimaces' as well as 'House of Echoes' and may well have been host to both, as there was a settlement here for more than two millennia – from approximately 600 BC

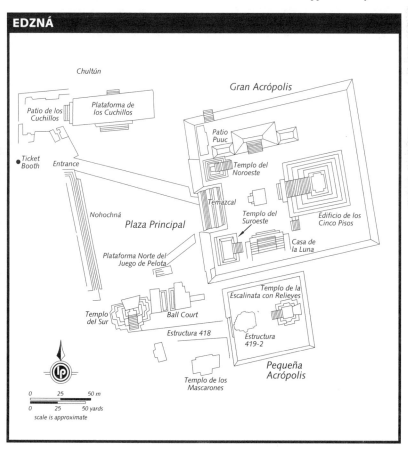

EDZNÁ

Chultún

Gran Acrópolis

Patio de los Cuchillos

Plataforma de los Cuchillos

Patio Puuc

Templo del Noroeste

Ticket Booth

Entrance

Temazcal

Templo del Suroeste

Edificio de los Cinco Pisos

Nohochná

Plaza Principal

Casa de la Luna

Plataforma Norte del Juego de Pelota

Templo de la Escalinata con Relieves

Templo del Sur

Ball Court

Estructura 418

Estructura 419-2

0   25   50 m
0   25   50 yards
scale is approximate

Templo de los Mascarones

Pequeña Acrópolis

CAMPECHE STATE

to 1500 AD. Most of the carvings visible at the site date from 550 to 810 AD.

Though a long way from such Puuc Route sites as Uxmal and Kabah, Edzná's architecture is similar to Puuc style. However, archaeologists believe Edzná was an independent kingdom. What led to its decline and gradual abandonment remains a mystery.

Although the archaeological zone covers 2 sq km, the best part is the main plaza, 160m long and 100m wide, surrounded by temples. Every Mayan site has huge masses of stone, but at Edzná there are cascades of it, terrace upon terrace of bleached limestone.

The major temple here, the 30m-high **Edificio de los Cinco Pisos** (Temple of Five Levels), often referred to as the Five-Story Palace, is to the left as you enter the plaza from the ticket kiosk. Built on a vast platform, it rises five levels from base to roofcomb, with vaulted rooms and some weathered decorations of masks, serpents and jaguars' heads on each level. A great central staircase of 65 steps goes right to the top.

The temple wasn't erected in one construction period, but rather five different ones. What's visible today belongs primarily to the Puuc architectural style. Scholars generally agree that the temple is a hybrid of a pyramid and a palace. The impressive roofcomb atop the temple is a clear reference to the sacred buildings at Tikal in Guatemala.

Often overlooked but worth a look is the **Templo de los Mascarones** (Temple of the Masks), where it's possible to see portrayals of the sun god. The central motif is that of the head of a Mayan man whose face has been modified to give him the appearance of a jaguar.

The **Plataforma de los Cuchillos** (Platform of the Knives), near the entrance of the site, takes its name from the offering of flint knives found within it. On top of the platform it's still possible to see several walls that once formed rooms which archaeologists suspect were used by high-ranking figures. Another noteworthy structure at Edzná is the **Nohochná** (Big House), located on the main plaza. The structure was topped by four long halls that likely served administrative tasks, such as the collection of

Those Noble Headdresses

Mayan noblemen distinguished themselves from common folk with intricate headdresses. Typically, the frames were custom-made from wicker or wood and were held in place by chin straps. Animal skins, semi-precious stones, and feathers from quetzals, parrots and other colorful birds were fastened to the frames in brilliant displays. Some of the headdresses were worn with matching masks that resembled jaguars, snakes or gods. As befits a civilization that placed great importance on rank, the most elaborate headdresses belonged to the regional rulers, the least elaborate to the lowliest aristocrats. Stone images of Mayan chiefs indicate that the flashiest headdresses were often as tall and twice as wide as the men who wore them.

tributes and ministering of justice. The built-in benches facing the main plaza clearly were designed to serve spectators of special events in the plaza.

On the opposite (right) side of the plaza as you enter is a monumental staircase 100m

wide, which once led up to the Casa de la Luna (House of the Moon), one of the site's numerous temples. At the far end of the plaza is a ruined temple that may have been the priests' quarters.

The site is open 8 am to 5 pm daily. Admission costs US$4, free on Sunday.

Getting There & Away Picazh Servicios Turísticos (☎ 816-4426, fax 816-2760), Calle 16 No 348, between Calles 57 and 59 in Campeche, runs tours to Edzná from Campeche. For US$15 per person, they'll drive two or more people to the Edzná ruins and back. For another US$5 per person, they'll give you a guided tour in Spanish or English. Entry to the site is not included in these prices. Join the tour at the plaza next to the Puerta de Tierra in Campeche. Tours depart daily at 9 am and 2 pm.

The Picazh tours are worth the money for convenience, but you can do it more cheaply by bus. Catch a 2nd-class village bus early in the morning headed for Edzná (66km) from near the Sindicato del Campesino in Campeche, on Av Central, south of Av Circuito Baluartes; it may be a bus going to Pich, 15km southeast of Edzná, or to Hool, 25km southwest. Either bus will drop you at the access road to the site.

Coming from the north and east, get off at San Antonio Cayal and hitch or catch a bus 20km south to Edzná.

A sign just north of the Edzná turnoff on Hwy 261 says, 'Edzná 2km,' but the ruins are just 500m beyond the sign, only about 400m off the highway.

When you leave you'll have to depend on hitching or buses to get you to San Antonio Cayal, from where you can hitch or catch a bus west back to Campeche or east and north to Hopelchén, Bolonchén and ultimately Uxmal.

Hopelchén, Bolonchén de Rejón & Xtacumbilxunaan

By heading 40km east from San Antonio Cayal, you'll reach Hopelchén, where Hwy 261 turns north. The town contains no attractions, but it does offer travelers a decent hotel, *Hotel Arcos*, with rooms for US$5/7

single/double. The hotel is on Hwy 261 as it passes through town. Also in town is a bus station that is served exclusively by 2nd-class Autobuses del Sur. There are 12 buses daily to Campeche from 4:45 am to 7:45 pm (US$2); four to Mérida (7:35 am and 1:35, 4 and 6:30 pm, US$4); eight buses to Dzibalchén from 8:30 am to 8 pm (US$1); two to Chencoh (8:30 am and 6:15 pm, US$1.20); and one to Xpujil (8 pm, US$5.10). The next town to appear out of the flat, dry jungle is Bolonchén de Rejón, after 34km. The local festival of Santa Cruz is held each year on May 3.

Bolonchén is near the Grutas de Xtacumbilxunaan ('SHTAA-koom-beel-shoo-NAHN'), about 3km south of town. You can visit the cavern by taking a 30- to 45-minute tour with the guide/caretaker for the price of a tip. The cave is 'open' whenever the caretaker is around, which is most of the time during daylight hours. There are no objects or art in the cave, few stalactites and stalagmites, and it's very wet and slippery. From a trail that winds through the cave there appears to be a bottomless pit. The guide will tell you there's a cenote at the bottom of it, and there may well be but it's not presently accessible.

Hwy 261 continues into Yucatán state to Uxmal, with a side road leading to the Puuc Route ruin sites (see Yucatán State chapter).

CAMPECHE TO CIUDAD DEL CARMEN

Hwy 180 from Campeche to Ciudad del Carmen clings to the coast its entire length, infrequently passing sand dunes and marshlands along the way. The road is occasionally winding and always dangerous to travel at night due to bandits that are said to operate along it after sundown. There's also a military checkpoint at the turnoff to Sabancuy most nights; expect to have your vehicle thoroughly searched there if you're foolish enough to be on the road after sunset. Motorists should also be aware that the local and federal police from Campeche to Ciudad del Carmen seem to hone in on cars sporting decals identifying them as rental vehicles. This writer was once stopped three times in

Panama hats are made and sold in Becal.

18th-century Iglesia de San Francisco, Hecelchakan.

The impressive monster-mouth doorway of Hochob's principal palace.

Detail of the steps at the Palace at Edzná.

Restored temple at Hochob in Campeche.

Pro-conquest propaganda in Campeche.

The Edificio de los Cinco Pisos (Five-Story Palace) at Edzná and the surrounding ruins.

a single day, in each instance accused of speeding (which he wasn't) and told to hand over a total of $480; the author negotiated the sum down to $190. The police in Sabancuy will stop a foreigner traveling more than 20km/h in town, though the posted speed limit is 30km/h.

Champotón

This seaside fishing town is most memorable for its lovely river, but it's also home to a one-story Franciscan church that dates from the 17th century, and to the ruins of a fort that dates from the 18th century. Neither the fort nor the church are worth a special stop, but travelers should be aware that there are several good-value *hotels* here, all on or near the highway and south of the river (Champotón is a small community; walking from one hotel to another is a five-minute affair). This town of 22,000 is most enjoyable from November 30 to December 8, when its inhabitants celebrate the Immaculate Conception with processions, regional food contests, fireworks, dances and even waterskiing displays.

Because of its location near a major highway intersection, Champotón has a lively bus station, which is on a main road 50m from Hwy 180 and south of the river. The station is served by the 1st-class carrier ADO and 2nd-class Sur and, to a much lesser extent, the 1st-class carrier TRP.

ADO serves Campeche (7, 8, 9, 10:30 am, noon and 4, 6, 8:30 and 10:15 pm, US$2.40), Cancún (10:15 am, US$22.00), Ciudad del Carmen (9 and 10 am and 1:45, 4, 5:30, 7:30 and 9:40 pm, US$5.30), Chetumal (1 pm, US$11.70), Escárcega (1 and 9 pm, US$2.80), Mexico City (TAPO, 8 pm, US$46), Mérida (9 am, noon and 4 and 10:15 pm, US$8.60), Playa del Carmen (10:15 pm, US$23), Veracruz (9 pm, US$28.50), and Villahermosa (11 am and 1:45 and 8 pm, US$12.50).

Sur serves: Campeche (every 30 minutes, US$1.60), Sabancuy (6:30 and 7:30 am, noon and 1:15 and 2:20 pm, US$1.70), Ciudad del Carmen (same as Sabancuy, US$4.20), Escárcega (every half hour, US$1.80), Xpujil (6:15 and 9:45 am and 11:15 pm, US$5.50), Candelaria (7, 9 and 11:15 am and 1:30, 2:45 and 3:15 pm, US$4.50), Chetumal (1:50 am and 11 pm, US$9), Villahermosa (10:30 am and 1:15 and 3:30 pm, US$10.30) and Mérida (12:30, 4:30 and 6:30 pm, US$6.50).

TRP provides service to Campeche, Ciudad del Carmen, Escárcega, Mérida, Sabancuy and Villahermosa.

Sabancuy

There's little reason to stop in Sabancuy, a small town 2km from Hwy 180 on the road to (or from) Escárcega. It's mentioned here primarily because weary travelers finding themselves in its vicinity when night falls would be wise to get off the road, and there are far worse places to spend the night than Sabancuy. That's because Sabancuy is home to the *Hotel Bella Vista* (10 clean rooms, several with air-con, all with private bathroom, US$10 to US$14 per room, no phone), which offers very good value and is often full. The hotel is located beside the town's main plaza, which itself is located beside the road that passes through town. If the Bella Vista is full, there's another budget hotel behind the police station (the station faces the main plaza). There's also a bus station beside the main plaza, with frequent buses departing during daylight hours for Ciudad del Carmen, Champotón, Escárcega, Campeche and Mérida.

CIUDAD DEL CARMEN
☎ 9 • pop 150,161

Located on the southern tip of Isla del Carmen, and connected to the mainland at both ends by long bridges that span the two mouths of the Laguna de Términos, Ciudad del Carmen attracts few foreign visitors. Not to be mistaken for lovely Playa del Carmen on the Caribbean coast, Ciudad del Carmen is a bustling, unattractive city whose visitors are generally involved with the extraction of crude oil, the city's No 1 industry.

Before oil, it was the area's precious dyewoods that appealed to people of many nationalities, including pirates from England, Holland and France who initially used the island as a base of operations from which to launch raids on ships that plied the Gulf of Mexico and towns along the Gulf Coast. As

CAMPECHE STATE

time wore on, a number of the pirates tried to make their living a more honorable way – by exploiting the island's dyewoods and exporting them to Europe.

The Spanish were the first white men to find the island, arriving in 1518, and not long after pirates took to using the island as a springboard for attacks. Indeed, pirates inhabited the long and narrow island from the mid-16th century until 1718, when a Spanish force drove the pirates from the island forever. Ciudad del Carmen was founded in 1722; previous to then the town was know as the Isla de Tris.

Today, Ciudad del Carmen is laid out in a grid pattern and its finest attraction is its main plaza, located near the intersection of Calles 31 and 22. The Parque General Ignacio Zaragoza, as the plaza is called, contains many mature shade trees and dozens of benches that are filled with people day and night. A church, the Iglesia de Nuestra Señora del Carmen, overlooks the plaza. It was built in 1856, but its altar was redone in 1998 and looks, frankly, ridiculous. The centerpiece is a mannequin in a wedding dress. It's supposed to resemble the Virgin, but it looks more like a life-size Bride Barbie doll. There are numerous banks, travel agencies and hotels within a two-block radius of the plaza. The best value of the host of hotels is the *Hotel Victoria* (☎ 382-9302, fax 832-0286, Calle 24 No 32), at Calle 27, which has 22 air-con rooms with fan, TV and hot-water private bathroom. Cost is US$35 per room. The bus station, about 15 blocks from the plaza, on the corner of Avs 20 de Noviembre and Colosio, is where you can catch frequent buses to Mérida (US$13.90), Campeche (US$7.70), Champotón (US$5.30), Frontera (US$3.50) and Escárcega (US$4.50).

ISLA DEL CARMEN

This 37km-long island with a bay on one side and a large lagoon on the other must look beautiful from a plane. The bay is the color of imperial jade and the lagoon a deep blue. Most of the island is still covered in mangrove, which from a flying hawk's perspective resembles a healthy forest.

But unlike the beaches at and near Playa del Carmen in northern Quintana Roo, the ones here aren't covered in soft white sand. Instead, it seems that for every grain of its salt-and-pepper sand, there's a tiny shell. There must be trillions of them, and they are unpleasant to step on. Which is why, despite the numerous beaches on the island, few people use them.

As for Isla de Aguada and Isla Cañon, near the northern tip of Isla del Carmen and looking oh-so intriguing on a map, they are poverty-stricken and unattractive fishing communities. There's one hotel on Isla de Aguada, the *Hotel La Cabaña*. It's worn and infrequently visited, and rooms go for US$12.

ESCÁRCEGA

☎ 9 • pop 25,209

Most buses between Villahermosa in Tabasco and the Yucatán Peninsula stop in Escárcega to give passengers a refreshment break, but there is no other reason to stop in this town at the junction of Hwys 186 and 261, 150km south of Campeche and 301km from Villahermosa. Indeed, as most buses arrive in town full and depart in the same condition, you may find it difficult to get out of Escárcega if you break your trip here.

The town is spread out along 2km of Hwy 186 toward Chetumal. It's 1.7km between the ADO and Autobuses del Sur bus stations. The ADO station is located at the junction of the highways, whereas the 2nd-class bus station is situated on Hwy 186 on the west side of the intersection. Most hotels are nearer to the Autobuses del Sur bus station than to the ADO; most of the better restaurants are near the ADO bus station.

Places to Stay & Eat

The best accommodations in this crossroads town is the *Hotel Escárcega* (☎ 824-0188, fax 824-0187), on Hwy 186 about 400m east of the junction. The hotel offers 70 rooms, most with air-con, TV, hot-water private bathroom and firm beds. Rates are US$16/18 for a single/double with fan only, and US$4 more for air-con.

There are slightly less appealing places for slightly less money. One's opposite the 2nd-class bus station while the other is about another 150m east of the Hotel Escárcega on Hwy 186.

The best place to eat is the **Restaurant La Teja**, which is about 100m west of the junction. La Teja is open 24 hours and has a rather extensive menu, ranging from the usual *antojitos* (burritos, tacos, quesadillas and sandwiches) to lots of chicken and beef dishes. There's seafood as well, but seafood is not their strong suit. Few items cost more than US$4.

Getting There & Away

Again, you want to try to avoid switching buses in Escárcega if you can, because they often arrive full and depart that way. First-class ADO and TRP buses leave from the ADO station. Several carriers serve the 2nd-class station. You best bet for a seat is the ADO station.

Together, ADO and TRP serve: Acayucan (12:30 and 4:15 am and 10:30 pm, US$18), Balancan (1:45 am, US$6), Chetumal (1, 4:30, 5, 8:30 and 10:30 am and 12:30 pm, US$9), Campeche (1:30, 4:30, 5:30 and 11:30 am and 1, 2, 4:15, 5 and 11:35 pm, US$5.25), Cancún (1, 2, 4:45 and 10:30 am and midnight, US$21), Champotón (5:30 am and 2 pm, US$2.50), Xpujil (4:45 am and 2:30 pm, US$5), Mérida (1:30, 4:30, 5:30 and 11:30 am and 1, 2, 5 and 11:35 pm, US$15), Palenque (4 am and 1 pm, US$7), Playa del Carmen (1, 2, 4:45 and 10 am and midnight, US$19), Veracruz (10:20 and 10:30 pm, US$26) and Villahermosa (1, 2:30, 4:15 and 6 am and 1, 4, 2:30 pm, US$10).

ESCÁRCEGA TO XPUJIL

Hwy 186 heads due east from Escárcega through the scrubby jungle to Chetumal in the state of Quintana Roo, a 271km, three-hour ride. The largest town between Escárcega and Chetumal – and the only one with accommodations – is Xpujil ('ISH-pu-HEEL'), which is located on Hwy 186 about 20km west of the Campeche-Quintana Roo state border. The only gasoline station between Escárcega and Chetumal is located about 5km east of Xpujil.

Between Escárcega and Xpujil are numerous archaeological sites, all of which were being restored at the time of writing. The most significant of the group historically is Calakmul, which also is the most difficult to reach. From the highway to the ruins it's a 60km trip each direction on a paved road that winds through some light rain forest. It is not reachable by bus, but it's possible to hire a taxi in Xpujil, which is home to two reasonably priced hotels and one excessively priced place.

Balamku

Discovered only in 1990, Balamku is famous for the exquisite façade of one building. The façade is decorated with a well-preserved bas relief stucco stylized figure of a jaguar flanked by two large mask designs, and topped with designs of other animals and humans. This elaborate, unusual design bears little resemblance to any of the known decorative elements in the Chenes and Río Bec styles, and has mystified archaeologists.

Balamku is 60km west of Xpujil junction (less than 3km west of Conhuas), then just under 3km north of the highway along a paved road. Admission costs US$1. A round-trip taxi ride from Xpujil with a one-hour visit costs US$30.

Calakmul

Most Mayanists agree that Calakmul is a very important site (and size-wise it's larger than Tikal in Guatemala), but at this writing only a fraction of its expanse has been cleared and few of its 6500 buildings have been consolidated, let alone restored. But like Tikal, these ruins are set amid a veritable sea of rain forest, which is best viewed from the top of one of the site's several pyramids (indeed, Calakmul means 'Adjacent Mounds').

The ruins were discovered in 1931 by American botanist Cyrus Lundell. Today, we know that Calakmul was the leading city in a vast region known as the Kingdom of the Serpent's Head from about 250 through 750 AD. Its perpetual rival was Tikal. Indeed, Calakmul's decline began with power struggles and internal conflicts that followed

Project: Maya World

Visible in many parts of the Yucatán Peninsula are blue-and-white road signs with a Mayan design and the words 'Mundo Maya' (Maya World) on them. The signs are part of a tourism project launched during the early 1990s by Mexico, Guatemala, Belize, Honduras and El Salvador to promote the entire world of the ancient Maya.

With a US$1 million grant and technical advice from the European Community, the five countries have agreed on the need to restore the Mayan cities of yesteryear, to preserve much of the region's natural beauty and to facilitate travel throughout the region. It's for this reason that most of the Mayan ruins that have been discovered are reachable by road, and it explains why numerous national parks and biosphere reserves have recently opened in this area once occupied by the legendary civilization.

the defeat by Tikal of Calakmul's King Garra de Jaguar (Jaguar Claw).

As at Tikal, there are indications that construction occurred over a period lasting more than a millennium. Beneath Edificio VII, archaeologists discovered a burial crypt and a funerary offering of some 2000 pieces of jade. Other jade offerings were found beneath other structures. Calakmul also has a surprising number of carved stelae – 120 have been located to date – many eroded.

Calakmul is open 8 am to 5 pm daily. It can be reached via a 60km forested road running south from Conhuas. Admission costs US$2.50. Be advised there's a 500m walk from the parking lot to the ruins, and that no drinks were available at the time of writing (bring some water with you). A roundtrip taxi ride from Xpujil with a two-hour visit costs US$50.

Chicanná

Almost 12km west of Xpujil junction and 800m south of the highway, Chicanná ('House of the Snake's Jaws') is a mixture of Chenes and Río Bec architectural styles

buried in the jungle. The city flourished about 660 to 680 AD, and today is open 8 am to 5 pm for US$1.50 admission.

Enter through the modern palapa admission building, then follow the rock paths through the jungle to Grupo D and Edificio XX (750-830 AD), which boasts not one but two monster-mouth doorways, one above the other, the pair topped by a roofcomb.

A five-minute walk along the jungle path brings you to Grupo C, with two low buildings (Edificios X and XI) on a raised platform; the temples bear a few fragments of decoration.

The buildings in Grupo B have some intact decoration as well, and there's a good roofcomb on Edificio VI.

At the end of the path is Chicanná's most famous building, Edificio II (750-770 AD) in Grupo A, with its gigantic Chenes-style monster-mouth doorway. If you photograph nothing else here, you'll want a picture of this, which is best taken in the afternoon.

A roundtrip taxi ride from Xpujil with a one-hour visit costs US$10.

Becán

Becán ('Path of the Snake' in Mayan) sits atop a rock outcrop. It is well named, as a 2km moat ('becan' in Mayan) snakes its way around the entire city to protect it from attack. Seven causeways once crossed the moat (fosse), providing access to the city. Becán was occupied from 550 BC until 1000 AD. Today the site, 400m north of the highway, is open 8 am to 5 pm daily; admission costs US$1.50 (free Sunday).

This is among the largest and most elaborate sites in the area. The first building you reach, Edificio I on the Plaza Sureste (Southeast Plaza), has the two towers typical of Río Bec style. Climb a stairway on the east side of the building to get to the Plaza Sureste, surrounded by four large temples and a circular altar (Edificio III-a) on the east side.

Arrows direct you to a path which leaves the plaza's northeast corner and descends a flight of stairs, then turns left (west) and passes along a rock-walled walkway and beneath a corbeled arch. At the end of the path is a huge twin-towered temple with

cylindrical columns at the top of a flight of steps. This is Edificio VIII, dating from about 600 to 730 AD. The view from the top of this temple is good in all directions.

Northwest of Edificio VIII is the Plaza Central, surrounded by the 30m-high Edificio IX, the tallest building at the site, and the better looking Edificio X.

More ruins await you in the jungle. The Plaza Oeste (West Plaza), west of Edificio X, is surrounded by low buildings, one of which is a ball court.

A roundtrip taxi ride from Xpujil with a one-hour visit costs US$10.

XPUJIL

The hamlet of Xpujil, at the junction of the east-west and northern highways, is growing into a village, but services are still few and basic. There still is no bank or laundry, and the nearest gas station is, oddly, 5km east of town.

Xpujil is not much of a destination in itself, but it makes for a great base from which to visit the area's numerous architectural sites. In this town of several hundred people (mostly, it would seem, soldiers and police assigned to the border), there's a bus station, several restaurants, three hotels and

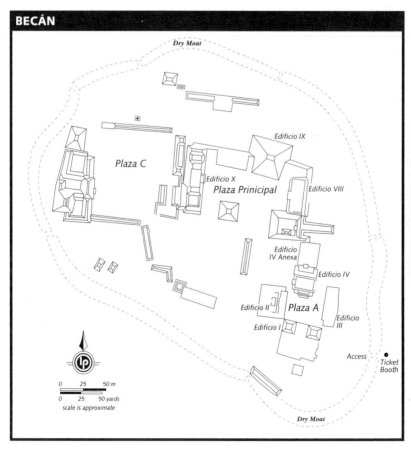

BECÁN

Dry Moat

Edificio IX

Plaza C

Edificio X

Plaza Prinicipal

Edificio VIII

Edificio IV Anexa

Edificio IV

Edificio II

Plaza A

Edificio III

Edificio I

Access

Ticket Booth

0   25   50 m
0   25   50 yards
scale is approximate

Dry Moat

a taxi stand near the bus depot. From the taxi stand, it is possible to hire drivers to take you to any of the archaeological sites along or off Hwy 186, including Calakmul. The drivers charge very reasonable fares, but be sure to agree on the fare before you depart to avoid any surprises later.

From the junction, the Xpujil ruins are 1.5km west; Becán is 8km west, Chicanná is 11.5km west and Balamku is 60km west.

Ruinas Xpujil

Xpujil ('Place of the Cattails' in Mayan) flourished during the Late Classic period from 600 to 900 AD, though there was a settlement here much earlier. The site, 200m north of the highway, is open 8 am to 5 pm and admission costs US$1.50. A roundtrip taxi ride with a one-hour wait costs US$5.

Edificio I in Grupo I, built about 760 AD, is a fine example of the Río Bec architectural style with its lofty towers (see the Río Bec section, later in this chapter, for a description of this style of architecture). The three towers (rather than the usual two) have traces of the impractically steep ornamental stairways reaching nearly to their tops, and several fierce jaguar masks (go around to the back of the tower to see the best one).

About 60m to the east is Edificio II, an elite residence.

Xpujil is a far larger site than may be imagined from these two buildings. Three other structure groups have been identified, but it may be decades before they are restored.

Places to Stay & Eat

There are two good-value hotels in Xpujil. The one closest to the bus station (about 100m west of it) is the *Mirador Maya* (☎ 9-871-6028, fax 9-871-6005). There are nine bungalows and two rooms. The rooms were built in 1999 and each includes air-con, fan and private bathroom with hot water. The rate is US$30 per room. Two of the bungalows look very rustic from the outside but they're quite OK, with fan, private bathroom and two beds in each. They go for US$20. The seven other bungalows are rather rustic inside and out and have shared bathroom; they rent for US$15.

About 400m west of the bus station, the *Hotel Calakmul* (☎ 9-871-6029) has four rooms, which were built in 1999, with air-con, private bathroom, and TV – very comfy – for US$25. The hotel also has nine cabins with four shared bathrooms for US$12 each. There's a restaurant at this hotel and at the Mirador Maya, and they represent the best eateries along the highway.

Xpujil has upscale accommodations in the form of the *Ramada Chicanná Eco-village Resort* (☎/fax 9-876-2233), Hwy 186 at Km 144, 12km west of Xpujil junction, then 500m north of the highway. Large, airy rooms with private baths and ceiling fans are grouped four to a bungalow and set amid well-tended grass lawns. The small dining room and bar serves decent meals at fairly high prices. Room rates are an excessive US$75 to US$95.

Getting There & Away

Xpujil is 183km south of Hopelchén, 152km east of Escárcega and 119km west of Chetumal. There are seven buses daily between Xpujil and Campeche, four between Xpujil and Chetumal. No buses originate in Xpujil, so you must hope to find a vacant seat on one passing through. The bus station is 100m east of the highway junction in Xpujil, on the north side of the highway. The Xpujil ruins are within walking distance of Xpujil junction.

AROUND XPUJIL
Hormiguero

Hormiguero (Spanish for 'anthill') is an old site, with some buildings dating from 50 to 250 AD, though it flourished during the Late Classic period.

Located 22km southwest of Xpujil junction (6km beyond the village of Carrizal), Hormiguero has one of the most impressive buildings in the region. The 50m-long Edificio II has a huge Chenes-style monster-mouth doorway, with much of its decoration in good condition. Though similar to the huge monster-mouths at Hochob and Chicanná, Hormiguero's is even bigger and bolder. You'll also want to see Edificio V, 60m to the north, and Edificio E-1 in the Grupo Oriente (East Group).

Admission costs US$1.50. A roundtrip taxi ride from Xpujil with a one-hour wait costs US$20.

Río Bec

Río Bec is the designation for an agglomeration of small sites, 17 at last count, in a 50-sq-km area southeast of Xpujil. Of these many sites, the most interesting is certainly Grupo B, followed by Grupos I and N. These sites were difficult to reach at the time of this writing, and require a guide; most taxi drivers will perform this service for an additional fee.

Río Bec gave its name to the prevalent architectural style of the region, characterized by long, low buildings that look as though they're divided into sections, each with a huge serpent-mouth for a door. The façades are decorated with smaller masks, geometric designs and columns. At the corners of the buildings are tall, solid towers with extremely small and steep nonfunctional steps, topped by small temples. Many of these towers have roofcombs as well.

The best example of Río Bec architecture is Edificio I at Grupo B, a Late Classic building dating from around 700 AD. Though not restored, Edificio I has been consolidated and is in a condition certainly good enough to allow appreciation of its former glory.

At Grupo I, look for Edificios XVII and XI. At Grupo N, Edificio I is quite similar to the grand one at Grupo B.

A roundtrip taxi ride from Xpujil with a one-hour wait costs US$20.

El Ramonal

These fairly impressive ruins are within walking distance of the Ejido 20 de Noviembre collective farm, reached by a road 10km east of Xpujil junction. Look for signs, turn south and follow an unpaved *ejido* (cooperative) road for 5km to the farm and its **U'lu'um Chac Yuk Nature Reserve**. As you come into the Spartan village with its free-roaming livestock and thatched huts, look for the 'museum,' the fourth building on the right-hand side of the road. Ask here for guides to show you the sites of El Ramonal.

Guides from the ejido can also show you the various sites of Río Bec, about 13km away. Admission costs US$1.50. A roundtrip taxi ride from Xpujil with a one-hour wait costs US$20.

Language

Pronunciation

Pronunciation of Spanish is not difficult, given that many Spanish sounds are similar to their English counterparts, and there is a clear and consistent relationship between pronunciation and spelling. Unless otherwise indicated, the English words used below to approximate Spanish sounds take standard American pronunciation.

Vowels Spanish has five vowels: **a**, **e**, **i**, **o** and **u**. They are pronounced something like the highlighted letters of the following English words:

a	as in 'f**a**ther'
e	as in 'm**e**t'
i	as in 'f**ee**t'
o	as in 'h**o**t'
u	as in 'p**u**t'

Diphthongs A diphthong is one syllable made up of two vowels, each of which conserves its own sound. Here are some diphthongs in Spanish, and their approximate pronunciations:

ai	as in 'h**i**de'
au	as in 'h**ow**'
ei	as in 'h**ay**'
ia	as in '**ya**rd'
ie	as in '**ye**s'
oi	as in 'b**oy**'
ua	as in '**wa**sh'
ue	as in '**we**ll'

Consonants Many consonants are pronounced in much the same way as in English, but there are some exceptions:

c	is pronounced like 's' in 'sit' when before 'e' or 'i'; elsewhere it is like 'k'
ch	as in 'choose'
g	as the 'g' in 'gate' before 'a,' 'o' and 'u'; before 'e' or 'i' it is a harsh, breathy sound like the 'h' in 'hit.' Note that when 'g' is followed by 'ue' or 'ui' the 'u' is

silent, unless it has a dieresis (ü), in which case it functions much like the English 'w':
guerra 'GEH-rra'
güero 'GWEH-ro'

h	always silent
j	a harsh, guttural sound similar to the 'ch' in the Scottish 'loch'
ll	as the 'y' in 'yellow'
ñ	nasal sound like the 'ny' in 'canyon'
q	as the 'k' in 'kick'; always followed by a silent 'u'
r	a very short rolled 'r'
rr	a longer rolled 'r'
x	like the English 'h' when it comes after 'e' or 'i,' otherwise it is like English 'x' as in 'taxi'; in many Indian words (particularly Mayan ones) 'x' is pronounced like English 'sh'
z	the same as the English 's'; under no circumstances should 's' or 'z' be pronounced like English 'z' – that sound does not exist in Spanish

There are a few other minor pronunciation differences, but the longer you stay in Mexico, the easier they will become. The letter **ñ** is considered a separate letter of the alphabet and follows 'n' in alphabetically organized lists and books, such as dictionaries and phone books; in many cases, this is also true for **ll** and **ch**, though this is not always the case.

Stress There are three general rules regarding stress:

- For words ending in a vowel, 'n' or 's,' the stress goes on the penultimate (next-to-the-last) syllable:

naranja	na-RAHN-ha
joven	HO-ven
zapatos	sa-PA-tos

- For words ending in a consonant other than 'n' or 's,' the stress is on the final syllable:

estoy	es-TOY
ciudad	syoo-DAHD
catedral	ka-teh-DRAL

- Any deviation from these rules is indicated by an accent:

México	MEH-hee-ko
mudéjar	moo-DEH-har
Cortés	cor-TESS

Gender

Nouns in Spanish are either masculine or feminine. Nouns ending in 'o,' 'e' or 'ma' are usually masculine. Nouns ending in 'a,' 'ión' or 'dad' are usually feminine. Some nouns take either a masculine or feminine form, depending on the ending; for example, *viajero* is a male traveler, *viajera* is a female traveler. An adjective usually comes after the noun it describes and must take the same gender as the noun.

Greetings & Civilities

Hello/Hi.	*Hola.*
Good morning/Good day.	*Buenos días.*
Good afternoon.	*Buenas tardes.*
Good evening/Good night.	*Buenas noches.*
See you.	*Hasta luego.*
Good-bye.	*Adiós.*
Pleased to meet you.	*Mucho gusto.*

How are you? (to one person)	
¿Como está?	
How are you? (to more than one person)	
¿Como están?	

I am fine.	*Estoy bien.*
Please.	*Por favor.*
Thank you.	*Gracias.*
You're welcome.	*De nada.*
Excuse me.	*Perdóneme.*

People

I	*yo*
you (familiar)	*tú*
you (formal)	*usted*
you (pl, formal)	*ustedes*
he/it	*el*
she/it	*ella*
we	*nosotros*
they (m)	*ellos*
they (f)	*ellas*
my wife	*mi esposa*
my husband	*mi esposo,*
	mi marido

my sister	*mi hermana*
my brother	*mi hermano*
Sir/Mr	*Señor*
Madam/Mrs	*Señora*
Miss	*Señorita*

Useful Words & Phrases

For words pertaining to food and restaurants, see the Food and Drinks sections of the Facts for the Visitor chapter.

Yes.	*Sí.*
No.	*No.*
What did you say?	*¿Mande?*
(colloq)	*¿Cómo?*
good/OK	*bueno/a*
bad	*malo/a*
better	*mejor*
best	*lo mejor*
more	*más*
less	*menos*
very little	*poco/a* or
	poquito/a

I am… (location or temporary condition)	*Estoy…*
here	*aquí*
tired (m/f)	*cansado/a*
sick/ill (m/f)	*enfermo/a*
I am… (permanent state)	*Soy…*
a worker	*trabajador/a*
married	*casado/a*

Buying

How much?	*¿Cuánto?*
How much is it worth?	*¿Cuánto vale?*
I want…	*Quiero…*
I do not want…	*No quiero…*
I would like…	*Quisiera…*
Give me…	*Dame…*
What do you want?	*¿Qué quiere?*
Do you have…?	*¿Tiene…?*
Is/are there…?	*¿Hay…?*

How much does it cost?	
¿Cuánto cuesta? or *¿Cuánto se cobra?*	

Nationalities

American (m/f)	*(norte)americano/a*
Australian (m/f)	*australiano/a*
British (m/f)	*británico/a*

LANGUAGE

Canadian (m & f) — *canadiense*
English (m/f) — *inglés/inglesa*
French (m/f) — *francés/francesa*
German (m/f) — *alemán/alemana*

Languages
I speak… — *Yo hablo…*
I do not speak… — *No hablo…*
Do you speak…? — *¿Habla usted…?*
  Spanish — *español*
  English — *inglés*
  German — *alemán*
  French — *francés*
I understand. — *Entiendo.*
I do not understand. — *No entiendo.*
Do you understand? — *¿Entiende usted?*

Please speak slowly.
  Por favor hable despacio.

Crossing the Border
birth certificate — *certificado de nacimiento*
border (frontier) — *la frontera*
car-owner's title — *título de propiedad*
car registration — *registración*
customs — *aduana*
driver's license — *licencia de manejar*
identification — *identificación*
immigration — *inmigración*
insurance — *seguro*
passport — *pasaporte*
tourist card — *tarjeta de turista*
visa — *visado*

temporary vehicle import permit
  permiso de importación temporal de vehículo

Getting Around
street — *la calle*
boulevard — *el bulevar, boulevard*
avenue — *la avenida*
road — *el camino*
highway — *la carretera*
corner (of) — *la esquina (de)*
corner/bend — *la vuelta*
block — *la cuadra*
to the left — *a la izquierda*
to the right — *a la derecha*
forward, ahead — *adelante*

straight ahead — *todo recto* or *derecho*
this way — *por aquí*
that way — *por allí*
north — *norte (Nte)*
south — *sur*
east — *este*
east (in an address) — *oriente (Ote)*
west — *oeste*
west (in an address) — *poniente (Pte)*
Where is…? — *¿Dónde está…?*
  the bus station — *el terminal de auto-buses/central camionera*
  the train station — *la estación del ferrocarril*
  the airport — *el aeropuerto*
  the post office — *el correo*
  a long-distance phone — *un teléfono de larga distancia*
bus — *el camión* or *el autobús*
minibus — *el colectivo* or *la combi*
train — *el tren*
taxi — *el taxi*
ticket sales counter — *la taquilla*
waiting room — *la sala de espera*
baggage check-in — *(el recibo de) equipaje*
toilet — *el sanitario*
departure — *la salida*
arrival — *la llegada*
platform — *el andén*

left-luggage room/checkroom
  la guardería (or *la guarda*) *de equipaje*
How far is…?
  ¿A qué distancia está…?
How long? (How much time?)
  ¿Cuánto tiempo?
short route (usually a toll highway)
  vía corta

Driving
gasoline — *la gasolina*
fuel station — *la tienda gasolinera*
unleaded — *sin plomo*
fill the tank — *llene el tanque; llenarlo*
full — *lleno* or *'ful'*

oil	*el aceite*
tire	*la llanta*
puncture	*el agujero*

How much is a liter of gasoline?
: *¿Cuánto cuesta el litro de gasolina?*
My car has broken down.
: *Se me ha descompuesto el carro.*
I need a tow truck.
: *Necesito un remolque.*
Is there a garage near here?
: *¿Hay un garaje cerca de aquí?*

Highway Signs

Though Mexico mostly uses the familiar international road signs, you should be prepared to encounter these other signs as well:

road repairs	*camino en reparación*
keep to the right	*conserve su derecha*
do not overtake	*no rebase*
dangerous curve	*curva peligrosa*
landslides or subsidence	*derrumbes*
slow	*despacio*
detour	*desviación*
slow down	*disminuya su velocidad*
school (zone)	*escuela (zona escolar)*
men working	*hombres trabajando*
road closed	*no hay paso*
danger	*peligro*
continuous white line	*raya continua*
speed bumps	*topes* or *vibradores*
road under repair	*tramo en reparación*
narrow bridge	*puente angosto*
toll highway	*vía cuota*
short route (often a toll road)	*vía corta*
have toll ready	*prepare su cuota*

one-lane road 100 meters ahead
: *un solo carril a 100 m*

Accommodations

hotel	*hotel*
guesthouse	*casa de huéspedes*
inn	*posada*
room	*cuarto, habitación*
room with one bed	*cuarto sencillo*
room with two beds	*cuarto doble*

room for one person	*cuarto para una persona*
room for two people	*cuarto para dos personas*

double bed	*cama matrimonial*
twin beds	*camas gemelas*
with bath	*con baño*
shower	*ducha* or *regadera*
hot water	*agua caliente*
air-conditioning	*aire acondicionado*
blanket	*manta, cobija*
towel	*toalla*
soap	*jabón*
toilet paper	*papel higiénico*
the check (bill)	*la cuenta*
What is the price?	*¿Cuál es el precio?*

Does that include taxes?
: *¿Están incluidos los impuestos?*
Does that include service?
: *¿Está incluido el servicio?*

Money

money	*el dinero*
traveler's checks	*cheques de viajero*
bank	*el banco*
exchange bureau	*la casa de cambio*
credit card	*la tarjeta de crédito*
exchange rate	*el tipo de cambio*
ATM	*la caja permanente* or *el cajero automático*

I want/would like to change some money.
: *Quiero/quisiera cambiar dinero.*
What is the exchange rate?
: *¿Cuál es el tipo de cambio?*
Is there a commission?
: *¿Hay comisión?*

Telephones

telephone	*el teléfono*
telephone call	*la llamada*
telephone number	*el número telefónico*
telephone card	*la tarjeta telefónica*
area or city code	*la clave*
prefix for long-distance call	*el prefijo*
local call	*llamada local*

long-distance call
llamada de larga distancia
long-distance telephone
teléfono de larga distancia
coin-operated telephone
teléfono de monedas
card-operated telephone
teléfono de tarjetas telefónicas
long-distance telephone office
la caseta de larga distancia

tone	*el tono*
operator	*operador(a)*
person to person	*persona a persona*
collect (reverse charges)	*por cobrar*
dial the number	*marque el número*
please wait	*favor de esperar*
busy	*ocupado*
toll/cost (of call)	*cuota/costo*
time & charges	*tiempo y costo*
don't hang up	*no cuelgue*

Times & Dates

Monday	*lunes*
Tuesday	*martes*
Wednesday	*miércoles*
Thursday	*jueves*
Friday	*viernes*
Saturday	*sábado*
Sunday	*domingo*
yesterday	*ayer*
today	*hoy*

tomorrow (also at some point, or maybe)
la mañana
right now (meaning in a few minutes)
horita, ahorita

already	*ya*
morning	*la mañana*
tomorrow morning	*la mañana por la mañana*
afternoon	*la tarde*
night	*la noche*
What time is it?	*¿Qué hora es?*

Numbers

0	*cero*
1	*un, uno* (m), *una* (f)
2	*dos*
3	*tres*
4	*cuatro*
5	*cinco*
6	*seis*
7	*siete*
8	*ocho*
9	*nueve*
10	*diez*
11	*once*
12	*doce*
13	*trece*
14	*catorce*
15	*quince*
16	*dieciséis*
17	*diecisiete*
18	*dieciocho*
19	*diecinueve*
20	*veinte*
21	*veintiuno*
22	*veintidós*
30	*treinta*
31	*treinta y uno*
32	*treinta y dos*
40	*cuarenta*
50	*cincuenta*
60	*sesenta*
70	*setenta*
80	*ochenta*
90	*noventa*
100	*cien*
101	*ciento uno*
143	*ciento cuarenta y tres*
200	*doscientos*
500	*quinientos*
700	*setecientos*
900	*novecientos*
1000	*mil*
2000	*dos mil*

Modern Mayan

Since the Classic period, the two ancient Mayan languages, Yucatecan and Cholan, have subdivided into 35 separate Mayan languages (Yucatec, Chol, Chorti, Tzeltal, Tzotzil, Lacandon, Mam, Quiché, Cakchiquel, etc), some of them unintelligible to speakers of others. Writing today is in the Latin alphabet brought by the conquistadors – what writing there is. Most literate Maya are literate in Spanish, the language of the government, the school, the church, radio, TV and the newspapers; they may not be literate in Mayan.

Pronunciation There are several rules to remember when pronouncing Mayan words and place names. Mayan vowels are pretty straightforward; it's the consonants that give problems. Remember:

c   is always hard, like 'k'

j   is always an aspirated 'h' sound. So *jipi-japa* is pronounced HEE-pee-HAA-pah and *abaj* is pronounced ah-BAHH; to get the 'HH' sound, take the 'h' sound from 'half' and put it at the end of ah-BAHH

u   is 'oo' except when it begins or ends a word, in which case it is like English 'w'. Thus *baktun* is 'bahk-TOON,' but *Uax-actún* is 'wah-shahk-TOON' and *ahau* is 'ah-HAW'

x   is like English 'sh,' a shushing sound

Mayan glottalized consonants, those followed by an apostrophe (b', ch', k', p', t'), are sim-ilar to normal consonants, but pronounced more forcefully and 'explosively'. However, an apostrophe following a *vowel* signifies a glottal stop, *not* a more forceful vowel.

Another rule to remember is that in most Mayan words the stress falls on the last syllable. Sometimes this is indicated by an acute accent, sometimes not. Here are some pronunciation examples:

Abaj Takalik	ah-BAHH tah-kah-LEEK
Acanceh	ah-kahn-KEH
Ahau	ah-HAW
Dzibilchaltún	dzee-beel-chahl-TOON
Kaminaljuyú	kah-mee-nahl-hoo-YOO
Oxcutzkab	ohsh-kootz-KAHB
Pacal	pah-KAHL
Pop	pope
Tikal	tee-KAHL
Uaxactún	wah-shahk-TOON
Xcaret	sh-kah-REHT
Yaxchilán	yahsh-chee-LAHN

Glossary

Words specific to food, restaurants and eating are listed in the Menu Guide that follows this glossary.

abrazo – embrace, hug; in particular, the formal, ceremonial hug between political leaders

alux, aluxes – Mayan for gremlin, leprechaun, benevolent 'little people'

Apartado Postal – post office box, abbreviated *Apdo Postal*

Ayuntamiento – often seen as *H Ayuntamiento (Honorable Ayuntamiento)* on the front of Town Hall buildings, it translates as 'Municipal Government'

barrio – district, neighborhood

billete – bank note (unlike in Spain, where it's a ticket)

boleto – ticket (bus, train, museum, etc)

caballeros – literally 'horsemen,' but corresponds to 'gentlemen' in English; look for it on toilet doors

cacique – Indian chief; also used to describe provincial warlord or strongman

cafetería – literally 'coffee-shop,' it refers to any informal restaurant with waiter service; it is not usually a cafeteria in the American sense of a self-service restaurant

cajero automático – automated bank teller machine (ATM)

callejón – alley or small, narrow or very short street

camión – truck; bus

casa de cambio – currency exchange office; it offers exchange rates comparable to banks and is much faster to use

caseta de larga distancia – long-distance telephone station, often shortened to *caseta*

cazuela – clay cooking pot, usually sold in a nested set

cenote – large natural limestone cave used for water storage (or ceremonial purposes) in Yucatán

cerveza – beer

Chac – Mayan god of rain

chac-mool – Mayan sacrificial stone sculpture

chapín – a citizen of Guatemala; Guatemalan

charro – cowboy

chingar – literally 'to rape' but in practice a verb with a wide range of colloquial meanings similar to the use of 'to screw' or 'to fuck' in English

chultún – artificial Mayan cistern found at Puuc archaeological sites south of Mérida

Churrigueresque – Spanish baroque architectural style of the early 18th century, with lavish ornamentation; named for architect José Churriguera

cigarro – cigarette

cocina – cookshop (literally 'kitchen'), a small, basic restaurant usually run by one woman, often located in or near a municipal market; also seen as *cocina económica* (economical kitchen) or *cocina familiar* (family kitchen); see also *lonchería*

colectivo – jitney taxi or minibus (usually a *combi*, or minibus) that picks up and drops off passengers along its route

comida corrida – set meal, meal of the day

completo – full up, a sign you may see on hotel desks in crowded cities

conquistador – Explorer-conqueror of Latin America from Spain

correos – post office

curandero – Indian traditional healer

damas – ladies, the usual sign on toilet doors

dzul, dzules – Mayan for foreigners or 'townfolk,' that is, not Maya from the countryside

ejido – in Mexico, communally owned Indian land taken over by landowners but returned to the original owners under a program initiated by President Lázaro Cárdenas

encomienda – Spanish colonial practice of subjecting Indians to the 'guardianship' of landowners, akin to medieval serfdom

estación ferrocarril – train station

ferrocarril – railroad

galón, galones – US gallons (fluid measure of 3.79 liters)

gringo/a – a mild Mexican pejorative term applied to a male/female North American visitor; sometimes applied to any visitor of European heritage

gruta – cave

guayabera – man's thin fabric shirt with pockets and appliquéd designs on the front, over the shoulders and down the back; often worn in place of a jacket and tie at formal occasions

guardarropa – cloakroom, place to leave parcels when entering an establishment

hacienda – estate; also 'Treasury,' as in *Departamento de Hacienda*, Treasury Department

hay – pronounced like 'eye,' meaning 'there is,' 'there are'. You're equally likely to hear *no hay*, 'there isn't' or 'there aren't'

henequen – agave fiber used to make rope, grown particularly around Mérida

hombre/s – man/men

huipil – woven white dress from the Mayan regions with intricate, colorful embroidery

IMSS – Instituto Mexicana de Seguridad Social, the Mexican Social Security Institute; it operates many of Mexico's larger public hospitals

IVA – the *impuesto al valor agregado* or 'ee-vah' is a value-added tax which can be as high as 15% and is added to many items in Mexico

Kukulcán – Mayan name for the Aztec-Toltec plumed serpent Quetzalcóatl

larga distancia – long-distance telephone, abbreviated as Lada; see also *caseta de larga distancia*

lavandería – laundry; a *lavandería automática* is a coin-operated laundry (laundromat)

lista de correos – general delivery in Mexico; literally 'mail list,' the list of addressees for whom mail is being held, displayed in the post office

lonchería – from English *lunch*; a simple restaurant which may in fact serve meals all day (not just lunch), often seen near municipal markets

lleno – full (fuel tank)

machismo – maleness, masculine virility; an ever-present aspect of Mexican society

malecon – waterfront boulevard

manzana – apple; also a city block. A *supermanzana* is a large group of city blocks bounded by major avenues. Ciudad Cancún uses manzana and supermanzana numbers as addresses

mariachi – small ensemble of Mexican street musicians; strolling mariachi bands often perform in restaurants

más o menos – more or less, somewhat

mestizo – a person of mixed Indian and European blood; the word now more commonly means 'Mexican'

metate – flattish stone on which corn is ground with a cylindrical stone roller

Montezuma's revenge – Mexican version of 'Delhi-belly' or travelers' diarrhea

mordida – 'bite,' or small bribe that's usually paid to keep the wheels of bureaucracy turning. Some say that giving a *mordida* to a traffic policeman may ensure that you won't have a bigger traffic fine to pay

mudéjar – Moorish architectural style

mujer/es – woman/women

Palacio de Gobierno – building housing the executive offices of a state or regional government

Palacio Municipal – City Hall, seat of the corporation or municipal government

palapa – thatched, palm-leaf-roofed shelter with open sides

parada – bus stop, usually for city buses

pisto – colloquial Mayan term for money

Plateresque – 'silversmith-like'; the architectural style of the Spanish renaissance (16th century), rich in decoration

Porfirato – name given to the era of Porfirio Diaz's 35-year rule (1876-1911) that preceded the Mexican Revolution

PRI – Institutional Revolutionary Party, the controlling force in Mexican politics for more than half a century

propino, propina – a tip, different from a *mordida*, which is really a bribe

puro – cigar

Quetzalcóatl – plumed serpent god of the Aztecs and Toltecs

rebozo – long woolen or linen scarf covering the head or shoulders

retablo – ornate gilded, carved decoration of wood in a church

retorno – 'return'; in Cancún, a U-shaped street which starts from a major boulevard, loops around and 'returns' to the boulevard a block away

roofcomb – a decorative stonework lattice atop a Mayan pyramid or temple

rutelero – a small bus with a regular route but an irregular schedule

sacbé, sacbeob – ceremonial limestone avenue or path between great Mayan cities

sanatorio – hospital, particularly a small private one

sanitario – literally 'sanitary'; usually means toilet

serape – traditional woolen blanket

stela, stelae – standing stone monument(s), usually carved

supermercado – supermarket, ranging from a corner store to a large, American-style supermarket

taller – shop or workshop. A *taller mecánico* is a mechanic's shop, usually for cars. A *taller de llantas* is a tire-repair shop

templo – in Mexico, a church; anything from a wayside chapel to a cathedral

tequila – clear, distilled liquor produced, like pulque and mezcal, from the maguey cactus

Tex-Mex – Americanized version of Mexican food

típico – typical or characteristic of a region; particularly used to describe food

topes – speed bumps found in many Mexican towns, sometimes indicated by a highway sign bearing a row of little bumps

viajero – traveler

vulcanizadora – automobile tire repair shop

War of the Castes – bloody Mayan uprising in Yucatán during the mid-19th century

zócalo – Aztec for 'pedestal' or 'plinth,' but used to refer to a town's main plaza

zotz – bat (the mammal) in many Mayan languages

Menu Guide

For a description of Yucatecan specialties, turn to the boxed text 'Food of the Yucatán' in the Mérida – Places to Eat section of the Yucatán State chapter.

ANTOJITOS

Many traditional Mexican dishes fall under the heading of *antojitos* ('little whims'), savory or spicy concoctions that delight the palate.

burrito – any combination of beans, cheese, meat, chicken or seafood, seasoned with salsa or chile and wrapped in a wheat-flour tortilla

chilaquiles – scrambled eggs with chiles and bits of tortilla

chile relleno – *poblano* chile stuffed with cheese, meat or other foods, dipped in egg whites, fried and baked in sauce

empanada – small pastry with savory or sweet filling

enchilada – ingredients similar to those used in tacos and burritos wrapped in a corn tortilla, dipped in sauce and then baked or fried

enfrijolada – soft tortilla in a frijole sauce with cheese and onion on top

entomatada – soft tortilla in a tomato sauce with cheese and onion on top

gordita – fried corn (maize) dough filled with refried beans, topped with cream, cheese and lettuce

guacamole – mashed avocados mixed with onion, chili, lemon, tomato and other ingredients

machaca – cured, dried and shredded beef or pork mixed with eggs, onions, cilantro and chiles

papadzul – corn tortillas filled with hard-boiled eggs, cucumber or zucchini seeds and covered in tomato sauce

quesadilla – flour tortilla topped or filled with cheese and occasionally other ingredients and then heated

queso fundido – melted cheese served with tortillas

queso relleno – 'stuffed cheese,' a mild yellow cheese stuffed with minced meat and spices

sincronizada – a lightly grilled or fried tortilla 'sandwich,' usually with a ham and cheese filling

sope – thick patty of corn dough lightly grilled then served with green or red salsa and frijoles, onion and cheese

taco – a soft or crisp corn tortilla wrapped or folded around the same filling as a burrito

tamale – corn dough, stuffed or not, wrapped in corn husks and steamed

torta – Mexican-style sandwich in a roll

tostada – flat, crisp tortilla topped with meat or cheese, tomatoes, beans and lettuce

SOPAS (SOUPS)

birria – a spicy-hot soup of meat, onions, peppers and cilantro, served with tortillas

chipilín – cheese and cream soup in a maize (corn) base

gazpacho – chilled tomato-vegetable soup spiced with hot chiles

menudo – popular soup made with the spiced entrails (tripe) of various four-legged beasts

pozole – hominy soup with meat and vegetables (can be spicy)

sopa de arroz – not a soup at all but just a plate of rice; commonly served with lunch

sopa de lima – 'lime soup,' chicken stock flavored with lime and filled with pieces of crisped corn tortilla

sopa de pollo – bits of chicken in a thin chicken broth

HUEVOS (EGGS)

huevos estrellados – fried eggs

huevos fritos – fried eggs

huevos motuleños – local dish of the Yucatecan town of Motul: fried eggs atop a tortilla spread with refried beans, garnished with diced ham, green peas, shredded cheese and tomato sauce, with fried bananas (platanos) on the side

huevos rancheros – ranch-style eggs: fried, laid on a tortilla and smothered with spicy tomato sauce

huevos revueltos estilo mexicano – 'eggs scrambled Mexican-style' with tomatoes, onions, chiles and garlic

huevos revueltos – scrambled eggs; *con chorizo* (chor-REE-so) is with spicy sausage, *con frijoles* is with beans

PESCADO, MARISCOS (SEAFOOD)

The variety and quality of seafood from the coastal waters of Yucatán and Belize is excellent. Lobster is available all along Mexico's Caribbean coast, and Campeche is a major shrimping port, with much of its catch exported.

All of the following types of seafood are available most of the year in seafood restaurants. Clams, oysters, shrimp and prawns are also often available as *cocteles* (cocktails).

abulón – abalone

almejas – clams

atún – tuna

cabrilla – sea bass

camarones – shrimp

camarones gigantes – prawns

cangrejo – large crab

ceviche – raw seafood marinated in lime juice and mixed with onions, chiles, garlic, tomatoes and cilantro (fresh coriander leaf)

dorado – dolphin fish *(not* the marine mammal)

filete de pescado – fish fillet

huachinango – red snapper

jaiba – small crab

jurel – yellowtail

langosta – lobster

lenguado – flounder or sole

mariscos – shellfish

ostiones – oysters

pargo – red snapper

pescado – fish after it has been caught (see *pez)*

pescado al mojo de ajo – fish fried in butter and garlic

pez – fish which is alive in the water (see *pescado)*

pez espada – swordfish

sierra – mackerel

tiburón – shark

tortuga or *caguama* – turtle

trucha de mar – sea trout

CARNES Y AVES (MEAT & POULTRY)

asado – roast

barbacoa – literally 'barbecued,' but by a process whereby the meat is covered and placed under hot coals

birria – barbecued on a spit
bistec – beefsteak; sometimes any cut of meat, fish or poultry
bistec de res – beefsteak
borrego – sheep
cabro – goat
carne al carbón – charcoal-grilled meat
carne asada – tough but tasty grilled beef
carnitas – deep-fried pork
cerdo – pork
chicharrones – deep-fried pork skin
chorizo – pork sausage
chuletas de cerdo – pork chops
cochinita – suckling pig
codorniz, la chaquaca – quail
conejo – rabbit
cordero – lamb
costillas de cerdo – pork ribs or chops
guajolote – turkey
hígado – liver
jamón – ham
milanesa – crumbed, breaded
milanesa de res – crumbed beefsteak
patas de puerco – pig's feet
pato – duck
pavo – turkey, a fowl native to Yucatán that figures prominently in Yucatecan cuisine
pibil – Yucatecan preparation: meat is flavored with *achiote* sauce, wrapped in banana leaves and baked in a pit oven, or *pib*
poc-chuc – slices of pork cooked in a tangy sauce of onion and sour oranges or lemons
pollo – chicken
pollo asado – grilled (not roast) chicken
pollo con arroz – chicken with rice
pollo frito – fried chicken
puerco – pork
tampiqueño, tampiqueña – 'in the style of Tampico,' with spiced tomato sauce
tocino – bacon or salt pork
venado – venison

FRUTAS (FRUIT)

coco – coconut
dátil – date
fresas – strawberries; any berries
guayaba – guava
higo – fig
limón – lime or lemon
mango – mango
melón – melon

naranja – orange
papaya – papaya
piña – pineapple
plátano – banana (suitable for cooking)
toronja – grapefruit
uva – grape

LEGUMBRES, VERDURAS (VEGETABLES)

Vegetables are rarely served as separate dishes, but are often mixed into salads, soups and sauces.

aceitunas – olives
calabaza – squash, marrow (zucchini) or pumpkin
cebolla – onion
champiñones – mushrooms
chícharos – peas
ejotes – green beans
elote – corn on the cob; commonly served from steaming bins on street carts
jícama – a popular root vegetable that resembles a potato crossed with an apple; eaten fresh with a sprinkling of lime, chile and salt
lechuga – lettuce
papa – potato
tomate – tomato
zanahoria – carrot

DULCES (DESSERTS, SWEETS)

flan – custard, créme caramel
helado – ice cream
nieve – Mexican equivalent of the American 'snow cone': flavored ice with the consistency of ice cream
paleta – flavored ice on a stick (Popsicle)
pan dulce – sweet rolls, usually eaten for breakfast
pastel – cake
postre – dessert, after-meal sweet

CAFÉ (COFFEE)

café con crema – coffee with cream served separately
café con leche – coffee with hot milk
café negro or *café americano* – black coffee with nothing added except sugar, unless it's made with sugar-coated coffee beans
café sin azúcar – coffee without sugar. This keeps the waiter from adding heaps of sugar

to your cup, but it doesn't mean your coffee won't taste sweet; sugar is often added to and processed with the beans

Nescafé – instant coffee; the name is used generically

CONDIMENTS & OTHER FOODS

achiote – a mild, tart spice paste colored red with annato seed and used widely in Yucatán cooking

azúcar – sugar

bolillo – French-style bread rolls

crema – cream

guacamole – mashed avocados mixed with onion, chile sauce, lemon, tomato and other ingredients

leche – milk

mantequilla – butter; intestinal upset from butter gone rancid in this hot climate has generated its jocular colloquial name 'meant-ta-kill-ya'

mole poblano – a popular sauce from Puebla, Mexico, made from more than 30 ingredients, including bitter chocolate, various chiles and many spices; often served over chicken or turkey

pimienta negra – black pepper

queso – cheese

sal – salt

salsa – sauce made with chiles, onion, tomato, lemon or lime juice and spices; also, any kind of sauce

AT THE TABLE

la copa – glass

la cuchara – spoon

la cuchillo – knife

la cuenta – bill

la lista – menu (short for *lista de comidas*); also see *menú*

el menú – fixed price meal, as in *menú del día*; also see *la lista*

el plato – plate

la propina – the tip, 10 to 15% of the bill

la servilleta – table napkin

la taza – cup

el tenedor – fork

el vaso – drinking glass

LONELY PLANET

Guides by Region

Lonely Planet is known worldwide for publishing practical, reliable and no-nonsense travel information in our guides and on our web site. The Lonely Planet list covers just about every accessible part of the world. Currently there are fifteen series: travel guides, Shoestrings, Condensed, Phrasebooks, Read This First, Healthy Travel, Walking guides, Cycling guides, Pisces Diving & Snorkeling guides, City Maps, Travel Atlases, Out to Eat, World Food, Journeys travel literature and Pictorials.

AFRICA Africa on a shoestring • Africa – the South • Arabic (Egyptian) phrasebook • Arabic (Moroccan) phrasebook • Cairo • Cape Town • Cape Town city map • Central Africa • East Africa • Egypt • Egypt travel atlas • Ethiopian (Amharic) phrasebook • The Gambia & Senegal • Healthy Travel Africa • Kenya • Kenya travel atlas • Malawi, Mozambique & Zambia • Morocco • North Africa • Read This First Africa • South Africa, Lesotho & Swaziland • South Africa, Lesotho & Swaziland travel atlas • Swahili phrasebook • Tanzania, Zanzibar & Pemba • Trekking in East Africa • Tunisia • West Africa • Zimbabwe, Botswana & Namibia • Zimbabwe, Botswana & Namibia travel atlas • World Food Morocco

Travel Literature: The Rainbird: A Central African Journey • Songs to an African Sunset: A Zimbabwean Story • Mali Blues: Traveling to an African Beat

AUSTRALIA & THE PACIFIC Auckland • Australia • Australian phrasebook • Bushwalking in Australia • Bushwalking in Papua New Guinea • Fiji • Fijian phrasebook • Healthy Travel Australia, NZ and the Pacific • Islands of Australia's Great Barrier Reef • Melbourne • Melbourne city map • Micronesia • New Caledonia • New South Wales & the ACT • New Zealand • Northern Territory • Outback Australia • Out to Eat – Melbourne • Out to Eat – Sydney • Papua New Guinea • Pidgin phrasebook • Queensland • Rarotonga & the Cook Islands • Samoa • Solomon Islands • South Australia • South Pacific • South Pacific Languages phrasebook • Sydney • Sydney city map • Sydney condensed • Tahiti & French Polynesia • Tasmania • Tonga • Tramping in New Zealand • Vanuatu • Victoria • Western Australia

Travel Literature: Islands in the Clouds • Kiwi Tracks: A New Zealand Journey • Sean & David's Long Drive

CENTRAL AMERICA & THE CARIBBEAN Bahamas, Turks & Caicos • Bermuda • Central America on a shoestring • Costa Rica • Cuba • Dominican Republic & Haiti • Eastern Caribbean • Guatemala, Belize & Yucatán: La Ruta Maya • Jamaica • Mexico • Mexico City • Panama • Puerto Rico • Read This First Central & South America • World Food Mexico • Yucatán

Travel Literature: Green Dreams: Travels in Central America

EUROPE Amsterdam • Amsterdam city map • Andalucía • Austria • Baltic States phrasebook • Barcelona • Berlin • Berlin city map• Britain • British phrasebook • Brussels, Bruges & Antwerp • Budapest city map • Canary Islands • Central Europe • Central Europe phrasebook • Corfu & Ionians • Corsica • Crete • Crete condensed • Croatia • Cyprus • Czech & Slovak Republics • Denmark • Dublin • Eastern Europe • Eastern Europe phrasebook • Edinburgh • Estonia, Latvia & Lithuania • Europe on a shoestring • Finland • Florence • France • French phrasebook • Germany • German phrasebook • Greece • Greek Islands • Greek phrasebook • Hungary • Iceland, Greenland & the Faroe Islands • Istanbul city map • Ireland • Italian phrasebook • Italy • Krakow • Lisbon • London • London city map • London condensed • Mediterranean Europe • Mediterranean Europe phrasebook • Munich • Norway • Paris • Paris city map • Paris condensed • Poland • Portugal • Portugese phrasebook • Portugal travel atlas • Prague • Prague city map • Provence & the Côte d'Azur • Read This First Europe • Romania & Moldova • Rome • Russia, Ukraine & Belarus • Russian phrasebook • Scandinavian & Baltic Europe • Scandinavian Europe phrasebook • Scotland • Slovenia • Spain • Spanish phrasebook • St Petersburg • Switzerland • Trekking in Spain • Ukrainian phrasebook • Venice • Vienna • Walking in Britain • Walking in Ireland • Walking in Italy • Walking in Spain • Walking in Switzerland • Western Europe • Western Europe phrasebook • World Food Italy • World Food Spain

Travel Literature: The Olive Grove: Travels in Greece

LONELY PLANET

Mail Order

Lonely Planet products are distributed worldwide. They are also available by mail order from Lonely Planet, so if you have difficulty finding a title please write to us. North and South American residents should write to 150 Linden St, Oakland, CA 94607, USA; European and African residents should write to 10a Spring Place, London, NW5 3BH; and residents of other countries to PO Box 617, Hawthorn, Victoria 3122, Australia.

INDIAN SUBCONTINENT Bangladesh • Bengali phrasebook • Bhutan • Delhi • Goa • Hindi/Urdu phrasebook • India • India & Bangladesh travel atlas • Indian Himalaya • Karakoram Highway • Kerala • Mumbai • Nepal • Nepali phrasebook • Pakistan • Rajasthan • Read This First: Asia & India • South India • Sri Lanka • Sri Lanka phrasebook • Trekking in the Indian Himalaya • Trekking in the Karakoram & Hindukush • Trekking in the Nepal Himalaya
Travel Literature: In Rajasthan • Shopping for Buddhas • The Age of Kali

ISLANDS OF THE INDIAN OCEAN Madagascar & Comoros • Maldives • Mauritius, Réunion & Seychelles

MIDDLE EAST & CENTRAL ASIA Bahrain, Kuwait & Qatar • Central Asia • Central Asia phrasebook • Dubai • Hebrew phrasebook • Iran • Israel & the Palestinian Territories • Israel & the Palestinian Territories travel atlas • Istanbul • Istanbul city map • Istanbul to Cairo on a shoestring • Jerusalem • Jerusalem city map • Jordan • Jordan, Syria & Lebanon travel atlas • Lebanon • Middle East • Oman & the United Arab Emirates • Syria • Turkey • Turkey travel atlas • Turkish phrasebook •Yemen
Travel Literature: The Gates of Damascus • Kingdom of the Film Stars: Journey into Jordan • Black on Black: Iran Revisited

NORTH AMERICA Alaska • Backpacking in Alaska • Baja California • Boston • California & Nevada • California condensed • Canada • Chicago • Chicago city map • Deep South • Florida • Hawaii • Las Vegas • Los Angeles • Miami • New England • New Orleans • New York City • New York city map • New York condensed • New York, New Jersey & Pennsylvania • Oahu • Pacific Northwest USA • Puerto Rico • Rocky Mountain States • San Francisco • San Francisco city map • Seattle • Southwest USA • Texas • USA • USA phrasebook • Vancouver • Washington, DC & the Capital Region • Washington, DC city map
Travel Literature: Drive Thru America

NORTH-EAST ASIA Beijing • Cantonese phrasebook • China • Hong Kong • Hong Kong city map • Hong Kong, Macau & Guangzhou • Japan • Japanese phrasebook • Japanese audio pack • Korea • Korean phrasebook • Kyoto • Mandarin phrasebook • Mongolia • Mongolian phrasebook • North-East Asia on a shoestring • Seoul • South-West China • Taiwan • Tibet • Tibetan phrasebook • Tokyo
Travel Literature: Lost Japan • In Xanadu

SOUTH AMERICA Argentina, Uruguay & Paraguay • Bolivia • Brazil • Brazilian phrasebook • Buenos Aires • Chile & Easter Island • Chile & Easter Island travel atlas • Colombia • Ecuador & the Galapagos Islands • Healthy Travel Central & South America • Latin American Spanish phrasebook • Peru • Quechua phrasebook • Rio de Janeiro • Rio de Janeiro city map • South America on a shoestring • Trekking in the Patagonian Andes • Venezuela
Travel Literature: Full Circle: A South American Journey

SOUTH-EAST ASIA Bali & Lombok • Bangkok • Bangkok city map • Burmese phrasebook • Cambodia • Hanoi • Healthy Travel Asia & India • Hill Tribes phrasebook • Ho Chi Minh City • Indonesia • Indonesia's Eastern Islands • Indonesian phrasebook • Indonesian audio pack • Jakarta • Java • Laos • Lao phrasebook • Laos travel atlas • Malay phrasebook • Malaysia, Singapore & Brunei • Myanmar (Burma) • Philippines • Pilipino (Tagalog) phrasebook • Read This First Asia & India • Singapore • South-East Asia on a shoestring • South-East Asia phrasebook • Thailand • Thailand's Islands & Beaches • Thailand travel atlas • Thai phrasebook • Thai audio pack • Vietnam • Vietnamese phrasebook • Vietnam travel atlas • World Food Thailand • World Food Vietnam

ALSO AVAILABLE: Antarctica • The Arctic • Brief Encounters: Stories of Love, Sex & Travel • Chasing Rickshaws • Lonely Planet Unpacked • Not the Only Planet: Travel Stories from Science Fiction • Sacred India • Travel with Children • Traveller's Tales

LONELY PLANET

You already know that Lonely Planet produces more than this one guidebook, but you might not be aware of the other products we have on this region. Here is a selection of titles which you may want to check out as well:

Mexico
ISBN 1 86450 089 1
US$24.99 • UK£14.99 • 179FF

Diving & Snorkeling Cozumel
ISBN 0 86442 574 0
US$14.95 • UK£8.99 • 110FF

Healthy Travel
ISBN 1 86450 053 0
US$5.95 • UK£3.99 • 39FF

World Food Mexico
ISBN 1 86450 023 9
US$11.95 • UK£6.99 • 95FF

Guatemala
ISBN 0 86442 684 4
US$16.99 • UK£10.99 • 129FF

Latin American Spanish phrasebook
ISBN 0 86442 558 9
US$6.95 • UK£4.50 • 50FF

Available wherever books are sold.

Index

Text

Bold indicates maps.

Boxed Text

MAP LEGEND

BOUNDARIES

- International
- Province

HYDROGRAPHY

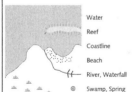

- Water
- Reef
- Coastline
- Beach
- River, Waterfall
- Swamp, Spring

ROUTES & TRANSPORT

- Freeway
- Toll Freeway
- Primary Road
- Secondary Road
- Tertiary Road
- Unpaved Road
- Pedestrian Mall
- Trail, Track
- Walking Tour
- Ferry Route
- Railway, Train Station
- Mass Transit Line & Station

ROUTE SHIELDS

- Mexico Highway
- Mexico Toll Highway
- State Highway

AREA FEATURES

- Building
- Cemetery
- Ecological Reserve
- Golf Course
- Park
- Plaza

- ✪ **NATIONAL CAPITAL**
- ◉ **State, Provincial Capital**
- ● **LARGE CITY**
- ● **Medium City**
- ● Small City
- ● Town, Village
- ○ *Point of Interest*

- ■ Place to Stay
- ▲ Campground
- ⬔ RV Park
- ⛺ Refugio (Shelter)

- ▼ Place to Eat
- ◗ Bar (Place to Drink)

MAP SYMBOLS

- ✚ Airfield
- ✈ Airport
- ∴ Archaeological Site, Ruins
- ⑨ Bank
- ◗ Baseball Diamond
- ⫪ Beach
- ✛ Border Crossing
- ◗ Bus, Ferry or Colectivo Stop
- ▦ Cathedral
- ⌂ Cave
- ✝ Church
- ◼ Dive Site
- ◷ Embassy, Consulate
- ⊁ Footbridge
- ➤ Fish Hatchery
- ❖ Garden
- ⛽ Gas Station
- ✛ Hospital, Clinic
- ❶ Information
- ⚱ Lighthouse
- ☼ Lookout

- ♛ Mine
- ⚑ Monument
- ▲ Mountain
- ⛫ Museum
- ⌒ Observatory
- ← One-Way Street
- ⚘ Park
- ℗ Parking
-) (Pass
- ⊼ Picnic Area
- ★ Police Station
- ⌣ Pool
- ▣ Post Office
- ❖ Shopping Mall
- ♭ Snorkeling
- ⛫ Stately Home
- ☎ Telephone
- ▣ Tomb, Mausoleum
- ⚐ Trailhead
- ⚲ Winery
- ⛭ Zoo

Note: Not all symbols displayed above appear in this book.

LONELY PLANET OFFICES

Australia
PO Box 617, Hawthorn 3122, Victoria
☎ 03 9819 1877 fax 03 9819 6459
email talk2us@lonelyplanet.com.au

USA
150 Linden Street, Oakland, California 94607
☎ 510 893 8555, TOLL FREE 800 275 8555
fax 510 893 8572
email info@lonelyplanet.com

UK
10A Spring Place, London NW5 3BH
☎ 020 7428 4800 fax 020 7428 4828
email go@lonelyplanet.co.uk

France
1 rue du Dahomey, 75011 Paris
☎ 01 55 25 33 00 fax 01 55 25 33 01
www.lonelyplanet.fr

World Wide Web: www.lonelyplanet.com *or* AOL keyword: lp
Lonely Planet Images: lpi@lonelyplanet.com.au

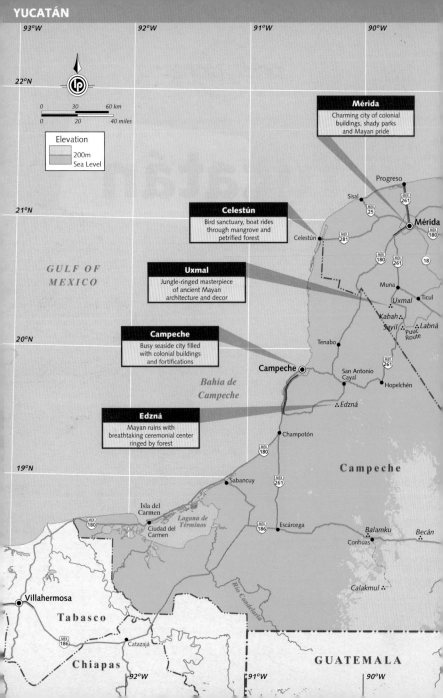

Yuc

Scott Doggett

LONELY PLANET PUBLICATIONS
Melbourne • Oakland • London • Paris